Giant in the Shadows

What a responsibility to live a worthy life as the son of such a man.

—F. Lauristan Bullard, on the death of Robert T. Lincoln

Giant in the Shadows

The Life of Robert T. Lincoln

JASON EMERSON

Southern Illinois University Press
Carbondale and Edwardsville

Printed in the United States of America

Frontispiece: Sketch of Robert Lincoln, age seventy-eight, made from life by his granddaughter Mary "Peggy" Beckwith, September 9, 1921. Courtesy of Hildene, The Lincoln Family Home, Manchester, Vermont.

Library of Congress Cataloging-in-Publication Data
Emerson, Jason, 1975–
Giant in the shadows : the life of Robert T. Lincoln / Jason Emerson.
p. cm.
Includes bibliographical references and index.
ISBN-13: 978-0-8093-3055-3 (cloth : alk. paper)
ISBN-10: 0-8093-3055-5 (cloth : alk. paper)
ISBN-13: 978-0-8093-9071-7 (ebook)
ISBN-10: 0-8093-9071-X (ebook)
1. Lincoln, Robert Todd, 1843–1926. 2. Children of presidents—United States—Biography. 3. United States—Politics and government—1865–1933. 4. Ambassadors—United States—Biography. 5. Lawyers—United States—Biography. I. Title.
E664.L63E48 2011
973.7092—dc22
[B] 2011008852

Printed on recycled paper. ♻
The paper used in this publication meets the minimum requirements of American National Standard for Information Sciences—Permanence of Paper for Printed Library Materials, ANSI Z39.48-1992. ♾

For my wife, Kathleen,

who has assisted, encouraged, and endured me
and my years of work on this book
far beyond my ability to ever thank her enough.

As I wrote of her thirteen years ago and still believe:

Her muse sustains my luminous faith,
sovereigns love, profounds my bliss,
Kathleen . . . my sweet Kathleen . . .
she is my happiness.

Contents

Illustrations

Acknowledgments

Any author who spends nearly a decade traveling across the country, visiting and researching in numerous archives, museums, and historic sites, speaking to countless groups, meeting scores of interesting and helpful people, and ultimately creating a biographical tome (with a first draft of more than twelve hundred manuscript pages) hopes and intends to be definitive and will become indebted to a long list of people who assisted in various ways. I have done my best through the years conscientiously to keep my list, but if I have omitted anyone's name, I apologize profusely. I offer a blanket statement of sincere gratitude to everyone who has aided me along the way. More particularly, I thank:

The entire staff at Robert Lincoln's Hildene, the Lincoln Family Home, Manchester, Vermont, for their assistance and enthusiasm. I especially thank director Seth Bongartz for making me Hildene's first scholar-in-residence for the year 2010, and again for 2011; deputy director Laine Dunham for scanning so many photos and illustrations from the Hildene collections; former curator/historian Brian Knight and his interim replacement, lead historic interpreter Gary Sloan Jr., for their generous research assistance and for allowing me unparalleled access to the Hildene archives and collections.

The staff at the Abraham Lincoln Presidential Library, Springfield, Illinois, especially Lincoln curator James Cornelius, whose assistance and generosity was incalculable, Jennifer Ericson, Cheryl Schnirring, Glenna Schroeder-Lein, and Gwenith Podeschi.

Lynn Ellsworth, executive director, Harlan-Lincoln House, Iowa Wesleyan College, Mount Pleasant, Iowa.

Edouard L. Desrochers, assistant librarian and academy archivist, Phillips Exeter Academy, Exeter, New Hampshire.

Debbie Vaughn, director of research and access and chief librarian, Chicago History Museum.

Keith Housewright, librarian, Sangamon Valley Collection, Lincoln Library, Springfield, Illinois.

Jane Westenfeld, curator, Ida M. Tarbell Collection, Pelletier Library, Allegheny College, Meadville, Pennsylvania.

Elizabeth B. Dunn, Rare Book, Manuscript, and Special Collections Library, Duke University, Durham, North Carolina.

Tim Townsend, historian, and Susan Haake, curator, Lincoln Home National Historic Site, Springfield, Illinois.

Gwen Thompson, director, and the entire staff of the Mary Todd Lincoln House, Lexington, Kentucky.

Chris Winter, curator, Batavia Depot Museum, Batavia, Illinois.

Olga Tsapina, Norris Foundation Curator, American Historical Manuscripts, Huntington Library, San Marino, California.

Don McCue, curator, Lincoln Shrine, Redlands, California.

Jason Meyers, curator, Museum of Funeral Customs, Springfield, Illinois.

Nan Card, curator of manuscripts, Rutherford B. Hayes Presidential Center, Spiegel Grove, Fremont, Ohio.

Barbara L. Krieger, archives specialist, Rauner Special Collections Library, Dartmouth College Library, Hanover, New Hampshire.

Alex Rankin, assistant director for acquisitions, Howard Gotlieb Archival Research Center, Boston University.

Margaret Downs Hrabe, reference coordinator, Albert and Shirley Small Special Collections Library, University of Virginia, Charlottesville.

Martha Briggs, Lloyd Lewis Curator of Midwest Manuscripts, Newberry Archives, Newberry Library, Chicago, Illinois.

Holly Snyder, Patricia Sirois, and Ann Morgan Dodge of the John Hay Library, Brown University, Providence, Rhode Island.

Susan Halpert, reference librarian, Houghton Library of the Harvard College Library, Cambridge, Massachusetts, for helping me find my way through the labyrinth of the Houghton's vast holdings.

Michelle Gachette and Kyle DeCicco-Carey, reference assistants at the Harvard University Archives, Pusey Library, Harvard Yard, Cambridge, Massachusetts.

Diane P. Rofini, librarian, Chester County Historical Society, West Chester, Pennsylvania.

Bill Marshall, curator of manuscripts, Margaret I. King Library, and Laura Hall, reference services, Reference Commons, University of Kentucky, Lexington.

Ron Keller, curator, Lincoln College Museum, Lincoln, Illinois.

John Sellers, former Lincoln Librarian, and the entire staff of the Manuscript Division, Library of Congress.

Jill M. Abraham, archives specialist, old military and civil records, and Sharon Fitzpatrick, Congressional relations specialist, National Archives and Records Administration, Washington, D.C.

Rick Peuser, assistant chief, NWCT2—Reference, Archives II, National Archives at College Park, Maryland.

Dottie Hopkins-Rehan, senior archival conservator Illinois State Archives, for finding and photocopying documents related to Abraham Lincoln's 1901 reburial.

Lee Whittlesey, park historian, Yellowstone National Park.

Cindy Van Horn, Lincoln librarian, formerly of the Lincoln Museum and now of the Allen County Public Library in Fort Wayne, Indiana.

Eric Brooks, curator, Ashland: The Henry Clay Estate, Lexington, Kentucky.

Tara Zachary Laver, curator of manuscripts, Special Collections Library, Louisiana State University.

James S. Brust, MD, chairman of the Department of Psychiatry and medical director of the psychiatric unit at Providence, Little Company of Mary Medical Center, San Pedro, California, and assistant clinical professor of psychiatry David Geffen, School of Medicine at University of California, Los Angeles.

Ophthalmologists James W. Rosenberg, MD, of Chestnut Hill, Massachusetts, and Tay Weinman, MD, of San Pedro, California.

Richard E. Hart, Springfield, Illinois, for sharing his research on Robert Lincoln's childhood teacher and schooling.

Karen Needles, from Lincolnarchives.com, who assisted me in a pinch by helping with Library of Congress research.

For their advice and support through the years, historians Mike Burkhimer, Michael Burlingame, Tom Craughwell, Harold Holzer, Michael W. Kauffman, Donna McCreary, Rodney Ross, Frank Williams, and Douglas L. Wilson.

I especially thank Wayne C. Temple, that dean of Lincoln studies, whose advice, assistance, and friendship have been invaluable to me through many years.

Phil Stephensen-Payne and Monte Herridge for helping me find and acquire the elusive writings of Patrick D. Tyrrell in *Flynn's* weekly detective magazine.

R. Emmett Tyrrell, for his friendship, support, and sharing of family items regarding Patrick D. Tyrrell.

T. J. Heronimus, of Grundy Center, Iowa, for finding and sending me copies of land lots that Abraham, Mary, and Robert T. Lincoln bought, owned, and sold.

John Norton, Augustana Historical Society, for sharing his notes regarding the diary of Lars Paul Esbjörn.

John R. Paul, Prairie Archives bookstore, Springfield, Illinois, who always was able to find books and articles I needed in my research.

David Patrick, Plattsburgh, New York, for sharing with me the unpublished memoirs of Charles W. McLellan.

Jonathan Mann, publisher of *The Railsplitter*.

Chuck Hand, proprietor of LincolnBooks.net.

Fred Towers Jr., Judy Reemtsma, and Dorcy Burns, the children of Frederic N. Towers, the Lincoln family attorney, for their support and assistance.

The staffs at the Rappahannock Regional Library, Fredericksburg, Virginia, and Cazenovia Public Library, Cazenovia, New York, for all their help with my numerous interlibrary loan requests.

Steven K. Rogstad, Lincoln Fellowship of Wisconsin, for his hospitality and his generosity in opening his vast Lincoln periodical archive to me.

Jack Bales, reference and humanities librarian, University of Mary Washington, Fredericksburg, Virginia, for his wonderful research assistance.

Richard F. Bales, of Wheaton, Illinois, for helping me understand real estate and insurance law.

My good friends: Drew and Trisha Long, for their hospitality on my many trips to Washington, D.C., and for Drew's help with research at Duke University, which I know he found thrilling; Joel and Jennifer Van Haaften, who gave me a place to sleep on research visits to Chicago and helped with research; Jonda and Rick Anderson for their support, their love of Lincoln, and their hospitality on research trips.

Aby and Blake Bethem, owners of Bistro Bethem in Fredericksburg, Virginia, and the entire Bistro staff who worked with me during the years I served tables to help pay the mortgage while I wrote this book. Their support and tolerance of my Lincoln-related conversations were truly heroic and appreciated.

Paul Lewis, a true friend and intellectual inspiration and also director of the Fredericksburg Athenaeum, Fredericksburg, Virginia, which likewise is a source of intellectual, artistic, and spiritual inspiration.

Mark Johnson and Cat Mancuso, longtime friends who not only supported and assisted my historical research through the years but were some of the first people—especially Cat, who was the first—to introduce me to and encourage me in the wonderful history of Abraham Lincoln and his family.

My in-laws, Manny and Pam Rio, for their continued love and support and all the days of staying with my daughter Olivia while I was on the road.

My Aunt Emily Gronberg and cousin Michelle Gronberg, for allowing me to stay with them on research trips.

My editor Sylvia Frank Rodrigue, for her support, flexibility, understanding, and excellent constructive criticism. Her keen eye made this book infinitely better.

And, as always, to my girls, Kathleen and Olivia, who endured and supported the years of travel, research, and writing I put into this book and without whom nothing is possible—or even worthwhile.

Giant in the Shadows

Introduction

In 1888, Robert Todd Lincoln, the only surviving child of Abraham and Mary Lincoln, was in serious danger of becoming president of the United States. This is not idle speculation, for "danger" is exactly what Robert Lincoln considered it to be. "I have seen too much of the wear and tear of official life to ever have a desire to reenter it," he told a reporter in 1887, two years after finishing his term as secretary of war. "The Presidential office is but a gilded prison. The care and worry outweigh, to my mind, the honor which surrounds the position."[1] Yet, he was the ideal candidate. At that time, the forty-five-year-old Lincoln was a prominent Chicago attorney, an active Republican, former supervisor of the town of South Chicago, and former secretary of war under Presidents James A. Garfield and Chester A. Arthur. And Robert was a Lincoln.

In fact, just four years earlier, Lincoln nearly became the Republican vice presidential nominee, second on the ticket to James G. Blaine. Lincoln thought the speculation about him was nonsense, but when it became evident he was going to be nominated that time, he immediately telegraphed the Republican convention and forbade his name to be presented. As Robert wrote to an admirer in May 1884, "I have discouraged all use of my name and have no other wish than that the convention will calmly select a man who will unite all our people and enable us to take advantage of the present situation of our opponents. I hope that no such responsibility will be thrust upon me."[2] By 1888, Lincoln had four more years of age, political activism, and legal experience to add to his already impressive résumé. More important, the Republican Party had no clear front-runner for its presidential nomination. Blaine stated that he, as a failed candidate, would not run again. The rest of the party was broken among regional factions. Lincoln became the "dark horse" possibility over whom Republicans salivated and Americans adulated.

In the end, Lincoln's reluctance and political inactivity allowed him to escape nomination and a most probable election. Yet, Lincoln's own worth, in addition to further experience as President Benjamin Harrison's minister to Great Britain and as president of the multi-million-dollar Pullman Company, coupled with his illustrious name, would have his party continue to seek his ascendancy to his father's old office three more times during his life. As the *Chicago Tribune* stated in 1890, "There is one quiet man, not now much talked of, whom all the Presidential aspirants want to keep their eyes on, and that man is Robert T. Lincoln. His name in connection with the Presidential nomination . . . is like a motion to adjourn—it is always in order."[3]

Robert Todd Lincoln was the oldest of Abraham and Mary Lincoln's four children, all sons, and the only son to live to maturity. Robert graduated from Harvard College, served on Ulysses S. Grant's staff during the last months of the Civil War, and afterward undertook the practice of law in Chicago. He became one of the most prominent attorneys in the city during the late nineteenth century. He accepted prestigious civil service positions in the U.S. government and became a captain of industry as the leader of the Pullman Palace Car Company. He was a family man, a businessman, and a philanthropist; he was a self-made man who died a multimillionaire.

Robert T. Lincoln (he never used his middle name, only his middle initial) also was the preserver, protector, and defender of his father's ever-growing reputation, as well as the owner of his father's letters and personal artifacts. In this capacity, which Robert never flaunted, he was besieged by historians, collectors, museums, historical societies, politicians, and the general public, all seeking souvenirs, access, and contact with the surviving link to the Great Emancipator. Robert's attitudes toward the papers and artifacts always remained consistent—he never gave full access to anyone. His relationship with his father's legacy, however, was more complex. He revered his father's memory and agreed with the hagiographical style of biography prevalent at the time, but he was publicly reticent and strove not to insert himself into his father's apotheosis. As Robert aged, his patience thinned, and he eventually became a more outspoken advocate for the purity of his father's memory.

The son of Abraham Lincoln, however, did not allow his father's legacy or memory to control his life, although it imbued it. He did not trade on his name, but others traded for him. He did not seek publicity or public adoration, but such exposure was thrust upon him. Nor did he live under an inferiority complex due to his father's apotheosis and to the expectations of the masses, but such judgments often were made about him.

Robert was a disciplined, hard-working man; he was strong, confident, and self-aware; he was intelligent, witty, kind, gentlemanly, proper, and generous.

Yet he was also impatient: with laziness, with ignorance, with lies and deception, with dishonorable and selfish people; and, once offended, he knew how to hold a grudge, like many of his mother's family. Robert had a great many successes in his life, tempered by failures, setbacks, and controversies. He was a successful attorney, public servant, and businessman with a loving family and good friends. Yet he failed his first attempt to gain entrance to Harvard; he was compelled to commit his mother to a sanitarium; and he lost three brothers, a father, and his only son to early deaths. Robert T. Lincoln was an accomplished man, one of the exemplars of his generation, who, beyond being the son of Abraham Lincoln, should and must be recognized for his independent achievements. On top of all that, Robert's life, from 1843 to 1926, spanned one of the most innovative, impressive, and dynamic eras in American history. During his almost eighty-three years of life, Robert Lincoln witnessed the achievement of major inventions from photography to phonographs to telephones to automobiles to airplanes and multitudes of others.

Robert's life is a fantastic journey through a rich period of American history, and it has been unexamined since John Goff's 1969 biography, *Robert Todd Lincoln: A Man in His Own Right*. Goff's book, long out of print, is an admirable work, but its 286 pages yield a more general overview of Robert's life rather than an in-depth analysis. It is a strong starting place, as is Ruth Painter Randall's 1955 book, *Lincoln's Sons*, but more is available and required for a full understanding of Robert T. Lincoln's life story. Unfortunately, because he was Abraham Lincoln's son, Robert Lincoln long has been subsumed under the "Lincolniana" heading—more than that, he has been often ignored, usually misunderstood, and typically maligned by Lincoln scholars. He is regarded as a Todd rather than a Lincoln, a stuffed shirt, a cold and reclusive man, a superficial snob embarrassed by and disdainful of his common-clay father.

Robert's poor historical reputation has certain causes, the most prevalent of which is the sheer lack of readily available information about who he was and how he lived. This book strives to fill in these gaps. In addition to the typical aspects of his life such as his personality and character, this volume presents his family and social life, his business and political dealings, myriad new facts—unknown and unused in previous Lincoln-related works. These involve famous events such as President Lincoln's assassination, Mary Todd Lincoln's commitment to a sanitarium, the 1876 attempt to steal the body of Abraham Lincoln, the assassination of President Garfield (at which Robert was present), Robert's role in breaking the infamous Pullman Strike of 1894, the accused "slavery" of the Pullman Company towards its porters under Robert's leadership, and the true story about what Robert kept and destroyed of his parents' papers. The more obscure events are his three brushes with death—twice by accidents and once as a target for assassination—his relationship with his father during the Civil War, his stewardship of the Lincoln legacy, the life and death of his only son Abraham "Jack" Lincoln II, and the real reason Robert is buried in Arlington National Cemetery and not in the Lincoln Tomb in Springfield.

Robert Lincoln never wanted to be the subject of a biography and if he were alive today would most certainly have opposed such an endeavor. He more than once told journalists he was "too unimportant a person" to be the subject of an interview or article, and he disliked public speaking.[4] As a carefree college student in 1860, he wrote to his mother, imaging himself laid bare before a large and eager audience, "Just phancy my phelinks mounted on the rostrum, holding 'a vast sea of human faces,' etc. I stop overwhelmed."[5] Whether he would like it or not, his story is the story of American achievement, of Gilded Age success, and of the endurance of the Lincoln legacy.

1

"I Was Born in the Globe Tavern"

The town of Springfield, just west of the geographic center of the state of Illinois, was a pristine, untilled, lonely prairie in the early nineteenth century. It was set within the midst of nine hundred square miles of Sangamon County, on part of territory originally claimed by Kickapoo and Pottawatomie Indians and far from the major American settlements of Chicago and St. Louis.[1] The early pioneers of Springfield began filtering into the Sangamon Valley of central Illinois in 1819, not long after the end of the War of 1812, and less than one year after Illinois officially became a state of the American Union. Settlers were lured by the descriptions of miles of "gently undulating" prairie with rich quality soil interlaced by numerous branches of the Sangamon River.[2] One early settler marveled at the heavy forests on the prairie's edges "festooned with grape vines and fringed with plum and haw bushes, crab-apples, hazelnuts, elders and blackberries, and encircled by millions of strawberry vines."[3]

By 1843, Sangamon County had a population of about sixteen thousand settlers, while Springfield, by then the county seat as well as the state capital, had about three thousand inhabitants.[4] Just four years earlier, one traveler's directory had lauded how "the rough and unseemly cabin is giving place to comfortable framed or brick tenements," and Springfield soon would be the richest, most populous city in the west.[5] The town, comprising nearly thirty blocks and a town square, boasted dozens of stores, groceries, and public houses; numerous lawyers' and physicians' offices; and industrial sites for mechanics and trades of various descriptions, including printing offices for two weekly newspapers. The town's public buildings included a courthouse, jail, market house, several schools, and six churches of various denominations.[6] Into this Illinois city, what easterners considered a frontier town, was born the oldest child of Abraham and Mary Lincoln on August 1, 1843.

The Lincolns were a well-known couple in Springfield. Abraham was a friendly, gregarious attorney, known for his devotion to Whig politics and renowned for his ability as a raconteur. Lincoln also had been a member of the state legislature for four terms and was one of the leading forces behind getting the state capital moved to Springfield from Vandalia in the late 1830s. He moved to Springfield from the little hamlet of New Salem in 1837, the year Springfield officially became the capital. Mary Todd was a Kentucky belle, daughter of Robert Smith Todd, a wealthy banker and politician from Lexington. She moved to Springfield in 1839 and lived with her sister Elizabeth Edwards, the wife of Ninian Edwards, son of the former Illinois governor. The Edwardses were the social leaders of the town, presiding over the soirees of the town's most influential people, known as the Springfield "coterie."

Abraham was well liked in town, and while accepted into the coterie, he was not considered a social equal of the town's more aristocratic members. He was from the backwoods, tall, gaunt and gawky, poor, uncouth, self-educated, and dressed in ill-fitting clothes. Lincoln was "cold" and "abstracted," not social, said his sister-in-law Elizabeth Edwards; he "could not hold a lengthy conversation with a lady, was not sufficiently educated and intelligent in the female line to do so."[7] Mary, on the other hand, was an enchantress, full of charm, culture, and grace, with a high intelligence, a quick wit, and a noticeable beauty.[8] "She is the very creature of excitement," one young lawyer wrote in 1840; Mary's brother-in-law Ninian Edwards said of her, "She could make a bishop forget his prayers."[9] She intoxicated the bachelors of the town and counted among her suitors a grandson of Patrick Henry, future U.S. Senators Stephen A. Douglas, Edward D. Baker, James Shields, and Lyman Trumbull, and, of course, Abraham Lincoln.

Abraham and Mary met at one of the Edwards's many parties. As their niece described it years later, the two made eyes at each other across the room until Lincoln approached and said, "Miss Todd, I want to dance with you in the worst way"; and Mary, after the party, "with a roguish smile and twinkle in her eyes," told her cousin, "[a]nd he certainly did."[10] Most of the townspeople thought the pairing of Abraham Lincoln and Mary Todd an incongruous one. Yet, the two had much in common. They both loved poetry and literature, both believed in Whig political principles and idolized Henry Clay (whom Mary knew personally), both loved children, and both suffered the death of their mother at an early age.[11] Some have contended, both then and today, that Mary chose Abraham over her other suitors because she saw in him his potential greatness. "She loved show and power, and was the most ambitious woman I ever knew," Elizabeth stated years later. "She used to contend when a girl, to her friends in Kentucky, that she was destined to marry a President."[12]

Abraham and Mary became engaged in 1840, despite Elizabeth's admonition against it. Lincoln, however, broke it off either due to self-doubts about his worthiness to be a husband or his interest in another woman.[13] After an eighteen-month hiatus in their relationship, accompanied by much emotional pain on both sides, the two were reunited by mutual friends. Abraham and Mary wed, again against the protests of Elizabeth and Ninian Edwards, on November 4, 1842, at the Edwards home.[14] Lincoln had the phrase "Love is Eternal" inscribed on the inside of Mary's wedding band, and the marriage was, by most accounts, based on a foundation of love.

The Lincolns did not "keep house" after their wedding but boarded at the Globe Tavern, an L-shaped structure a few blocks west of the Springfield public square. They paid $4 per week.[15] The Globe boardinghouse was not a paltry place, and beginning married life there was not an embarrassment. In fact, two other members of the Todd family began their married lives there: John Todd Stuart, Mary's cousin and Lincoln's first law partner, in 1837, and Dr. William S. Wallace and Mary's sister Frances, in 1839.[16] The Lincolns actually followed the Todd family precedent so much that they inhabited the Wallaces' vacated rooms.

As they settled into their new roles of husband and wife, both Abraham and Mary had to acclimatize. "Nothing new here, except for my marrying, which to me, is a matter of profound wonder," Lincoln wrote just days after the nuptials.[17] Mary certainly had the more difficult time as a new wife. Coming from a wealthy Kentucky family, Mary had always had servants to care for her. Now, as the wife of a middle-class lawyer, Mary had to learn to do things such as cooking and cleaning. As a proper daughter of privilege, she already knew how to sew, and not long after her marriage, she began putting those skills to work.

The approaching wonder of parenthood quickly proceeded the wonder of marriage. The first known intimation of the coming event appears in March 1843, when Lincoln wrote to his friend Joshua Speed, "About the prospect of your having a namesake at our house cant say, exactly yet."[18] In May, Lincoln refused an invitation to visit Speed in Kentucky that year, citing poverty, attending to business, and "those 'coming events'" that he suspected "would be somewhat in the way."[19] By July, the Lincolns were eagerly awaiting the birth. "We are two, as yet," he wrote to Speed.[20] The delivery came, attended by two physicians, August 1, 1843, three days short of exactly nine months after the Lincoln marriage.[21] Mary later reminisced on the day "my beloved husband, was bending over me . . . with all the affectionate devotion, which a human being is capable of," when their first son was born.[22] The Lincolns named the boy Robert Todd, after his maternal grandfather, who visited Springfield not long after. "May God bless and protect my little namesake," he had prayed.[23] Baby Robert was short and round—physically more like a Todd than a Lincoln—with gray eyes and brown hair. He also had one lazy eye, like his father, which would later cause him both physical and social troubles. Abraham was said to be relieved that the baby had equal length appendages, telling friends, "I was afraid it might have one leg [long] like mine and one leg [short] like Mary's!"[24]

Interestingly, Robert himself was not certain where he was born. "I seem to recollect having heard as a boy that I was born in the Globe Tavern," Robert wrote to a friend in 1886, "but I have also in later years seen such a newspaper statement and therefore was inclined to think otherwise. It is probably true, however, for what it is worth."[25] Only two written records of Robert's first days exist. A neighbor girl, Sophie Bledsoe, wrote seventy years later that Mary had no nurse to help care for the child or for herself after the birth, so Sophie's mother went over every day to assist. Six-year-old Sophie went along and acted as "amateur nurse" because she loved babies: "I remember well how I used to lug this rather large baby about to my great delight, often dragging him through a hole in the fence between the tavern grounds and an adjacent empty lot, and laying him down in the high grass, where he contentedly lay awake or asleep, as the case might be. I have often since that time wondered how Mrs. Lincoln could have trusted a particularly small six year old with this charge."[26] The second account of Robert as a baby stated he was a "delicate" infant who had "summer complaint," for which his mother would drive around the streets of Springfield every day in the cool of the morning with him on a pillow to help him get well.[27]

The addition of a new baby led the Lincolns to realize that more room was needed for their growing family. In November, they rented a small three-room frame cottage at 214 South Fourth Street. In January 1844, Lincoln contracted with Charles Dresser, the reverend who married him, to purchase Dresser's three-room frame cottage at the corner of Eighth and Jackson Streets. Lincoln paid $1,200 in cash plus a lot on Adams Street he jointly owned with his law partner, Stephen T. Logan.[28] The sale was completed, and the family assumed residence of the Dresser house in May. This house, in which the Lincolns lived for seventeen years and enlarged in 1856, was the only home they ever owned and the place of Robert's upbringing.

Here, the Lincolns settled into their living routines. Mary stayed at home, watched Robert, made his clothes, cooked the meals, and tended house. Sometimes a neighbor girl would come over to help, or the Lincolns would hire a girl. By the time he purchased his house in the spring of 1844, Abraham, twice a junior law partner, had just become the senior partner of his own law firm, hiring William H. Herndon as his junior man. Lincoln divided his time between working at his Springfield office and riding the Eighth Judicial Circuit.[29] By 1845, he was making an annual income of between $1,500 and $2,000, which afforded a modest, but in no way impoverished, scale of living.[30]

Due to their unhappy childhoods, both Abraham and Mary adored and indulged their children. Whether Robert, as the firstborn, was the most spoiled of the Lincoln children or the least spoiled due to his father's frequent absences while on the circuit is impossible to say. It seems as though all the Lincoln boys were given the same upbringing. The parental philosophy of the Lincolns was, "Let the children have a good time."[31] Mary Lincoln later admitted her husband was extremely indulgent to the children: "chided or praised for it he always said, 'It is my pleasure that my children are free, happy and unrestrained by parental tyranny. Love is the chain whereby to lock a child to its parents.'"[32] Mary also reportedly once said that her children never required disciplining, that "a gentle, loving word, was all sufficient with them."[33] Harriet Hanks Chapman (daughter of Lincoln's cousin Dennis Hanks), who lived in the Lincoln home from 1842 to 1844 and worked as a domestic while attending school in Springfield, once told about an instance from Robert's childhood in which Lincoln sanguinely corrected the boy for some misdeed, despite Mary's attempt to supersede him. "She then tried tongue lashing but met with the same fate, for Mr. Lincoln corrected his child as a father ought to do, in the face of his wife's anger and that too without even changing his countenance, or making any reply to his wife."[34]

Much of what is known today about Lincoln and his family, however, comes from Herndon's inimitable research; and his opinion of the Lincolns' parenting skills was not high. He considered Lincoln an overindulgent parent. "His children did much as they pleased. Many of their antics he approved, and he restrained them in nothing. He never reproved them or gave them a fatherly frown."[35] This is not necessarily true, as Chapman's recollection shows, and, besides, Herndon's dislike of the Lincoln children stems more from his later experiences with Willie and Tad than with Robert. One of Herndon's most famous stories tells how Willie and Tad would come to the law office with Lincoln on Sundays and while there were "absolutely unrestrained" in their amusement. They pulled books off shelves, bent the points of pens, overturned inkstands and ash buckets, scattered papers all over the floor, and threw the pencils in the spittoon.[36] During all this, Lincoln was undisturbed, much to Herndon's ire. "Had they s—t in Lincoln's hat and rubbed it on his boots, he would have laughed and thought it smart," Herndon wrote.[37] Although the Lincoln's child-rearing apothem today typically is remembered and applied to the antics of the two youngest Lincoln boys, it applied just as well to Robert, who was raised in the same manner. Commenting once on Tad's boisterousness and lack of schooling during the White House years, Lincoln compared Tad to

Robert, saying, "Let him run, he has time enough yet to learn his letters and get pokey. Bob was just such a little rascal, and now he is a very decent boy."[38]

For all the examination of Abraham Lincoln as a father and of Mary Lincoln as a wife, there is little talk of Mary as a mother. In fact, her role as mother was probably the most important role in Robert's life and growth, as she raised him, much of the time, alone. Abraham even began calling her "Mother" after Robert was born, replacing his previous nickname for her of "Molly." Abraham would ride the judicial circuit and travel for political purposes for six to eight months of the year. Lincoln's sister-in-law later wrote that Lincoln was "the very best kindest father I ever saw," yet even Robert admitted that his relationship with his father was rather distant, stating, "During my childhood and early youth he was almost constantly away from home, attending court or making political speeches."[39] One biographer referred to Mary quite simply as a "single parent."[40] As a consequence, Mary had the primary responsibility to teach her boys manners, social etiquette, reading, writing, and all the other life lessons that parents early instill in their children.[41]

As a child, Robert clearly was showered with an illimitable amount of love from both his parents. Harriet Hanks Chapman remembered that Lincoln was "kind and affectionate" with Robert and was "remarkably fond" of children: "One of his greatest pleasures when at home was that of nursing and playing with his little boy."[42] James Gourley, a Lincoln neighbor, said the same and recollected that Lincoln liked to walk with his children out into the woods and "talk to them, explain things carefully, particularly."[43] Chapman also told how Mary Lincoln once refused to invite her cousin to a party because the cousin had "intimated that Robert who was a baby was a sweet child but not good looking."[44] Gibson William Harris, a law clerk in Lincoln's office between 1845 and 1847, recalled Lincoln telling him about three-year-old Robert falling down the stairs after trying to walk in his father's boots. "You ought to have seen him, Gibson—he looked *so* comical with the boot-legs reaching clear up to his little body," Lincoln said, laughing heartily and breaking into laughter over the incident multiple times for the rest of the day.[45]

Before Robert was three, a second son, Edward Baker, named for Lincoln's political friend Edward D. Baker, was born to the Lincolns. In late 1846, in a revealing letter about his children, Lincoln told of the new addition and gave an insight into Robert's early world:

> We have another boy, born the 10th of March last. He is very much such a child as Bob was at his age—rather of a longer order. Bob is "short and low," and, I expect, always will be. He talks very plainly—almost as plainly as

> any body. He is quite smart enough. I some times fear he is one of the little rare-ripe sort, that are smarter at about five than ever after. He has a great deal of that sort of mischief, that is the offspring of much animal spirits. Since I began this letter a messenger came to tell me, Bob was lost; but by the time I reached the house, his mother had found him, and had him whip[p]ed—and, by now, very likely he is run away again.[46]

A former domestic in the Lincoln house, Margaret Ryan, claimed in later years that Mary would "whip Bob a good deal."[47] Lincoln's cavalier attitude about Robert's "whipping"—most likely a spanking—seems as though this was typical of the nineteenth-century upbringing of "spare the rod and spoil the child." Mary later insisted that neither she nor her husband ever whipped the boys, although such disciplining seems in line with her famously mercurial temper.[48]

The 1840s were formative years for Abraham Lincoln and, as such, greatly influenced his family. He was building a solid and lucrative law practice and professional reputation while also becoming politically well known, respected, and in demand for speeches and rallies. In 1844, he sought his party's nomination to run for a seat in the U.S. House of Representatives but failed. Two years later, he tried again, secured the nomination, and was elected congressman from the Seventh District of Illinois—the only Whig in the state to win an otherwise Democratic national victory. To become a member of the U.S. Congress was an aspiration Lincoln cherished, yet its fulfillment he later found had "not pleased me as much as I expected."[49] Mary, of course, was elated at the promise of recognition, respect, and acceptance into Washington society, things she once knew as a Todd and had longed for since.

Shortly prior to Lincoln's election, Mary became homesick for her childhood home. As a consequence, the Lincolns decided that their trip to Washington for the start of the Thirtieth Congress would first detour for a three-week vacation at the Todd home in Lexington, Kentucky.[50] Not only would it be a homecoming for Mary to see the family she remembered but she also had numerous half-brothers and half-sisters whom she had never met, and nobody in her Lexington-based family other than Robert Todd had ever met her husband or children. The Lincolns rented out their house, and on October 25, 1847, Abraham, Mary, four-year-old Robert, and eighteen-month-old Eddie set out for Lexington.[51] They took a carriage ride to St. Louis, then a steamship to Frankfort, and finally a train to Lexington, in what was a typical, although exhausting, journey for the time. They arrived at the Todd home more than one week later, around November 2.[52]

Emily (also spelled Emilie) Todd Helm, Mary's younger sister, later told an amusing incident that illustrates what an indulgent father Lincoln was and what type of childhood Robert had. Mary's cousin Joseph Humphreys had traveled on the same train as the Lincolns, although he did not know who they were. While the Lincolns waited for their luggage at the Lexington station, Humphreys walked from the railroad to the Todd home, where he told Mary's stepmother of the ordeal of his train ride. "Aunt Betsy, I was never so glad to get off a train in my life," he began. "There were two lively youngsters on board who kept the whole train in a turmoil, and their long-legged father, instead of spanking the brats, looked pleased as Punch and aided and abetted the older one in mischief." When the Todd carriage appeared at the door moments later carrying the troublesome family, Humphreys, seeing them out the window, exclaimed, "Good lord, there they are now." He ran away and was not seen again during the Lincolns' visit.[53]

Robert Smith Todd's home, a two-story, brick building on West Main Street, was a "gentleman's city estate" of fourteen hundred square feet with fourteen rooms and ten fireplaces; outside, the property contained stables and a carriage house, spring house, wash house, kitchen, slave quarters, conservatory, and formal garden. Upon the Lincolns' arrival, the entire Todd family—including the house slaves at the rear of the entrance hall—gathered at the door to welcome Mary home. Mary walked in first with Eddie in her arms, followed by Abraham holding Robert. Eleven-year-old Emily Todd later recalled her "romps on the floor" with her nephew Bob and how her giant brother-in-law, absorbed in reading books from the extensive Todd library, was never disturbed by their boisterous play.[54]

The Todd house and property were a new and impressive world to young Robert. This also probably was the first time the boy encountered slaves and the condition of slavery. What impact this made on him is unknown, but it is known that the Todd family was good to their slaves and that Robert S. Todd himself was a man who "deplored" the existence of slavery.[55] After three weeks of visiting, the Lincolns continued to Washington.[56] Robert later wrote in his Harvard autobiography, "I followed the usual pursuits of infancy and childhood . . . until I was four years old, when I was taken by my parents to Washington D.C., my father being at that time a Member of the House of Representatives. Of my life at Washington my recollections are very faint."[57]

The city of Washington in 1847 was a contradictory place both wondrous and fearsome to a four-year-old boy from Illinois. Robert's first experience in the city was arriving at the rail station at Pennsylvania Avenue and Second Street, contemporarily described as a "mere shed of slight construction, designed only for temporary use, a disgrace both to the [railroad] company and the city," where idle and objectionable people gathered.[58] The family then took a hotel omnibus ride—practically the sole and also very dangerous means of public transportation—to Brown's Hotel.[59] The city, comprising more than six thousand dwellings, numerous private businesses, and government buildings, was described by one resident as "an ill-contrived, ill-arranged, rambling, scrambling village."[60] The houses—a "strange jumble of magnificence and squalor," with mansions and shanties standing side-by-side—all had privies, pigsties, cow sheds, and geese pens in the back yards, although the animals roamed the city streets and alleys freely, rooting among the piles of garbage littered there.[61] Only two streets in the entire city were (poorly) paved, and none were lighted, except a part of Pennsylvania Avenue, and that only during sessions of Congress. Few sidewalks were paved outside the center of the city, being instead made of gravel and ashes ridged in the center.[62] Despite the jumble of buildings in the center of the city, stretches of vacant spaces and sparsely settled areas extended between the Capitol and the White House and out into the suburbs, which contained rural farms.[63]

The city was the national capital, however, and the government buildings and the road and sidewalk leading between them were anything but neglected and dirty. Pennsylvania Avenue, which connected the Capitol to the White House, was laid with large cobblestones, and on the north side of the avenue was a brick sidewalk that extended from the foot of Capitol Hill for more than one mile.[64] The Capitol itself was grand and white (though unfinished, with the temporary dome made of wood and the two congressional wings not yet begun), surrounded by stone steps, monuments, and large shade trees.[65] The Treasury Department was only partly erected, while the State, War, and Navy Departments had separate brick structures. The foundations of the original red-brick Smithsonian Museum were only recently laid and the walls being built.

Within this infrastructure, Robert saw a city teeming with people. Washington had a permanent population of a little less than thirty thousand white residents, eight thousand free black people, and over two thousand slaves. That number vastly multiplied when Congress was in session. A common sight, and one a four year-old boy would not miss, would have been the gangs of slaves chained together, led down the street to a slave trader's business—basically a warehouse for humans—awaiting sale and/or shipment down south. Although Robert had seen slaves at his grandfather Todd's house in Lexington, this may have been the first time he had seen groups of black people chained together and led down the street like a train of animals.

The Lincolns arrived in Washington on December 2, and after a few days of temporary lodging at Brown's Hotel, they took up residence at Mrs. Ann G.

Sprigg's boardinghouse on Capitol Hill.[66] The Sprigg house was the fourth of a row of houses known as Carroll Row, situated on the east side of First Street, between A Street and East Capitol Street.[67] The four Lincolns shared one large room and from their windows had a view of the U.S. Capitol. Besides the Lincoln family, Mrs. Sprigg had eight gentlemen boarders—five of whom were Whig Members of the House—and one other family. One of the boarders, Dr. Samuel C. Busey, remembered Congressman Lincoln as a popular, amiable fellow who was "very simple and approachable in manner, and unpretentious," while Robert "was a bright boy . . . [who] seemed to have his own way."[68]

Despite the success of Abraham's election to Congress, life in Washington was not exactly what the Lincoln family expected. Abraham felt the presence of his family hindered him in attending to business, while Mary felt lonely and contained within the boardinghouse.[69] The Lincolns attended Marine Band concerts on the Capitol grounds on Saturday afternoons, but as newcomers to Washington, they were not embraced within the city's social circles and therefore not invited to gatherings or parties.[70] With her husband constantly busy and she having little female companionship, Mary was rarely seen by the other boarders except at mealtime.[71] Between Mary's self-confinement and her need to care for baby Eddie, who was not yet two years old, Robert's time in Washington was likely spent mostly playing by himself around the boardinghouse. Mary took the boys for walks to the Capitol, the White House grounds, or down to the racetrack on the outskirts of town, if the weather was amenable, or down the "fashionable promenade" of Pennsylvania Avenue during the afternoon social time after the government offices had closed for the day.[72] The custom was for friends to meet and gather, divide and subdivide into various groups, and end with invitations to tea at various homes. Mary had no known acquaintances during this time in Washington, and so her promenades would have been spent with the boys, observing the gaiety, wishing to be included.

One event Robert fondly remembered during his time in Washington was when his father took him to visit the model room of the U.S. Patent Office, one of the wonders of early Washington.[73] The Patent Office building was an immense marble and columned structure covering two city blocks, with an immense Model Room containing about two hundred thousand models of American inventions as well as priceless items of historic interest and curiosity. Models could be inspected anytime by anyone, and, according to one history of the Patent Office, the model-room gallery was visited yearly by thousands of people.[74] Lincoln and son, amazed at the number of inventions they saw, there decided that man's ingenuity and mastery over nature were so great that there was nothing new left to discover.[75] Ironically, only one year later, Abraham

Lincoln himself contributed another new invention to the world and a new model to the collection of the patent office.[76]

While Robert was young to appreciate his surroundings, life in Washington in 1847–48 was a notable time. The country was in the midst of the Mexican War, which had turned the capital into a gigantic fortress surrounded and imbued by military encampments, fortifications, parade grounds, hospitals, wagon yards, mule pens, "and other munitions of warfare."[77] The streets were constantly filled with moving troops, as well as with that inevitable concomitant to war: contrabands, refugees, camp followers, tramps, scalawags, money changers, and office seekers. There was vociferous opposition to the war, including resolutions and a House floor speech by Robert's father, Congressman Lincoln, who believed the war to be illegally begun by Democrat President James K. Polk for the sole purpose of territorial expansion. Lincoln condemned the war and demanded to know the exact spot of land on which the conflict started.[78] Then in February 1848, while in the midst of a House session, former President John Quincy Adams, then a representative from Massachusetts, collapsed in his seat and died two days later.[79] Lincoln was appointed to the "committee of thirty" to superintend the funeral ceremonies and marched in the funeral procession. On July 4, 1848, the cornerstone was laid for the Washington Monument, a tribute to General George Washington, a ceremony that Congressman Lincoln would have attended.[80]

Robert and the rest of the family, however, did not see this momentous event. By the early spring of 1848, Mary had had enough of life in a Washington boardinghouse, so she and the boys returned to Lexington. There they stayed until September in the comfortable Todd house on West Main Street and also at Buena Vista, the Todd summer home. Buena Vista, a tall, frame house with a double portico in the front and a long porch on the side, was connected to two stone slave cabins. Large locust trees surrounded the house, which was situated on a knoll and punctuated at its base by a tiny brook. Robert enjoyed great freedom and fun during his spring and summer in Lexington, in weather much warmer than Washington, with freedom to leave the house and play outdoors with little brother, Eddie, and resuming his relationship with little Emily, with whom he had had such good romps on his first visit.[81]

There also was more specific excitement for the boys. In August, two circuses came to Lexington and paraded down Main Street—right in front of the Todd home—with music, a multitude of exotic animals, clowns, harlequins, acrobats, pantomimes, and "many other wonderful and impressive objects collected from remote parts of the Globe."[82] That same month, the county was in an upheaval as word spread that seventy-five slaves had escaped from their masters and were headed, armed and dangerous, toward the Ohio River. Residents, in an angry furor, decrying abolitionists who enticed slave insurrections, held a fiery mass meeting to organize pursuit of the fugitives. The sixteen masters whose slaves had fled offered a $5,000 reward ($100 to $200 per slave) for the slaves' capture. The businesses and parlors of Lexington echoed with angry and fearful talk, while on the streets hundreds of possemen scoured the countryside on horse, on foot and with dogs, by daylight and by lantern and torchlight, in search of the band, all of whom were quickly captured.[83] Once again, as with the chain gangs of slaves on the streets of Washington, slavery revealed its violent face to Robert.

During the Lincoln family's stay in Lexington, Abraham and Mary wrote many letters, although few of them have been preserved.[84] The letters show a great love between the Lincolns and a great love for their children, whom Lincoln referred to affectionately as "the dear codgers" and "the dear rascals."[85] In April 1848, about one month after his family went to Kentucky, Lincoln was obviously sad and lonely. He told his wife, "In this troublesome world, we are never quite satisfied. When you were here, I thought you hindered me some in attending to business; but now, having nothing but business—no variety—it has grown exceedingly tasteless to me. I hate to sit down and direct documents, and I hate to stay in this old room by myself."[86] This letter also shows Lincoln's paternal tenderness. He went shopping for plaid stockings for "Eddy's dear little feet" and was worried, due to a dream he had had, about Robert: "I did not get rid of the impression of that foolish dream about dear Bobby till I got your letter written the same day. What did he and Eddy think of the little letters father sent them? Don't let the blessed fellows forget father."[87]

In May, Mary wrote a letter to her husband as clearly loving as his, assuring him, "How much, I wish instead of writing, we were together this evening, I feel very sad away from you." She also had an anecdote about the boys.

> Uncle S[amuel Todd] was to leave there [Springfield] on yesterday for Ky—Our little Eddy, has recovered from his spell of sickness—Dear boy, I must tell you a story about him—Bobby in his wanderings today, came across in a yard, a little kitten, *your hobby*, he says he asked a man for it, he brought it triumphantly to the house, so soon as Eddy, spied it—his *tenderness*, broke forth, he made them bring it *water*, fed it with bread himself, with his *own dear hands*, he was a delighted little creature over it, in the midst of his happiness Ma came in, she you must know disliked the whole cat race, I thought in a very unfeeling manner, she ordered the servant near, to throw it out, which, of *course*, was done, Ed—screaming & protesting loudly against the

> proceeding, *she* never appeared to mind his screams, which were long and loud I assure you.

Mary also suggested that she and the boys might return to Washington in July, accompanying her uncle on his way from Lexington to Philadelphia. "You know I am so fond of sightseeing, and I did not get to New York or Boston, or travel the lake route," she wrote, teasing her husband that she, in fact, may linger on the road before arriving in Washington.[88] An excited Abraham replied, "Come on just as soon as you can. I want to see you, and our dear—*dear* boys very much. Everybody here [in the boardinghouse] wants to see our dear Bobby."[89] Mary, however, did not travel with her uncle and did not return to the capital until late July or early August. After Congress adjourned on August 14, the Lincolns stayed in Washington until early September while Abraham worked on campaign mailings.[90]

Congressman Lincoln then was invited to speak at the Massachusetts Whig State Convention at Worcester on September 12, and the family used the opportunity for some sightseeing in Boston, just as Mary had desired in her previous letter.[91] They left Washington on September 5 for New York City; after a few days sightseeing there, the family headed for Boston on September 9.[92] Mary and the boys then stayed in Boston while Abraham spent the next ten days campaigning for the Whig party across Massachusetts. The stay in Boston lasted longer than planned, as the family was "detained by the illness of our little boy [Eddie]," Mary later wrote.[93] The Lincolns then traveled first to New York City and on their way to Buffalo, where, on September 26, they fulfilled Mary's desire to "travel the lake route" when they boarded the steamer *Globe* for the ten-day trip to Chicago. From Chicago, they spent five more days, first by canal, then by stagecoach, traveling to Springfield.[94]

By the time he was five years old, Robert had become a well-traveled boy. In one year, he had journeyed more than one thousand miles—by stage, rail, canal boat, and lake steamer—from Illinois to Washington and back again in a circular route traversing nine states and four Great Lakes.[95] He had visited wealthy relatives and witnessed the southern slave culture of Kentucky. He had lived in the nation's capital for almost four months and experienced the political and cultural experiences it offered, as well as the wartime events and slave trading that occurred in the streets. He had seen the major cities of New York and Boston and traveled nearly fifteen hundred miles across the Great Lakes. Robert was a precocious boy, and the impact of this year was palpable. Not only that but seeing the respect with which his congressman father was treated and witnessing him working on important national matters also was impressive. Indeed, this trip, plus a boy's natural idolization of his parents and Abraham's frequent absences, had a profound impact on Robert and one that led him to work diligently to be an impressive and admirable son.

When the Lincolns returned to Springfield on October 10, they could not return to their little cottage at the corner of Eighth and Jackson Streets because it still was under rental contract. Instead, the family lodged downtown at the Globe Tavern—returning to Abraham and Mary's first marital residence and Robert's birthplace. The Globe had changed owners since the Lincolns' first stay there in 1843, and the building had been much expanded and improved.[96] Lincoln had to return to Washington at the end of November, and instead of having Mary care for children and a house by herself, he extended the rental of his house until February 1849, and Mary stayed on at the Globe.[97]

Abraham Lincoln left Springfield to return to Washington for the next session of Congress in late November, but he did not go alone. He took five-year-old Robert with him. Traveling the same route as they had on their first journey to Washington in 1847, father and son traveled to Lexington so Robert could spend the winter with his grandfather.[98] During Robert's four months in Lexington—from late November 1848 to late March 1849—he resumed his friendships with his Aunt Emily and Uncle Alec, perhaps was tutored along with the Todd children, and certainly suffered stringent lessons about morals and manners of his stepgrandmother, Betsey Todd. Robert also spent time with his grandfather, visiting the cotton business in which Robert Todd was a partner or visiting the state legislature where the elder Todd was active in politics. Historian Ruth Painter Randall states that Robert's winter at the Todd home made an enormous impression on his five-year-old psyche and that there he assumed the Todd family's aristocratic airs that made him, in her mind, so un-Lincoln:

> The Todd relatives had so much to offer in contrast to the modest household of his odd lawyer father who had grown up in the backwoods. The Todd ancestors had a distinguished record, they had occupied positions of trust and honor, they were intelligent, gifted, determined people, excellent fighters as soldiers, and patriotic citizens. The Todd kin whom Robert knew had the things he liked, high standards of social correctness, prosperity and the comfortable type of living that goes with it. It is easy to see how he could have come under their influence and looked at matters through their eyes.[99]

Robert S. Todd probably did make an imprint of respectability and propriety on his grandson, impressing little Robert with his education, achievements, and public service, but this time would only have been the substratum of Robert's later character change at college. No, what truly made Robert's time in Lexington so important was that it was the cementing of a relationship with his Aunt Emily that would span the next seventy-eight years. This would be one of the closest relationships of Robert's long life, with the exchange of many visits and hundreds of letters.[100] It also created a kinship with the entire Todd clan that Robert never ignored, especially in later years when he helped his relatives out with loans of money and with assistance obtaining government positions.

When Abraham Lincoln returned to Springfield from Washington in March 1849 at the end of his congressional term, he stopped in Lexington to bring Robert back to Springfield. They returned to Mary and Eddie at the Globe Tavern—and the threat of a cholera epidemic in Springfield—on March 31, 1849.[101] Abraham Lincoln's time in Congress has been termed a failure by historians, and, upon his return from Washington, even Lincoln thought it was so. As the Springfield Whigs had agreed to rotation in congressional office, Lincoln was not nominated for a second term in the House. His opposition to the Mexican War and his "spot resolutions," however, damned the Whigs as unpatriotic, and they lost the seat entirely in 1848, despite Zachary Taylor's presidential win. Lincoln's services to the party, especially his New England speaking tour, earned him respect but not the appointment he desired as commissioner of the General Land Office. He was offered both the secretaryship and the governorship of the Oregon Territory but declined.[102]

The Lincolns chose to stay in Springfield. There, they resumed their pre-Washington life. Lincoln focused on his law practice, politics, and his family; Mary resumed the domestic roles of housekeeper, cook, and seamstress; Robert began attending school. Times were happy, but just eleven months later, death would strike the Lincoln house in a tragedy that would leave an indelible impression on young Robert.

2

"Is Bicarb a Swear Word?"

By the time the Lincoln family resumed occupancy of its house on the corner of Eighth and Jackson Streets in April 1849, Robert was nearly six years old. He returned to life in a house lit by candles and heated by fireplaces, where water was pumped from wells or rainwater collected in a cistern, where to be clean was to bathe once a week with every family member taking a turn in the used water. It meant privies and bedpans, the endless chopping of firewood, caring for horses in the barn and milking the family cow; it meant homemade clothes and patched clothes; it meant simple foods such as corn bread and salted, smoked pork, whatever fruits and vegetables were in season, and to drink only coffee, tea, milk, or water.[1] In this world, children relied on their imaginations for entertainment, playing games, reading or being read books, creating their own stories.

The Springfield in which Robert grew during the late 1840s and 1850s was a vibrant, rapidly growing mid-Western city. In 1849, the population was approximately four thousand inhabitants, a number that would practically double over the ensuing decade, while the downtown area contained sixty-one local businesses of every conceivable profession.[2] By the early 1850s, a free public school district had been established, as had the Illinois State University; the Chicago-Alton railroad line had come to town, and a regular county fair had been created.[3] The more prominent characteristics of the town to Robert's preteen eyes, however, were more likely the dusty streets that turned into deep quagmires of inky, black mud when it rained, the few and uneven plank sidewalks, the sound of horses hooves and jangling carriages on the streets, the smells of the horses and their manure in the road, the sight and smell of pigs freely roaming the city and rooting in the ground, and the miles and miles of prairie that began literally in his backyard.[4] Wagon trains of pioneers would sometimes pass through Springfield on their way farther west to the promise of California. During the spring gold rush of 1849, eager parties left Springfield every few days, with the total exodus estimated at nearly 150 people.[5]

Ex-Congressman Lincoln resumed his law practice—disappointed and embarrassed that none urged him to run for a second term in the House—going to the office every morning, visiting friends in the drugstore or on the street, and telling his famous stories. Mary resumed the duties of a housekeeper, cooking meals, making clothes for the family, cleaning the house. She was again near family and friends and had company during the days. She also returned to the familiarity of attending her own church on Sundays and on every Thursday hosting a sewing group to make clothing for the poor.[6] Being in charge of an entire house again also meant the hiring of a girl to help her keep the house. One black woman who worked as a nurse for the Lincolns at this time, Ann Ruth Stanton, remembered that life in the Lincoln home at this time was modest but not impoverished. She recollected how the affluent children in town would avoid or tease Robert because he wore blue-jeaned pants that his mother made and patched when he wore holes in them. "The children, Robert, 5 years old, and [Eddie], a few years younger, were very good boys," she remembered. "We would play around the streets of Springfield, and the white children would throw stones at the colored children." Stanton stated that she would scrub the floors and wait on the table and help Mary clean the dishes and do the washing, and Mary did all the upstairs work, made clothes for Robert and Eddie, and cooked the meals. "Mrs. Lincoln was a very nice lady," she said.[7] Of course, not all of Mary's hired girls thought so highly of her. In later years, due to his wife's mercurial temper, Lincoln had to secretly pay girls extra money to keep them around.[8]

Here, the Lincolns were happy. They had returned to a place of familiarity, populated with family and friends. They could visit these people during the days or have or attend parties at night. Family evenings in the Lincoln home consisted of reading and of playing games such as blind man's bluff, chess, and checkers.[9] "Mr. Lincoln's home life was all happiness and content so far as I could even know," remembered one neighbor. "He seemed to idolize his wife and boys and they one and all sincerely loved him."[10]

Unfortunately, life is such that even in the midst of happiness, as Mary once wrote, "[T]rouble comes soon enough."[11] On July 17, 1849, Robert S. Todd died from a cholera outbreak that hit Lexington.[12] To make matters worse, Mary's youngest brother, George Todd, contested the will. Abraham Lincoln became the legal adviser to Mary and her three Springfield sisters. The Lincolns returned to Lexington in November 1849 to settle the business.[13] Not long after the Lincolns return from Lexington, Eddie, always a sickly boy, turned ill again with what later was determined to be tuberculosis. From this illness, unlike previous times, he could not recover. While worrying about their youngest boy, the Lincolns were informed of the death of Mary's maternal grandmother, Elizabeth Parker, on January 22, 1850.[14] This was a severe blow to Mary, especially after her father's death, for Elizabeth Parker was Mary's childhood relief from a stepmother she disliked. The biggest loss for the Lincoln family, however, was yet to come. Just six days later, on February 1, 1850, after a fifty-two-day struggle, Eddie died. It was one month before his fourth birthday.[15]

The death of Edward Lincoln had a profound impact on the Lincoln family. Mary's emotional nature, especially at the death of a loved one, has become well known. But adding the death of her baby to those of her father and grandmother was egregious. Mary was so distraught that she shut herself in her room for days and refused to eat or sleep, forcing Lincoln finally to plead, "Mary, you must eat, for we must live."[16] Lincoln himself suffered a profound grief at Eddie's death but "resolved to keep his feelings under a firm sway."[17] Lincoln's only written mention of his loss, simple and painfully controlled, came three weeks later when he informed his stepbrother, "We lost our little boy. . . . We miss him very much."[18]

Funeral rites of the day required that the dead boy be laid out overnight before burial. His body would have been washed and dressed and "sat up with" until morning, most likely by Mary's sisters.[19] The Reverend James Smith, of the First Presbyterian Church, visited the Lincolns at their home. He prayed with them and for them and prayed over Eddie's corpse.[20] Robert would have witnessed these things. Then, dressed in a little suit, he would have participated in his brother's funeral, the short procession to Hutchinson's Cemetery a few blocks west, and the burial, finished by Dr. Smith's eulogy. Returning home, the full impact of life without Eddie—to Robert and his parents, collectively and as individuals—became more pronounced in the grim, muted, funereal pall.

A few weeks after Eddie's death, the Lincolns returned to Lexington so Abraham could settle the estate of Grandmother Parker and continue work on the estate of Robert Todd.[21] Once the litigation was finished, Abraham returned to Springfield to attend to business while Mary and Robert lingered in Lexington for a "more extensive visit" at the Todd summer home, Buena Vista.[22] Here, Robert resumed play with his Aunt Emily and his Uncle Alec, and the two boys "scampered about on ponies, slid down the ice-house roof and romped with the dogs," Emily later remembered.[23] While Mary herself was glad to be home and gossiping about family and old friends, she was often "very sad, and grieving for her little dead baby and for our father."[24]

Back in Springfield in the spring of 1850 after Eddie's death, the Lincoln family changed somewhat not only by grief but through a deeper devotion to religion.[25] Dr. Smith's ministering after Eddie's death touched the Lincolns so much that Mary left the Episcopal church to join his First Presbyterian Church congregation. Abraham, at this time, was more a deist than a subscriber to any particular denomination. But in the midst of his anguish, perhaps wanting to find a deeper faith, he found solace through a book he discovered in the Todd home during the spring 1850 visit. *The Christian's Defense* was a retort to atheist arguments against the truth of the Bible. To Lincoln's surprise, the author was none other than Reverend James Smith, the pastor whose words had so soothed the Lincolns' pain after their son's death. Upon returning to Springfield, Lincoln sought out Dr. Smith for an interview, where the pastor found him "much depressed and downcast at the death of his son and without the consolation of the gospel."[26] Following his discussion with Smith, Lincoln finished reading *The Christian's Defense*, which, according to multiple witnesses, changed his view on the Christian religion, led him to rent a pew in Smith's church, and to attend services regularly with Mary whenever he was home from riding the circuit.[27]

Religion was a large part of Robert's childhood, although his own religious beliefs are as mysterious as some consider his father's.[28] Robert as a toddler attended Sunday school at the Episcopal church and continued the practice later when the Lincolns joined the Presbyterian church.[29] Mary took Robert to Presbyterian revival services, held sewing circles every week comprising fellow church members, and attended other church events.[30] While Abraham's religion was not so overt as his wife's, he frequently read the Bible and also owned John Bunyan's *Pilgrim's Progress*—which was one of the first "large books" that Robert ever read—as well as "a few" other religious works.[31] In addition to religious observances, Robert also learned morality and charity from his parents' examples, such as his father's simple honesty and integrity in everything he did, his mother's weekly sewing for the poor, and a now-famous incident in which the Lincolns helped nurse a neighbor's baby when the mother was too sick to do it.[32] As a grown man, Robert, while a Presbyterian church trustee in Chicago but not a member, was also a kind, conscientious, and charitable man. Religion, however, was not the anodyne for a not-quite-seven-year-old boy that it was for his parents. Indeed, with Abraham attending to business at his office and on the circuit, and Mary overwhelmed with grief, Robert was likely lonely and morose. He had lost his only sibling, which would later leave him in a sense set apart from the family circle. Robert was seven years older than the third Lincoln boy, William Wallace, called Willie by the family, and nine years older than Thomas, known as Tad; and although the two young boys were close companions, Robert lived a separate life. As physician and historian W. A. Evans wrote about the disparity in 1932, "Those men with whom I have talked of their Lincoln associations have referred to themselves as playmates of Robert or playmates of Willie and Tad, but never as playmates of Robert *and* the younger boys. Had Edward lived, he would have bridged this gap."[33]

Robert also was a cognizant, precocious seven-year-old who recognized his parents' reaction to the death. Most immediate to Robert was his mother's anguish. Although Abraham and other friends and neighbors and family would have comforted her, the real burden fell to Robert. He was the only child left, doted on and coveted for his survival, and old enough to understand his mother's grief and seek to make her happy and comforted. When Abraham left the house to go to his office, Robert would have been alone with his mother, enduring her suffering, avoiding it, or trying to comfort it. When Abraham left the house to ride the judicial circuit—which he did from April 3 to April 22 and again from April 25 to June 3—Robert was Mary's only day-to-day support.[34] This is likely the underpinning for the close relationship Robert and Mary enjoyed for decades to come. It also was likely the beginning of Robert's lifelong devotion to protecting his mother, both from her own extreme emotionalism and self-centeredness and from the actions and opinions of others. It was a duty he continued throughout his entire life.

As always, in the midst of death there was also life. Just one month after Eddie's passing, Mary became pregnant with the Lincolns' third child—an attempt to alleviate some of the parents' grief. William Wallace Lincoln was born on December 21, 1850, and the fourth boy, Thomas "Tad" Lincoln, was born April 4, 1853. The addition of two babies into the house, when Robert was seven and nine years old, respectively, changed the family dynamic and added to Robert's responsibilities. He surely would have helped his parents, especially his mother, care for the new additions. When Abraham was gone from home, Robert did the male chores, such as chopping firewood, milking the family cow, and taking it to and from the pasture. He also helped his mother by going to the downtown stores to purchase necessities for her.[35]

Robert's life in the 1850s was rather normal, full of ups and downs, pleasure and pain; his childhood was one of friends, fun, and childish devilry. Isaac R. Diller, a friend of the Lincoln boys and son of Springfield druggist Roland Diller, stated that Mary would not let her boys use "rough language." He remembered:

> One day when Robert was small he came to my father's drug store on an errand and spotted a label reading "Soda Bicarb."
>
> "Mr. Diller," he inquired, "is Bicarb a swear word?" "Why no, Robert, it's the abbreviation for bicarbonate," father answered.
>
> "Well then," said Robert, happy in having at last found a means of expressing himself, "I'm going to Bi-carb our old horse all over town!"[36]

Robert was reported by a childhood friend to be "considered by his mates somewhat wild" during his boyhood years in Springfield: "A circus exhibition in Springfield once lured him away, and when his friends found him, Bob was almost in the costume of a Texan, i.e. with nothing but hat and boots. A good drubbing soon took the romance out of him." A neighbor remembered, "Bob used to harness cats. Bob and my boy used to harness up my dog and they would take him and go out into the woods and get nuts."[37] One Springfield resident recalled Robert and a friend filching a quantity of lead pipe from a house undergoing construction and then selling the pipe at the downtown hardware store. A shocked Lincoln marched his son down to the store, made Robert admit his crime, paid for the pipe, and then returned it to the owner.[38]

One of Robert's more infamous shenanigans occurred when he and his friends, inspired by the visitation of a "wild animal" show to Springfield, attempted to wrangle cats and dogs and put on a show of their own in the Lincoln barn. The boys tried to train two big dogs to be lions and stand on their hind legs and growl. As the dogs were heavy and uncooperative, the boys decided to put ropes around each dog's neck, sling the ropes over the barn rafters, and then hoist up the dogs. A neighbor heard the dogs' howls and the boys' screams, ran to Lincoln's law office, and told him a crowd of boys was hanging animals in his barn, and two of the animals were already dead. Lincoln, who despised cruelty to animals, rushed to the barn with a barrel stave in his hand, rescued the poor creatures, and scolded and swatted any boys not smart enough to run away.[39]

Robert, just like Willie and Tad, emulated his father in his love of stories, jokes, and pranks. As a young man, he often was characterized as a worthy son to the famous raconteur. One childhood friend said Robert liked to tease his mother: "He delighted in tormenting his mother. I've seen her fly into a rage at his pranks."[40] Robert also was remembered as the "head of pranks" during his four years at the Illinois State University in the late 1850s, leading the other boys in mischief such as covering the school's prayer-room floor with manure and other sweepings and even buying a horse skeleton to leave in the doorway of the Latin professor, who, when he opened the door, had to catch the falling bones![41] Yet, despite his impish ways, Robert was also a polite and rather disciplined young boy, due not only to his mother's careful training but no doubt also to Betsey Todd's strict discipline during his visits to Lexington. Robert's Aunt Emily, who, as a sixteen-year-old girl, visited the Lincolns for six months during 1854–55, recalled Robert as "quite a little Chesterfield," who "would help us out of the carriage" and gather wild flowers and "carry home great armfuls."[42]

Robert's childhood, while full of fun, was not free from danger or injury. Once, as a small boy barely able to walk, Robert's adventurous and inquisitive nature led him to the lime box in the backyard beside the privy. Finding her son with a little of the poisonous powder in his mouth, Mary ran into her front yard hysterical, screaming, "Bobbie will die! Bobbie will die!" A neighbor ran over and washed out the baby's mouth, and no damage was done.[43] Robert also was bitten by a rabid dog as a boy, and Abraham took his son to Terre Haute, Indiana, to be healed with a mad-stone, a common folk remedy for rabies.[44] "Great apprehension was felt for the young hopeful's escape from hydrophobia," wrote Ward H. Lamon. "Mr. Lincoln more than anyone else feared for the life of his first born."[45] The aftermath of the incident is unknown, so either the dog was not rabid or Robert's immune system was able to fight off the infection.

Robert's major medical problem as a child, which he actually endured his entire life, was a condition called right esotropia, a common form of strabismus, in which the right eye turns inward. Abraham Lincoln's left eye turned upward (called a left hypertropia). Although strabismus tends to run in families, it is not clear whether the gaze defects of father and son were related.[46] This defect caused Robert ridicule as a child, as his peers and playmates teased him with the nicknames Cockeye and Cross-eyed Bob.[47] Conjecture has been that Robert may have undergone surgery in an attempt to correct his gaze defect, but the evidence is scanty and speculative.[48] For such a procedure, the surgeon would have gone behind the eye and either cut a tendon and then either lengthened or shortened it to force a straightening or else adjusted the weak eye muscle causing the convergence.[49] Such surgery was a last resort, rarely done on children at that time because the operation was delicate, the recovery extremely painful, and the affected eye susceptible to deformities.[50] Most cases of strabismus, then and now, were fixed through orthoptic exercises, usually by covering the good eye to strengthen the weak eye.[51] One early biographer of Robert stated the boy stared through the keyhole of a door to cure his affliction, although there is no proof to justify the statement.[52]

Whether Robert underwent surgery or peeped through keyholes or wore a special orthoptic mask cannot be firmly established. What is known, however, is that Robert eventually became blind in his right eye. "I have been pulling along with only one eye for many years, in a lopsided way, like a cab-horse in Vienna," he wrote in 1894.[53] Such vision loss is a common occurrence of uncorrected strabismus, what one physician labeled a "natural suppression" of vision, without which the afflicted person would suffer double vision.[54] One source stated it was "an imperfect operation" that caused Robert's blindness.[55] Either way, Robert rarely mentioned his vision loss, and his only stated regret about it was being unable to enjoy the sport of shooting.[56] He worried that sight in his good eye may not last his life, but it did, and as an old man he spent much time reading.[57] The teasing Robert suffered as a boy may have caused him to become self-conscious about his "squint," as it is sometimes called, but there is no evidence that his condition made him a shy or reserved person, as all his classmates, associates, and friends recalled him as a sociable, gregarious, charming boy and man.

Besides his eye, one of the great trials of Robert's childhood was dealing with his mother, who suffered from anxiety and what was most likely bipolar disorder.[58] During the Springfield years, it was familiarly stated that Mary was "always either in the garret or the cellar."[59] Stories abound of Mary's love for her children, her intelligence and charming wit, her sweet disposition and social graces. One neighborhood boy remembered that Mary was never impatient with all the boys playing at her house: "Instead of being harsh with us when we were too boisterous in her house or in her yard she would give us cookies and other good things to eat and in other ways was motherly and kindly, and always had the regard of the boys, although not to the extent that her husband had."[60]

Yet, Mary also was childish, petty, selfish, frequently mean, and often high-strung. She suffered bouts of depression and migraine headaches, both of which would have incapacitated her. In her anxiety, if she ever could not find Robert (which was almost every day), she would shriek from her front yard, arms waving, "Bobbie is lost! Bobbie is lost!" when often he was simply at a neighbor's house.[61] Mary was terrified of being alone in the house, especially at night. She feared burglars and fires and, especially, thunderstorms. Gibson William Harris, a law clerk in the Lincoln-Herndon law office in the late 1840s, stated that Mary was "unusually timid and nervous during a thunderstorm and whenever one threatened[,] her husband made it a point to leave whatever he was engaged upon and go home and stay with her till it passed over."[62] Abraham or Mary often would engage a neighbor man or boy to sleep at the Lincoln home while Lincoln was away until Robert was old enough to act as protector.

In addition to headaches, depression, and irrational fears, Robert also witnessed his mother's infamous temper, which would cause her to lash out at anyone in her path, although she usually was contrite once her anger passed.[63] Stories of her screaming at Abraham, chasing him with a butcher's knife, throwing firewood at him, and locking him out of the house have become legendary.[64] Robert witnessed and endured this aspect of his mother until he left home at age sixteen (and, later, as an adult). Her many troubles probably made Robert simultaneously attached and detached to her—seeking to protect her from herself as well as others, as he did after Eddie's death and would for her entire life, but also embarrassed and, at times no doubt, injured by her anger. As he grew older, Robert may have wished his father would take his mother more firmly in hand to suppress her outbursts and would have recognized how peculiar and deft any handling of her moods had to be.

Mary's temper actually had the tangential effect of creating more time between Robert and his father by more than once driving them out of the house. One neighbor recalled seeing the outcast Lincoln and Robert eating breakfast at a saloon on Monroe Street when, at the end of the meal, Lincoln supposedly said, 'Well, Bobby, this ain't so very bad after all, is it? If ma don't conclude to let us come back we will board here all summer.'"[65] Lincoln's law partner William H. Herndon remembered:

> Many and many a time have I known Lincoln to come down to our office, sometimes Bob with him, with a small lot of cheese, crackers, and "bologna" sausages under his arm; he would not speak to me, for he was full of sadness, melancholy, and I suppose of the devil; he would draw out the sofa, sit down on it, open his breakfast, and divide between Bob and himself. I would as a matter of course know that Lincoln was driven from home, by a club, knife, or tongue, and so I would let down the curtain on the inside, go out, and lock the door behind me, taking the key out with me. I would stay away, say an hour, and then I would go into the office on one pretense or another, and if Lincoln did not then speak, I did as before, go away, etc. In the course of another hour I would go back, and if Lincoln spoke, I knew it was all over, i.e., his fit of sadness, etc.[66]

But these forced retreats were not the only time Robert spent with his father. Indeed, Robert and Abraham seemed as close as father and son could be, given Lincoln's constant absence from home and, later, Robert's time away at school. A solid indication of what Abraham was like as a father to Robert can—and should—be taken from his interactions with Willie and Tad. More is known about the two younger Lincoln boys, who were covered more in the press as Lincoln became known on the national stage, but it is likely that Lincoln treated his first son nearly the same if not exactly the same as he did his third and fourth sons. Accounts of Lincoln and his last two sons relate that Lincoln indulged his children, played with them, loved their pranks and ideas, and was rarely seen on the streets of Springfield without one or the other sitting on his shoulders. Lincoln took his boys with him most places when he could, and he loved their company. One neighbor remembered Lincoln was fond of horses and enjoyed the races at the county fair, to which he would go, in attendance "always by some of us boys," including his oldest son.[67] Robert once recalled traveling alone with his father through a region Lincoln realized he had surveyed as a young man. "On several occasions he stopped the buggy, and laughingly asked me to go a little distance in the woods where I would find a blazed tree, which he described, which he had marked as a survey corner. . . . He did this several times and never made a mistake once."[68]

Robert also accompanied his father on important occasions, such as the dedication of town of Lincoln, Illinois, in 1853. It is the only town named for Abraham Lincoln during his lifetime. In an 1884 campaign speech in Lincoln, then–Secretary of War Robert Lincoln stated, "This is a city in which I have always taken a kind and personal interest, not only because it bears the name of my father, but because I myself was here about thirty years ago when the only building on this ground was a covered wagon."[69] Tradition states that Abraham Lincoln christened the town by selecting two watermelons from a merchant's covered wagon, squeezing the juice of one into a tin cup and pouring the juice on the ground, then sharing the watermelons with the three town fathers who were present.[70] "The youngest American on the ground shall feast with me on the christening watermelon," Lincoln supposedly said, in what was perhaps a reference to sharing the watermelon with his ten-year-old son.[71]

During the 1850s, Robert was not only a growing adolescent and an eldest son but also an older brother. One story by George T. M. Davis illustrates Robert as a typical big brother who occasionally took advantage of his younger siblings. One incident Davis liked to tell was to show how Abraham Lincoln instilled the "cardinal virtues" into his boys.

> I made a visit on business one summer to Springfield, where Mr. Lincoln resided. While I was standing on the sidewalk, on the shady side of the hotel where I was stopping, Mr. Lincoln came along with his youngest pet boy, Tad, who was holding on the tip of the tail of father's frock coat. We drew up chairs in the shade and at once engage in talking politics. Tad changed his position by taking refuge between his father's knees, and remained there a silent listener during our conversation. In a short time Bob, who was considerably older than Tad, came along, and, noticing us, also stopped and joined our circle. In a side conversation that ensued between the two brothers, the purport of which I had not noticed, something was said that induced the father to pause for a moment in his talk with me, and, turning to the boys, he exclaimed:
>
> "Tad, show Mr. Davis the knife I bought you yesterday," and, turning to me, he added, "it's the first knife Tad ever had, and it's a big thing for him."
>
> Tad hesitating and making no reply, his father asked, "You haven't lost your knife, have you?"
>
> "No, but I ain't got any," the boy replied.
>
> "What has become of it?" inquired Mr. Lincoln in his quizzical and usual smiling, pleasant way. There was another momentary pause on the part of Tad, when he replied to his father, in the fullness of his childish simplicity, and the truthfulness which was a prominent element of his birthright:

"Bob told me if he was me, he'd swap my knife for candy."

At this Mr. Lincoln gave one of his good natured laughs, and turning to Bob—who by this time bore somewhat of the semblance of slight embarrassment—but without the slightest change in either his merry tone or manner, asked:

"Bob, how much did you pay for the candy?"

Bob, naming the price, his father said to him, "Why Tad's knife cost three bits (37½ cents); do you think you made a fair trade with Tad?"

Bob, in a prompt and manly tone, which I shall never forget, answered the father, "No, sir," and taking the knife out of his pocket, said "Here, Tad, is your knife," which Tad, with evident delight, took back, but without a word of comment. Their father, however, said to the eldest:

"I guess, Bob, that's about right on your part, and now, Tad, as you've got your knife, you must give back to Bob the candy he gave you for the knife."

Tad exclaimed, "I can't, 'cause I ate up all the candy Bob gave me, and I ain't got no money to buy it."

"Oh!" said Mr. Lincoln, "what will you do then? Bob must have his candy back to make things square between you."

Tad was evidently in a quandary, and was at a loss how to get out of it, but his father, after waiting a few moments, and without making the slightest comment, handed Tad a bit (12½ cents). Tad looked at it with a good deal of satisfaction and shrieked out in his boyish glee:

"Come on, Bob, I'll get your candy back for you."

Both the father and I joined in a hearty laugh, and as the boys started off Mr. Lincoln called out to them:

"Boys, I reckon that's about right between you. Bob, do you take Tad right home as soon as he had paid you the candy."[72]

One night toward the end of the decade, Abraham and Mary were to attend a party, while Robert was to stay home with the younger boys. Willie and Tad, recently returned from a candy pull and completely smeared with molasses, threw apoplectic fits because they wanted to go to the party. Abraham convinced Mary to allow it only after the boys promised to behave themselves. Robert and a hired girl then rushed to clean and dress the boys (putting Tad's pants on backwards as a result), who went first with Abraham; Robert then dressed himself and escorted his mother.[73]

In 1856, as the boys in the Lincoln family grew bigger and older, and Abraham grew more prominent and affluent, Mary decided to enlarge their house to two full stories. The addition not only served to showcase the Lincolns' growing social and financial prominence but also gave thirteen-year-old Robert his own bedroom. Tradition holds that Mary ordered the construction done while Lincoln was away on the judicial circuit, and when he returned to a two-story house, he inquired of his neighbor, "Stranger, do you know where Lincoln lives?"[74]

Mary Lincoln loved to entertain, and the enlarged house helped the Lincolns hold their own parties as well. These ranged from a few dinner guests, to strawberry parties of fifty or so, and to the coup de grace, in February 1857, a party for five hundred invited guests, "yet owning to an *unlucky* rain, three hundred only favored us by their presence," Mary lamented.[75] Herndon recalled that the Lincoln boys often were present at their parents' entertainments. "It was the habit, custom, of Mrs. Lincoln, when any big man or woman visited her house, to dress up and trot out Bob, Willie or Tad and get them to monkey around, talk, dance, speak, quote poetry, etc., etc. Then she would become enthusiastic and eloquent over the children, much to the annoyance of the visitor and to the mortification of Lincoln."[76] Of the Lincoln's parties, one frequent visitor recalled, "[A]ll the young people were assured a good time" at their house. "Mrs. Lincoln was a charming hostess, and the boys full of fun and Mr. Lincoln the prince of entertainers. If there was a party on hand he would appear generally early in the evening, and 'start the ball rolling' as he would afterwards say that there were no wallflowers or bashful boys in corners."[77]

Since the Lincolns belonged to the higher-class society circles in Springfield, Robert attended balls, soirees, and strawberry parties at residences besides his own, where he often was confronted by that bane and joy of teenage boys: dancing with girls. In January 1856, the governor held a ball at his new residence—newly furnished with gas lighting—for the young teenagers of Springfield. "The house was full of boys and girls," John Todd Stuart, Mary Lincoln's cousin and Abraham's first law partner, wrote his daughter. "The gas was in full operation—the band was in attendance—all the rooms were thrown open, and all the children danced or at least hopped around. John [Stuart Jr.] danced all evening *in his way*. Next day he and Bob Lincoln were hunting up the dancing master."[78]

In the spring of 1858, Robert joined the Springfield Cadets, a "military company" of young men ages sixteen to twenty, who learned military marching and "tactics" and marched in parades and at meetings, festivals, and other special events. The uniform of the company was a dark-blue coat, fashioned after the U.S. military uniform, gilt-lace trim, white pants, and a glazed cap. Robert was a fourth corporal.[79] Belonging to the cadets would have been similar then to a high school student today being a member of a sports team. It provided friendship and camaraderie, puffed the boys up with pride in their uniforms and their skills, earned them respect from adults, and probably not more than a little attention from girls. One newspaper announcement for the Cadets' Festival in January 1859 stated that the cadets "deserve the smiles of the belles and the encouragement of the citizens."[80]

Being a cadet gave Robert the duty to observe the final senatorial debate between his father and Stephen A. Douglas in Alton, Illinois, on October 15, 1858. The cadets, along with Merritt's Coronet Band, accompanied a delegation of Springfield citizens and paraded through the town's streets. "We are sure they need not fear comparison with any company in the state," the *Alton Courier* declared a few days later. "The beauty of their uniform, their general neatness of appearance, the certainty and rapidity with which they moved at the word of command, all combined to make them justly worthy of admiration and praise."[81]

Robert lived in the western roughness of Springfield until he was sixteen years old. At that time, he determined to attend Harvard College, the oldest and most prestigious university in America. Robert said he decided this himself, but secondary sources say his father decided it for him.[82] It probably was a mutual understanding, and even expectation, that Robert would attend a respected university. Robert's two closest friends both attended eastern ivy-league schools—Clinton Conkling to Yale University and John Hay to Brown University—and such boyhood camaraderie and/or social peer pressure certainly had an influence on Robert's decision.[83] His parents encouraged the choice. Abraham wanted his son to have the best schooling, something he never had; Mary did have the best schooling while growing up—twelve years' worth—and she wanted the same for Robert.[84] So in the summer of 1859, after ten years of local schooling in Springfield, Robert set out for Cambridge, Massachusetts, to take the entrance examinations to Harvard College. His failure that summer was monumental.

3

"The Most Profitable [Year] of My Life"

An educated mind was an important achievement in antebellum America, but it was especially so for the oldest son of Abraham and Mary Lincoln. Both Lincolns had great intellects and loved reading, writing, and discussing current events. In fact, one of the many influences that brought Abraham and Mary together as a couple was their shared adoration for poetry, literature, and politics. "You could not say too much of his love for books," Robert once wrote about his father. "I do not remember ever seeing him without a book in his hand."[1] This literary sharing continued after the Lincoln marriage, when Mary would read to Abraham in the evenings or summarize for him a book that she had been reading.[2] The Lincolns both were great writers as well, something that comes from good reading. Mary dabbled in poetry, wrote an infamous parody for the local newspaper that ended with Abraham nearly fighting a duel, and was an indefatigable letter writer. Lincoln wrote multiple poems, some of which still exist, and he belonged to a short-lived poetry society in 1838–39.[3] Of course, Lincoln also was a great student of politics and oratory, read contemporary newspapers, and researched and wrote political speeches. He also had an especially analytical mind, evident in his love and mastery of math, surveying, astronomy, and other sciences. His passion of the scientific led him to create an original invention and to write and deliver a lecture on "Discoveries and Inventions."[4] So much intellectual enjoyment and curiosity by both his parents must have stimulated and inspired their oldest son.

Robert's general education began at home with Mary and, to a lesser extent, from Abraham. The mere example of his parents reading and writing would have had an influence on young Robert. Mary herself had more formal schooling than most American woman at the time. One school friend remembered that Mary was a studious girl with "a retentive memory and a mind that enabled her to grasp and thoroughly understand the lessons she was required to learn."[5] She began Robert's education by reading him the Bible, classic literature, and poetry, and as Robert was later fluent in speaking and writing French, his fluent mother most likely taught him the beginnings of that language as well.

Mary's sister Emily Todd offered one example of the impact of Mary's literary influence during her 1854 visit to the Lincoln home. That spring, Mary had been reading the novels and poems of Sir Walter Scott to her sons. One day, Mary and Emily heard "sounds of strife" outside and ran to the window to investigate. They saw Robert and a friend "having a battle royal," enacting scenes of Scott's poem "The Lady of the Lake," Emilie recalled. "Bob, with his sturdy little legs wide apart, was wielding a fence paling in lieu of a lance and proclaiming in a loud voice, 'This rock shall fly from its firm base as soon as I.' Mary, bubbling with laughter, called out, 'Grammercy, brave knights. Pray be more merciful than you are brawny.'"[6]

Abraham's influence, though less than his wife's due to his necessary absences from home, was still palpable. He always read out loud as a better way to grasp the material, which also would have gone into Robert's ears.[7] Lincoln's niece and former domestic, Harriet Hanks, remembered that her uncle preferred to turn a chair down on the floor and put a pillow on it and would sit there "for hours" and read.[8] One neighbor boy remembered that Lincoln "insisted . . . on the importance of learning, in early life, sentiments expressed in verse. In effect he said that as a man grows older lines which he learned because of their pleasant sound come to have meaning; just as old saws show their truth in later life."[9] Lincoln's scientific leanings led him to study mathematics, grammar, philosophy, science, and astronomy, which, according to William Herndon, Lincoln did most intensely beginning in 1849 after his failure in Congress and return to Springfield.[10]

Robert's formal education began in 1849, not long after Abraham's return from Congress. "I dimly recall being under the slipper-guardianship of a school mistress," Robert wrote.[11] This would most likely have been a simple day school where the mistress used her slipper to inflict punishment and ensure discipline. Robert's time at that school lasted less than one year, and in 1850 he became a student at Abel Estabrook's Springfield Academy, where he remained for the next three years. The Estabrook Academy was a private, subscription-based school, common in Illinois before free public schools were created in 1855.[12] One schoolmate of Robert's during that time stated, "[Robert's] character as a student was irreproachable. He was generally at the head of his class," while another later stated Robert was the best Latin scholar in the class.[13] Robert's attendance proves that the Lincolns' finances were solvent enough to allow their son an education, something many families could not afford. "In the beginning of the period, 1850–1880, numerous private schools were in operation [in Illinois] but there were very few schools open to the poor," according to one scholar; and these schools were dependent upon the initiative of individuals for their location as well as for their support.[14]

Most academies prior to the free-school period were established by religious denominations, the Presbyterians in particular. These schools were not only created to teach reading, writing, and mathematics but also were a source of moral education. Both the private schools, and later the free schools, contained much religious instruction, including prayer, hymn singing, and Bible reading.[15] The Springfield Academy's specific curriculum is unknown but most likely included the classical training in Greek, Latin, mathematics, composition, and declamation. It probably contained religious instruction as well, as Estabrook was associated with the Presbyterian church.[16] Once public schools were created, private academies, such as Estabrook's, fell out of favor and went out of business. Often, the schools gave their buildings to the new state schools, and the administrators and instructors became teachers at the public schools.[17]

It was not the free schools but the creation of Illinois State University that lost Estabrook the Lincolns' son and subscription in 1853. The university began in 1847 in Hillsboro, Illinois, as the Literary and Theological Institute of the Evangelical Lutheran Church. In 1852, prominent citizens convinced the Hillsboro Institute trustees to move the school to Springfield and change the name; the new university opened in April 1852, with an enrollment of seventy-nine students.[18] It offered a four-year course of instruction, broken into two sessions, as well as a preparatory department. The object of the university was to establish an institution "fully capable of furnishing to all the great interests and pursuits of man, the rich blessings of learning, science and skill can impart."[19] The school sought to influence educational and moral development in its students but did not require pupils to be members of the Lutheran church, only that their deportment be imbued with Christian moral principles acknowledged by all denominations.[20]

While Abraham Lincoln did not become a member of the university's board of trustees in 1852 (as many of his friends did), he recognized the importance of the institution and purchased a $300 "perpetual scholarship" for his oldest son in October 1852. The scholarship provided permanent privilege of attendance for one student at the university without further charge of tuition.[21] Robert entered the preparatory department of Illinois State University in the fall of 1853, at age eleven. There he studied reading, writing, arithmetic, geography, English grammar, spelling, history of the United States, declamation and composition, Greek and Latin grammar and reading, the classics, algebra, ancient geography and history, and bookkeeping.[22] Two years later, after passing the entrance examination, he entered the freshman class of the university, one of fifty-two students. "This university had, I believe, four instructors," Robert wrote. "The government was very easy, and we did just what pleased us, study concerning only a very small portion of our time."[23] Robert later verified the school's lack of impression on him when he declared that he could not recall "anything of interest" about his time there.[24]

Robert's first recorded grades—from his junior year in 1858—show him to have been an average student. He received 85 in Greek, 80 in mathematics, 75 in chemistry, and 60 in a subject not designated, which was probably composition and declamation, a required course.[25] These grades show Robert to have been more interested in math and science than the humanities, although one of Robert's schoolmates stated that Robert was "especially brilliant in the Greek class."[26] Robert's achievements in the analytical studies may have been so high due to the fact that his father actually studied with him during these years as a way to gain the "elements of [formal] education" the father failed to receive as a child.[27] This makes sense, as Abraham Lincoln's period of intensive study after returning from Congress coincided with Robert's entrance into the university.

As a sophomore in 1856, Robert was elected a member of the Philomathean Society, an organization dedicated to weekly debates and declamations, readings of original essays, and critical analyses. "One must admit that these students [in the society] displayed a remarkable degree of intelligence and capacity," stated one historian. "The subjects for discussion ranged from deep philosophical problems to the political issues of the day." Yet, consistent with Robert's poor grades in composition and declamation, he also was a poor participant in the club. Society records show he was once fined for failure to attend meetings. His reluctance to participate continued even after he was elected recording secretary for the group in 1858. He recorded only two meetings, failed to attend for the next two months, and then requested an "honorable dismissal" from the society. At the next meeting, Robert withdrew his request for dismissal, yet still failed to attend the meetings. He was thereafter given the honorary dismissal, and not long after, he left the university to attend school in New Hampshire.[28]

Life in Springfield in the 1850s, while Robert was acquiring his early education, was an edifying and exciting place for a young boy. As the state capital, Springfield teemed with local, state, and national politicians; in addition to the meetings and speeches of the state legislature, cultural events were continuously offered, such as lectures, plays, music, and sociables. As Abraham Lincoln rose to political prominence, Robert also was exposed to people, places, and events he otherwise may not have been. In fact, the school historian of Illinois State University stated that Robert was often absent from classes because of attending his father's political rallies outside of Springfield.[29] But, as with nearly every young person, one of the most enduring aspects of Robert's 1850s adolescence was in his friendships. He had many friends at this time, but two in particular stand out in the closeness of their affection and the duration of their friendships, Clinton Conkling and John Hay.

Clinton Conkling was the son of James Conkling and Mercy Levering Conkling. James was a close friend and political ally of Abraham Lincoln, and Mercy had been a close friend of Mary Lincoln since their girlhood days. Robert and Clinton probably were acquainted since they were babies, due to their closeness in age and parents' friendship. Clinton also did his preparatory work at Illinois State University, one year behind Robert, and then his degree at Yale University. He returned to Springfield, was admitted to the bar, and joined his father's law firm. He and Robert remained friends until Robert's death in 1926.[30] Clinton also acted as Robert's agent in Springfield on matters such as the rental of the Lincoln home, the administration of the Lincoln tomb, and the centennial Lincoln celebration in 1909 and as a conduit to Robert in Chicago for state legislative news, as well as social news and gossip.

John Hay was from Warsaw, Illinois, and moved to Springfield in 1852 at age fourteen to attend Illinois State University. Hay was a quick, likeable, witty boy who was full of life and thoroughly enjoyed the social pleasures of parties, picnics, and dances. He also was highly intelligent and is said to have read six books of Virgil and learned Latin, some Greek, and a speaking knowledge of German by the time he was twelve.[31] "His schoolmates envied his capacity for getting his lessons without apparently any study," according to one biographer.[32]

Hay was five years older than Robert Lincoln, so their initial contacts as fellow students at Illinois State University were minimal.[33] "I barely knew him, but greatly admired him," Robert later wrote.[34] This admiration for the older boy may have been Robert's inspiration to join the university's Philomathean Society, of which Hay was a member. Hay, however, left Springfield in 1855 to attend Brown University in Providence, Rhode Island. He returned to Springfield in spring 1859 to clerk in his uncle Milton Hay's law office, and it was at that time that he and Robert became friends. "I was only fifteen years old but was fortunate enough to be allowed to see something of him and a very small party of fellows of his age and my liking for him became very great," Robert remembered.[35] Hay biographer Tyler Dennett believes Robert admired John more as an older brother than as a friend, and, certainly, the cultured, urbane, and college-educated Hay would have been an impressive role model.[36] The friendship developed through the White House years, where Hay was one of President Lincoln's private secretaries, and continued until Hay's death in 1905.

Robert's grades at Illinois State University may not have been exceptional, but he clearly had intellect. In addition to the schoolwork required of him, he also was an enthusiastic recreational reader. Between 1857 and 1858, Abraham and Mary gave their oldest son a twenty-four-volume biographical series of books titled *Abbott's Illustrated Histories*, which Robert enjoyed his entire life and eventually passed on to his own son.[37] Robert also made good use of the Illinois State Library as a teenager, withdrawing twenty-seven books between April 1858 and July 1859.[38] He later remembered the state library as "a very good miscellaneous library," as well as social club, which his father used often in times of leisure.[39] Robert's reading records show him to have read books across the humanities spectrum, including novels, poetry, history, biographies, and essays. He had a penchant for the literature of Charles Dickens, Washington Irving, and James Fenimore Cooper; he read Sir Walter Scott's *Poetical Works*, Mary Shelley's *Frankenstein*, Victor Hugo's *Hunchback of Notre Dame*, Homer's *Iliad*, a story of Mexican War campaigns of Winfield Scott, volume 1 of a work on women in the American Revolution, and, later in early 1861, the plays of Aeschylus.[40] Robert also was a rapid reader, taking typically two to four days to read and return each, although some of the heftier works he borrowed for two weeks.

Robert's use of the library at this time shows a love of literature, imbued by his parents, especially Mary, who enjoyed good fiction. It also may show, perhaps, a determination to be well read in preparation for applying to college. Indeed, by the spring of 1859, Robert said that he "became aware that I could never get an education in that way [at Illinois State University] and resolved to enter Harvard College."[41] Like so many teenagers, Robert's self-confidence and self-esteem erroneously convinced him of his infallibility, making him believe his acceptance to Harvard would be a foregone conclusion requiring the mere formality of the entrance exams. Perhaps the perceived impact of his father's fame, as the man who famously debated U.S. Senator Stephen A. Douglas across Illinois the year before, contributed to his overconfidence. Robert soon discovered, however, and later admitted, that his flippancy over the entrance exams was "very much mistaken."

In August 1859, sixteen-year-old Robert, with his friend George C. Latham, and also one whole cooked ham, traveled to Cambridge, Massachusetts, to seek admission to Harvard College.[42] Mary Lincoln, in a natural motherly way, felt "quite lonely" because of her oldest son's leave-taking and wrote that "it almost appears as if light and mirth, had departed with him."[43] It was related by Edward Everett Hale at the end of the nineteenth century—and repeated by every historian since—that Robert carried with him a letter of introduction from Senator Douglas, presenting Robert as the son of his friend Abraham

Lincoln, "with whom I have lately been canvassing the state of Illinois."[44] This story, while a good one, is untrue. Robert even told Hale, twice, that his facts were incorrect, stating the second time, "I certainly never told the story to you, because I do not believe it to have any foundation whatever."[45] Robert thought it "quite impossible" that he carried a letter from Douglas, for, even though the elder Lincoln and Douglas had known each other well, "I do not think they were ever what can be called friends." Robert also said he was "quite sure" that the relations of the two men after the 1858 senatorial campaign "were not such as to permit that my father should have asked of Senator Douglas a letter of introduction for me to anybody. More than that, Senator Douglas had been from early manhood away from the New England States, and I think it very unlikely that he had such relations as to authorize him to give a letter of introduction to anyone at Cambridge."[46]

Robert actually did carry a letter of introduction with him that summer, written by a clerk in the Lincoln & Herndon law office, Charles B. Brown. Brown was an 1856 Harvard graduate, whose letter introduced Robert to Brown's former classmate William W. Burrage. "I saw Mr. Burrage upon my arrival, and he posted me sufficiently as to the steps I should take in regard to submitting myself to the examination," Robert wrote.[47] Bearing such an introduction, being the son of the nationally known Illinoisan who was by then mentioned as a possible presidential candidate, and full of his own vanity, Robert walked into the entrance-exam room full of confidence. He was confronted by subjects such as Latin and Greek—translations and grammar—history, geometry, algebra, trigonometry, and economics. He faced questions such as, "Describe the rivers of Italy and Cisalpine Gaul," "What appears inconsistent in the acts of Pompeii?" "How many faces, edges, plane angles, solid angles has a cube? If it lies upon a horizontal surface, how many of the edges will have a horizontal, and how many a vertical position?" and "Translate into Greek: 'These men say that there is nothing more unjust than rumor,' and 'Do not injure those who are doing good to the state.'"[48] By the time he left, he was humbled by the reality of life, having failed to gain entrance, failing what one historian has claimed were fifteen of the sixteen tests.[49] This catastrophe was a combination of a clearly lackluster personal performance in general, inadequate instruction at Illinois State University and, perhaps most important, the fact that Harvard prided itself on having the most difficult entrance exams in America.[50]

There is no known communication from Robert to his parents that day explaining his failure, but Abraham Lincoln did write a fatherly note of advice to Robert's friend and Illinois State University classmate George Latham one year later after he failed the same exams a second time.

> My dear George,
> I have scarcely felt greater pain in my life than on learning yesterday from Bob's letter, that you had failed to enter Harvard University. And yet there is very little in it, if you will allow no feeling of *discouragement* to seize, and prey upon you. It is a *certain* truth, that you *can* enter, and graduate in, Harvard University; and having made the attempt, you *must* succeed in it. "*Must*" is the word.
>
> I know not how to aid you, save in the assurance of one of mature age, and much severe experience, that you *can* not fail, if you resolutely determine, that you *will* not.
>
> The President of the institution, can scarcely be other than a kind man; and doubtless he would grant you an interview, and point out the readiest way to remove, or overcome, the obstacles which have thwarted you.
>
> In your temporary failure there is no evidence that you may not be a better scholar, and a more successful man in the great struggle of life, than many others, who have entered college more easily.
>
> Again I say let no feeling of discouragement prey upon you, and in the end you are sure to succeed.[51]

This letter is so full of conviction and life experience that there can be little doubt its contents about perseverance, self-confidence, and success are lessons Lincoln taught his own sons. Certainly, this advice, to a boy whom Lincoln treated as a son after Latham's father died, was similar to the advice Lincoln gave Robert in 1859. This is evident in Robert's own account of his failure: "On being examined I had the honor to receive a fabulous number of conditions which preceded my admission. [However,] I was resolved not to retire beaten." Instead, he secured an interview with Dr. James Walker, president of Harvard, and asked his advice on how best to proceed to prepare for admission the next year. Walker suggested a year of preparatory work and named numerous possible schools, out of which Robert chose Phillips Academy, in Exeter, New Hampshire.[52]

Robert's choice of Phillips Exeter Academy could not have been more appropriate. The school, founded by John Phillips in 1781, was the premier preparatory school in America by 1859, boasting, among other alumni, former Senator Daniel Webster and former President Franklin Pierce. The academy focused on the humanities, with a prominence in Latin and Greek studies. The school's founding charter established an academy, "For the education of Youth in the English, Latin, and Greek Languages; in Writing, Arithmetic, Music, and the Art of Speaking, Practical Geometry, Logic, and Geography, and such other of the Liberal Arts and Sciences or Languages as opportunity may hereafter permit, and as the Trustees hereinafter provided shall direct."[53] More than its reputation and educational theory, however, Phillips Exeter matched its curriculum closely to Harvard's entrance requirements, making it the leading supplier of academy-prepared students to Harvard's freshman class.[54] As one historian explains, after 1845, preparing for college at Exeter "of course meant Harvard."[55]

Coming from the rugged West of Illinois to such bastions of New England culture as Cambridge, Massachusetts, and Exeter, New Hampshire, must have been a simultaneously frightening and exhilarating experience for young Robert, full of exotic social and cultural experiences. Besides being the home of the famous Phillips Academy, Exeter in August 1859 was a thriving, bustling seaport with schooners, wherries, and gundalows traveling back and forth from the Atlantic Ocean. The town had been settled in 1638 around the waterfalls where the freshwater Exeter River meets the tidal saltwater Piscataqua River, offering the ideal river amenities of sustenance, power, and transportation. Although Springfield, Illinois, was settled near the Sangamon River, the scale of Exeter's nautical commerce would have been nothing like Robert had ever seen. Exeter also was a center of land-based industry. The area surrounding Exeter boasted large meadows and stands of timber for agriculture and livestock grazing, while the falls were covered with the water-driven manufacturing of sawmills, gristmills, carding mills, starch mills, paper mills, chocolate mills, and even a gunpowder factory. The town had about two thousand inhabitants of multiple races, colors, and nationalities, all drawn by the commercial opportunities of sea and land industries. The streets were made of dirt, and candles were used for light, but there were a public library, a bank, and a police force, as well as the major Exeter Manufacturing Company.[56]

The campus of Phillips Academy was only steps from downtown Exeter, down Court Street. It was just a few blocks of walking for Robert to get to the campus from his rooming house. The school had only 134 students during the 1859–60 academic year.[57] Boys spent their idle time walking through the woods, playing sports on the campus, tramping through the town, and visiting places such as Lovering's bookstore or riding to the nearby towns of Rye and Hampton.[58]

Inexperienced as Robert certainly was, far from home and preparing his own living for the first time in his life, he was not alone. George Latham also entered Phillips Academy in 1859 with the same hopes of attaining sufficient knowledge to pass the Harvard exams the following year. Robert also had a mentor/guardian of sorts to whom he could turn in times of need. Amos Tuck, a congressional colleague of Abraham Lincoln in 1847–49, lived in Exeter. Although no letters are known to exist from Abraham Lincoln to Tuck for that time, the father may have informed his friend of his son's arrival and asked him to keep an eye on his boy. One source claimed that Robert actually spent his first few nights in Exeter at the Tuck home until he found permanent lodging.[59]

Robert and George eventually roomed together at the residence of Mrs. S. B. Clarke at the corner of Pleasant and High Streets for two dollars per week, not including lights or fuel.[60] Off-campus living was normal for young men with families of adequate means. Phillips Academy had three instructors and one principal during Robert's year there. Tuition was eight dollars per term, for three terms of the year. Robert went to Exeter hoping to enter the class preparing to enter college the next July as sophomores. The principal, Dr. Gideon Lane Soule, convinced Robert of "the vanity of my aspirations," and instead he entered the subfreshman class.[61]

Robert's year at Exeter was the seminal time of his adolescence. He referred to his affection for the school and his time there many times during his life, most poignantly stating in 1881, "I look back upon my year at Exeter as the most profitable one of my life."[62] Robert's time in Exeter, and subsequently at Harvard, undeniably changed him from a Midwestern boy into a proper, well-dressed, articulate New England gentleman, imbued with all the traits of the Victorian-era social codes and mores. This was not an accident. In fact, it was a staunch resolve of Principal Soule to rely on the uprightness and honor of his boys and help make them men. Soule was "a thorough gentleman" who was "courteous, high minded, just, and generous in his treatment of all." He governed the students' conduct with "an unwritten code of propriety and honor which is recognized as the fundamental principle of every moral and enlightened community."[63] He began each term with a speech in which he told the students what was expected of them; he recited the few rules that governed them, most famously his injunction that any student who "crossed the threshold" of a billiard parlor—a den of iniquity for gentleman—crossed the threshold of the school for the last time.[64] As one school historian notes, all of Soule's rules were "summed up in the injunction that they were to behave as gentlemen,—and then added that he should trust to their honor, and that the honor of a gentleman was inviolable."[65]

One former Exeter student said in 1883 said his greatest lesson at the school was manners, which taught him to be a "cultivated gentleman and polished scholar." Another former student said in 1903, "Exeter training and life stood for Obligation. Whatever of friendship, whatever of training I took from there, I took, above all, the belief—it was more than a belief, it was a sense—that that which is required of you, must be done."[66] This belief in the tenets of manly duty and honor was a pillar of Gilded Age masculinity, a trait that Robert exhibited throughout his entire life.

"Bob Lincoln was a very popular young fellow, a gentleman in every sense of the word; quiet in manner, with a certain dignity of his own," one classmate recalled. "He was a very good fellow, however, and always ready for any good time and clean fun. He was very popular with the girls of the town as well as with the boys. He was what would be called nowadays a 'good dresser,' and always looked as well as acted the part of a gentleman."[67] Robert's character as described here can be viewed as a perfect melding of his two childhood influences: his mother and his father. Mary taught Robert proper social etiquette: how to be a gentleman, how to behave toward ladies, and the respectability that comes from good dress and grooming. Abraham's influence was more in Robert's character. Like his father, Robert was a companionable boy who told good stories and jokes, was a talented athlete, and was always up for having fun; he was also an honest boy with a great respect for truth and law. Through the influence of both his parents, Robert assumed a quiet dignity and self-respect, as well as an inquisitive and talented mind. Robert's grades during his time at Exeter bear out these qualities. During his three terms at the academy, his average "Deportment" was 10 out of 10 every term; while his "average of scholarship" for recitations, compositions, and declamations in Latin, Greek, and Mathematics, out of a possible score of 10, was 8.9, 9.3, and 9.3, respectively, for each term.[68]

In later reminiscences, Robert recalled some of his teachers with respect and fear. He called mathematics professor George Albert Wentworth "the most thorough instructor I ever saw" and also remembered how Dr. Soule, the Latin teacher as well as the principal, would constantly call boys up, using a lottery system, to the front for recitation: "The little tickets were carefully placed downward in a tin box, and delicately picked out, one by one, with the moistened tip of his finger, and laid aside until the name of the fellow he was after was reached."[69] Robert later characterized his year at Exeter as "devoid of excitement, and full of hard work."[70] That, however, is not entirely true. Robert spent ample time playing sports. One classmate even labeled him an "outstanding" athlete in his performances in track (standing and running broad jump), football, and baseball (called "round ball" before the Civil War).[71] The end of his final semester also offered plenty of excitement, which he recalled as "a flight from Justice in the shape of a policeman all over the flourishing village, for having, in company with others, committed sundry depredations on the property of various denizens."[72]

This incident occurred at the close of the academic year in 1860, when Robert and some friends went through the town and unhinged and carried off numerous fence gates and signposts. Their "flight from justice" did not last long before being apprehended. Stories differ as to the outcome. One says the boys were brought before a local justice of the peace, while another says they were brought before the principal, Dr. Soule. Both stories agree, however, in that Robert's name was removed from the list of offenders because of the prominence of his father, who had recently been nominated as the Republican candidate for president. They also agree that Robert refused such immunity and insisted on his inclusion in the blame and the punishment.[73] "Filthy lucre, also the root of all evil, proved a great blessing in the present case, and we all got off by paying damages," Robert whimsically recounted.[74] This outlaw incident illustrates both a young man's moral flaws and virtues: easy fraternity and eagerness for fun, as well as a lack of respect for the property of others. It also illustrates his nascent manly qualities and endeavoring to emulate his father's honest character.

Another exciting incident at Exeter that year was a visit from Abraham Lincoln—an event that Robert later boasted made his father president of the United States but one that almost did not happen. In 1856, the elder Lincoln was nearly named John C. Fremont's vice presidential running mate, and in 1858 Lincoln verbally dueled Senator Douglas around the state of Illinois in a series of debates that garnered Lincoln national attention. By 1859, while the oldest Lincoln son was away at school in New Hampshire, Abraham Lincoln was enlarging his national reputation. He was at the peak of his law career, was in great demand as a political speaker, and was openly being mentioned as possible presidential material. Despite all this political success, Lincoln was still a normal man with everyday problems. The main trouble was money. After his self-financed debates with Douglas, Lincoln found himself in such financial straits as to declare himself "absolutely without money now for even household expenses."[75] He immediately returned to the judicial circuit and a greater legal load and gave himself limited time for political travel and speeches.

Added to Lincoln's expanses of law office, home, and family were also Robert's school tuition and expenses. The Lincolns had to outfit Robert with the necessary items for his time at school, including things such as light and heavy clothing, gloves, towels, soap and other toiletries, and a watch guard.[76] In addition to the two dollars per week for Robert's room, the tuition at Phillips Exeter Academy was twenty-four dollars per year, not including books and other expenses. Lincoln also sent Robert money at least once a month, ranging anywhere from ten to fifty dollars, for a total of $150 from November 1859 to May 1860.[77]

Abraham and Mary certainly took more interest in their oldest son's life and education than merely paying the bills. In October, Mary told a friend, "I miss Bob, so much, that I do not feel settled down, as much as I used to." She also stated that she and her son had already made plans to spend some time in New

York City and a week in the White Mountains of New Hampshire during the summer of 1860.[78] These two letters, plus a third in which Mary apologized to a friend for writing such a short letter because she just had written such a long letter to Robert, show that the relationship between mother and oldest son was extremely close. Abraham missed his son as well, so when in October 1859 an invitation came to speak at Reverend Henry Ward Beecher's church in Brooklyn, New York, he accepted.[79] The trip would not only allow him to visit Robert but would advance his presidential prospects in the east and was a guaranteed $200 payment to defray expenses.[80]

Lincoln set off for New York from Springfield in late February. His original itinerary was to speak in Brooklyn and then travel to Exeter. Abraham Lincoln's February 27, 1860, speech at the Cooper Union Institute in New York City is now unanimously characterized as the event that led to his presidential nomination by spreading his political genius beyond the Midwest. Or, as one historian more simply, yet very aptly, states, the speech was "the most pivotal public appearance of [Lincoln's] career."[81] In it, he explored the history of American slavery going back to the Founders' original thoughts and beliefs on the subject and showed not only that slavery's national extension was wrong but also that it—plus the Dred Scott decision that allowed such nationalization—was politically espoused on "assumed historical facts which were not really true."[82] The speech was such a great success that speaking requests deluged him during his entire eastern trip. Immediately after completing his Cooper Union speech, he was beseeched to speak in Providence, Rhode Island, the very next day; while in Providence, he received an invitation to speak at Exeter during his visit to his son.[83] Robert also received a letter that day from the Dover, New Hampshire, Republican Committee, asking if his father could be persuaded to speak in that city while in the area. Robert responded that he would give the letter to his father, who would answer it himself, "though I have no doubt he will be happy to comply with your kind invitation should his time permit."[84] Emissaries from the Dover Committee then met Lincoln on his arrival to Exeter and secured a promised speech from him for March 2.

Robert was reunited with his father in Exeter on February 29 and spent the evening with him; Robert's friend George Latham joined them. Lincoln may have spent the night in the home of his old congressional colleague Amos Tuck, although it is unknown, and the next day took the boys with him on a two-day speaking tour, stopping first at Concord, New Hampshire, and then at Manchester, New Hampshire.[85] On March 2, Robert and George returned to Exeter to attend to their studies, while Lincoln spent the night in Dover for his promised speech.[86] Robert had lunch with his father the next day, March 3, and gave him a walking tour of the town of Exeter. That evening, Lincoln spoke in the Exeter Town Hall to a crowd of about 850 people, including most of the 134 academy students.[87]

The general feeling that night was an eagerness to hear the famed Illinois lawyer speak but then shock and even embarrassment at his ill-kempt and uncouth exterior. One student recalled Lincoln's rumpled hair, "his neckwear was all awry, he sat somewhat bent in the chair, and altogether presented a very remarkable, and, to us, disappointing appearance;" while another student "could not help noticing his lankness of stature, and an occasional uncouth posture or gesture."[88] But once Lincoln began to speak, and the audience was carried away by his arguments and speaking style: "There was no more pity for our friend Bob: we were proud of his father."[89]

For the remainder of Saturday night, and all day Sunday, March 4, Robert and his father enjoyed each other's company. Local lore relates that on Sunday morning, Lincoln rose early at the Front Street home of Amos Tuck and walked up to Pickpocket Falls, where he stopped a few minutes to chat with a fisherman.[90] Father and son then attended the Second Congregational Church on Robert's "orders" and spent the rest of the afternoon together.[91] Lincoln "entered with real zest into the boy's interests and his companionships with the other students," according to one historian. "Lincoln appears in these contacts with the boys and with the townspeople he ran across to have been ever simple and sociable, a man thoroughly enjoying his brief snatches of holiday."[92] Sunday evening, Robert's friends called at his room to meet his father. When Robert told his father that one friend played the banjo, Lincoln enthusiastically suggested the boy run and get it. After an exhibition of his talent, Lincoln told his son, "Robert, you ought to have one."[93] The entire visit appears to have been an enjoyable and meaningful time of bonding between a father and son not often allowed such personal time together.

Lincoln stayed at Exeter Sunday night and left on the morning train. On his way home to Springfield, he made a number of other political stops, making a total of ten speeches during his eastern trip, although he originally had only intended to make the one in New York.[94] Such a busy schedule caused him to tell his wife, "I have been unable to escape this toil. If I had foreseen it I think I would not have come East at all."[95] Robert found this comment by his father "interesting in view of the effect which was being made upon his future career without thought of it by him, by his unanticipated speeches, which would not have been made but for his visit to a school boy."[96]

The prominence of his father, as well as the grand impression Abraham Lincoln made during his Exeter speech, made Robert even more popular at school than he already was. This did not seem to affect his character, however, as all known accounts point to Robert being an unassuming young man.

Upon the announcement of Abraham Lincoln's Republican nomination for the presidency in May 1860, one of Robert's friends, Albert Blair, hurried to the local bowling alley to find Robert, who was a frequent player. "Bob, your father has got it," Blair announced as he held up the *Boston Journal* to show the news. "Good!" Robert replied, "I will write home for a check before he spends all his money in the campaign."[97] In later years, Robert liked to say that his failure to enter Harvard had made his father president.[98]

Robert graduated from Phillips Exeter Academy not long after his father's nomination as the Republican presidential candidate. On July 16, he again attempted the Harvard entrance exams, and this time passed easily.[99] "After the commencement in 1860, I was able to inform my father that I had succeeded in entering College without a condition, quite a change from the previous year," Robert wrote.[100] Abraham was pleased to brag about his son's achievements. He wrote to a friend, "Our oldest boy 'Bob' has been away from us nearly a year at school. He will enter Harvard University this month. He promises well, considering we never controlled him much."[101] Abraham Lincoln was not the only person to notice his son's promise. His friend Amos Tuck wrote in August 1860 that Robert "has behaved himself [at Exeter] as the son of Abraham Lincoln might be expected to do. He stands at the top of the ladder as a scholar, and is a singularly discreet, well-behaved, brilliant and promising young man. His good sense is severely tested, by the attentions he receives from everybody, but he stands it all. He is a member of our 'Wide Awakes,' and was out in full uniform a few evenings since, with the rest of the 'Boys' to attend the raising of a Lincoln and Hamlin banner."[102]

In August 1860, Robert moved to Cambridge, Massachusetts, to begin the next stage in his life. He arrived at the famous town and hallowed institution as a college student, but within three months, he was to become the oldest son of the president of the United States.

4

"Robert Lincoln Has Been Dubbed the Prince of Rails!"

During the hiatus between leaving Phillips Exeter Academy and entering Harvard, Robert did not return home to Springfield. Instead, he spent the summer of 1860 in Exeter, presumably with friends. In June, his mother wrote a friend that after Robert's absence of "almost *a year*, a *long year* . . . at times I feel *wild* to see him." No doubt this sadness at missing Robert—her oldest boy and the only one who every day for sixteen years had shared her joys, griefs, and fears while Abraham Lincoln was away on business—was augmented by the death of Mary's ten-year-old nephew from typhoid, an event redolent of little Eddie's death ten years prior.[1] But her sadness was tempered with pride when Robert was invited to deliver the Fourth of July oration at the annual celebration at Portsmouth, New Hampshire.[2] He replied to the invitation by saying he would do it "if father is willing," to which Abraham Lincoln replied, "Tell Robert to take every occasion to read that immortal document, and the bigger the crowd the louder he must holler." Robert's first public speech, done before more than one thousand people, "went off very well," one witness recounted.[3]

In late July, Robert tasked his father to do what every parent dreams and fears: begin to pay for the boy's college. Robert sent Abraham a blank bond for the payment of college dues to the amount of $400 to be signed by him and a citizen of Massachusetts as a surety.[4] Lincoln sent the bond to Julius Rockwell, a Whig Congressional colleague from the Thirtieth Congress and a later U.S. Senator. "I think of you more readily than any other citizen of Massachusetts, as one who would probably be willing to oblige me," Lincoln wrote.[5]

With the bond signed, Robert officially became a student of Harvard College.[6] It was an achievement that he had earnestly sought and one that would serve him well throughout his life. The education, life experiences, friendships, and connections attained by Robert at this time cannot be underestimated. Harvard in 1860 was considered the most prestigious college in America, and an education from there would open any door. The children of America's wealthiest and most influential citizens attended there, a fraternity to which Robert Lincoln—despite being from a merely above-average Midwestern family—fit in well, thanks to his year at Phillips Exeter Academy. Of course, by the time of Robert's acceptance, his father had become the Republican presidential nominee, and Robert himself, as Lincoln's oldest son, was a known and marked boy.

One classmate remembered that there was "considerable satisfaction" on campus when it was known that Robert had passed the entrance exams and was "safely landed" in the class of 1864: "His father had just received the Republican nomination of 1860, which fact, together with the good opinions of his classmates from Exeter, gave him a good vantage-ground of popularity."[7] Not long after the beginning of the fall 1860 semester, members of the sophomore class, intent on upholding the Harvard tradition of hazing freshman, decided it a good idea to haze the son of the prominent Illinoisan. A group of sophomores roused Robert from his bed one night for an "inquisition." Robert, standing in his nightshirt, surrounded by bullying sophomores most likely in masks, was interrogated: "Are you the son of the Mr. Lincoln who is named by the Republicans for the presidency?" Robert admitted that he was. It was then demanded: "What manner of man is this father of yours?" Robert, very coolly and honestly, said, "Father is the queerest old cuss you ever saw." One of the sophomores later recalled, "Robert Lincoln was neither fresh nor pompous nor scared nor peevish" but was admirable to give "a boy's frank estimate of his father instead of trying to impress the company with his father's importance or greatness."[8]

During the first term of his freshman year, Robert studied Greek, Latin, composition, mathematics, and religious instruction (ethics).[9] While highly intelligent and well read, Robert at Harvard was not a bookworm. He was above average in class rank, but as he wrote during his senior year, "I have studied enough to satisfy myself without being a 'dig.'"[10] In fact, while Robert did not ignore his studies, he seems to have spent more time participating in school-sponsored extracurricular activities, as well as chumming around with his friends.

Unfortunately, Robert's closest friend and Exeter roommate, George Latham, once again failed the Harvard entrance exams and retreated to Phillips Academy to continue studying for another try in 1861. This left Robert without a roommate, as he and Latham planned to room together again in Cambridge.[11] But Robert made another good friend in his new roommate, Frederick P. Anderson, son of the wealthy Larz Anderson II, of Cincinnati, Ohio, and nephew of Major Robert Anderson of later Fort Sumter fame. The two lived in a rooming house at "Pasco's, corner of Main and Linden Streets" during their freshman year and then in campus housing for their final three years in Stoughton 22 and Hollis 25.[12] Their room was "more of a resort for the elegant young gentlemen of leisure of the Class than for hard students," one classmate remembered.[13] Indeed, during his four years at Harvard, Robert was repeatedly admonished by the faculty for rule breaking, and the president of Harvard even sent a letter to Abraham Lincoln, warning him of Robert's neglected studies and his need to "guard against good-fellowship."[14] The first of these transgressions was recorded at the October 1, 1860, faculty meeting, where it was voted to fine Robert two dollars for "writing on settees in Mr. Bates's room."[15]

It is clear from the existing testimony that Robert was a level-headed boy who easily made friends and liked to have a good time. He did not take himself too seriously and did not feel entitled to special treatment simply because of his father's fame.[16] This says much about Robert's character because by the fall of 1860 his father's name and face were ubiquitous around the country. As the lone Republican facing a Democrat party divided into three sectional candidates—Stephen A. Douglas for the Northern Democrats, John Breckinridge for the Southern Democrats, and John Bell for the Constitutional Union Party—the outlook for Abraham Lincoln's victory was nearly certain. The election of 1860 also was unlike any other in that it was understood to be a showdown over the issue of slavery. As soon as Lincoln—whom southerners called a "Black Republican" who supposedly wanted to steal their slave property and make black persons equal to white persons—was nominated by his party, a number of southern states threatened to secede from the Union if he were elected.

Aside from the contentious political issues of the day, Lincoln's family and life in Springfield also were a focus of many newspapers and magazines. Articles detailing the antics of Willie and Tad, Mrs. Lincoln's clothing and homemaking, the Lincoln house itself, and how the candidate spent his days were numerous. As one newspaper editorialized, "Mr. Lincoln is unfortunate. If he ventures to whistle, the echo comes back to him from a thousand partisan journals, and his friends forthwith urge in his favor that he is a good whistler. The most trivial actions of his life are made affairs of moment."[17] Robert, as the oldest son of Lincoln, was not immune to such publicity, although mentions of him in the newspapers were short and few. As the son of the "Railsplitter" candidate, Robert was, however, given the nickname the "Prince of Rails" by the press in October 1860—a reference to the American visit of the English Prince of Wales, Albert Edward, who began a short tour of New England in September 1860.[18]

As early as October 12, the *(Springfield) Illinois State Journal* had reported that Robert spent a few days in the White Mountains of New Hampshire, where the local citizens "gave him a reception as the 'Prince of Rails.' A procession was formed to escort the 'Prince,' and speeches were made, to which he made a happy reply." The paper also stated of Robert, "They say that for story telling and wit, he is a chip off the original rail."[19] It was most likely in reference to this story that Mercy Levering Conkling, a long-time friend of Mary Lincoln, wrote her son only eight days later, "Bob Lincoln you have doubtless seen, has been styled the *Prince of Rails*!"[20] It was a name constantly connected with Robert by the press until his father's inauguration in March 1861, and one that Robert's friends seemed to get a good laugh out of on occasion, as when Harry Gourley in February 1861 addressed a letter to Robert as, "to His Royal Highness the Prince of Rails."[21] Robert himself, with his growing sense of Victorian propriety and gentlemanliness, endured the publicity well but not without frustration.

During the fall campaign, speeches, parades, and torchlight processions were common occurrences around the country. In Springfield, Illinois, a great wigwam was erected to host political rallies and social events. On August 8, 1860, the city hosted a stentorian political rally that drew fifty thousand people.[22] In New England, Lincoln was the nearly unanimous choice of the voters—indeed, he carried every northern state on election night except New Jersey. In Cambridge, Massachusetts, Lincoln Club No. 1 (a group of supporters working out of a vacant store) on Brattle Square was open every day in support of the Republican ticket, and every night the streets were afire with the torches of Wide-Awake clubs, political groups that supported the ticket.[23] On October 16, a huge, impressive torchlight procession was held in Boston in favor of Hannibal Hamlin, the vice presidential nominee, and Abraham Lincoln, in which Robert, the newly minted "Prince," most likely participated, as he had done at Exeter.[24]

On election night, November 6, Lincoln won the popular vote over his closest rival, Stephen A. Douglas, by a half million votes, although a united Democrat Party candidate would have beaten him by over one million. When the news of Lincoln's election was confirmed in Cambridge, where Robert was among the throng eagerly awaiting the results, a group of Robert's friends put him on a fence rail—in allusion to his rail-splitter father—and "bore him around in triumph, accompanied by torches and uproarious demonstrations."[25] The next day, another group of students called on Robert—in a less-boisterous and more formal way—to congratulate him on his father's election. "The young man is said to be a worthy scion of the old stock, and is quite popular among his fellow students," one newspaper reported of the occurrence.[26]

The victory celebrations in the north soon were overshadowed by the rage of southern citizens who decried the election of a Black Republican. "The South shall be surrounded by a cordon of fire, so that her institutions will be destroyed," the Jackson *Weekly Mississippian* warned. "People of Mississippi read and reflect, and decide if you are prepared to submit to the rule of a Government to be controlled for your RUIN and DEGREDATION?"[27] In Aiken, South Carolina, as in other southern towns, Lincoln was burned in effigy, and the *Charleston Courier* called for a southern confederacy.[28] On December 20, 1860, a convention of South Carolina state delegates voted to secede from the Union. In January, Mississippi, Florida, Alabama, and Louisiana followed this bold step, as did Texas in February. President James Buchanan did nothing, believing he had no constitutional power to act; while in Springfield, Illinois, president-elect Lincoln stayed silent. He would add nothing to his previous statements about his intentions toward slavery and referred all questions to those statements. One Springfield neighbor and friend wrote that Lincoln was waiting patiently to take office, "though it is hard to wait 63 days powerless to do good while treason is raging openly and with a determination to dissolve the Union."[29] Meanwhile, Lincoln followed political events in the newspapers, formed his cabinet, received visitors, attended to his vast correspondence, and composed his inaugural address.[30]

Little is known of Robert's life during these harrowing months. He attended to his studies and became a more popular and well-known fellow as the son of the president-elect. He also may have received jeers and angry stares from the southern students, a number of whom left Cambridge in indignation after the election.[31] What is known of his life at this time shows him to be a typical college freshman, filled with the self-centeredness of youth. His first-term grades were respectable, considering his notoriety, his penchant for social activities, and his decision to study enough but not too much. School records show that, out of 100 percent, Robert scored 96 in ethics, 87 in freshman mathematics, 79 in Latin and Greek composition, 78 in freshman Greek, and 68 in freshman Latin; he finished the term ranked thirty-eighth in his class of 125 men.[32]

During the winter break in late November to early December 1860, Robert traveled to Exeter with his friend Richard McConkey and enjoyed a "constant round of dissipation" including dinners, dances, and teas. He was enjoying himself but not fully embracing his celebrity status. "Ain't you beginning to get a little tired of this constant uproar?" he playfully wrote to his mother. He even more light-heartedly informed her of his own trials avoiding the hullabaloo:

> You will remember I wrote to Father about a fellow who is boring me considerably. He capped the climax lately. There was a Republican levee and supper at Cambridge to which I was invited. I did not go, for I anticipated what really happened.
>
> I was sitting in my room, about 9½, when two boys came up and handed me an admission ticket on the back of which this fellow had written, asking

> me to come over as they were calling for me. I wrote him a note excusing myself. He must be the biggest fool in the world not to know that I did not want to go over, when if I did, I would be expected to make a speech! Just phancy my phelinks mounted on the rostrum, holding "a vast sea of human faces," etc. I stop overwhelmed.[33]

The first term at Harvard ended on Wednesday, January 16, 1861, after which the students enjoyed six weeks of winter vacation.[34] Mary Lincoln, eager to see her son, took the opportunity to meet Robert in New York City the following Saturday.[35] Robert and George Latham met Mary in New York and spent a few days there with her while she shopped for clothing for her tenure as first lady, after which they all traveled together back to Springfield, arriving on January 25.[36] Abraham Lincoln, eager to see his wife and oldest son but not informed of their arrival day, waited three consecutive nights at the train depot in the cold and snow to receive them.[37]

Robert's return to Springfield was his first visit home in nearly eighteen months. The city had grown and changed since his departure in 1859, and so had the boy who left. Friends and family noticed a substantial difference in Robert. "The heir apparent of the President elect has been the observed of all the observing Springfield girls today," one newspaper reported of Robert's first day in town. "The effect of a residence within the improving influences of genteel, well dressed and well behaved Boston is plainly noticeable in his outward appearance, the comparative elegance of which certainly presents a striking contrast to the loose, careless, awkward rigging of his Presidential father."[38] Family friend Mercy Conkling wrote a similar sentiment, that the young ladies of Springfield "say that Bob has greatly improved, and that he is much more gentlemanly." She also admired his beaver hat (also called a stove-pipe hat).[39]

Back at home, Robert talked, walked, and took carriage rides with his mother, played with brothers Willie and Tad, and spent time with friends old and new. It was at this time that Robert became reacquainted with John Hay, whom he had so idolized at Illinois State University and befriended in 1859. By 1861, Hay, then age twenty-two, was informally assisting president-elect Lincoln's personal secretary, John G. Nicolay, in his daily work and was formally hired to the job in February.[40] Robert's previous acquaintance with Hay, as well as Hay's proximity to the elder Lincoln, facilitated a deeper friendship between the younger Lincoln and Hay.

The main purpose of Robert's return to Springfield at this time, however, was to assist and accompany his father to Washington. As Mercy Conkling wrote in anticipation of Robert's visit in November 1860, "Bob . . . will be here about the 20th of January and remain *with Mr. Lincoln* till after the inauguration."[41] In February, Conkling wrote that "Bob figures quite largely" in the day-to-day life of the president-elect. Exactly what he did or did not do to assist his father is unclear. Had Robert been a college graduate at this time, his father may have made him a presidential secretary or assistant, much as other members of Lincoln's cabinet did with their sons. As it was, Robert was the only member of the Lincoln family to accompany Abraham from the beginning of the inaugural journey.

As the March 4 date of Abraham Lincoln's inauguration approached, the secession crisis grew worse. Fear, anger, resentment, and worry roiled the country. With the inaction and ineptitude of Buchanan's last days, the populace looked to Springfield for comfort, but Lincoln offered few words. Privately, he told politicians that he would follow the Republican platform and leave slavery alone where it existed but not allow it to spread west. "Do the people of the south really entertain fears that a Republican administration would, *directly*, or *indirectly*, interfere with their slaves, or with them, about their slaves?" Lincoln asked in a letter to Alexander H. Stephens, a former congressional colleague and future Confederate vice president. "The south would be in no more danger in this respect, than it was in the days of Washington. I suppose, however, this does not meet the case. You think slavery is *right* and ought to be extended; while we think it is *wrong* and ought to be restricted. That I suppose is the rub, it certainly is the only substantial difference between us."[42] In November 1860, Lincoln had tried to help assuage southern worries by declaring his respect for states' rights and each state's power to protect its property. His words, spoken by U.S. Senator Lyman Trumbull of Illinois during a Springfield speech, did nothing to alleviate southern fears, however. Lincoln expected they would not.[43]

The southern hostility to the president-elect showed itself not only in the angry editorials and letters printed daily in southern newspapers but also in death threats. As early as mid-November 1860, the *New York Herald* had reported, "Letters threatening [Lincoln's] life are daily received from the south."[44] In January, Mary Lincoln received a late Christmas gift from South Carolina in the form of a painting of her husband dangling from a tree with a noose around his neck, his feet chained, and his body tarred and feathered.[45] The mounting danger caused many to worry over the Lincoln family's safety during their planned train journey to Washington in February. A number of Mary Lincoln's concerned family members and friends, as well as General Winfield Scott, head of the U.S. Army, wanted Mary and the younger Lincoln boys to stay at Springfield until after Lincoln had arrived safely in Washington. Lincoln himself preferred to have the family meet him and Robert in New York. But Mary rebuffed suggestions of not accompanying her husband, and at the last minute Scott changed his mind, deciding that having the family with the president-elect might actually be a safer arrangement. She and the two younger boys, therefore, were going to leave Springfield on a separate, later train and meet Lincoln and Robert at Indianapolis, Indiana.[46]

On February 6, as the days drew closer to their departure, the Lincoln family held a final grand farewell reception at their home. "And such a crowd I seldom, or ever saw at a private home," wrote a friend. "It took about twenty minutes to get in the hall door. And then it required no little management to make your way out."[47] *New York Herald* correspondent Henry Villard wrote that the farewell party "was the most brilliant affair of the kind witnessed here in many years." Hundreds of people came to wish the Lincolns farewell, but the limited size of the house (and no doubt the size of the women's hoop skirts) created a "slight jam" of the receiving line. "Every room on both the first and second floor was densely packed with a fashionable multitude. The President and lady received their guests in the parlor on the first floor. They stood close to each other nearly all the evening in order to facilitate presentations. Mrs. Lincoln's splendid toilette gave satisfactory evidence of extensive purchases during her late visit to New York."[48] Robert, ebullient and carefree, approached his father in the receiving line that night and said, "Good evening Mr. Lincoln!" at which the father gave him a "gentle slap across the face."[49]

During the following days, the Lincolns sold much of their furniture, packed their belongings, and rented their house.[50] The family spent their last few nights in Springfield at a hotel. At the Great Western depot the next day, huge crowds turned out to wish Lincoln good-bye, despite the rain. The presidential party consisted of the Lincolns, along with brothers-in-law Lockwood Todd and Dr. William S. Wallace, presidential secretaries John Nicolay and John Hay, and family friends David Davis, Norman B. Judd, Latham, and Colonel E. Elmer Ellsworth, as well as Colonel E. V. Sumner, Major David Hunter, Captains George W. Hazard and John Pope, Ward Hill Lamon, J. M. Burgess, William S. Wood, B. Forbes, and journalist Villard. A number of Springfield friends also traveled with the party to the first overnight stop at Indianapolis.[51]

The morning of February 11 dawned rainy and dreary. Spirits were dampened by the weather. Despite the rain, hundreds of people turned out to say good-bye. Robert and his father arrived at the depot with their luggage and said good-bye to Mary, Willie, Tad, and numerous friends and associates. The president-elect had not intended to speak and had even told the press that there would be no address but at the last moment, overcome by emotion, Lincoln, standing at the back of the train, said a few extemporaneous words of farewell.[52] The moment was "quite affecting," wrote Lincoln's friend and neighbor James Conkling to his son. "Many eyes were filled to overflowing as Mr. Lincoln uttered those few and simple words which you will see in the papers. His own breast heaved with emotion, and he could scarcely command his feelings sufficiently to commence. He is now fairly on his way for the weal or woe of the nation."[53]

Abraham Lincoln's inaugural journey by train was not only a necessity by the limits of transportation in 1861 but also was intended as a public-relations tour. Lincoln wanted his fellow citizens who had read his words but never seen his face to see him. His journey was scheduled to take him through the major cities of Indianapolis, Cincinnati, Columbus, Pittsburgh, Cleveland, Buffalo, Albany, New York City, Philadelphia, Harrisburg, and Baltimore and into Washington, D.C. The exultation that must have been Robert's is difficult to comprehend. He was the oldest son of the president-elect, a college freshman aboard a train full of family, friends, statesmen, dignitaries, and journalists. At every stop, the party was feted by crowds, bands, more journalists, and local dignitaries. Robert himself was consistently found by the local youths and treated to drinks, cigars, flattery, and pageantry fit for a true prince. As both Nicolay and Villard observed, Lincoln was sober, but Robert, along with Willie and Tad, were jubilant at the celebratory atmosphere of the trip.[54]

This revelry got Robert into some serious trouble after only one day into the journey, when he nearly lost his father's inaugural address. According to Lamon, law associate and self-appointed bodyguard of the president-elect, it was the only time he had ever seen his patient, jovial friend Abraham Lincoln so angry.[55] Lincoln had worked diligently and stealthily on his inaugural address, understanding the importance of his words on the deteriorating national situation. He hoped his speech would reassure angry southerners and perhaps recall them to the Union, but he knew just as well that if he offended anyone, especially those in the Border States, it could make the situation even worse.

Using only a copy of the Constitution, Senator Daniel Webster's reply to Senator Robert Hayne, and Andrew Jackson's proclamation on nullification, Lincoln worked on his speech in the second-floor storeroom of his brother-in-law's store, far from the prying eyes of the press and the eager hordes of office seekers and well-wishers. Once completed, the inaugural was entrusted to William H. Bailhache, editor of the *(Springfield) Illinois State Journal*, who locked himself and one typesetter in the composing room of the newspaper and printed a dozen copies. These were distributed to various friends and associates of Lincoln for review and feedback. By the time of the departure for Washington, the inaugural had been revised three times and reprinted. Yet, despite such care and secrecy involved in its composition, for its security on the journey Lincoln merely put it in a black oilcloth handbag, gave it to his oldest son, and told him to "Take care of it" but did not tell him what it contained.[56]

When the inaugural train reached Indianapolis that first night, it was greeted at the station by what Nicolay estimated at fifty thousand people.[57] The crowds were large and poorly controlled; most of the presidential party had to carry their own luggage and walk to the Bates House, where they were spending the night. Along the route, Robert was besieged by local youths who carried him off in raucous celebration. Abraham Lincoln, reaching the hotel long after Robert and only after a ceremonial tour through the streets and speech from the hotel balcony, was anxious about his black bag. Robert, however, could not be found for some time. When finally he appeared before his father, Robert was anxiously interrogated on the whereabouts of the satchel. Robert, unaware of the need for such anxiety, replied "with bored and injured virtue" that since he had no room assigned him on his arrival at the hotel, he knew of nothing better to do than give it to the hotel clerk, as any traveler would.[58] The rest of the incident is best described by Nicolay, who was present and who also was friends with Robert for the next forty years:

> "And what did the clerk do with it," asked his father.
>
> "Set it on the floor behind the counter," answered Robert complacently.
>
> A look of stupefaction passed over the countenance of Mr. Lincoln, and visions of that Inaugural in all the next morning's newspapers floated through his imagination. Without a word he opened the door of his room, forced his way through the crowded corridor down to the office, where, with a single stride of his long legs, he swung himself across the clerk's counter, behind which a small mountain of carpetbags of all colors had accumulated. Then drawing a little key out of his pocket he began delving for the black ones, and opened one by one those that the key would unlock, to the great surprise and amusement of the clerk and bystanders, as their miscellaneous contents came to light. Fortune favored the President-elect, for after the first half dozen trials, he found his treasures.[59]

Lincoln carried the bag back to his room, this time told Robert what it contained, handed it back to his son, and said, "Now you keep it!" "You bet I did," Robert later related, adding reminiscently, "Father did not scold. He never alluded to it again."[60]

Entire volumes have been, and will continue to be, written about Lincoln's inaugural journey. Mary, Willie, and Tad joined Abraham and Robert in Indianapolis on the morning of February 12.[61] Once the entire family was together, the train continued the rest of the journey east. Lincoln's secretaries, Nicolay and Hay, summed up the journey succinctly in their biography of Lincoln: "A proper description of the Presidential tour which followed [the Springfield departure] would fill a volume. It embraced two weeks of official receptions by committees, mayors, governors, and legislatures; of crowded evening receptions and interminable hand-shakings; of impromptu or informal addresses at every ceremony; of cheers, salutes, bonfires, military parades, and imposing processions amid miles of spectators."[62]

Seventeen-year-old Robert, at the height of his adolescence, experienced the journey as a typical teenager: he had as much fun as he could and availed himself of every opportunity for such. It was reported that his jovial, colloquial ways contributed daily to the general good feelings of the train party. Robert, twenty-two-year-old Hay, twenty-nine-year-old Nicolay, and twenty-four-year-old Ellsworth, were the four youngest men on board and spent much time together. Most of Robert's chumming, in the form of socializing, drinking, smoking, and flirting with girls, was with Hay alone, as Nicolay was shy and extremely busy as Lincoln's secretary, and Ellsworth, head of the Springfield Zouaves, was full of a military dignity and abstemiousness. In Cincinnati, Robert was fawned over and feted with a special supper by seventy-five young Republicans.[63] On the trip from Buffalo to Albany, Robert rode "on the engine" of the train most of the trip and "expressed himself as highly gratified at the new sensations experienced."[64] In New York City, Robert visited P. T. Barnum's American Museum, where he observed Aztec children and the "lightning calculator"; he also wanted to consult the museum's fortune-teller about the future of the country, but as she had extremely southern attitudes, "she rather favored secession."[65]

Also typical of young men, Robert noticed and was noticed by girls. On February 4, in Springfield, he accompanied nineteen-year-old Anna Ridgely to a meeting of the Reading Society, most likely for a poetry reading.[66] In Columbus, he had his head turned by a local beauty, and the party's departure from that city the next morning left him with a heavy heart, and in New York, Mary reportedly made a quip about how much Robert was "fond of the girls."[67] It was later stated that during his college years, Robert was "somewhat of a ladies man," especially whenever he was in Washington; indeed, by the end of February, after sufficient time for Robert to have participated in numerous soirees around the city, the *New York World* reported, "Young Bob has been extensively lionized, and a good deal of regret is expressed by the ladies at his approaching departure for Harvard."[68]

Unlike his father, Robert was not a teetotaler. Journalist Villard reported that while on the train, from the very beginning of the trip, Robert "adhered closely to the refreshment saloon, the gayest of the gay."[69] Villard later marveled at Robert's drinking prowess, after he emerged from a night of drinking sparkling Catawba "with which the Republican youths of Cincinnati had plied him so liberally" without any obvious aftereffects.[70] Robert also had a penchant for smoking, and it was reported from Albany, New York, that he "thinks of nothing just now but segars . . . and indulged in all sorts of uproarious merriment" in the forward saloon car.[71] Some newspapers, especially those run by Democrats, characterized Robert as quite a partier, or "fast." The *New York Tribune* sought to rebut these statements by declaring him "a young man of fine abilities and much dignity of character" and stating that reports to the contrary were "no less painful to him than to his excellent parents, to whom he has ever been a dutiful and affectionate son."[72] As dutiful and affectionate as Robert was, it is not incorrect to reveal his great desire and ability for smoking cigars, drinking, and carousing, which only increased during his college years.

Aside from revelry and merrymaking, Robert had a public part to play as well. At every stop, the curious looked for and pointed out "the Prince of Rails," and he was called on often to give speeches. The first call for his appearance occurred in Indianapolis. Robert responded to the vehement calls for a speech by him simply with "a graceful waving of his hand."[73] He repeated the performance in Cincinnati, where the *New York World* reported that rumors of his presence made the Burnet House hotel "wild." Robert "with a fine display of pluck declined to make a speech. He waved his hat, however, bowed, and retired, his debut being a pronounced success. . . . [Robert] seems to inherit the paternal energy, is visible everywhere simultaneously, and wears the plume of his new title, 'the prince of rails,' with jaunty self possession and grace."[74]

Another one of Robert's probable duties was, along with the rest of the male members of the inaugural train party, the protection of his father. Nicolay wrote his fiancée that the reception at every city where they stopped was so immense that "it has been a serious task for us of his escort, to prevent his being killed with kindness."[75] In Buffalo, New York, the crowds were so ferocious that Major Hunter had his arm dislocated; likewise in Albany, the crush was so great and annoying that one reporter stated the Lincolns left the city "with feelings of gratitude for their safe deliverance and with resolutions never to return hither again."[76] But being killed by kindness was not the only death Abraham Lincoln—or the members of his party—had to guard against.

As the inaugural train proceeded farther east, rumors were afloat of trouble brewing in Baltimore, a city with strong secessionist feelings and ties. Detective Allan Pinkerton, while investigating the possibility of sabotage to the railroad lines, discovered a plot to murder Lincoln as his train stopped to change engines in the city nicknamed since 1835 as "Mobtown." Only a few days after Pinkerton notified Lincoln of this plot, Frederick Seward, son of William Seward, the secretary of state–designate, brought a message that his father and General Scott had also uncovered a separate assassination plot in Baltimore.[77] At the dire urgings of Pinkerton, Seward, and Lincoln's other trusted advisers, the president-elect agreed to undertake a secret journey through Baltimore one night ahead of his published schedule.[78] Accompanied only by his friend Lamon and detective Pinkerton, Lincoln traveled through Baltimore on the midnight train and arrived in Washington in the early morning of February 23.

Few people in the presidential party knew of the president-elect's secret midnight run: Davis, Lincoln's friend and campaign manager, and the three military men in the party, Sumner, Hunter, and Pope. Despite the need and desire for the utmost secrecy, Mary Lincoln also was told of the plan. "This [Lincoln] said he could not avoid, as otherwise she would be very much excited by his absence," Pinkerton later related.[79] Robert had no idea his father had gone until he heard the news the next morning.[80] The public reaction to this change of plan was mixed. Some understood the need for safety, especially in such an incendiary town as Baltimore, while others decried it as cowardice. Whatever the feelings of the presidential party, the absence of the president-elect left a gloomy residue inside the train. There was little conversation during the ride from Harrisburg to York, Pennsylvania. At York, about two thousand people were waiting at the station. When it was announced that Lincoln was not on the train, the crowd was unbelieving. Wood, the choreographer of the inaugural journey, then presented Robert Lincoln to the crowds as a substitute for the president-elect. Robert had only a moment to wave, however, before the train lurched forward to continue towards Baltimore.[81] When the train crossed the Maryland state line, Robert led the party in singing the "Star-Spangled Banner," which raised everyone's spirits.[82]

A new and different kind of pall was about to descend on the group at Baltimore, however. Lincoln's absence on the train did not alleviate the antipathy of the waiting phalanx of citizens. Some people did not believe he was already in Washington. When the inaugural party reached Baltimore, vast crowds surrounded the cars, and as detective Pinkerton later described, "[T]hey met with anything but a cordial reception."[83] Pinkerton's language can be called euphemism to say the least. True to the warnings, the crowd comprised mostly secessionists, full of resentment and violence, who shouted and cheered for the south and Jefferson Davis. The *Baltimore Sun* reported that as soon as the presidential train stopped, "the crowd leaped upon the platforms and mounted the tops of the cars like so many monkeys, until, like a hive of bees, they swarmed upon them, shouting, hallooing, and making all manner of noises."[84] The *New York Times* reported that members of the mob (whom the newspaper called "plug-uglies") thrust their heads into the windows of the presidential car looking for Lincoln and shouting, "Trot him out," "Let's have him," "We'll give you hell," "You bloody Black Republicans."[85] Some men forced their way into the car and were promptly and forcibly pushed out by Hay, who then locked the door. One of the members of the presidential party, guest Margaret Williams, remembered that once the crowd realized that Lincoln was not on the train, a shout went up for "Bob" to show himself, who, "with courage commanding admiration from all, including the mob, appeared in the platform." Williams also stated that Robert, Hay, and Nicolay all were armed with revolvers "in case of need."[86]

After about thirty minutes of enduring the epithets and obscenities, the party was taken by carriage to the Eutaw House for dinner and afterwards taken to a different train depot for the final leg of their journey. Once again, with the cars stationary on the tracks and waiting to start the journey, a mob surrounded the presidential train. The "ill-bred men and boys" shouted at them with foul language, leered in at the windows, and forced open the windows that were shut. One mobster, face pressed against the car window, leered at Robert Lincoln and asked, "How's your old man?" Robert, "annoyed" by the crowd, tried to be unaffected and nonchalant as he smoked his cigar.[87] The entire experience in Baltimore was of such an impressive character that Robert in 1910 wrote, "I remember very well the trip from Harrisburg to Washington."[88]

The presidential party arrived in Washington in the early evening of February 23 and proceeded to Willards Hotel.[89] Abraham Lincoln had spent the day with soon-to-be Secretary of State Seward, visited Capitol Hill, met with politicians, and discussed the military and security situation with Scott. Scott, a Mexican War hero known as "Old Fuss and Feathers," had the security of Washington and of the inauguration well in hand, according to the newspapers. Angry at the possibility that secessionists may try to prevent the inauguration or even assassinate Lincoln, Scott was positioning troops and cannons around the city and identifying which regiments were loyal to the Union and which were not. As early as February 3, Julia Trumbull, wife of Senator Trumbull, wrote that Washington "begins to present a warlike appearance," with troops in Judiciary Square and near the Capitol and the White House.[90] Also during these tense days before March 4, a Peace Commission of politicians had met and offered proposals for the solution of the looming internecine conflict. The proposals made headlines, but nobody expected the south to accept the proposition, and Lincoln had already said he would not deviate from the platform on which he was elected.

Abraham Lincoln was constantly occupied during those tense days between February 23 and March 4, but his family had few commitments. Robert spent his days seeing the Washington sights and socializing. One of the first places he visited was the model room of the U.S. Patent Office—repeating the visit (one of Robert's earliest and fondest memories) he and his father made in 1847 during Abraham Lincoln's single term in Congress—and where president-elect

Lincoln had a model of his own patented invention.[91] In the evenings, the presidential party had cheerful times at Willard's Hotel, eating, talking, and dancing. Nicolay wrote that the hotel was so crowded with people, especially ladies in the parlor, that it seemed like they were "having a party every night."[92] One party member recalled that Robert and Hay were very enthusiastic revelers, who continually tried to draw out the socially shy Nicolay and Ellsworth.[93]

Robert's time in Washington was not entirely consumed by society; he also assisted his father. The complete extent of this aid is unknown, but it is known that on February 25, Robert accompanied his father on a long walk around Washington "that there might be a physical stratum on which to rest the mental labors of the day."[94] Robert also may have served as a sounding board for his father as the president-elect read aloud his address the night prior and morning of the inauguration.[95]

While the presidential party endured the tenseness and excitement that morning of March 4, General Scott had the city prepared for trouble. "Washington is full of soldiers, and every possible precaution has been and is being taken by Gen. Scott to protect the public property and the lives of the citizens," one visitor remembered. "I rode through a short street this morning, along which were mounted cannon on both sides, and artillery men to each piece, all ready to fire. A fine company of regulars from West Point are here, the Sappers and Miners, and also two or three companies of cavalry. They are stationed all over the city—some at the corners, on the house roofs, in private yards, and I even saw a sentinel pacing backward and forward in yard of the young ladies institute."[96]

At 10 A.M., the inaugural procession began at the White House, driving President Buchanan to Willard's to pick up the president-elect. The two rode in an open carriage down streets flanked with soldiers to the Capitol, while Lincoln's family rode behind in a separate carriage. The cortege walked through the Capitol out on to inaugural platform filled with generations of luminaries and dignitaries. Robert watched from the diplomatic gallery as his father took the oath from moribund U.S. Supreme Court Chief Justice Roger B. Taney, the man who had written the Dred Scott decision. Lincoln's vanquished challenger Senator Douglas offered to hold and held the new president's hat during the delivery of the inaugural address. Sitting on the platform, observing the vista of thousands of people listening to his father's words, wondering whether it would be—as Lincoln originally wrote but then deleted from his remarks—peace or the sword, Robert heard his father declare in his high-pitched voice: "In *your* hands, my dissatisfied fellow countrymen, and not in *mine*, is the momentous issue of civil war. The government will not assail *you*. You can have no conflict, without being yourselves the aggressors. *You* have no oath registered in Heaven to destroy the government, while *I* shall have the most solemn one to 'preserve, protect and defend' it."[97] The shouts of approval for Lincoln's speech were loud and long.[98] No violence occurred during the event; the closest thing to a disturbance during the day was a man who climbed atop a tall tree in front of the Capitol and made a long political diatribe in which he claimed to be the rightful president of the United States.[99] "We had a gratifying and glorious inauguration," Nicolay wrote the next day; General Scott is reported to have heaved a sigh of relief and said, "Thank God, we now have a government."[100] After the ceremony, former President Buchanan took President Lincoln to the White House, where Robert witnessed Buchanan give the new president the door key.[101] Robert may or may not have witnessed another scene between the outgoing and incoming presidents that occurred in the President's Room of the Capitol on inauguration day. Buchanan took Lincoln aside to a corner of the room near Hay, the young secretary who, eager and certain to hear some "momentous counsels" from the elder statesman, listened as Buchanan said, "I think you will find the water of the right-hand well at the White House better than that at the left," and other details of the kitchen and pantry.[102]

The inaugural ball held that evening was described as elegant and tasteful, "very successful and brilliant," attended by about one thousand people.[103] The presidential party, including Robert, entered the ball at about 11 P.M. Dancing continued until about 4 A.M. Mary Lincoln left shortly before the finish, while fun-loving Robert probably stayed until the end. President Lincoln had departed only a few hours after arriving, harrowed by the secession crisis.

Robert returned to Harvard on March 6, two days after his father's inauguration. The spring semester had begun on February 28, but Robert was allowed a late arrival in order to attend his father's inauguration.[104] Once the ceremonies were completed, Robert was eager to return to Cambridge and to the friends, the girls, the smoking and drinking, and (possibly) the education he had been away from for seven weeks. In addition to these reasons, and perhaps even more than these reasons, Robert had had his fill of being the Prince of Rails. His distaste for being a celebrity had been sorely tried during his vacation—the attention, the finger-pointing, the well-wishers and sycophants, the journalists and politicians, and, perhaps, the strain of watching his father prepare for a monumental task, had all made him weary. "He is sick of Washington and glad to get back to his college," one newspaper reported.[105] Eleven-year-old Willie Lincoln perhaps best voiced the feelings of the Lincoln sons when he said, "I wish they wouldn't stare at us so. Wasn't there ever a president who had children?"[106] But for Robert, the oldest and an able-bodied young man who did not join the Army after the war began in April, the attention on him had only just begun.

5

"He Is Only Mr. Robert Lincoln, of Cambridge"

Back at Harvard, Robert—known to friends as Bob—returned to his boarding room and roommate Frederick P. Anderson and easily settled back into college life. His second-term classes kept him studying Greek, Latin, mathematics, and composition, while history and elocution replaced his first-term ethics course.[1] Every day as he crossed Main Street to enter the college campus, he would pass under the stone arch engraved with the maxim "ENTER TO GROW IN WISDOM." Of course, there was no better place than Harvard to gain such wisdom. The college had assembled a roster of some of the most brilliant professorial minds in the country, including naturalist Louis Agassiz, botanist Asa Gray, poet and essayist James Russell Lowell, and physician and poet Oliver Wendell Holmes Sr.

Friends and classmates later stated that Robert was an able student and a voracious reader, but his first known letter after returning to Cambridge from Washington was written not about anything he had learned but about that universal male constancy of interest: women. Writing to John Hay, Robert first whimsically lamented the departure of a girl he called "the Star of Boston and vicinity," who was leaving to spend a month or two in New York; he went on to discuss letters he received from admiring girls in Ohio and Indiana. Of the latter he wrote, "The writer had a baby, she had named after me (!) and requesting me to send said baby a dress or a pair of boots (size not stated). It commenced: 'Sir. You have a baby here,* my child, which is a namesake of yours.' She signed her name: 'Miss ______.' Somebody must have been '*mis-staken*.' (goak)." In his starred note at the bottom of the letter, he humorously added, "*At this point, I nearly fainted from an excess of supposed paternal dignity. The close however cleared up my fears."[2] Robert, still and ever the

Prince of Rails to the public, also received numerous gifts in the mail. Some were tokens of appreciation for him, some were "gifts" in an attempt to curry favor with the president. Robert received so many offerings, in fact, that one friend recalled how Bob's friends would help him go through it all.[3]

As the above illustrates, even in college in Massachusetts the oldest son of President Lincoln was not immune from the attentions of the eager populace.[4] A more interesting anecdote of Robert's trials also occurred during his Spring 1861 term, when an office seeker asked Robert to intervene with the president to get him an appointment as Cambridge postmaster. In the first time "Bob" sought a political favor from his father, the president quickly and tersely replied, "If you do not attend to your studies and let matters such as you write about alone, I will take you away from college." Robert thereafter carried his father's letter in his pocket and on many occasions afterwards pulled it out when accosted by other aspiring office seekers.[5] This did not mean that Robert never helped anybody and never asked his father for appointments, but it seems he thereafter limited his recommendations to his personal friends.[6]

Despite his fame, Robert Lincoln was universally remembered by friends and classmates as a modest, amiable person, never one to trade on his father's name or position. "Of course his parentage gave him celebrity, but in the democratic community of Cambridge that was all," wrote one classmate. "It fixed all eyes on him, but it was a very insignificant factor in determining his essential importance."[7] Another classmate recalled how Robert was a "sturdy, whole-souled, modest fellow, of strong affections and friendships, and to his closer friends he was without reserve and delightfully entertaining"; another remembrance was of young Lincoln "as he hied with nimble and elastic step across the college campus, the shrewd, good-natured glance of his eye, the quick and abrupt nod to the right and left as he greeted passing friends, his cheery voice as he hailed some crony or another with some old nickname of his own coinage."[8] One newspaper editor praised Robert's "modesty and self-control" during his years at Harvard, stating that when his life "was surrounded by temptations that might have turned an older head," instead of yielding to these natural temptations, "he was the most unassuming, unpretending private citizen in the country."[9]

Robert's outer calm may or may not have belied an inner anxiety for the fate of the country his father now led. Ever since South Carolina had seceded from the Union in December, the nation had been on a path to war. Robert saw this firsthand while with his father in Springfield and Washington, but the tension and anxiety were just as palpable at Harvard. "The year opens & continues with anxiety & uncertainty as to the movements of the Southern States towards secession," Harvard College librarian John Langdon Sibley wrote in his diary in January. "Newspapers are filled with all manner of statements."[10] Most of the talk centered on the standoff between the federal government and the state of South Carolina pertaining to the ownership and manning of the federal forts in Charleston Harbor. In his inaugural address, President Lincoln had declared that he would hold all government property; but the state of South Carolina considered the fort its property, on loan to the federal government.

The impasse and uncertainty over whether the state would forcibly take the forts or the Lincoln administration would attempt to resupply them was heightened when Major Robert Anderson, the commanding U.S. military officer at Fort Moultrie in Charleston Harbor, secretly moved his garrison of eighty-five men across the harbor to Fort Sumter on December 26. It was a brilliant tactic that transferred his vulnerable troops to a more defensible position in the face of growing agitation and militarism from the South Carolinians on the surrounding shores. After nearly four months of what amounted to a siege at Sumter, during the transition from the old Democrat president to the new Republican one, after fruitless negotiations for surrender, South Carolina batteries opened fire on the fort on April 12. The *Boston Daily Journal* reported that news of the bombardment "was received with mingled feelings of sorrow and burning indignation" in the city, and crowds gathered on corners and at newspaper offices to hear the latest news.[11] When Major Anderson evacuated his troops after thirty-six hours of shelling, Harvard librarian Sibley wrote in his diary, "Fort Sumter surrenders; it is said at Boston. If so, there will be a dreadful, bloody, civil war."[12]

And he was correct. President Lincoln immediately called for seventy-five thousand militia troops for three months' service. The response from the loyal states was so overwhelming that volunteers far outnumbered the president's initial call. In Boston, patriots with eagerness redolent of the spirit of 1776 lined up for service and were some of the first troops to enter and defend Washington; in Cambridge, the patriotic feeling of the young men was even more pronounced, and "the College sprang into warlike action."[13] Within days of the news, the Cambridge company of volunteers was organized, and two members of Harvard's junior class had left the college to muster in at Boston.[14] On Saturday, April 20, two Harvard alumni were sent off to muster in at Boston as commissioned officers of the fifth regiment, with a grand ceremony in front of Lyceum Hall in Harvard Square. A huge collection of enthusiastic people attended the event, including Robert Lincoln, who was inveigled to give a speech. Sibley summed up the mood of the college in his diary: "The college is full of the spirit of war & indignant at the treatment of the country's flag. Very little studying going on."[15]

The students of Harvard quickly formed drill companies, the faculty provided arms and instructors, the playing field was turned into a marching and drill ground, the octagonal gymnasium was utilized as an armory, and the book *Hardee's Tactics* "bulged from every pocket."[16] When rumors began circulating in late April that rebel sympathizers would blow up the state arsenal on Garden Street, the student corps set themselves to guard duty. As one student reminisced, "Are there not some still with us who can recall the Gymnasium turned into an armory, the Delta glittering with bayonets, and the gallant squad of Harvard Cadets marching up to the defense of the Arsenal? The relief of the guard there on duty, and the three days of danger, picket-duty, fun and frolic?"[17] Librarian Sibley recorded that the guard on the arsenal was "maintained night and day in true military style," and a drenching rain all day and night on April 28 "brought hard experience to military tyros."[18] By fall 1861, when the Harvard faculty lost interest in assisting the student body in military drilling, the students took it into their own hands and formed the Harvard Drill Club.

The town was further shocked to hear that one of their Boston regiments was attacked on its way through Baltimore to protect the capital—blood shed exactly eighty-six years to the day after the first Massachusetts casualties of the Revolution. Interestingly, for all their patriotic bluster, very few Harvard students actually enlisted in the army. The fighting men of Cambridge and Harvard—most famously the Twentieth Massachusetts—were Harvard graduates, not undergraduates.[19] School historians say the students did not enlist because they felt it beneath the dignity of a Harvard gentleman to enlist as a private. The young men sought instead to finish their degree and then be commissioned as regimental or staff officers.[20] As Charles Francis Adams Jr. later arrogantly wrote of one Harvard graduate, but it serves as a synecdoche of typical Cambridge thinking at the time, "[T]he previous training of the typical Harvard man specially qualified him for efficient work [as a staff officer]. He had but to familiarize himself with his duties."[21]

Robert Lincoln, like most young men at the time, ardently wanted to enlist. "In those days, a young man . . . had an unpleasant feeling if he could not take some part in the War," he later wrote.[22] It is unclear, however, whether he intended to enter the ranks as a private (so anathema to Harvard men like Adams) or seek a commission as a staff officer. Robert always had been enticed by military matters: hearing as a young boy his father's stories of his enlistment during the Black Hawk War, living in Washington during the Mexican War, and then serving in the Springfield Cadets as a teenager. (It is unknown whether he served in the Harvard Drill Club, although it is unlikely, as membership of the president's son certainly would be mentioned in later reminiscences of the club, which he was not.) Both Robert's aunt and his mother's seamstress recalled how keenly he sought to join the army.[23] Yet, despite his enthusiasm, and his father's egalitarianism, Robert's eagerness for military service was blocked by his parents—or, more specifically, by his mother.

Mary Lincoln is one of the more interesting women in American history, especially in the pantheon of First Ladies. Her seamstress, Elizabeth Keckly, later wrote, "I never in my life saw a more peculiarly constituted woman. Search the world over, and you will not find her counterpart."[24] She had extreme emotional shifts from happy to sad, euphoria to depression. In the White House, William O. Stoddard, presidential secretary, wrote, "It was not easy, at first, to understand why a lady who could be one day so kindly, so considerate, so generous, so thoughtful and so hopeful, could, upon another day, appear so unreasonable, so irritable, so despondent, so even niggardly, and so prone to see the dark, the wrong side of men and women and events."[25] Mary also was plagued with paranoia and intense anxiety, especially over the health and safety of her husband and children. By 1861, as the country mobilized for war, Mary suffered a dire terror of death. She never had handled death well, each grief being compounded with the last, beginning with her mother, then her father, grandmother, and four-year-old son Eddie in a span of six months between 1849 and 1850. After Lincoln was elected to the presidency, the continual death threats and the Baltimore assassination plot unnerved her and increased her worry.

Now, Mary's oldest son wanted to go to war. She was convinced he would never survive, so she refused to allow him to go. Publicly, her reason—similar to those of the Harvard student body—was so Robert could finish his education, stating that "an educated man can serve his country better than an ignoramus"; but privately she told her husband, "We have lost one son, and his loss is as much as I can bear, without being called upon to make another sacrifice."[26] While the president argued that many mothers had lost all their children and Mary should not be so selfish, Lincoln, aware of his wife's frailties and anxieties, in fact a father figure to her in many ways, found himself unwilling to impose this burden of fear on her and forbade Robert to join the army.[27]

In addition to his wife's fears, however, Abraham Lincoln had fears of his own about Robert's enlistment. He was afraid his political enemies would use or abuse his soldier son as a way to cause him public embarrassment or interfere with his public duties. Such men had attempted similar plans in regards to the spending habits and personal life of the president's wife, and Lincoln, a shrewd politician, knew the game. In October 1860, he had vowed "to not unnecessarily put any weapons" in the hands of men "who are eager for something new upon which to base new misrepresentations" of him.[28] In fact, in later life, Robert cited this as his father's main reason for preventing his enlistment, more than his mother's fears.[29]

Robert's civilian status caused both the president and his son much embarrassment and harassment. Newspapers excoriated Lincoln as a hypocrite willing to let other men's sons die but not his own, and even members of Congress criticized the situation.[30] Robert was not immune from criticism. Newspapers, unaware of the real reason for his military absence, called him either a shirker or a coward. Robert resented his parents' decision, but as a dutiful and conscientious son, the only thing he could do was to continue his education and hope his parents would change their minds.

Harvard's fall semester extended from late August or early September to mid-January, with a break for Thanksgiving. Winter vacation was given for six weeks, with the spring semester beginning in late February or early March and continuing until early July, with a five-day recess in late May. At the end of his first year of study, Robert spent his spring break in Washington.[31] He had only been gone from the White House for two months after having attended the inauguration, but now that his family had settled in, it was a new home and a completely different atmosphere.

The Washington to which Robert returned was a different place. It had changed from a country town to a roiling garrison engorged with soldiers from numerous states and all their necessary panoply. In late April, John Nicolay stated that about ten thousand troops were in the city, with about one new regiment arriving every day.[32] Soldiers drilled and trained on grounds all over the city, and a large encampment was settled on the grounds between the White House and the War Department, while the Navy Yard wharf was filled with all sorts of ships. But for all the preparation, the reality of war had not truly set in. Military bands held numerous concerts to which citizens and cabinet members happily attended; promenades along the Mall were common; soldiers attended their drilling with a fun-loving attitude that belied the seriousness of the situation. Attitudes changed, however, when the state of Virginia officially seceded from the Union on May 23, 1861.

The reality of rebel sympathizers and soldiers just across the river from the capital city was a sobering truth. On May 24, eleven regiments of Union soldiers invaded Virginia and occupied the countryside across the Potomac River from Washington, D.C. The Federal troops easily drove off the few rebel pickets in Arlington, Virginia, occupied Robert E. Lee's estate on Arlington Heights, and made it a military command post, while two Union regiments—the First Michigan and Eleventh New York Zouaves—crossed the river into Alexandria. The Zouaves, led by the dashing twenty-four-year-old E. Elmer Ellsworth, a personal friend of Abraham Lincoln, quickly secured the railroad station and telegraph office.[33] But in attempting to remove a Confederate flag from atop the Marshall House inn, Ellsworth was shot and killed by the proprietor.

The military success of the operation was clouded by Ellsworth's death, which brought great sorrow to President Lincoln.[34] Ellsworth's body was placed in state in the East Room of the White House on May 25.

This was the situation to which Robert returned to Washington. He, too, knew Ellsworth and had spent much time with him, as well as presidential secretaries Nicolay and Hay, on the inaugural journey in February. Eager, as many young men are and have always been, to see the front lines of battle into which he could not march, Robert journeyed by horseback with Nicolay and Hay to the captured Virginia country after only a few days back in Washington. The three young men crossed the Long Bridge into Virginia, past the soldiers busy constructing defensive earthen breastworks at the various approaches to the bridge, and up to Arlington Heights. The Heights was the ancestral home of the Custis family (who married into the Lee family), who were related to George Washington. Nicolay, with a patriotic and Unionist fervor, described the old mansion as "in its day a proud affair, and its arrangement, furniture, pictures, etc., at once carry one back to the good old 'first family' days of Virginia, before her social decay bred and engendered the treasonous reptiles that now wallow in the slime and mire her political and moral corruption." In the mansion gardens, the three men met an old slave who was born at Mount Vernon before Washington's death. "We asked him many questions, delighted him with introducing 'Bob,' the president's son, in whom the old darkey expressed a lively interest, and furnished him with a gift of small change," Nicolay wrote.[35]

Whenever he was in Washington during the war, Robert spent much of his time in visiting with Nicolay and Hay. He had known them briefly in Springfield, spent much time together—especially with Hay—during the inaugural journey, lived together in the White House, and were all near the same age. The White House years, in fact, cemented a lifelong friendship between the three young men. Robert also visited with his family, with most of his time recorded as being spent with his mother. Throughout the war years, he accompanied her on shopping trips to New York, Boston, and Philadelphia and on vacations to various locations such as the White Mountains of New Hampshire and Vermont, and she often visited him in Cambridge.

Mary's first visit to Robert at school occurred in May 1861, after a week of shopping in New York and Philadelphia for items to refurbish the dilapidated White House. Robert spent two days with his mother and her cousin Elizabeth Todd Grimsley in Boston where "everything [was] arranged for a charming reception at the Revere House [by Senator Charles Sumner], dining and drives, and we met many of the most distinguished men of Boston and Harvard," Mrs. Grimsley later wrote.[36] This trip was but one of many shopping excursions undertaken by Mary Lincoln to spend her $20,000 congressional appropriation to upgrade the internal appearance of the White House.[37] As with so much of her shopping during the war years, Mary Lincoln's spending was done to impress not only visiting dignitaries but also the Washington society whom she knew did not respect her. But, as the editors of Mary's collected letters astutely observe, "It was the very people Mary Lincoln desired to impress who were the loudest in criticizing her extravagance."[38]

Rumors also were vicious and rampant in 1861 of Mary Lincoln's floundering as mistress of the White House, her uncouthness, her clumsy actions, her attempts to influence presidential appointments. Charles Francis Adams wrote in his diary how "all manner of stories about her were flying around," especially about her wanting to put the White House on an "economical basis" and firing the servants. Adams also recorded how Sumner, in discussing cabinet gossip, said that Mary Lincoln "wanted to make a Collector of the Port of Boston, on account of her son 'Bobby,' and *had* made a naval officer."[39]

President Lincoln, meanwhile, was occupied to distraction first trying to prepare for and then win a civil war, to say nothing of arranging the bureaucracy of his administration during its first months. Then on July 21, after three months of a nearly bloodless war, the first major battle began near Manassas, Virginia, when Brigadier General Irving McDowell marched from Washington against Confederate troops near Centreville. After hours of fighting and with early momentum on their side, the Federal troops were driven back into a retreat that quickly deteriorated into a rout. As Washingtonians watched the shattered remnants of their army trickle back into the city, they expected to be overrun and captured at any moment. But the moment never came. The Confederates were as surprised and disorganized in their victory as the Federals had been in their defeat. But still, President Lincoln stayed awake all that night, and General Winfield Scott encouraged Mary to take Willie and Tad up north until the capital could be secured from invasion, which she refused.[40] In the blame and embarrassment of the North's first defeat, McDowell was relieved of command of the Union army and replaced by Major General George B. McClellan, who set about reorganizing and training the troops. While President Lincoln brooded and realized this would not be a short, easy war, his son in college heard the news of the battle and worried about the possibility of the capture of Washington.

Mary Lincoln was worried at this time as well, not only for her family in Washington but also for her son who was supposed to be on his way. On July 17, Robert's semester had ended, and he was supposed to be returning to Washington for the summer. With armies on the move near the capital and her boy en route, Mary's usual anxiety caused her to telegraph Robert about his plans. She became extremely alarmed when he did not respond, causing

Abraham Lincoln to query the Cambridge Telegraph office, "Mrs. Lincoln is very much alarmed, has her trunks packed to leave. Did you receive message for Robert T. Lincoln of this morning. Why no answer—."[41] Robert this time replied with the news that he had the mumps, although he was "not sick at all" and would come to Washington in a few days.[42] He arrived in Washington on July 23, just after McDowell's troops regrouped in the city.

The Prince of Rails then spent his six-week summer vacation with his family, arriving in time to attend the August 3 White House reception for another prince, Napoleon of France.[43] Little more than one week later, Robert left with his college friend Richard McConkey and presidential secretary Hay for the resort town of Long Branch, New Jersey, where Mary Lincoln had planned a family vacation of sorts. "The increasing hospitalities of the White House, continued through the Summer, preclude the usual residence at the Old Soldiers' Home during the hot weather, but Mrs. Lincoln finds it absolutely necessary to her health that she should enjoy a release from her arduous responsibilities in the more invigorating air of the sea shore," the *New York Times* reported.[44]

Robert and his friends arrived in Long Branch on August 15, one day before Mary Lincoln and her "suite" of family and friends, including the two young Lincoln boys, Willie and Tad. Eager crowds thronged Robert's party on the drive to the fashionable Mansion House; and for the entirety of the next day, until the first lady's arrival in town, Robert and John Hay "were the objects of all interest and curiosity."[45] Yet despite the regal sound to the news reports of their vacation, it is clear that Robert (and for the most part Mary) were intent simply to have a quiet and restful vacation. Robert and his friends stayed in a small cottage separate from the Mansion House Hotel. They attended balls and hops (and had a good time observing, being observed by, and flirting with the young coquettes, all of whom were "aflutter to be introduced to, to dance and talk with" Robert), went fishing and "chowdering" and accompanied Mary Lincoln and her suite to a "life-saving station" on the beach (a small building full of men, boats, and other paraphernalia used to save shipwrecked mariners).[46] Mary stayed mostly in her room with her sick friend Hannah Shearer.

Despite the ubiquitous attention and adoration, Robert, as was his wont and character both at college and at Washington, was simply another young man on vacation. The "Jenkin" (slang for reporter) from the *New York World* who followed the presidential parties' movements could not help but express his admiration for Robert's modesty. "A more moderate, easy, quiet sort of young gentleman you never saw," he wrote after two days at Long Branch. "He does everything well, but avoids doing anything extraordinary. He doesn't talk much; he doesn't dance differently from other people; he isn't odd, outré nor strange in any way. . . . In short, he is only Mr. Robert Lincoln, of Cambridge, and I believe he desires to be only that. He does nothing whatever to attract attention, and shows by every gentlemanly way how much he dislikes this fulsome sort of admiration, but it comes, all the same."[47] Hay, who stayed at Long Branch only for two days before returning to Washington, more bluntly criticized the beach crowds as "a sort of queer half-baked New Jersey confectionery, with a tendency to stammer when spoken to, and to flatten its nose against our windows while we ate."[48]

After nine days in Long Branch, Robert made a short stop back at the White House—his father was at that time in Virginia reviewing the troops with Secretary of State William H. Seward—then returned to Harvard to begin his sophomore year.[49] During both terms, he took courses in Greek, Latin, math, rhetoric, elocution, and chemistry and added a course in botany during his second term.[50] While this classical education sounds daunting to a twenty-first-century reader, it was not as overwhelming as one might think. Harvard College in mid-nineteenth century was not the educational polestar it has since become, although it still was the best college in America. Henry Adams, a graduate of the class of 1858, stated that Harvard "taught little, and that little ill, but it left the mind open, free from bias, ignorant of facts, but docile."[51] Life at Harvard in the 1860s was one of rules and routines, clubs and socializing, and then classes and study. Students were required to attend chapel every morning and twice on Sundays and if off-campus, to attend with their family and return with a certificate of church attendance signed by their parent. Church absences were punished by demerits. Students were required to wear "a black coat with black buttons" every Sunday and on commencement day, exhibition days, and all public occasions; freshmen were not allowed to sport a cane before Christmas, wear a high hat, smoke cigars, or frequent the local smoke and billiard parlors. Smoking in public was forbidden to all students.[52]

Harvard in the 1860s, according to one historian, was the "heyday of class spirit." One reason was that the class of 1860 was the first in school history to have more than one hundred students. Athletic contests—most specifically, boating and baseball—caused great camaraderie among the students, as did the various class outings and class dinners. There also were numerous clubs for students to join, such as the famed Hasty Pudding Club and the Institute of 1770, along with fraternities such as Delta Kappa Epsilon and the Porcellian Club. As was (and is) typical of most universities, the numerous rules and penalties for rule breaking were symbiotic with a culture of drinking, smoking, and little study. In 1863, President Thomas Hill lamented in his annual report that the frequency of horsecars traveling between Cambridge and Boston made it "practically impossible" for the administrators to "prevent our young men from being exposed to the temptations of the city." This was not long after the writer Artemus Ward famously declared that Harvard College was "located in the Parker House bar."[53]

Robert himself was not immune from such distractions. As one of his classmates wrote, "if his own stories about himself were true, he had considerable ground sowed to wild oats during a part of his course."[54] As previously stated, Robert's college dorm room was considered for four years to be more of a salon than a room of study, and as a great socializer, he was a "universally popular" classmate.[55] While on vacation at Long Branch, New Jersey, the *New York Herald* reporter noted that Robert was happier smoking a pipe and "doing his share in a good laugh" than in anything else—two characteristics he showed on the inaugural journey and continued throughout his entire life and the latter, of course, so similar to his father.[56] Harvard classmates also recollected Robert's camaraderie extended to the sporting fields. He was a good bowler, and it is known that while at Phillips Exeter, he was an avid athlete, especially of baseball, so he probably participated in pickup games on "the Delta," the Harvard playing fields.[57] During his second year, he joined the Institute of 1770, a social club for sophomores that still retained some of its original purpose to promote public speaking, and was editor for one term; he also joined a "secret society."[58]

But Robert's fun-loving ways also got him into trouble. He was mentioned multiple times in the faculty meeting minutes for his rule breaking. As previously stated, he was fined two dollars when a freshman in October 1860 for "writing on settees on Mr. Bates's room"; as a sophomore and again as a junior, he was privately admonished and punished by the recitation of ten prayers for a transgression not stated.[59] None of these infractions or punishments were unusual or excessive, Harvard faculty minutes show, indicating that the president's son was a common and flawed college student, same as the rest.

Robert's worst offense, however, occurred during his junior year in late 1862 when he was caught smoking in public—a serious transgression. He was privately admonished for it in September, but when caught again in December, he was publicly admonished with a letter sent to his father by the college president: "The faculty last evening voted 'that Lincoln, Junior, be publicly admonished for smoking in Harvard Square after being privately admonished for the same offense.' The word 'publicly' simply makes it my duty to inform you of the admonition, and I trust, sir, that you will impress upon him the necessity not only of attention to matters of decorum, but of giving heed to the private admonitions of his instructors."[60] This was not the first letter President Lincoln received from Harvard administrators regarding his oldest son. In January 1862, college president Cornelius C. Felton wrote Lincoln to warn him that Robert had become intimate with "some of the idled persons in his class," and as a consequence, his studies had suffered, especially in chemistry, where "his failure has been complete." Felton did not believe Robert was deserving of censure but that he must "guard against good-fellowship" and turn himself around: "He is a good, ingenious, frank and pleasant young man, with the ability to do well in every department. . . . I have no doubt a word or two from you will set everything right; for I feel quite sure that he has no bad habits as yet."[61]

Although there are no records about it, it seems logical to assume that Lincoln discussed this letter with his oldest son during the winter break, for which Robert returned to the White House on January 18.[62] This talk may have had an impact on Robert, for his grades steadily improved from then on, and no other letters from the college to his father are known. Unfortunately, during this same break in the winter of 1862 a tragedy befell the Lincoln family that also had a great impact on Robert, perhaps causing him to sober up and work harder to please his parents—the death of his eleven-year-old brother, Willie.

Willie Lincoln was the third Lincoln son, conceived immediately after little Eddie's death in February 1850, and born in December of that same year. Sixteen-year-old Julia Taft (whose father was Horatio Nelson Taft, an examiner at the U.S. Patent Office) knew the Lincolns in Washington and described Willie as "the most lovable boy I ever knew, bright, sensible, sweet-tempered and gentle-mannered."[63] He was a great reader and lover of books, especially poetry, just like his parents; he even composed an original poem on the death of his father's good friend Edward D. Baker.[64] Like his father, Willie also had a curious mind, drawn to math; he drew up railroad timetables for fun and, as his mother recalled, was a "most peculiarly religious child." But Willie was also the fun-loving playmate and confederate of his younger brother, Tad, and the two boys terrorized and amused White House staff and visitors with their antics.

In February 1862, however, both boys became terribly ill with what is now known to have been typhoid fever, due to contaminated drinking water. Willie was sick for nearly three weeks, beginning just before Mary Lincoln's grand February 5 reception to show off the newly refurbished White House. Abraham and Mary continually left the party to check on their sick boy, but the family doctor assured them Willie would be fine. Over the next two weeks, Willie declined, and little Tad also became ill, causing both parents even more anxiety. When Willie died on February 20, it "was not altogether unexpected," Nicolay sadly wrote.[65]

Much has been written about the reactions of Abraham and Mary Lincoln at Willie's death, the second time they had to bury a child. Abraham was devastated by the loss, turned more toward religion for solace, and, it is reported, frequently closed himself in Willie's room and wept.[66] Mary was inconsolable, staying confined to her room for weeks and banishing all items connected to Willie from the White House.[67] Her son's death also initiated Mary's fascination with Spiritualism—the belief that the dead could communicate with the living through a medium—a belief many people considered insane.[68] Mary's grief was so overwhelming, in fact, it prompted the president one day to point to the lunatic asylum visible from a White House window and say to his wife, "'Mother, do you see that large white building on the hill yonder? Try and control your grief, or it will drive you mad, and we may have to send you there.'"[69] Tad, too, was devastated, having lost not only his brother but his best friend.[70] Robert's reaction, however, has gone unnoticed and unexamined in history, yet it must certainly have had a shocking impact on him. He had been home and had witnessed the entirety of Willie's sickness, probably sat with his brother in the sick room, and had assisted in receiving guests at the February 5 White House ball while his parents anxiously and continuously excused themselves from the party to check on their son in his room; Robert also was in the White House when his brother died.[71]

The extended illness and slow decline, the apprehension and anxiety of both parents, the hushed worries and clouded faces were redolent to Robert of the similar circumstances surrounding Eddie's death from tuberculosis twelve years prior. Robert was older this time and could appreciate the loss of his brother even more, but the horrendous bereavement of his parents was the same, perhaps worse, and the ministrations to his mother's debilitating reaction were as oppressively similar. Rather than offering strength and solace to her remaining children, Mary was the emotional invalid needing tending. Robert was so worried about his mother, in fact, that he wrote "very imploringly" to his Aunt Elizabeth Edwards, Mary's older sister, in Springfield, and requested that she come to Washington to comfort his mother.[72] Elizabeth wrote to her daughter in March that Mary was confined to her room, was "utterly unable to control her feelings," "gives way to violent grief," and "is so constituted, and the surrounding circumstances will present, a long indulgence of gloom."[73] Mary did not attend Willie's funeral in the East Room of the White House on February 21, although she, Abraham, and Robert did spend half an hour alone with Willie's body to say good-bye.[74] Robert attended the funeral with his father and accompanied him to the Georgetown cemetery where Willie was placed.[75]

Willie's death not only saddened and sobered Robert and brought him closer to his youngest brother, Tad, but also affected his desire to join the army. As a dutiful son in 1861, he had stayed in college and out of the war due partly to his mother's fears and feelings. After his brother's death, Robert not only had a greater filial duty to his parents but his mother was even more agitated about the possibility of her oldest son being killed in the war. He must have known this, perhaps he and his father even discussed it, but it did not end his desire for service. In March 1862, it is known that Robert was reading *Cadet Life at West Point* and probably other such books as well.[76] By the summer of 1862, the Union cause was not as strong militarily as many had hoped. There had been hard-earned victories at Shiloh and New Orleans in April, and the battle of the ironclads USS *Monitor* and CSS *Virginia* (formerly the USS *Merrimack*) had ended in a draw in March in Hampton Roads, Virginia, but April through August also saw the disastrous Peninsula Campaign, which resulted in General McClellan's removal from command. Robert certainly kept abreast of the military campaigns as a young man and as the president's son and also as a Harvard student, for the deeds of the "Harvard Regiment," the Twentieth Massachusetts infantry, were much discussed around campus. Sons of Boston scions with names such as Crowninshield, Revere, Lowell, and Holmes were officers of the regiment and did their families, their city, and their alma mater proud. The Harvard Regiment fought in every major battle of the war, beginning at Ball's Bluff in October 1861.

Robert returned to Washington for summer break again in 1862. "Robert will be home from Cambridge in about six weeks and will spend his vacation with us," his mother wrote in anticipation in May to a friend. "He has grown and improved more than any one you ever saw."[77] Robert and his mother continued to have the close bond they shared during Robert's childhood, and he was conscientious about spending portions of every school vacation with her. He accompanied his mother and brother, Tad, for a weeklong excursion to New York City in July and spent the rest of his vacation at the White House and Soldiers' Home with his family.[78] As the summer neared its end, Mary lamented to a friend, "I shall dread when he has to return to Cambridge," stating that her son was "very companionable."[79] In early November, after spending more than two weeks in New York with Tad, Mary again visited Robert at Cambridge.[80] In the midst of Mary Lincoln's travels with Tad and Robert's schooling and visits with his mother, the battle of Antietam had been fought in Maryland, President Lincoln had issued his preliminary Emancipation Proclamation, and he had survived a "cabinet crisis" created by one of his cabinet members while the horrible Union defeat at the battle of Fredericksburg loomed on the horizon. And the war continued.

Robert remained in college.

During his upper-class years, Robert hit his academic stride at Harvard. As a junior, he took classes in chemistry, physics, Greek, Latin, declamations (first term), themes (first term), French (elective, both terms) and rhetoric (second term); as a senior, his courses included history, physics, forensics, philosophy, political economy, and, as electives, Italian and Spanish. Aside from his electives, Robert's undergraduate course of study was "the usual one" comprising mainly required courses.[81] His typical week consisted of multiple hours of recitations for each course, as well as numerous oral tests.[82] Robert had a class ranking of 43 (out of 125) at the end of his sophomore year. Over the next four terms, his grades steadily improved, and his class rank rose from 36 to 34 to 32 to 30 by graduation. His overall class ranking for his entire undergraduate course work was 32 out of a class of approximately 100.[83]

Robert's academic prowess may have improved due to his parents' admonitions, his own increasing maturity, or perhaps simply a growth in intellectual curiosity. College students in the early 1860s lived and studied in an exciting academic period. In 1859, Charles Darwin published his groundbreaking book, *The Origin of the Species*, and Harvard professors were leaders in the vociferous debate between creationists and evolutionists.[84] Classic literature such as *Great Expectations* by Charles Dickens (1861) and *Les Miserables* by Victor Hugo (1862) were published, while Boston Brahmins such as Ralph Waldo Emerson, Henry David Thoreau, and Henry Wadsworth Longfellow lived in Boston only a stone's throw from Harvard. Inventions flourished during the 1860s—some because of the war, some not—such as Richard Gatling's gun and Western Union Telegraph's transcontinental telegraph line, both in 1861, and Louis Pasteur's invention of pasteurization in 1864.

One of Robert's "most highly cherished experiences" while at Harvard was learning Dante under distinguished academic James Russell Lowell, professor of modern languages and belles lettres. Lowell was a renowned poet, scholar, humorist, essayist, critic, and, later, Republican politician. "Our duty was to prepare ourselves to translate the text, and Mr. Lowell heard our blunderings with a wonderful patience, and rewarded us with delightful talks on matters suggested in the poem," Robert wrote. "With us he was always conversational, and flattered us and gained us by an assumption that what interested him interested us. When I now take up my Dante, Mr. Lowell seems to be with me."[85] Lowell was famous for inviting students to informal gatherings once a week in his office, and Robert Lincoln was "one of a gang of insurgents" who needed extra help with his lessons.[86] Lowell later wrote to a friend, "I do not wonder that you like Mr. Lincoln. I have known him since he was a boy and always thought well of him. He was in one of my classes at Harvard. I don't think he distinguished himself as a scholar—perhaps that may have been my fault as much as his—but he was always an honest fellow with no harm in him and I was sure he would turn out well."[87]

Dr. John Gorham Palfrey, an ordained minister who was heavily involved in politics, history, and literature, also befriended Robert during his undergraduate work. Palfrey had been a former Whig colleague of Abraham Lincoln during the Thirtieth Congress and served as postmaster of Boston during the Lincoln administration. He was also, like Robert, an alumnus of Phillips Exeter Academy and had graduated from Harvard in 1815.[88] Charles Francis Adams wrote of Palfrey, "I have never in my life known a more truly estimable character."[89] Palfrey began his association with Robert with an invitation to dinner in late 1860, according to Robert. The correspondence that survives between the two shows that Robert was a welcome visitor and dinner guest of Palfrey, who entertained the young undergraduate at the Union Club in Boston and even invited him to join his circle of friends on Thanksgiving day in 1863.[90] "He was very kind to me while I was an undergraduate," Robert recalled years later.[91] While Palfrey's kindness may have been a pretext for ingratiating himself with the new president in order to obtain a civil-service appointment—which he did request and receive—his continued friendship after his appointment as Boston postmaster, and Robert's continued kind feelings, suggest otherwise.[92] Indeed, as a man of great kindness and intelligence, with experience in politics, literature, and history, he would have been an ideal mentor and intellectual stimulus for the eager, young college student.

As Professor Lowell remarked, young Lincoln was no great intellectual; Robert was, like his father, a social animal. He enjoyed good company, good cigars, and good times. In pursuance of those ends, Robert joined a "secret club" during his junior year, the fraternity Delta Kappa Epsilon, which was ostensibly a literary and social society.[93] DKE lore states that Robert wrote his father for permission to join the fraternity and that the president wrote back with his assent.[94] That the fraternity had a predilection for drinking under the guise of its moral and intellectual endeavors and that Robert whole-heartedly participated in the events are attested to by Robert's own words. "Don't get me into that DKE scrape," Robert wrote to Hay in 1874, in what appears to have been an invitation to a reunion. "For more than eight years have I been earnestly struggling to build up a reputation for sobriety and to be considered as having long passed the follies of youth. My memories of the classical literary exercises which took up so much time at the meetings (perhaps they were called 'symposia,' I have forgotten) of the 'Chapter' to which I belonged, make me think that an essay of the kind you mention would ruin me for sure. Recall that I have to set an example to a daughter and a son, to say nothing of Isham [Robert's law partner]."[95]

Robert also became a member—and vice president during his first term of senior year—of the famed Hasty Pudding Club, a society for juniors and seniors dedicated to the production of dramatic skits and farces.[96] Through the years, other men of historical note to have joined the Hasty Pudding ranks include Oliver Wendell Holmes Jr., J. P. Morgan, Theodore Roosevelt, Owen Wister, and George Santayana.[97] Robert Lincoln was remembered as "one of the choicest spirits" at their regular Friday night meetings in room 32 of Stoughton dormitory, where he "put to good use his familiarity with the attic stage, and no array of 'all the talents' on a play night was complete without his stellar radiance. And to this day tradition speaketh loud under the Cambridge elms of how Lincoln used to enact the villany of Old Daddy Wylie, in Hardwicke's 'Bachelor of Arts,' or illustrated the swinging passion of that cruel parent Russet, in the 'Jealous Wife.'"[98] Handbills of the club show Robert performed in the comedies *The Serious Family* in November 1862, *To Oblige Benson* in May 1863, *The Jealous Wife* in December 1863, and the drama *Babes in the Wood* and the comedy *Cool as a Cucumber* in May 1864—the last performance for the men of the class of 1864—for which he also acted as stage manager.[99]

As Robert grew older and became his own man, he had his own plans and schedules for his free time away from school. He often visited friends in various places during vacations, such as Clinton Conkling at Yale, but he also always spent at least a few weeks visiting his family, although he later stated, "I was very little in Washington while [my father] was there."[100] It was during one of Robert's travels to Washington that one of the arguably more bizarre coincidences in American history occurred, namely, that Robert was saved from being crushed by a train by Edwin Booth, the brother of John Wilkes Booth, Abraham Lincoln's assassin. The story itself has been told numerous times over the past century and a half, beginning with a *New York Times* article in 1865, although the story and its mythos continually evolved as the decades passed.[101]

In 1863 or 1864, Robert, on vacation from Harvard, was traveling from New York to Washington and waiting at a train station in Jersey City, New Jersey. While standing in line for tickets on a station platform, Robert was pressed by the crowd against the waiting train—which then began to move forward—and he fell into the narrow space between the train and the platform. He was helpless to escape when a hand grabbed his coat collar and pulled him up onto the platform. Robert turned to find his rescuer to be Edwin Booth, America's most revered stage actor, who was traveling to Richmond, Virginia, with his friend John T. Ford (owner of Ford's Theater in Washington, D.C.), to fulfill an engagement. Robert recognized the actor and thanked him by name.[102] "I was probably saved by [Mr. Booth] from a very bad injury if not something more," Robert later wrote.[103] Had Robert been maimed or even killed by the train that day, the effect upon his parents would have been incalculable, especially after the death of young Willie Lincoln in 1862. Strangely, there is no record that Robert even told his parents about what happened. He may have assumed his father had enough worries on his mind, and perhaps he feared, or just wished to avoid, his mother's probable hysterical reaction to the story. Robert later wrote that although he never again met Edwin Booth in person, he always had a "most grateful recollection of his prompt action on my behalf."[104]

Robert often spent his vacations traveling with his mother to New York or other major northern cities, although their favorite destinations were the mountains of New England. Robert went with his mother and younger brother to the White Mountains of New Hampshire in 1863 and to the Green Mountains of Vermont 1864; he planned to return with his entire family (including the president) to the mountains in Manchester, Vermont, in summer 1865.[105] These mother-son jaunts were not only a shared joy but, to the first lady at least, a seasonal necessity. Mary needed (like every other Washington resident) to escape the horribly humid summer months in the capital city; she also loved seeing new sights, being feted everywhere she went, and finding new places to shop. The president never accompanied his family on these vacations simply because he was too busy directing a country at war. His vacations were either visiting the troops in the field or spending the summer months at the Soldiers' Home three miles outside of Washington.

When Robert did return home, his visits were always a welcome and exciting event in the White House. Presidential secretary Stoddard remembered that Robert "was liked by everyone; and by his sincerity of manner, unassuming deportment and general good sense, won a degree of good will and respect."[106] Robert's visits to the White House are by no means uninteresting events. In fact, Robert personally experienced his father's reactions to important moments, and his statements are some of the only eyewitness recollections that survive. Unfortunately, most of Robert's testimony has been ignored under the erroneous assumption that he spent little time in Washington during his father's administration. But a look at his life and papers shows fascinating vignettes about his father and life in the White House—it also shows that despite his later statement that he "scarcely ever had two minutes quiet talk with [my father] during his Presidency," Robert in fact was his father's confidant during many of the most trying times of the administration.[107]

Probably the most notable recollection from Robert was witnessing his father's anguished reaction to the aftermath of the 1863 Battle of Gettysburg and the failure of General George Gordon Meade to finish off Lee's Army of Northern Virginia and end the war. After the Union repulse of Pickett's Charge on the third day of battle, the Confederate army began a slow retreat out of Pennsylvania and back to Virginia. Lee's supply lines and trains of wounded stretched for miles. Meade pursued, yet, despite the fact that he had the momentum and morale of victory on his side, he followed cautiously, wary of Lee's ability to continue fighting. At the time, and ever since, Meade has been criticized for failing to finish off the victory begun on the fields of Gettysburg. "Never again in the campaign would Meade be able to maneuver his opponent into such a tight corner" as during the first days of pursuit, historian Edwin B. Coddington wrote in his definitive study of the battle.[108] For the next ten days, Meade, following Lee's retreat, consolidated his army but refused to engage in another battle. President Lincoln, at first, was pleased with Meade's performance. On July 4, he issued an announcement complimenting the "great success" of the Army of the Potomac at Gettysburg.[109] On July 7, Lincoln telegraphed General-in-Chief Henry Halleck of the surrender of Vicksburg: "If General Meade can complete his work, so gloriously prosecuted thus far, by the literal or substantial destruction of Lee's army, the rebellion will be over."[110]

As each day came without news of a major attack by Meade, Lincoln became impatient and began to detect a whiff of McClellan's old procrastination in Meade's excuses. Once Lee reached the Potomac and found it swollen and impassable due to heavy rains, Lincoln saw Meade's opportunity to finish the war. When no battle occurred and Lee escaped across the river on July 14, Lincoln was "distressed immeasurably" at the news. "I do not believe you appreciate the magnitude of the misfortune involved in Lee's escape," the president scolded Meade in a letter he decided not to send. "He was within your easy grasp and, to have closed upon him would, in connection with our late other successes, have ended the war. As it is, the war will be prolonged indefinitely."[111]

Robert was in Washington during this time and remembered clearly his father's anguish. He later recalled going into his father's office and finding him "in much distress, his head leaning upon [his arms upon] the desk in front of him, and when he raised his head there were evidences of tears upon his face." The president told his son that he had believed that Meade could have dealt the "final blow" to Lee's army while it was trapped with its back to the swollen river, but the general had refused all entreaties to act. The president also told his son about the letter of rebuke he wrote to Meade the day before but did not send.[112] Some historians have questioned Robert's recollection, unsure if he was even in Washington at that time. It is known, however, that after Mary Lincoln's July 2 carriage accident, during which the driver lost control of the horses and the first lady had to leap from the runaway carriage to save herself, the president telegraphed Robert at Cambridge not to worry, "Your mother very slightly hurt by her fall."[113] When Mary's minor head injury became infected, the president telegraphed his son, who was in New York, to come to Washington. When Robert did not respond, his father irritably telegrammed, "Why do I hear no more of you?" Robert, who was en route home, arrived at the White House the next day, July 15.[114] Hay's diary in fact shows that Robert was home then, for on July 15 he recorded, "R. T. L. says the Tycoon is grieved silently but deeply about the escape of Lee. He said, 'If I had gone up there, I could have whipped them myself.' I know he had that idea."[115]

Robert again discussed Meade's passivity with his father in mid-October, when Lee's army was once again with its back to a river, this time the Rapidan in Virginia. Lincoln instructed his general to attack, stating that if he won, Meade could take all the glory, but if he lost, the president would take all the blame.[116] "I remember the contents [of the telegram] because father read it to me before he sent it," Robert stated. "Father sent just such an order over to Meade by the government wire and the receipt of it was acknowledged."[117] Once again Lee escaped and Lincoln was disappointed.

Another event during the Lincoln administration that Robert experienced was the issuance of the now-famous "Pomeroy Circular." The circular, which Kansas Republican Senator Samuel C. Pomeroy issued on February 20, 1864, decried the ineptitude of the Lincoln administration and called for a new presidential candidate for the party in 1864, specifically, Treasury Secretary Salmon P. Chase. Pomeroy's missive was a follow-up to a similar document titled "The Next Presidential Election," which the Organization to Make S. P. Chase President issued on February 9, 1864. This was but the latest event in a series of treacherous machinations by Chase since 1861 to oust Lincoln from the presidential chair. Chase, convinced of his superiority to Lincoln, used his patronage powers as a cabinet member to win supporters and earn favors from numerous and powerful politicians. As presidential secretary Nicolay wrote at that time, "The Treasury rats are busy night and day becoming more and more unscrupulous and malicious" in their advocacy of Chase.[118] The Treasury secretary himself continually sought to undermine Lincoln, his most famous attempt being the manipulation of several Republican Senators who called for the removal of Secretary of State Seward—Chase's political enemy—from the cabinet. During this "cabinet crisis" in 1862, both Seward and Chase tendered their resignations, but Lincoln's political adroitness placated the senators, embarrassed Chase, and preserved both secretaries. (Lincoln, in fact, also discussed the entire event with his oldest son, when Robert came home a few weeks later for winter recess.)[119] By February 1864, Chase and his supporters saw a good opportunity to advance his presidential candidacy after Lincoln announced his proclamation of amnesty and reconstruction on December 8, 1863, the leniency of which angered many radical Republicans.

Once the Washington *National Intelligencer* published Pomeroy's circular on February 22, the corridor outside the oval office was thronged with people anxious to see the president about it. While passing through the crowd, Robert was approached by Simon Hanscomb, editor of the Washington *National*

Republican newspaper, and was entreated to help the newsman get in to see the president, which Robert did. That night after dinner, the president entered Robert's bedroom to show him a letter he had just received from Chase denying any knowledge of the circular and offering his resignation.

> My father asked me to lay out writing materials for him, and at my table he wrote a short note to Mr. Chase in which he said in substance, "that he knew of no reason why he should not remain in the Cabinet." Upon his showing this note to me I expressed surprise at that part of the note above specified, and asked him if he had not seen the circular. He stopped me and said he didn't know anything about it; that a good many people during the day had tried to see him and tell him something which he supposed was some new piece of Chase's deviltry, and it did not suit him to know anything about it, and that therefore the remark in his letter declining to accept his resignation was strictly true. Thereupon at his request I called a messenger, and the note to Mr. Chase was sent.[120]

Robert's memory here is a bit faulty about the date, but that does not make his recollection untrue. President Lincoln did write a short note to Chase that night, in which he said he would answer his letter more fully at a later time. Lincoln's letter in which he refused Chase's resignation was then sent on February 29, a full week later. Robert was actually in Washington on both of those dates, so probably did witness both letters and simply mingled the memory.

In January 1865, Robert also had a discussion with his father about the events leading up to the February 3 Hampton Roads conference between President Lincoln and Secretary of State Seward and three representatives of the Confederate government. The meeting was conceived by Republican elder statesman Francis P. Blair, who went to Richmond and met with Confederate President Jefferson Davis about ending the war. Blair's idea was to reunite the two sections in a war against France in Mexico to oust French puppet Emperor Maximilian and enforce the Monroe Doctrine. Confederate Vice President Alexander H. Stephens, Senator Robert M. T. Hunter, and Assistant Secretary of War John A. Campbell traveled to Lieutenant General Ulysses S. Grant's headquarters at City Point, Virginia, asking to pass through the lines to go to Washington and meet with Lincoln. After weeks of telegram communications among Lincoln, Union army officers, and the Confederate agents, Lincoln sent Major Thomas Eckert as his envoy to straighten out the situation.

"I remember my father telling me one evening all that had occurred up to that time in the matter," Robert recalled, "and his indicating to me that he was not feeling quite comfortable as to the way in which the matter was being handled at Army Headquarters at City Point; and that, therefore, he had that day sent 'Tom Eckert,' as he affectionately called him, with written instructions, to handle the whole matter of the application of these visitors from Mr. Davis to get into our lines." Major Eckert was chief of the War Department telegraph office and was well known and liked by the president, who spent many hours sending and receiving dispatches. In fact, Robert recalled his father telling him that he trusted Eckert implicitly because "he never failed to do completely what was given him to do, and to do it in the most complete and tactful manner, and to refrain from doing anything outside which would hurt his mission." The president was "so emphatic in expressing this reason for sending Major Eckert that it made a deep impression upon me," Robert remembered, "and I never see General Eckert without thinking of it."[121] Lincoln eventually sent Seward and then went himself to Fort Monroe, where he and his secretary of state met with the Southern commissioners aboard the president's boat *River Queen*. The meeting lasted four hours, but no agreements were reached. The rebels wanted a peace between two sovereign countries, while Lincoln insisted on a complete surrender of rebel forces, the reuniting of one common country, and emancipation for all slaves. The main effect of the conference was to convince the Confederates that Lincoln would not compromise and that their only hope of ending the war on their terms would have to be achieved by victories by Lee's army.[122]

It was also in January 1865, during Robert Lincoln's visit to Washington, that he learned his father frequently would walk to the War Department telegraph office from the White House late at night and unaccompanied. Robert remonstrated against such trips and told his father not to go out at night without him. "Accordingly, it is my memory, that on a number of occasions he came to my room after I had fallen asleep, and said that he wanted to go over, whereupon I dressed myself hastily and accompanied him," Robert later recalled.[123] What is important to note about the Gettysburg, cabinet crisis, Pomeroy Circular, telegraph office, and Hampton Roads Conference events is that they show a close relationship between Robert Lincoln and his father that has long been obfuscated. These were all major events in Lincoln's administration—and one can be sure they were considered of even greater import at the times they occurred—and for the president to have discussed them with Robert and in two cases to have shown his son his letters of response show that the president had a definite regard for his son's opinions.

There are other stories of Robert's interaction with his father in the White House that while they may not give evidence of major historical events are important in that they show the day-to-day aspects of the father-son relationship. One disagreement between the two occurred in the summer of 1864 when Robert "with a flushed face" entered Nicolay's room and declared he had just had "a great row with the president of the United States." That day, Secretary of War Edwin M. Stanton had commissioned eleven-year-old Tad a lieutenant, upon which the boy promptly had muskets sent to the White House, discharged the guard, and mustered all the gardeners and servants into service. He gave them guns, drilled them, then put them on guard duty. "I found it out an hour ago," Robert told Nicolay and artist Francis B. Carpenter, "and thinking it a great shame, as the men had been hard at work all day, I went to father with it; but instead of punishing Tad, as I think he ought, he evidently looks upon it as a good joke, and won't do anything about it!" Tad, however, soon went to bed, and the men were discharged. Thus the White House was unguarded for a full night during the war.[124]

Earlier that year, in February 1864, Robert and his father had a legal discussion due to the burning of the White House stables. Six horses were killed, and all the personal possessions of one of the stablemen, Jehu Cooper, were destroyed. The next morning, Robert entered his father's office and said he "had a point of law which he wished to submit." Cooper had lost hundreds of dollars in U.S. greenbacks in the fire, and Robert and Nicolay were arguing as to the liability of the government for its notes where it could be shown they were burned or otherwise destroyed. The president thought for a moment and then said that a citizen cannot sue the government and, therefore, "I don't see but that it is a dead loss for Jehu." It was also a bitter loss for little Tad, who was in tears over the deaths of his two ponies.[125]

Robert's visits to Washington also included much time spent with presidential secretaries Nicolay and Hay, traveling to the front lines and attending social events in the capital. In July 1863, Hay offered evidence of just what good times he and Robert had together when he told Nicolay, "Bob and I had a fearful orgy last night on whiskey and cheese."[126] Robert also was a frequent guest of the Seward family and, that same summer, accompanied the secretary of state's family on a trip to Fortress Monroe in Norfolk, Virginia.[127] It also appears that Robert, like his mother, or perhaps with his mother, visited wounded soldiers in the hospitals when he was in Washington. In particular, Robert spent much time with an injured French soldier named Charlemagne who could not speak English and was from a New York regiment. Robert, fluent in French, would talk and read to the soldier, bring him newspapers and fruit, and translate for the doctors when necessary. "He was certainly very badly wounded and very low spirited in his isolation and I tried to help him along," especially after the amputation of a leg, Robert remembered.[128]

Of course, as a famous, fashionable, gregarious, and modest young man, Robert's interests for and from the young ladies of Washington and Cambridge cannot be ignored. One newspaper termed Robert "somewhat of a lady's man" during his college years.[129] Fanny Seward, daughter of the secretary of state, described Robert on her first meeting with him as "ready and easy in conversation having, I fancy, considerable humor in his composition." She was impressed at his unassuming ways, declaring him to be "Robert Lincoln—rather than the son of the President of the United States. Agreeable, good-natured and intelligent."[130] In fact, Robert was so polished, well-dressed, and graceful in his manners that his mother was afraid he was "getting too much attached to Cambridge and New England, and would become a yankee."[131]

But perhaps that is what the girls in Washington and Cambridge were looking for. The earliest girl associated with Robert at college was Alice M. Huntington, whose father was a dry-goods and lumber merchant in Springfield, Illinois, but who often stayed with family in Boston. Robert invited her to a play in 1861, sent her his photograph in 1862, and invited her to his college graduation in 1864.[132] Robert may have had a crush on the beautiful Carlota Wilhelmina Maria von Gerolt, daughter of the Prussian minister to the United States. According to Hay, when the girl got married in August 1863, "Bob was so shattered by the idol of us all . . . that he rushed madly off to sympathize with nature in her sterner aspects"—alluding to Robert's trip with his mother to the White Mountains of New Hampshire.[133] Robert's most infamous female association was his supposed romance with Lucy Hale, daughter of New Hampshire Senator John P. Hale and later fiancée to John Wilkes Booth. The legend has survived for more than a century that the president's son and the famous actor were rivals for the young girl's affections—even that Booth's hatred of the father stemmed from his jealousy of the son. The story was first printed widely in 1878 in a gossipy Chicago newspaper based on the "memories" of an unidentifiable person—a fabrication that Robert Lincoln immediately, unequivocally, and publicly denied.[134]

The Washington belle who caught Robert's eye more than any other, however, was Mary Eunice Harlan, oldest daughter of Iowa U.S. Senator James Harlan. Mary was a beautiful, blonde, blue-eyed coquette, intelligent and cultured and apparently quite admired by the young men of the capital. Letters from her friend Minnie Chandler show young Mary was quite flirtatious and had numerous beaus.[135] She and Robert met at a hop in the Metropolitan Hotel, although it was said that Mary Todd Lincoln worked fervently to match the young couple up herself. One of Robert's cousins later wrote that President Lincoln once said to Secretary of War Stanton, "Mary is tremendously in love with Senator Harlan's little daughter, I think she has picked her out for a daughter-in-law. As usual, I think Mary has shown fine taste."[136] The first lady often invited the entire Harlan family on outings with her as a way to get Robert and Mary together.

Robert's four years at Harvard, accomplished in the midst of a civil war in which his father was the president, were busy. After an inauspicious start, interspersed by some minor malefactions, Robert finished his undergraduate education ranked in the top third of his class. One of his final duties as an undergraduate was to serve as chairman of the Class Day Committee, an undertaking that took more work than he expected.[137] Class Day, on Friday, June 24, consisted of oration services in the church, then music, dancing, and fraternizing on the grounds, followed that night by more music and socializing on the common and a grand illumination by Chinese lanterns.[138] Robert's mother and brother, Tad, traveled to Boston for the Class Day activities, although the president did not.[139] Robert wanted to invite Mary Harlan to the festivities as well but did not know where to send her invitation.[140]

At some point during his upper-class years, Robert decided his profession after graduation would be the law, just like his father.[141] That does not mean, however, that he stopped enjoining the president to allow him to enter the army. On his return to Washington after his graduation, Robert again approached his father about enlisting. Now that he had a degree, he wanted a commission "as an officer and at close range [to see] something of the work in the Army" before the war was over.[142] Even newspaper correspondents assumed the president's son would join now that he had a degree, and his enlistment constantly was expected.[143]

Unfortunately for Robert, Abraham Lincoln continued to support his wife, who still refused her permission; yet, according to Robert, the president still feared that his son's presence in the army could in some way embarrass him politically, especially as his reelection campaign approached. Robert vented his frustration to his father that summer when the president asked about his future plans and the son retorted that since he could not join the army, he would go back to Cambridge to the law school. Robert recalled his father saying, "If you become a lawyer, you will probably make more money at it than I ever did, but you won't have half the fun."[144] Robert, chagrined, returned in the fall to Harvard. Little did he know that his parents soon would change their minds, or that, by the end of April 1865, he would be witness to two of the most important events in American history.

6

"A Very Dreadful Night"

Robert Lincoln began law school in 1864 as his father sought reelection to the presidency. No records survive to indicate young Lincoln's prowess as a law student, his feelings about being at Harvard, or his thoughts or actions supporting a second term in office for his father.[1] He watched the contest as did the rest of the country, eagerly, because Abraham Lincoln's reelection was not as inevitable in 1864 as it seems today. No president had been renominated by his party since 1840, and none had been reelected since Andrew Jackson in 1832. Lincoln himself long believed he would not win and with good reason. The country showed signs of disenchantment—such as the New York draft riots—with a four-year war with few major victories, a continuous shifting of commanding generals, high soldier casualties, and suspension of some civil liberties. Abraham Lincoln was, in fact, during his first term, one of the most reviled presidents in American history. It should be no surprise then that Lincoln prepared both himself and his administration for defeat. In late August 1864, six days before the Democrat Party officially chose General George B. McClellan as its presidential candidate, Lincoln had his entire cabinet blindly sign a letter he had written that, he showed them all later, pledged to "so cooperate with the President-elect as to save the Union between the election and the inauguration; as he will have secured his election on such ground that he cannot possibly save it afterwards."[2]

Lincoln may have underestimated himself and overestimated McClellan here, for, on election day, Lincoln won in a landslide. His victory was helped immeasurably by General William Tecumseh Sherman's capture of Atlanta in September. Interestingly, Robert Lincoln later told a friend that what pleased his father more than anything else during the campaign was the support of the soldiers. Union prisoners in Libby Prison held their own election on

November 4, 1864, and Lincoln defeated McClellan 3–1. When the president heard of this vote months later, he referred to it as "the most satisfactory and encouraging episode in the Presidential campaign. His words were in effect: We can trust the soldiers."[3]

By the beginning of 1865, with Union victories in Atlanta and Savannah, Sheridan cleaning out the Shenandoah Valley, Grant laying siege to Petersburg, and the end of the war apparently in sight, Robert made a renewed effort to enlist. He returned to the White House in January 1865 for his winter break specifically to "press upon my father my wish to see some military service before the close of the war."[4] Finally, the president relented, but it was not a complete concession for Abraham Lincoln as a father. He still wanted to protect his son, both for his wife's emotional sake and for his own political fears. Mary Lincoln's reaction to or part in this decision is unknown.

On January 19, 1865, President Lincoln wrote to Lieutenant General Ulysses S. Grant to ask if the Union commander could place Robert on his staff as a volunteer aide-de-camp. "I do not wish to put him in the ranks, nor yet to give him a commission to which those who have already served long are better entitled and better qualified to hold," Lincoln wrote. "Could he, without embarrassment to you, or detriment to the service, go into your military family with some nominal rank, I, and not the public, furnishing his necessary means?" Lincoln clearly was embarrassed by this request, as is evident not only in proposing to pay Robert's salary himself but also by asking Grant to read and answer the letter "as though I was not the President, but only a friend" and to feel free to refuse his request "without the least hesitation."[5] One historian even concludes that in asking for special favors for his son, "Lincoln veered slightly from his usual moral and ethical path."[6] While Lincoln did use his position to influence his son's appointment, the majority of military commissions during the war were achieved due to political connections. Yet unlike many political appointees, Robert, as a Harvard graduate, was qualified for such a post. Grant responded two days later that he would be "most happy" to have Robert join his staff. He rejected the notion that the president's son not receive a full commission and be a volunteer and instead suggested the rank of captain with the appropriate emoluments.[7]

Finally, after nearly five years of wanting to join the army, Robert's desire was fulfilled. "I have been informed by my father this morning, of your kindness in allowing me to become one of your Staff, and I desire to express to you both his and my own hearty thanks for it," Robert wrote to Grant on January 22. "As I have been living at Cambridge for nearly five years, and left there with the expectation of returning, it will be necessary for me to go back and arrange my affairs before going to City Point; and as I also very much desire to be present at the Inauguration, unless I can in any way be useful before, I would request your kind indulgence until after that time, when I will have the honor to report to you in person."[8] Any response from Grant is unknown; and although Robert was given time to settle his affairs in Cambridge, he did not wait until after the inauguration to report to City Point. His mother told a friend that Robert was "anxious" to be with Grant when the general captured Richmond and feared that if he waited until after the inauguration he would miss it.[9]

Robert's commission as an assistant adjutant general of volunteers with the rank of captain was nominated to the War Department on Saturday, February 11, 1865, and then to the U.S. Senate on Tuesday, February 14, 1865.[10] His father paid for his outfit and equipment and also bought him a new horse.[11] Robert officially entered the army on February 20, 1865, and on that day accepted his commission, signed the oath of office, and left Washington to report for duty at General Grant's headquarters in City Point, Virginia.[12]

City Point (today the city of Hopewell) was a harbor at the junction of the Appomattox and James Rivers, surrounded by high bluffs on which lay a small town. Once Grant decided to make the place his headquarters, "City Point, which had been the sleepiest of riverside hamlets, had become one of the world's great seaports," historian Bruce Catton observes.[13] Wharves lined the waterway for more than a mile with hundreds of vessels coming, going, tied up, or anchored every day. Grant used the small group of houses atop the bluff as his headquarters, while warehouses, bakeries, blacksmith shops, wagon repair shops, soldier barracks, civilian quarters, and a ten-thousand-man army hospital quickly spread around the houses. Grant also had built a huge railroad connecting headquarters to the front lines at Petersburg. City Point therefore also boasted freight yards, coal docks, roundhouse, repair shops, and all the other necessary outbuildings for a railroad depot.[14]

President Lincoln's anxiety (or maybe his wife's) at his oldest son riding off to war is evident in the fact that only a few days after Robert left Washington, the president telegraphed Grant asking if his boy had arrived. Grant reassured him that Robert had reported for duty on time, arriving at City Point on February 22; he was assigned to duty on February 23.[15] "The new acquisition to the company at headquarters soon became exceedingly popular," wrote Horace Porter, at that time a brevet colonel of volunteers on Grant's staff. "He had inherited many of the genial traits of his father, and entered heartily into all the social pastimes at headquarters. He was always ready to perform his share of hard work, and never expected to be treated differently from any other office on account of his being the son of the Chief Executive of the nation."[16] Captain Lincoln was, however, the president's son, and, as he had requested upon hearing of his acceptance into Grant's staff, he was given leave to attend his father's second inauguration on March 4, despite having been on active duty for less than two weeks.

The second inauguration of Abraham Lincoln as president of the United States occurred on a day that began dreary and rainy. The streets were quagmires of mud, and it was feared the inauguration would have to be performed inside the Senate chamber. Regardless of the weather, an estimated forty thousand people were massed at the Capitol, the White House, and on the sidewalks in between to witness the event. When the ceremonies began and the presidential family and administration members left the White House to parade to the Capitol, President Lincoln was not among the group. He was already in the Capitol, signing bills Congress passed that morning. The *New York Herald* called the grand procession down Pennsylvania Avenue minus the president, "the play of Hamlet with Hamlet left out."[17]

The inaugural ceremonies began around noon in the U.S. Senate chamber. Members of Congress, military personnel, and administration officials filled the floor; representatives from foreign legations packed the diplomatic gallery, while the visitor galleries—crowded, humid, smelling of packed bodies and wet cloth—were thronged with women in their elegant and colorful dresses all damp and stained with mud. Outgoing Vice President Hannibal Hamlin gave a farewell speech; but the opening event, both then and now, was marked by the drunk and incoherent remarks of the new vice president, Andrew Johnson, who had taken three shots of whiskey to ameliorate an illness and steady his nerves prior to the ceremony. Navy Secretary Gideon Welles recorded in his diary that Johnson's "rambling and strange harangue" was listened to "with pain and mortification by his friends," while the new vice president's conduct was thoroughly criticized by the newspapers the next day.[18] It was feared Lincoln's oath-taking and inaugural address would have to be delivered in the Senate chamber as well, but the weather cleared.

Noah Brooks, a reporter for the *Sacramento (CA) Union* and *New York Herald*, recalled that when the president and other dignitaries appeared on the platform on the east front of the Capitol, "a tremendous shout, prolonged and loud, arose from the surging ocean of humanity around the Capitol building." Many witnesses that day estimated the crowds to be at least twice as large as on Lincoln's first inauguration. When the president, tall and gaunt in his black broadcloth suit, advanced to give his remarks, "a roar of applause shook the air, and, again and again repeated, finally died away on the outer fringe of the throng, like a sweeping wave upon the shore."[19] Lincoln's inaugural address that day was anticipated to be, like previous second inaugurals, a declaration of victory and political vindication with humble thanks for reelection and perhaps some statements regarding reconstruction and black citizenship.

Instead, Lincoln encompassed the entire country in his remarks—much like he did in his Gettysburg Address in 1863—blamed both North and South for the war, extended his hand of peace and friendship to both sides, and once again showed his magnanimity in the face of victory. Lincoln began:

> On the occasion corresponding to this four years ago, all thoughts were anxiously directed to an impending civil war. All dreaded it—all sought to avert it. While the inaugural address was being delivered from this place, devoted altogether to *saving* the Union without war, insurgent agents were in this city seeking to *destroy* it without war—seeking to dissolve the Union, and divide effects, by negotiation. Both parties deprecated war; but one of them would *make* war rather than let the nation survive; and the other would *accept* war rather than let it perish. And the war came.[20]

Captain Robert Lincoln, in full military dress uniform, after hearing Johnson's inebriated remarks in the Senate chamber, listened to his father's second address with mingled pride and sadness.[21] How different a day compared to March 1861! Back then he was a seventeen-year-old boy, just starting college, fresh from a triumphal inaugural journey across the country; and four years later he was a twenty-one-year-old college graduate, now a captain in the army on the staff of the commanding general. It had been four years of loss, beginning with his friend Ephraim Elmer Ellsworth, his father's dear friend Edward D. Baker, and then his little brother Willie. Robert had witnessed the Harvard campus prepare for war and read the stories of the Boston boys who fought and died at all the major battles, while he was forced to sit it out. More than everything else, he saw the heavy toll the war had taken on his parents, especially his father: the loss of young life, the political intrigues, the public criticisms and scrutiny, so much of which his father had shared with him. He witnessed his father physically change from the robust, clean-shaven man he had known as a boy to the weary, aged, bearded president who stood on the platform.

Robert watched his father that day at the pinnacle of his glory, the war nearly ended, the adulation of thousands, and a firm yet forgiving intention to reunite the country. His father said, in part, "With malice toward none; with charity for all; with firmness in the right, as God gives us to see the right, let us strive on to finish the work we are in; to bind up the nation's wounds; to care for him who shall have borne the battle, and for his widow, and his orphan—to do all which may achieve a just and lasting peace, among ourselves, and with all nations." Cheers went up at times during the speech and at its conclusion, but while the second inaugural is considered by many Lincoln's greatest speech, at the time something other than his words caught people's attention. Just as Lincoln stepped forward to begin speaking, the clouds that had hung heavy, dark, and malevolent all morning suddenly parted, and the sun burst through and illuminated the entire scene. More than one person remarked on this inspiring occurrence, seeing in it an omen that four years of darkness were now to be dissipated by peace.[22] As reporter Brooks later wrote, "Chiefly memorable in the mid of those who saw that second inauguration must still remain the tall, pathetic, melancholy figure of the man who, then inducted into office in the midst of the glad acclaim of thousands of people, and illumined by the deceptive brilliance of a March sunburst, was already standing in the shadow of death."[23]

When the ceremonies were completed, Robert rode with his father in the presidential barouche from the Capitol to the White House.[24] This arrangement, the same as all of the confidences bestowed from father to son throughout the war, again shows a closeness between Abraham and Robert. It illustrates a manly bond between the two that had been growing since 1860 and is in keeping with President Lincoln's great pride in his son's academic achievements and now military standing. One Congressman's son later remembered President Lincoln boasting, "You know, my boy here has just been made a captain on Gen. Grant's staff."[25]

That night, Captain Lincoln attended the inaugural reception at the White House. Two nights later, Monday, March 6, he again dressed in his military dress uniform to attend the inaugural ball being held at the spacious U.S. Patent Office.[26] When the presidential party entered the ball at about 10:30 P.M., President Lincoln walked with Speaker of the House Schuyler Colfax, Mary Lincoln was escorted by her friend Senator Charles Sumner, and reporters and social gossips all noticed that the former Prince of Rails and now dashing young army captain Robert Lincoln escorted Miss Mary Harlan, the pretty daughter of U.S. Senator James Harlan of Iowa.[27]

Washington rumor long had connected Robert and Mary as an item, and their appearance together at the inaugural ball publicly affirmed their relationship. The actual details of their wartime courting, however, are turbid. They exchanged letters while Robert was in Cambridge and socialized when Robert was in Washington. Their relationship apparently blossomed in late 1864, when, as previously stated, Robert wanted to invite Mary to his college graduation. In January 1865, Robert probably attended a parlor hop Mary and her mother sponsored at the National Hotel, to which both John Hay and John Nicolay (Robert's constant Washington companions) were invited.[28]

The morning after the inaugural ball, Tuesday. March 7, Robert left Washington to return to his post at City Point.[29] Back on military duty, the president's son was once again simply Captain Lincoln. One of his earliest assignments, sometime in early March, was to escort two women from Fortress Monroe, Virginia, as far as the flag of truce boat would proceed, which was near Petersburg. When Robert boarded the boat, he was surprised to find that he knew one of the two ladies he was to escort. "Well, if it isn't my aunt Emily!" he said as Emily Todd Helm simultaneously exclaimed, "Robert! Oh, how glad I am to see you!" Robert had not seen his aunt—who in reality was only a few years older than he and who used to play with him when he was a boy—in about nine years, since her visit to Springfield in 1856. She was going to Richmond with her friend Mrs. Bernard Pratt to see about an investment of cotton she feared might be lost.[30]

Not long after seeing his aunt, Robert wrote a humorous letter to Hay about his military life at City Point. "I was sitting here on my lovely watch, (that is figurative: my watch is really in my vest pocket & not in the seat of my breeches) thinking cusses that I was not in my couch. Just why I ain't is because Kelly and Crook got took off by a Cavalry raid sometime ago and because the sentries will go to sleep sometimes." He mentioned that he had gone out to talk with Confederate soldiers under a flag of truce and seemed impressed by their appearance. "There have been lots of pretty girls down here lately," he closed. "If you want to do a favor, send some more and oblige."[31]

Robert's service on Grant's staff, occurring towards the end of the war, allowed him to see and experience some of the seminal final moments of the four-year struggle. It is known that General James W. Forsythe sent Captain Lincoln as a courier to General Philip Sheridan in White House, Virginia, that he took part in the operations that led to the evacuation of Petersburg by the Confederates, and that he stayed with Grant at the front up to the final surrender at Appomattox Court House.[32]

Many of Robert's duties, actually, involved his father. By the beginning of March 1865, Grant still was laying siege to Petersburg and preparing to make his final push into Richmond. The newspapers constantly reported the exhausted state of the president, who was not only weary from the toll of the war but also so sick with the flu that he limited his office hours and then spent one day in bed. Julia Grant, reading about the president's exhaustion, asked her husband why he did not invite his commander down to City Point for a visit—"so many people were coming and the weather was simply delightful," she wrote in her memoirs. But the general did not think it his place to extend such an invitation, believing if the president wanted to visit army headquarters, he would simply do so. When Mrs. Grant asked Robert about it, the young captain replied that he thought his father would visit if he was certain he would not be intruding.[33] Perhaps, too, Lincoln stayed away not wanting to be seen as meddling in military affairs, as newspapers had criticized him for doing throughout the war.

General Grant, understanding this, telegraphed an invitation to the president and Mrs. Lincoln on March 20, suggesting the trip would be restful and beneficial. Lincoln generally accepted, and the next day Robert telegraphed his father, asking, "Will you visit the army this week? Answer at City Point."[34] That same day, March 21, Gustavus V. Fox, assistant secretary of the navy, telegraphed and offered the president use of his ship, the *Bat*.[35] Besieged by invitations, Lincoln telegraphed both his son and his commanding general that he would leave on March 23 to visit headquarters.[36]

The party of President and Mrs. Lincoln, Tad, an unnamed maid, and the president's bodyguard Captain Charles B. Penrose arrived at City Point at about 9 P.M. the next day, March 24. Because of the addition of the first lady to the traveling party, the trip was made on the steamer *River Queen* instead of the *Bat*, the former being more comfortable for ladies. Captain Lincoln met his family at the dock and then went to inform General and Mrs. Grant of the party's arrival and escort them to the president's boat.[37]

The presidential visit was a family reunion, but it was primarily about business, and the business of the day was war. Every morning the president would go directly to the adjutant general's office and hear all news of the front received during the night, and then he would have long conferences with Grant and other commanders about prospective operations.[38] At the time of Lincoln's arrival at City Point, Lee was trying to break his army through Grant's siege lines at Petersburg, and on the morning of March 25, a small battle occurred at the front near Fort Stedman. "Robert just now tells me there was a little rumpus up the line," the president telegraphed Secretary of War Stanton before riding to within five miles of the scene.[39] Perhaps recalling Lincoln's coming under fire and near miss by a bullet at Fort Stevens in July 1864, Stanton urged Lincoln to be careful: "I hope you will remember General [William Henry] Harrison's advice to his men at Tippecanoe, that they 'can see as well a little farther off.'"[40]

On March 26, the presidential party took another foray to the front lines to inspect the troops, and on the twenty-seventh, Robert accompanied his father on a trip to the observation tower at Point of Rocks and there watched the armies at the front. That evening, the president had a council of war with Grant, General Sherman who arrived that day, and Admiral David Porter.[41]

This March trip to City Point was memorable not only for the actions and engagements of the armies and the president but also has become infamous due to the actions of Mary Lincoln. The vagaries of the first lady—her erratic temper, her vice, her selfishness, her emotionalism, and her aristocratic attitudes—by this time were well known to and criticized by Washington society. And she put them on full display at City Point. As newspaper correspondent Sylvanus Cadwallader later stated, "Mrs. Lincoln seemed insanely jealous of every person, and everything, which drew [her husband] away from her and monopolized his attention for an hour."[42]

During a review of General Edward O. C. Ord's Army of the James on March 26, Mary threw a fit when she saw General Ord's young and beautiful wife riding next to the president. Mary unleashed such a verbal harangue on Mrs. Ord that the younger woman broke down in tears. The first lady then unleashed her venom on her traveling companion, Mrs. Grant, and later on her husband at a military staff dinner, to the embarrassment of all at the table.[43] As the story was repeated in later years, so it was gossiped about at City Point when it happened and embarrassed Captain Lincoln in front of his peers. Mary—who typically switched from anger to contrition in a flash—was also so humiliated by it that she stayed in her cabin on the *River Queen* for the next few days and then returned to Washington alone on April 1.[44]

On March 29, Grant began his final push against Lee's army and moved his staff and headquarters closer to the front. It was during this time that Robert Lincoln participated in the fall of Petersburg and Richmond. It is unknown exactly what Robert did during these days, but as the fighting was continuous, with troops ever attacking and defending, advancing and shifting position, with cavalry raids, artillery shelling, pursuit of the retreating Confederates, and relentless sending of dispatches between commanders, it is certain that Robert, like all the junior officers on the headquarters staff, would have been in constant motion by direction of his commanders, would have heard and seen blood and battle, and would have had little rest for days. The president, like any father, was anxious about his son's welfare during the final fighting, and only when he saw Robert again in Petersburg on April 3 did he find relief.[45]

After visiting both Petersburg and Richmond, President Lincoln telegraphed his wife, "Petersburg and Richmond are both in our hands; and Tad and I have been to the former and been with Bob four or five hours. He is well and in good spirits."[46] After Lincoln returned to City Point, Grant and his staff followed the Army of the Potomac on its final push against Lee's Army of Northern Virginia, which ended on Sunday, April 9, with Lee's surrender at Appomattox Court House, Virginia.

The meeting between the two commanding generals that day and the surrender of the seemingly indomitable Robert E. Lee have been historically marked for various distinctions, such as General Lee's polished and gentlemanly appearance contrasted with that of General Grant's rumpled clothes and muddy boots, as well as the ironic fact that the land on which the war ended was owned by the same man who owned the land in Manassas on which the war began, Wilmer McLean. It is not generally known, however, that a third distinction could be claimed in that Captain Robert Lincoln, the son of President Abraham Lincoln, as a member of Grant's staff, was personally present. No other son of a sitting president has ever participated in and then witnessed a scene so colossal and historic. No other son of a sitting president ever has been personally introduced to the defeated commander at the scene of surrender. In later years, in the early twentieth century, Robert Lincoln would live so old as to be recognized not only as Abraham Lincoln's son, as a respected public servant, as a great captain of industry but also as the last living person who was present at the Appomattox surrender.

Robert wrote or spoke about his experience at Appomattox numerous times throughout his life and explained how when Grant entered the McLean house, the majority of the general's staff—especially the junior members, of which Robert was one—waited on the large front porch. Once the conference between Grant and Lee was completed in the front parlor and the capitulation agreements written and signed, the officers were presented to the Confederate commander.[47] "Looking back into history, the events on that day form a page that can never be forgotten, especially by those who were present on that occasion," Robert told a newspaper reporter in 1881. But when pressed for more details of the dramatic nature of the scene, Robert, then President James A. Garfield's secretary of war, somewhat anticlimactically said, "As I recall the scene now, it appeared to be a very ordinary transaction. . . . It seemed just as if I had sold you a house and we had but to pass the titles and other conveyances."[48]

This sober reflection sixteen years later may belie Robert's reaction in 1865. At the time, Union soldiers were jubilant at the surrender, while Confederates were distraught; local citizens were angry at the pillaging done by the two armies in their necessary foraging; and McLean was enraged after his house was literally looted for artifacts by soldiers wanting a piece of the house in which the war ended. Robert was likely as lighthearted as his compatriots at the event, as well as eager to return to Washington and tell his father all about it. In fact, the young captain left with General Grant and cortege the next morning for the four-day journey to Washington.[49]

The general's boat pulled into the Washington shipyard on the morning of April 14 greeted by the city's joyous din of celebration: "As we reached our destination that bright morning . . . every gun in and near Washington burst forth—and such a salvo!—all the bells rang out merry greetings, and the city was literally swathed in flags and bunting," Julia Grant wrote.[50] Indeed, the city of Washington had been celebrating since the April 2 fall of Richmond with illuminations, bands, bells, crowds, cannons, and flags. The April 9 surrender at Appomattox was a cause for even more intense revelry, and April 14, the four-year anniversary of the surrender of Fort Sumter, was to be commemorated with the reraising of the flag over the fort. Robert was included in the heroes' welcome given for Grant and his retinue, but like his commanding general, Captain Lincoln was impressed but aloof from the parades and pageantry. He simply mounted his horse and rode directly from the wharf to the White House that fateful morning, eager to rejoin his family, whom he found at breakfast.

After four years of a terrible war, the loss of family and friends—including the death of eleven-year-old Willie—the Lincoln family was happier then than during their entire sojourn in Washington. Mary Lincoln would comment later on how her husband's great cheerfulness that morning surprised her.[51] When oldest son, Robert, came into the breakfast room that morning, fresh from the front, sleep-deprived yet exulted and still in his rumpled and muddy blue uniform, it was a joyous family reunion. Robert was the first person to give his father an eyewitness account of Lee's surrender. The son even brought his father a photograph of the Confederate commander, to which the president, after thoughtful scrutiny of the portrait, said, "It is a good face; it is the face of a noble, noble, brave man. I am glad the war is over at last."[52]

After breakfast, Robert spent a few hours talking alone with his father, recounting to him the final days of the campaign.[53] The president was so eager to spend time with his oldest son, in fact, he postponed his morning cabinet meeting—a meeting in which General Grant was to attend and the group was to discuss the important subject of reconstruction—for two hours in order to "see something of [Robert] before I go to work."[54] At 11 A.M., the president met with his cabinet and victorious commanding general to discuss the aftermath of the war. In the afternoon, the president and first lady had a date of sorts. A few days previous, Abraham had written his wife a playful yet tender letter asking her to go for a carriage ride. "He was to Mrs. Lincoln as chivalrous on the last day of his life as when he courted her," one contemporary wrote.[55] As they rode, they discussed their plans for life after his presidency. They would travel across America to visit California, then to Europe, and Lincoln wanted to visit Jerusalem.[56] They considered whether they would return to their house in Springfield or live in Chicago upon Lincoln's retirement from the White House.[57] "During the drive he was so gay," Mary said, "that I said to him, laughingly, 'Dear Husband, you almost startle me by your great cheerfulness,' he replied, 'and well I may feel so, Mary, I consider *this* day, the war, has come to a close."[58]

How Robert spent his day is unknown. After two weeks with practically no rest, he probably took a bath, put on clean clothing and had his uniform washed. He almost certainly spent time with his mother and little brother, recounting to them the events of the final campaign. He may even have called upon Mary Harlan, his date for the inaugural ball, whom he had not seen since that night's celebration more than one month before.[59] He later stated that he did not see his father again until dinner.[60]

One thing Robert did not learn until later was a story his father told his cabinet during their meeting that day. When the talk turned to the news of Sherman's army and whether he had yet defeated the army of Confederate General Joseph Johnston, still at large, Lincoln said he was certain good news would come soon. "I had," the president remarked, "this strange dream again last night, and we shall, judging from the past, have great news very soon." This dream, the president said, he had had preceding nearly every great and important event of the war, including Fort Sumter, Antietam, Gettysburg, Stone River, and Vicksburg. He was in "some singular, indescribable vessel" and was moving "with great rapidity toward an indefinite shore."[61]

That night, the Lincolns and the Grants were scheduled to attend the play *Our American Cousin* at Ford's Theatre. The Grants, however, eager to return to their children in New Jersey, declined that morning to go. Others were invited to the theater in their place, such as Speaker of the House Colfax and Major Thomas Eckert of the War Department Telegraph Office, but none could go.[62] Finally, the Lincolns found success in the couple of Miss Clara Harris, daughter of New York U.S. Senator Ira Harris, and her fiancée, Major Henry Rathbone.

After dinner that evening, the president went to Robert's room and asked him some more questions about the surrender of Lee. "He came into my room just before going to the theater and talked with me, but I do not recall that it was anything of importance," Robert later stated. The president also invited his son to accompany him to the theater. Robert, tired after two weeks in the field, having not slept in a bed or with his uniform off during all that time, told his father he wanted to stay home and go to bed early.[63]

The president and first lady left for the theater a little after 8 P.M. Tad had left earlier to see a children's play at the National Theatre. Robert stayed in his room, and he and his friend, presidential secretary Hay, who had probably been too busy to see Robert during the day, visited and sat gossiping.[64]

As the president left the White House for the theater that Good Friday, he was accosted by a group of men who wanted a word. Lincoln declined, citing that he was late, but wrote a note to allow the men an appointment the next morning.[65] Legend states that as he left, the president bid farewell to his longtime bodyguard William H. Crook but, instead of saying "good night" as he always did, he said, "Good bye, Crook," which the bodyguard thought strange.[66]
At about 10:15 P.M., during act 3, scene 2, of *Our American Cousin*, as lead character Asa Trenchard uttered what was considered one of the play's funniest

lines—"Don't know the manners of good society, eh? Well, I guess I know enough to turn you inside out, old gal—you sockdologizing old man-trap"—the firing of a single-shot Derringer pistol was barely audible above the delighted uproar of the audience.

"About 10:30 I heard the clatter of horses coming up the drive to the White House," Robert Lincoln later stated in the only known interview or reminiscence he ever gave about the events of that night. "I thought someone was coming to get a reprieve for some poor soldier who was going to get shot the next morning and they would be disappointed because the president was not there."[67] Instead, a great commotion occurred in the foyer, and suddenly someone burst into Robert's room with the news that his father had been shot. He and Hay ran downstairs and, finding a carriage waiting at the door, immediately took off for the theater on Tenth Street. Already rumors were flying around the city about who had been shot, how, and where. Robert first heard his father had been shot in the arm; then a friend told him and Hay, just as they were leaving the White House, that Secretary of State Seward and most of the cabinet had been murdered. The two young men had little time to digest this information in the few minutes it would have taken their carriage to race the seven blocks from Pennsylvania Avenue to Tenth Street. "The news was all so improbable that they could not help hoping it was all untrue," Hay later wrote. "But when they got to Tenth Street and found every thoroughfare blocked by the swiftly gathering thousands, agitated by tumultuous excitement, they were prepared for the worst."[68]

As with so many events connected with the life and death of Abraham Lincoln, multiple people in subsequent years claimed to be the one and only person to run to the White House and notify Robert of his father's assassination. Alexander Williamson, tutor to both Willie and Tad in the White House, stated that he was interrupted while preparing for bed and told by his son of the assassination, who was present at Ford's Theatre that night. "I pulled on my clothes and hurried first to the President's House to find Robert. On the stairs I met little Tad, in charge of one of the messengers. . . . I hurried upstairs to Mr. Robert Lincoln's and Major John Hay's rooms and informed them of what happened, on which they hastened to the theater."[69]

Thomas F. Pendel, a doorkeeper/usher at the White House, said the arrival of Senator Sumner at the White House that night presaged the news of President Lincoln's assassination. When the news came, Pendel ran up to Robert's room, where he found the captain holding a vial in one hand and a teaspoon in the other, as if he were about to take a dose of medication. "I shall never forget, even to my dying day, the expression that overspread his face as I shrieked out my fearful news. He had looked up in surprise as I burst into his room, and, as I told my errand, he unconsciously let the bottle drop from one hand and then the spoon from the other. I could say nothing more, but gazed in a sort of fascination as the medicine slowly gurgled out over the carpet." Robert told Pendel to get Hay, who was in his own room, and then the two young men ran out the door.[70]

C. C. Bangs, a delegate to the U.S. Christian Commission, offers some corroboration to Pendel's statement. Bangs stated that upon hearing the news of the assassination, he hurried to the Petersen House—the building across the street from Ford's Theatre where the doctors took the president's wounded body—where he saw Mrs. Lincoln standing in the doorway looking for a messenger to tell Robert what had happened. Bangs volunteered. Inside the White House, he found "several gentlemen" in the front room who had not heard of the events at the theater. "Taking aside one of the ushers I quickly made known my errand. He at once took me to Robert Lincoln's room. He was partially undressed, but quickly made ready and came with me to the room below." Senator Sumner was one of the gentlemen waiting in the front room, and at Robert's request, he, Robert, and Bangs jumped in a carriage and rushed to the Petersen House, Bangs stated.[71]

Sumner's longtime secretary, Arnold B. Johnson, also corroborated these accounts. He recollected that on the night of the assassination, Sumner was dining at the home of California U.S. Senator John Conness. When news of Lincoln's assassination reached them, Sumner, doubting the story, rushed to the White House, where no news had yet been received. "Robert Lincoln, of whom inquiry was made, accompanied Mr. Sumner" to the Petersen House, Johnson later wrote.[72] Sumner himself, according to his earliest biographers, told the same story to Charles Dickens in 1868; yet in an 1874 statement to a journalist, said simply, "I was with Mr. Lincoln all night and in the morning saw him breathe his last."[73]

When asked in later years who exactly had notified him that night of his father's assassination, Robert stated he did not know. "I remember distinctly a number of the early incidents of that evening, but I cannot recall the name of any one except John Hay, whom I saw before I left the President's Home," Robert wrote.[74] In fact, Robert's response suggests that more than one person came to his room that night and therefore perhaps Williamson, Pendel, Bangs, and Johnson all were correct in general, even though some of their stories have implausible aspects and absurd dramatic touches. "In response to your inquiry I regret to say that I cannot definitely answer whether or not Mr. Sumner was *one of those* who suddenly came to my room at the time you mention," Robert wrote in 1909.[75]

Arriving at the Petersen House, fighting through the surrounding throng of onlookers and soldiers, rushing up the stairs to the first-floor apartment, Robert and Hay (and perhaps Sumner with them) were met at the door by Dr. Robert K. Stone, the Lincoln family physician, whom Mary Lincoln had immediately sent for on reaching the house. There, in the foyer, Stone told Robert Lincoln there was no hope for his father's recovery.[76] "After a natural outburst of grief," John Hay later wrote, "young Lincoln devoted himself the rest of the night to soothing and comforting his mother."[77] In fact, Robert spent the night alternating between comforting his frantic mother and watching his dying father.

William Petersen's home at 453 Tenth Street was a three-story house often rented to lodgers, especially actors. Renter Henry Safford had seen the crowd carrying the president's limp body out of the theater and looking for a place to take him and shouted, "Bring him in here!" After ascending a short stairway from the street, Lincoln's body was taken the ten feet down a narrow hallway—large enough only to go single file—to the back bedroom, occupied by William T. Clark, a War Department clerk, who was not then at home. Lincoln's body was laid diagonally across Clark's bed, which was too short to fit the president's tall frame. The bedroom itself was very small, 9½ by 17 feet, and contained the bed, a dresser, and two chairs. A door on the left side led to a back porch. Despite the fact that the small room could hold only eight to ten people comfortably, dozens of people came and went throughout the night, paying their respects, taking one last look at the president, including fourteen physicians.[78]

Immediately to the left of the front door was the parlor, which fronted the street and contained a sofa, chairs, and table. It was in this room that Mary Lincoln spent most of the night in shock and anxiety, attended by her friend Elizabeth Dixon, Dixon's sister Mary Kinney and daughter Constance Kinney, and Clara Harris.[79] Mrs. Lincoln would leave the room about once an hour to go to her husband's side, crying, begging for him to speak to her.

Attached to the front parlor was a second parlor, with a bed, tables, and chairs. This room was used by Secretary of War Stanton to direct the manhunt for the president's assassin. This room was connected to the hallway by a door adjacent to the entrance to the back bedroom, and couriers, messengers, and soldiers came and went all night, bringing in information and witnesses who gave their accounts of the evening. Stanton's room was separated from the front parlor by a door, certainly closed, but no doubt everyone was still able to hear the wails and cries of Mrs. Lincoln in the front room.

For nine hours that night, Robert Lincoln was surrounded by the subdued maelstrom of people and events swirling within the confines of those three rooms. "I remember with great vividness, it seems to me, all the details of that dreadful time," he later wrote.[80] Years afterward, just before the centennial anniversary of his father's birth, Robert Lincoln was asked by Richard Watson Gilder, editor of the *Century* magazine and longtime friend, to write an article detailing his reminiscence of the assassination. Robert not only declined but also asked that Gilder not publish any article about it. "It was a very dreadful night," Robert wrote him, "and I personally should not like to read again an account of it."[81]

During that dreadful night, Robert spent most of his time in the front parlor with his mother, comforting her, listening to her wonder why this happened, calling for her own death, calling for Tad to be brought, who, she was convinced, could make his father wake up because his father loved him so much. Once again, as after the deaths of his brothers Eddie and Willie, Robert found himself forced to comfort his hysterical mother and suppress his own anguish; once again mother and son switched roles of (somewhat) stolid nurse and devastated sufferer—yet, this time Robert had no father with whom to share his burden; the duty was his alone. "Capt. Robert Lincoln bore himself with great firmness, and constantly endeavored to assuage the grief of his mother by telling her to put her trust in God, and all would be well," one witness reported. "Occasionally, being entirely overcome, he would retire to the hall and give vent to the most heart-rending lamentations. He would recover himself and return to his mother, and with remarkable self-possession try to cheer her broken spirits and lighten her load of sorrow. His conduct was the most remarkable exhibit of calmness in a trying hour that I have ever seen."[82]

Robert watched as the military personnel rushed in and out of the house all night long, reporting events to Stanton shut in the second room, bringing in eyewitnesses for testimony. Robert also spent time in the room with his father, being comforted by his friend Hay and his family friend Sumner, listening to the talk in hushed tones, watching the surgeons observe his father's condition, watching the generals and politicians come and go, each one eager to pay respects, listening to his father's stertorous breathing. Surgeon General Joseph K. Barnes, Assistant Surgeon General Charles Henry Crane, Dr. Stone, Dr. E. W. Abbot, and Dr. Charles S. Taft stayed with the president, monitoring his condition through the night. Secretary of the Navy Welles spent the night in a chair at the foot of the bed. "The surgeons and members of the Cabinet were as many as should have been in the room," Welles wrote in his diary, "but there were many more, and the hall and other rooms in the front or main house were full."[83]

President Lincoln's clothes had been removed, his body covered in mustard plaster and covered with a blanket. Blood and brains continually oozed from his head wound where Booth had shot him, causing the pillow to be constantly changed, while his face under his right eye and around his right cheek bone was swollen and turning black from the wound. He never regained consciousness.[84] "Except for his breathing, and the sobbing of his wife, son, and devoted servant, not a sound was to be heard in that chamber for hours," one witness later wrote. "The night wore on, long and anxious, and finally the gray dawn of a dull and rainy morning began to creep slowly into the room. And still the martyr lived—if living it could be called."[85] Everyone in the house just stayed there waiting, waiting for the death they all knew to be inevitable. Outside, hundreds, perhaps thousands, of people gathered in Tenth Street outside the Petersen house, waiting for some word of the president's condition. Both Lincoln's pulse and breathing continually fluctuated during the night, but it was not until about 7 A.M. the next morning that his breathing and pulse weakened.

Mary then made her final visit to her husband. Robert also came in and stood with Sumner behind the headboard of the bed. The young captain "bore himself well, but gave way on two occasions to overpowering grief and sobbed aloud, turning his head and leaning on the shoulder of Senator Sumner," Welles recorded in his diary.[86] Robert Lincoln later told his cousin Katherine Helm he felt "the interminable agony of [that] night would never end, the hopeless watching, the anguished weeping, finally, the utter, peaceful stillness of death."[87] At 7:22 A.M., President Abraham Lincoln breathed his last. The Reverend Dr. Phineas Gurley, the Lincolns' friend and pastor who had been with Mary Lincoln most of the night in the front parlor, immediately knelt by the bed and led everyone in a prayer. Just before the present cabinet members assembled in the back parlor to sign a letter officially informing Vice President Andrew Johnson that he was now the president, Secretary of War Stanton, more distraught at the murder of his friend than subsequent historians have given him credit, uttered the now-famous phrase about his chief, "Now he belongs to the ages"—and Robert Lincoln's world was changed forever.

7

"I Feel Utterly without Spirit or Courage"

One witness to the death of President Abraham Lincoln characterized the grieving twenty-one-year-old Robert at the time as "only a boy, for all his shoulder straps."[1] Whether a correct statement or not, there is no doubt that Robert found himself in a new and overwhelming position once his father died. Robert Lincoln was now, in the Victorian custom, the head of the Lincoln family, and, as such, it was his duty to manage family business and to care for his mother and youngest brother. Robert knew his own limitations and so immediately telegraphed an old family friend and political ally of Abraham Lincoln, David Davis, who was then an associate justice of the United States Supreme Court, "Please come at once to Washington and take charge of my father's affairs."[2] Davis's wife, Sarah, who was with her husband at the time in Chicago, wrote her children of their father's errand, adding, "I feel reluctant to have him go, and yet cannot refuse the family of Mr. Lincoln."[3] And Robert certainly needed help. Not only was he dealing with his own grief but also had to assume the father-figure status for twelve-year-old Tad and to continue ministering to his debilitated mother.

In a daze after the president's death, Robert escorted his mother from the Petersen House back to the White House, where they reunited with scared and stricken little Tad, who kept asking, "Where is my pa?" and "Who has killed papa?"[4] Who indeed? By early Saturday morning, Robert long would have known that the actor John Wilkes Booth had been the assassin but little more. Booth was still on the run from the army, and no other conspirators had yet been captured. It is unclear how much Robert told Tad or even how much Robert cared, considering the weight now resting on his shoulders. While the newspapers reported all the details of the murder, the manhunt, and the scenes at the Petersen House, Robert was in the White House with his family.

"Returning to Mrs. Lincoln's room, I found her in a new paroxysm of grief," Mary's seamstress, Elizabeth Keckly, later wrote of the scene that morning in the White House. "Robert was bending over his mother with tender affection, and little Tad was couched at the foot of the bed, with a world of agony in his young face."[5] There, Mary had only Keckly, Elizabeth Dixon, and Mary Jane (Mrs. Gideon) Welles to comfort her.[6] The Lincolns received numerous telegrams that morning from family and friends offering sympathy and assistance. Robert received missives from his cousin Emily Todd Helm, his uncle Clark M. Smith, and his close friend Clinton Conkling.[7] Elizabeth Edwards, despite a three-year feud with her sister stemming from patronage desires, telegraphed Mary "as a sister and mother" and offered her assistance and her home for the duration of the funeral services in Springfield.[8] But it was actually to her cousin Elizabeth Todd Grimsley that Mary reached out that day, asking her to come immediately to Washington.[9]

As for Robert, "He suffered deeply, as his haggard face indicated, but he was ever manly and collected when in the presence of his mother," Keckly wrote.[10] The nation may have lost its leader, but Robert Lincoln had lost his father. "In all my plans for the future, the chief object I had in view was the approbation of my father," he wrote two weeks after the assassination, "and now that he is gone and in such a way, I feel utterly without spirit or courage. I know that such a feeling is wrong and that it is my duty to overcome it. I trust that for the sake of my mother and little brother that I will be able to do it."[11]

One of Robert's later friends, Nicholas Murray Butler, suggested that perhaps the greatest effect of the assassination on Robert was the overwhelming guilt it caused him, in that he never forgave himself for his absence at Ford's Theatre that night. As the youngest member of the presidential party, Robert would have sat at the back of the box, closest to the door. According to Butler, Robert always felt that had he been there, "Booth would have had to deal with him before he could have shot the president."[12]

The city of Washington mirrored Robert's own agonized feelings. John Nicolay, who had gone to South Carolina to witness the flag raising above Fort Sumter, returned to Washington on April 17 and was immediately impressed by the "air of gloom" that hung over the city: "Almost every house was draped, and closed, and men stood idle and listless in groups on the street corner. The Executive Mansion was dark and still as almost the grave itself. The silence, and gloom, and sorrow depicted on every face are as heavy and ominous of terror, as if some greater calamity still hung in the air, and was about to crush and overwhelm every one."[13] The *New York Times* stated more simply, "Strong men weep in the streets."[14]

On Tuesday, April 18, President Lincoln's embalmed body was placed in the East Room of the White House for public viewing. Newspapers estimated twenty-five thousand people passed through to pay their last respects. It was also being reported that Lewis Paine, who attacked Secretary of State William Seward, and a number of other conspirators, including a woman, Mary Surratt, had been arrested that morning.

The next day, Wednesday, April 19, Lincoln's funeral was held in the East Room. Robert was the official family representative since his mother was too distraught to attend; he sat at the foot of his father's coffin with friends Hay and Nicolay.[15] All government buildings and agencies were closed, and all civil servants walked in the funeral procession, as did vast military contingents and foreign and American diplomats. Mourners lined the streets on both sides for the procession's entire one and a half miles from the White House to the Capitol. As one civil servant wrote after seeing Lincoln in the Capitol rotunda, "Seeing him lying there, dead, and all the funeral trappings, I biled with indignation."[16] This anger, as well as a sense of dread for the future, was not uncommon. Major General John J. Peck, commander in New York, responded to the news of Lincoln's death: "His death at this crisis is the greatest national calamity that could befall us."[17] More than one ex-Confederate stoutly declared that when Lincoln was murdered, the South lost its best friend. Even Robert E. Lee called the assassination of President Lincoln "a crime previously unknown to this country, and one that must be deprecated by every American."[18]

The president's body lay in state in the Capitol rotunda until Friday morning, when the funeral train, with the addition of the body of little Willie Lincoln, who had died in 1862, left Washington for its twelve-day, six-state, seventeen-hundred-mile journey back to Illinois for burial. Robert saw the train off from Washington but was not a passenger during any part of its trip.[19] He stayed in the capital to continue closing up his father's affairs and help care for his frantic mother, who was being comforted daily by Mary Jane Welles. Robert received callers, responded to gifts his mother received, wrote to President Johnson thanking him for his indulgence to Mary's distress, and even was forced to expel a number of female Spiritualists from the White House, who, as one contemporary wrote, "nearly crazed" the widow as they "poured into her ears pretended messages from her dead husband."[20] Mary later characterized her final six weeks at the White House as "a bed of illness & many days & nights of almost positive derangement."[21] The Washington *National Intelligencer* reported that Mary Lincoln was in such anguish as to be under the care of family physician Dr. Robert K. Stone, while Robert Lincoln "has deported himself in a manner that has at once commanded the respect and excited the sympathy of those who have seen him since his father's death."[22]

One of Robert's first actions in those dark days was to resign his army commission, believing his foremost duty to be to his family.[23] Robert also wrote, along with his mother, to the Sangamon County, Illinois, court to request letters of administration for his father's estate to be granted to David Davis, as no will could be found for the late president.[24] Finally, Robert began what would be a lifelong task of caring for his father's papers and guarding his father's legacy. He asked the presidential secretaries, Nicolay and Hay, to box up all the White House papers for storage and even helped then in their endeavor.[25] The boxes were sent, under direction of Secretary of War Edwin M. Stanton, to Davis's hometown of Bloomington, Illinois, where they were deposited in a vault in the National Bank.[26] It did not take long, however—less than two weeks—for historians and would-be biographers to begin asking Robert for information and access to his father's belongings.

On April 27, a letter came from Cambridge, Massachusetts, suggesting Robert allow the renowned scholar Charles Eliot Norton to write the president's biography. Robert replied with thanks but that it would be "impossible" for a complete life to be written at that time because many of the documents necessary for such a work would be "damaging" to men then living. "The papers have been carefully collected by the Private Secretaries, and sealed, and deposited in a safe place," Robert wrote. "At sometime within the next three or four years, I propose, in conjunction with the Secretaries and one or two friends of my father, on whose judgment I rely, to open the boxes, and to glean out what is useless and to classify the remainder in some sort. No one will have access to them before that time."[27] Robert made a similar response to historian James Parton on May 10, adding, "As to who shall do the work [of a biography], when it is time, I have taken no thought. If I should find that some personal friend of my father had conceived the idea and have made preparations, I should, I own, be prejudiced in his favor, but I do not as yet know of any such."[28] Robert may have been speaking in half-truths here, as he certainly knew Nicolay and Hay were contemplating a biography; and on June 10, Robert told would-be biographer Josiah G. Holland that he had heard William H. Herndon, Abraham Lincoln's former law partner, also intended to write a biography.[29]

It should be noted that while Robert was distraught about his father's death, he was not without support. Davis, whom Robert later referred to as a "second father," was there, as were friends Hay and Nicolay.[30] Mary Harlan may even have offered him some comfort. Yet, Robert had another bastion of support during this time who is rarely mentioned in subsequent histories—Edwin Stanton. Stanton had, and still has, the reputation of a gruff, unfriendly, nearly apathetic individual who handled the night of the assassination and following days with a cold, stolid, steely hand. Some even have accused him of complicity in the assassination plot.[31] Yet, Stanton's love for Lincoln and great sense of loss at his death are clear in the many descriptions of him as breaking down into tears after his chief's death. Stanton also showed a great inner compassion and support towards Robert after the assassination. "Your ideas of [Stanton's] different characteristics agree entirely with my own," Robert explained in a 1911 letter to historian David H. Bates. "His gruffness and complete absorption in the great work he had at hand were the most prominent characteristics to the public of course; but like yourself I knew personally of many things which indicated the great warmness of his heart. I would not care to have it published, but I will tell you that for more than ten days after my father's death in Washington, he called every morning on me in my room, and spent the first few minutes of his visits weeping without saying a word."[32]

Two of the most important things Robert and his mother had to decide in those first days after the assassination were where the family would live once they left Washington and where Abraham Lincoln would be buried. The first was rather easy, as Mary had been intending for years to live in Chicago once her husband finished his second term as president, even though he intended to return to Springfield or perhaps even settle in California.[33] Mary, in fact, told her son on April 15, the day her husband died, and on subsequent days, that she did not want to return to Springfield but would rather live in Chicago. Both Robert and Davis thought Mary should return to where she had family and friends, not to mention a fully paid house in which to live.[34] But just as she never again entered the White House bedroom in which her son Willie died in 1862, so Mary could not bear the thought of ever again stepping foot inside the family's old Springfield home.

The more difficult question for the family was to decide where to bury their patriarch. It was not so much a decision as it turned out to be a battle—a battle that Mary Lincoln, steely willed despite her grief, was determined to win. Since Abraham Lincoln was the people's president, savior of the Union, and the first martyred president, everyone seemed to have an opinion on where he should be buried. Some thought he should be placed in the crypt under the U.S. Capitol that had been prepared for George Washington but never used or perhaps even next to Washington's body at Mount Vernon. Some thought that if it had to return to Illinois, it should be placed in the major city of Chicago rather than the small hamlet of Springfield. The leaders of Lincoln's hometown, however, went beyond thoughts and into immediate action.

Within hours of Lincoln's death, the citizens and city council of Springfield, Illinois, held a mass meeting at which it was decided to request of Mary Lincoln that her husband's body be buried in the town he so loved.[35] A committee—that included Mary's cousin and Lincoln's friend and first law partner John Todd Stuart, as well as other Lincoln friends Ozias M. Hatch and James C.

Conkling—was appointed to make all the arrangements for Lincoln's funeral and burial. Although the committee visited Oak Ridge Cemetery on April 17 and was offered by the proprietors a beautiful lot for Lincoln's tomb, most of the citizens of Springfield—as can be seen in newspaper reports, diaries, and letters—preferred a place more centrally located for both Lincoln's—and the town's—glory. To this end, the committee decided instead to bury the president on the Mather place, a six-acre lot in the middle of the city.[36] "The last resting place of Mr. Lincoln will be the Mecca of millions of people, and for all time the spot will be looked on as almost holy ground," the *Chicago Tribune* reported in giving the reasons for the decision. "This grove is in the heart of the city, and accessible to all classes of people, rich and poor, while Oak Ridge is distant about three miles, and many times during the year very hard to reach."[37] While this decision was perhaps understandable, it has gone down ignominiously in history for the way in which it was made, namely, without the least thought for or consultation with the wishes and intentions of the Lincoln family.

While the Springfield committee had moved immediately, in those first days after the assassination Mary Lincoln had not made any decision on the location of her husband's burial. U.S. Senator Orville H. Browning from Illinois recorded in his diary that Mary was, at first, "vehemently opposed" to burial in Springfield, even though her son Robert, her husband's estate executor, Davis, and Browning himself all thought it appropriate. Mary preferred Chicago but was persuaded to change her mind, and when the funeral train left Washington for Illinois on April 21, it was generally understood that Oak Ridge Cemetery in Springfield was the final destination.[38] In later years, Mary related to one biographer that her husband had specifically asked her, during their last trip to Virginia in the spring of 1865, to bury him in "some quiet place" when he died.[39] Perhaps the tranquil, bucolic setting of Oak Ridge on the outskirts of Springfield, so in harmony with her husband's request, was the deciding factor in Mary's final decision. She certainly was familiar with the area, having been present, with her husband, at the new cemetery's dedication on May 24, 1860.[40]

When, however, Mary read in the Springfield newspaper on Friday, April 28 (one day after the news of John Wilkes Booth's death was reported), that the city committee had decided to bury the president on the Mather place—indeed, that they had already received five hundred subscriptions, spent more than $50,000, and nearly completed building the tomb—she was outraged.[41] Mary felt Oak Ridge "would be better in accord with her husband's Republican tastes, than the center of a noisy city," according to her close friend Anson G. Henry. In addition to that—and perhaps even more important to Mary, who always knew how to hold a grudge—she felt "a strong repugnance to having those who had abused and vilified him while living and who always considered his elevation to the Presidency a personal injustice to themselves, assuming to decide where his remains should depose, and taking so prominent a part in doing honor to his memory."[42]

Immediately, both Mary (through her cousin John B. S. Todd) and Secretary of War Stanton telegraphed the committee head Stuart in Springfield and insisted that the president's remains be buried in Oak Ridge Cemetery and nowhere else.[43] On Sunday, Stuart telegraphed that the entire committee agreed with him that arrangements on the Mather lot had "gone too far to be changed"; Mary replied that they must be changed or she would remove her husband's body to Chicago for burial.[44] On Monday, May 1, Robert wrote to Illinois Governor Richard J. Oglesby, "There seems to be a disposition at Springfield to disregard my mother's wishes in regard to the interment. Both the temporary and final interment must take place in the Oak Ridge Cemetery. We have reasons for not wishing to use the Mather place for either purpose and we expect and demand that our wishes be consulted."[45] Also that day, Mary's cousin John B. S. Todd and her friend Henry wrote at her request to prominent Springfield men that her husband must be buried in Oak Ridge and reiterated her intention to bury her husband in Chicago if ignored.[46]

The threat of moving Lincoln's body out of Springfield had the desired effect on the committee, and they finally relented—much to their chagrin, as well as the chagrin of many Springfield area residents. "The excitement in Springfield at that time was very high and much feeling in the matter was displayed," one resident later recalled.[47] The nearly completed work on the Mather lot tomb was immediately halted, and new work quickly begun to prepare the cemetery and the public receiving vault for the May 4 funeral. The city was already fully dressed in black, every public building, private business, and home. The statehouse was draped all the way up to the top of its dome. Lincoln's old home at the corner of Eighth and Jackson Streets was also mournfully hung inside and out, with an arch of evergreens over the front gate, two national flags draped over the front door, and a large colored photograph of Lincoln over the middle of the doorway between the two parlors.[48] In the days surrounding the funeral, tens of thousands of people passed through the house in a reverential pilgrimage. Robert, accompanied by Nicolay, left Washington on May 1 to attend the funeral. He was the only member of the immediate family present, as his mother could not bear the thought of burying her husband, and she insisted Tad stay in Washington with her. Robert arrived in Springfield on May 3, where he and Nicolay stayed at the home of John Todd Stuart.[49]

Abraham Lincoln's body arrived in Springfield on Wednesday, May 3, and was placed in state in the capitol and allowed for public viewing until the funeral began the next day. "This was one of the most magnificent and solemn scenes ever witnessed on this continent," wrote one witness. "Language is tame and inadequate to describe or convey a correct idea of the scene."[50] The immense funeral procession left the capitol to travel the one and a half miles north to Oak Ridge Cemetery on the edge of town. Robert rode in the family carriage, accompanied by Elizabeth Grimsley. The obsequies at the cemetery took a little more than an hour, at the end of which time the military guard of honor locked the receiving vault and gave the key to Robert Lincoln; he in turn gave it to Stuart for safekeeping.[51] One newspaper at this time described Robert as "solemn and thoughtful, and bore himself with manly courage throughout."[52] Another newspaper stated his "bearing and conduct during the obsequies of his lamented father have been full of Christian nobleness."[53] After the funeral, young Springfield resident Julia Kirby went to Stuart's house and there met Robert, whom she found so despondent that "my heart ached for him."[54]

Robert telegraphed his cousin John B. S. Todd after the funeral and said it was "all as I wished," and he would return to Washington in a few days.[55] Robert stayed in Springfield for the next three days. On May 5, he and Davis went out to Oak Ridge Cemetery and selected a six-acre piece of land to be the site of the permanent Lincoln tomb.[56] What else Robert did in Springfield is unknown, other than visit with family and his good friend Clinton Conkling. Robert probably spent much time with Davis going over President Lincoln's affairs and discussing the future of the Lincoln family, especially Tad, who would, for the first time, begin attending school in Chicago. Robert may have gone to the Lincoln homestead to go through his father's belongings left in the second-floor storeroom in 1861.

When Robert returned to Washington on Monday, May 8, he found his mother "feeling much better" and also pleased with the lot selection for the permanent Lincoln tomb in Oak Ridge.[57] Mary's letters at this time belie Robert's perceptions, however, using phrases such as "utter desolation," "bowed down as I am with my great sorrow," and "doubting the goodness of the Almighty."[58] In this state, Mary Lincoln, surrounded by her sons and a few friends, continued to languish in the White House. President Andrew Johnson, living in his own house and working out of an office in the Treasury Department, allowed Mary much latitude in her bereavement. It was in fact more than one month after the assassination, on May 22, 1865, that the Lincoln family finally vacated the White House.[59] "I go hence, broken hearted, with every hope almost in life—crushed," Mary wrote Charles Sumner before her departure.[60]

Robert Lincoln, like his mother, suffered deeply in the months after his father's assassination. Besides grief, however, Robert was battling with anxiety over the uncertainty of his own future.[61] Robert, now head of the family, chief comforter and supporter of his mother, older brother and now mentor to young Tad, also had to immediately get started on a career. Yet, in accordance with the rules of Gilded Age masculinity, Robert kept his emotional pain to himself. "Poor Robert, has borne his sorrows, manfully, yet with a broken heart," his mother wrote to a friend three months after the assassination.[62] And why shouldn't he be full of sorrow? He not only suffered his father's murder, which came only three years after his young brother's death, but also the complete altering of the course of his life.

Robert's postwar life plans are unknown, other than that he intended eventually to become a lawyer, but it can be logically surmised that he either planned to return to Harvard or, more likely, to apprentice at a law firm in Washington.[63] In the 1860s, the path to practicing law was either through study at an accredited law school or, more usually, professional apprenticeship. He also may have stayed in the army for months or years after the active campaigning of the war closed or even sought some government position. He or his father may even have considered a place on the presidential staff, just as other politicians had placed their sons under them as aides. Instead, Robert resigned his army commission and moved with his family to Chicago, thereby eschewing Harvard and Washington and leaving behind not only the eastern friends and life he so enjoyed but also Mary Harlan, the young woman he was courting.

Robert's decision to accompany his mother and brother back to Illinois was, as he saw it, his duty. Existing records and correspondence show no equivocation or doubt on his part about this course of action. Robert was a devotee of the contemporary Victorian-era social mores: for him, Honor, Respect, and, most important, Duty—capitalized and moralized—were the guiding principles of a gentleman's life.[64] One of the most famous, and pejorative, stories about young Robert's developing social character was the White House visit of the well-known dwarf Charles S. Stratton, known as General Tom Thumb, in February 1863. Mary Lincoln not only delighted in the prospect of hosting the diminutive circus entertainer and his dwarf bride but, according to her seamstress, also believed it her duty as first lady. "Tom Thumb had been caressed by royalty in the Old World, and why should not the wife of the President of his native country smile upon him also?" Mary supposedly asked. To Robert, however, the entertainment was undignified, even ridiculous, and he refused to attend. "My notions of duty, perhaps, are somewhat different from yours," he told his mother. Seamstress Elizabeth Keckly declared, "Robert had a lofty soul, and he could not stoop to all the follies and absurdities of the ephemeral current of fashionable life."[65] Robert's predilection for social propriety, gentlemanly duty, and self-respect led some people to see him as a snob in his later life.

As one social historian has written, however, it was not fashion but contribution to society and fulfillment of duty on which men were judged during this era. The ideal man "performed his duties faithfully, governed his passions rationally, submitted to his fate and to his place in society, and treated his dependents with firm but affectionate wisdom."[66] But duty does not always come without self-interest, regret, or even resentment. It is clear that Robert was unhappy as the family began their new life in Chicago. They stayed first at the fashionable Tremont House in the city, but after only one week, Mary decided to move to the less-expensive Hyde Park, a summer resort seven miles south of Chicago.[67] Robert spent the first day there arranging his room, unpacking his books, and conversing with Keckly, who accompanied the family to Chicago. Upon her remark that the new accommodations were "delightful," Robert retorted, "Since you do not have to stay here, you can safely say as much about the charming situation as you please. I presume that I must put up with it, as mother's pleasure must be consulted before my own. But candidly, I would almost as soon be dead as be compelled to remain three months in this dreary house."[68]

It was a difficult time for the Lincoln family. Mary Lincoln's letters are filled with statements about the desolation and bereavement all three suffered. But there was more to their suffering than just the death of their patriarch. Very real emotional issues centered around money, living conditions, publicity, and respect. The money problems—both real and perceived—may have been the most onerous. Mary Lincoln always had been a contradictory woman in regard to financial affairs, both in Springfield and in Washington. She had the reputation of stinginess in domestic affairs but extravagance when it came to her own wardrobe. She was accused of accepting bribes and padding expense accounts as first lady (accusations that history has proven correct). Davis called her an outright kleptomaniac.[69] Her reputation was so bad that when she left the White House with fifty-five trunks of personal possessions, she was accused of looting the place.[70] This weakness—the compulsion to spend money and acquire possessions—had a great impact on Mary in the months after her husband's death; it also severely impacted oldest son, Robert, who was often embarrassed by and angry at his mother's continued and negative publicity.

Mary constantly complained of her destitution and moved her residence three times in three months believing it financially necessary (moving from the Hyde Park Hotel to the residential hotel Clifton House in August). Her financial situation made her simultaneously panicked and angry. She was panicked because of the huge debts she had accumulated as first lady that were coming due—debts that she had kept secret from her husband and then from her son Robert and estate administrator Davis—and she was angry because of the American people's seeming indifference to her financial plight. She felt entitled to a public endowment for her future living, which never came to fruition. This failure was exacerbated by the fact that General Ulysses S. Grant was being lavished with gifts, especially of houses, all over the country. "Roving Generals have elegant mansions, showered upon them, and the American people—leave the family of the Martyred President, to struggle as best they can!" Mary complained after her third move.[71]

Abraham Lincoln's estate had amounted to a little more than $83,000, but it was mostly in real estate and bonds, and so the family had only the yearly interest off which to live.[72] That interest amounted to only about $1,500 yearly each for Mary and Robert, which was enough to live modestly but nothing more. Tad, as a minor, received only enough to pay for his own expenses. The postwar period was one of high prices and high inflation, and Robert (after consulting with his mother) told Davis in late June that it was not possible for the family to either purchase or rent and furnish "a suitable home" in Chicago or any other city. Robert also marveled at the rumors he had been hearing that he and Tad each had private fortunes, Robert's coming from military contracts during the war. "I should be glad to know where drafts on those funds would be housed," he sarcastically wrote.[73] The issue of personal finances eventually would lead to trying times for Robert, full of consternation and worry, as his mother's personal debts and later public antics would humiliate him, invigorate the press, and embarrass the American public. The press, in fact, was unrelenting in its curiosity of the Lincolns. "Anything, *we do* is seized on—an especial way, of 'being cared for, by the American people,'" Mary wrote that summer.[74]

Robert's main goal as soon as the family settled in Chicago was to prepare for his career. This was, of course, something he had to do anyway, but his role as male head of the family, along with the family's meager finances, gave the endeavor added urgency. Robert long had known he wanted to be a lawyer, and his father had encouraged him. As Robert once told a visiting Englishman, "[h]e had been from the first brought up for the law, and he had not allowed his studies to be interrupted a single day by his father being president. The only pause had been when, like other young men, he had served in the army."[75] Perhaps his father gave him the same advice he gave another aspiring lawyer in 1860. The way to obtain a thorough knowledge of the law, Abraham Lincoln had advised, is "very simple, though laborious, and tedious. It is only to get the books, and read, and study them carefully. . . . Work, work, work, is the main thing."[76] And this Robert conscientiously did.

On the advice of Davis, Robert resumed his legal studies in June through reading law in the offices of Scammon, McCagg, & Fuller in downtown

Chicago and also in taking law courses at the University of Chicago.[77] Robert could have done little better for his apprenticeship than the firm he chose. Scammon, McCagg, & Fuller was one of the most respected firms in Chicago. All three partners had known and worked with Abraham Lincoln and Davis, and the connection gained Robert's entry into the firm. As mentors, the three partners had much to teach young Lincoln. All were able, devoted, and conscientious lawyers, successful businessmen, and accomplished cultural men with interests in literature, music, and science.

Jonathan Young Scammon, the firm's senior member, was one of the premier citizens of Chicago, highly respected as a lawyer, journalist, financier, philanthropist, and intellectual. He began practicing law in Chicago in 1835 and there remained until his death in 1890. While he was not directly engaged in the day-to-day affairs of the office while Robert clerked there from 1865 to 1866, he was involved, and his influence on the young man may have been profound. As one associate and historian later wrote of him, "Mr. Scammon's friendship to young men just starting in life was exceedingly valuable. For all such he had a kindly word of advice under any circumstances and he was generous with substantial encouragement when the occasion seemed to demand such aid."[78] Scammon may have paid Robert Lincoln more attention than other clerks, however, given his parentage. Scammon was an ardent Republican in 1860 and one of the most enthusiastic supporters of Abraham Lincoln's presidential campaign. He published and distributed much of the literature of that campaign at his own expense. Looking at Scammon's life and interests at this time, one can see a great similarity to Robert Lincoln's own endeavors in his later life, such as his interests in business, especially real estate, which would become Robert's legal specialty, railroads, philanthropy, and even Robert's later passion of astronomy.[79] Robert's first law partner, in fact, was Charles T. Scammon, his mentor's only son.

Ezra B. McCagg joined Scammon in partnership in 1849. McCagg's reputation was that of a sound and careful lawyer, a smart businessman, a great reader, and a world traveler. McCagg also was an extremely wealthy man who lived in great luxury—one historian claimed his style of living had "few or no equals in Chicago"—yet also had a great public spirit that earned him a general social respect. "No one at the bar had a more varied experience than Mr. McCagg. No lawyer at the Chicago bar traveled so much as he, and none had such opportunities to make himself well informed and well read as he," wrote one historian.[80] Upon McCagg's leaving for Europe in 1856, Samuel W. Fuller took charge of the office. Fuller was a lawyer with a thorough comprehension of the law. "He has a very excellent knowledge of law, but not sufficient to make him devoted to its letter in contradistinction to its spirit," according to one history. "He has a very thorough comprehension of legal principles, and the knowledge of books requisite to give those principles authoritative force." Fuller also was a great reader and thinker in subjects other than the law.[81] On McCagg's return to Chicago in 1857, the firm became Scammon, McCagg, & Fuller, with the latter two partners running the office.

Robert took the train into the city every morning to go to work at the law office on Lake Street (about a thirty-minute ride).[82] The editors of the *Chicago Legal News* watched Robert during this time, noticing how he "took his place with the other young men in the office, and studied as faithfully, diligently, and profitably for nearly two years, as any young man that ever came under our notice. He was always at his place, kind in manner, and energetic in business, never afraid to perform any duty that devolved upon him as a student. The writer of this has seen him as a law student going to and returning from our courts laden with law books for the firm with whom he was studying, with the same willingness that the son of one of our humblest citizens would have done."[83] Two historians later aptly characterized Robert's days at this time, vigorously studying law, eschewing personal pleasures, and simultaneously being the "beloved brother and devoted son" his mother admired:

> The company of young people such as [Robert] had known in Cambridge and Washington (among them, Mary Harlan, the girl he loved) was lost to him for the duration. There was no more gay little excursions, no more parties, dances, and talk sessions, none of that exhilarating sense of participation he had known during his brief war service. Each evening he would return wearily to the Hyde Park apartment, where two people depended on him for strength he could not always summon.[84]

Just as the Lincolns were getting settled into their new life, trying to heal their emotional wounds, the controversy over Abraham Lincoln's tomb resurfaced in early June. While Robert and his mother thought the plans had all been settled in May—that is, that President Lincoln's burial place and tomb, as well as any subsequent monument to his memory, would all be placed in Oak Ridge Cemetery—the members of the Lincoln National Monument Association had different plans. In fact, the association seems to have had different plans from the beginning, but it was in June that Mary and Robert learned the association was going to erect the monument to President Lincoln not over his burial site but on the old Mather block, the original site decided by the citizens of Springfield for the tomb. The association had in fact already begun construction and was actively soliciting donations to help defray costs.[85] Once again, both Mary and Robert were outraged at the indifference with which the monument committee treated their understood wishes.

Mary Lincoln immediately wrote to Governor Oglesby, stating that if the monument to her husband was not placed over his tomb in Oak Ridge, she would remove his body out of the state entirely and back to Washington.[86] Members of the association traveled to Chicago to speak with the former first lady personally about her wounded and threatening letter. Robert, who, as he had written in his previous letter to Oglesby, supported his mother's position about the tomb, met the men upon their arrival. He bore another letter from his mother in which she declared her determination to be "unalterable" and added the condition that no one except the Lincoln family and its descendants ever be buried in the Lincoln tomb.[87] The commissioners spoke with Robert, after which he took them to the Hyde Park Hotel, but Mary, after consulting with Robert for some minutes, refused to see them. After meeting such an impenetrable wall as erected by Mary and Robert, the association finally relented and agreed to Mary's terms.[88]

One little known fact about this incident—an incident that two historians dubbed the "battle of the gravesite"—is that the National Lincoln Monument Association nearly ignored the Lincoln family's wishes altogether and only acquiesced to Mary's demands by a majority of one during the vote of the full board of directors.[89] What Mary would have done had that one vote gone the other way is, of course, unknown. Given her vehemence about the monument plans being in Oak Ridge, however, her clear exasperation at the association for continually ignoring her wishes, and her general vindictiveness at those she deemed her enemies, it is not unlikely she indeed would have had her husband's remains sent back to Washington, as she threatened. Robert's specific opinions are unknown, although he likely would have assisted and defended his mother in her decision, as he had during the entire imbroglio, but the avalanche of publicity would have been embarrassing and distasteful to his Victorian character, especially at a time when he was endeavoring to start a legal career.

Indeed, Robert felt it his duty to be diligent in learning the law and therefore quickly being able to begin generating an income. A good example of his acquiescence to duty is his refusal in October 1865 to accompany his good friend Edgar T. Welles (son of Gideon Welles, Abraham Lincoln's secretary of the navy) on a trip to Havana, Cuba. The vacation would have been a great relief from Robert's previous six months of emotional hardships, but after consulting both Davis and McCagg, Robert declined, believing his first responsibility to be to his studies. "I regret very much the opportunity of seeing Cuba and of laying in cigars for the next year or so, but biz is biz and must be attended to," he jocularly wrote.[90] A letter by Mary Lincoln, however, shows a more serious side of Robert's decision. She told Edgar's mother that she "almost marveled" that Robert refused such an offer. "In consideration, of our recent afflictions, pressing so heavily upon us, Robert, thinks it best, for the present, to be quiet, and attend to his studies."[91] Upon Edgar's return, Mary reiterated, "[I]t is quite a trial to me, when I reflect, on the pleasure, *such a trip*, would have afforded my poor sad boy, Robert. He was conscientious, in what he considered his duty, to remain at home, for the present."[92]

As 1865 wound on, Robert and his family adjusted to their new lives while trying to move past their family tragedy. It was not easy; the aftermath of the war was ubiquitous. Before they had even left Washington, the trial of the assassination conspirators began in the Old Arsenal Building in downtown Washington, the proceedings of which were constantly in the news and on the public tongues. On May 23, the day after Robert and his family left Washington, as the Lincolns were in the midst of their fifty-four-hour train ride to Chicago, the great review of the victorious Army of the Potomac marched in awesome procession of eighty thousand men through the streets of Washington, D.C.—streets that only a few weeks before had been the scene of Abraham Lincoln's funeral. The next day, the armies of the Tennessee and of Georgia, totaling sixty-five thousand men, had their own march down Pennsylvania Avenue.

A few weeks later, on June 29, the nearly two-month-long trial of the conspirators concluded, with the verdicts and sentences announced the following day. On July 6, Secretary of War Stanton telegraphed the news to Robert Lincoln that four of the conspirators were to be executed, three had received life in prison, and one got six years' hard labor.[93] Articles, pamphlets, and books about the life and death of America's first martyred president began to be published immediately after the assassination, and the Lincolns watched as their patriarch's memory took hold in a great national apotheosis.[94] Would-be historians continued to ask Robert for access to his father's papers, but Robert still was collecting them. In August, he traveled to Springfield for the unhappy task of sorting through his father's papers at the Lincoln & Herndon law office and possibly at the house on Eighth and Jackson.[95]

The year 1865 ended with the removal of Abraham Lincoln's body from the receiving vault at Oak Ridge Cemetery to the temporary vault a few hundred feet up the hill. Both Robert and his mother went to Springfield to approve the site of the vault, but Mary was unable to endure the moving ceremony, which Robert attended alone.[96] Mary's egregious emotionalism and overwrought show of Victorian mourning caused her to take to her bed for multiple days thereafter. And although Mary complained of being homeless and near penniless, and Robert, distressed and frustrated at his mother's emotional state, urged her to live rent free at the old home at Eighth and Jackson Streets in Springfield, Mary declared that the visit to the state capital that December convinced her more than ever that the only way to maintain her sanity was to live far away from that place of painful memories.[97] Robert himself feared for his mother's sanity whatever her distance from her old hometown and worried what might happen in the future.

But as the pain of 1865 turned to the hope of a new year, Robert may have imagined that better times must lie ahead. On January 1, 1866, he moved out of the apartment he had been sharing with his mother and brother and rented his own rooms in downtown Chicago to "begin to live with some degree of comfort—a thing not known in my present quarters."[98] But sadly—and one could even say inevitably, looking back at the ongoing tragedies of the Lincoln family—the hope of peace was not to be. In addition to the daily toils of his own life, his legal training, and career and financial worries, Robert found himself increasingly concerned about his mother's erratic behavior and mental state. The largest issue concerned money and how much of it his mother not only spent but demanded she needed. Robert also began to get more involved in his father's legacy and, specifically, having to endure the stories being told by his father's old law partner, William Herndon—stories that were to Robert not only socially improper but at times libelous. In fact, while one might think the traumatic events of 1860–65, with the trials of the civil war, the murder of his father, and the death of his brother, would be the low point in young Robert's life, the next ten years could be argued to be the most difficult he would ever have to endure.

8

"One of the Most Promising Young Men of the West"

An old adage says that men are attracted to women who remind them of their mothers. The possibility of such attraction in regards to Robert Lincoln is an interesting one. Robert and his mother had a very close relationship, and, as such, he acquired many of her likes, dislikes, and traits. Like Mary, Robert was well and professionally educated, and he had a passion for literature and music, was fluent in French, and loved to travel. Mary Lincoln was, it is well known, highly intelligent, cultured, witty, attractive, and engaging, having numerous beaus as a young woman in Springfield. Such a description applies equally well to the girl Robert was courting, Mary Eunice Harlan. Mary, three years younger than Robert, was a highly regarded belle of Washington during the Civil War, when her father served as a U.S. Senator from Iowa. She had ten years of sporadic schooling, beginning in Iowa in 1854 at age eight and continuing through the Civil War years in Washington.[1] She was bright and charming, intelligent and cultured, and very musical. She and Robert both played the piano, and it was said by one of her schoolmates that Mary Harlan played the harp "divinely."[2]

Despite their years of acquaintance and courting, what happened to their relationship during the first years after Robert moved with his family to Chicago in May 1865 is unknown. None of Robert's correspondence from Chicago mentions anything about Mary Harlan—in fact, about any woman. Robert's clear intentions and actions to study law, begin a solid legal practice, care for his mother and brother, and manage his father's estate suggest that he simply had no time for such extracurricular activities as courting. In his grief over his father's death and his duty to accompany his family halfway across the country, perhaps he decided, or he and Mary agreed, that whatever relationship they had created should be put on hold. Unfortunately, this is mere speculation.

At the time, of course, there was also gossip. In April 1866, the Washington correspondent of the *Nashville (TX) Republican Banner* wrote that it was universally known in the capital that Robert and Mary had been engaged in 1865 but that Mary had jilted him after the assassination—the reason being that with the president dead and her father safely appointed to the cabinet as secretary of interior, she, like a female mercenary, had no more use for young Bob. "The lady wavered, the nuptials were postponed; and finally, as visions of a gay career and better match began to flit across her beautiful blue eyes, she resolved that she was not so much in love as she had been."[3] The story was run in newspapers across the country, with some declaring that while the reasoning may be false, there was at least the "foundation in fact" that Robert and Mary had been engaged.[4]

Whether Robert and Mary suffered a broken engagement only to reconnect later—just like Robert's parents—is uncertain. Correspondence between Mary Harlan and her friend Minnie Chandler in 1866 and 1867, however, does offer some clues to the relationship, as well as to Mary Harlan's coquettishness in general. It seems Minnie thought Mary to be "a great flirt" with "quantities of beaux" and in one letter even listed five young men and wondered to which Mary was referring.[5] The attentions of Robert Lincoln to Mary Harlan in 1865, although unknown, seem to have been minimal and therefore upsetting to Mary. When she told Minnie that Robert finally wrote to her in early 1866, her friend replied, "Now that you have received a letter from B. L. you like him as well as ever."[6] Perhaps there was a lull in their correspondence that made Mary wonder about Robert's true feelings. If so, it seems the January letter was the beginning of a rapprochement, for by early March, Mary was "so truly happy" that it makes one wonder if perhaps an admission of love or even an understanding of marriage had taken place.[7] When writing to Mary later about the broken engagement gossip, Minnie said she told questioners that Mary had in fact been engaged during "the first part of the winter, but whether to the man in the moon or not they don't know." She told people she "didn't believe a word of it, if you had ever been engaged to [Robert Lincoln] you were now." But while Minnie knew Mary's secret, she seems not to have known to whom Mary was engaged and even asked if it was "Major Herbert."[8]

By the end of 1866, Minnie wrote that she had been asked "several times this year" if Mary and Robert were engaged but always replied that she did not know.[9] A closeness between the two certainly was progressing, and Mary's letters show that she visited Robert in Chicago and saw him whenever he visited Washington.[10] In January 1867, one of the senior partners of Scammon, McCagg, & Fuller was going to Washington, and Robert had "some little inclination to accompany him" but decided against the idea.[11] Whether Robert's inclination was a girl named Mary Harlan is possible but uncertain.

By this time, Robert was nearing the end of his apprenticeship, preparing to take the bar exams, and speculating about his future. He considered a trip to Europe "for a couple of months before settling down to practice [law] as I expect to do next fall" but did not go.[12] Shortly thereafter, he passed the bar. He was licensed as an attorney in Chicago on February 22, 1867, and certified to practice law four days later.[13] As was common, the newspapers were full of gossip about this milestone in Robert's life, with the *Chicago Tribune* reprinting an article stating Robert intended to move to Cincinnati to practice law there.[14] This was incorrect, and just weeks earlier, he had told John Hay he intended to stay in Chicago and open a practice there, "for I like it very much"—a sentiment he also told his mother the previous October.[15]

Robert launched his legal career by becoming the junior partner of Charles T. Scammon, son of Robert's mentor Jonathan Young Scammon. How this partnership came about is unknown, whether Scammon the elder arranged it or Robert and Charles created it. It certainly had a promising future being composed of the son of the martyr president and the son of one of Chicago's leading citizens, both fathers being highly successful attorneys. The firm of Scammon & Lincoln, located in room 1 in the Marine Bank Building at 154 Lake Street in downtown Chicago, specialized in insurance and real-estate law.[16] Robert apparently found this focus through exposure at Scammon, McCagg, & Fuller, especially since two of the three partners preferred the same specialty.

Scammon and Lincoln hung out their shingle in March 1867, almost immediately after Lincoln achieved his law license. According to one newspaper article, Robert, always a good raconteur like his father, liked to tell the story of his first legal fee.

> Old Judge Logan, under whom he read law, had always told him not to be afraid to charge big fees for his services. "People don't respect a cheap lawyer," said the Judge.[17]
>
> One day, soon after Mr. Lincoln had been admitted to practice, he sat alone in his office, when a messenger brought a note from the Chicago agent of one of the wealthiest insurance companies in America, asking to have the title to a certain piece of property looked up. The young lawyer spent about half an hour looking into the title, and then sent his report to the insurance office. Pretty soon the messenger came with another note. This one requested Mr. Lincoln to send his bill by the bearer. The young lawyer had no idea

what to charge. At first he thought it would be good policy not to charge anything, "for," said he to himself, "I should like to get that company's work regularly." But he knew Judge Logan would not approve that sort of thing, and he did not want the judge to think that he was heedless of his advice. So he figured it that, since he had worked only half an hour, $10 would be a good stiff price, for it would be at the rate of $200 a day of ten hours. The words of Judge Logan, however, rang in his ears, and, with a stroke of audacity that almost frightened him, Mr. Lincoln finally made the bill for $25. He felt that this was an outrageously high fee, and was hesitating as to whether he would give it to the boy or make out another for $10, when Judge Logan chanced to come in.

"You are just the man I want to see," said Mr. Lincoln, and he told him of his dilemma.

Judge Logan took the bill and tore it up.

"I knew it was outrageously high," said Mr. Lincoln, "but, Judge, you always told me to make high bills, and I did this more to please you than myself."

"Nonsense," said the Judge, "give me a pen." He sat down, wrote another bill, and gave it to the boy.

In a few minutes the boy returned with the insurance agent's check for $250, and a little note to Mr. Lincoln thanking him for his promptness, and saying the company's other work of this character would be sent to him.

"Great scott!" said the young lawyer to the old one, "did you make out a bill for $250?"

"Of course I did," answered the old Judge; "you don't want to be a d____d eleemosynary institution for insurance companies, do you?"[18]

Robert thereafter charged fees comparable to other attorneys in Chicago. Of course, this differs quite widely from what is known about Abraham Lincoln's professional fees, and it is a comparison often made. Yet, father and son lived in different times, under different circumstances, in different cities and had different specialties. Abraham Lincoln was a general practitioner in a small Midwest town who rode the Eighth Judicial Circuit and took whatever cases came before him. This was not uncommon and was a lifestyle that Abraham thoroughly enjoyed. He grew up poor, and although he sought to better himself, which he did, he was never terribly concerned about money. "I don't know anything about money; I never had enough of my own to fret me," Lincoln said.[19] David Davis, Lincoln's friend and presiding judge on the circuit, said he had never known a lawyer with so much experience and ability to have so little money.[20]

But as Harry Pratt, the premier historian of Lincoln's finances, writes, wealth was not the goal of Lincoln's ambition.[21] Lincoln even explained his theory of legal fees while preparing notes for a law lecture: "The matter of fees is important, far beyond the mere question of bread and butter involved. Properly attended to, fuller justice is done to both lawyer and client. An exorbitant fee should never be claimed. As a general rule never take your whole fee in advance, nor any more than a small retainer. When fully paid beforehand, you are more than a common mortal if you can feel the same interest in the case, as if something was still in prospect for you, as well as for your client. And when you lack interest in the case the job will very likely lack skill and diligence in the performance."[22]

Lincoln also advised young attorneys to above all be honest; "and if in your own judgment you cannot be an honest lawyer, resolve to be honest without being a lawyer."[23] As an attorney, Robert emulated his father in this and other of Abraham's noblest traits. He was honest, intelligent, diligent, savvy, and, also like his father, unpretentious. The prestigious *Chicago Legal News* lauded these traits in Robert in an 1868 feature article: "We have always thought, considering that he was the son of an honored President of the United States, and had been subjected to many temptations and trials in early manhood, growing out of his relation to many distinguished men in all departments of public life, that his modesty of manner, and sobriety, and industry of habit, were very remarkable, and worthy of the highest praise."[24] Robert's humility is evidenced in the fact that he was the junior partner in his law firm. It may seem logical considering he was newly licensed, but certainly the magical name of "Lincoln" heading a firm's sign, with people knowing it was the Great Emancipator's son, would have drawn more attention, and a more conceited or supercilious man might have insisted on headlining the partnership. But Robert was not that way, as an interesting observation from a visiting Englishman in September 1867 shows.

> There is nothing in [Robert Lincoln's] manner to indicate that his father had occupied a higher position than any other citizen. He cheerfully accepted our invitation to breakfast with us at our hotel next morning. He was with us at an early hour on Tuesday; for his business had to be attended to. He is about five-and-twenty; modest, quiet, and utterly unassuming. No one seemed to regard him as possessing any rank, by reason of his father having been president, nor did he so regard himself. He laughed heartily at a joke of ours about his being called "His Royal Highness the Prince Robert."[25]

Robert Lincoln appears to have been a truly humble, although confident, man in these opening years of his professional life; but that does not mean he never made mistakes or learned valuable lessons. One story of Robert's earliest days as a lawyer offers an example of how he and others handled his famous parentage and how he learned a lifelong lesson.

> A man named Hume wanted to lease a house. Lincoln, with his usual caution, determined to learn something of the applicant's character, and so sent for Fernando Jones, an old friend of his father's, who had been Hume's landlord. Jones obeyed the summons, and walked up two flights of stairs to the young lawyer's office. "You have sent for me and here I am. What can I do for you?" said the caller, who was a prominent and wealthy citizen. Lincoln had only begun his inquiry concerning Hume, when Jones interrupted him:
>
> "I like your zeal Mr. Lincoln," he said, "and I think you are starting out well in thus making inquiries concerning the character of your proposed tenants. But even if you are the son of a martyred president, don't you think that when you want to see a gentleman, particularly an elderly man, on business, in which you are interested and he is not, it would be better for you to make the call, instead of summoning the other to your office? I bid you good day, Mr. Lincoln."
>
> Fifteen minutes later Robert Lincoln was at the office of Fernando Jones.
>
> "I have come, Mr. Jones," he began, "to apol"—
>
> "Not another word, Robert. As for this man Hume, he is a safe tenant. He pays promptly. By the way, how about that railroad case of yours!"
>
> And the old gentleman led the conversation as far as possible from the object of the young lawyer's visit. But this visit was one which Robert Lincoln never forgot.[26]

In October 1867, after eight months of practicing law before state and local courts, Robert was admitted to practice law before the federal courts in Chicago. The Chicago *Evening Journal* commented on the news by calling Robert "one of the most promising young men of the West" and who resembled his father in all his best attributes. Robert "devotes nearly all of his time to the business of his profession and to literary studies—is a quiet, unassuming and courteous gentleman, and enjoys the personal esteem of his fellow citizens."[27] In 1868, the *Chicago Legal News* applauded "his virtue, his honesty, his modesty, his industry, and his close application to business, as an example to be followed by all young men who seek to make themselves distinguished at the bar, and honored by the community in which they live."[28] In 1871, a collection of portraits of Chicago lawyers included a mention of Robert T. Lincoln, calling him a "very worthy, estimable member of the Chicago bar." It said he was known to be "an excellent manager, possessed of good ability, quiet, shrewd, unostentatious, and with a thorough devotion to the profession of law."[29] In short, Robert was becoming exactly the professional man his father wanted him to be. Abraham wanted his son to have the schooling and opportunities he never had as a young man, which is why Robert went to Harvard and, for one term, Harvard Law School. It also has been speculated that Abraham intended, or at least hoped, that his son would become his law partner once he retired from the presidency, and the two perhaps would practice in Chicago.[30]

During these first two years after his father's death, Robert worked diligently and modestly to fulfill his familial duties. Of course, he also had personal desires and ambitions. One of his prerogatives was, like his mother, an inclination for travel. In August 1866, he went to the lakeshore in Mackinaw City, Michigan, for a short vacation, and in October, he joined in "the Grand Excursion" to the farthest reaches of the Union Pacific Railroad, 275 miles west of Omaha, Nebraska, into what was still the wild and untamed West.[31] The purpose of the excursion was to advertise and promote the advancement of the transcontinental rail line to the public and also to show the financiers and members of Congress that the construction was progressing satisfactorily. About one hundred people participated in the excursion, which left New York City on October 15, went through Chicago and Council Bluffs, Iowa, and then arrived at Omaha on October 22. Robert and a party of about twenty people left separately from Chicago and joined the full excursion at Omaha.

The weeklong round trip from Omaha to the end of the rail line in the Great Platte Valley on the one hundredth meridian resembled "an old-fashioned traveling show" with its bands, caterers, six cooks, three barbers, photographers, artists, sleight-of-hand performers, and even a printing press. There were feasts, dances, concerts, lectures, displays of fireworks, buffalo and antelope hunts, and even a mock Indian raid that was so realistic some ladies fainted in fear. The point of the excursion, of course, was for the visitors to see the efficient manner in which the track was laid and the railroad operated, and in this it was considered a universal success.[32] Robert had a grand time "bumming on the vast plains" as he told Hay; his jocular letter suggests that Robert finally was beginning to recover his vivacity and sense of humor with his friends, which his father's assassination had so sobered eighteen months before. He wrote to Hay, "We had on our trip a Frenchman Marquis de Chambrun who had an idea that he could talk English. One evening on the Plains we elected him into a burlesque club and the fellow thought he was a member of Congress or something and gave us a long speech in which everything from Adam to A. J. was brought in. Don't send any more of them out here. Large amounts of valuable time are thus taken from drinks."[33]

The trip for Robert was not only fun and personal but perhaps also professional as well—at least in the form of networking. The excursion was peopled with businessmen, financiers, socialites, journalists, and politicians. Celebrities such as Senator Benjamin Wade, railroad pioneer and General Grenville M. Dodge, *Chicago Tribune* editor Joseph Medill, and industrialist George M. Pullman were there, no doubt eager to meet, if not to befriend, the son of Abraham Lincoln. This trip may have in fact introduced Robert to George Pullman, a relationship that would ultimately help direct the course of Robert's life, for by 1879 (if not sooner) young Lincoln was acting professionally on behalf of the Pullman Palace Car Company—the company for which he would eventually become special counsel, president, and chairman of the board.[34]

In May 1867, Robert took another trip, this time to Washington. He stayed at the home of his close friend Edgar, son of Gideon Welles, and most likely visited with Mary Harlan as well. On his return to Chicago, Robert wished he was back in Washington.[35] Not long afterward, he traveled to St. Louis to attend the wedding of his college roommate Fred Anderson. After hearing that Robert was at the wedding, Hay teased him, "How long are you going to hang around like a dead leaf, the last of its clan? Marry, Bob, . . . You will be my age some of these days and will have given up the pursuit. Be warned in time."[36] After recent time spent with Mary Harlan and then being caught up in the midst of a happy wedding, who knows what thoughts were circumnavigating young Lincoln's mind?

Hay's advice was either prescient or coincidental. Robert returned to Washington in June 1867 and stayed until early July as he and Tad had been summoned to be present at the trial of John Surratt, one of the Lincoln assassination conspirators.[37] The Lincolns stayed at the Welles home. Robert and Edgar traveled to New York City on July 17, and the Lincoln boys returned to Chicago on July 27.[38] This was no ordinary trip for Robert, however. After years of acquaintance and courtship with Mary Harlan, closeness and separation, silence and communications, he had something on his mind. While in New York, Robert had gone to Tiffany's and purchased a 3.5-carat, rose-cut, solitaire-diamond engagement ring, and on his return to Washington, he asked Mary to be his wife, and she accepted.[39]

Whether Robert and Mary had a previous promise or agreement of marriage, although not an official proposal, as Minnie Chandler's letters seem to suggest, is uncertain. But this time it was official, and on his return to Chicago, Robert immediately wrote to Mary's father, Senator James Harlan, to ask his consent to the engagement. "My attachment for [Mary] began with an acquaintance and I have now no dearer wish than that she should become my wife," Robert wrote. "If you can trust me it will be the object of my life to ensure her happiness and I hope and feel that you will never have cause to regret a favorable answer."[40] Six days later, what must have been an anxious Robert received Senator Harlan's response and consent. "I shall take care that you never regret having given it," Robert wrote back, also promising soon to visit his future father-in-law in person to explain his present circumstances and future prospects. This he did with a trip to Mount Pleasant, Iowa, in September.[41] "I will only say now," Robert wrote to Harlan, "that I have every encouragement to go on in the profession I have chosen—and with this additional incentive I now have to labor I must succeed."[42]

Robert's personal potential to succeed in the law may have been bright, but his partnership with young Scammon was off to an inauspicious beginning. Robert soon learned that his partner was an alcoholic. He reported in July 1867 that Scammon had been "on a succession of sprees" since early May, and, by August 1, the senior partner in the firm of Scammon & Lincoln was under detoxification treatment in the east for an indefinite period of time. This left the newly licensed junior partner doing twice the work while also worrying that his partner's behavior was injuring the firm's—and his own—reputation. Robert's former employer Samuel W. Fuller suggested Robert dissolve the partnership, and Davis seems to have been of the same opinion. Robert was clearly leaning that way, when he wrote to Davis that Scammon was "utterly worthless and I cannot tell to what extent his debaucheries damage me personally." Two years after his father's murder, Robert was still a bit cynical about the vagaries of life, adding to Davis, "I suppose my experience is that of most men, sometimes smooth and sometimes rough sailing—though I think I have too much of the rough."[43]

Young Lincoln decided not to make a decision until speaking to J. Y. Scammon, his former mentor and his partner's father, who convinced Robert to give his partner another chance. Whether the elder Scammon offered to assist Robert in his law work while his son was in treatment is unclear, but Robert worked alone under the sign of Scammon & Lincoln for the next five months. Scammon returned to the firm in January 1868 apparently sober, and Robert decided to stick with him unless and until he fell back to his alcoholic ways.[44]

In addition to the law and his personal life, Robert had his hands full in the late 1860s with family business. In the two years following his father's death, Robert wrote twenty-eight letters and two telegrams to Davis, executor of Abraham Lincoln's estate, seeking advice and guidance on multiple issues. In later years, Robert stated that after his father's death, he went to Davis as a second father, and this Davis was until his death in 1886. Indeed, Robert asked Davis for advice on issues about his legal partnership, his finances, his mother, his father's papers and estate, and his brother's finances and education. Davis certainly was a father figure to Robert, despite his own brood of children, and Robert appreciated this immensely. The most immediate and important role that Davis played after the assassination, however, was as executor of Abraham

Lincoln's estate. This was no small task, as President Lincoln had been distracted by the war and rather disinterested in his own finances and had not even cashed four pay warrants before his death. Davis found Abraham Lincoln's estate to be worth a little more than $83,000 in cash and bonds.[45]

Davis had determined to settle Lincoln's estate by the time two years had passed from the president's death, and in this he was successful.[46] Between 1865 and 1867, Davis paid and collected debts, invested estate assets, and gave the family members their monthly interest allowances and other necessary withdrawals. By the end of Davis's administration, Lincoln's estate had increased by more than $27,000; Davis also saved the family another $6,600 by refusing his lawful 6 percent fee, employing no attorneys for his work, and making no charges for personal expenses. Robert tried to convince the judge to at least accept reimbursement for personal expenses, but Davis refused.[47] While Davis and Mary Lincoln did not always get along, and Mary often fulminated against the judge for not giving her what she thought was a sufficient amount of allowance every month, in the end she praised his work on the estate: "[I]n no hands save your own, could our interests have been so advantageously placed."[48]

Whether Mary realized it or not—and she probably did—Davis did not work on the estate alone. He had much help from Robert Lincoln. Davis biographer Willard King states that Robert kept the accounts, prepared drafts of the reports to the court, and generally did most of the work of the estate administrator—a statement that Robert's letters to Davis prove. "Robert Lincoln could hardly have shown himself to better advantage than in his correspondence regarding his father's estate," King declares. "His letters to Judge Davis are models of precision and propriety."[49] Robert's reasons for this were not simply an effort to relieve Davis of an unexpected burden but, again, were notions of duty. While Robert knew he was not experienced enough to take full control of the estate, he also knew he could help and believed it his duty to do so. Every year that Robert gained knowledge and experience with finances and legal work during his own legal apprenticeship and practice, his participation in administering the estate grew. But Robert also did not want to impinge upon Davis's generosity, and his letters to the judge during this time continually refrain with Robert's desire to "give you as little trouble as possible."[50]

This desire of Robert's not to take advantage of Davis's goodwill also concerned decisions regarding his brother. Young Thomas "Tad" Lincoln seems to be posterity's favorite Lincoln son. Stories of his antics before and during the White House years are legendary in their boisterousness, comicality, and even charm. Mary called Tad her "troublesome little sunshine"; and Robert later recalled his brother as "the mischievous, charmingly affectionate little boy who was such a comfort to my father."[51] Not everyone in the White House enjoyed his outbursts, of course, and the Lincolns' lack of parental discipline was well known. This freedom caused Tad to neglect any sort of formal education, and even though he had a tutor in the White House, he still could not read or write by the time his father died. Tad also had a speech impediment that made his words difficult to understand. The entire family understood Tad's particular situation and shortcomings, but it was the assassination that was the catalyst for change. Even Tad realized it was time to settle down. "Pa is dead. I can hardly believe that I shall never see him again. I must learn to take care of myself now," Tad said to his nurse just days after his father's death.[52]

Tad was correct; and not only did his personal life change but so did the family dynamic. As Tad was his father's solace after Willie's death in 1862, so he became his mother's emotional bulwark after his father's death in 1865. For Abraham Lincoln was more than just a husband to Mary, he was her everything. As she wrote in 1869, "He was . . . from my eighteenth year—Always—lover—husband—father & *all all to me*—Truly my all."[53] Once Abraham was gone, it was Tad who replaced him as Mary Lincoln's bastion of support, and for the next six years, she barely let her youngest son out of her sight. At first, understanding his mother's emotional needs, Robert did not disagree with her clinging to Tad. He deferred to her needs and desires, such as when they moved to the dreary Hyde Park resort in May 1865.

But while Mary clung to Tad, Tad clung to Robert. He wanted to emulate Robert and make his older brother proud; for his part, Robert adored Tad and sought to be not only his older brother but also a mentor and role model. A good example of Robert's tender feelings occurred in November 1865, when a neighbor gave Mary Lincoln a copy of Henry J. Raymond's book *The Life and Public Services of Abraham Lincoln* to borrow and read. When Mary told Robert, in Tad's presence, that it was "*the most* correct history, of his Father, that has been written," Tad immediately said he would save all his money to buy himself a copy. Robert, in what can be seen as a heart-warming (and heart-breaking) moment, told his little brother not to worry about saving the money, as he would buy him a copy.[54]

Interestingly, at this time, eleven-year-old Tad could not read, and so Mary immediately decided to become his tutor and begin his lessons. At first Tad rebelled, but when Robert told him he needed to be prepared for school in the fall, Tad immediately set to work, eager to please "Brother Bob" as he called him.[55] Tad was enrolled in school in Chicago that fall, and although he was eager to learn, in September 1866 Robert wrote that Tad "still has not learned to write."[56] Eventually, Robert took charge of Tad's education and sent him to Northwestern University and was impressed with how "diligently" his brother worked.[57] "I have put Tad into a very good school where he appears to be learning very fast," Robert wrote Davis in January 1868.[58]

Robert also sought to fix Tad's speech impediment, which was caused by a lisp and bad teeth—some have theorized even a cleft palate—rather than any sort of mental retardation as has been sometimes posited.[59] Mary had taken Tad to a dentist in late 1867 who said the boy's malformed teeth should be forced into a proper position by means of a spring frame in his mouth. Robert was away in Washington at the time and upon his return found Tad very unhappy and uncomfortable with the device. "He could hardly speak so as to be understood," Robert wrote to Davis, "and to keep him talking in that way for a year I thought, with his present bad habits of speech, to be risking too much." Robert consulted another dentist who said the spring frame was unnecessary, so Robert stopped Tad's use of it. Instead, Robert hired an elocutionist to help Tad improve his pronunciation, which worked well.[60]

Since Tad was still a minor after the assassination, his mother and brother decided it was necessary to designate someone as Tad's guardian. Only a guardian could receive Tad's share of the Lincoln estate and pay out money for the boy's expenses. Without a guardian, Mary and Robert had been paying these costs themselves for nearly a year and then asking Davis for reimbursement. As both Mary and Robert had minimal income from the estate interest, they—especially Mary—wanted Tad's bills to be paid with Tad's money. Robert's first thought was to assume guardianship himself—if possible, given his age, relationship to Tad, and ability to produce collateral security worth double Tad's estate—only until Davis could take his place. On second thought, however, Robert decided he would prefer someone else, that when Tad "needed advice or restraint, some older person should have authority to give it to him"—someone like Judge Davis.[61] Davis declined the offer, seeing no need for such an appointment but agreed thirteen months later, in July 1867, after a renewed appeal from Robert.[62]

These postwar years were times of excitement, tumult, and frustration in America. With the conflict ended and a new president in the White House, the government was arguing its way toward a reconstruction policy. How to reconstitute destroyed Southern cities and local governments, disband groups of marauding Southern mercenaries, and educate and embolden black people in their new civic rights were the major issues of the day.[63] But President Andrew Johnson and the radical Republicans in the Congress were at loggerheads over reconstruction, with the former seeking the generous policy espoused by Lincoln and the latter seeking one more vengeful. The radicals also sought immediate and sweeping civil rights for freed slaves, while Johnson, a southern former Democrat, had little or no interest in a race of people he clearly saw as inferior. These angry disagreements eventually led to Johnson's impeachment in the House of Representatives—the first ever of an American president—and acquittal in the Senate by only one vote.[64] A postwar boom in the economy saw prices inflating to high levels, land speculation booming, westward expansion increasing, and Northerners traveling south to take advantage of the Southern destitution and need for renewed infrastructure.

It was an exciting time to be a young man in America, especially in a city as thriving as Chicago. The war had made possible all sorts of technological advances in photography, medicine, travel, and communications, to name a few. In Chicago itself, multiple colleges and universities were being founded, and advances in medicine were being discovered. The city was a central hub of railroad transportation. Citizens were agitating for the modernization of the city's superstructure, including deepening of canals, construction of a lake tunnel, new buildings for waterworks, new schools, improvements in the city sewage system, widening of the river, and improvements in city pavements.[65] Republicans dominated Chicago politics in the late 1860s, branding Democrats as Copperheads and disunionists.

Robert was, like his father, a stout Republican always interested in politics and, as a man of business, also interested in current events. Robert also caught the westward land fever so common in postwar America. With the railroads extending west and the Midwest areas growing, land speculation still was a reliable means of accumulating wealth. Abraham Lincoln owned multiple properties in Illinois and Iowa (two from land bounties and two to pay off debts owed to him), and Robert's later mentor Davis made his fortune in land speculation. As a young man in a booming city, Robert was not immune to such enticements. He began looking at investments in February 1866 and asked Davis for $3,000 to buy property outside Chicago, although upon the judge's advice, he dropped the idea. Robert asked a few months later for $2,000 to invest, although it is unknown if he followed through on his intention.[66] He may have decided to await such speculation, being advised to let his understanding as well as his finances mature first. After settling a debt still owed Abraham Lincoln in 1867 worth $5,400, Robert sent the money to Davis to deposit in the Lincoln estate account rather than keep it for himself. When Davis asked him why, Robert replied that he had no need of it. "My business as it is running now does not fall very far short of supporting me and I want my head a little longer before speculating," he wrote.[67]

Robert may have been young, but he was still a grown man; and more than that, he was Abraham Lincoln's son. As such, he could not escape the limelight no matter how much he wanted to. Newspapers continually reported on him and his family, and the American people were eager to read the news. Politicians had their eyes on Robert, and he was a target of both parties because of his surname. Although Robert absolutely refused to trade on his father's name and accomplishments, his parentage certainly opened doors for him as a young attorney—doors his own innate capacity kept open. One immediate opportunity came from Hay, then secretary of legation at the U.S. embassy in Paris. In July 1866, he told Robert he was thinking of resigning and offered to recommend him as replacement to Secretary of State William Seward.[68] While this offer was more an act of friendship than politics as a way to help Robert forget his troubles, there is no doubt it would have been an automatic appointment for Abraham Lincoln's son. Robert refused.

By 1868, newspapers were predicting Robert's entry into politics, with one stating that Robert would be a member of Congress "within five years."[69] On the other side of the political spectrum, the Democrat press sought in August 1868 to embarrass Republican presidential nominee Ulysses S. Grant by stating that Robert Lincoln supported the Democrat candidate, New York Governor Horatio Seymour, for president. Robert was "very much annoyed" by these reports, but said one close friend, "His nature is retiring and he shrinks from appearing in the papers, even to deny these downright lies about him."[70] In an arrangement typical of Victorian propriety, Robert wrote a private rebuttal letter to a correspondent, and his friends arranged to have the letter published. In it, Robert declared the story false and that "no one more earnestly desires the success of Gen. Grant and the Republican Party than myself."[71]

Despite other people's hopes and expectations about Abraham Lincoln's oldest son following in his father's political footsteps, Robert was not interested in elective office. He was focused on his career and his family, trying to gain a solid reputation in the city he had chosen for his home—a reputation separate from that of his illustrious father. Robert, as such, disliked publicity and determined to stay out of the public eye as much as possible. As he wrote in September 1867, after declining an invitation to deliver one or more lectures to the Soldiers Lecture Society in Monmouth, Illinois, "Besides doubting my ability to interest your society, I have no taste for any greater publicity than is necessary incident to my professional duties."[72]

Robert's reserve was made difficult, however, by the increasingly bizarre and embarrassing actions of his mother. After her public argument with the Lincoln Monument Commission in 1865 and then her demands and even begging for money from Congress ever since the assassination, Robert found his mother's behaviors embarrassing to her, to himself, and to his father's memory.

And as often as she obtruded herself upon the American public in those years, her actions were generally benign until she decided to sell a collection of her old White House clothing and jewelry in New York in the fall of 1867. The ensuing scandal was not just mortifying to Robert, a young lawyer trying to gain respect in a large city, but it also was the beginning of a period of intense anxiety about his mother's health, both mental and physical, that would lead him in less than a decade to have her declared insane.

Robert Lincoln's 1864 Harvard class photo.
Courtesy of Hildene, The Lincoln Family Home, Manchester, Vermont.

Robert Lincoln (*top row, fourth from left*) with other members of the Hasty Pudding Club, a Harvard society for juniors and seniors dedicated to the production of dramatic skits and farces. Robert was remembered as a good actor and "one of the choicest spirits" of the club. Courtesy of Hildene, The Lincoln Family Home, Manchester, Vermont.

"The Lincoln Family in 1861," one of many depictions of the Lincolns while residents of the White House. The family never actually posed together, and such representations are composites of multiple separate images. Also misleading in the print is that Robert did not grow his mustache until the late 1860s. Courtesy of Library of Congress, Prints and Photographs Division.

Mary Harlan Lincoln on her wedding day, September 24, 1868. Courtesy of Hildene, The Lincoln Family Home, Manchester, Vermont.

Portrait of Mamie Lincoln, age twenty-one, painted in 1890 in London while Robert Lincoln was serving as U.S. minister to the Court of St. James's. A year later, Mamie married Charles Isham. Courtesy of Hildene, The Lincoln Family Home, Manchester, Vermont.

Portrait of Abraham "Jack" Lincoln II at about age sixteen, painted around 1890. Robert and Mary Lincoln commissioned this painting after their son's death. Courtesy of Hildene, The Lincoln Family Home, Manchester, Vermont.

Portrait of Jessie Lincoln, age fourteen, made in London around 1890. Courtesy of Hildene, The Lincoln Family Home, Manchester, Vermont.

"President Garfield and His Cabinet," originally printed with a feature article of the same title by George Alfred Townsend in *Frank Leslie's Popular Monthly*, May 1881. Secretary of War Robert T. Lincoln sits third from the right, next to Secretary of State James G. Blaine. President Garfield is at the head of the table, far right. Author's collection.

President Arthur and party at Upper Geyser Basin, Yellowstone National Park, 1883. Secretary of War Robert Lincoln is seated second from right; President Arthur, seated middle; General Phil Sheridan, seated second from left. Photographer Frank Jay Haynes accompanied Arthur's party and photographed the trip. His photos, plus army press releases to the Associated Press, were later compiled in a book, *Journey through the Yellowstone National Park and Northwestern Wyoming, 1883*, the creation and publication of which Secretary Lincoln oversaw. Courtesy of Library of Congress, Prints and Photographs Division.

“King Chester Arthur’s Knight(cap)s of the Round Table,” a political cartoon ridiculing the Arthur administration for sleeping on the job. Originally published in *Puck* magazine, February 1882. Secretary of War Lincoln sits second from the right. Courtesy of Library of Congress, Prints and Photographs Division.

Political cartoon lampooning Secretary of War Lincoln and Secretary of the Navy Chandler for their ignorance and apathy concerning the fate of Lieutenant Adolphus W. Greely's doomed arctic expedition. Originally published in *Life* magazine, September 1883. Author's collection.

"Tannhauser at Chicago: The Grand Tournament of Song for the Presidency," depicting candidates for the 1884 Republican presidential nomination in a singing contest to win selection. The cartoon is a parody of Richard Wagner's opera *Tannhäuser and the Singers' Contest at Wartburg*. The favorite candidate, James G. Blaine, is the singer in the middle with the large plume in his hat. The singer second from the right with a sash saying "business endorsement" is President Chester Arthur. Robert Lincoln is fourth from right holding a paper that says, "Le Sabre de Mon Pere" (the sword of my father). Courtesy of Library of Congress, Prints and Photographs Division.

9

"I Am Likely to Have a Good Deal of Trouble"

In October 1867, Robert wrote his fiancée Mary Harlan that he believed his mother was "sane on all subjects but one"—money. Ever since he was a child, he had witnessed his mother's love for shopping—especially during the war years when he shopped with her—but it was not until late 1865 that he began to understand the depths of his mother's mania. It was at this time, as Congress finished its debate on Mary's request to be paid the remainder of her husband's second-term salary, that one House member informed Robert that numerous payment claims against his father's estate had exercised a "deleterious influence" on deliberations. "All this is very mysterious to me," Robert wrote David Davis. "I was not aware there were any claims, and even if there were, in what way they could be deleterious. You of course will exercise your own discretion in telling me, if you know anything of the matter."[1] In fact, Davis did know, as he had received multiple bills regarding Mary's overdue accounts.[2]

Robert soon learned that his mother had acquired huge debts while first lady, which she hid from her husband, assuming she could pay them off quietly during his second term. But with the president's death, creditors immediately came calling for payments that Mary did not have. The exact amount she owed is unknown, but estimates range from $6,000 to $70,000.[3] Mary thought she could keep these bills secret from her son and from estate executor Davis, which she could not. In the end, Mary liquidated the debt herself by returning many of the goods she had purchased on credit and paying off the rest.[4]

These Washington debts were only the beginning of Robert's troubles with his mother during the ensuing ten years. While not all of the issues involved money, most of them did, a circumstance that only strengthened Robert's belief and fear that his mother was growing increasingly irrational. While Robert,

Mary, and Tad were living only off the interest allowances doled out by Davis from Abraham Lincoln's estate, Mary continually demanded more and more money. Robert agreed with his mother that the family was living in limited circumstances, but it was in no way as close to poverty as Mary believed. But no matter how much he remonstrated with her on this topic, she simply would not agree with him.

Despite her fear and angst over shortened finances, Mary continued to purchase material goods for her own wardrobe that Robert found unnecessary and troublesome. In 1866, Mary decided to purchase and furnish a home at 375 West Washington Street in Chicago using the $22,000 Congress had given her as the remainder of President Lincoln's 1865 salary. Robert advised his mother against the move, believing her income not enough to sustain the house, but she did not listen. After just one year in the house, Robert was proved correct, and Mary was forced to vacate, rent it out, and return to boarding.[5]

Dejected by her failure to live comfortably, Mary Lincoln had an idea on how to raise funds that would lead to the most infamous event in her life and one that would completely humiliate Robert. Taking a cue from European royalty, specifically Empress Eugenie of France, Mary decided to sell her old White House dresses and jewelry in New York City as a way to raise money to alleviate her "common" circumstances. This she did anonymously to avoid newspaper exposure, but her ruse was quickly discovered and plastered in newspapers across the country. As if the secondhand sale was not embarrassing enough, Mary also wrote men whom her husband had given public offices and "suggested" they purchase some of her articles to help relieve the want of their dead benefactor's widow. When these people refused, Mary's solicitors forwarded the letters to the press. Once Mary's plot was publicly revealed, numerous gawkers came to see her items on exhibition but not to buy. In the end, hardly anything was sold, but the sale became a sort of carnival sideshow and was viciously ridiculed in the newspapers as an embarrassment to the memory of the martyr president created by a "vulgar" and "dreadful" woman.[6]

Robert, a Victorian gentleman who believed in the sanctity of family privacy and public propriety and who was attempting to build a solid social and legal reputation in Chicago at that time, was mortified when he read about his mother's actions in the newspapers. "R[obert] came up last evening like a maniac, and almost threatening his life, looking like death, because the letters of the [*New York*] *World* were published in yesterday's paper," Mary wrote, unable to understand why her actions were so castigated.[7] One newspaper reported at the time that Robert "is said to be as much astonished by the conduct of his mother as the greatest stranger can be; and the only theory he can suggest in her defense is, that she is insane."[8]

Robert was not the only person to feel this way. One Springfield, Illinois, newspaper reported that friends and family of Mary Lincoln in both Chicago and Springfield had believed her not "entirely in her right mind for several years."[9] Davis had a much simpler reaction to Mary's antics: "The selling of her clothes was an act of insanity. . . . On my remonstrance to her, she plead that she had to do so as she was in danger of becoming a pauper. She really had the insane delusion that poverty stared her in the face."[10] Strangely, no correspondence exists between Robert and Davis discussing the scandal. One person Robert did unburden his feelings to at this time, however, was his fiancée, and his letter to her shows he was not only humiliated, angered, and astonished but also was worried:

> I suppose you have seen some of the papers so there is no need of detailing what I was told they were full of. I did not read them. The simple truth, which I cannot tell anyone not personally interested, is that my mother is on one subject not mentally responsible. I have supposed this for some time from various indications and now have no doubt of it. I have taken the advice of one or two of my friends in whom I trust most and they tell me I can do nothing. It is terribly irksome to sit still under all that has happened and say nothing, but it has to be done. The greatest misery of all is the fear of what may happen in the future. This is, of course, not to be foreseen and is what troubles me most. I have no doubt that a great many good and amiable people wonder why I do not take charge of her affairs and keep them straight but it is very hard to deal with one who is sane on all subjects but one. You could hardly believe it possible, but my mother protests to me that she is in actual want and nothing I can do or say will convince her to the contrary. Do you see that I am likely to have a good deal of trouble in the future, do what I can to prevent it.[11]

This letter reveals many interesting and intimate aspects of Robert Lincoln. It shows that he previously suspected the deterioration of his mother's sanity and that he had a great prescience in fearing what her vagaries may lead to in the future. It gives further evidence of Robert doing his best to fulfill his duty as oldest son and head of the family by consulting two trustworthy friends about his mother. And it shows his forbearance in that he decided not to take any sort of precipitous action despite his mother's bizarre behaviors. But still he was worried, worried what this might mean and into what this might culminate.

Only one month after Mary Lincoln's clothing scandal, Davis finalized settlement of Abraham Lincoln's estate. Robert, Mary, and Tad each received $36,991.54 from the $110,974.62 estate.[12] Although this settlement date coincided with Davis's previously expressed two-year time frame, Mary Lincoln felt he and Robert had conspired to hurry the division of the estate to "*cross* my purposes."[13] No direct evidence suggests this, although Mary's estate income certainly would have been a good persuasion for her to stop the New York—or any future—clothing sale and was something Robert and Davis certainly would have calculated. Despite the money and her profession to Robert that she was "perfectly satisfied with the distribution," just four days later she was scheming again to print money-raising circulars and distribute them while Robert was on a trip out west to Wyoming.[14] She had learned enough to keep her activities secret from her son, and when she heard that her New York solicitors planned to send her clothing on an exhibition tour of Europe, she quickly stopped them. "Robert would go *raving distracted* if such a thing were done," she wrote. "R would blast us all if you were to have this project carried out."[15]

Despite her delusions of poverty and, concomitantly, her continued fund-raising, Mary decided in late 1867 to buy another house. She still owned the property at 375 West Washington Street and was renting it out (which paid solely for its taxes and upkeep) but now was interested in a cheaper house at number 462 on the same street. Robert did not think this investment to be a good idea and believed his mother was once again being taken in by hucksters and charlatans intent on defrauding the gullible widow to enrich themselves. Robert was beginning to see a pattern in the way his mother was buffaloed by people pretending to have her interests at heart when really they had only their own. His mother had fallen victim to this multiple times as first lady, then in being convinced to buy her first Chicago house in 1866, by allowing her New York solicitors to go publicly exhibit and advertise her "anonymous" clothing in 1867, and, to Robert's mind, by her continued consorting with Spiritualists.

In this latest real-estate idea, the man named Cole in whose house she was boarding (at 460 West Washington Street)[16] had apparently convinced Mary that his neighbor's house was available for a decent price—whether as a place to live or as an investment to resell for a profit is uncertain. (There is no mention of money for Cole himself, but he certainly would get a finder's fee at the very least.) This house was going to cost Mary $6,300, of which Robert was advancing her $4,950 of his own money as well as creating and filing all the appropriate deeds and paperwork.[17] Robert was so concerned about his mother's impending deal that he investigated the property's sale history, and he found that Cole was not being fully honest—and apparently this was not the first time. Robert wrote his mother, "The property you now propose to buy was sold by Cole in July. The amount expressed in the deed was $2,700 and it was stamped for that value. Cole may persuade you, but he cannot do so with me, that the price was $3,900. I am surprised after what you said to me yesterday, that you have allowed him to blind you again, but I am done with wasting time in urging you to beware of the advice of those who must possess such a deep interest in your welfare."[18]

Robert's aggravation is obvious, as is his sarcasm, and it is clear that he had lost patience with his mother's bad judgment in people and finances, which he had been directly witness to for three years and certainly aware of long before that. Yet, despite his exasperation, Robert continued to help his mother with her real-estate deal. He told her in the same letter to have Tad bring him the deeds and tell him the amount of money for the bank transfer, and he reminded her that she would be responsible for certain interest payments. Robert also sought to protect his mother by withholding part of the purchase price until the current owner paid his yearly taxes and back interest on the mortgage and in personally meeting with the seller to finalize the deal.[19]

Exactly why Cole thought he could use a shady real-estate transaction to hoodwink a woman whose son was a real-estate lawyer is unknown. Mary's gullibility and susceptibility to flattery were no secret, and perhaps Cole thought Robert too young to matter. Something happened, however, and the deal was never finalized. None of Robert's or Mary's correspondence says anything further about this matter, although the record is clear that Mary never bought a second house in Chicago.[20] A likely conclusion is that when Robert met the seller to complete the deal, he brought up his concerns about the disparity of the current value versus the previous value and then either pulled out of the deal or insisted on a better price that the seller refused to accept. Either way, Robert saved his mother from what appears to have been a suspicious investment, again doing his duty as her son to protect her from her own poor judgment.

Robert, of course, was not flawless, and he had learned his own hard lesson about the trustworthiness of people about one year before his mother's business with Cole. Robert's great lesson—and lifelong aggravation—came in the form of Mr. William H. Herndon, a man who has become both famous and infamous in Lincoln lore. Robert had known Herndon since he was a boy, due to the latter's position as Abraham Lincoln's junior law partner in Springfield, but they were never more than acquaintances. Herndon had tried to initiate a correspondence with "Bob" while the boy was a student at Harvard, which went nowhere. Years later, when the two men mutually despised each other, Robert ridiculed Herndon's letters to him as "absurd pseudo philosophical" babble.[21] But before Abraham Lincoln's death, and in the immediate months afterwards, there is no evidence to suggest Robert saw Herndon as anything more or less than a friend and colleague of his father. He may not have had any great respect for Herndon—after all, how could he not be at least minimally influenced by his mother's lifelong aversion to the man she called a drunk and mere office drudge?—but he seems to have held no ill will.

In 1865 and 1866, Robert had minimal dealings with Herndon that were mostly benign. In August 1865, Robert traveled to Springfield to clean out his father's papers and possessions at the Lincoln & Herndon law office and in December was in town for the removal of his father's remains to the temporary tomb.[22] The only known disagreement between Robert and Herndon at this time concerned property in the law office. When Robert tried to clean out his father's possessions, Herndon politely refused and said his partner gifted everything in the office to him. Robert knew this was a lie but decided not to make an issue of it despite the fact that he, as an aspiring lawyer, had hoped to take possession of at least some of his father's law books, which would have saved the son thousands of dollars.[23] But in general it was not a major disagreement and one that Robert could not disprove.

During his two visits, Robert may even have answered some questions about his father for Herndon, who was, by that time, preparing some biographical sketches and lectures on Lincoln. As the dead president's law partner for nearly twenty years, Herndon became a magnet for historians, journalists, and simple curiosity seekers, all looking for information about America's first martyred leader. Herndon cultivated this relationship into a lifelong study of Abraham Lincoln. But in 1865, Herndon knew only what he witnessed and experienced himself. These observations and thoughts he turned into a two-part lecture titled, "Analysis of the Character of Abraham Lincoln," which was delivered in Springfield, Illinois, on December 12 and 27, 1865.[24] Herndon's goal was to reveal to the public Abraham Lincoln "where he in fact and truth and question belongs."[25] Both lectures were received with great applause and admiration by newspapers across the country, as well as by many of Lincoln's old friends.

Mary Lincoln, however, seems to have taken exception to the lectures. She apparently chastised Herndon in a letter, to which he responded with two letters to Robert, accusing him of being the true author. Robert's response is very interesting, not just in his handling of Herndon but because it also reveals Robert's lifelong philosophy of dealing with historians, journalists, and other contributors to Abraham Lincoln's legacy.

> I was not aware that my mother had written you and so of course I did not compose the letter you have received. I had seen a synopsis of your lecture and I assure you I saw nothing in it at which to take umbrage. In the first place, I would not judge a discourse by an abstract of it, but more than all, even when I differ with anyone in his views of my father's character, etc., unless it were something flagrantly wrong, I would not discuss the subject.
>
> While it is true that the details of the private life of a public man have

> always a great interest to the minds of some, it is after all his works which make him live, and the rest is but secondary.
>
> I am extremely sorry to perceive that you seem to think that I bear ill will towards you from the correspondence which arose out of a misunderstanding. I beg you to believe that nothing could be further from the truth. My feelings towards you are of the kindest and I wish I had some means of proving them.[26]

Robert may not have taken "umbrage" at Herndon's lectures, but he did not find them completely innocuous either. In a letter to Judge Davis, Robert called them "rather odd literary efforts. . . . I hope he will stop it."[27] But still, Robert and his mother seem to truly have held no resentment toward Herndon after this and even contributed to his historical research. Robert allowed him access to some of his father's papers and answered his questions in letters, and both Robert and his mother spoke to Herndon personally in Springfield.[28]

Herndon permanently damaged the relationship, however, with his third lecture on Abraham Lincoln, delivered in November 1866 and titled, "A. Lincoln, Miss Ann Rutledge, New Salem, Pioneering, and *The Poem*." This lecture was audacious in its declarations that Abraham Lincoln had a love affair as a young man in New Salem with a girl named Ann Rutledge and that after her death he never truly loved another woman again—including his termagant wife—and was therefore forever miserable at home.[29] Herndon actually intended this to be a defense of both the Lincolns and what he believed to be their "loveless" marriage; for if the world knew of Lincoln's permanent emotional pain, he couldn't be blamed for his marital apathy nor she for her unrelenting shrewishness.[30] To Herndon's mind, it was better for one of Lincoln's friends to reveal the story than one of his enemies. For Robert, this lecture may have been the catalyst for his later reticence in dealing with information seekers about his father's life, for if he couldn't trust one of his father's friends to tell the truth, how could he ever trust anybody?

Herndon's lecture was widely anticipated, publicized, and believed, due to his longtime position as Lincoln's professional partner. This time Robert did take umbrage, for the lecture was offensive on multiple levels. As he told Davis, whether true or not (and Robert did not think them true), Herndon's statements were completely improper for public revelation. This was a time in America when social etiquette dictated that women's names appeared in the newspapers only at their marriages and their deaths, and anything else was an invasion of privacy. But more than that, Herndon's accusations were painful and humiliating to Robert's mother, from whom it threatened to rob her of her memories, her dreams, and even her identity. Robert did not tell his mother about the lecture when he found out, hoping to shield her from it. (She actually did not find out about it until its publication four months later.)[31] But Robert did immediately write to Davis and vent his frustration: "Mr. Wm. H. Herndon is making an ass of himself in his lectures. I am getting seriously annoyed at his way of doing things." Robert asked Davis his advice on whether or not to confront Herndon, which he worried might actually make matters worse considering that Herndon was such a "singular character."[32] In the end, he decided to risk it and went to Springfield.

The meeting appears to have been quite cordial. "We talked everything over in a very good natured way," Robert wrote to Davis on his return from Springfield, "and I found that he really had no idea of conveying the impressions he does in his lecture and that the main trouble comes from his heaping words on words without much care of their selection."[33] Herndon himself admitted as much in an 1886 memoranda: "In delivering my lectures I did not always follow the written words, but as ideas would come up I would orally state the ideas in unwritten words."[34] Subsequent correspondence between Robert and Herndon shows that the latter continually assured Robert that his intentions were noble, but perhaps his verbal expressions were faulty. For his part, Robert repeated that he believed him: "I have never had any doubt of your good intentions." Yet, Robert's mistrust of this pseudophilosophical, self-righteous, publicity-seeking man was clear, and he felt the need to caution Herndon: "Your opinion [of my father] may not agree with mine, but that is not my affair. All I ask is that nothing be published by you, which after *careful consideration* will seem apt to cause pain to my father's family, which I am sure you do not wish to do."[35]

Robert's responses to Herndon's letters make clear that the older man was bending over backwards to assure Robert of his good intentions, but Herndon's letters to others show that he had no intention of modifying his words or thoughts or handling Lincoln demurely: "Mr. Lincoln must stand on truth or not at all," he declared in one letter.[36] It is clear that in his own feelings of intellectual superiority and historiographical acumen, he placated Robert as one would a naïve and ignorant child. In that vein, he remembered his 1866 meeting with Robert somewhat differently. He said Robert came down "raging to be somehow satisfied," that he "wanted a fight, but I kept my temper and he couldn't fight, because he had no one to fight with."[37] This was written years later, after the two men had nothing but contempt for each other, and Herndon thought Robert "a d——d fool," "a wretch of a man," "a little wee bit of a man," and "a little bitter fellow of the pig-headed kind, silly and cold and selfish."[38] Herndon's memory of the meeting is almost certainly hyperbole, especially when compared with Robert's letters written at the time of the visit, but it is consistent with Herndon's perpetual condescension and disrespect for anyone who disagreed with him.

Herndon's guiding principle in his Lincoln work was to show the Truth—capital "T"—about Lincoln, not gloss it over and write hagiography, which he believed was what most biographers at that time were doing, or as he more viscerally put it, "nice, dainty, financial, kid-gloved asses who loved smooth literature with no admixture of truth to it, no robust truth."[39] Herndon honestly believed that what he was telling the world was the absolute truth but that few people understood or could understand his motives: "I felt it my religious duty to tell all I knew about Lincoln. . . . I did this to benefit my fellow man."[40] His later writing partner, Jesse Weik, felt the same about Herndon as Herndon did about himself. "Herndon had his weaknesses," Weik wrote in 1917, "but deviation from the truth was not one of them."[41]

Robert was beginning to see through Herndon's cleverness and half-truths, however, and had lost his patience. He wrote a letter to Herndon—cordial but certainly more forceful than his previous letters—again asking him to respect his family's privacy, especially his mother's, in Herndon's anticipated book-length biography of Abraham Lincoln.

> I *infer* from your letter, but I hope it is not so, that it is your purpose to make some considerable mention of my mother in your work. I say I hope it is not so, because in the first place it would not be pleasant for her or for any woman, to be made public property of in that way. With a man it is very different, for he lives out in the world and is used to being talked of. One of the unpleasant consequences of political success is that however little it may have to do with that success, his whole private life is exposed to the public gaze. That is part of the price he pays. But I see no reason why his wife and children should be included—especially while they are alive. I think no sensible man would live in a glass house and I think he ought not to be compelled to do so against his will. I feel very keenly on the subject, for the annoyance I am subjected to sometimes is nearly intolerable. I hope you will consider this matter carefully, my dear Mr. Herndon, for once done there is no undoing.[42]

Again, Herndon placated Robert in his reply, but the damage had been done. There are only a handful of known letters from Robert to Herndon after this, all in 1867 and all short, professional, and about minor topics.[43] Robert never again aided Herndon with any information about his father or any other topic, and he certainly had lost whatever modicum of respect or goodwill he had had for his father's former partner.

For Mary Lincoln, Herndon's early lectures were the final straw in the amount of seemingly relentless public humiliation she could endure. She was enraged, agitated, incredulous, and deeply emotionally wounded. She called Herndon a "dirty dog" and even threatened him physically in letters she wrote to Davis.[44] Robert understood his mother's feelings but also was worried by them. He sensed in his mother's reactions to Herndon's lectures a further deterioration in what he increasingly saw as her delicate mental balance. After suffering the apathy of the American people, the disdain and penury of Congress, the unremitting criticism of the press, and now the accusations of her husband's former partner, Mary was beyond distress. Her feeble health (along with her undoubted hypochondriasis) suffered, and her physician advised that she go abroad to Europe for a change of air.[45] She intended to leave on August 1, 1868, but Robert asked her to postpone. He wanted her and Tad to be present at his wedding.

It is nearly overwhelming to consider the myriad trials and tribulations that Robert Lincoln had to cope with at this point in his young life. In addition to the general issues of food, clothing, and shelter, he was endeavoring to create a reputable and lucrative legal practice in a major American city despite having an alcoholic partner; he had to deal with a spendthrift and increasingly agitated and irrational mother and all of her private and public needs and deeds; he was overseeing his younger brother's education and general welfare; he was taking a major role in managing his father's estate; and he was dealing with his father's historical reputation—and the public scrutiny and curiosity that concomitantly attached to himself—from writers in general and from William Herndon in particular. To say that Robert had a lot on his plate is an understatement. Yet, despite all of this responsibility, obligation, and stress, his personal letters do not read as though he was overwhelmed. In later years, he would be repeatedly praised for his outstanding management abilities, and perhaps he began learning how to balance multiple issues at this time. Robert did also have his friends with whom to communicate, and his letters to them are infused with conviviality and optimism, but more than that, Robert had also found his great happiness in love.

After at least four years of courtship and one year of engagement, Robert Lincoln and Mary Harlan were married on Thursday, September 24, 1868. The marriage of the son of Abraham Lincoln at that time was like the marriage of John F. Kennedy Jr. in the twentieth century: the entire nation was interested in facts and gossip, and had the details of the event been publicly known, it certainly would have turned into a circus. The wedding actually had been intended for later in the autumn but was rescheduled; newspapers stated it was to accommodate Mary Lincoln before her European trip, the biographer of James Harlan, Mary's father, stated it was to coincide with the senator's trip to Washington for a special session of Congress.[46] Whatever the reason, the bride and groom kept the event private and, coinciding with their own personalities, modest by inviting only thirty or so immediate friends (word-of-mouth for they did not issue paper invitations) to attend the event at the spacious Harlan home at 303 H Street in Washington, D.C.[47]

The parlors of the Harlan house were decorated with rare flowers in pyramids and bouquets, and on one wall was a monogram of roses forming the letters "M. R." for the bride and groom's first initials. The guests began arriving around 7:30 P.M. and included politicians (and their wives) such as cabinet secretaries Hugh McCullough and Gideon Welles, U.S. Senator Alexander Ramsey of Minnesota, and U.S. Representative William Loughridge of Iowa. Former Secretary of War Edwin M. Stanton was not able to attend due to business in Ohio, but his wife was there, along with her son, Robert's close friend Edwin L. "Ned" Stanton. Robert's other close friends Edgar T. Welles and college chum W. Robeson were there, and Mary's friends Cora Bean and Miss Caleb also attended.[48] Senator and Mrs. Harlan were present, as well as Mary's younger brother Willie Harlan; and, despite her "terror" and "horror" at the thought of returning to the city of her husband's murder, Mary Lincoln (still in her widow's weeds) was present, as was fifteen-year-old Tad.[49]

Shortly after 8 P.M., the bride and groom appeared in the parlor to begin the ceremony officiated by Bishop Matthew Simpson of the Methodist Episcopal Church. Mary wore a rich white silk dress, trimmed with white satin and pearl ornaments, made with high corsage and long sleeves, a train and overskirt, and belt and fan-shaped bow behind. She had a full white veil, fastened under her blonde hair with a small wreath of orange blossoms. Robert, always a fashionable young man, was dressed in a suit of black broadcloth, with a solitaire adorning his necktie, and white gloves. The *Washington Star* newspaper wrote that Mary's wedding gown "although plain, was exceedingly tasteful and rich," while the *Washington Express* described Robert as "the very personification of joy." After the short, Methodist ceremony, the new couple was congratulated all around and then all had an elegant catered supper and an hour-and-a-half of conversation and light refreshments accompanied by vocal music, until the guests departed. The bride and groom, as well as Mary Lincoln and Tad, stayed overnight at the Harlan house.[50]

In the morning, the newlyweds, accompanied by Robert's mother, the groomsmen, bridesmaids, and the caterer, took a special train to New York City for a honeymoon tour of the north. Mary Lincoln left the party at Baltimore (Tad had stayed in Washington with the Harlans), and the rest of the party continued to New York. The complete details of the honeymoon after that are unknown, although Robert and Mary spent at least part of their time at the Hoffman House in New York City. After a two-week getaway, the newlyweds returned to Washington to spend a few days with the Harlans before leaving for Illinois.[51]

When Robert returned to Chicago with his new bride in late October, it was the beginning of a new epoch in his life. This beginning was even more revolutionary for him because he was, for the first time in his life, living entirely on his own terms. On October 1, his mother and brother had sailed out of Baltimore to Europe, where they would spend almost three years. While they and Robert and Mary Harlan kept in close communication through letters, Robert finally could focus his energies almost exclusively on himself and his new family.

The Robert Lincolns settled into Robert's apartment in Chicago in late 1868 but in less than one year bought a small house at 653 Wabash Avenue—a moderately priced but respectable neighborhood on the south side of the city.[52] Robert returned to his legal practice after weeks away to find that his partner Charles Scammon (who did not attend the wedding, whether to keep the office open or for some other reason is unknown) had relapsed back into his alcoholic ways.[53] By January 1869, Robert had had enough and finally severed ties and dissolved the partnership. He kept the office at room 1 in the Marine Bank building on Lake Street and opened his own practice, something not terribly difficult or new since he had been doing nearly all the work of the Scammon & Lincoln firm anyway.

Robert continued to focus on insurance and real-estate law, often assisting family and friends with property transactions. In addition to advising and assisting his mother, Robert also took charge of multiple land lots he and his brother jointly owned in Illinois and Iowa. Robert's correspondence about the management of these parcels of land is sizeable and shows him to be a knowledgeable, engaged, and shrewd businessman.[54] He did some business for his father's longtime friend James C. Conkling and also worked for nearly ten years for President Lincoln's friend and Secretary of the Navy Welles.[55] Beginning in 1869 and continuing until at least 1877, Robert took charge of mortgage loans Welles made to a Chicago resident named Mrs. Grand and all the concomitant issues (Robert also worked for Mrs. Grand in litigation cases); by 1877, Robert appears to have been Welles's general business agent in Chicago.[56]

One of the more interesting cases Robert took up in 1868–69 involved a real-estate transaction and subsequent financial delinquency of Father Sebastian

Duroc, the Roman Catholic priest in charge of the Escanaba parish in Michigan. Duroc was the first pastor of Marquette, Michigan, from 1855 to 1864, after which he went to Escanaba, a small port town on the north shore (Upper Peninsula) of Lake Michigan.[57] The case required Robert to travel more than three hundred miles from Chicago to Escanaba, first by train to Green Bay, Wisconsin, and from there, two days north (120 miles) by sledge. Robert was not aware of it at the time, but he learned years later that while in Michigan, he nearly shared his father's fate by meeting with an assassin's bullet from a member of the Booth family.

In late 1868, not long after his wedding and honeymoon, Robert Lincoln was engaged by Edmond Carrey, the French vice consul in Chicago, to travel to Escanaba and attempt to reconcile the Duroc matter.[58] Succinctly, in 1857, Duroc had persuaded on a personal visit two men from Vosges, France, to send him a draft for thirty thousand francs with which to purchase land, primarily as a speculation on their part. When Duroc cashed the draft, it was valued at only $5,700 due to the American financial crisis of that year, and two years later, another $1,100 of the money was lost by the failure of the bank in Detroit where the money was on deposit. Duroc therefore was responsible for about $4,600, but his investors never heard from him again. Apparently, the priest used the money to buy land in his own name, some of which he sold and kept the profits for himself.

Robert arrived in Escanaba on January 13, 1869, where he stayed at the home of Eli P. Royce, the oldest and most distinguished resident of the town.[59] The young lawyer immediately conferred with everyone in town with knowledge of the situation, including Duroc himself, who "made no denial of his bad conduct," "seemed to care nothing about the scandal of the situation at all," and "determined to get out as cheaply as he could." Robert soon learned that Duroc had sold the land he had bought with the entrusted money for $6,000 and had nothing left of it but five unpaid bank notes for $1,000 each, bearing 7 percent interest, payable respectively in one, two, three, four, and five years. Robert concluded Duroc had received only about $3,000 of the total thirty thousand francs he was given, the rest having been lost by the bankruptcy troubles in Detroit; Duroc, in fact, claimed he paid for part of the land in question with some of his own money. "After considering the cost of a lawsuit in that rough country where court was held twice a year for a week at a time, and that a suit would have to be managed either from Chicago or Detroit, and after much discussion with Duroc I agreed to take the last four notes [payable in 1870, 1871, 1872, and 1873 with 7 percent interest] . . . and an assignment of the mortgage, letting Duroc keep the fifth note," Robert later related. In the end, the two French investors recouped "a considerable part" of their original investment but lost ten years' worth of interest as well as some of the principal from the financial troubles of 1857. The business agent for the French investors in Escanaba and vice consul Carrey both "thoroughly approved" of Robert's resolution of the matter.[60]

When Robert was asked decades later by the Delta County Historical Society in Escanaba to relate the Duroc business for their historical records, at first he wanted to know why they would care about such mundane affairs. The vice president of the society responded, "[T]he inquiry was made for the purpose of getting the exact data of what came so nearly to be a repetition of the terrible tragedy that caused the death of your father." He then explained that the wife of Robert's Escanaba host, Eli Royce, had an invalid sister also staying in the house. The Royces had hired as a nurse "a young lady who was very pretty, accomplished and refined." When the nurse was asked to wait upon table at dinner and told that they had Mr. Lincoln as a guest, "The young lady flew into a passion and said she would wait upon the table with a pistol in her hand. She was a niece of Wilkes Booth, who assassinated your father. It is almost unnecessary to say that she was immediately dismissed."[61] Robert was very interested in the story and admitted that he had no idea then or later of the threat.[62]

If Robert had been assassinated in 1869—just as if Edwin Booth had not saved him from injury or death by the moving train in Jersey City in 1863—the influence of his absence on American history would have been palpable. Robert's impact as lawyer, businessman, public servant, and family curator certainly were pervasive but, perhaps more important to some, were Robert's position and influence as patriarch. Shortly after his return from Escanaba, Robert and Mary learned they were going to have a baby—the inauguration of the next Lincoln generation.

The news was joyous to everyone in both families, but Mary Todd Lincoln especially was thrilled. She had been enamored of Mary Harlan since she first met the young girl in Washington during the war and was immensely proud and pleased when the younger Mary became her daughter-in-law. "I consider this marriage a great gain," Mary wrote one month before the wedding. "A charming daughter will be my portion and one whom my idolized husband loved and admired, since she was very young." Of course, anything connected to her dead husband became sentimental to Mary, but her fondness for her future daughter-in-law was cemented when the younger Mary told the older that she was "only passing from one mother to another."[63] Such flattery—certainly truthful expression but flattering nonetheless—always had an enormous impact on Mary Lincoln, who craved admiration her entire life.

The two Marys had a continuous correspondence while Robert's mother was in Europe. Mary Harlan kept her mother-in-law updated on the state of her marriage and her pregnancy, telling the widow in December 1868 how she was "so happy" as a wife and in late October 1869 that she and Robert "are *more* in love, with each other than ever."[64] Young Mary's pregnancy appears to have been typical and free from any sort of dangerous health complications. Only once did she tell her mother-in-law that she was ill, to which the older Mary replied, "[G]o out *every day* and enjoy yourself—you are so *very young* and should be as gay as a lark. Trouble comes soon enough, my dear child, and you must enjoy life, whenever you can."[65] As the birth approached, young Mary told her mother-in-law that she "never imagined *such* devotion" as she received from Robert.[66]

When Mary Harlan's "confinement" finally occurred, she endured eight hours of labor during which she was attended by her mother, her doctor, and a nurse. Robert stayed up all night although it is unlikely he participated in the birth, as a father's presence in the birth room was not a typical occurrence in the nineteenth century. The baby was born on October 15, 1869. She was named "Mary Lincoln," after her maternal grandmother, but was nicknamed "Mamie" by the family.[67] Robert informed his mother of her new grandchild in a letter written just four hours after the birth and told his "second father" David Davis of it first by word-of-mouth through his old mentor Samuel Fuller and then by letter three weeks later. "The young lady . . . is as fat and hearty as one could wish," Robert wrote, and his wife had "progressed towards her complete recovery very rapidly and is today in all appearance as well as ever."[68] James Harlan visited his new granddaughter for three days in late November and was "delighted" with the new addition. Robert told his friend Edgar Welles, "We are all flourishing in the highest possible way."[69]

The birth further cemented the already close relationship between the Robert Lincolns and their absent matriarch. Grandmother Lincoln constantly wrote letters and sent gifts, especially baby clothes, while Robert and Mary Harlan continually wrote their mother and encouraged her and Tad to return to America and live with them in Chicago.[70] When the Lincolns reunited in spring 1871 after more than two years apart, Robert and his wife rejoiced at the event and insisted that Mary and Tad stay at their home. Unfortunately, Mary Lincoln's previous admonition to her daughter-in-law that in the midst of happiness "troubles comes soon enough" came back to haunt the bereaved widow, for Tad soon became seriously ill.

10

"I Am in Better Shape Than Most"

Tad Lincoln had grown up much since his carefree days as the ten-year-old tyrant of the White House. The assassination, and his position as his mother's emotional support, had subdued him considerably. During the nearly three years in which Tad and his mother had been in Europe, the boy gained much culture by traveling the Continent, and he apparently gained a deep reverence for religion, but he spent the majority of his time in study, and he conquered with great patience his childhood speech impediment. Robert, who had administered the majority of Tad's financial affairs as well as supervised his young brother's education in America, was eager to see the boy and quite impressed by the eighteen-year-old young man he beheld in May 1871. "Poor Tad was a good boy and extraordinarily affectionate and firm in his friendships," Robert later wrote to journalist Noah Brooks, a frequent visitor to President Lincoln's White House in the 1860s. "After you knew him he studied diligently and overcame entirely the defect in his speech. This he did by reading aloud as a regular exercise and as it was done mainly while he was in Germany and under a German (English speaking) tutor, he came home . . . articulating properly, but with deliberation—speaking German perfectly but in English owing to his practice in reading he had a slight German accent."[1]

Mary and Tad stayed at Robert's house on Wabash Avenue.[2] The joyous family reunion was, however, quickly clouded. First, Mary Harlan was called to Washington to stay with her sick mother while her father campaigned for reelection in Iowa.[3] She took baby Mamie with her (this became a common occurrence during the Lincoln marriage—Mary nursing her invalid mother in Washington or back in Mount Pleasant, Iowa, always taking the children with her, and Robert needing to stay and work in Chicago). Then in late May or early June, Tad became seriously ill, whether as a result of the trip across the Atlantic

Ocean or a worsening of a previous condition is unknown. His illness kept him bedridden and forced his and his mother's planned removal from Robert's home to the Clifton House hotel—decided because Robert's house was too small—to be postponed.[4] Tad's health fluctuated but never completely recovered. His lungs filled with fluid, a condition doctors then called "dropsy of the chest."

Drs. Charles Gilman Smith and Hosmer Allen Johnson were called in to care for Tad, and when his symptoms worsened, they consulted Dr. Nathan Smith Davis, a renowned physician and lung specialist. On June 8, the doctors said the boy was recovering, but a few nights later, "through an imprudence in changing his clothing in our treacherous Chicago climate, he was suddenly stricken by a pleuristic attack," Robert explained.[5] Pleurisy is an inflammation of the membrane that surrounds the lungs and lines the rib cage. The condition causes shortness of breath but likewise can make breathing extremely painful, and it reduces the ability of the sufferer to move freely. Tad's lungs became so filled with fluid that eventually he was forced to both rest and sleep in a chair with a bar across the front, put there to keep him upright so he would not drown. Robert described Tad's illness as "long and painful" and "torturous," lasting from early June through mid-July.[6] "Such suffering I never saw but it was all born with marvelous fortitude," Robert wrote.[7] He spent so much time caring for Tad those two months that he neglected his legal practice.[8]

Robert wrote often to his absent wife to update her on the fluctuations of Tad's health. Tad and his mother by this time had removed to the Clifton House hotel. On July 11, Tad seemed to be improving, but by July 14, Robert reported that Dr. Davis expected the boy could not live for more than a few days. That night, however, Tad "seemed to rally" and by 11 P.M. was "sleeping nicely," so Robert went home. He was awakened at 4:30 A.M., rushed to the hotel, and saw that his brother was failing fast. "He was in great distress and laboring for breath and ease but I do not think he was in acute pain," Robert wrote his wife. "He lingered on so until between half past seven and eight, when he suddenly threw himself forward on his bar and was gone."[9]

Funeral services for Tad were held at Robert's residence on Wabash Avenue.[10] One attendee said the services in Robert's house were "simple, quiet, and unostentatious but deeply impressive and very pathetic. . . . Mrs. Lincoln looked truly the woman of sorrow that she was."[11] Robert sat with his mother on a couch during the service, comforting her, again, as he had done during the deaths of his other brothers and his father. She looked to him for support; the American public looked to him as the last surviving son of Abraham Lincoln.

Robert accompanied Tad's body to Springfield for burial in the newly completed Lincoln tomb in Oak Ridge Cemetery—the same journey he had made in 1865 with his father's body. He traveled without his wife, who was still in

Washington, or his mother, who was too distraught to go, but with his father-in-law, James Harlan; his "second father," David Davis; and a few close friends to give him support.[12] On his return home, he found his mother doing about as well as he expected. For Mary Lincoln, however, this was not good at all. Tad's death was yet another slap against her, beating her down after she had finally began to recover from the traumatic loss of her husband. The *New York Times* reported that Mary Lincoln was "almost completely prostrated by her affliction"; while the *Chicago Tribune* called the boy's death "a fearful blow" to Mary and reported that "her physician dreads that it may produce insanity."[13] Robert encouraged his mother to travel to Springfield and spend some time with her sister Elizabeth Edwards, believing such a visit to the woman who was more a mother figure than sibling could benefit her greatly.[14] Mary, however, was not disposed to end the feud with Elizabeth that began during the Civil War over government appointments. She decided to stay in Chicago.

Robert was emotionally and physically exhausted by his brother's death. "I will not attempt to tell you all that has happened in the last ten days, for I am a good deal used up," he wrote to his wife.[15] He did not crumble in the face of tragedy as did his mother, but the pain was still as sharp. Tad "was only eighteen when he died but he was so manly and self reliant that I had the greatest hopes for his future," Robert lamented.[16] Due to his distress, his doctor advised him to take a month-long holiday to the Rocky Mountains—a typical nineteenth-century prescription for exhausted gentlemen—which he did from late July to mid-August.[17]

Despite his own exhaustion, Robert went to great lengths to look after his mother before, during, and after his trip. After his encouragement for her to visit the Edwards home in Springfield failed, Robert arranged for his close friend and Chicago neighbor Norman Williams to spend nights in the spare bedroom so his mother would not be alone during his four-week absence. Mary reciprocated her son's care by staying in Chicago rather than leaving for a spa or a Spiritualist resort so Robert would not worry about her. "My son's health required that he should leave town," Mary told a friend. "I promised him that I would remain in his house."[18] Robert wrote letters to his mother while he was gone and may have hired a nurse to stay with her or retained the nurse who stayed with her while he attended Tad's funeral. Robert returned from his trip feeling "very much refreshed" and ready to commence his fall work.[19] His wife and daughter still were with Mrs. Harlan in Washington (soon to accompany her to Mount Pleasant in October), and although his mother had previously declined a permanent place in Robert's house, now he insisted.

In September, Robert traveled to Springfield yet again, this time to be present at the removal of the remains of his father and brothers Eddie and Willie from the temporary vault to the permanent Lincoln family vault in Oak Ridge Cemetery, there to rest beside Tad.[20] While in the state capital, Robert filed papers with the Sangamon County Court regarding Tad's death and his estate, which was valued at approximately $37,000, for which he and his mother were the heirs. State law gave Mary Lincoln two-thirds of her son's estate and gave Robert Lincoln one-third. Mary, however, insisted that it be divided equally between her and her last surviving son. "This is very generous on her part," Robert wrote to David Davis, "as it makes a difference of about $7,000."[21]

Robert may have gained an unexpected amount of money, but he also was about to lose an unexpected amount—as were thousands of other people in Chicago. On the evening of Sunday, October 8, 1871, a fire started in the barn of Mr. and Mrs. Patrick and Catherine O'Leary on the city's West Side. Due to high winds, dry weather, and the prevalence of cheap wooden buildings in proximity to each other, what is now known as the Great Fire quickly spread out of control. On Monday, it raged through the central business district, destroying hotels, department stores, the opera house and theaters, churches and printing plants, City Hall, and eventually the city waterworks. Residents were in a panic, fleeing for their lives, some hurrying to save possessions, others looting abandoned stores and homes. As the fire spread north and even jumped over the Chicago River, residents fled before it seeking refuge in Lincoln Park and on the shores of Lake Michigan. By the time the conflagration burned itself out on Tuesday morning, October 10, it had burned a swath through downtown Chicago of thirty-four blocks, or more than three square miles. Approximately three hundred people had died, one hundred thousand were left homeless, and $192,000,000 in property was destroyed in one of the largest U.S. disasters of the nineteenth century.[22]

Both Robert Lincoln and his mother were in Chicago during the fire (Mary and Mamie were with the Harlans in Mount Pleasant), although the Lincoln home on the south side of the city was never in danger. Robert's law office in the Marine Bank building on Lake Street, on the other hand, was directly in the fire's path. On Sunday, the first night, Robert hurried to his office and "had only time, before being driven out by the dense smoke, to throw some valuable papers into the vault, and to leave his law library, valued at $10,000, to its fate," reported one newspaper. The next morning, Robert returned the Marine Bank building ruins to discover his law books safe, except for a few that had been left open on tables and were wet.[23] His vault also was intact, but, taking no chances, Robert "opened the vault and piled upon a table cloth the most valuable papers, then slung the pack over his shoulder, and escaped amid a shower of falling firebrands," wrote John Hay, Robert's friend and now a journalist for the *New York Tribune*, who accompanied Robert that morning.[24]

Robert himself later wrote, "Our fire has left us in a very bad condition as you can imagine but so far as I can learn I am in better shape than most of my confreres as my vault stood the fire."[25]

The contents of his vault were legal documents, not his father's papers. Those still were in Davis's bank vault in Bloomington, Illinois, and so were never in danger. Robert's personal collection of family memorabilia and heirlooms, however, is another matter. He later said that the few letters he owned in his father's handwriting—presumably letters to Robert at college—burned in the fire.[26] Despite losing little property, Robert said the fire not only caused him an immense amount of professional work settling insurance claims but it also "embarrasses me *very* much in some real estate matters and I am in need of some money to meet engagements," he told Davis.[27] Robert observed of the fire's aftermath, "There is no use in trying to disguise the fact that things are very gloomy here. So long as our people only compare themselves with each other, they can laugh but when a man thinks where he was a month ago, it isn't so funny."[28]

Chicagoans were not a people to sit around idly and complain, however. They began rebuilding the city even as the last embers died out. The renovations and modernizations spurred Chicago's development into one of the most populous and economically important cities in America. Robert, true to his Victorian beliefs in honor and social duty, as well as his rising social status, did his part to help. In December, he sent a plea to the lawyers of New York State, asking assistance to replace the city's law books because the library of the Chicago Law Institute, as well as many private legal libraries, had been destroyed in the fire.[29]

Robert may not have lost his office vault in the fire, but he did lose his office building, as did thousands of other attorneys in the city. This turned out to be a blessing in disguise. It became common courtesy at the time for lawyers with offices intact to allow their more unfortunate brethren to share their office space until more became available. It was in this way that Robert Lincoln became acquainted with his future partner Edward Swift Isham.

Isham, a little more than seven years Robert's senior, was born in Bennington, Vermont, in 1836, the oldest son of a distinguished lawyer and judge. He did preparatory work at Lawrence Academy in Massachusetts, matriculated at Williams College in Massachusetts from 1853 to 1857, and studied law at Harvard Law School. After apprenticing in his father's law office, Isham was admitted to the Vermont bar in 1858 but soon traveled west and settled in Chicago. In 1864, Isham was elected to the state legislature and during his term served on the judiciary committee. From 1865 to 1866, he toured Europe, and on his return to Chicago set up his own law practice. By the time of the

Great Fire in 1871, Isham held a prominent position at the bar and was highly respected for his superior legal acumen and abilities; lucrative business "came to him freely." Isham was also a highly cultured man, with interests in literature, history, and music.[30]

It appears Robert did not know Isham personally, perhaps only socially through membership in the Chicago Club, but after the fire, he approached the distinguished lawyer about the possibility of temporarily sharing his office.[31] "He was a young lawyer, with matters pressing hard upon him, as you may well imagine they might upon any lawyer after such a fire, and particularly a lawyer with large insurance interests," Isham later recalled. "Making new relations after the fire, Mr. Lincoln and myself got to understand each other, and went into business together."[32] The partnership of Isham & Lincoln was officially formed in February 1872. While Robert specialized his legal career up to that time in insurance and real-estate matters, Isham ranged further afield. He undertook work on personal trusts, corporate affairs, equity cases, and railroad interests and litigation. Both Isham and Lincoln had occasionally been engaged in jury cases involving general legal issues, which they continued to do as a partnership.

The early records of the firm show that as the junior member, Robert did most of the everyday work, correspondence, arguing cases in court, and the like, and Isham handled the more important matters. Robert referred to himself as "the mechanics lien man of the firm," meaning he specialized in real-estate liens, which result from someone (such as a contractor) doing work on property and not getting paid.[33] Robert's association with Isham would prove to be a watershed moment in his life, both professionally and personally; the firm of Isham & Lincoln ultimately became one of the most respected law firms in Chicago.

On a more personal level, Robert's wife and daughter returned to Chicago in early 1872, after about eight months away. Robert had visited them periodically while they stayed with Mrs. Harlan in Washington and Iowa—Mount Pleasant was only a few hours' train ride from Chicago and an easy weekend trip—but to have his wife and two-year-old daughter home again was a delight. With his mother also living in the Wabash Avenue house, Robert had his entire family together. Unfortunately, Mary Todd Lincoln was not an easy woman to live with, and life at the Lincoln house soon became unpleasant.

It appears that shortly after Mary and Mamie's return, Robert's mother, who was capable of immense self-centeredness, sanctimony, and imperialism, tried to dominate the running of the household and the raising of her granddaughter. Mary Harlan Lincoln, who could be as strong and steely as her mother-in-law, refused to tolerate such interference, and the two had a heated argument.

Robert's only explanation was that there was a "misunderstanding" between the two women, and his mother became angry at his wife "for some trifle." Robert had to "break up housekeeping" to end the trouble—a Victorian-era euphemism meaning he kicked his mother out of the house. After that, the two Marys did not meet again for nearly ten years, "but when my wife has sent our children to see her," Robert explained in 1875, "she has driven my servants out of the room by her insulting remarks concerning her mistress and this in the presence of my little girl."[34]

When Mary Todd Lincoln left her son's home in spring 1872, she became an itinerant woman, traveling across the United States in search of health spas to relieve her myriad physical indispositions and also visiting Spiritualist communities to help her contact her dead children and husband.[35] Robert remained concerned about his mother's health and rationality, especially after his attempts to watch over and care for her in his house had failed, and so he hired a full-time nurse to travel with his mother, care for her, and be her constant companion.[36] Robert also wrote his mother letters and visited with her whenever she stopped in Chicago.

That same summer, Robert took his family across the ocean for a six-month European tour. This was the beginning of the Lincolns' annual family vacations, a tradition they would continue for the rest of their lives. It was also a trip Robert had desired ever since attaining his law license in January 1867, when he wanted to tour the Continent for a few months before settling into his professional career. Five years later, he had the same intention, this time a family vacation before settling down to work at his new firm of Isham & Lincoln.[37] The only fact known about this trip is that while in London, Robert accompanied Benjamin Moran of the U.S. legation as representatives of the United States to the annual dinner given by the sheriffs of London and Middlesex.[38]

The Lincolns returned from Europe in November and traveled directly to the Harlans in Mount Pleasant for a short visit.[39] Back home in their Wabash Avenue house in Chicago, the Lincolns resumed their previous routines. Robert settled firmly into the work of his new law firm, where he quickly enhanced his already positive reputation as an enthusiastic and astute lawyer, and he and Isham became complementary partners as well as great friends.

Robert received an early Christmas gift that year when Mary announced she was pregnant. The Lincolns' son Abraham Lincoln II was born on August 14, 1873. He was promptly nicknamed "Jack" by his father, apparently because Robert felt "Abraham" too long and formal a name for a young boy, and he disliked the moniker "Abe," just as his father had.[40] In later years, it would be said that Jack was in looks, temperament, and intelligence practically a reincarnation of his martyred grandfather. Whether true or not, Robert was immensely proud of his boy and happy to be a new father. Robert now had two children, Mary and Abraham Lincoln, named after his parents.

It was about this time that Robert found himself yet again confronted by impertinent and outrageous historical statements about his father by men who were supposed to have been the president's friends. The issue of his father's legacy was never far from Robert's mind. In the seven years since Abraham Lincoln's murder, a number of books had been published, and more were on the way, and while Robert occasionally corresponded with some of these historians, he universally refused to allow anyone access to his father's papers in Bloomington. The reasons for this were multiple. First of all, Robert and Davis needed to find correspondingly available free time to go through the papers together to assess their importance and to weed out items that were either insignificant or of a purely private nature—and, of course, he would not allow anyone to look through the papers before he did himself. Robert also wanted his friend and former presidential secretary John Nicolay to be present for the review, believing he would understand better than anyone "the purport of all of them."[41] Robert had planned to spend part of the summer of 1871 in Bloomington surveying the papers, but Tad's illness and death and Robert's need for a western retreat postponed the trip.[42] Besides being busy, Robert was loathe to take this first step because he knew that once he opened the trunks, a multitude of people would descend upon him asking to view, borrow, or purchase the contents, and Robert simply, and understandably, did not want to deal with the annoyance.

Robert's sense of Victorian propriety was another roadblock to his decision to share his father's papers. He believed it inappropriate to allow the publication of materials pertaining to living people, information that could embarrass or annoy them. This was a prerogative he fervently held and assiduously exercised his entire life. The most important issue for Robert, however, was that of his own family's privacy. He planned to weed out anything purely personal, but even the most mundane or professional of papers could offer glimpses into a man's private life. Robert understood the historical elevation his father had achieved, and he was extremely proud of it, but he did not feel the personal aspects had any place in a man's reputation. The last thing Robert wanted was for his mother, his brothers, and himself to become public fodder as well (at least any more than they already were).[43]

Still, Robert knew he had to attend to the papers sooner rather than later. But as 1871 turned into 1872 and 1873, the job remained undone. One of the people eager to search through the boxes was Abraham Lincoln's old friend Ward Hill Lamon, who was writing his own Lincoln biography. Lamon had known Lincoln since their days in the 1850s riding the judicial circuit together. When president, Lincoln had appointed Lamon as marshal of the District of Columbia; Lamon also declared himself the president's unofficial bodyguard. Robert Lincoln had denied Lamon's research request in Bloomington in 1869 and later that year learned the former bodyguard had purchased all of Herndon's Lincoln research materials for $4,000 and was going to use them as the basis of his work. "What sort of a book Mr. Lamon proposes to put up I do not know," Robert wrote to David Davis, "but I confess I am afraid of his impulsive way of doing things generally and the pecuniary value he puts on Herndon's stuff is not agreeable to think of under the circumstances." In his wariness, Robert asked Davis if he would take an interest in Lamon's work and influence him to do the noble thing "in case he is bent on any mischief."[44]

It turned out that Robert was right to worry. Lamon took Herndon's materials at face value and used them all. Friends of Abraham Lincoln such as Davis, Leonard Swett, and Isaac N. Arnold urged him to omit some of the materials, which he largely did not do. Instead, he repeated Herndon's most outrageous statements from the 1866–67 lectures, including the Ann Rutledge love story and the accusation that Lincoln never loved Mary Todd, and went even further to declare Lincoln the illegitimate child of an unmarried couple—a devastating accusation in the nineteenth century. Moreover, the entire book was an attack on Lincoln's public policies, labeling them at best misguided and at worst ignorant. It soon was revealed that Lamon used a ghostwriter for his book, a fervent Democrat and Lincoln critic named Chauncey F. Black, whose father had been a cabinet member in the Buchanan administration.[45]

When Lamon's *Life of Abraham Lincoln* was published in 1872, it caused a sensation. Robert later admitted that upon the advice of his friends he did not read it, but he had heard about its contents and was outraged. It was an affront he would not forget and was the basis for a great confrontation with Lamon ten years later. As if the Lamon book wasn't enough, in December 1873 William Herndon emerged from his six-year hiatus and again offered up his spectacular assertions as to the private life of Abraham Lincoln in a lecture called "Lincoln's Religion."

Whereas Herndon claimed in his 1866–67 lectures that Lincoln never loved his wife, in 1873 he claimed, citing his own 1865 interview with Mary Lincoln as a source, that his former law partner was an atheist.[46] Such an assertion infuriated Robert Lincoln, not just because it was false but because disbelief in religion was anathema to society's religious standards of the time and a humiliation to the Lincoln legacy.[47] Years later, Robert wrote to a correspondent the conclusion he had reached about Herndon's outrages against his father's memory.

> It may not surprise you to know that my regard for Herndon or anybody connected with him is not great. It was very difficult for me to understand him at first, but soon after my father's death, I became convinced that he was actuated by an intense malice, and was possessed of a most ingenious imagination. The malice arose, I am quite sure, from the fact that my father could not see his way, in view of Herndon's personal character, to give him some lucrative employment during the war of the rebellion. Those who knew Herndon personally could well understand the reasons for that. I have endeavored for my own piece of mind to refrain from thinking much about him.[48]

In December 1873, however, Robert could not ignore it. "Herndon has so clearly falsified the record that I think it time he was squelched," Robert angrily wrote to his friend John Nicolay, then marshal of the U.S. Supreme Court in Washington (a position Robert had recommended him for in a letter to Associate Justice David Davis).[49] Robert had written a rebuttal to Herndon's accusations and asked Nicolay to rewrite it in his own hand, modify if necessary, get Judge Davis's approval, and publish it in the Washington *Chronicle* (the editor and proprietor of which in 1873 was Robert's father-in-law, James Harlan) under his own name, "for I do not wish to personally enter the controversy."[50] It seems Davis and other of Robert's friends opposed his plan, and Robert's subsequent letters to Nicolay suggest that it was never carried out.[51] This may have also partly been because of the negative press coverage Herndon's lecture was receiving. Unlike Herndon's previous Ann Rutledge lecture, which was lauded by newspapers across the country in 1866, his lecture on Lincoln's religion was universally vilified by journalists, which both surprised and pleased Robert. In a subsequent letter to Nicolay, Robert enclosed a clipping of one such article that called Herndon a "false friend" and stated, "In his present effort to make a sensation, he has played the part of a traitor in the household and a ghoul at the grave of a friend."[52]

Although Robert vented his anger in letters to friends, he never personally publicly challenged any historian with whom he disagreed, even the nefarious Herndon. Mary Todd Lincoln, on the other hand, was not so reserved. Her response to Herndon's lecture was first to publicly deny the interview with Herndon ever occurred, then to admit it but call him a liar.[53] Herndon slyly refused to condemn Mary but used her own words against her and suggested the poor woman was incompetent and untrustworthy as a witness.[54] The episode made Mary look foolish and, being redolent of the Old Clothes Scandal, caused newspapers and regular citizens to be embarrassed for and about Mary for once again "obtruding herself before the public" in such a pitiful and improper way.[55]

Robert, too, was embarrassed by his mother's public display and also worried about her emotional reaction to Herndon's accusations.

Mary's public clash with Herndon only worsened her fragile mental state, which had been degrading since Tad's death. Just months before Herndon's lectures, homeopathic surgeon Dr. Willis Danforth had begun treating Mary for "fever and nervous derangement of the head." Danforth later testified that Mary's symptoms included the continued physical complaints of severe headaches, joint and muscle pains, incontinence, swelling, insomnia, and her mental symptoms worsened to a general debility of the nervous system, anxiety, melancholia, depression, delusions, and hallucinations.[56]

Mary's personal nurse verified these symptoms and stated the widow suffered from "periods of mild insanity" and "had strange delusions" in the years between 1871 and 1875. Mary thought gas was the invention of the devil and often would use nothing but candles for lighting; at other times, she would draw the shades and sit in the darkened room.[57] "From that time [of Tad's death], Mrs. Lincoln, in the judgment of her most intimate friends, was never entirely responsible for her conduct. She was peculiar and eccentric, and had various hallucinations," stated family friend Isaac N. Arnold.[58]

Mary's growing psychosis culminated in spring 1875. In March, while wintering in Jacksonville, Florida, she became inexplicably convinced that Robert was deathly ill. "My dearly beloved son Robert T. Lincoln rouse yourself and live for my sake all I have is yours from this hour. I am praying every moment for your life to be spared to your mother," she telegraphed to Robert via his law partner.[59] As soon as Robert was informed of his mother's behavior, he wired the telegraph station manager to discretely inquire "if Mrs. Abraham Lincoln now at Jacksonville is in any trouble mentally or otherwise"; the manager responded that Mary appeared "nervous and somewhat excited" and that her nurse "thinks Mrs. L should be at home as soon as possible."[60] Mary boarded the first available train for Chicago. Robert was so worried that he monitored his mother's condition along her entire journey by having telegraph-station managers observe her behavior and report to him at every stop.[61]

Robert, anxious but in perfect physical health, met his mother at the Chicago train station. He took her to the Grand Pacific Hotel for dinner and a room since she refused to stay at his house, despite his invitation. During their meal, her conversation was so delusional that Robert, in his concern, took a room next to his mother's, where he stayed for more than two weeks.[62] Every night Robert was awoken by his mother's restlessness, her knocking on his door, and eventually her requests to sleep in his room for fear of being alone. Robert called Dr. Ralph N. Isham, his personal physician and kin to his law partner, Edward Isham, to attend his mother.[63]

Mary's behaviors over the next two months grew increasingly bizarre and worrisome. Besides her growing delusions and hallucinations, or perhaps because of them, Mary was spending more and more money on items such as clothing, jewelry, and household goods that she neither wore nor used but kept in their original packaging.[64] Robert thought them all useless since she had no home to decorate and never wore anything but black clothing without jewelry, so he returned many of the items.[65] Then he learned that his mother was so afraid of getting robbed that she decided the safest thing was to carry all her money on her person, so she walked the streets of Chicago with $57,000 worth of government bonds in her pockets. Robert was terrified by this, afraid his mother would get injured or killed by someone trying to rob her. For this reason, in the beginning of May, he hired the Pinkerton Detective Agency to have agents follow, observe, and protect her (without her knowledge) at all times.[66] The Pinkertons were there to protect her from street thugs as well as what her son considered her unsavory Spiritualist associates. These so-called communicators with the dead were largely reviled at this time as thieves preying on gullible, weak-minded, and grieving people. Robert shared in this popular view and was worried because his mother was spending increasing amounts of time and money on these charlatans.

Robert's concern about his mother's finances was not a selfish one, although it certainly was not without self-interest.[67] He saw his mother's indefatigable need to spend money and acquire possessions (psychiatrically considered a form of monomania) as a continued symptom of her increasing insanity. As her oldest and last surviving son and as the head of the family, it was Robert's familial and social obligation to protect his mother from financial ruin, whether caused by her own actions or those of others such as thieves or Spiritualist con artists. Personally, if his mother bankrupted herself, it would be his personal duty to assist her financially, which he could not afford to do at that time. His law practice in 1875 was lucrative but not sumptuously so; he had professional bills to pay, money tied up in investments and in bonds, he had a home mortgage and a family of wife and two children and, Robert and his wife discovered in spring 1875, a third child on the way. Also, in lieu of living expenses, he could not have his mother live with him and his family—the aftermath of Tad's death in 1871 had proven that beyond a doubt.

Robert had anticipated, however, that one day his mother's sanity might finally break; after receiving her initial telegrams from Florida, he had written to his mother's cousin Elizabeth "Lizzie" Grimsley Brown to inform her of the situation and broach the possibility of her coming to Chicago to stay with Mary.[68] By May 1875, after two months observing his mother's strange behaviors, Robert "was so distressed in mind that I did not dare to trust to or act upon my own judgment."[69] He called in Mary's previous physicians Drs. Isham and Danforth and also consulted with Dr. Richard J. Patterson, proprietor of the highly respected private institution Bellevue Place Sanitarium in Batavia, Illinois, and one of the region's leading mental-health experts.[70]

Robert also sought advice from his mother's cousin (and his father's first law partner) John Todd Stuart and, as always, consulted David Davis.[71] At the suggestion of Davis, Robert also called upon Chicago attorney Leonard Swett, a friend and associate of Abraham Lincoln and one of the premier trial lawyers of the Midwest.[72] From then on, Robert made no decisions about his mother without consulting these advisers. "Whatever was done then was done not upon my own judgment alone nor by myself done but upon the most thorough consultation with and [illegible] consideration of the persons who I felt were nearest my father, to [my mother] and to me and to whom under the distressing circumstances I could and ought to trust for counsel and assistance," he later explained.[73]

Stuart, Davis, and Swett all had known Mary Lincoln for more than twenty years, and all agreed (as did cousin Lizzie Brown) that the poor widow had gone insane. After a "protracted consultation" about what should be done, Robert agreed with his advisers that his mother needed personal restraint and medical care in a sanitarium.[74] Yet, all four men knew that the proud and strong-minded Mary Lincoln would never admit of mental illness or voluntarily submit to psychiatric treatment. Robert's only recourse then, if he truly wanted his mother to receive help, was to the law.

On Swett's advice, Robert hired attorney B. F. Ayer, one of the most prominent members of the Chicago bar, who immediately held a meeting with Robert, Swett, and six physicians to determine the state of Mary Lincoln's mental health and the legal actions available to her concerned son.[75] Robert told the gathered men the entire history of his mother's bizarre behaviors. Most of the physicians present also had either treated or at least observed Mary Lincoln and shared their experiences with the group as well: Drs. Isham and Patterson could attest to their treatment of Mary since April; Drs. Johnson, Smith, and Davis all had cared for Tad during his final illness and death in 1871 and could state their observations (and any possible treatments) of Mary at that time. Only James Stewart Jewell, chair of Nervous and Mental Diseases at Chicago Medical College and one of the country's foremost experts on mental and nervous diseases, had never previously met or treated Mary Lincoln.[76]

The result of the medical counsel was the agreement that Mary Lincoln was not only insane and in need of professional medical care but also that she was in danger. Robert already feared his mother could be mugged or even murdered on the streets of Chicago for the large sums of money she carried in her pockets, but, more important, the physicians were extremely concerned over Mary's fear of and delusions concerning fire. Robert had explained how ever since the Great Fire in 1871, his mother suffered constant anxiety that buildings or entire cities were either on fire or about to be. She often pointed to nearby chimney smoke and exclaimed that the city was burning down, and in April 1875, she sent eleven trunks of possessions to Milwaukee because she was convinced Chicago was about to be consumed in flames.[77] The doctors told Robert that any person, man or woman, with such a delusion might, at any moment, suddenly leap out of a window, thinking the building to be ablaze. "They were pronounced and earnest that the time had come when her personal safety had to be assured," Robert later wrote.[78] He also explained to his friend John Hay and to his mother's close friend Sally Orne that the council of physicians told him every delay in his mother's treatment was making him "morally responsible for some very probable tragedy, which might occur at any moment."[79]

Under the Illinois state lunacy statute, a person could be involuntarily committed to medical care only after a jury trial.[80] So on May 19—four days after meeting with his advisers and physicians—Robert Lincoln filed a petition in Cook County Court to have his mother arrested and brought to trial to answer the charge of insanity.[81] Under the law, sheriff's deputies were to go to Mary's hotel and arrest her, place her in handcuffs, and bring her to court in the police wagon. Robert was going to allow this to occur until Swett convinced Robert to allow him to go to Mary's hotel himself and convey her to court in his personal carriage. This serious mistake Robert almost made would not be his last when dealing with his mother's situation.

Robert's decision to take the public step of an insanity trial in open court shows the depth of his concern over his mother's health and welfare. To eschew his ingrained sense of privacy and family decency was not an action to take lightly and was one that caused him immense pain. But he saw it to be his filial duty—as did most of society. As one newspaper opined, "There was reason to apprehend that in [Mary Lincoln's] restless, troubled state of mind she might have received personal injury, and at last, when longer delay would really be cruelty and neglect of duty, her son was compelled to the painful proceeding."[82] This belief in manly duty was typical and ubiquitous. Both Davis and Swett believed it was their duty, as friends of Abraham Lincoln, to help Robert and Mary through their time of difficulty.[83] Isaac Arnold, a friend of Abraham Lincoln and the man who defended Mary during her trial, also considered it his duty to Lincoln and to the law to act on Mary's behalf in court, even though he considered her insane.[84]

The insanity trial of Mary Todd Lincoln lasted three hours, during which time eighteen witnesses testified to her derangement. These witnesses included physicians, hotel employees, Chicago merchants, and her only son.

Robert explained his mother's mental history over the past ten years, beginning with the impact of his father's assassination. He told of his mother's fear of his illness and imminent death in March but could not explain it as he had not been sick in ten years; he told the events of her sleepless nights in the Grand Pacific Hotel and his attempts to relieve her anxiety, the stories of her delusions of fire, of her paranoia of being followed and poisoned, and robbed by a "Wandering Jew." He recounted an event detailing her increasingly paranoid and agitated state, when she tried to descend the hotel elevator half-dressed. Robert called the elevator back and sought to induce his mother to return to her room. When she refused to leave the elevator, Robert, with the help of a hotel employee, "gently forced her out," to which she screamed, "You are going to murder me!"[85]

Robert, pale and weepy-eyed, told the court he had instituted the trial "in the interest of his mother" to protect her from herself and from other people and that he "feared some harm might befall her unless she is placed under restraint." He said his mother always had been exceedingly kind to him, but he had "no doubt" that she was insane: "She has been of unsound mind since the death of father; has been irresponsible for the past ten years." He regarded her as "eccentric and unmanageable," meeting with strange people, spending lavishly on useless items, and ignoring his advice. "She has long been a source of much anxiety to me," he concluded amid unstoppable tears and after breaking down twice in the witness chair.[86]

The Chicago press and the public in general all shared in Robert's pain and humiliation. The major Chicago newspapers all stated that the former first lady's mind had been prey to a growing madness since her husband's assassination, her mental vagaries were no secret to anyone, and her final breakdown had been inevitable. "Some of the testimony was of the most startling nature, and served to show a great degree of forbearance and patience on the part of her son and her friends," and Robert "discharged his delicate and unhappy task with filial thoughtfulness," opined the *Chicago Times*.[87] The *Atlanta Constitution* declared along with numerous other newspapers that Mary Lincoln's "relatives and friends have delayed this step as long as was considered prudent, but finally agreed that nothing else would suffice."[88]

While Robert's duty made it necessary for him to legally commit his mother and even testify against her, it was also his duty to protect her and his family's reputation. This was why, in order to minimize public exposure and embarrassment, Robert allowed his lawyers to present only the barest minimum of evidence necessary to establish the case.[89] From a historical perspective, this decision leaves one wondering just how much Robert kept private and how much documentary evidence he later destroyed, as he admittedly did.[90]

One thing not said during the trial but stated in Robert's correspondence was that his mother once suggested to a lady the idea of kidnapping Robert's five-year-old daughter, Mamie.[91] Such a revelation makes clear that Mary Lincoln's mental illness went much deeper than a simple mania for shopping. It also highlights the degree to which Robert's previously intimate relationship with his mother had declined in the years after Tad's death—certainly from the self-containment of his own adult life and responsibilities, from his mother's growing irrationality, and possibly as a direct result of her feud with his wife. Mary Todd Lincoln's appalling plot was just one of many such incidents Robert had endured, symptoms of her insanity that was the result of the "shock" of his father's assassination, and that, as he had told a family friend a few years earlier, "I find an excuse for a great many things which have given me intense pain."[92]

The jury in the trial of Mary Lincoln took less than ten minutes to return with a verdict of insanity.[93] Although Illinois law assumed placement for "lunatics" in the State Hospital for the Insane, Robert had arranged to send his mother to Bellevue Place Sanitarium.[94] Mary was to be taken there the next day.

As part of the verdict, Mary was deemed incapable of controlling her property, and the court appointed Robert the conservator of his mother's estate.[95] He now had sole power to collect her income, pay her debts, and spend her money. The day of the trial, Robert filed an inventory of Mary's estate totaling $73,454.18.[96] Mary, however, was indignant at the prospect of relinquishing her property, and at first she refused to surrender her $56,000 in bonds. "And you are not satisfied with locking me up in an insane asylum, but now you are going to rob me of all I have on earth. My husband is dead, and my children are dead and these bonds I have saved for my necessities in my old age; now you are going to rob me of them," she screamed.[97]

Up to this point in her life, Mary Lincoln's actions had rarely, if ever, been violent. But because of the fear that she would jump out of a window to escape an imaginary fire, Robert hired a nurse to stay with her that night in the hotel room and had a guard posted outside her door. Mary was so angry and dejected by the verdict, however, so certain her last surviving son and the men her husband trusted above all others had robbed and betrayed her, feeling so alone and rejected by society, and now to become a prisoner in a mental hospital, that she tried to kill herself.

The next morning, she evaded her nurse and the guard outside her door and descended to the hotel drugstore to get a concoction of poison to drink. Luckily, the druggist knew about her condition and gave her a placebo; he also warned other druggists on the block not to give her any medicines and sent for Robert Lincoln. Robert and Swett soon arrived and brought Mary back to her hotel room.[98] "It is perfectly frightful to think how near she came to poisoning herself," Swett wrote David Davis.[99] John Hay, writing anonymously in a *New York Tribune* editorial, bespoke the general contemporary perception that the suicide attempt "was a terrible confirmation of the justice of the decree of the Court."[100]

Robert accompanied his mother to her new home at Bellevue Place. She had apparently submitted to her fate and was even quite "cheerful and kind" in her demeanor.[101] Robert later said her anger at him after the jury verdict "really lasted for a moment only" and that by the time of her their departure, they were on cordial terms.[102] David Davis wrote to Robert immediately after the trial, "Some good comes out of almost everything and the necessity of confining your mother in an asylum will go very far toward removing the unfavorable impressions created by her conduct since your father's death. . . . The terrible strain on you will be removed and you can go back to work."[103]

After one month of treatment at Bellevue Place, Mary Lincoln's doctor said she was one of the best, quietest patients he had ever had. There was no way Robert could have anticipated his mother's coming and virulent relapse, or known that although her trial was over, his was only just beginning.

11

"I Have Done My Duty as I Best Know"

In 1879, four years after having his mother declared insane, Robert Lincoln wrote, "If I could have foreseen my own experience in the matter, no consideration would have induced me to go through with it, the ordinary troubles and distresses of life are enough without such as that."[1] The institutionalization of his mother, in fact, not only ruptured his relationship with his mother for half a decade but also put his life in jeopardy.

Robert checked his mother into the sanitarium on May 20, 1875.[2] Bellevue Place was located in the beautiful Fox River valley in Batavia, Illinois, about a ninety-minute train ride from Chicago. The facility was established in 1867 as a retreat for the treatment of nervous and mental diseases for "a select class of lady patients of quiet unexceptionable habits" and used only the most modern method of "moral" psychiatric treatment: rest, diet, baths, fresh air, occupation, diversion, change of scene, minimal medications, and the least restraint possible.[3]

Part of the treatment included exercise on the grounds: twenty acres of secluded and manicured lawns containing numerous shady trees, flowers beds, and ornamental shrubs, all interwoven by concrete walks and driveways. The property included forty thousand square feet of greenhouses, also with wide walks, and offered carriages and sleighs for patients to use for daily outings.[4]

The main building of Bellevue Place was a three-story limestone structure built to be welcoming and spacious and decorated to give a "bright, cheerful and homelike expression" in order to "create an atmosphere of home, with its restfulness, freedom and seclusion."[5] Bellevue Place had twenty inmates during Mary Lincoln's stay; it also housed Dr. Patterson and his family, along with about a dozen attendants and nurses.[6] Mary Lincoln had her own private suite of two rooms on the second floor (including a private bath), which she shared with a personal attendant—a young former schoolteacher selected for the position "on account of her kindness and intelligence."[7]

Robert Lincoln traveled to Batavia usually every week to visit his mother. Often he brought along his five-year-old daughter, Mamie, his mother's beloved little namesake, which he knew gave the widow pleasure. Robert found his mother typically amiable but depressed on his visits. "While she will not in words admit that she is not sane, still her entire acquiescence in absolutely everything, while it arises in part from the plain enfeebled condition of her mind, makes me think that she is aware of the necessity of what has been done," he wrote in early June.[8]

The public reaction to Mary Lincoln's commitment predominantly supported Robert's actions and commiserated with the poor widow.[9] There was, of course, criticism, which Robert expected.[10] As he wrote to John Hay two weeks after the trial, "I knew that on the next day after my action the whole country would be flooded with criticisms, kind or unkind as might happen, but all based on a short press dispatch, which could not sufficiently give the facts." It would be "impossible" for anyone to understand "the distress and anxiety of my mind for the two months before that time," he added.[11]

Yet, although Robert anticipated the censure—which he found annoying and "impertinent"—he noticed a general misunderstanding of his mother's situation. In all the letters he received, there was an impression that his mother was locked in a veritable prison, "the writers using the word 'asylum,' with a notion of straightjackets, cells and brutal keepers." He and Leonard Swett both felt it necessary to correct this public misperception, and so he asked his friend Hay, an editor at the *New York Tribune*, if he would publish a clarifying article (anonymously written by Robert) in the form of a letter from the newspaper's Chicago correspondent. "It will be a 'triumph of journalism' for there isn't a lie in it," Robert wrote, showing his lifelong distrust of sensationalist reporting, "but you must not tell the personal column man so, or he wouldn't touch it with a pair of tongs."[12]

Robert's anonymous editorial explains that his action was taken only after consultation with family friends and medical experts. It describes Mary's situation as pleasant, with private rooms, friendly attendants, and personal freedom. "Such has been the influence of the quiet and pleasant surroundings that nothing whatever has occurred to render necessary anything more than a prudent supervision, and this is given by pleasant companionship, without any appearance of restraint," the editorial states. "At present her derangement exhibits itself mainly in a general feebleness and incapacity, and it is not yet possible to give an opinion as to her restoration."[13]

During Mary Lincoln's first five weeks at the sanitarium, Robert was pleased by his mother's treatment and apparent improvement. "My mother is, I think, under as good care and as happily situated as is possible under the circumstances," he wrote his mother's concerned friend Sally Orne. "She is in the private part of the house of Dr. Patterson and her associates are the members of his family only. With them she walks and drives whenever she likes and takes her meals with them or in her own rooms as she chooses, and she tells me she likes them all very much. . . . Indeed my consolation in this sad affair is in thinking that she herself is happier in every way, in her freedom from care and excitement, than she has been in ten years."[14] Orne responded, "It is a great comfort to hear from your own self, of the loving care and wise guidance which your dear Mother is under. Not that I ever had one doubt of that, for I know too much of your goodness as a son from her own lips to ever allow the first thought or suggestion to have any influence over me."[15]

Robert may have believed his mother was content, but in reality she was harboring a deep pain, humiliation, and resentment. She had told him after the trial that a breach now was between them that would never be closed and that he "was no longer her son who would thus treat the mother who bore him and loved him."[16] And while she thereafter hid her antipathy from him and from her doctor, it festered inside her until she had to let it out.

In early July, after weeks of quiet, treatment, and a self-imposed social isolation, Mary gave an interview to a Chicago reporter who wanted to update the public on the former first lady's condition and circumstances. Dr. Patterson, who believed his patient to be "quite satisfied with her surroundings," did not object. The reporter found Bellevue Place a beautiful retreat, Dr. Patterson an impressive doctor, and Mary Lincoln a poor widow with a clearly shattered mind. During the conversation, the reporter said she was acquainted with some of Mary's Chicago friends (which may have instigated her visit), after which the widow "alluded very feelingly" to her Chicago neighbors James and Myra Bradwell.[17]

The Bradwells were well-known and influential Chicagoans. James B. Bradwell was an attorney, a former county judge, and a current member of the state legislature. Myra Colby Bradwell was an abolitionist, a feminist, a women's suffragist, and the founder and editor of the *Chicago Legal News*, the most widely read legal newsletter in America. She had passed the Illinois bar exam with high honors in 1869 but had been denied a license to practice law by the Illinois bar because she was a married woman.[18] Mary Lincoln had been friends with the couple since her move to Chicago in 1865, lived on the same street, and visited them often in the days after Tad's 1871 death.[19] James Bradwell also acted occasionally as her attorney.

Mary's interview apparently made her realize that her friends still were thinking about her; and so on July 15, after a visit from Robert and Mamie, Mary suddenly told Dr. Patterson she wanted to live with her sister Elizabeth Edwards in Springfield, Illinois. On Robert's next visit two weeks later, Mary told her son the same thing. Robert was caught somewhat off-guard by his mother's statement. He had been encouraging her for years to bury the past and reconnect with her older sister, but always he was rebuffed.[20] Seeing his mother's request as a positive development, he suggested she write to Elizabeth and request a visit to her home. Robert left Batavia that day encouraged that his mother finally planned to make amends with her family. He soon learned, however, that his mother had deceived him in what turned out to be the beginning of her campaign to free herself from Bellevue Place sanitarium.

Instead of writing to her sister as she claimed, Mary Lincoln wrote to James and Myra Bradwell and asked them to come to Batavia and to bring with them friends, influential citizens, and even a journalist.[21] When the Bradwells, as well as John Franklin Farnsworth, a Civil War general, attorney, and former congressman, arrived the next day, Mary told them she was oppressed by her incarceration and wanted their help in her release. Farnsworth told Dr. Patterson, "*she does not talk like a sane woman* but still she would hardly be called insane by those who used to know her"; he suggested Mary be set free but Robert maintain control of her money and property. Myra Bradwell told Dr. Patterson that even though she believed Mary was "not quite right," she thought the widow should be allowed to "be at home and have 'tender loving care.'"[22]

The Bradwells then wrote letters to Mary's sister Elizabeth and cousin John Todd Stuart in which they claimed Mary was suffering terribly as prisoner in a horrible place where she lived "behind grates and bars." They also suggested she be allowed to visit Springfield.[23] Stuart did not respond, but Elizabeth agreed with the Bradwells' objections to Mary's commitment. She did not think her sister was sane but considered it improper to place her in a sanitarium. She thought her sister simply needed a personal attendant and companion. "The judgment of others must now, I presume, be silently acquiesced in, for a time, in the hope, that ere long, her physical and mental condition, will be improved, by rest and medical treatment," Edwards wrote.[24]

Robert learned of his mother's machinations only after Dr. Patterson showed him Elizabeth Edwards' letter to Myra Bradwell. Robert took the opportunity to explain his actions to his aunt. "There is no need of my rehearsing ten years of our domestic history. If it has caused you one tenth of the grief it has caused me, you will remember it," Robert wrote about his relationship with his mother. He considered it a "blessing" to put his mother at Bellevue, the facility and superintendent of which he described at length. Robert also criticized the interference of Myra Bradwell, saying he felt the peace and quiet of the sanitarium had improved his mother's condition. He and Dr. Patterson, however, were afraid that the Bradwells' visits and manner would "tend to undo the good that has been accomplished."[25]

"What trouble Mrs. Bradwell may give me with her interference I cannot foretell," Robert wrote his aunt. "I understand she is a high priestess in a gang of Spiritualists and from what I have heard it is to their interest that my mother should be at liberty to control herself and her property." But more than his mother's finances, he feared for her safety, saying that if she was freed, she would immediately go to Europe, "and such a thing in her present state of mind would be productive of the most disturbing events to us all." Robert reiterated that he had no objection to Mary's visit to Springfield, in fact he thought it would be beneficial, and he invited his aunt to visit Bellevue and see the place for herself, rather than rely on the word of Myra Bradwell.[26] "Rightly or wrongly I consider that I alone must assume the entire and absolute charge of her unfortunate situation and I must deal with it as my condition allows me to do. I am alone held responsible and I cannot help it. If you can and will take any part of the burden from me I will be only too glad and grateful to you for it," Robert wrote. "I have done my duty as I best know and Providence must take care of the rest."[27]

After reading Robert's letter, Elizabeth apologized to her nephew for her comments to Myra Bradwell. She also demurred at the suggestion of Mary moving into the Edwards' home. "The peculiarities of her whole life have been so marked and well understood by me, that I have not indulged the faintest hope, of a permanent cure. The painful excitement of the *past years*, only added to the malady, [which was] . . . apparent to her family for years," she wrote. "I am unwilling to urge any steps, or assume any responsibility, in her case. My present feeble health [from a recent operation], causing such nervous prostration, as would render me, a most unfit person, to control an unsound mind. I am now satisfied, that understanding her propensities, as you do, the course you have decided upon, is the surest and wisest."[28]

Robert had convinced his aunt that his actions were appropriate, but his mother's previous equanimity (as Robert and Dr. Patterson believed it to be) was diminishing rapidly. She was becoming increasingly restless and unhappy in her situation, due to the Bradwells' influence. Shortly after Myra Bradwell's first visit to Batavia, Mary lamented to her friend, "It does not appear that God is good, to have placed me here. . . . I have worshipped my son and no unpleasant word ever passed between us, yet I cannot understand why I should have been brought out here."[29] A few days later, Mary told Myra that Robert seemed coldly determined to stop her from leaving the sanitarium. "I rather think he *would* prefer *my* remaining *here* in his heart," she angrily wrote.[30]

In an attempt to resolve the situation, Robert had a "long talk" with Myra Bradwell in early August to hear her thoughts and to clarify his reasons and positions regarding his mother's situation.[31] Myra conceded that Mary was "not entirely right" but repeated her contention that Mary should not be confined to a sanitarium. Robert wryly noted in a letter to his aunt, "How completely recovered my mother really is is shown by Mrs. B's saying she was to take out to her samples of dress goods she wants to buy. She has with her *seven* trunks of clothing and there are stored here *nine* more. I told Mrs. Bradwell that the experiment of putting her entirely at liberty would be interesting to those who have no responsibility for the results. They can afterwards dismiss the matter with a shrug of the shoulders."[32]

Despite her apparently cordial conference with Robert on August 10, Myra continued to assist Mary Lincoln in her campaign for release. The two women next arranged for a long interview of Mary by Franc B. Wilkie, the principal writer for the sensationalist *Chicago Times* newspaper. The interview was conducted at the sanitarium on a day when both women knew Dr. Patterson would be out of town and Robert would not be visiting.[33]

When he learned of the devious interview, Robert was furious that Myra had brought a man to visit his mother who was not only a complete stranger to him but a journalist as well. He "characterized her introduction of Mr. Wilkie . . . as an outrage" and called Myra "a pest and a nuisance." He had Dr. Patterson bar her from visiting his mother without his approval, especially if accompanied by a stranger.[34] "I visited my mother on yesterday and I could not help observing with pain, a renewal in the degree of the same appearances which marked her in May and which I had not noticed in my last few visits," Robert subsequently wrote to his mother's friend. "I do not know of any outside cause for this unless it is the constant excitement she has been in since your first visit." His time with his mother convinced him that Myra's visits had created "a partial destruction of the good accomplished by two months and a half of quiet and freedom from all chance of excitement."[35]

Robert perceived his mother was reverting to her previous nervousness, and perhaps he even realized her growing resentment. He wrote her a tenderly worded letter explaining that her sister Elizabeth was too ill to consent to a visit, but he would try to arrange it soon, as there was nothing he thought would do her more good. "You must trust me that I can and will do everything that is for your good and you must not allow yourself to think otherwise, for in that way you will only retard the recovery I am looking for," he concluded. "Your stay with Dr. Patterson has plainly benefited you and you must not undo all that has been done."[36]

Robert completely miscalculated his mother's strength of mind and resolve here, as well as Myra's tenacity. Despite his discussions, rebukes, and limitations on their relations, the two women did not relent in their campaign. Rather, they went on the offensive, with Myra continuing to badger Dr. Patterson and writing renewed entreaties of help to Elizabeth Edwards and courting Chicago newspapers for favorable coverage of the widow's suffering and plight.

Suddenly, Dr. Patterson, who had previously doubted Mary Lincoln would ever recover her sanity, told Robert that Mary was "both mentally and physically greatly improved," and he saw no reason medically why she should not be allowed to leave Bellevue and go live with her sister in Springfield.[37] Elizabeth Edwards also had an abrupt change of heart, writing her nephew—who was at this time at Rye Beach, New Hampshire, taking his annual family vacation—that he had misunderstood her previous letters: "It may be that a refusal, to yield, to her wishes, at this crisis, will greatly increase her disorder. . . . I now say, that *if you will bring* her down, *feeling perfectly willing*, to make the experiment, I promise to do all in my power, for her comfort and recovery."[38]

On the same day that he received his aunt's capricious letter, Robert received an upsetting telegram from Dr. Patterson stating that Judge and Mrs. Bradwell spent an hour meeting privately with Mary Lincoln, and they claimed that "improper influences" were brought to bear on Elizabeth Edwards, which had caused her to previously reject her sister's plea for sanctuary. "If Mrs. E. shall change her [illegible] purpose, shall I remand the patient to her?" Patterson inquired.[39]

Finally, Robert Lincoln had had enough. He responded to Dr. Patterson with a terse telegram: "Contents of letters sent by you show that your patient must not be allowed to leave you now. Cut off absolutely all communication with improper persons. I write today to you and Mrs. Edwards."[40] Upon receiving Robert Lincoln's telegram, Dr. Patterson immediately wrote to James Bradwell and courteously informed him that at least until Robert's return in early September from New Hampshire, the Bradwells would not be allowed to visit Mary Lincoln. He said that the possibility of Mary's removal from Bellevue never should have been discussed with her, and promises should never have been made, especially by people not in control of the situation. Such conversations have put Mary's mind in a "constant ferment."[41]

Bradwell replied by saying he believed "that such confinement is injurious to her in the extreme, and calculated to drive her insane." He closed his letter with a threat: "Should you not allow her to visit Mrs. Edwards, and insist on keeping her in close confinement, and I should be satisfied that the good of Mrs. Lincoln required it, as I certainly shall unless there is change in her condition,

I, as her legal advisor and friend, will see if a habeas corpus cannot open the door of Mrs. Lincoln's prison house."[42] The private affair of Mary Lincoln's situation then became a public exhibition when the Bradwells subsequently fed stories, gave interviews, and published this letter in the Chicago newspapers. They did not attack Robert Lincoln for his actions in committing his mother, instead leveling all their accusations of false imprisonment and undue restraint at Dr. Patterson—a smart move since public sympathy was on Robert's side.

Then on August 24, Franc Wilkie published in the *Chicago Times* the account of his July interview with Mary Lincoln. The headline read, "REASON RESTORED: Mrs. Lincoln Will Soon Return from the Insane Asylum: For Her Physicians Pronounce Her Sane as Those Who Sent Her There: And She Is Only Awaiting Robert's Return from the East to Set Her Free Again." The story purported to be an independent analysis of Mary's health and that the reporter went to Bellevue Place "not as a newspaper man but as a gentleman who knew her history and took a friendly interest in all that pertained to her welfare."[43] Of course, Wilkie was invited there by Mary Lincoln and Myra Bradwell to carry out a specific agenda as a reporter to condemn the sanitarium and exonerate the beleaguered widow.

The story contained an interview with Myra Bradwell, who said that by late August she considered Mary recovered. "She is no more insane than I am," Myra declared. She also mendaciously added that Robert told her he would allow his mother's release and that Elizabeth Edwards was prepared to receive her sister into her home; all that was needed for the removal was Robert's return from New Hampshire. Myra added that she had "no reason in the world to doubt Mr. Robert Lincoln's word."[44] By thus praising him as an honorable man, she made it impossible for Robert to oppose his mother's freedom without dishonoring himself and opening the floodgates of media criticism.

When Robert Lincoln returned to Chicago on September 1, he was confronted by what he called "the extraordinary performances of the Bradwells." He had not even had time to "digest" them, however, before writing a letter to Dr. Patterson to ask the physician's opinion on the safety of moving Mary Lincoln to Springfield.[45] This was apparently an idea Robert had been considering for the entire two weeks of his vacation, as he had received his aunt's letter saying she would accept her sister as a houseguest not long after he arrived in New Hampshire. Robert's ultimate change of mind was not the result of embarrassing publicity or James Bradwell's legal threats but his belief that the quietude of Bellevue Place had been permanently destroyed. Mary was now constantly agitated by the promise of Springfield and would only continue to be agitated, even if all communication with the Bradwells was stopped. In such a state of constant ferment, her health would fail to improve and perhaps would decline. Dr. Patterson, clearly affected by the negative publicity he was receiving, ultimately told Robert, "Now that so much is said about Mrs. Lincoln's removal to Springfield, I think it would be well if she could go at once."[46]

Before making his final decision, Robert sought a second opinion on the prudence and safety of removing his mother from treatment at Bellevue Place. "As a guest of her sister, I do not think it possible that the same restraint could be exercised over possible irrational acts, should they occur as if she remained under the care of Dr. Patterson," Robert wrote Drs. Andrew McFarland and Alexander McDill, two of the Midwest's top mental-health experts, "but I am anxious that she should visit my aunt, if it is not probable that harm to her may come of it."[47]

McDill could not assist, but McFarland arrived at Batavia four days after receiving Robert's letter.[48] He found the condition of Robert's mother such as to cause him "grave apprehensions as to the result [of transfer] unless the utmost quietude is observed for the few ensuing months." McFarland did not think it wise to let Mary go to Springfield unless she was under the constant care of an attendant, but even then he saw "no good results likely to follow beyond gratifying an ardent desire to go, in which she seems to have been prompted by others. My fears are that a desire for further adventure will take possession of her mind, as soon as beyond the control of the present guardians of her safety, that may be attended with hazard if gratified."[49]

This was exactly Robert's fear as well. Yet, despite McFarland's opinion, Robert decided to allow his mother to travel to Springfield immediately—for a visit, not a relocation as his mother and the Bradwells wanted. He told Dr. Patterson to prepare his mother for the journey and allow her to bring only three trunks of possessions.[50] When Mary Lincoln arrived in Chicago on September 10, 1875—a little less than four months after her trial and commitment—Robert met her at the train station. He spent the night with her, presumably at a hotel rather than in his house, and the next morning accompanied his mother to the Edwards home in Springfield, where he had a female attendant waiting for her.[51]

While Elizabeth Edwards told Robert she thought it would be good and productive of healing for her sister to visit with family and friends in Springfield, her nephew did not expect any positive results. He often said his mother could do or say anything to achieve a desired end, and he saw in her desire for Springfield a route to escape, not socialize. "I cannot have any confidence in her sincerity in this and I do not believe that if her object was accomplished, she would receive a call from any one of her sisters. Keep this letter and see if I am not correct," he admonished.[52]

To his surprise and chagrin, he was not correct. After three days in Springfield, Mary was happy and agreeable, willing to take walks and rides, and overall "delighted" to visit friends and family. "I can truly say, that she never appeared to better advantage than she does now," Elizabeth wrote.[53] Robert's aunt also revealed exactly why, after ten years of estrangement, she accepted her sister into her home. "Insanity, although a new feature, in our family, first appeared within my knowledge, in the case of my own daughter, at the early age of thirteen," she confided.[54] In fact, psychiatric illness ran deeply in the Todd family—a revelation that may have given Robert pause.[55]

On September 20, ten days into Mary's visit, Robert requested Dr. Patterson's opinion on his mother's condition and on the safety of her permanent removal to Springfield. "I am not able to report much change," the physician wrote. "I do not hesitate to say that as a result of her intercourse with Judge and Mrs. Bradwell, she became worse; and since they have ceased their visits, she is again better and improving." As to her permanent removal to Springfield, since she had complied with all the conditions placed upon her to achieve the move, "I suppose the experiment ought to be made," Patterson said.[56] After this letter, the widow's return to Bellevue Place was postponed indefinitely.

Robert may have hoped his concession to the Springfield plan would ease his mother's aggravation, but it actually made it worse. She still was legally insane, and Robert still was her court-appointed conservator. This situation—the fact that her traitorous (she now believed) son controlled her money—infuriated Mary, constantly ate at her mind, and inflamed her bipolarity. She was cheerful, polite, affectionate, and agreeable unless and until the subject of her property came up, after which she was impatient and incensed.[57] "I am convinced, that the only alternative in this case, for the sake of peace and quietness, will be to yield your mother the right to control her possessions," Elizabeth wrote Robert in mid-November. "You will understand, that she is now pressing this matter, until the unpleasantness is such, that I am constrained to make the plea." Mary had even suggested that if returned to her, she would leave her bonds in possession of Jacob Bunn, a prominent Springfield banker, "to be undisturbed during her life."[58]

This last was Robert's main concern. He did not trust his mother's judgment in financial matters and would not allow her the "power of impoverishing herself."[59] As her son and her conservator, he was responsible for her conduct and physical and financial security. "There is no person upon whom lies the responsibility and duty of protecting her when she needs it, except myself," Robert wrote his uncle. But he agreed that he wanted "every liberty and privilege" restored to his mother as soon as it was safe to do so. "I want to do everything I can which is really for her happiness and I have no wish to interfere with her expenditures further than to ensure her having money to expend as long as she lives," Robert continued. "But if there is danger of her expending her capital and we should countlessly ignore it or imprudently contribute to it and she should impoverish herself we would be severely censured."[60]

Not simply emotional issues were involved in changing his mother's situation but financial, legal, and social issues as well. First of all, it was not even clear if Robert legally could return his mother's power of possession to her. The entire point of the conservatorship was to keep the responsibility away from those declared insane. Second, Robert had posted a bond as conservator, backed financially by two suretors for $150,000. This was insurance against his mother's estate. If the conservator spent all his ward's money, that $150,000 bond would repay the loss. Robert was concerned that if Mary regained control of her estate while he was still conservator, she could spend her entire fortune before she was legally released from the conservatorship. If that happened, Robert and his friends would be obligated to repay that bond to Mary.[61]

Not only could the widow bankrupt herself due to her mental illness but Robert knew that in her exasperation at him, she also could do it out of spite.[62] Her anger towards Robert was undeniable by this time, and what better way to make him pay for her commitment than to publicly humiliate him by bankrupting him and his friends? Third was the social issue of Robert's duty to his mother. He could not allow her to impoverish herself nor, more simply, to make a public spectacle of herself as she had done numerous times in the past. Such a spectacle would embarrass Robert, his mother, and his father's memory.

Faced, again, with a complicated and stressful situation, Robert turned once more to his advisers, David Davis, Leonard Swett, and John Todd Stuart. "You know the whole story and you can judge as well as anyone what would be the consequences to my mother of erroneous action on my part at this time," he wrote to Stuart.[63] To Davis, Robert decried the naïvety of his aunt's misunderstanding of the severity of his mother's condition. That his mother had resumed making large purchases at stores in Springfield, without any rebuke from Elizabeth Edwards, was a clear indication to him that "no radical change has taken place since last Spring but only opportunity is wanting to develop the same trouble."[64] It was his responsibility, he told Davis, to care for his mother, and he could not, as his aunt suggested, turn a blind eye to the situation.[65]

Davis agreed. "You cannot escape responsibility if you wanted to, and it would be esteemed by the world bad conduct if you should try," he advised. He recommended that Robert remove all restraints on his mother's travel and residence, return all her personal effects, and pay her the monthly income from her bonds. "If she had remained undisturbed at Batavia there might have been a chance for her recovery, but I fear the intermeddling will prove disastrous to her, as it has already added to your trouble," Davis wrote. "I think your mother would rest satisfied, if unrestrained and paid her income in monthly installments."[66]

Robert took this advice and gave his mother everything she requested of him (including eleven trunks of clothing and a box of jewelry), except the power to control her bonds.[67] But this did nothing to lessen her anger or excitability. "Your mother for the last two or three weeks has been very much embittered against you," Ninian Edwards, Elizabeth's husband, told Robert, "and the more you have yielded the more immeasurable she seems to be."[68] What concerned the Edwardses most was that Mary was giving away money and possessions that either belonged to Robert or would be part of his eventual inheritance. Both Ninian and Elizabeth were shocked by this and mentioned in separate letters they believed Robert should not be robbed of his future.[69]

This did not concern Robert. He said multiple times that he had no interest in his mother's property and assumed she had already arranged to cut him out of her will.[70] "I do not desire that any interest of mine or my children in the ultimate disposition of her property should be consulted and the only object I wish attained by any plan is her own protection," he explained.[71] Five months later, when Robert was told his mother planned to bankrupt herself to prevent her son's inheritance, he suggested that a more "sane" action would be to cut him out of her will.[72] This was further proof to Robert that his mother was not recovered and that he could not be remiss in continuing to look after her needs. "She has always been exceedingly generous to me," he told his Uncle Ninian. "I am exceedingly gratified to her for it all and shall never hesitate to acknowledge it but being grateful merely will not discharge my duty to her even if necessary against her will."[73]

By the end of the year, the subject of her bonds threw Mary into fits. "It is impossible to reason with her on the subject," the Edwardses wrote Robert. "She is much exasperated against you."[74] In all other ways, they said, she was cheerful, gregarious, social, and active, although her amount of shopping was increasing. They both repeatedly told Robert that only restoring his mother's bonds to her possession would calm her. Yet, Robert was constrained by the law, which mandated a minimum of one year for a conservatorship; and his efforts to transfer the job to someone else had failed.[75]

Then in mid-January, Robert received the news that his mother wanted to kill him.

"I am sorry to say that your mother has for the last month been very much embittered against you, and has on several occasions said that she has hired two men to take your life," Ninian warned. "On this morning we learned that she carries a pistol in her pocket. . . . She says she will never again allow you to come into her presence. We do not know what is best to be done."[76] Robert's sardonic response was to say that he was concerned "not for myself but I fear that something unforeseen may happen [to my mother]." He added in a rather

I-told-you-so manner at the Edwardses' meddling, "The doctors whom we consulted last spring were very urgent in expressing their opinion that no one could foretell the possible freaks which might take possession of my mother and that she should be placed where no catastrophe could happen."[77]

Robert saw his mother's worsening spending mania and her devolution to threats of murder as a deterioration of her condition. He also had heard from one of his Springfield friends that his mother was making large and unnecessary purchases and incurring debts with various Springfield merchants.[78] As these actions had worried Robert in March, they now worried him again as evidence of impending trouble. "I am afraid the present situation will as it did last spring move from bad to worse," he wrote. "If it would get better it would relieve me from an anxiety which is overwhelming. She was removed from the care of Dr. Patterson against my judgment as to the safety of such a step and she remains out of professional care contrary to my judgment. No catastrophe has yet occurred, but remembering what was told me by the physicians last spring, I live in continual apprehension of it."[79] Robert also suggested—indirectly to his uncle and directly to his aunt—that if his mother's condition did not improve, he may have to return her to Bellevue Place. "If your influence cannot restrain her what are we to do?" he peevishly asked.[80]

As the first anniversary of Robert's conservatorship approached, he decided not to block his removal as conservator and his mother's reinstatement to control her own estate. His entire reason for instituting the 1875 trial—medical treatment for his mother—had been thwarted and made innocuous, and her continued status as a conservatee only proved to worsen her condition. To allow his mother her freedom was the only way to appease her—and the only way to extricate himself from the onus of his responsibility and her antipathy. Robert's mentor Davis supported the plan. "I have after mature reflection come to the conclusion that it is better for your happiness to give a free consent to the removal of all restraint on her person or property and trust to the chances of time," Davis advised.[81]

On June 15, 1876, at 2 P.M. in an unpublicized hearing, Robert Lincoln, as his mother's conservator, Leonard Swett as Robert's attorney, and Ninian Edwards as a witness on his sister-in-law's behalf attended a hearing to decide Mary Lincoln's fitness to control her property. This was not a trial to declare her sane; it was a hearing to remove her conservator and to restore her rights and property. As was typical of Robert's private nature, he asked the judge and court clerk—and his Uncle Ninian—to keep the hearing a secret to prevent "a large crowd of loafers [who] would be on hand expecting some sensation."[82]

The hearing actually took less time than the empanelling of the twelve-member jury. Swett offered a statement, Edwards read statements from Mary

Lincoln and from himself, and Robert "waived process," which allowed for his immediate discharge as conservator rather than imposing the usual ten-day wait.[83] The jury declared Mary Lincoln "restored to reason and . . . capable to manage and control her own estate."[84] Robert presented to the court his official accounting of his mother's estate, which totaled $81,390.35 in cash, stocks and bonds, and personal possessions—an increase of nearly $8,000 under his stewardship.[85]

The next morning, Robert went to Springfield to personally return his mother's bonds to her. He found no welcome from the woman he had tried to honor and protect, only anger. He was accosted and accused by this small woman still in widow's weeds with bringing false charges against her in order to steal her money, with causing her broken heart and her gray hair by his traitorous conduct, and with creating his own heavenly rejection and exile from the rest of the family—especially his sainted father.[86]

Three days later, Robert received a vicious, hurtful letter in which his mother denounced him as a treacherous thief and demanded return of all her property in his possession, specifically enumerating laces, jewelry, engravings, and books.

> I am now in constant receipt of letters, from my friends denouncing you in the bitterest terms, six letters from prominent, *respectable*, Chicago people such as you do not associate with. . . . Two prominent clergy men, have written me, since I saw you—and mention in their letters, that they think it advisable to offer up prayers for you in Church, on account of your wickedness against me and High Heaven. In reference to Chicago you have the enemies, and I chance to have the friends there. Send me all I have written for, you have tried your game of robbery long enough. On yesterday, I received two telegrams from prominent Eastern lawyers. You have injured yourself, not me, by your wicked conduct.[87]

For weeks after that, mother and son fought a war of words and accusations, using Ninian Edwards and Leonard Swett as proxies. The subject, still, was Mary's property. Her bonds had been returned to her, but she was demanding the return of everything she considered her property in Robert's house—this included every present she ever gave Robert and his wife, which Mary was now claiming they had stolen from her. She also declared she would take him to court and publicly ruin him.

Robert was wounded deeply by his mother's accusations, but after more than one year of tolerating her accusations, schemes, and irrationalities, his forbearance was at an end. He showed her letters to Swett, and the two decided that Robert would not comply.[88] The items she demanded did not belong to her, they belonged to Robert, Swett told Ninian Edwards.

> While of course, owing to her condition of mind, this unkindness is to be forgiven and forgotten, the fear of being misunderstood by strangers has induced Robert—and I think wisely—in reference to the things referred to in your letters, not to return them, demanded as a matter of right, accompanied with the assertion that they were obtained improperly. Therefore if Mrs. Lincoln shall desire these things under the terms named in my first letter, she must ask for them, recognizing the fact that they were given to her children, and that they are rightly in their possession.[89]

Swett also added a personal note indicating the depth of his own anger over Mary's threats against her son after all Robert had done and sacrificed for her. If Mary tried to sue and ruin Robert, as she threatened, "I shall, as a citizen, irrespective of Robert, or any one, . . . have her confined as an insane person, whatever may be the clamor or consequences," Swett concluded.[90] His threat worked, for Mary promised that she would "neither bring suit against Robert nor make any attacks on him."[91] She also, however, refused to speak to him.

Four months later, Robert Lincoln learned that his mother had left Springfield and gone to Europe—the exact action he had feared she would do if released from Bellevue Place sanitarium. Mary's "resentful nature" made it necessary for her to "place an ocean" between herself and her son, Elizabeth Edwards told her nephew four weeks after his mother had sailed from New York.[92] The trip was concealed from the newspapers in order to keep it secret from Robert, whom Mary believed would stop her and try to commit her again.[93] It would be four years before Mary returned to America and five years before Robert saw or spoke to his mother again.

The entire affair had not only caused Robert Lincoln immense stress and anxiety but also vast amounts of emotional pain. Over the ensuing years, he wrote how he would forgive his mother and think nothing of the past, but she refused to speak to him.[94] He even answered one query asking for her address by saying she was "somewhere in Europe," but he did not know where because she would not speak to him.[95] Robert was heartbroken and also frustrated. One small consolation, however, was that his mother continued to send presents to Mamie, her little namesake, despite the rift with her son. This gave Robert a hope that one day his mother's animosity towards him would end. "I am very anxious that it should," he told his Aunt Elizabeth. "Its existence has been very distressing to me."[96]

In the maelstrom of life, events—significant or otherwise—do not typically occur singularly, or linearly, or predictably. While the thirty-two-year-old Robert was dealing with his mother's institutionalization in 1875, as well as with all the events concerning her in the years preceding and succeeding it, he still was a husband, father, attorney, businessman, and active Chicago citizen.

Robert's family finished growing with the birth of daughter Jessie in November 1875. She, two-year-old Jack, and six-year-old Mamie were the next generation of Lincolns and were, as Robert once whimsically wrote, "of 'assorted sizes' as the merchants say, all hearty and well."[97] The Lincolns adored their children, but Mary may have doted on them. Robert once complained to a friend that his wife "gives too much care to her babies," for which he often chided her.[98] Mary liked to bring the children to Mount Pleasant to visit her parents as much as possible, especially in the summers, and to play in the clean Iowa air, and she and the children also spent much time with the Harlans in Colorado Springs, Colorado, due to health reasons. Both Mary Harlan Lincoln and her mother were constantly sickly (they were called "invalids" at the time because of their frail health, regardless of the degree of illness) and frequently in need of care and healthy climates.

Robert understood and encouraged his wife's travel with the children. He hired a nurse to accompany them, and it was typical nineteenth-century American lifestyle that the wife cared for the children while the husband made a living. Robert spent his bachelor time at the law office and socializing over cigars and billiards. His personal letters often included information, stories, and vignettes about his children, such as in 1870 when he told his friend Edgar Welles that six-month-old Mamie "gets fuller and fatter every day and is immeasurably proud of her one tooth which stands solitary and proud like a lonely sentinel in the Mammoth Cave."[99] Robert was immensely proud of Jack, who was extremely precocious and would eventually endear himself to the entire country. Jessie, the youngest, was the wild child of the three and as she grew older caused quite a bit of family drama.

Robert, not only a father, was also a son and constantly involved in his father's legacy. In April 1874, he had purchased his mother's half share of the old Lincoln Homestead in Springfield at the corner of Eighth and Jackson Streets for $500, making him the sole owner. He owned, rented, preserved, and allowed public tours of the house for the next thirteen years, and it gave him more than a few headaches.[100] Later that same year, Robert was present and spoke at the unveiling of the Lincoln monument at his father's tomb in Springfield.[101] The last Lincoln son rarely spoke publicly about his father or attended events in honor of his father, but in addition to the tomb dedication, he also read the Emancipation Proclamation at a Fourth of July celebration in Aurora, Illinois, in 1871.[102] A few years later, however, Robert refused invitations to speak on the private lecture circuit, saying, "I have always studiously endeavored to avoid even the appearance of turning to profit my relationship to my father and have always declined invitations to lecture which I felt assured were given me for no merit of my own."[103]

As a lawyer, Robert and his firm of Isham & Lincoln were flourishing just as well as his family. As one member of his law firm later wrote, Robert "was a studious and able lawyer" and "devoted himself actively and prodigiously to the practice of the law."[104] He was nationally lauded in 1871 for having a reputation as "an excellent manager, a shrewd and capable lawyer, and systematic man of business."[105] He became acquainted with such of Chicago's legal luminaries as Mark Skinner, future U.S. Supreme Court Associate Justice John Marshall Harlan, and future Chief Justice Melville Weston Fuller, among others, all of whom held him in high regard. Justice Harlan once said, "Robert Lincoln argued a case more clearly and had more promise of the future than any man in his circuit."[106]

Robert also impressed people with his resolve to be his own man. "No man ever made a more determined effort to avoid the use of a name as capital than did he, and no lawyer ever worked more conscientiously along the slow way to sure success," wrote one journalist.[107] Of course, comparisons to his father were inevitable, and in Robert people found an inherited honesty, decency, and sincerity in all he did. As one colleague recalled:

> He inspires one immediately with perfect faith in his uprightness and honesty. The result of this is seen in the perfect confidence placed in him by his clients, and also in the great consideration and weight given to his statements by the courts. He is not only scrupulously accurate and just in all his doings and statements, but his whole moral sense is so keen that the slightest irregularity on the part of others meets with the severest condemnation. I remember on one occasion he had concluded a foreclosure suit, and the time for redemption had expired. It transpired that the mortgagor, when about to lose possession of his property, had leased portions of it to various tenants, and by liberal discounts had induced them to pay rent for several months in advance. The poor victims, when notified by the mortgagee that they should pay their rents to him, came with their stories, and by him were referred to Mr. Lincoln. As the third or fourth man came to make his complaint, Mr. Lincoln grew actually livid with rage, and stormed about the office as if he himself were the subject of the outrageous swindle.
>
> These qualities win the respect of everyone who knows Mr. Lincoln; and the cordial and gracious manner with which he meets all who have occasion to address him make him personally popular.[108]

The son was similar to the father not just in his morality and legal ability but also in his great wit. A story from the trial of Arthur W. Windett illustrates both. Windett apparently was a man who was hopelessly insolvent but full of grand schemes and boisterous talk; he was ultimately sued for failure to repay numerous loans. While the defendant was on the stand, Robert addressed him during the cross-examination with the accent on the first syllable of the man's last name. Windett corrected him, saying, "Mr. Windét, if you please sir, Mr. Windét," accenting the last syllable. Lincoln replied very quietly, "I beg your pardon sir; but I think that I am to be excused for not knowing whether to associate more of wind or debt with you."[109] Isham & Lincoln grew steadily, taking cases out of state and then out of the country. They argued cases in local, state, and federal courts and eventually worked for such corporate clients as Pullman Car Company and Commonwealth Edison Company.

Robert Lincoln was not just a lawyer; he was also a businessman. Like most men of his time, location, and stature, he sought to add to his income through land and property speculation. His father had done this on a limited basis, and Robert's mentor David Davis amassed a fortune through his own investing. Robert's letters in the 1860s and 1870s show that he had many ideas and opportunities, some of which came to fruition and some that did not. In December 1868, he had asked his mother for a loan worth more than $50,000 to invest in a plan to build twenty-eight houses on the north side of Chicago; six years later, he paid his mother $100 for a forty-acre plot of Iowa land, originally owned by Abraham Lincoln, which he then sold in February 1875 for $500.[110] In early 1872, Robert joined a group of Chicago businessmen to incorporate the Western Land Improvement Company. The purpose of the company was to "improve, settle, and colonize lands in the Territories of the United States, and especially to open up and develop the resources thereof by the construction of rail, wagon and other roads and telegraph lines in connection therewith; to purchase, sell and mortgage any lands in said Territories." The company also would have the right-of-way through public lands in order to improve the land two hundred feet on each side of the railroad tracks to be granted for such purpose. A bill to allow the creation if this company was introduced in the Illinois state senate in April 1872 but apparently came to nothing.[111]

Robert certainly knew his business when buying and selling property and took it seriously. In 1870, he and his close friend Edgar Welles discussed forming a partnership in land and property speculation, in which Robert stated he would "make it a rule not to loan on any but good City property at not more than half its cash value." The real-estate demand was so high at the time that Robert said they could ignore any applications they received that seemed undesirable. His reputation must have been solid, for he also told Edgar to inform prospective clients that "I shall attend personally to seeing that the record of the month is correct and during the continuance of the loan that all taxes are paid and insurance kept up."[112] If this joint venture ever came to fruition, it must have been short-lived, as no further records of such a partnership have been found.

In spring 1872, Robert owned eight adjoining lots on Holt Street in Chicago and sold them just before he left for his summer trip to Europe. When offered the opportunity to buy one lot back in 1873, Robert scoffed at the high price of $250, stating he would not make such a purchase unless he could make some sort of profit from it. "There is no earthly reason why I should turn a business matter into a charity," he wrote and offered $100 instead.[113] He also was not above playing hardball when his clients failed to pay, threatening to send the police to arrest one man until he came to Robert's office to sign a lease and pay the rent as he promised and rebuking another that his late payments forced Robert to advance money himself, which he could not regularly afford to do.[114]

Robert worked hard, but at this time he was in no way the wealthy man he would later become, and the financial Panic of 1873—which turned into a depression and lasted until 1878—affected him as it did the rest of the country. (Robert, in fact, contributed to the Panic and ultimate depression by being one of the myriad speculators throughout America whose exuberant actions contributed to banking failures, which led to a stock-market crash, railroad and then small business failures, and ultimately mass unemployment.) In May 1874, Robert admitted he was "a little hard up just now" for money and added that "real estate is exceedingly dull here at this time and it is a great risk to touch anything with our enormous taxes."[115] At the end of 1876, he requested an advance payment from the mortgagee of his land in Lincoln, Illinois; in mid-1877, he arranged for a new home loan for $6,000 with the bond signed by his father-in-law; by late 1878, he was in debt at least $10,000.[116]

Like his senior law partner, and perhaps due in part to his influence, Robert also had an active cultural and social life. In May 1873, Robert was a general manager for a Grand Jubilee Ball at the Pacific Hotel, done to commemorate the rebuilding of Chicago after the Great Fire.[117] Robert also belonged to a number of social organizations in Chicago. His first was as a founding member in 1869 of the Chicago Club, and he and his friends ate lunch and transacted business there every day at noon for years. Robert's regular luncheon group consisted of him, his law partner, Edward Isham, and friends Norman Williams and Henry W. Bishop. In later years, their group came to be called "the millionaire's table," not because Robert and his friends were rich but because later members included millionaires George Pullman, Marshall Field, and John Crerar.[118] Robert also was a founding member of the Chicago Bar Association in 1874, joined the Chicago Literary Club in 1876 (the club acquired the reputation of being the most exclusive and difficult to access of any in the city), served as vice president of the Chicago Historical Society in 1876 and 1877, was a member of the Chicago Commercial Club, and was a trustee (but not a member) of the Second Presbyterian Church from 1879 to 1889.[119]

Perhaps Robert's social prominence is best shown in that he was included with various soldiers, statesmen, lawyers, preachers, and journalists in an 1879 newspaper feature article concerning "a subject of great importance to mankind . . . feet." Robert T. Lincoln was listed as having a pair of the "Best-Known Chicago Feet," along with such men as his mentor David Davis, his friend and attorney Leonard Swett, and Civil War General Philip Sheridan. It was written that "Bob" Lincoln wore a lace shoe, size 9½, and not too tight—and there was even a drawing of Robert's foot (along with twenty-seven other feet) copied from the records of haberdasher Richard Melcher & Company.[120] Whether Robert and the other subjects of the story gave permission to reproduce their podiatric drawings is unknown, but such a story certainly could not have changed in any way Robert Lincoln's disdain of the press and belief in its utter vacuity.

As Robert's prominence grew, his name more often was mentioned for numerous political possibilities. He was an ardent Republican who was knowledgeable on all the issues and political scuttlebutt of the day. He often discussed politics in letters to friends, who was running for office, and how public affairs would impact citizens. Robert had supported Ulysses S. Grant for president in 1868 and 1872, but by 1874, he was "not interested" in giving Grant a third term in the White House, as many Republicans were. He was, however, afraid of Democrats who were "virulent non-fighting rebels" during the Civil War. "You and I will yet pay taxes to compensate for the loss of slaves, I am afraid," he wrote Gideon Welles. "If the effect of the [1874 midterm congressional] elections shall be to divorce the Republican party from Grant and make a more patriotic Union man President in '76 then will none rejoice more than I."[121]

The party ultimately found its man in Ohio Governor Rutherford B. Hayes. Robert, for the first time, took an active part in the campaign, speaking across the Midwest in support of the Republican ticket. His public political emergence was followed with praise and excitement by the press. His first speech of the campaign was given in September in Indiana. It was reported as being given "with the tremor of a novice," but "in the grasping of great issues and plain force in argument, [he] showed himself a chip off the old block."[122] Democrats were nervous about Robert's sudden activism and even planted stories that Honest Abe's son supported Democrat presidential candidate Samuel Tilden.[123] Despite his zeal for public affairs, Robert had absolutely no interest in running for political office or seeking political appointments. When his friend John Hay suggested in 1874 that he accept appointment to a diplomatic post, Lincoln quickly demurred.[124] Choices that were more difficult came his way, however, which led him in 1876 to accept a local political appointment while declining a national appointment in 1877.

In the midst of these, however, in fact on the very night of the 1876 presidential election, November 6, another momentous event in Robert's life would take place and overshadow them all. An event more dastardly than Robert ever could have imagined, one hardly to be believed, and one in which he would be intricately involved—the attempt by a small and desperate group of criminals to steal the body of Abraham Lincoln from its Springfield tomb.

12

"I Could Have Stopped This Scheme with Little Trouble"

By late October 1876, thirty-three-year-old Robert Lincoln's life was returning to normal after an eventful and not entirely pleasant year. His travails with his mother had recently ended, and she had only weeks before sailed for Europe; his twenty-four-year-old brother-in-law, Willie Harlan, had died, and the Lincoln family had traveled to Mount Pleasant for the funeral (Mary and the children stayed for two weeks); Robert had only days before finished campaigning for the Republican presidential candidate, Rutherford B. Hayes, in the upcoming national elections; and with the birth of his third child, Jessie, in November 1875, his wife was preparing for the girl's approaching first birthday.

A strange incident had occurred that summer as well. Robert heard that a group of men in Lincoln, Illinois, supposedly planned to steal his father's body from the Lincoln tomb on the night of July 4, hide the casket underwater in the Sangamon River, and demand a ransom for its return. As rumors of the plot began to circulate around Logan and Sangamon Counties, Springfield Police Chief Abner Wilkinson informed the Lincoln Monument Association of the possible threat, urged them to place guards at the tomb, and then began an official investigation. The plotters quickly abandoned the area and the scheme.[1]

The rumors caused little excitement at the time, seeming too depraved and bizarre to be true. The local and regional newspapers ignored the story. Even members of the Lincoln Monument Association—the men tasked to preserve and protect the Lincoln tomb—did not believe it and so did nothing for added security. Robert Lincoln, however, when he found out about it, had no time to worry or take action, if he even believed it. It was more than one month before a Chicago newspaper stated the Logan County Plot—as it has come to be called—was "quietly followed up" but was "possibly a sensation."[2]

Nearly four months later, on the morning of October 27, a U.S. Secret Service agent visited Robert Lincoln at his Chicago law office. The agent, a thickset, square-jawed, steely-eyed Irishman, introduced himself as Chief Operative Captain Patrick D. Tyrrell and said he had uncovered a verified plot by a gang of counterfeiters to steal the remains of Abraham Lincoln from the Springfield tomb and hold it for ransom. He was there not only to inform Robert of the discovery but also to ask his permission to let the plot proceed so he could catch the crooks red-handed. Robert was incredulous. "It's impossible," he supposedly told Tyrrell. "I simply can't believe such a vile plot could come from the mind of a man, no matter how vicious."[3]

Body snatching, however, certainly was not a new idea in 1876. Grave robbers, or, as they were called in the nineteenth century, ghouls or resurrectionists, commonly prowled America's graveyards in search of the freshest bodies. Typically, the corpses were taken to the nearest medical school and sold as cadavers for experiment and dissection, but sometimes the ghouls were out for robbery. The practice was so prevalent, in fact, that families of the dead often kept vigilant watch in the graveyard for days until the body was old enough to be out of danger.[4] One of the most sensational grave-robbing cases in nineteenth-century America occurred in 1830 when a fired gardener at George Washington's home, Mount Vernon, tried to steal the first president's skull but ended up with the bones of a distant relative instead.[5]

The Lincoln tomb plot was nothing so simple or pedestrian, Tyrrell explained.

During the Civil War, the rise of a national paper currency, commonly called greenbacks, led to a simultaneous rise in counterfeiting. By 1865, the problem was so pervasive and injurious to the Union war effort that Treasury Secretary Hugh McCullough, with the assent of President Lincoln, created the U.S. Secret Service, whose sole job was to find and arrest counterfeiters. The irrepressible William P. Wood was appointed the Service's first chief, and within one year more than two hundred counterfeiters had been arrested and sent to prison.[6] Although the new effort certainly hindered the counterfeiting business, it did not stop it; by the early 1870s, fake money was again flourishing. It was estimated that half of all national paper currency in the Midwest was phony.

In the world of counterfeiting, the general term for criminals who dealt in counterfeit money, or coney, was *coney men* or *coniackers*. This criminal enterprise had multiple levels of involvement, sometimes performed by one individual but usually done by a gang. "Engravers" cut the counterfeit plates and sold them to "dealers" who used the plates to print the fake money. The dealers used shovers to disseminate the phony bills. By the 1870s, the market price for good quality coney was seventeen cents on the dollar.[7]

While counterfeiting had a certain separation between eastern and western coniackers, the operations were not necessarily independent. "The connections between East and West crossed and interlaced, until they formed a figurative freemasonry of counterfeiting, reaching from ocean to ocean and from Canada to the Gulf," Tyrrell explained.[8] It was this interconnectedness that prompted current Secret Service Chief Elmer Washburn to attempt to "break the back" of counterfeiting in the spring of 1875 by focusing agency efforts on the two most important coney men in America: Benjamin Boyd and Nelson Driggs. Boyd was the most expert engraver of counterfeit plates in the United States, and Driggs was the most extensive dealer in counterfeit money. The two were believed to be at that time working together in the Midwest. Tyrrell conducted the operation out of the Secret Service's Midwest headquarters in Chicago.

Tyrrell was one of the service's most outstanding operatives and later in his career would be considered one of the most distinguished law-enforcement officers in the country. He was born in Dublin, Ireland, in 1835 but at age three moved with his family to America. He grew up in Buffalo, New York, and as a young man worked as a carpenter and shipwright. In 1856, he became a police officer in Dunkirk, New York; one year later, he became a detective for the Erie Railroad, then returned the next year to the Dunkirk police force as deputy sheriff. In 1869, Tyrrell made his way to Chicago, where he worked for a time as a private detective until he joined the city police force and was quickly made a detective by then Police Chief Elmer Washburn.

As a police detective, Tyrrell established himself as one of the department's top men. He began by solving the mysterious Winnetka murder case that had stymied the other detectives; he then solved a bond robbery case and broke up a gang of burglars who had been robbing freight cars. When Washburn was appointed chief of the U.S. Secret Service in 1874, he brought Tyrrell with him and made the Irishman head of the Chicago regional office. There, Tyrrell again distinguished himself as a top operative by shutting down and arresting numerous counterfeiters and gangs, operations large and small.[9]

The Boyd-Driggs case began in February 1875 when Washburn traveled to Chicago to give Tyrrell the assignment. "If you can get them dead to rights you will break the backbone of counterfeiting in American," Washburn said.

"Are they as important as that?" Tyrrell asked.

"Yes," answered the chief, "they are the most important coney men in existence today."[10]

The service had by then expended $5,000 in trying to locate the men but still knew nothing about the criminals but their names and various aliases. Tyrrell decided to stake out the town of Nauvoo, Illinois, a known counterfeiting hub. He eventually discovered that Driggs visited the town to court a local woman. Months of patient and careful surveillance of Driggs eventually disclosed the location of Ben Boyd and the identification of two other men and four women in the gang. On the morning of October 21, 1875, Tyrrell and his men arrested Boyd and his wife at their home in Fulton, Illinois; Washburn and his men were immediately telegraphed and moved to arrest Driggs, his wife, and four other accomplices at a house in Centralia, Illinois. The arrests also netted the gang's printing presses, ink, paper, seventeen sets of plates, and more than $130,000 in counterfeit money. It was the most important counterfeiting arrest the Secret Service had made in years. Boyd was tried and sentenced to ten years in in the Joliet, Illinois, penitentiary, while Driggs received fifteen years.[11]

Robert Lincoln certainly had read the Chicago newspaper reports.

The incarceration of the Boyd-Driggs gang in early 1876—especially of America's top coney engraver Boyd—crippled counterfeiting in America, especially in Illinois, as Washburn predicted.[12] Never again would so much coney be circulating throughout the Midwest. Regional counterfeiters, in fact, were so hobbled in their operations with the loss of Boyd they were desperate to find a solution. There then began "a series of conferences of the coniackers in Chicago, St. Louis, and Lincoln [Illinois] at which was discussed the prospective serious effect on the counterfeiting business of the locking up of its best plate cutter," Tyrrell related.[13] These three cities were the main gathering places—and the road between them the main artery—for Illinois/Midwest counterfeiting. The Hub saloon at 294 West Madison Street in Chicago, owned by known coney men James B. "Big Jim" Kinnely and Terrence Mullen, was the general Chicago rendezvous for counterfeiters in the Central West; a similar saloon in St. Louis owned by Fred Biebush, one of the most extensive coney dealers in the world, was the southern headquarters. The halfway station between these two points was a saloon in Lincoln, Illinois, kept by Robert Splane and used as headquarters for a band of counterfeiters in and around Lincoln. The men in these cities were all associated with each other, as well as with Boyd and Driggs, and their businesses were interlaced.

Kinnely, in particular, was one of the top men in the region; he once lived in St. Louis but moved to Chicago in 1875. His legitimate occupation was as a horse dealer, but he was known to the Secret Service as a central figure in Midwestern counterfeiting. He had been arrested in 1865 for passing fake notes in St. Louis, but after that he was more of a dealer than a passer. Kinnely (also spelled Kineally and Kennally) certainly had the air of the man he was: a mastermind behind criminal operations. He stood nearly six feet tall, had a long mustache and full beard, a ruddy face, and a missing front upper tooth. A slight brogue betrayed his Irish lineage. He dressed well, walked purposefully, and spoke emphatically, often gesticulating with one hand while the other was in his pants pocket; he was likely to finish up a sentence by saying, "by the eternal Jesus." He never crossed a street or turned a corner without looking back over his shoulder and frequently would stop and look all around. "He has the appearance of a live, wide awake businessman, of the ever ready sort, never astonished at anything that takes place."[14]

Kinnely realized that breaking Boyd out of prison was impossible but also that Lincoln's body was a national treasure. So in March 1875, he hatched the Logan County plan to steal the body of Abraham Lincoln and trade its return for Boyd's release and payment of $200,000. He may have found inspiration for his plan from a supposed 1867 plot to steal Lincoln's body by a Springfield lawyer.[15] When members of the gang investigated Lincoln's tomb in spring 1875, they found it shockingly vulnerable: the casket was above ground, encased in a marble sarcophagus in the middle of the burial chamber, protected only by a gate with a single padlock, and no guard or night watchman. After the plot was discovered, Kinnely did not give up the idea; he simply changed his location and his crew.

He traveled to his saloon, the Hub, in Chicago to plan a second attempt. There he recruited Mullen and Jack Hughes into the plot. Mullen was the proprietor of the Hub. In 1876, he was about twenty-seven years old, had black hair, dark gray eyes, and a black mustache and beard. He was described as "always looking about, has that peculiar indescribably notion of the eyes which takes in everything at a glance, often seen in convicts."[16] Hughes was also part of the Midwest counterfeiting gang and had been arrested in 1870 in Philadelphia for passing counterfeit coins.[17] In fact, he had been indicted for counterfeiting in 1874 and was on the run from the Secret Service.

Mullen and Hughes decided they could succeed in stealing Lincoln's body where the intemperate and garrulous Logan County gang had failed. They kept generally to the previous plan with the same amount for the ransom: the release of Ben Boyd from Joliet Prison and $200,000. They decided to steal the body the night of November 7, presidential election night, knowing the entire town of Springfield would be in the city square anxiously awaiting the returns. It was "a damned elegant time to do it," the counterfeiters believed. They also decided that instead of sinking the coffin in a river, they would cart it to Indiana and bury it in the sand dunes where the shifting sand would erase all traces, and only their own map would lead to its recovery.[18]

Kinnely would not be actively participating in the robbery, so Mullen and Hughes agreed they needed a third man with them. They brought in Louis C. Swegles, a known criminal and horse thief and frequenter of the Hub. Swegles convinced the duo that he was the man for the job, calling himself "the boss body snatcher of Chicago" and evincing a knowledge of the grave-robbing business. He soon learned all their plans and was appointed to secure the driver and wagon that would transport the coffin to Indiana.

What Mullen and Hughes did not know was that in addition to being a criminal, Swegles also was a "roper"—an informant for the Secret Service—and had been sent to the Hub by Captain Tyrrell to infiltrate the counterfeiting gang. Tyrrell had no idea of the Lincoln tomb plot, but he did know the gang was desperately searching for a plan to spring Boyd. He had traced his fugitive Hughes to the Hub and wanted to catch the band in the act and arrest them all. Instead of the gang's latest counterfeiting plan, Swegles had uncovered the body-snatching plot.

The day Swegles learned of the counterfeiters' scheme, he left the Hub to inform Tyrrell, but the captain was not in Chicago. Instead, Swegles told an attorney he knew, C. W. Dean, of the robbery plans in general (he saved the particulars for Tyrrell). Dean then told his friend Leonard Swett, who informed Robert Lincoln.

When Tyrrell learned of the scheme from Swegles the next day (and from a second roper he had operating at the Hub, James K. McClaughrey),[19] he immediately requested from his superiors to be allowed to act against the attempt even though it was technically not within Secret Service jurisdiction. Such a "damnable act" was of "national importance," he fumed, and would be a "national disgrace" if allowed to succeed.[20] Tyrrell then went to see Robert Lincoln.

When Tyrrell arrived at Robert Lincoln's law office on the morning of October 27, Robert already had decided he would be intricately involved in protecting his father's remains.[21] He also had arranged that Leonard Swett be his adviser in the matter and authorized him to act in his name, if necessary, during the affair. Robert previously had praised Swett for his "earnestness, tact and resources" in dealing with Mary Lincoln's institutionalization and its aftermath over the previous year, and when once again faced with a major situation having not only personal but national implications, Robert was in need of those same qualities again.[22]

That morning, Tyrrell had a "long conversation" with Robert and Swett (who was with Robert when Tyrrell arrived) and laid out the entire body-snatching plot in intimate detail. He asked that instead of preemptively (and most likely only temporarily) scaring the criminals off their plans, such as in the Logan County plot, Robert allow the scheme to move forward. The Secret Service then could catch the ghouls in the act and send them to prison for the robbery. Robert was hesitant at first, unwilling to risk damage to the tomb or the bodies it contained, but feeling indebted to Tyrrell for uncovering the plot and encouraged by Leonard Swett that only stopping the theft in the act would assure his father's safety, he agreed. He attached the conditions that his father's body in no way be allowed to be removed from the tomb or desecrated by the robbers and that the government assume full responsibility for both the task and the cost of the criminals' convictions. Robert and Swett then telegraphed John Todd Stuart, president of the Lincoln Monument Association, and informed him of everything.[23]

With permission to proceed obtained from both Robert Lincoln and the Secret Service chief, Tyrrell instructed Swegles to continue participating in the plot and inform him of every development. Tyrrell told Robert Lincoln on the morning of November 6 that the robbery was set to take place the next night. They arranged to meet again later that afternoon. On his return, Tyrrell brought his former chief Washburn (who only recently had been replaced as head of the Secret Service) and met with Robert and Robert's law partner Edward Swift Isham. Robert assured Tyrrell of his support and assistance and requested that Washburn be a part of the Springfield operation, to which Tyrrell gladly agreed.

Tyrrell knew he needed more men, however, but had no time to request additional Secret Service agents from another city. Robert suggested and arranged for him to borrow two agents from the Pinkerton Detective Agency, a company with which Robert had a long history and a good relationship.[24] He then telegraphed John Todd Stuart in Springfield and asked him to meet Tyrrell at the train station and to assist and coordinate in the Secret Service sting operation at the tomb.

That night, Monday, November 6, after spending much of the day assisting in Tyrrell's program, Robert Lincoln met the captain at the Chicago train station to finalize plans before the group of lawmen departed for Springfield.[25] Filled with anxiety, he watched the train leave for his old hometown.

Tyrrell called November 7 "one of the most unfortunate nights I have ever experienced," and after learning the events that transpired at the Lincoln Tomb, Robert Lincoln easily could understand why.[26] That morning, Tyrrell met both with Stuart and Lincoln Tomb custodian John Carroll Power. Tyrrell toured the monument structure and the grounds with Power and instructed the custodian not to betray any knowledge of the plot when the robbers came to ask questions and inspect the tomb themselves, which they did at about 3 P.M. The crooks verified then, as the Logan County gang had discovered in July, the tomb had no night guard and only one padlock for protection.

At 7 P.M., one hour after sunset, Tyrrell, Secret Service Agent John McDonald, Washburn, journalist John English (Washburn's former private secretary),

Pinkerton agents John McGinn and George Hay, and tomb custodian Power hid themselves inside Memorial Hall at the front (south end) of the tomb. Lincoln's crypt was at the back (north end) of the tomb about 150 feet away, where Mullen, Hughes, and Swegles arrived at around 9 P.M. The three robbers sawed off the padlock and broke open the marble sarcophagus, but they could not remove Lincoln's lead-lined coffin from the sarcophagus because the coffin's five-hundred-pound weight was too heavy. Mullen, figuring all four conspirators could lift the coffin out, sent Swegles out to fetch the wagon and driver (neither of which existed, being a fiction Swegles told his co-conspirators). Swegles used this opportunity to run to Memorial Hall and whisper the password, "WASH," through the door as the signal for Tyrrell and his men to spring their trap.

The officers had all removed their shoes during their three-hour wait in Memorial Hall, afraid the clicking of their heels on the marble would reveal their presence. As they cautiously moved out the door and around the side of the tomb toward the rear, every man drew his revolver. Unfortunately, when Pinkerton Detective Hay cocked his pistol, it accidentally discharged. Tyrrell later wrote, "[T]he detonation was not loud and I paid little attention to it," but at the time, it alarmed them enough to make a rush to the crypt entrance.[27] Tyrrell stopped at the door frame and shouted for the ghouls to surrender but was met by silence. He lit a match and saw "the marks of their Devilish work plainly visible": the sawed-off padlock on the floor, tools scattered around the room, the marble sarcophagus pried open, Lincoln's casket pulled nearly two feet out of its container—and Mullen and Hughes gone.

He shouted at his men to search the grounds. Tyrrell himself ran back to Memorial Hall to get his shoes, then ascended one of the four staircases leading up to the tomb's terrace sixteen feet above ground level. Suddenly, Tyrrell saw men in the shadows at the other end of the terrace and fired his revolver. The men fired back, and a brief shooting match ensued around the Lincoln monument statuaries. Tyrrell called out to his detectives on the grounds to assist him immediately: "The Devils are up here!" One of the men Tyrrell was shooting at then shouted, "Tyrrell is that you?" Thinking it a trap, since Hughes knew his voice from a previous encounter, he did not respond but again shouted for assistance from his men. Again came a shout, "Tyrrell for God sake is that you?" It was then that Tyrrell realized the two Pinkerton agents had returned from inspecting the grounds as he had been putting on his shoes. They went up on the terrace from the other side of the monument, and it was them he had been shooting at. "Thus for a time the most serious and dastardly plot ever devised turned into a farce," Tyrrell later recalled.[28] In his official report later that night, however, Tyrrell, much more soberly, wrote, "God protected us in doing right, the encounter on President Lincoln's Monument shall ever be remembered by me; the escape from Death most miraculous, and thank *God* from the bottom of my heart."[29]

In the melee, however, the robbers had escaped. It is unknown why Mullen and Hughes were not in the crypt when Tyrrell sprang his trap. The discharge of Hay's revolver certainly scared them away, but tomb custodian Power later stated, "[I]t was afterwards learned" that Hughes and Mullen had gone about one hundred feet away from the tomb and hid in the trees while they waited for Swegles to return with the wagon. This was merely a precaution, but when they saw the scrum of officers running toward the vault, they decided the police had found them out.[30] Tyrrell later confessed, "It is not known to this day why Mullen and Hughes left the tomb after Swegles went after the team," but cited both theories as being possible.[31] Whatever the reason the two thieves left the crypt chamber, when they ran off into the night, they had no idea it was their man Swegles who had betrayed them.

Tyrrell and his men, realizing their trap had failed, standing in the dark outside the Lincoln Tomb, some still probably in their stocking feet, were disappointed, embarrassed, and upset. They consulted on a course of action and decided that four of them would return to Chicago while the other three stayed in Springfield. Tyrrell reached Chicago the next morning and went to Leonard Swett's law office. There, he related to Swett and Robert Lincoln the previous night's events and declared that even though the trap had failed, he was confident it was "only a question of time" before Mullen and Hughes were caught. Robert declared himself completely "satisfied" with what had been done.[32]

"HORRIBLE: Dastardly Attempt to Despoil the Lincoln Monument," newspapers cried the next day; "Sacrilege," wrote one; "Atrocious Vandalism" declared another; "A Dastardly Desecration" echoed a third.[33] Although the story was somewhat overshadowed by the presidential contest between Hayes and Samuel Tilden—the results of which were in doubt on election night and would remain so for months afterwards—it was never an overlooked or ignored story. The outrage against the perpetrators and the praise for the Secret Service in most papers were accompanied by doubt from others. The Chicago *Inter Ocean* specifically claimed the story was false: a "put up job" by Republicans to sway public opinion in their favor for the contested presidential contest; a "plant" concocted by Washburn in his attempts to get rehired as Chicago chief of police; a "put up" by Swegles, who was the true robber and a liar.[34]

Tyrrell and Washburn actually help create and contribute to this disbelief—in a plan sanctioned by Robert and Swett—by telling newspapers the plot was nothing serious. The idea was to reassure Hughes and Mullen it was safe to return to Chicago and come out into the open, thus ensuring their arrest. The ruse worked perfectly, and when Hughes and Mullen returned to the Hub about one week later, they were immediately arrested.[35]

Mullen and Hughes were transported back to Springfield for their indictments and trial in mid-November, although the latter did not begin until March 1877 and did not conclude until May. They proclaimed their innocence, declared that they were victims of a frame-up by the police; but they ultimately were found guilty of conspiracy and attempted larceny of property of the National Lincoln Monument Association worth $75 (Lincoln's coffin). They were not tried for attempted grave robbing because the state of Illinois at that time did not have a statute for the crime. Both men were sentenced to one year in prison. Through further investigation after the arrests, Tyrrell discovered that "Big Jim" Kinnely was the mastermind behind both the Logan County and the Chicago plots, but Tyrell had no evidence to prove it.[36] Ironically, Kinnely was arrested in early 1877 for attempting to procure "straw bail"—a worthless bond used to jump bail—for Mullen, although he was ultimately acquitted of the charge.[37]

For Robert Lincoln, the arrests of Mullen and Hughes were not the end of the Lincoln Tomb incident but only the beginning of a new, much more infuriating, chapter. For although lawyer Lincoln, son of the Great Emancipator, had been assured by the Secret Service that the U.S. government would assume full legal and financial responsibility for prosecution of the conspirators, the government soon reneged.[38]

After the arrests of Mullen and Hughes, Robert arranged for Charles H. Reed, a respected assistant U.S. attorney in Chicago, to be appointed special prosecutor for the case and be paid $500 for the job. It also was determined that Tyrrell's two informants, Swegles and William Neely (another roper who had given information to the Secret Service after the November 7 attempt that led to the arrest at the Hub) needed $2.50 a day for living expenses in order to ensure their availability to testify at the trial. Robert paid most of this per-diem cost himself, expecting to be reimbursed, but also because it was an immediate necessity to keep the ropers around that could not wait to go through bureaucratic red tape. Robert later met with Assistant Secretary of the Treasury Charles F. Conant in Washington to verify these arrangements. Conant agreed with everything Robert had done and told him the expenses would be paid out of the Secret Service budget.[39]

These arrangements stayed as they were until March 1877, when the government officers suddenly changed their minds.

The first hitch was when what everyone thought would be a speedy trial of Mullen and Hughes did not come to fruition. The men were indicted three days after their arrests, on November 20, but a trial could not be scheduled until the next court term began in February because the defense attorneys were not prepared. The trial was set for March 14. During this hiatus, Robert continued to pay the expenses of the witnesses, which, for the two men, amounted to $5 per day (roughly $100 in today's money) for more than one hundred days. This was a major expense at the time but especially during the deep national economic recession that had begun in 1873 and would not end until 1878. Robert was at the time making only a modest middle-class income, had a family with three children, and as a businessman and investor had numerous loans and debts to repay. The monetary expense of the case was a pressing issue for him. In fact, after the postponement, it appears that Robert and Leonard Swett sought to help defray these prosecution expenses by soliciting donations through the Lincoln Monument Association.[40]

By early March, Robert not only had not been reimbursed for anything but he also was informed by Tyrrell five days before the start of the trial that no repayment was coming and U.S. Attorney Reed was pulled off the case by the Treasury Department. Robert immediately telegraphed Conant to inquire about both issues and request that the government stick to its deal with him. "Need money instantly," he wired in one telegram.[41] When he received no reply, he wrote a letter to David Davis, then a U.S. Senator, explaining the entire situation and asking for his assistance. "I think you understand my situation. I could have stopped this scheme with little trouble and no expense, but allowed it to go on at their request. Now they leave me in the lurch, and I am compelled to continue the prosecution at my own expense, and I cannot well pay ten or fifteen hundred dollars for such a thing, if I can help it," he wrote.[42]

Once again, as when dealing with his mother's institutionalization, Robert found himself in a situation where his honor and duty were at stake as much as were his personal interests. If the government failed to pay for the trial, Robert would be forced to fund the prosecution, because if he did not, he would fail in his duty as a man and as a son to prosecute the men who tried to defile his family tomb. After he wrote to Davis, Robert was informed by Tyrrell that James J. Brooks, Secret Service chief, had authorized him to pay the expenses of the two trial witnesses but not necessarily to reimburse Robert Lincoln for the monies he had thus far expended. Robert immediately wrote to Conant, "I assented to the plot being allowed to proceed understanding that the secret service department would take care of the punishment of the offenders. . . . When I left you at Washington I understood you recognized the peculiar situation in which I had been placed by having allowed this matter to go on at the request of the government officers here, and that now my own personal situation was such that I had to carry the prosecution on, if necessary, at my own expense to save my reputation. . . . It is with great difficulty that I can myself bear the expenses, and for the reasons which I gave you when I saw you I really think I ought not to do so."[43]

The March trial of Mullen and Hughes was again postponed until May 17 due to defense requests. This gave Robert more time to advocate his position with the government, but it also continued to cost him daily expenditures. He wrote to Brooks and to the assistant solicitor of the U.S. Treasury and regularly talked with Captain Tyrrell.[44] The Treasury Department and the Secret Service chief moved slowly in responding to Robert's multiple letters. His correspondence and Tyrrell's daily reports show that Chief Brooks was not impressed by Lincoln's arguments and was not inclined to pay him money out of the Secret Service budget. Rather than argue against the issue directly, however, more than once he told Robert that the expense receipts submitted by both Robert and Tyrrell were insufficient and needed revising before any remittances were made. Then, due to Tyrrell's continued assistance to Robert Lincoln in communicating and remitting the paperwork and his advocacy for Robert's cause in his daily reports, Chief Brooks officially censured Tyrrell for supposedly overstepping his authority. Robert responded to this with a letter to Brooks absolving Tyrrell of any wrongdoing. "There was no bargain made between us as to the prosecution," Robert explained. "My trouble was that I took too much for granted, for which I do not blame Mr. Tyrrell at all, but only myself." Robert called Tyrrell "an active and good officer" and declared, "I should not excuse myself if I were in any way the means of injuring him."[45]

The conclusion of this episode is unfortunately unclear. Swegles and Neely were present at the May trial to testify, and Mullen and Hughes were found guilty. Robert ended up paying $643 (roughly about $12,000 in today's money) out of his own pocket to ensure the witnesses' appearance.[46] There is no evidence currently known to show whether Robert was ever reimbursed. A letter from him to Brooks on June 26, 1877, written to clear up more expense discrepancies (according to Brooks), is the last letter in Robert's personal records; Tyrrell's daily reports stop mentioning the subject after reporting on June 26 that he spoke to Robert Lincoln, who said he would write to Brooks.[47] It may be assumed that Robert was eventually paid or else he would have continued his correspondence on the matter.

The attempt to steal Abraham Lincoln's body, although ultimately a failure, had multiple ramifications. Robert was so grateful to Tyrrell for protecting his father's body that he gave the captain a framed portrait of President Lincoln and years later recommended Tyrrell for the position of chief of the Secret Service.[48] Tyrrell wrote in his memoirs that the Lincoln tomb robbery was directly responsible for the successful grave robbing of the body of millionaire

A. T. Stewart in 1878, and the plot apparently was hatched by some of the same men.[49] Conspirator Mullen, after his release from prison, went out west, only to be arrested in 1887 for land fraud. During his trial in the U.S. District Court in Santa Fe, New Mexico, the prosecutor turned on Mullen and thundered, "Were you not arrested, tried, and convicted for stealing the dead body of Abraham Lincoln from its tomb?" To this Mullen answered yes, which caused a sensation in the courtroom. Undoubtedly, the prosecutor hoped the revelation would help him get a guilty verdict, which did not happen.[50]

The most immediate ramification of the episode, of course, was the measures subsequently taken to prevent another robbery attempt, measures in which Robert Lincoln again was perpetually informed and involved. To protect Abraham Lincoln's remains, his coffin was placed in the basement of the tomb in a shallow ditch and hidden under a pile of old, rotting wood. Three years later, it was moved to a different part of the basement and fully buried under the ground. In 1882, Mary Lincoln's remains joined her husband's in the basement at her son's request. There the two coffins stayed until 1887, when they were moved to a different part of the catacombs as a more fitting and final resting place. When the monument was revealed to be crumbling in 1899, the bodies again were moved to a temporary crypt until permanent reburial in 1901. Robert requested at that time—still being concerned twenty-three years after the 1876 theft attempt—that "proper protection" be provided for his family's remains, telling the Illinois governor he would pay for it if the state either could not or would not.[51]

After a complete reconstruction of the tomb, the State of Illinois had decided to place Abraham Lincoln's body back in the exact marble sarcophagus in the same room with again only one padlock from where it was nearly stolen in 1876. In May 1901, Robert traveled to Springfield to tour the reconstructed tomb and was stunned by its failure to protect the bodies it held. He objected to the plan and instead suggested that his father's coffin be surrounded by a steel frame structure and encased within ten feet of concrete—just as Robert's old friend and mentor George M. Pullman's body had been in 1897. Robert was so adamant about this, in fact, that he said he would pay for the adoption of this plan (estimated to cost about $500) if the state could not afford it. Illinois Governor Richard Yates agreed with Robert's proposal as the only way to ensure the body's safety.[52]

In September 1901, the final reburial of Abraham Lincoln took place, at which the coffin was opened to "verify" that the remains of Lincoln still were inside. This was the seventeenth time the body was moved and the sixth time it was exposed and viewed since 1865.[53] A great brouhaha erupted over the 1901 viewing because it was not only deemed a despicable act but it also was not authorized by Robert Lincoln. In fact, a number of newspapers claimed the Pullman-style, steel-and-concrete burial demanded by Robert was not so much to protect his father from grave robbers as it was from his overzealous admirers.[54]

After thirty-six years of dealing with events concerning his father's tomb—the history of which one newspaper called "a sort of burlesque"—Robert never again had to worry about it. Abraham Lincoln was finally and permanently at rest. The entire affair, however, was only one small piece of the vast Lincoln legacy—a legacy that would occupy, satisfy, and very often aggravate Robert his entire life.

13

"I Don't Want to Be Minister to England or Anywhere Else"

For a man with no interest in pursuing political jobs, Robert Lincoln lived a remarkable life of public service. There were two main reasons for this. First, citizens and politicians all were exuberant at the idea of the son of Abraham Lincoln entering politics and perhaps even continuing where his father left off in the White House, and so their encouragement of his political advance was relentless. Second, Robert held a deep respect for the duty of a man and an American citizen to set aside his personal preferences and accept public service when called upon by the people. This notion of civic duty—instilled by his parents, his New England schooling, and his overall Victorian values system—more than anything else is what ultimately led Robert from local to regional to national and even international political responsibilities. Along the way, he was more than once urged—and quite nearly drafted—into running for president himself.

Robert Lincoln's political emergence occurred in late 1876, when he campaigned in support of Republican Rutherford B. Hayes for president. The GOP had changed somewhat since the days of Robert's father. The party still believed in its policies of transforming the south and protecting southern black citizens, but as Reconstruction dragged through its tenth year, Republicans began to lose interest in actively governing the southern states. The scandals of President Ulysses S. Grant's administration and the Democrat gains in the 1874 congressional elections caused Republicans to begin championing civil-service reform. But the main focus of the party turned to economic issues. The financial Panic of 1873 and its ensuing (and ongoing in 1876) depression caused the Republicans to focus more on fiscal responsibility and to support American businesses to a greater degree through federal tariffs and other subsidies. Out on the stump, the party of Lincoln continued to brand all Democrats as traitors who caused the late war and criminals bent on pillaging the public coffers.

Robert Lincoln was an ardent Republican—not merely because it was the party his father helped to found but because he truly believed in the principles for which it stood. His active support for Hayes and the entire national Republican ticket in 1876 was out of the belief that Republican policies were best for the country, while Democrat policies were likely to destroy it. But as with so many politicians, the true catalyst for Robert's transformation from political observer to active participant was a local issue.

For years, Democrats had controlled Chicago city elective offices. They won their jobs through intimidation and voter fraud and practiced shameless and well-known corruption while in office. The citizens of the city, however, were never sufficiently outraged to mount a serious electoral challenge to the party incumbents, despite the increased taxes and the decreased public spending.

Abraham Lincoln characterized corruption in government as "the bane of our American politics" and said that "he could not respect, either as a man or as a politician, one who bribed or was bribed."[1] Robert Lincoln felt the same and had watched for years as the politicians in his town of South Chicago promulgated corruption and stole elections. As one newspaper wrote, "Since 1872, these elections, whose importance has not been appreciated, have been turned over to the rabble, the regular political parties only once entering the field."[2] According to the *Chicago Times*, this held true in 1876: "If there is a pimp, a sneak thief, a blackleg, a highway robber, or a confidence man in the city who did not help to swell the ranks of that mongrel, leprous, lecherous, treacherous gang [of Democrats], it was because he overslept himself."[3]

On April 4, 1876, the elections for North, South, and West Chicago occurred to choose the town supervisors, assessors, collectors, and clerks. The previous year, the four positions in South Chicago went to Democrats who won by ballot stuffing, then shamelessly engaged in corruption, embezzlement, bribery, and personal aggrandizement. Their greed left the town near bankruptcy and yet collecting increasing amounts of personal taxes. Both Democrat and Republican newspapers urged voters to oust the "bummers," as they were called, in 1876; and the voter turnout was the largest in years. The Democrats attempted to threaten and physically prevent Republicans from voting in at least one precinct, but their efforts failed, and the early predictions were of a large Republican dominance. Of the approximately fifteen thousand votes on the South Side, the Republican candidates had a clear majority after the first day's counting.[4] The official tallying was postponed two days, however, by disputed ballot boxes in two wards. During the interim, all the ballot boxes were locked in the town offices and supposedly guarded by police. Democrat operatives, including the incumbent town clerk, entered the office (apparently assisted by the police guards), destroyed the legal ballots, and replaced them with false ballots with Democrat votes. The break-in was witnessed by numerous people and reported in the newspapers, but the election was certified an incumbent victory from the illegal ballots nevertheless.[5]

The community was outraged. A mass meeting of "businessmen, taxpayers, and citizens generally, without distinction of party" was called for the evening of April 8 to challenge the election results. Robert Lincoln attended and listened as his friend and mentor Leonard Swett, one of the leaders of the meeting, declared the occasion to be a fight for liberty: "The question is not whether we are to drift to anarchy and be ruled by a mob, but whether, being under a mob, we can emancipate ourselves." It was subsequently determined that the South Town election results were but a smaller piece of a citywide pattern of corruption. Chicago Mayor Harvey D. Colvin, surrounded and supported by a cadre of corrupt aldermen, used a new city statute to declare himself continued in office without the need for his participation in the upcoming election.[6]

This circumstance led to a mass meeting on April 11 that fifty thousand people attended—the largest political meeting in Chicago since a Stephen A. Douglas rally in 1859. "The meeting was literally the assembled city," reported the *Chicago Times*.[7] Robert Lincoln attended the second rally as well, along with a number of his friends and mentors such as Norman Williams, Ezra B. McCagg, John Young Scammon, Melville Weston Fuller, Marshall Field, Potter Palmer, Isaac N. Arnold, and Swett.

The assemblage voted to support a number of resolutions, which included the mayor's resignation, a united body of voters to elect a new mayor, the appointment of honest public servants to city offices, the creation of polling place and ballot-box observation committees, and an overturning of the South Town election results. A committee of 150 citizens was appointed to call upon the common council of the city and demand action on the resolutions; a Committee of Twenty-Five was appointed specifically to approach the South Town board and demand the resignation of the incumbents, or, failing that, a call of meeting of citizens to protest and support the cause. Robert Lincoln was appointed a member of both the Committee of 150 and the Committee of Twenty-Five.[8]

The Committee of Twenty-Five wasted no time in fulfilling its mandate and after extensive legal research and strategizing forced a meeting of the South Town Board of Appointment on April 15 to confront the charge of election fraud. A mass of citizens, led by committee member Swett, put forth their case to the board and demanded action. Board member and South Town Justice of the Peace L. B. Otis—who also was chairman of the Committee of Twenty-Five—made the motion to hear the petition, which was accepted. The subsequent meeting was in effect an ad hoc civil trial to determine whether the town board members had been fraudulently elected on April 4. Swett took the lead for the committee and offered testimony by numerous witnesses to the ballot stuffing and also multiple legal precedents to bolster the case of fraud and the need to overturn the election. After hearing the evidence, current and newly reelected Town Supervisor P. K. Ryan resigned, declaring he had no part in the fraud and would not retain his office under such circumstances. Robert Lincoln then was nominated to fill the vacant post of supervisor and was appointed by unanimous vote. Further evidence and testimony was then taken, and the Board of Appointments—a body of seven justices of the peace—ultimately declared the contested election fraudulent, the results void, and the positions vacant. The committee put forth its nominees—all Republicans—for clerk, assessor, and collector, and all were appointed and sworn in.[9]

That Robert Lincoln attended the rallies and meetings and accepted appointment to committees and as supervisor shows his commitment to his community, his political principles, and his Victorian code of duty; but the fact that he was not a speaker or a leader in any of these events or groups is another example of his personal aversion to political leadership but his acquiescence to public duty. In fact, Supervisor Ryan resigned his office not only because of the evidence of fraud but also because of the Committee of Twenty-Five's assurance that Robert Lincoln would be his replacement. Lincoln did not seek the appointment but when consulted replied, "I will say that if I am elected, I will serve."[10] The *Chicago Tribune* lauded Lincoln's election to town supervisor as the "notable incident" of the entire election affair:

> He has been noted heretofore for his aversion to political life, and for the quiet resolution with which he has refused to permit his friends to put him forward for nomination or appointment to any office. Since his admission to the Bar, some ten years ago, he has resisted all solicitations to embark on a political career, and has closely and successfully applied himself to the practice of his profession. But the while he has not suffered himself to lose sight of his duties as a citizen, and upon the perpetration of the treasonable frauds . . . he threw aside his scruples, came to the front, and accepted the rather humble office.[11]

Thus was the son of Abraham Lincoln elected and inaugurated into active political life—not a popular election of general voters to be sure but an election by their chosen representatives on the Committee of Twenty-Five and the South Chicago Town Board of Appointments.

The rectitude of the fraudulent South Town elections were not over, however, but, for Supervisor Lincoln, were only just beginning. The three ousted politicians—Town Clerk James Gleason, Town Collector Mike Evans, and Town Assessor Ed Phillips—fought against their removal at the meeting and afterward through legal challenges. Lincoln acted not only as supervisor but also assisted as legal counsel for the town board in the courts. Phillips sought an injunction to prevent his replacement as assessor to undertake his job, which was declined by the Cook County Circuit Court. Evans brought suit in criminal court to regain his position as town collector. The courts decided his ouster illegal and proclaimed him duly elected, but Supervisor Lincoln thereafter refused to certify two bonds offered by Evans, declaring both insufficient to authorize the tax collection according to statute.[12] Approval of the bond was necessary for Evans to be certified as town collector.

Evans then twice sued Robert Lincoln to get the circuit court to approve his bond, which was refused both times. The judge in the second decision stated, "I may have differed with the supervisor on the question whether the bond tendered was ample . . . but it is not my opinion or judgment that controls. It is the supervisor. Inasmuch as the law vests judgment and discretion in him."[13] Evans then changed tactics and applied to the circuit court for an overturning of the injunction that prevented the county clerk from turning over the collector books to Evans. Once again, he lost.[14] In all of these cases, Evans argued that Supervisor Lincoln was acting arbitrarily and illegally, intent to refuse Evans his place based on his own suppositions as to the 1876 election fraud. In every legal decision, however, the courts declared that Supervisor Lincoln had acted according to his reading of the law, a reading they declared accurate and legal. The *Chicago Tribune* seemed to verify, or at least agree with, Evans's interpretation, when it praised, "The Supervisor, Mr. Lincoln, is not acting as a mere officeholder. He represents that public opinion which Evans defies."[15] Robert himself wrote that he would "fight this thing out" as long as it took to prevent the "danger" of either Evans becoming the town collector or the town going bankrupt because of lack of revenue.[16]

In terms of the political actions of the town board (with Lincoln as its head), it reduced taxes, reduced board expenses and salaries, brought the town's accounts back to solvency, and eradicated the graft and corruption that had permeated the town board for years. Specifically, the board reduced town expenses from an average of $25,000 during the previous three years to barely more than $3,000 in 1876–77. This was achieved by cutting extraneous expenses, reducing board member salaries, and by lawfully collecting the town collector's surplus commissions for the town coffers, something previously ignored in order to enrich the holder of the post. Robert himself accepted only $50 as salary where previous supervisors had taken $2,500. The board also reduced town taxes from $37,700 in 1875 to $10,200 in 1876, which became $0 in 1877 and 1878.[17]

"We think one of the most remarkable instances of political reform, and the potency of self-government when the better classes assert themselves, is to be found in the Town of South Chicago," the *Chicago Tribune* declared at the end of the 1876–77 term.[18] The paper estimated that the town board had saved the citizens roughly $33,000 through its "honest and economical management."[19] It also lauded Robert Lincoln's tenure as supervisor by stating that he "added greatly to [the] dignity and importance [of his office] in the way he exercised its functions for the protection of the taxpayers. He fought the bummers with a skill and pertinacity that showed he was a 'chip off the old block.' . . . Mr. Lincoln made more reputation and won more encomiums in his year's fight with the tax-eaters and ballot-box stuffers than did the whole Cook County delegation in Congress."[20]

When the next town elections were held in April 1877, the Republican candidates easily swept up the votes and remained in control of the town government. Robert Lincoln was not retained as town supervisor, however, because he did not run in the election. No paper trail exists to explain why he refused what would have been an easy election, but a knowledge of Robert's previous actions and beliefs leads to an obvious conclusion: he had no desire for the post. Robert was not a politician and did not want to be. He accepted the supervisor position as a public duty to oust a gang of crooks and return the town to fiscal and political solvency. This he and the town board accomplished, and therefore he had no reason to run for reelection. He may even have made it a condition of his election in 1876 that he would not run for reelection, although that is speculation.

During the final meeting of the 1876–77 town board, Supervisor Lincoln was "tendered a vote of thanks for his efficient services during the past year."[21] In later years, Robert's tenure as supervisor would come to be repeatedly praised, mostly as proof of his fitness for higher elective office. One magazine, trying to whip up popular support for a Lincoln presidential run in 1884, praised his integrity for relentlessly fighting for the public good, even after the public had lost interest in all of the legal challenges he faced in 1876–77: "His pluck, pertinacity and legal ability all attracting marked attention, and showing more clearly than anything else had done, the real character of the man. Some of those who had counted him only a soft complacent man of society awoke to the fact that they had failed rightly to take his measure. He . . . had a stubborn courage in doing what seemed to him right."[22] Another magazine declared that Robert's first public position showed "how great was his skill and accuracy in business management."[23]

Robert was proud of the job he did as town supervisor—not only of ousting and keeping out the Democrat bummers but also in implementing an honest administration based on Republican principles. He was so proud of it, in fact, that he kept a scrapbook of newspaper clippings about his tenure as supervisor and his legal battles with Evans—an action that could almost be seen as vain by a man so publicly reserved and unassuming.[24] Lincoln's pride turned to frustration in later years, as the previous abuses and illegal salaries began to creep back into the town by the turn of the decade.[25]

During his time as town supervisor, perhaps even because of the notable job he was doing in South Chicago, the governor appointed him to the Douglas Monument Commission. It was a group of nine men charged with arranging and supervising the erection of a monument atop the Chicago tomb of Senator Stephen A. Douglas, Abraham Lincoln's old political rival, who had died in 1861. Robert held this position until the work was completed in 1881 and resumed his position in 1902 when the monument needed repair.[26] One historian has stated that without Robert Lincoln, the monument never would have been completed: Lincoln was able to unite state Republicans behind the project that had been languishing without their political support (due to hard feelings against Democrats in the aftermath of the Civil War) for ten years.[27]

Six months after leaving town office, Robert's political possibilities jumped to an entirely new level when Secretary of State William M. Evarts, on behalf of President Hayes, offered Robert the position of third assistant secretary of state. It was just such an administration position that Robert's friend John Hay, himself a former state department diplomat, had been urging on Lincoln for years and may even have had a role in procuring. Robert took several days to consider the unexpected offer but ultimately declined to accept. His decision was "compelled by the necessity of dedicating myself to my profession for at least some years yet to come," he wrote to President Hayes.[28] To Secretary Evarts, he was more expansive.

> I am however compelled to refrain from accepting the place for the reason that which I regard its acceptance as a duty which should outweigh an ordinary immediate loss to myself, I would find it impossible to accept it without abandoning in too great a degree the advantages of a professional association and position here which are now exceedingly gratifying to me and which it is my ambition to retain and improve.
>
> Without considering only the immediate comfort and welfare of my family, for which I am almost wholly dependent upon my business, it has long seemed to me and still does seem after the consideration I have given your very kind letter, that my duty lies, at least during my earlier years, in devoting myself entirely to the profession, with no deviation from which a

> change of purpose could be implied until such time as the satisfaction of a proper political aspiration will not seem inconsistent with professional ambition. That time has not arrived in my case.[29]

In a time before major civil-service reforms began to occur in 1883, political offices typically were handed out to party faithful, political supporters, and personal friends regardless of qualifications. Robert Lincoln was certainly faithful to his party, and he had earned patronage by campaigning for Hayes in October 1876; but there can be little doubt he was offered the assistant secretary position because of who his father was. Robert even alluded to this in his response to Evarts: "The interest in me personally manifested by your note leads me to say that the work I am now in, with such expectations for the future as may reasonably be entertained, make the attainment to a fair measure of professional success *dependent only on my own faithfulness* and in this trust I shall not be wanting."[30]

Robert's resolve to earn his own plaudits shows he did not live under an inferiority complex because of his surname. He knew his own worth, and he had no qualms about accepting political appointments that he knew he was qualified to hold, that would enhance his reputation and his business prospects, and that would not impinge upon his legal practice and his ability to generate an income. Such a position was not far in the future, but first Lincoln refused even more offices. It was reported in August 1878 that he declined to run for Congress from Chicago and that "he says he made up his mind in early youth never to enter actively into politics."[31] His friend John Hay continued to urge him to take a government post and again offered to assist him. In late 1879, Robert responded to Hay's newest suggestion by writing, "I don't want to be minister to England or anywhere else," and instead he asked for patronage assistance for a friend.[32]

It was the presidential election of 1880 that vaulted Robert Lincoln onto the national scene. The Civil War and its aftermath left the Republicans firmly in control of national politics, but the party itself was divided by the issue of patronage. The multiple corruption scandals of President Grant's administration such as Credit Mobilier and the Whiskey Ring had caused some Republicans to oppose the spoils system of patronage and instead champion civil-service reform. In his single term in office, President Hayes had himself supported reform and even ousted corrupt party bosses in various posts. Hayes's one-term pledge left the 1880 party nomination completely open, and it turned into a fight between former President Grant, whose supporters were seeking his return for a third term, and James G. Blaine, arguably one of the most important Republican politicians in the late nineteenth century.

Despite his previous disdain for a third term for Grant in 1876, Robert Lincoln supported the movement in 1880. There is no direct evidence to explain this change of heart, only that he, like many Americans, wanted a strong man returned to the White House who would deal decisively with issues such as the economic depression and labor strikes affecting the entire country. Grant's stature as a statesman also had risen after his presidency while he undertook a two-year world tour. As his longtime friend Adam Badeau later explained, Grant's time abroad had opened his mind to a greater understanding of micro and macro political issues and vastly improved his statesmanship. Adding this to his innate strength of will and character, Grant was "never so fit to be president" as he was in 1880.[33]

As early as 1879, a group of distinguished social, business, and political leaders in Chicago began advocating Grant's return to the White House. In November 1879, wealthy businessman Potter Palmer hosted a dinner at his home to celebrate the ex-president's return to America. Among the guests were Mr. and Mrs. Robert Lincoln.[34] By April 1880, the fervor for Grant's reemergence was being called a "boom" in Chicago. A gathering of important state Republicans was held at the Palmer House hotel on April 11 to organize a mass meeting on April 15 in support of Grant as the Republican presidential candidate. Robert Lincoln was elected chair of the April 11 meeting and subsequently named chair of the April 15 mass meeting. Stephen A. Douglas Jr. was named secretary.[35] At the April 15 meeting, Chairman Lincoln gave a rousing speech in favor of Grant that was printed in full in the Chicago newspapers. He opened:

> Ladies and Gentlemen, we meet here tonight on the eve of one of the most important political contests which has been witnessed by this generation. The Democratic party has by fraud and violence established for itself a majority in the National Senate and House of Representatives, and in order that it may attain complete ascendancy in every part of the government, is now engaged in the repeal of the provision of law by which the purity of the ballot box is attempted to be guarded. What are their ultimate intentions are no longer a mere conjecture. We must judge of the future by the past.[36]

Lincoln recalled with anger the suppression of the black vote in the south over the previous decade and even of the Chicago city elections of 1876 in which he took part. He lauded the Republican Party's extirpation of slavery from America and said, "[A]s we gave freedom to the slave, we will give freedom to the ballot." He said the party needed a proven leader as its candidate in 1880, one who was brave and resolute, such as was General Grant. The *St. Louis Globe-Democrat* newspaper called Lincoln's emergence into national politics "notable as well as significant," praised his modesty and self-control, and decreed that "he knew his own mind, and that he had a mind worth knowing."[37] The people at this meeting were later dubbed the "Palmer House delegates," and they pushed earnestly at both the Illinois state party convention in Springfield and the national Republican convention in Chicago for Grant's nomination.

The 1880 Chicago convention was a raucous affair, a battle among the three factions of the party: the Stalwarts, who supported Grant and generally favored political machines and the spoils system of patronage; the Half-Breeds, who supported Blaine and advocated civil-service reform and a merit system; and the members who opposed both other factions and united behind Treasury Secretary and former Ohio Senator John Sherman. "In strategy, in bitterness, in dramatic oratory and in its surprising result, no convention of any party ever exceeded the Republican convention of 1880," wrote journalist Henry L. Stoddard.[38] The first thirty ballots changed little in their deadlock among Grant, Blaine, and Sherman, but none could gain a majority of votes. By then, talk of introducing a "dark horse" candidate into the mix began to gain momentum, and on the thirty-fourth ballot, Senator-elect James A. Garfield of Ohio began receiving votes. When Blaine realized that if he withdrew his name from contention, Grant was assured the nomination, he threw his delegates to his friend Garfield, who triumphed on the thirty-sixth ballot. Chester A. Arthur of New York was chosen for the vice-presidential candidate to placate the Grant Stalwarts and the powerful New York State party boss, Roscoe Conkling.[39]

The Democrat party nominated for its ticket Civil War General Winfield Scott Hancock for president and former Indiana Congressman William Hayden English for vice president. The Democrats had not won a presidential election since 1856, and Hancock was an inexperienced and uninspiring candidate. The two parties differed on few issues other than the protective tariff, which Hancock favored minimally only for revenue, and Garfield embraced as a form of protectionism. In the November election, Garfield won by less than ten thousand votes but more than fifty electoral votes.

If Robert Lincoln did any campaigning for the Republican ticket, it must have been minimal. The major newspapers seem devoid of mentions of him, and in responding to an August 1880 invitation to speak, which he declined, he said that he was so busy as to be unsure how much, if any, work he would do for the Republican canvass.[40] He certainly was a busy man at this time. His children were now ages eleven, seven, and five; his wife was often ill and either recuperating at home or a health retreat in another state (always accompanied by the children and a nanny); his law practice was one of the biggest in Chicago; and during the summer of 1880, he was appointed by the governor as a trustee of the Illinois Central Railroad, although he resigned this position after only a few months on the job.[41] His resignation letters do not explain his reason, but it seems as though he was avoiding a possible conflict of interest, because he ran for election in November as a Republican presidential elector—the only time in his life he would actively run for an elective position. He received the highest popular vote of any state Republican candidate: 318,037.[42] When it came time for Robert to travel to Springfield to cast his electoral vote for the party ticket, he joked in a letter to John Hay, "I have about made up my mind to vote for Garfield and Arthur but it would be fun to be constituted and do something else."[43]

This letter to Hay is actually more interesting for a statement it contains in which Robert commented on how, for the third time in his adult life, he narrowly escaped a premature death. Like his encounter with Edwin Booth in 1863, the incident in 1880 also concerned a train. As Robert explained the day after the event, he was riding in a railway passenger car from Washington to Chicago when the car he was in "collided with two opposing trains a few second apart." One newspaper reported that Robert "sustained bruises which made him unconscious for half an hour"; he declared that he suffered multiple bruises and bleeding wounds. "My escape from death appears to me almost miraculous," he wrote.[44] A few months later, Robert told Hay that the accident was "too close a call to be amusing," and he was treated with plaster and liniment for a week or two as a result: "It left me with a pain in the back which was pretty severe at first but now reminds me of its existence only when I get a jar."[45]

After the election, President-elect Garfield stayed at his home in Mentor, Ohio. His only two jobs until the inauguration in March were to write his inaugural speech and to form a cabinet. Both were more difficult than he expected.[46] Selecting cabinet members in the nineteenth century was a deft political balancing act that would not only assure that each region of the country (especially the large, politically powerful states) would be equally represented but also that would mollify party bosses and candidates defeated at the convention. Such a game was difficult enough, but Garfield also had to emolliate the various party factions—headed by three of the party's brightest stars—especially the Stalwarts, who very nearly triumphed in Chicago.

The entire country presumed, correctly, that the preeminent cabinet post of secretary of state would go to Speaker of the House Blaine, who not only was a leading candidate in Chicago but also Garfield's close friend. The other positions were much more problematic for the president-elect. In the end, his cabinet consisted of Blaine, secretary of state; William Windom, secretary of the Treasury; Wayne McVeigh, attorney general; Samuel J. Kirkwood, secretary of the Interior; Thomas L. James, postmaster general; William H. Hunt, secretary of the navy; and Robert T. Lincoln, secretary of war.

Exactly how Garfield came to choose a man so young and politically inexperienced as Robert Lincoln for a cabinet post was influenced by the usual political considerations and, of course, by the Lincoln name. Specifically though, it began because of the imperative for Garfield to name a Stalwart to the cabinet. J. Donald Cameron, John A. Logan, and Roscoe Conkling were the "triumvirate" of leading senators backing Grant at the 1880 Republican convention. Each was extremely influential in the party and needed to be consulted about cabinet appointments. Cameron was senator from Pennsylvania and also the Republican National Committee chairman. Logan was a distinguished Civil War general who was elected senator from Illinois in 1880. Conkling was senator from New York and state party boss.

Apparently Logan, in seeking both a Stalwart and an Illinoisan to recommend for the cabinet, urged Robert T. Lincoln's name on Garfield. Logan's wife remembered that her husband gathered support for the appointment from other prominent Illinois men and first mentioned it to Garfield during a February 1881 visit to the president-elect's home in Mentor, Ohio.[47] Garfield's diary, however, shows that it was Logan's colleague Senator Cameron who first brought it up during his December 29, 1880, visit to Mentor.[48] This may have been a previously discussed strategy by Cameron and Logan, because on December 30, Logan wrote to Lincoln informing him of the possibility of a cabinet nomination. Robert responded on January 10 by saying he wasn't interested but could probably be talked into accepting a position:

> In the principal matter I am somewhat in doubt. I have strong faith that General Garfield's character, influenced by his broad culture and great political experience, will make his administration a marked one and that under it we may hope for an abatement of the subjects which have so long made our political contests discreditable to the country and for that reason I would certainly be glad to be associated with the administration. My own conviction however is that situated as I am, I could not in justice to my family take any office which interfered with my present means of livelihood. This is perhaps not a patriotic way of looking at things and would not be justifiable in a situation where which might arise but is not likely to do so again in one day. Mr. Isham and I have been together for eight years and our professional business is I think probably the largest in Chicago. I am 37 years old, in good health and am in receipt of a professional income which not only enables me to live in comfort but added to my other small resources encourages me to think that by handling my affairs properly I may be able to make a reasonable provision for my children. I like my present way of life and think I would not like a political career. If I should go into such a career, I think I

> would have to make up my mind to look to it for my future. In such a place as you mention my income would be considerably reduced and my expenses largely increased and the outcome of the whole matter in its relation to those dependent on me would be a constant source of anxiety. Such positions are highly honorable of course and are proper objects of ambition but they seem to me to be in the nature of luxuries which can only be properly enjoyed by men of some fortune.
>
> I am at the age in life at which I can best do the things I must do and I am not so old but that I could ten or twelve years later enjoy an honorable political place as well as now and I think it would not be more difficult to obtain then than now if I should be in a position to take it.
>
> I think it very likely that you might be able to argue me out of my present notions by keeping my attention to the attractive side of the picture but sitting here coolly I think I am judging correctly for my own case. Feeling as I do now I should be compelled to decline any appointment and I think that inasmuch as my name has been mentioned to Gen. Garfield, he ought to know my feelings.[49]

In his efforts to gather other Illinois men to support him, Logan wrote to ex-President Ulysses S. Grant (on whose staff Robert served during the war), *Chicago Tribune* editor Joseph Medill, and prominent Chicago businessman J. D. Harvey, among others. Grant replied, "There is nothing that I could consistently do for Robert Lincoln that I would not do. I believe it would strike the public most favorably to see him in the Cabinet, and no one more so than myself." Grant advised, however, in that letter and another in February, that being so young, a cabinet position might damage Robert's livelihood; and if he was offered a place, it should be one that would assist his career, such as attorney general.[50] Medill agreed with Grant that both the state of Illinois and the entire nation would welcome Robert's nomination; he added that "unless this be done the chance of an Illinois man going into the Cabinet is hardly worth considering."[51] Harvey replied, "If Lincoln goes in, I think it will be a popular choice; it will please the young men of the party and Bob will be a credit to his state and name."[52] Logan also convinced every Republican member of the Illinois Congressional delegation to sign a petition to Garfield in support of Lincoln for a cabinet post.[53]

Garfield, meanwhile, was favorably impressed with the idea of Robert Lincoln in his cabinet from the moment Cameron mentioned it on December 29, 1880. Shortly after receiving the Illinois delegation petition, he wrote in his diary that if he were compelled to make a cabinet that day, Lincoln would be in it.[54] "The talk about Lincoln seems to have been spontaneous in many quarters," he wrote to Hay in late January.[55] But while he was an experienced politician attuned to public sentiment, Garfield also was an intelligent and practical man. He may have wanted the name of Lincoln in his cabinet, but he also wanted to ascertain whether or not the son of the Great Emancipator had any managerial or political ability. He invited Senator Logan to Mentor to discuss the Illinois cabinet position and after the meeting found himself "incline[d] to think favorably of Robert Lincoln."[56] Garfield also wrote to Illinois U.S. Senator David Davis for his opinion as to Lincoln's fitness for the job. Davis, Lincoln's mentor and "second father" since 1865, replied in an extremely professional manner—indeed so professional and dispassionate as to appear that Davis was no more intimate with Lincoln than he would be with a young professional colleague—that Robert "has good ability, and fine executive talent; he is upright, has excellent habits; is industrious, and I believe, both from his traditions, and for his own sake, the suggested honor would be acceptable to the state."[57]

As these movements and machinations went on in and between Illinois, Washington, and Mentor, Robert himself had no idea what would happen. His letters at the time show that he was receiving callers, inquiries, and congratulations about his possible prospects, all with more than a tincture of uncertainty. On February 7, he wrote to Hay that if President-elect Garfield did make him an offer, it would embarrass him. "I have not only great misgivings as to the way in which I should acquaint myself in a place of such responsibility, but the gravest concern on the prosaic bread and butter question," Robert confided. "It is likely that I would be compelled to use up in living a large part of my tangible assets and at the end would find myself with no money and no business, but with a wife and three pretty well grown up children wanting to know whether then this moveable parent can keep them up in proper style and if not, why not. Of course, such a place is a great honor and in itself I would so much like it that it is very probably that when the opportunity came I would throw business prudence to the winds."[58]

Three weeks later, after having been to Washington, D.C., on business, Robert indicated he knew an offer was coming and so would have to seriously consider the question and his answer. "I am more reconciled to the idea of accepting the right thing if it is offered but I feel that if I do so I commit an error," he wrote to Hay. "My excuse to myself would be that the seduction is so great that an error in that direction would seem more venial than in the other."[59] The very next day, Garfield wrote to Lincoln his intention to nominate him for secretary of war.[60] Robert received the letter two days later while he was in Springfield on business for the Pullman Company. He wrote his reply in the office of Governor Shelby M. Cullom: "I appreciate highly this distinguished mark of your confidence and I accept it with the earnest hope that in the performance of the duties of this important office, I may be able to meet my own wishes and your expectations."[61]

Garfield's inauguration as the nation's twentieth president on March 4, 1881, occurred without incident and with a lackluster presidential speech. He spoke of the end of sectional strife, stating, "Let all our people, leaving behind them the battlefields of dead issues, move forward and in their strength of liberty and the restored Union win the grander victories of peace." He also mentioned a host of other issues such as black rights and citizenship, free and untainted elections, illiteracy and education, monetary issues, and civil-service reform. The new president's cabinet nominations all were sent to the Senate and approved on March 5, and every member except Robert Lincoln was sworn into their respective offices on March 7.[62]

Lincoln had business in Springfield on March 4 and also had to prepare his business and personal affairs in Chicago before he left for the east. One of these tasks involved hiring a repairman to fix a leak in the house after son, Jack, broke a gutter pipe while cleaning snow off the roof.[63] As it was, he could not arrange his children's "affairs" (most likely their schooling) in time for his departure, so they stayed temporarily in Chicago while Robert and his wife traveled to Washington on March 9. The day before, a group of about thirty of Robert's friends and colleagues held a lunch for him at the Union League Club. He was reported to be in good spirits, but he told the group that a few days previous he had been "one of the unhappiest men" to think of the associations he would have to sever for four years and the magnitude of his new and unfamiliar duties.[64]

Robert and Mary arrived in Washington on March 10 and stayed at Wormley's hotel.[65] When the new war secretary appeared at the White House to take the oath of office that day, it was an old friend who swore him in. "Why, hello, Colonel!" Robert genially said to William H. Crook, executive clerk, and President Lincoln's former bodyguard. "How are you Mr. Secretary?" Crook said, to which Lincoln replied, "I'm not that yet."[66] Crook later wrote that it felt it good to hear the name Lincoln in the White House again, and he was not alone in this sentiment. Newspapers around the country were pleased and excited by his appointment. "We predict that Mr. Lincoln's administration of the War Department will not only be able and efficient, but that he will become, on general matters, one of the most trusted and valuable advisors of the President," the Chicago *Inter Ocean* declared on March 7.[67] The general feeling and editorial statements were that Bob Lincoln every year grew more and more like his father, that he had had great ability and character yet was modest and unassuming.[68]

While Robert Lincoln was given his cabinet appointment because of necessary political concerns, there is no doubt he would not even have been considered if not for his parentage and his surname. Some newspapers objected to his appointment for that very reason, saying he was too young and inexperienced—a small man with a big name.[69] Still, his tenure as secretary of war would be so well administered and so positively reviewed that by 1884, he would begin to step out of his father's immense shadow and find himself being talked of and even voted for as a potential national candidate. But first, and perhaps partly as a consequence, the country would endure the assassination of its second president in sixteen years; and this time, Robert Lincoln would not be in the White House when the shot was fired but standing only a few yards away.

14

"How Many Hours of Sorrow I Have Passed in This Town"

Secretary of War Robert T. Lincoln entered into his new position with goodwill and high expectations from the public but a nagging anxiety and self-doubt from himself. Could he perform his job to his own high standards, standards influenced by his father's legacy? Did he make the correct decision to accept the appointment, move his family to Washington, and leave his highly satisfying and lucrative law practice? These questions would be answered in due time, and in the end, his reputation would be that of an excellent administrator—a talent that would serve him well throughout the rest of his life. In fact, the responsibility of the secretary of war in the late nineteenth century was less about war and more about handling the routine administrations within the vast bureaucracy of the War Department. This included issues such as military appointments, promotions, and transfers; civilian employee examinations, appointments, transfers, and discharges; yearly department appropriations and publications; land surveys; improvements to bridges, harbors, rivers, and canals; government acquisition of land; and issues regarding Indian reservations and military campaigns.

"On that first morning in office he was simply lawyer Lincoln, of Chicago; unabashed, unobtrusive, seeming to lack some element of self-assertion, and yet asserting himself in a way to leave impressions of sharp individuality on the hundreds who called to offer congratulations," recalled one journalist.[1] Robert's first days and weeks on the job were filled with routine and mundane affairs. The first five letters in his letterpress books from his time in the cabinet were, in fact, requests for his autograph.[2] The most immediate job he had to face, however, was to make civilian employee appointments. In a time before permanent civil-service employment, every new administration fired and hired thousands of new employees and therefore was deluged with seemingly endless requests for jobs. Robert received letters from strangers, colleagues, Republican Party faithful, personal friends, and family members. Being the son of a former president, he also received numerous requests and even demands for jobs from people who claimed to have assisted his father's elections, administration, and military victories by their stint as soldiers and therefore found it proper—even necessary—that the son remunerate them. Robert dealt with these requests and appointments conscientiously but also politically. He was not averse to handing out spoils to family, friends, and party faithful; yet, he never removed, replaced, or overstepped an existing employee to make room for an inexperienced political appointment.

Robert at this time received requests for favors and appointments from people such as former President Ulysses S. Grant, Senator David Davis, his friend and mentor Leonard Swett, his father-in-law, James Harlan, his law partner, Edward Isham, and his Aunt Elizabeth Edwards.[3] The requests he received from Todd family members, in fact, made up such a large portion of his incoming mail that he had to begin refusing them. As he explained to his cousin:

> Shortly before I came here, but when I had been informed that I was to occupy my present place, I was urged by my cousin, Mrs. Ella Canfield, the widowed daughter of my mother's brother, Levi Todd, who was in a temporary clerkship here, to get her a place in one of the departments here. I could not see my way to have her in the War Department, and, with a good deal of difficulty, I arranged to have her made a clerk in the State Department, where she now is.[4] Her brother, Robert S. Todd, is a clerk in the Treasury (not through me) and is urging me to help him to promotion. Their young sister, now in Lexington, is also anxious to come here in government employment, but I was obliged to write that, both on her own account, and on my own, I felt compelled to withhold my assistance for such a purpose. During the presidency of Mr. Hayes, it came in my way to give some help by which another cousin, Miss Mattie Todd, of Cynthiana, Ky., (daughter of my uncle, George Todd) was made postmaster at that place, which office she still holds, and, I am told, administers well. Now, I am being pressed to urge a sister of my mother [Emily Helm] for another post office in [Elizabethtown] Kentucky. I have a great regard for her and want to do anything proper in my power to aid her.[5] The Governor of your state has written me to aid in getting a post office in Missouri for another cousin, Miss Boyd. Another cousin, a son of Gen. J. B. S. Todd, of Dakota, urges me to get him a commission in the Army; and Mrs. Gen. Todd wants to be given the post office in Yankton.

> Now, I confess, these things have bothered me to reply to. I would be very glad to see any or all of these wished gratified, for I know it would do good; but it is simply impossible for me to put myself forward and use my official influence in this way. If I had the courage to try it, I would be ridiculed out of office.[6]

Robert finally became so impatient with the number of requests he was receiving that his irritation began to come out in his letters. He responded to one woman on April 11 by saying, "My failure to answer your letter of some two weeks ago, did not arise, as you seem to think, from my desire not to give you the 'common courtesies of every day life,' but from a feeling on my part that I have some public duties to attend to other than to answer the innumerable applications for office which are poured in upon me."[7] Years later, Robert characterized his cabinet responsibility to deal with appointments as "the greatest possible bore."[8]

Due to the deluge of job requests, as well as the simple task of becoming acquainted with his new job and an overabundance of work to be done, Robert more than once during his first months in office stated he was "overwhelmed" with it all. "He has had, each day, several hundred requisitions to examine and sign," wrote Robert's personal secretary Charles Sweet, after only one week in the War Department. "The reception rooms and corridors are crowded with visitors from nine to five."[9] In the beginning, Robert clearly was not enjoying his new position. He wrote to a friend in April, "I am getting along here after a fashion, but would rather be in Chicago or New York."[10] By the end of May, Robert declared, "I prefer practicing law to performing my duties here, but now that I am in it, I must keep on, for a while, at least."[11]

In April, Robert and Mary traveled to Chicago to gather the children, pack the family possessions, and prepare the house for rental. A reporter from the Chicago *Inter Ocean* called at his house on Wabash Avenue to see how the new secretary was getting along. "Packing boxes stood about, some looking hungry and waiting to be filled, while others seemed over-satisfied and hardly able to contain their gorge. Books and pictures were scattered about the floor, and in the midst of the generally-confused household sat the Secretary and two or three friends enjoying a quiet chat over their cigars." Robert, ever the gentleman, welcomed the journalist into his home but refused to be interviewed on any official business.[12]

When the entire Lincoln family returned to Washington, they moved into a rented house on Massachusetts Avenue fronting on Thomas Circle, just a few blocks from the White House. Robert had an office created on the second floor where he spent many evenings "with a box of Henry Clay cigars at his elbow, for he is an almost incessant smoker, running over papers from the department and the news of the day."[13] Life in Washington was familiar to Robert and Mary, both of whose fathers had previously worked for years in the capital, and they readily took to life in Washington, made new acquaintances, and reconnected with old friends. Marian Adams, wife of Henry Adams, found the new War Secretary, whom she met through John Hay, "a quiet, gentlemanly, attractive man."[14] Washington socialite Mary Abigail Dodge found Mary Harlan Lincoln to be "very sweet, and simple, and attractive. . . . She has almost everything to make her handsome but health." She said Mrs. Lincoln told her she would like the new war secretary, "that he is thoroughly good, and honest, and noble."[15]

For the Lincoln children, Washington was a new world. By 1881, Mamie was twelve, Jack was eight, and Jessie was six. They had their own pony and cart in which to drive around their neighborhood, and they quickly became friends with President Garfield's children: James (age fifteen), Mary (called "Mollie," age fourteen), Irvin (age ten), and Abram (age eight). The White House soon resounded with the noises of boisterous play, such as when Willie and Tad Lincoln lived there during the Civil War.[16]

Unlike the previous generation of Lincolns, however, Mamie, Jack, and Jessie were well-behaved and proper young children—raised much differently than their father and his brothers. Robert and Mary were both quiet, reserved, and socially proper people, and they taught and influenced their children to be the same. Mary Harlan Lincoln, especially, as the mother and homemaker, had the largest influence and reared her daughters and son in the more disciplined and structured Harlan style as she had been. Mary's friend Minnie Chandler—whom she had not seen since 1868 and reconnected with on her 1881 return to Washington—was amazed at the three young Lincolns. "Mary, do you realize what lovely children you have? Mamie is a most fascinating little woman, with her hearty cordial kiss. . . . And Jack! I looked at him with perfect astonishment, seated straight in a chair with his feet down. My three young men behave very differently . . . Jessie . . . what a sweet, shy, graceful manner."[17]

For as much as the political rise of Abraham Lincoln's son excited the country in 1881, it was probably Robert's son, Jack, who captured the public's imagination the most. To have a Lincoln work in the White House was one thing, but to have an Abraham Lincoln around the White House again was something else. The press continually reported on his progress and antics and loved to describe how similar he was in looks, manner, intelligence, and temperament to his grandfather and namesake. One 1882 article reported, "Jack Lincoln, son of Secretary Lincoln, is a very bright and interesting little fellow, and affords a considerable amount of entertainment to the clerks and visitors to his father's office. The other day he was amusing himself by copying the names of the presidents, and, pausing, looked up from his work, and, with great naiveté, remarked: 'Why, ever so many of the presidents were named after streets in Chicago!'"[18]

Secretary Lincoln, like his own father, was a dedicated and affectionate family man, but during his first months in his new cabinet position, he was, as he said many times, overwhelmed with his new duties. In addition to the avalanche of appointments that threatened to bury him, Robert had numerous other items requiring his attention. One was to review and reorganize the various military departments. For this, he ordered Lieutenant General Philip Sheridan, commander of the Department of Missouri, to Washington to be consulted along with General of the Army William T. Sherman.[19] Under a previous act of Congress, Secretary Lincoln was in charge of preparing for certain aspects of the centennial celebration of the surrender of Lord Cornwallis at Yorktown, Virginia, scheduled for October 19, 1881. The secretary of war was responsible for appointing commissioners and expending monies for the erection and dedication of a monument and for arranging the military encampment and exercises. Lincoln selected Major General Winfield Scott Hancock to take command of the twenty thousand troops at the event and to direct all military movements during the celebration.[20]

Robert also began to inspect—sometimes by letter and sometimes in person—various military schools, forts, and outposts across the country to examine their effectiveness, preparedness, and circumstances. It was, in fact, during a trip to inspect Fort Leavenworth, Kansas, in May 1881 that Robert stopped in Springfield, Illinois, and saw his mother for the first time in five years. Ever since Mary Lincoln had been "restored to reason" by a Chicago jury in June 1876 and had been returned the power over her own finances, she had refused to speak to her only surviving son. She had fled to Europe in a self-imposed exile and lived mainly in Pau, France.

Mary returned to America in late 1880, at age sixty-one, due to her rapidly declining physical health; she went back to Springfield and lived once again in the Edwards home. She did not inform Robert. Not only was she still angry with him but she also was afraid he would immediately have her arrested and recommitted. This was the main reason she had not returned to the United States sooner. When Robert learned this from his Aunt Elizabeth, he asked her to assure his mother that "under no possible circumstances" would he do so. "I have no reason to think that such interference is now or will hereafter be proper but that whatever I might think hereafter, I would under no circumstance do anything," he stated.[21]

By April 1881, as Robert was preparing his trip to Fort Leavenworth, he probably knew—through newspaper reports and Aunt Elizabeth—that his mother was again living in Springfield. Also at this time, he learned that his cousin Fannie Wallace, daughter of his Aunt Frances Todd Wallace, was ill. He wrote his Aunt Frances that he hoped to visit her and Fannie in Springfield as he traveled through Illinois in mid-May.[22] The shocking news that his cousin, whom he thought was recovering, died in early May, may have made Robert's plans to visit Springfield definite in order to visit his bereaved relatives.[23]

Secretary Lincoln, traveling without his family because he was on official War Department business, stopped in Springfield from May 26 to May 27 on his way west.[24] While there, in addition to calling on the Wallace family, he spent an entire day with his mother at the Edwards home.[25] The origin of this meeting is unknown. Robert may have decided to call upon his mother out of simple hopefulness of a meeting, but the more likely scenario is that Elizabeth Edwards devised the reunion. She was the mother figure who understood her stubborn younger sister and the matriarch who respected Robert and always regretted the mother-son rift. Elizabeth was, in fact, probably the only person who *could* have brought them together; she had for years had been urging both sides to mend fences. While Robert had been willing, Mary never was. But by spring 1881, sick, lonely, missing her granddaughter, and perhaps finally softening in her anger at her son, Mary Lincoln relented.[26] Whatever occurred at this meeting has gone unrecorded, but it resulted in Mary's forgiveness. After this reunion, during which Robert found his mother in poor health and learned she had not left her room in six months, he and his family visited her every few weeks for the rest of her life.[27]

While reuniting with his mother certainly was a milestone at this point in Robert's personal life, the major political issue confronting him at this time was the preparation for a government-sponsored arctic expedition being run under the aegis of the War Department. This event would begin well but ultimately become the bane of Robert's entire tenure as secretary of war and continue to be argued over for many years.

The Lady Franklin Bay Expedition, as it was officially named, was part of the United States' participation in the first International Polar Year—a dozen countries cooperating in a joint scientific venture to explore the arctic. The year was set for 1882–83, from summer to summer, although the inception of the Polar Year idea itself dated to 1879. Although Captain Henry Howgate of the U.S. Signal Corps began pushing for his own arctic expedition in that year and again in 1880, it was not until March 3, 1881—the close of the congressional session and the day before President James A. Garfield was inaugurated into office—that the U.S. Congress approved it as an official government venture under the direction of the War Department's chief signal officer. The expedition to Lady Franklin Bay (one of two expeditions authorized and sent under the legislation) was tasked to leave in summer 1881 and carry on meteorological observations for two years in the high Canadian arctic, near the northwest tip of Greenland. The second year would coincide with the International Polar Year.[28]

The expedition consisted of twenty-five men and was commanded by thirty-seven-year-old Lieutenant Adolphus W. Greely of the Fifth Cavalry. Greely, according to one historian, "seemed to embody the combination of scientific and soldierly qualities that formed the twin pillars of the expedition."[29] He had long been fascinated by the arctic, had read every book about polar exploration he could find, and was an accomplished scientist and military commander. The official War Department orders, as drawn up by Greely and Chief Signal Officer General William B. Hazen, provided for a resupply ship to be sent to the expedition in summer 1882 and for the men to be returned to the United States by ship in summer 1883. The expedition was equipped with supplies to last two years, in case the 1882 resupply ship failed to arrive. If the 1883 relief ship failed to penetrate the icy waters up to Lady Franklin Bay, Greely's orders called for the men to travel south to meet at Smith Sound, a more accessible rendezvous point. Greely also planned to leave caches of supplies at various points above Smith Sound for his men to use if forced to make this overland trek.

While preparing for the expedition, Greely encountered a roadblock in the new Secretary of War. Robert Lincoln had inherited the arctic program when he entered his office, and he was not happy with it. Nor was President Garfield interested in it. Both men believed that whatever possible scientific knowledge would be gained from the perilous expedition—which they believed would be nominal—would be utterly inconsequential when compared to the American military lives that inevitably would be lost. So immediately upon entering his office, Robert ordered a review of the project to determine if it was feasible or practicable to actually undertake it. In the meantime, Greely had been attempting to assign personnel and contract for equipment, but he could not officially proceed until Lincoln signed the authorization papers, which the secretary refused for six weeks to do.[30]

In his frustration, Greely (along with General Hazen and U.S. Senator Omar D. Conger) began to incessantly badger the Secretary of War, Greely complaining that he could not move forward with his plans. Although Robert never explicitly stated his motives, it appears that he was purposely stonewalling Greely's preparation in order to prevent the expedition's departure before the arctic travel season closed. If Greely was forced to wait until 1882, perhaps Robert hoped he could quash the expedition over the ensuing year. In addition, part of the delay may have been caused by Robert's rising temper—an inherited Todd family trait—at Greely's petulance and brashness. By complaining at all but especially by going directly to Robert and also enlisting the support of a

U.S. senator, Greely had overstepped his bounds as an inferior military officer, something Robert never tolerated. (Such insubordination towards Robert, in fact, later led to the court-martial of General Hazen and a public argument with General Sheridan.) But Greely himself was not one to be disregarded, and he later confronted Secretary Lincoln about his "avowed hostility" to the expedition and accused him of thwarting the will of Congress by his lack of support. After this, Robert reluctantly gave the final orders to proceed, despite his "fear of disaster" befalling the expedition.[31]

On July 6, 1881, the expedition sailed from St. John's, Newfoundland, north toward Greenland. It arrived in Lady Franklin Bay quickly and easily on August 11. The uneventful passage north, due to a mild winter and early summer, in fact, belied the typical harsh conditions of the area. Robert later wrote, "The original voyage of Greely was so fatally easy that I confess I was not fully conscious of the peril into which he had put himself."[32] This peril became clear when both the 1882 supply ship and the 1883 relief ship failed to make it through the ice to reach Greely's party. The Lady Franklin Bay Expedition and the relief efforts ultimately became the story of failure, disaster, and horrible death that Secretary Lincoln had predicted and would have to confront for the next three years.

In these early days of the Garfield administration, Robert Lincoln impressed his peers, the press, and the public with his strong work ethic and administrative skills. "He is now a strong-looking young man, with plenty of beard, and grave yet prompt movement," lauded one journalist.[33] A Chicago newspaper editorialized, "He is not a genius, brilliant and erratic, but a man of talent, energy, conviction, dignity, and strong common sense. He is a growing man, and will be greater at the end of four years than he is now."[34] Robert himself eventually became familiar and adept with his duties and by May already was planning to escape his office and accompany General Sheridan and a party to Yellowstone National Park in Wyoming and also his annual family summer vacation to Rye Beach, New Hampshire.[35]

Saturday July 2, 1881, was a hot and sultry day. President Garfield woke early and spent the morning finishing up work and meeting separately with his cabinet members before leaving on a trip to New England.[36] Secretary of State James G. Blaine met with the president and accompanied him in his carriage to the Baltimore and Potomac Railroad Depot at Sixth Street and B Street NW. Some cabinet members and their wives were accompanying the president on his trip. Secretary Lincoln was scheduled to go but could not leave the city until the next day. Lincoln took his own carriage to the railroad station to excuse himself from the trip and arrived a few minutes after Garfield and Blaine. He was about forty feet away, walking toward the distinguished pair, who were in the ladies' waiting room on their way to the platform, when he heard two shots ring out through the station.[37] He heard someone cry, "The president is shot!" and he ran to Garfield's side. "I think I reached him in fifteen seconds," Robert wrote to his friend Norman Williams a few weeks after the shooting.

> He was lying on his back, his eyes closed and with a leaden gray look on his face. Mr. Blaine and one or two strangers were by him. I remembered that my driver was awaiting me and ran to him, told him to bring Dr. [D. W.] Bliss [the Garfield family physician]. By this time the President was surrounded by friends and by somebody's order was taken up stairs on a mattress. There was an enormous crowd gathering and threatening to lynch the assassin. I followed up stairs, ran across a telegraph room and it occurred to me that it would quiet things down to have one small force of troops here (four companies) show themselves and so I advised them to come with all speed. The doctors came (Bliss next after the Health officer whose office was near the depot) and a hasty examination was made. I was standing by the President as he lay on the floor upstairs on his mattress, when he opened his eyes, saw me and reached out his hand to me. His color had greatly improved and he was at once apparently the coolest man in the room, telling in a clear strong voice the location of his pains in answer to the surgeons. In about half an hour an ambulance was ready, he was taken down on his bed and put in it and with the doctors was driven at full speed to the White House. I followed with others, sent my carriage for Mary and by eleven o'clock all intruders were out of the grounds and a strong military guard on duty there and another at the jail to prevent lynching and a reserve between. From that time until Tuesday morning I was hardly out of the White House.[38]

Robert's actions to call for Dr. Bliss, call out troops, and evacuate and place a guard around the White House were decisively done, redolent even of his predecessor Edwin M. Stanton on the night of April 14, 1865. Robert also sent a veritable blizzard of telegrams to individuals and offices all across the country informing the appropriate people what had happened and giving continual updates on Garfield's medical condition.[39]

Garfield had been shot in two places. The first bullet had merely grazed the skin under his left arm; the second bullet went into his back just above the kidney and had perforated the liver. Dr. Bliss immediately declared the wound extremely serious. At the station, he said it was not necessarily a fatal wound, but in private he told Garfield and his cabinet ministers that the president may die within hours. For the first few days after the shooting, the doctors fluctuated between declaring the president in good shape and on the brink of death. Garfield himself was physically and mentally strong and kept a calm demeanor as a way to reassure his wife as well as the country. But those first two days were the worst. Robert later wrote, "I said that I did not believe that we were to have such singular coincidences as Adams and Jefferson dying on July 4, 1826, Monroe on Monday July 4, 1831, and Garfield on Monday July 4, exactly fifty years after to the day of the month and the week. This I figured out in the long hours of Sunday night."[40]

Garfield did not die on July 4 but remained convalescent in the White House, attended by a handful of the best doctors in the country. Vice President Chester A. Arthur was in New York, and although he did travel to Washington, he did not assert any claim to presidential power. Even his trip to Washington was undertaken with reluctance, fearing he would seem too eager to assume the presidency. Arthur believed the vice president had no power to do anything but await either the president's recovery or his death, although Garfield's clear inability to discharge his official duties, especially by mid-August, had many clamoring for Arthur to assert his Constitutional duty and take charge of the government. It was even reported that Postmaster General Thomas L. James and Secretary of War Lincoln supported the action. The issue in general and Arthur's actions in particular were widely covered and criticized by national newspapers.[41]

In those first few hours and days, in fact, Secretaries Lincoln and Blaine took immediate charge of the government. Lincoln used the military to control the situation and secure the president and the White House as well as send telegrams across the country explaining the event, while Blaine assured Americans abroad and foreign governments that the president had survived the attack. Lincoln and Blaine also undertook an immediate inquiry to establish whether the assassin, identified as Charles Guiteau, a forty-year-old lawyer and mentally disturbed, disgruntled office seeker, was the lone assassin or part of a large conspiracy.[42] It was determined Guiteau acted alone in order to rid the country of Garfield and replace him with Arthur. Guiteau, in fact, wrote letters of explanation in which he admitted the assassination was a "sad necessity" to unite the Republican party and save the country; he also said he was a Stalwart supporter of Grant and Arthur.[43] Robert later explained to a friend that after the turmoil of the event had concluded, the government simply ran itself, and each cabinet head maintained his own sphere. "Every man running his own department and thinking he is doing so well alone that he may be President some day. Sec. Kirkwood [Interior Department] and I have to confer about Indian matters but otherwise it is paddle your own course. I think it likely that all miss the hand-strengthening we used to give each other at our semi-weekly meetings and especially that we got always from our good chief but we are bound he shall find everything in good order when he takes the deck again."[44]

For all of the seeming ease with which Robert wrote about Garfield's assassination and its aftermath, it is impossible to think it did not seriously affect him and remind him of that dark and rainy night in April 1865 when the doctors huddled around his father on the too-small bed in the Petersen House, the politicians and soldiers coming and going to pay their last respects, when the little boarding room echoed with the hysterical cries and sobs of Mary Lincoln. The *New York Times* reported that, aside from Blaine, who was a close personal friend of Garfield, Secretary Lincoln seemed more affected by the current tragedy than anyone else, being reminded so vividly of his father's death. "My God," Robert exclaimed in front of the reporter on July 3. "How many hours of sorrow I have passed in this town." Postmaster General James replied, "Do you remember how often Gen. Garfield has referred to your father in the past few days?" "Yes," replied Robert, "and it was only night before last that I entered into a detailed recital of the events of that awful night."[45] But it was Mary Harlan Lincoln's friend Minnie Chandler who wrote what must have been on many minds at the time: "What an awful time these last two weeks must have been for your husband, with the all too vividly revived associations. Think how near he comes to our two great national tragedies."[46]

In addition to the slew of telegrams he sent across the country about the president's condition after the shooting, Robert wrote numerous multipage letters to friends and relatives telling of the attack and giving updates on the president's health.

On July 7, five days after the shooting, Robert wrote his father-in-law, James Harlan, stating encouragement about the president's condition. "For more than 48 hours there has been an entire absence of unfavorable symptoms. The wound however is a very dangerous one yet. Various things may happen, from which a fatal result may come. The president himself is very cheerful, and seems to be physically as strong as ever."[47]

The same day Robert wrote his former law partner Edward Isham three pages detailing the president's medical situation, as told him by the physicians, including aspects not publicly known or reported in the newspapers. The main secret was this: the president nearly died in those hours and days after the shooting, despite the positive public statements of recovery. "Sometimes our sense of this would be obliterated by the encouragement which came from his room that the dangerous symptoms were less pronounced than they had been, but when, as on Sunday morning, the bad symptoms began to develop very rapidly, we were all I think, without exception, discouraged to the last degree," he told Isham.[48]

On July 8, Robert wrote Lieutenant General Sheridan, relating his meeting at the White House with George Scoville, Charles Guiteau's brother-in-law. Scoville, a Chicago attorney whom Robert had known professionally for many years, asked Robert to procure him access to Guiteau in prison. Robert declined but introduced Scoville to the district attorney in charge of the case. Robert also instructed Sheridan to investigate Scoville's movements in Chicago on July 2 since the story he told in Washington was inconsistent with the known facts.[49]

On July 18, Robert wrote John Hay and expressed his concerns about Garfield. "I wish I felt better about the President. He is an awfully wounded man. I have not seen him since this Saturday afternoon but I am told he has changed a great deal and that the fight has left sad marks on him. Isn't the affair simply devilish?" Robert also used his inimitable humor to tell Hay a story:

> The other day a newspaper man says, says he, "I s'pose you can't go with Sheridan to the Yellowstone as you intended?" Says I "certainly not. I have telegraphed Sheridan to fill my place." Says he "what will you do?" Says I, "When the President gets well, if it is not too late, I may go to Rye Beach but I have no plans whatever now." Then he says to his paper that I am going to Rye Beach soon and the *New York World* of Saturday shudders at the heartlessness . . . etc. It reminds me of the old initiation into the Sons of Malta. The Candidate was asked, "would you lie in wait and steal upon the enemy?" "I would." "Record it! He would lie and steal!"[50]

While funny, this story reveals Robert's continuing distrust and even contempt of the press. Nor was it the first time regarding the assassination. Earlier in the month, Robert wrote Norman Williams, "The newspapers seem to have gone wild. Not one item in ten relating to talk and recurrences in the sick room have the slightest basis. . . . I especially advise you to put no faith in anything you may see in or from the *N.Y. Herald*. It finds room for all the stuff that anybody will insist and I am told that its Special [correspondent] here actually pays for any item in writing which may be brought him by anybody and puts it in his telegram."[51]

As the summer progressed, Garfield remained in his bed in the White House. His condition fluctuated, but he was generally lucid and calm and sometimes accepted visitors and played cards. An apparatus for blowing cold air from the basement of the White House through a pipe and into Garfield's room was installed to keep the president cool and comfortable.[52] The government continued working on its own momentum. Secretary Lincoln did not leave Washington that summer for a vacation as he expected but stayed close by the White House, as did the other cabinet members. By mid-August, Garfield seemed in no immediate danger, and Robert traveled to New York City to meet his law-partner-in-abeyance, Edward Isham, to discuss private business matters. While there, he received a telegram saying the president's condition had taken a drastic turn for the worse and urging the secretary to immediately return to Washington. "We have had a most anxious day," Robert wrote Hay on arrival in Washington on August 16. "At about one I received such information that I supposed the president would hardly live through tonight. We are now a little encouraged but there is no use in disguising the fact that the situation is very grave."[53] It was so grave, in fact, that that afternoon Robert assembled the cabinet to discuss possible presidential succession.[54]

The president's condition became a national obsession. Medical dispatches were released by Garfield's physicians every few hours and disseminated across the country via telegraph and newspaper.[55] They stated his temperature, his pulse and respiration, his level of pain, and his sleep habits, as well as his medical treatment. The doctors knew the bullet was lodged in Garfield's body somewhere, but they didn't know where, and they were afraid if they probed too much for it, the president would die.[56] The inventor Alexander Graham Bell even used his new metal detector on the president to try to locate the bullet, although Garfield's metal bed frame made the tool useless. The existing records do show, however, that Garfield's wound was continually probed by unsanitized metal instruments and even the physicians' fingers. Garfield's original wound was 3.5 inches long, but by September, the wound track was twenty inches long and oozing pus. The president was treated with doses of quinine and morphine and frequent sips of brandy. Garfield had chronic abdominal symptoms during his convalescence, and fearing his intestines had been pierced by the bullet, the doctors had Garfield fed rectally.[57]

By early September, with Garfield's condition not improving, his physicians decided he needed to be moved to a cooler, fresher climate than that of Washington. Through Secretary Lincoln's personal friendship and professional acquaintance with George M. Pullman, a special Pullman Company parlor car was arranged to take the failing president to the seashore at Elberon, New Jersey, on September 6.[58] He was accompanied by his family, his doctors, and his cabinet members. His condition continued to fluctuate, and on September 19, 1881, eighty days after being shot, President James A. Garfield died. Arterial hemorrhage along the track of the bullet was declared the official cause of death.[59] Medical historians today believe the wound actually was nonlethal, but Garfield died of infections caused by the unsanitary practices of the doctors.[60] Garfield's body was taken back to Washington, D.C., and a grand national funeral planned before the removal of the remains to his hometown of Mentor, Ohio. "Never was more tender solicitude, more deep personal feeling, apart from every selfish consideration, evinced than by members of General Garfield's Cabinet," declared the *Washington Post*. "They seemed rather to be the brothers of the prostrate man than counselors whom he had selected for the administration of government. During the entire three months preceding the assassination they had learned to love him."[61]

During Garfield's long convalescence, his assassin, Charles Guiteau, was in jail. He was indicted on October 8, 1881, for Garfield's murder. Guiteau pleaded not guilty at his trial by reason of insanity as well as malpractice, claiming it was medical incompetence that killed the president, not his bullet. After a two-month trial, the jury found Guiteau guilty. He was hanged on June 30, 1882.[62]

Just as historians have avoided examining Robert Lincoln's role during the assassination and aftermath, so, too, did contemporary reports. In fact, at Guiteau's trial, every person in or near the depot's waiting room during the shooting on July 2 (twenty-five witnesses total) was called to testify for the prosecution at the trial—everyone except Robert Lincoln. Likewise, newspaper reports at the time typically mentioned Secretary Lincoln's cabinet activities but also avoided detailed examinations of his recollections and of his experiences and feelings about the assassination. Given Robert's proximity and unparalleled access to the president during this entire period, his general omission from the scene is startling. It is possible that since he did not actually *see* the shooting, he was not called to testify; or the press and the Guiteau prosecutors sought to respect Robert's feelings and privacy at a time so reminiscent of his own personal tragedy twenty years before; or perhaps Robert avoided the press and specifically requested that he not be called to testify at Guiteau's trial, not only for personal reasons but also so the story did not change from one about the martyred Garfield to the unlucky secretary of war. No evidence is known to explain this circumstance or Robert's feelings about it.

On September 20, Secretary of War Lincoln officially informed the U.S. military of President Garfield's death and of Vice President Arthur's swearing in as president.[63] Arthur had spent most of the eighty days since the shooting at his home in New York City awaiting events. After Garfield's death, Arthur was sworn into office in his home and then traveled down to Elberon with former President Grant to accompany the dead president's body to Washington and attend the funeral.

Immediately after the funeral ceremonies were ended, the country exploded with wonder and speculation about Arthur's intentions as president, especially the composition of his cabinet. Which current members would leave, and which would stay? Would they resign or be asked to leave? It was generally assumed that the entire body would be replaced. The new president invited all of Garfield's men to delay their resignations until Congress convened in December. In the end, Arthur retained only one of Garfield's original advisers—Secretary of War Robert T. Lincoln.

15

"The Best Secretary of War since Jefferson Davis"

When he assumed the presidency in September 1881, Chester A. Arthur had no experience in national politics and absolutely no desire to be president of the United States. He was a part of New York State machine politics, a loyal partisan supporter of powerful state boss U.S. Senator Roscoe Conkling. In his youth, Arthur had been a teacher and lawyer in New York City and then served as quartermaster general of the State of New York during the Civil War, ending his service with the rank of brigadier general. In 1871, President Grant appointed Arthur collector of the port of New York, a lucrative and politically influential position. Arthur was an honest man who ran the Customs House well administratively, but as a firm believer in political spoils, he used his position to the utmost to reward Republican party loyalists with jobs and other emoluments. He was ousted from office in 1878 by President Rutherford B. Hayes's government reform efforts. Arthur's nomination as vice president in 1880 was an attempt to mollify the Stalwart wing of the Republican Party, loyal to Grant and Conkling, rather than a reward to Arthur. As one biographer wrote, "That happened less because of Arthur's skills and ambition than because he was acceptable."[1] In fact, after Garfield was shot, politicians and journalists were terrified at the idea that such an overt partisan and spoilsman as "Chet" Arthur might become president.

The new president surprised his critics and supporters alike, however, by being a respectable, nonpartisan leader who eschewed his previous cronyism and championed civil-service reform. But upon his ascension to office, he first had to create his own cabinet. A total overhaul of Garfield's cabinet was expected, although it was generally accepted that whatever Arthur decided, he would not dare remove the son of Abraham Lincoln. But did Robert Lincoln want to stay? He was unhappy as a politician and longed to return to the private life of a Chicago attorney; he even mused aloud if it would be in his family's best interest for him to resign. He told a reporter from the *Brooklyn Eagle* he was considering the financial aspects of the issue, saying he made $12,000 a year as an attorney compared to $8,000 as a cabinet member, and Washington was far more expensive to live in than Chicago.[2] But Robert Lincoln was a man who believed in civic duty and party loyalty, so when President Arthur asked him to remain at the War Department, he could not refuse.[3] Few people believed Secretary Lincoln was retained for anything more than his name; but true to his personal principles and dignity, Robert later wrote that he would have resigned if he felt Arthur had retained him for anything less than his job performance.[4] Yet, even after agreeing to stay in the Cabinet, he wrote to John Hay that he was in a "near rut" and having no fun. "I long for the independence of Chicago," he lamented.[5]

Robert Lincoln's tenure as secretary of war under President Arthur could, as with any and every presidential cabinet member, be the subject of its own book. In general, it is a record of unexciting administrative duties, although it does have certain interesting highlights. The most common question about Secretary Lincoln's term in office was his role in handling the western Indian wars. Despite his title of secretary of war, Robert Lincoln actually had very little to do with the issue. Indian policy was the purview of the Office of Indian Affairs in the Interior Department, not the War Department, and so Secretary Lincoln had little, if any, input on that policy.[6] He was in charge of the army, and as such he was responsible for sending troops and commanding officers out to the western territories to implement the policy decided by others in the government. In fact, Robert relied on his commanders in the field and General of the Army William T. Sherman to handle most logistics of western troops deployments, knowing they, as professional soldiers, understood it better than he, who had only four months of military experience in 1865. By 1883, the "Indian wars," as they were called, were over, and the army switched from fighting the Native Americans to protecting them and their reservation lands from encroachment by white settlers. Robert's papers include few mentions about Indian policy, other than one letter in which he declared that the Apache troubles "disturbed" him his entire tenure.[7]

During the final months of 1881, one of the most pressing issues for Secretary Lincoln was not professional but personal. His mother's health continued to decline. Nearly sixty-three years old in late 1881, Mary Lincoln had suffered numerous physical maladies for years—headaches, joint pains and swelling, incontinence, fatigue, frequent spells of cough and cold—and they only increased with age. In December 1879, she had fallen off a stool while hanging a painting and seriously injured her spine, causing her intense pain on her left side and difficulty walking. Then in June 1880, due to the pain and weakness in her left side, Mary fell down a flight of stairs, further injuring her back.[8] She consulted with a doctor in New York City on her return to America, and he told a newspaper reporter the widow suffered from inflammation of the spine, kidney trouble, and a "great mental depression."[9]

The shooting of President Garfield in July 1881 further affected Mary's health, especially mentally. She was enraged that another president had been shot; she was sympathetic to Mrs. Garfield; she was despondent in the recollections of her husband's murder; and she was terrified and paranoid that her son, as secretary of war, would be assassinated next.[10] But what upset her most came after Garfield died, when his widow, Lucretia, was flooded with sympathy—and money. Influential businessman Cyrus Field had immediately begun soliciting subscriptions to help Mrs. Garfield care for her five children and live a decent lifestyle as a presidential widow. The public responded quickly, and more than $300,000 was raised for the widow's benefit, while it also was understood Congress was going to give her a pension.[11]

After all the hardships, heartache, and indignities that Mary Lincoln suffered after her husband's assassination, especially the reluctance (and delay) with which Congress gave her any money at all, Mary was insulted and infuriated at the outpouring of sympathy for Mrs. Garfield. The financial aspects especially aroused Mary Lincoln, and her delusions of her own poverty suddenly and aggressively resurfaced. While she never believed the $3,000 per year she was granted in 1870 was enough for her to live comfortably on, by September 1881 she was complaining her income was far insufficient for her boarding payments and her necessary medical care.[12] While Mary Lincoln certainly was unwell and spending money on medical treatments, she also had a long history of hypochondria. Her son Robert knew this all too well and wrote to one of his mother's friends, "The reports you have seen about her are exaggerated very much. She is undoubtedly far from well . . . and she thinks she is very ill. My own judgment is that some part of her troubles is imaginary."[13]

By November 1881, Mary Lincoln roused herself for one last pension fight with Congress—no doubt much to the chagrin of her son Robert who, unlike in the late 1860s when he was a private citizen, was in 1881 a public figure. Mary's physician, Dr. Louis A. Sayre, announced to the country that Mary was living in near poverty, and her annual $3,000 congressional pension was inadequate to cover her living expenses, which included rent, board, medical advice and treatment, clothing, travel, and a personal attendant. He chastised Congress for its penury and said the former first lady suffered from Bright's disease of the kidneys and inflammation of the spinal cord. "Mrs. Lincoln is improving but her condition is such that she will need attention constantly for a long time, and possibly as long as she lives," he declared.[14] Mary also enlisted the help of her friend Noyes W. Miner to lobby Congress on her behalf. Unlike the Old Clothes Scandal in 1867, this time Mary was sensitive to her son's public position and instructed Miner, "*Do not* approach Robert T. Lincoln you will understand how he is situated."[15]

Like so many aspects of and events throughout his mother's life, Robert watched as the accusation that she was practically destitute created national headlines. Some newspapers accused Dr. Sayre of meddling in other's affairs, seeking only his own publicity; other newspapers accused Mary of succumbing again to the same embarrassing delusions of poverty that led to the Old Clothes Scandal in 1867.[16] Some people even accused Robert of filial neglect for not taking care of his mother. Mary herself refuted that allegation, telling a reporter that both Robert and his wife had repeatedly suggested they take care of her, but Mary refused and "insisted it was her duty to live upon her own resources."[17]

Unlike Mary Lincoln's previous headline-making behaviors, in 1881 Robert and his wife appear to have been little affected by the public clamor. No writings exist to suggest Robert was upset or embarrassed by his mother's publicity. Of course, with age, children, and experience come patience, or Robert may simply have become inured to it after a lifetime of experience. But Robert was far from apathetic. He and his family had resumed their pre-1875 close relationship with their matriarch and had been visiting her biweekly for the past year; and while Mary was in New York for medical treatment, the Lincolns visited her every week.

Robert and his wife were eager that their mother receive financial parity with Mrs. Garfield—not only for her financial security and medical care but for her tenuous mental balance as well. To that end, Mary Harlan Lincoln approached Cyrus Field—the man responsible for Mrs. Garfield's hugely successful subscription fund—and asked him to lobby Congress for an increase in her mother-in-law's government pension from $3,000 to $5,000 per year.[18] When legislation to achieve this increase was introduced in both the U.S. House and Senate in January 1882, it is likely that Secretary Lincoln had a quiet hand in it, especially since the Senate sponsor, John A. Logan of Illinois, was a longtime and close personal friend of Robert Lincoln.[19]

Congress supported the bill "for the relief of Mrs. Lincoln" without any controversy. The legislation not only raised Mary's pension by $2,000 but also paid her $15,000 in back payments.[20] The ease of its passage when compared to her 1865–70 pension battle had many reasons, not the least of which were her son's political position, reputation, and influence. Mary requested the $15,000 be sent to her immediately, as she believed—in her typical paranoia—her "enemies" in Washington would attempt to prevent her from receiving it.[21] Robert was satisfied that his mother would receive the extra income she so badly wanted and in many ways needed. But before her increased pension payments could begin, she died of a stroke in July.

Robert was living alone in Washington at the time his mother died; his wife and children had left the city in late May to spend the summer at the Harlan home in Mount Pleasant—a summer ritual that had begun in the early 1870s. Mary loved spending summers at her childhood home, "so very restful," she liked to say, "and so good for the children growing up"—and the Lincoln children loved it as well.[22] Mary also liked to visit and help care for her invalid mother and during this trip planned to accompany her parents to the mineral spas of Colorado Springs, Colorado, to improve her own health, which was delicate.[23] Robert had to stay in the capital to work but had been planning a trip out west to visit his family when he was informed by telegram on the morning of Sunday, July 16, that his mother was critically ill.

He immediately began to arrange his affairs at the War Department so he could leave Washington that night and be in Springfield with his mother by Tuesday morning. In the meantime, he asked to be updated hourly on her condition. Before he could leave that night, however, he was telegraphed that his mother had died.[24] Robert wired the news to his wife in Colorado Springs and asked her to meet him in Chicago, where they could then proceed to Springfield together for the funeral. The children stayed with the Harlans in Colorado.

Robert did not reach Springfield until the evening of Tuesday, July 18. He was unexpectedly delayed about twelve hours in Chicago because of his wife's poor health. She had made the trip from Colorado Springs, but the journey was so affecting that she was "confined to her room by ill health" and could not go down to Springfield with her husband.[25] Robert, instead, traveled with his law partner, Edward Isham, and a few other Chicago friends.

The funeral of Mary Todd Lincoln occurred Wednesday morning, July 19. It had been arranged by Elizabeth Edwards while her nephew was en route from Washington, and Robert finalized the plans on his arrival in Springfield Tuesday night.[26] As his mother had requested, Robert had her body laid out for private viewing by family and friends in the parlor of the Edwards home, the same room in which she was married.[27] The funeral was then held in her old parish, the First Presbyterian Church of Springfield, and was characterized as nearly the largest funeral in the city's history, second only to that of her husband.[28]

As Robert walked in the funeral procession from the Edwards home to the church, he saw a city in mourning, with flags draped at half mast, all business suspended for the day, and crowds of saddened people mulling outside the church. Inside, the church was filled with flowers, wreaths, and bouquets, and every pew was occupied. Robert sat in the front row, next to his mother's cousin Lizzie Grimsley and others of the Todd clan, and listened to the Reverend James A. Reed's eulogy extolling Mary Lincoln's virtues.[29] In what was perhaps to Robert's grieving mind the most personal and perspicacious statement—spoken or written—concerning his mother's postpresidential life, Reed likened Abraham and Mary Lincoln to two great trees whose roots were intertwined, and when one had been blasted away, the other also died, only much more slowly.[30] Mary's casket, accompanied by an enormous funeral cortege of citizens and admirers, then was conveyed to the Lincoln tomb in Oak Ridge Cemetery. There it was placed in crypt 4, alongside her sons Eddie, Willie, and Tad and her beloved husband.

Standing, once again, in the family tomb, surrounded by the names of his parents and brothers etched in marble, with only one crypt now remaining empty, what must Robert Lincoln have been feeling? Although his mother had been a great worry and burden to him for seventeen years, he loved her dearly and did not blame her for her mental vagaries. Did he remember most her insanity trial in 1875, or is it more probable that he remembered her affectionate maternity while he was growing up? Did he remember reenacting the stories of Sir Walter Scott in the front yard and hearing his mother cry in support out the window, "Grammercy, brave knights. Pray be more merciful than you are brawny"? Did he remember visiting her in the White House during his college breaks and traveling with her to New York City, New Jersey, and Vermont? And how much did he dwell on the palpable fact that he was now the last surviving member of his father's immediate family? No personal letters exist to offer a glimpse of his feelings. Only one newspaper account mentioned his reaction after the burial: "After viewing the scene and the tears of a loving people, old friends of his father and mother, and old soldiers when the former was commander-in-chief of the national forces, the modest son, the present War Minister of the Republic, Robert Todd Lincoln, turned away from the reminders of sad memories."[31]

The fact that a group of Robert's personal Chicago friends traveled with him from Chicago to attend the funeral suggests that Robert either wanted or needed their support. Robert himself was not a religious man and did not seek solace through a church or a pastor. He even eschewed any religious prayers or ceremony at the Lincoln gravesite, arranging such ministrations to occur only during the funeral in the church. Like his father, Robert Lincoln apparently believed in a higher power, but he did not subscribe to any particular religious denomination.[32]

Robert had spent his entire adult life trying to protect his mother from the selfish motives of untrustworthy people. He warned her about questionable business investments, shady Spiritualist mediums, and general unsavory companions. After her death, Mary's last surviving son had one final act of protection to undertake. The night before the funeral, Robert met with his mother's cousin John Todd Stuart, the man who was Abraham Lincoln's first law partner, who had stayed close to Mary Lincoln during her entire life and who also was the chairman of the executive committee of the National Lincoln Monument Association. Robert revealed that he feared for the safety of his mother's remains, feared someone would attempt to steal her body as they had attempted to steal her husband's six years earlier. He arranged with Stuart to have his mother's body secretly removed from the crypt and buried next to his father in the basement of the tomb.[33]

In 1876, after the attempt to steal Abraham Lincoln's body was thwarted, Stuart had gathered members of the committee, and together they buried Lincoln's coffin in the basement catacombs of the tomb. In 1879, the coffin was reburied in a different spot in the catacombs for further protection. At 10 P.M. on the night of July 21, two days after Mary Lincoln's burial, eight members of the Lincoln Guard of Honor—the men sworn to protect the remains of Abraham Lincoln—gathered at the Lincoln monument. They removed Mary Lincoln's coffin from crypt 4, carried it down into the catacombs of the Lincoln tomb monument, and buried it under the dirt floor beside the remains of her husband.

Upon learning that the reburial had been completed, Robert wrote a letter of thanks to the men of the Lincoln Guard of Honor, addressed to his longtime friend and guard member Clinton Conkling:

> My Dear Friend—On my return here [Washington] I find a letter from Major Stuart advising me that you and the other gentlemen of the Guard of Honor, have laid me under a great obligation by carrying out the wish I expressed to him that my mother's body should be placed beside my father's, so that there can be no danger of a spoliation. It is a great satisfaction to know that such an act is now impossible, and I think it will be best that no change should be made for a long time to come.
>
> I cannot adequately thank you and the other gentlemen for personally doing this, so that the object should be fully attained; but I beg you and them to be assured that I appreciate the kind act.[34]

Robert stayed in Springfield for nearly a week after his mother's funeral, attending to her estate, especially the packing and preparing of her sixty-four trunks of possessions for removal from the Edwards home. Despite the sheer volume of possessions, the one thing Robert did not find was his mother's will. He knew she had drawn one up between 1872 and 1873 with the assistance of her friend and sometime legal counsel James Bradwell, but the document itself was neither found nor brought forward.[35] Robert, therefore, as his mother's sole heir, applied to the Sangamon County Court for letters of administration in order to receive her estate, which totaled $84,035.[36]

Robert returned to his wife in Chicago, where he found her little improved but well enough to travel with him back to Washington. Why she did not return to Colorado Springs is unknown, but apparently she saw it as her duty—"like the Harlan she was and the Lincoln she had become," as her cousin said—to at least begin the job of examining and cataloguing all her mother-in-law's possessions, a collection she bemoaned as "this unconscionable accumulation."[37] Apparently, she did this from her sick room in Washington, around her daily doctor visits. Her health remained tepid, however, and a concerned Robert determined in early September "in trying to get her health restored" to take his wife the seashore at Atlantic City, New Jersey, where she could take the fresh air and medical cures.[38] By the time the Lincoln children returned to Washington in late October, Robert wrote a friend, "Mrs. Lincoln is no worse than when I saw you, but does not improve as rapidly as we could wish."[39]

Secretary Lincoln received the inevitable sympathy from the country for his mother's passing (and his wife's continual illness), but as each month went by, he also received greater respect as a cabinet administrator. In 1881, he was the only cabinet member to complete and submit his yearly budget request on time; and all of his yearly reports were able and intelligent documents. They showed that as secretary of war, Robert Lincoln was concerned with improving department management and reducing overall department costs, as well as improving army efficiency. "I do not see Bob often," former presidential secretary John Nicolay wrote to John Hay in early 1883, "but the Department seems to be running pretty smoothly and I judge he is making a good record."[40] In June 1883, one newspaper wrote a long and unusual encomium to the war secretary, explaining his personal friends and habits, his resemblances and differences with his illustrious father, and his excellent management of his department. "His administration has been a long and careful study of correct and useful methods of doing the public business," the article stated. "He is a tireless worker. . . . He has the strength and the enthusiasm for his work which make him able and willing to burn the midnight oil, when it is necessary, in order that he may fully understand the questions he is to decide or the advice he shall give to the President." The story also quoted Adjutant General Richard C. Drum, who said of his superior, "He is the best secretary of war we have had since Jefferson Davis"—a statement repeated by another admirer six months later.[41]

Since Arthur assumed the presidency, Robert had dealt with numerous important issues in his department. He had been responsible for overseeing relief efforts for the four hundred thousand victims of a massive Mississippi River flooding that spanned twenty-two thousand square miles and affected six states. Secretary Lincoln sent troops to the region, arranged for emergency shelters for displaced residents, disbursed $350,000 in federal aid, and served on the board of trustees of the Red Cross.[42] He oversaw the investigation of the value of Robert E. Lee's former lands in Arlington, Virginia, which led to the purchase of the land by the U.S. government and eventually became the Arlington National Cemetery.[43] Robert caused a small religious controversy when he refused to allow the building of a Catholic church on the Presidio Military Reservation in San Francisco. His refusal, endorsed by General of the Army Sherman, was based on his opposition to nongovernmental use of federal land without a sanctioning act of Congress.[44] Secretary Lincoln also confronted the thorny issue of race relations in the army in the form of courts-martial and removals of black soldiers and West Point cadets. In these cases, which Robert in one letter dubbed "nightmares," he consistently followed the code of army conduct and the military laws but clearly favored extending rights to black soldiers when he could.[45]

Another "nightmare" case for Secretary Lincoln concerned the court-martial of Sergeant John A. Mason, who, while on military guard of Charles Guiteau, President Garfield's killer, tried to assassinate the assassin. Mason was on duty outside the U.S. Jail in Washington, D.C., on September 11, 1881, when he fired a bullet through Guiteau's cell window, barely missing Guiteau's head. He was court-martialed for breach of military discipline (sixty-second Article of War), found guilty, and sentenced to a dishonorable discharge and eight years at hard labor in the penitentiary. Mason's case became a cause célèbre, and Robert was sent numerous petitions for Mason's pardon—since, after all, his target was only the president's assassin, so really he had done nothing wrong, according to his supporters—including one by the judge-advocate general of the army. Secretary Lincoln disagreed with calls for clemency and recommended to President Arthur that a pardon would be detrimental to the public interest and to military discipline and instead suggested a partial remittance of sentence. "I have been very much interested in having the law sustained in this matter, whatever may be the President's final action by way of clemency," Robert wrote. Arthur pardoned Mason in 1883.[46]

Robert also caused and caught a little controversy by securing his beloved Aunt Emily Todd Helm—an ardent and unapologetic Democrat and widow of a Confederate Civil War general—a federal job as postmistress of Elizabethtown, Kentucky, in 1883 and displacing a loyal Republican in the process.[47]

Robert's appointment of his aunt as postmistress—and the myriad other types of assistance he gave his Todd relatives and other friends—were not the only personal prerogatives he asserted as secretary of war. In early 1883, he asked the commissioner of agriculture to have his department examine and report on the quality of the silver in a mining claim he and his father-in-law, James Harlan, were thinking of investing in—such a request was not questionable at the time, although today it certainly smacks of conflict of interest.[48] Also in 1883, Robert used his official position in the cabinet to deny a federal job to a man who had offended him eleven years earlier—a clear indication of Robert's inheritance of the Todd family temper and proneness to holding grudges.

The offense related to Abraham Lincoln's former friend and legal colleague Ward Lamon, who had applied for the position of postmaster of Denver, Colorado. Lamon was the author of the sensational 1872 biography of his old friend that repeated so many of the offensive assertions of William Herndon that Robert Lincoln found impertinent and abhorrent. Eleven years later, when Secretary of War Lincoln heard about Lamon's application for postmaster, Robert sat down with Postmaster General Timothy O. Howe and told him such an appointment would be "personally offensive" to him and requested its refusal. When Lamon heard of his denial, he also heard rumors that the secretary of war was responsible. "If what is charged is true I can't understand it," Lamon wrote to Robert. "[I]t is so unlike anything your father ever did or was capable of doing that I can't and won't believe it until I know from you the truth or falsehood of it."[49] Robert, usually so smooth and diplomatic in his correspondence, replied with unapologetic vigor and explained his motives.

> The facts are that I observed in a morning paper here a statement that you were a candidate for the place in question. I took an early opportunity to say to the Postmaster General that your appointment would be personally offensive to me, and I explained to him, briefly, the reasons.
>
> They are that notwithstanding the especially kind consideration accorded to you by my father, from the time when he was in a position to benefit you, you, after his death, published a volume called "The Life of Abraham Lincoln," so offensive in its character that upon advice of several friends to avoid useless personal annoyance to myself, I have never until today opened it. I was made aware, however, by many newspaper paragraphs, which I could not easily avoid seeing, that it contained one insinuation which was especially offensive in itself, and made more so by the pretended effort to take away its force by a reference to mere neighborhood repute.[50] I refer to the first paragraph on page 10 of your book, which I have opened for the sole purpose of being definite in a matter which, to my amazement, you

> seem to have forgotten. The statement in lines 16, 17, and 18 of the paragraph was easily proved to be absolutely false,—more easily, as it chanced, than would be likely in nine cases out of ten.[51] I cannot believe you acted by inadvertence, merely using carelessly material bought from Herndon; for it was told me before the publication of your book that you had resisted the importunity of at least one good friend of my father, who begged you to omit some offensive statements which he had seen in proof the sheets, of which I believe this was one.
>
> I have no reason to believe that you did not know the statement to be without foundation when you made it; but however this may be, the burden of the paragraph has always appeared to me to be an astonishing exhibition of malicious ingratitude on your part towards your dead benefactor. I cannot say whether my action in this matter is, as you say, unlike anything my father ever did or was capable of doing. He was charitable and forgiving to the last degree, but I think that no man attempted while he was living to give him such a wound as you tried to deal when his friendship was no longer of practical use to you except to be advertised to increase the sale of your merchandise.[52]

Lamon was infuriated by Robert's letter and responded with a multipage diatribe defending the accuracy of his book and belittling the war secretary as a "knave" and a "fool." "You seem to form a melancholy contrast between yourself and your noble sire," Lamon retorted. "Judging from your letter to me if nobility of character has ever been presented to your mind it must have been only while you were thinking of the perfection of your father."[53]

Robert did not respond to Lamon's second letter and in no way regretted his own letter. He replied to a suggestion that he apologize to Lamon by saying he could not do so and keep his self-respect. "I have been for years indignant at Lamon's outrageous conduct towards my father after his death," Robert wrote. "[My letter to him] was not intended to be complimentary."[54] For the rest of his life, whenever the topic of Lamon's book was broached to him, Robert responded simply by saying it was "blackguardianism" fabricated from malicious and selfish motives. Lamon, on the other hand, could not let the insult go. He wrote letters to people such as David Davis and Leonard Swett ranting about his ill treatment, defending the book his friends resented, and berating Robert Lincoln.[55]

The major event of 1883, however, was undoubtedly the summer presidential trip to Yellowstone Park in Wyoming.[56] Summers were a slow political time in Washington with Congress on recess, so it was an excellent opportunity for the president to get out of the humid swampiness of the capital and see America's first national park. Along the journey, Arthur would accomplish a few official visits to U.S. military forts, as well as meet with Native American tribes and address Indian policy, but the primary reason for the trip was relaxation for a seriously ill president. Arthur was diagnosed with Bright's disease, a fatal kidney ailment, in 1882, although only Arthur, his physician, and a few confidants knew it. Symptoms of the disease included nausea, mental depression, and indolence, and the typically prescribed remedies were rest and relaxation. The 1883 Yellowstone trip was hoped to be a restorative.

The presidential expedition was under the auspices of Secretary Lincoln's War Department, specifically under command of General Philip Sheridan, commander of the western and southwestern military divisions of the army, who had made similar trips during the previous two years for military and scientific survey purposes. The 1883 trip, in fact, was a previously arranged survey mission, which the president decided to accompany. Arthur had attempted to go to Yellowstone in 1882, and Secretary Lincoln had attempted to accompany Sheridan in both 1881 and 1882, but events had intervened to prevent the plans.

The 1883 presidential party included in addition to Arthur, Lincoln, and Sheridan, U.S. Senator George C. Vest of Missouri, Montana Governor John Schuyler Crosby, a friend of the president, a few military officers, and a physician. Professional photographer Frank Jay Haynes also accompanied the group to officially document the excursion. By order of both the president and the secretary of war, no reporters were allowed to go, although many had petitioned for a spot in the party. (Arthur and Lincoln both felt that if a reporter was present, "our pleasure will be destroyed.") Instead, press releases were written by military personnel, approved by the president, and sent to the Associated Press.[57] The retinue was escorted by seventy-five men from Troop G of the Fifth U.S. Cavalry, and 175 pack animals carried supplies.

Arthur and his party left Washington on July 30 and traveled by special Pullman railroad car (probably arranged by Secretary Lincoln due to his personal friendship and previous professional relationship with George M. Pullman) to Louisville, Kentucky, where the president opened the Southern Cotton Exposition.[58] From there, the group traveled to Robert's hometown of Chicago where President Arthur and Secretary Lincoln both were badgered by reporters. Just before the train's departure for Cheyenne, a *Chicago Tribune* correspondent complained to Lincoln about the outlawed press coverage of the trip, "It is easier for a man to get a post office in Indiana than it is for a reporter to get on that train." Robert, true to his distrust and dislike of journalists, half jocularly retorted, "If one does get on he will be dropped through the trestle-work of the first bridge we reach."[59]

At Green River, Wyoming, after Arthur, Lincoln, and Vest made a few brief remarks to gathered citizens, the party traveled nearly two hundred miles by mule-drawn spring wagons to Fort Washakie. There, President Arthur undertook some Indian relations with the Arapahoe and Shoshone tribes. He watched five hundred Arapahoe warriors stage a mock battle for him, followed by twenty Shoshone braves performing a war dance. Arthur then met with the chiefs of both tribes to discuss the transfer of Indian affairs responsibility from the Interior Department to the War Department. It is unclear if Secretary Lincoln participated in this meeting, but he did attend to official duties by inspecting the fort and meeting with military officers.[60]

In yet another instance of false journalism that Robert Lincoln so disdained, the *Chicago Tribune* reported that Lincoln stayed behind at the fort for a few days of department business while the president and other party continued their journey. The official presidential press release, which was always approved by Robert and perhaps in this case even influenced by him, mocked the story and the "mythical personage" of the *Tribune* reporter, who was not part of the trip. "As the secretary has never been absent, it is a matter of much curiosity how the inventive genius of the fictitious correspondent could be able to restore him to us," the release stated. "As a matter of fact Mr. Lincoln has been one of the keenest daily observers of the country through which we are passing, and in constantly and pleasantly reminding us of his presence."[61]

From Fort Washakie, the presidential party set out on horseback for Yellowstone, traveling through country most Americans had never seen and that had only recently had been too dangerous to traverse due to the presence of renegade Indian war parties. For three weeks and more than three hundred miles, the party traveled through the "Yellowstone country" on horseback, rising every day at 5 A.M., traveling from 6 A.M. until noon, then encamping again. The afternoons were spent hiking, hunting, and fishing, the latter being the favorite activity of both the president and his secretary of war. Robert was an avid angler and during his tenure in the War Department took numerous fishing trips with the president and other government officials to places such as Pelee Island in Lake Erie, Ontario, Canada, and Governor's Island, New York. Lincoln did little or no hunting on the trip due to his nearly sightless right eye, the effects of his childhood strabismus.

During the journey, the party traversed difficult and dangerous trails, encountered hail, wind, and sandstorms, and endured multiple nights of below-freezing temperatures. They also saw some of the most beautiful and pristine country in the United States, including the Grand Tetons, the Titan Basin, Jackson's Lake, and "an old faithful geyser" that greeted the travelers shortly after their arrival with one of its hourly eruptions.[62]

The trip ended on September 1, when the party traveled to Livingston, Montana, and the main line of the Northern Pacific Railroad. They went to Minneapolis to participate in the Northern Pacific's celebration of its east-west transcontinental rail-line hookup—a major achievement in railway transportation.[63] Robert Lincoln, like all Americans, was impressed and fascinated by the expansion of railroads across the country, captivated not just by the ease of personal travel it created but also by the business possibilities it engendered. Unlike most of his fellow countrymen, however, Robert had traveled all over these new lines, understood the property and financial issues involved, inspected their operations, talked to the men responsible for building them, and was friends and colleagues with the businessmen who financed them. As a young boy in Illinois, Robert could remember the uncomfortable and tedious traveling by stagecoach and riverboat to Washington, D.C., with his Congressman father. During the Civil War, he traveled the rails for pleasure across the east with his mother and then witnessed the army construct new lines to move supplies. In 1866, he had traveled the Union Pacific Railroad to its western terminus in Omaha, Nebraska, and now he was witness to the completion of a northern transcontinental rail line.

From Minnesota, the presidential party traveled by rail to Chicago, where Secretary Lincoln had arranged for a huge political reception to greet the president. Newspapers reported that the intention of the event was to create a "boom" in the northwest for Arthur's nomination and election to the presidency in 1884.[64] On the way to Chicago, Robert had stopped for one day in Mount Pleasant to see his family, who were there on their annual summer visit; in Chicago, Robert probably visited his law partner, Edward Isham, to discuss the state of the law practice.[65] By September 7, the presidential party was back in Washington after more than one month away.

The Yellowstone trip was a mixture of business and pleasure for Lincoln and the other government officers in the party. After returning to Washington, Secretary Lincoln oversaw the creation of a memorial scrapbook/photo album of the entire trip containing the Haynes photographs and the military press releases given to the Associated Press.[66] Not long after his return, the other principal event of this year occurred: the failure of the second relief mission sent to return the twenty-five men of the Lady Franklin Bay Expedition back home. The relief ship *Neptune* in 1882 had failed to penetrate the ice and was forced to leave minimal supplies at a predetermined point near Littleton Island, more than two hundred miles from Greely's base at Fort Conger. This contingency had been planned, and the expedition had enough supplies to last the winter. The 1883 relief was imperative, however, because the men would run out of food and possibly be stranded on the open ice if they were not reached that year. In his 1882 annual report, Secretary Lincoln declared that the 1883 relief mission was essential and that an appropriation by Congress to fund the mission was "urgently recommended."[67]

The 1883 relief ship *Proteus* left Newfoundland on June 29, 1883, and, unlike the 1882 mission, was accompanied by a naval escort vessel, the *Yantic*. Like the *Neptune* the year before, the *Proteus* was stopped and trapped in the ice near Littleton Island; unlike the *Neptune*, which escaped, the *Proteus* was crushed, and the thirty-seven-man crew stranded on the ice. The naval ship *Yantic* had been delayed and following behind the *Proteus*. The thirty-seven survivors of the destroyed vessel—a group of naval personnel and a group of private northern whalers—set out south on foot in hopes of meeting the naval ship. More than one month and hundreds of miles later, the *Proteus* crew was rescued. Most of their resupply items for Greely, however, had sunk with the ship, and the *Yantic*, not equipped for plowing through ice fields, was determined too weak to risk a run up to the rendezvous point and instead turned for home.[68]

When news of the *Proteus* disaster reached Washington, Secretary Lincoln was faced with a dire decision. Should he send a second relief mission so late in the arctic sailing season and risk the deaths of the rescuers or wait until 1884? Greely's original orders provided that if the 1882 relief vessel did not penetrate Lady Franklin Bay, Greely and his men would retreat south by boat to Littleton Island no later than September 1, 1883, and there rendezvous with their relief. No instructions were given in case the 1883 ship failed to appear—Greely was expected to rely on his own judgment. He could either camp at Littleton Island or return to Fort Conger base camp until the next year. The problem for Secretary Lincoln was that Greely's party was so isolated and out of communication that he had no idea where they were or the amount and condition of their food and other supplies. It was assumed they had followed orders and traveled south towards Littleton Island, but upon finding no relief ship, did they stay there or retreat to Fort Conger?

Immediately upon his rescue and return to St. John's, Newfoundland, on September 13, Lieutenant Ernest A. Garlington, commander of the relief mission, informed Secretary Lincoln via telegraph of the *Proteus* wreck and failure. Lincoln consulted with Secretary of the Navy William E. Chandler, and the two men asked Garlington his opinion about sending another ship at once. Garlington replied the next day that it was too late in the season for another attempt. The two cabinet secretaries then telegraphed back asking for a fuller response from Garlington and *Yantic* Commander Frank Wildes. Both men replied that a second attempt was impossible so close to the onset of arctic winter. Lincoln and Chandler then solicited opinions from multiple arctic experts and previous successful arctic explorers about the feasibility of an attempt. All agreed it was impossible.[69]

Based on these consultations, Lincoln, supported by Chandler, decided not to allow a second relief attempt that year. He later reported to Congress, "The danger of wrecking a new relief party in its attempt to reach [Greenland] is far greater than should be incurred for the chance of rendering any aid to Greely." He stated that any such attempt would be not only "substantially hopeless" but "perilous in the extreme, if not foolhardy." Although it was impossible to know the condition of the expedition, it was believed there were enough supplies for their survival at Fort Conger and also cached at various points along the land route to Littleton Island. Greely "cannot fail to know that the most earnest efforts will be made to relieve him next year," Robert wrote.[70] Privately, Robert gave the same explanation to his friend Norman Williams but added a personal—and astute—addendum: "If I had taken that course [of a second relief mission] and the new party had been lost, this would have been attached to me as long as my name may be remembered or written, nothing but my folly in that regard."[71]

After the second relief expedition's failure, which was followed by relentless newspaper criticism, Lincoln opened a board of inquiry into Garlington's actions.[72] President Arthur convened a board of officers in December 1883 to consider and recommend to the secretaries of war and navy what steps to take for a successful relief effort in 1884. It was determined that no one but navy personnel would be allowed to participate—no civilian mariners or volunteers such as on the *Neptune* and *Proteus*, who were not subject to military discipline—and that two ships would be dispatched instead of one.[73] Congress also offered a bounty to any private ship that reached the expedition before the navy. This had the result not only of multiplying the number of ships looking for Greely but also hastened the preparations and movements of the naval ships.[74]

Greely and his men had indeed left Fort Conger, journeyed toward Littleton Island in 1883, and spent the winter camped on the ice at Cape Sabine. Their suffering was horrific. They had run out of food and eventually were forced to eat boiled strips of their sealskin clothing. When the rescue ship found them on June 22, 1884, only seven men were still alive out of the original twenty-five expedition members—although one man, Private Joseph Elison, died aboard the rescue ship *Bear* on the journey home. Greely and his men returned to the United States with a hero's welcome. The stories of their scientific achievements, courage, and sufferings were national headlines for days.[75]

Shortly after Greely's return from the arctic, Secretary Lincoln submitted his annual report to the Congress. To prepare his report, the secretary collected official reports from the chiefs of his subordinate offices, summarized these in his overall report, and attached the full statements in separate sections. Lincoln was surprised and angered to discover that Chief Signal Officer General William B. Hazen's report included not only disagreement with and criticism of the secretary's decision not to send a second relief mission in 1883 but also outright blamed Lincoln for the deaths of Greely's men. "That such disaster could have been averted, and that it was in no respect due to that commander of the expedition [Garlington], can be established by indubitable evidence," Hazen wrote.[76]

Lincoln included Hazen's full report plus his own detailed explanation of his actions and decision not to send a second ship. He included comments from Commander Winfield Scott Schley, the officer of charge of Greely's 1884 rescue, who stated that he learned the winter of 1883 in Melville Bay was the most severe experienced for thirty years, and had a second mission been sent, it certainly would have been totally lost.[77] Secretary Lincoln stated that he had never doubted his decision in 1883, which was based on the best information available at the time. Subsequent information, especially Schley's personal experiences and observations, made it clear, Lincoln wrote, that had he sent the second ship, "it is now hardly to be doubted that we would have had last summer the news of two Arctic calamities instead of one."[78]

Lincoln, however, in no way ignored the impropriety of Hazen's brazen—and public—comments.

> The expression of the Chief Signal Officer, above referred to, is an intrusion of an official opinion as to the propriety of the course of the Secretaries of War and of the Navy in not hazarding more lives in 1883 in a nearly hopeless adventure upon his telegraphic requests. This excursion into an official jurisdiction beyond his own, and his dictum upon the exercise of a superior responsibility which he was not invited to share are extraordinary in their time and place, and are hardly excusable even under whatever irritation may have been caused by the findings of the "Proteus" court of inquiry.[79]

Due to Lincoln's rebuke, as well as his universal vilification of Hazen, Hazen complained about his poor treatment and requested charges of court-martial against Garlington. His biggest mistake, however, was in attacking Lincoln directly. On February 17, 1885, in a long missive to the secretary of war, Hazen defended his actions and again blamed Lincoln's 1883 decision for the disaster of the Greely party. Robert responded that Hazen's opinion was not requested and therefore improper, as well as insubordinate. He warned that Hazen's accusation of "neglect of duty" would result in a court-martial if made public.[80] True to his self-righteous nature, Hazen shortly thereafter gave an interview with a *Washington Star* reporter, in which he alluded to his letter and repeated his accusations. Secretary Lincoln immediately court-martialed the chief signal officer for insubordination, for which Hazen was found guilty of "unwarranted and captious criticism of his superior officer" and officially reprimanded by the president.[81]

Hazen, however, was not Secretary Lincoln's only critic. In his 1886 memoirs, Lieutenant Greely criticized the ex-secretary for his decision not to send a second relief expedition in 1883, saying a second ship would have made it through. "The attempt of ex-Secretary Lincoln to defend his joint action in this matter must fall to the ground before the stern array of facts in the case," Greely wrote. In fact, Greely gave all the credit for the expedition's rescue to the "zeal and interest" of Secretary of the Navy Chandler—not Secretary Lincoln.[82]

The issue of the Greely expedition followed and irritated Robert Lincoln for years, especially after Greely's criticisms were published in his 1886 memoir. Subsequent histories of the expedition give little attention to Lincoln's role in the affair, other than to portray him as dangerously apathetic and ignorant of all that occurred. To this day, one of the few known events in Robert Lincoln's generally unknown life is how his refusal to send a second mission "caused" the deaths of most of Greely's men. At the time, however, nobody other than Hazen and Greely blamed Lincoln for the arctic disaster. The issue did nothing to damage Robert Lincoln's reputation or popular appeal, the latter of which, as the next presidential election approached, began to gather in momentum.

16

"I Am Not a Candidate"

The year 1884 was a presidential election year, and just as they do in the twenty-first century, potential candidates began jockeying for the nomination as soon as the previous election had ended—especially after the death of President Garfield. The leading contender for the Republican nomination was not the sitting president, Chester A. Arthur, but the "Plumed Knight," former Congressman and Secretary of State James G. Blaine. Blaine had actively sought the nomination in both 1876 and 1880 and saw 1884 as his year to win. He firmly disagreed with Arthur's political philosophy and had no qualms about challenging an incumbent. As for Arthur, although he never wanted to be and did not particularly enjoy being president, he also desired an election in his own right to avoid the label of "accidental president." He also felt that he deserved the nomination due to his incumbency as well as a career of loyal devotion to the party.

But it was Arthur's accidental status, his independent performance in office (during which he eschewed insular partisanism and instead focused on what he believed was best for the country), and the continued fracturing of the party between Stalwarts and Half-Breeds that led to a general free-for-all in potential candidates. Republican luminaries such as U.S. Senators George Edmunds, John A. Logan, and John Sherman, as well as Sherman's brother General William Tecumseh Sherman, either were mentioned as good possibilities or were actively considering running. There were murmurs here and there about Robert Lincoln for president, especially by blacks who looked upon his father, Abraham Lincoln, as their savior. There was even a song written in 1884 about black support for Robert in which the chorus went,

> O darkies come and join de song,
> For it fills de heart with joy;

We'se a gwine to hab for Presumdent,
Good old Massa Linkum's Boy.[1]

Mentions of Robert on the Republican ticket began in 1883, but just as Robert had quashed notions of him for Congress in 1878 and for Senate in 1882 and 1883, the son of Abraham Lincoln had no interest in running for national political office in 1884.[2] As early as 1882, he wrote to an admirer, "I believe I come as near as any man living to having no ambition for anything but a quiet and peaceful life."[3] In January 1883, U.S. Senator Preston B. Plumb of Kansas told the *Chicago Tribune* that Lincoln was an excellent secretary of war and would probably become a compromise nominee palatable to both Stalwarts and Half-Breeds.[4] By February, Robert was assuring an admirer of his "dislike" of his name being mentioned for president: "I have not the slightest ambition in that direction, and, on the other hand, if I thought such a mistake likely to be made by any considerable number of persons, I would take decisive means to put an end to it."[5]

Lincoln himself was solidly behind Arthur's nomination and reelection, believing that the president not only had earned it but also that he could actually win, particularly by carrying the votes in the imperative state of New York, while Blaine could not.[6] Despite Robert's numerous public disavowals of interest in national office, his popular appeal only grew as the June Republican convention approached. The *New York Times* found that "barbers, cardrivers and conductors, policeman, small tradesman of all kinds, who vote the Republican ticket are almost unanimous in the desire to see Mr. Lincoln secure the nomination. . . . Precisely what characteristic of Mr. Lincoln appeals most forcibly to the sympathy of the common people it is difficult to discover by talking with them. They seem to have a general admiration for the man, coupled with a veneration for the name which he bears, and the two feelings united point to him as the natural and proper candidate for the Republican Party."[7] The general humor and political satire magazine *Puck* also printed a poem about Robert's presidential prospects, praising his heritage and defending his relative youth as a positive rather than negative attribute for a candidate.[8]

Letters between politicos and aficionados at this time show that while Lincoln was not a universal choice, he could prevail as a dark-horse candidate. Republican Party operative A. Cowles wrote to Horace White, editor of the *New York Evening Post*, in May 1884, "[P]eople all along the line . . . are seriously considering the idea that both Mr. Blaine and Mr. Arthur will be unable to carry New York State and that it is necessary to find the 'Dark Horse' and that right off. I have it in Chicago, Cleveland and New York. I think they will run to Bob Lincoln."[9] One political observer told the *Boston Globe* that friends of

Arthur, Grant, and Logan, certain their candidates could not get the nomination, would unite behind Robert Lincoln as a way to defeat Blaine.[10] John Hay wrote in January 1884 that his friend "Bob" Lincoln was a serious contender for the nomination even though he had no organized following, "greatly to his annoyance as he is heartily for Arthur."[11]

Many politicians did not want Robert to become the nominee, thinking he had not earned it. The editor and publisher of *Opinion: A Weekly Literary and Political Paper* wrote to contender Senator John A. Logan in May 1884 that he would be at the nominating convention in Chicago to "work steadily to get the Kentucky votes on the break and to prevent any d——d Lincoln imbecility."[12] Former vice president of the United States Schuyler Colfax wrote, "[A] month or two ago, I thought Robert Lincoln had the best chance [to be the dark horse candidate]. But, as his spontaneous nomination all over the country for V.P. has so materially weakened Gen. Logan's chances for the Pres. nomination, his managers are striking back, and will evidently do so even more at the Conv."[13] What this striking back was is uncertain, but it is possible that Robert's foes would broach the subject of Mary Lincoln's insanity and Robert's part in committing her to an asylum in 1875.

As exciting as a Lincoln presidential candidacy would be, even Robert's admirers recognized he might be too young and inexperienced for the White House. This may be why Lincoln was, in some newspapers, found to be a strong choice for the vice-presidential nomination. In April 1884, a *New York Times* article mentioned the possibility—and the strength—of former President Ulysses S. Grant running again for the presidency with Robert Lincoln as his running mate.[14] Carl Schurz, a Civil War general and former secretary of the interior, wrote to Logan in February 1884, "To judge from what I see and hear, and from the expressions of sentiment which float through the press, there is in the Republican ranks an almost unanimous voice in favor of nominating Lincoln for the Vice-Presidency."[15] Even the eventual 1884 Republican presidential nominee, James G. Blaine, saw the practicability of nominating Lincoln for the second spot. His friend George S. Boutwell wrote in 1900 that Blaine told him he did not want the 1884 nomination; he wanted only to defeat the nomination of President Arthur. Blaine said that the ticket should be General Sherman and Robert Lincoln, a ticket that "most assuredly" would have been followed by their election.[16]

With only days to go before the convention, newspapers across the country—especially in his hometown of Chicago—reported that Lincoln would be on the ticket. "Every publication speaks of Robert T. Lincoln as the model candidate for the Vice-Presidency," declared the *Chicago Tribune*. "There is nothing more certain than if an Eastern man is nominated that he will have the second place on the ticket." The *Tribune* also stated that his "universal appeal" for the second place made him more likely to receive the presidential nomination as a dark horse if the convention becomes deadlocked over the major candidates.[17] The *Chicago Times* more directly reported, "It is conceded that Mr. Lincoln will be nominated for the vice presidency."[18]

Robert was neither deaf nor dumb to calls for his candidacy, but he so adamantly opposed it that in mid-March he wrote a letter to Leonard Swett and asked his old friend and adviser to forward it to both the *Chicago Tribune* and the *New York Times* for publication. "I am not a candidate for either President or Vice President, and therefore do not wish any clubs formed for me," the letter declared in Robert's public attempt to quell his supporters.[19] Still, the encouragements kept coming. "I am so sincerely not a candidate that in answer to your inquiry I can only say that I have no 'working friend' at Chicago," Robert wrote to an admirer in May 1884. "I have discouraged all use of my name and have no other wish than that the convention will calmly select a man who will unite all our people and enable us to take advantage of the present situation of our opponents. I hope that no such responsibility will be thrust upon me."[20]

Robert's wording in this letter is key—that no such "responsibility" would be "thrust" upon him—because in the nineteenth century, candidates often were chosen against their own desires. The Gilded Age was a time of manly honor and duty, and no honorable man could refuse his party or deny his duty to his country if called to serve in the White House. Robert said multiple times throughout his life that he would accept the presidential nomination if it devolved upon him, although he would not seek it out. The "duty" of a man to his party and his country is evident in the responses Robert's public disavowal received. The *Chicago Tribune* stated that Lincoln's determination not to be a candidate was "expressed very resolutely, but at the same time his candidacy is for the convention to determine rather than for personal decision. . . . If it should prove that the convention wants him to serve in either capacity, acquiescence would be a duty which he should perform and which the people would endorse."[21] This grand nineteenth-century political philosophy was not limited to the office of the presidency. When former Illinois Governor Richard J. Oglesby declared he was not a candidate for the U.S. Senate in 1887, one of his constituents wrote to him that any person who decides for himself that he is not a candidate "is not merely impertinent, but unpatriotic. . . . Whether a man announces himself as an active candidate is a matter of taste. . . . But . . . to declare he is not a candidate is to deprive the state of its lawful right of selection."[22]

When the Republican national convention began voting for candidates on June 6, 1884, it took four ballots to nominate James G. Blaine for president, although his nomination was never truly doubted. Arthur had too many political enemies and too little respect within the party as president for anyone to believe he could prevail. On all four ballots, Robert Lincoln took votes: four on the first, four on the second, eight on the third, and two on the fourth.[23]

Lincoln's support for the top spot was small, but true to popular sentiments, his name was prominent during the convention canvass for Blaine's running mate. Had Lincoln wanted the spot and urged his friends and supporters to work for it, there is no doubt that he would have received it. Yet, once his nomination seemed certain, he immediately telegraphed the convention and not only forbade his friends to present his name but also stated that he "would not take" the nomination.[24] While this seems to contradict Robert's numerous statements about civic duty, to him as to so many men of the day, the vice presidency was an empty, wasted position that served no real public interest; therefore, to refuse it really was not to compromise one's principle. In the end, the second spot went to another Illinoisan, Senator John A. Logan. "I am not at all disappointed" by avoiding a nomination, Robert wrote to an admirer two days later.[25]

President Arthur was embarrassed and discouraged by the rejection of his party. After telegraphing his congratulations and support to Blaine, he ordered a carriage and disappeared from sight. History has shown, however, that the president did not seriously want the nomination. He did not "bow out" of the contest, because to do so would raise suspicions about his health, cast doubt about his competence to handle the burdens of the presidency, and carry with it the implication of cowardice to both run on his record and to face possible defeat at the polls.[26] But his health was the reason for his inactive candidacy. Although publicly unknown at the time, Arthur knew his Bright's disease was in an advanced stage and being aggravated by the stress of the presidency, and that if elected, he probably would not live out a second term.

The knowledge of this fact makes it even more incredible to realize just how close Robert Lincoln actually came to being president. For, despite his disinterest in being the vice-presidential nominee, telegrams he wrote during the first day of the Republican National Convention show he was willing to accept the second place only if President Arthur was renominated. Lincoln, believing his name might be presented to the convention for vice-presidential contention, entrusted longtime friend Norman Williams with a telegram to U.S. Senator Shelby M. Cullom from Illinois. In it, Lincoln instructed Cullom to withdraw his name from contention for vice president if it was presented. Confidentially, Robert instructed Williams to deliver the telegram to Cullom "for his prompt action if any nomination for president is made by the Convention except President Arthur. . . . If that nomination is made, telegraph me for further instructions, as my relations to him require me to consider my proper course."[27] The missive makes clear that if Arthur had been nominated for the presidency, and he asked Lincoln to join the ticket, Robert would have assented out of respect and loyalty to his chief. Since Arthur died in early 1886, Vice President Lincoln would have become president.

Had Robert's intentions been known inside the convention hall during the balloting, it is likely it could have swung sufficient votes to enable Arthur to win the nomination. Robert, however, took extra care that his telegram would not be revealed. Instead of sending it to the telegram station in the convention hall, he sent it to the Western Union main office and had Williams pick it up there, rather than have it delivered to him. And, if Arthur truly wanted to receive the nomination, he could have approached Lincoln previously and announced Honest Abe's son as his running mate should he be nominated. With Lincoln on the national ticket, the Republicans would have had a much greater chance of winning the election.

The 1884 presidential contest has been called the dirtiest election in American history, now often termed the election of "rum, Romanism, and rebellion." The major political issues involved civil-service reforms and import tariffs, but the real arguments, campaign slogans, and mudslinging centered on the candidates' personal characters and private lives. Republican Blaine had long been seen as a corrupt plutocrat in the pocket of big business, while Democrat presidential nominee New York Governor Grover Cleveland's bane was having fathered a child out of wedlock, which, to his credit, he never denied but embraced. The Democrats countered that charge by stating that Blaine and his wife were married only three months when their first child was born. The Republican Party, fractured and fragile with Blaine as its candidate, feared its first loss of the White House in twenty-four years.

Secretary of War Lincoln, although disappointed in Arthur's rejection, was still a solid and loyal party man and faithfully advocated Blaine's election. In October 1884, Lincoln went on a three-week campaign stump through the Midwest for the Republican ticket. He spoke to immense crowds of tens of thousands of people in towns and cities across Illinois—Paris, Mattoon, Lincoln, Springfield, Bloomington, Aledo, Champaign, Burlington—and into Iowa. Robert was not a fanciful speaker full of flourishes and orotund dramatic rhetoric, rather, as the *Chicago Tribune* characterized, he presented facts, drew deductions logically, and appealed to the judgment and reason of the audience. He believed in the Republican program and was not afraid to jab at partisan emotions and wave the "bloody shirt"—he decried the Democrats as the party of corruption and rebellion, as the one seeking to give former Confederate soldiers a pension and to bankrupt American businesses and increase wages by lowering or eliminating the import tariff. He vilified the Democrat suppression of black votes—even shootings and hangings of black voters—in the southern states, saying, "I believe the time will come when we shall read the history of these bloody massacres as we read of massacres of the Spanish Inquisition. The Inquisition was employed to suppress the people by burning at the stake, just as Republicanism is now put down by the rope and bullet all over the South."[28]

The crowds erupted in applause for Secretary Lincoln at every stop he made, for he was not only a cabinet member but, perhaps more important to them, his father's son. At his first campaign rally in Mattoon, Illinois, it was reported that people felt "repaid for coming just by seeing the son of Abraham Lincoln"; every time Robert made a good point in his speech, remarks could be heard throughout the audience, "That's like Old Abe."[29] Secretary Lincoln toured Illinois to receptions like a modern movie star. After the rally in Bloomington on October 25, he was "seized by the crowd and carried away on the shoulders of yelling and cheering men."[30] At the end of his campaign circuit in Springfield on November 6, Lincoln said he felt confident of Blaine's election.[31]

The election results belied Lincoln's brave talk and shattered the Republican stronghold on the presidency. Blaine showed better than most expected, losing to Cleveland by the slimmest of margins—by slightly over one thousand votes in New York State, which lost him the state, which lost him the presidency.

Despite his position as a lame-duck president, Chester Arthur did not become an inactive chief executive. In fact, he focused his remaining months in office on creating a more aggressively expansionist foreign policy. He and his Secretary of State, Frederick T. Frelinghuysen, dispatched diplomats to help settle sectional strife between Chile and Peru and a boundary dispute between Mexico and Guatemala. They also sought to advance the construction of an interocean canal through Central America, preferably in Nicaragua, and engaged in creating reciprocity treaties with some Latin American countries, as well as Hawaii and Spain. One of President Arthur's final official acts was presiding over the dedication of the Washington Monument on February 21, 1885. Secretary of War Lincoln, whose father Congressman Abraham Lincoln had been present at the laying of the monument's cornerstone on July 4, 1848, also was present for the ceremony.[32]

Arthur left office proud of his performance and generally appreciated by America's citizens.[33] Publisher Alexander K. McClure recalled, "No man ever entered the Presidency so profoundly and widely distrusted as Chester Alan Arthur, and no one ever retired from the highest civil trust more generally respected, alike by political friend and foe."[34] Secretary Lincoln, too, admired his chief, writing, "It is a general feeling that the circumstances of Mr. Arthur's ascension were handled by him with a marvelous discretion, and this wise discretion in all his public acts, and an avoidance of mere political display, were the chief characteristics of his administration. Mr. Arthur was, in my judgment, guided by lofty ideas of his duties, and was gifted with great discretion."[35]

Secretary Lincoln's final months in office consisted of typical administrative duties—which included having his official War Department portrait painted in December 1884 by the renowned artist Daniel Huntington—as well as two (media-manufactured) controversies involving the chief of the army and the incoming Democrat president.[36] On November 1, 1883, General of the Army William T. Sherman retired from active duty, and Lieutenant General Philip H. Sheridan took his place.[37] Commanding military generals and civilian secretaries of war often had quarreled over the realms of their specific authorities, but Secretary Lincoln had worked well with Sherman and, as he was not only respected but personally friendly with Sheridan, no friction was expected. In September 1883, after hearing of his inevitable succession of Sherman, Sheridan sent a letter to Secretary Lincoln, suggesting changes in command assignments in the army. Lincoln gladly welcomed the suggestions and proposed some ideas of his own.[38]

An issue of authority did, however, occur between the two men at the end of 1884. After assuming his position as head of the army in November, Sheridan created a habit of issuing orders to certain War Department personnel who were not subject to his authority but, rather, to the secretary of war; Sheridan also had department personnel send reports directly to him instead of to the secretary, as was regulated. The result of these actions was officers' refusing to follow Sheridan's orders because they were subject to the secretary only, Sheridan then complaining about insubordination, and Lincoln threatening to court-martial officers who reported to Sheridan instead of him and therefore breaching the chain of command. On December 9, 1884, Lincoln sent Sheridan a letter clearly defining the limits of the general's authority and the extent of Lincoln's powers under existing law and precedent.

> I deem it my duty to point out to you that in my opinion your claim to command every officer in the Army under the terms of the assignment to duty under which you are now acting, is not tenable, and that if it were tenable, it would be an imperative duty on the part of the Secretary of War to recommend to the President such a change in the terms of your assignment to duty as would prevent the possibility of such a claim. The claim made is, so far as I am advised, without precedent in our history.

When no response was received, Lincoln sent a second letter on January 17.

> It is with much regret that I have felt myself forced to call attention to this matter again. I became aware soon after the assumption by you of your present duties that occasional orders, some unusual in form and others in substance as concerns the authority of the Secretary of War, were published from the Headquarters of the Army; but it was not until the endorsement which is the subject of this letter [orders given by Sheridan improperly to the commissary-general of subsistence], that I connected them with a purpose to adopt a course of action which is an assumption of functions either imposed on the Secretary of War by law, or reserved by him. . . . I have no wish to aggrandize my own exclusive functions, or to diminish your command. My personal friendship, as well as my high respect for you as an officer, would alike prevent such action; but it is a duty I cannot avoid to preserve intact the exclusive authority required by law, regulations and custom to be exercised by the Secretary of War, and to take such measures as will without fail accomplish that end. I trust this letter will be the only measure required for that purpose.[39]

Once again, as with the 1883 public insubordination that led to the court-martial of Chief Signal Officer William B. Hazen, Secretary Lincoln showed himself to be a strong and self-assured cabinet minister. Unlike the Hazen issue, the Sheridan confrontation was unknown outside the War Department at the time it occurred, which is how Lincoln wanted it to be—his was a forceful yet quiet administrative style. After Lincoln's successor, William C. Endicott, also had trouble in limiting Sheridan to his prescribed authority, however, Endicott sent copies of Lincoln's two letters to Sheridan to each division and department commander for his information. The national newspapers quickly picked up the story and made it public in August 1885, much to Robert's annoyance. The stories made much of Sheridan's belligerent feelings of superiority and Lincoln's need to put him in his place. Robert continually maintained that he never reprimanded Sheridan but merely clarified a misunderstanding, and the newspapers sensationalized the event to make headlines—a statement his papers and correspondence prove correct.[40]

Nearly the last official act of Secretary Lincoln was to finalize the bill placing former President Ulysses S. Grant on the army retired list, thereby restoring to him his rank of general (which he had given up upon being elected president in 1868) and giving him a $13,500 per year salary. Grant was by this time, early 1885, near death and impoverished, and the bill was universally applauded as proper justice to a faithful servant of the country. The bill passed the House in the final moments of the Forty-Eighth Congress on March 3, 1885. It immediately was sent to President Arthur, who submitted

Grant's nomination to the Senate a few minutes before midnight (after the clocks were turned back ten minutes to give him time to do so), making it his last official act as president. The Senate confirmed the appointment by unanimous vote.[41]

The next day, inauguration day for the first Democrat to win the White House since 1856, Secretary Lincoln drew up the official commission for Grant, expecting (and prepared to suggest) that President Cleveland and his incoming war secretary would make signing the commission their first official acts in office. Cleveland's cabinet officers were not immediately confirmed, however, and so Cleveland sent for Lincoln, still secretary, to bring the commission for immediate signature. Cleveland offered Lincoln the opportunity to sign the commission as his final official act (a rather poetic gesture since President Lincoln had signed the first commission appointing Grant General of the Army in 1864), but Lincoln demurred in favor of letting Endicott sign it the next day. "I plainly saw that it was an act of the new administration which should be completely so," Robert later wrote.[42]

The issue was simple and straightforward, yet, once again, a journalist falsified the story and created a typical government gossip scandal of the type Robert Lincoln abhorred. The journalist declared that Secretary Lincoln did not "appreciate his proper relations" to the new president and had overstepped his bounds by bringing the commission to Cleveland before Endicott was sworn into office. It said Lincoln was then "very cavalierly treated" by the Democrat president, who had no interest in hurrying to sign the commission and was portrayed as more interested in embarrassing the Republican Lincoln. The story was criticized and rebutted the next day by other newspapers as well as by Cleveland and Lincoln, but that did not alleviate Robert's irritation. He said he was "not a little annoyed" by the false newspaper article of the day before; one year later, he characterized the writer as "a malicious newspaper scribbler." This was certainly not a pleasurable way for Lincoln to leave office and only intensified his distrust and dislike of newspapers and their reporters.[43]

After a full four years as secretary of war, Robert T. Lincoln had earned an accomplished record and reputation as an able and judicious department head. Just as he had during his tenure as South Chicago town supervisor in 1876, Robert believed in and implemented his Republican-based philosophy of a thorough understanding of his department and duties, blunt common sense, business-like directness, administrative efficiency, appropriately frugal spending, independent decision making, and a modest yet forceful leadership style.

In addition to the major exigencies previously discussed, he began with a general reorganization of the department, transferring or eliminating incompetent political appointees; reformed the systems of army officers getting assigned to pleasure trips under the guise of official duties; recommended legislation to prevent and punish white intrusion upon Indian lands; recommended that the Weather Bureau be separated from the army; separated the Signal Service bureau from the army so that its expenditures would be separate from the army contingent fund (which saved the government more than $1 million per year); recommended an increase in pay for private soldiers as one way to discourage desertion; and proposed liberal appropriations to the states to support the formation of volunteer militia organizations.[44] Lincoln's two letters to General Sheridan enumerating the authority of the civilian war secretary over the general of the army served as a precedent for subsequent secretaries for more than decade.[45]

The truth of the often-repeated phrase that Lincoln was the "best secretary of war since Jeff Davis" is subjective. However, Lincoln certainly was one of the most respected, active, and accomplished secretaries of war of the eleven men who held the post between Davis and him. Of those eleven, the majority served terms of less than one year, were lax administrators, outright political partisans, and beholden to party cronyism. The two most accomplished secretaries during that period, Edwin M. Stanton (1862–68) and William Worth Belknap (1869–76), had their legacies tarnished by controversy: Stanton by being the War Secretary during the Civil War and the cause of President Andrew Johnson's impeachment; Belknap by accepting bribes in office and being impeached by the U.S. House of Representatives. In addition to the beneficial department reforms similarly instituted by both Lincoln and Davis, their comparison seems to rest on their thorough knowledge of the army and its management, and their desire to improve the efficiency and performance of the department, especially in the lives and working conditions of army personnel.

When his term as secretary of war ended in March 1885, Robert Lincoln returned to his home in Chicago. He had had his fill of political life in Washington and vowed never again to engage in it. "I am heartily tired of the annoyances of public life and when I get out it will be for good," he had written in 1884. "How any man can keep in it except for a living amazes me."[46] Once again, he was sorely mistaken, as his name continued to be broached as possible political appointee and presidential candidate. Letters suggesting his candidacy in 1888 began arriving only weeks after the 1884 election ended. He continued to answer that he had no ambition for such a place and would reject calls for his own nomination. "I think that time will only strengthen my dislike of the annoyances attending candidacy for, or holding of, public office," he replied to one newspaper editor.[47]

But Robert's life was filled with more than just politics. He was eager to focus his energies back on his law practice and to have more time with his family. Robert's family commitment was not just to Mary and the children. It also included the memory and legacies of his parents and even his grandparents. Overseeing this legacy, handling the family papers and heirlooms in his possession, and dealing with the historians, writers, and artists who sought his advice and assistance in how to portray his father in their respective arts were relentless responsibilities.

17

"I Expect Only the Greatest Satisfaction"

Abraham Lincoln supposedly disliked reading history, especially biography, because he felt such works lavished praise on their subjects and suppressed imperfections. They "commemorate a lie and cheat posterity out of the truth," he purportedly said. "History is not history unless it is truth."[1] Such a statement, of course, misses the notion that hagiographers consider their interpretations as much truth as do the harshest critics. William H. Herndon, the source of the above quote, thought only he himself, who included imperfections, told the truth about his former law partner's life and everyone else insularly perpetuated the pristine apotheosis of the Great Emancipator. Robert Lincoln, on the other hand, had no use for Herndon or any other interpretation that soiled his father's golden aura. But through the years, Robert, as the keeper of his father's legacy, dealt with adherents to both theories of biography.

Robert actually shared opinions, advice, and even documents with numerous biographers, some of whom he respected and helped more than others. To friends and colleagues of his father, he gave the most assistance—even to Herndon and Ward Hill Lamon before they betrayed his trust. But the men to whom Robert gave his full support and assistance were his father's former White House secretaries, John G. Nicolay and John Hay. Robert had faith in them not only because they were his personal friends but he also felt they were the only people intimately acquainted enough with his father's work to write a true history of his father's life and presidential administration.

The locus of any such study was Abraham Lincoln's papers, which had been stored in boxes in David Davis's bank vault in Bloomington, Illinois, since immediately after the assassination in 1865. This was done at Davis's suggestion to get them away from Washington and to protect them from "some persons" whom Davis did not want to allow access.[2] The plan was then to wait a few years before a thorough review and classification of everything by Robert and Nicolay, with the assistance of a few of Abraham Lincoln's intimate friends, certainly Davis and probably Leonard Swett, two men whom Robert trusted above all others.[3] The purpose of such a review was to keep everything of historical value and to destroy the rest. As Robert later told multiple historians, he sought to prevent the publication of any documents private to the Lincoln family and to embargo any that could be injurious to persons still living. This sentiment was typical of nineteenth-century social mores concerning personal privacy and public dignity, to which Robert Lincoln particularly subscribed.

But the job of "overhauling" his father's papers was one that Robert dreaded, and so it was one he continually procrastinated. "I confess to a great disinclination to looking over the papers, for I will have a host of people after one thing or another," Robert wrote in 1871 and repeated in 1873.[4] Part of the delay also was because Robert, Davis, and Nicolay could not coordinate any time—Robert figured the job would take at least one month—during which all three were available. By mid-1873, Robert had decided to transfer all the boxes from Bloomington to his law office in Chicago and go through them himself, but even this did not occur for nearly a year.[5]

It was not until late February 1874—nine years after the papers were deposited in Bloomington—that Robert decided it was "impossible" for him and Davis to coordinate their schedules, and he asked the judge to send the papers to Chicago, where Robert would store them in his office vault. "I think that I can make a hasty examination here so as to weed out anything purely private and let Hay and Nicolay have the rest for their use," Robert decided.[6] But after opening only one box, Robert was so overwhelmed by the enormity of the task that he decided to postpone the review until Nicolay could travel to Chicago and assist. Nicolay was pleased and relieved by Robert's decision. He exhorted, "I am also especially anxious—and I press this point particularly—that not a scrap of paper of any kind be destroyed. The merest memorandum, date, mark, signature, or figure, may have a future historical value, which we cannot now arbitrarily determine, and the only good rule is to *save everything*."[7] As far as the existing evidence shows, Robert followed Nicolay's wishes.[8] After Nicolay traveled to Chicago a few months later to see the papers, Robert allowed him to take them all back to Washington, where Nicolay stored them in the vault under the U.S. Capitol—a vault he had sole access to through his position as marshal of the U.S. Supreme Court.

With the papers in Nicolay's possession, he and Hay finally could begin their monumental work. They not only had the Lincoln papers but they also interviewed and examined the private papers of various cabinet officers and subordinate civilian employees, military officers, and other personnel in the

Lincoln administration; they also planned to examine the records of both the Union and Confederate governments. Robert helped them as much as he could by sending them newspaper clippings and articles he read, lending them family photographs to use, writing out his own reminiscences of certain events, and acquiring personal papers the secretaries did not have.[9] For example, in 1878, Robert approached his good friend Edgar T. Welles about letting Nicolay read through the diary of Edgar's recently deceased father, Gideon Welles, President Lincoln's secretary of the navy; in 1885, Robert acquired correspondence between his father and longtime friend Elihu B. Washburne, which he forwarded to Nicolay; and Robert did his own research on the Lincoln family history to help supplement the secretaries' findings.[10] "I think you both want it, as I do, to be the *one* book on the subject," Robert told Hay more than once.[11]

It took Nicolay and Hay more than ten years to complete *Abraham Lincoln: A History. Century Magazine* published it in forty excerpts between November 1886 and May 1890 and brought out in a ten-volume book set—dedicated to Robert T. Lincoln—in 1890. Robert believed it was the definitive work on his father, and he recommended it as such to inquirers for the rest of his life. "Many people speak to me and confirm my own feeling of it as a work in every way excellent not only sustaining but elevating my father's place in history," Robert wrote to Hay after the work's completion. "I shall never cease to be glad that the places you and Nicolay held near him and in his confidence were filled by you and not by others."[12] Reviews of the book were mixed. Many readers found it more about the Civil War than about Lincoln himself, while others found its overtly partisan tone discrediting. Some people criticized what they felt was a heavy-handed editing, even expurgating, by Robert Lincoln. A vehement critic of this was William Herndon, who raged that Nicolay and Hay knew the truth about Lincoln's life but refused to print it. They "handle things with silken gloves and 'a camel-hair pencil,'" he wrote, adding that they were afraid of Robert Lincoln and under his surveillance. "He gives them materials and they in their turn play hush."[13]

Robert Lincoln's role in the editing of Nicolay and Hay's work has long been criticized but not completely understood. As Robert wrote to David Davis, he gave the secretaries complete and unfettered access to everything he held, except letters "purely private" to the family. Robert later explained to the publishers of G. P. Putnam's Sons (after refusing to help them publish an anthology of Abraham Lincoln's papers),

> Many years ago I passed in the hands of Messrs. Nicolay and Hay all of my father's papers, for their use in preparing what I hope will be the standard history of his private and public life. These gentlemen have devoted years of

> time and labor in gathering material, and have gone very far in preparing the manuscripts of their work. . . . The demands upon my own time have always been of such a character, and so pressing, that it was never possible for me to undertake such a work, and it was not only with my sanction, but in accordance with my wishes and belief in their special fitness for the work, that Messrs. Nicolay and Hay have been engaged in it.[14]

It is clear that Robert completely trusted Nicolay and Hay with his father's legacy. As one history of the Lincoln papers correctly states, Robert "could depend completely on the discretion, conscience, and earnest purpose of these old friends. The loyalty they had brilliantly demonstrated to his father had now been transferred to him."[15]

Some historians have stated that Robert demanded the power of final review and editing of the book in exchange for access to his father's papers. The truth, however, is that Hay *offered* Robert the opportunity to "wield his blue pencil," and Robert accepted.[16] This would become Robert's policy toward other historians for the rest of his life: refusing to directly write anything about his father but agreeing to review manuscripts—not as an editor but as a fact checker of sorts, merely looking for errors. The first chapters by Nicolay and Hay were sent to Robert for review in January 1885. Hay wrote, "I need not tell you that every line has been written in a spirit of reverence and regard. Still you may find here or there words or sentences which do not suit you. I write now to request that you will read with a pencil in your hand and strike out everything to which you object. I will adopt your view in all cases, whether I agree with it or not, but I cannot help hoping you will find nothing objectionable."[17] The absence of any quid-pro-quo agreement is evidenced by part of Robert's response: "It is very good and thoughtful of you to put your work before me and I appreciate it. I know the spirit in which you have done the work and I expect only the greatest satisfaction in reading it."[18]

Robert, in fact, was "delighted" with the chapters, but he did have some suggestions. He thought the Lincoln family genealogy was "of little moment" except as a brief outline. He urged Hay to omit the story about his father helping to sew shut the eyes of a drove of wild hogs that a young Abraham and his crew could not corral onto their flatboat in the usual manner. Robert apparently thought the story too vulgar to include.[19] His major concern was in the depiction of his grandfather Thomas Lincoln, whom Hay labeled as a good-natured man, yet "idle, roving, inefficient," who "accomplished little," had "neither the will nor the intelligence" for any major accomplishments, and had no vices but also "no virtues" of which to speak.[20] "It is beyond doubt that my departed grandfather Lincoln was not an enterprising man and it is likely that your graphic assaults on him *passim* are not undeserved but I could not help feeling better if you 'let up' on him a little on a final revision," Robert wrote. "He did not have much chance to prepare to pose in the reflection of his son's fame and I feel sorry for him." Robert reiterated his feeling in a subsequent letter to Hay, "It was a rough life, the Lord knows, and my grandfather had so much of the roughness from the very start, and nothing else, that I don't want to see him sat down on."[21]

Hay responded to Robert's first criticisms by agreeing to make all suggested changes. "It is better, even as a matter of taste and without regard to your wishes which would, of course, be conclusive," Hay wrote.[22] Robert's reputation as a vehement—even overzealous—and distrustful benefactor and editor springs from Hay's subsequent letter to Robert in which he wrote, "I was very sorry to see by a letter you wrote to Nicolay the other day that you were still not satisfied with my assurance that I would make those first chapters right." Hay then obsequiously reassured him, "Since then, I have gone over the whole thing twice again, reading every line so far as possible from your point of view, and I don't think there is a word left in it that would displease you. But of course before final publication I shall give you another hack at it, with plenary blue pencil powers."[23]

Hay's comments support a critical view of Robert's editing; Robert's response, however, casts doubt on such a view. "I have a bad habit of talking of a thing—or writing—without saying all that ought to be said at the time," Robert explained. "I was not writing to Nicolay on the special subject of the early chapters but was sending him some copies of letters I got from Mr. Washburne, and as the other thing was in my mind I wrote about it without saying as I should have done, that I did so, not disregarding your assurances, but mainly to press as one will do, a matter of interest." Robert reassured his friend, "I have never had any doubt as to what you would do or how you would do it, but perhaps I have been unduly impatient to see the work out."[24]

Robert's faith in his friends' fidelity to their subject is proven further by his refusal later in the year to again review the page proofs and by his confident guarantee of support. "I do not care to see the proofs of what I saw in ms," he wrote Hay. "I know that you have noted what I suggested and that I would have nothing to say on your opening chapters. I mean nothing of criticism."[25] Robert's overall editing of Nicolay and Hay was relatively mild; Hay also edited much content in *anticipation* of Robert's possible disapproval but without actually showing it to him.[26]

Robert's faith in Hay's and Nicolay's devotion to his father was not misplaced. The secretaries wanted more than anything to tell the truth about the war and its leader. Responding to criticisms of "aggressive Northernism" in their work, Hay wrote to Nicolay, "We will not fall in with the present tone of blubbering sentiment, of course. But we ought to write the history of those times like two everlasting angels who know everything, judge everything, tell the truth about everything, and don't care a twang of their harps about one side or the other. There will be one exception," Hay continued. "We are Lincoln men all through."[27] Hay's prejudice he freely admitted to Robert as well, stating that the martyred president was "the one unapproachably great figure of a great epoch."[28] But Hay's most famous—and most poetic—praise for his dead benefactor he wrote to Herndon in 1866: "I consider Lincoln Republicanism incarnate—with all its faults and all its virtues. As in spite of some rudenesses, Republicanism is the sole hope of a sick world, so Lincoln with all his foibles, is the greatest character since Christ."[29]

Robert, too, adored and respected his father, and while his letters never outright state his feelings in such pious phrases as in John Hay's letters, they leave no doubt that the last Lincoln son believed in his father's greatness just as much as the secretaries and also wanted his father's legacy preserved and protected for future generations.

Once *Abraham Lincoln: A History* was finished, Robert suggested to Nicolay a new project.

> So you and Colonel Hay have now brought your great work to a most successful conclusion by the publication of your life of my father. I hope and request that you and he will supplement it by collecting, editing, and publishing the speeches, letters, state papers, and miscellaneous writings of my father. You and Colonel Hay have my consent and authority to obtain for yourselves such protection by copyright or otherwise in respect to the whole or part of such a collection as I might for any reason be entitled to have.[30]

Nicolay and Hay had, in fact, already decided to compile such a supplement, and published it, again with Robert's aid and encouragement, in 1894. Robert's letter was printed at the beginning of volume 1.

Nicolay and Hay were not the only biographers with whom Robert Lincoln had contact in the decades after his father's death. Historians and publishers constantly approached Robert seeking his assistance as well as access to the Lincoln papers. He aided only a small fraction of solicitors. Part of the reason, as Hay's biographer, Tyler Dennett, declared, was that Robert "had a simple sense of the dignity of his father's memory and did not wish to cheapen it with cheap books."[31] And during Robert's life—and especially since his death—there certainly have been numerous cheap books. Jay Monaghan's great bibliography spanning 1839 to 1939 shows 249 works published about Lincoln between 1866 and the 1890 publication of the Nicolay-Hay biography alone, not all of them, of course, deserving of merit.[32]

However, certain writers and historians Robert did assist. One of his earliest interactions was with Isaac Arnold, a legal associate of Abraham Lincoln and a Chicago congressman during the Civil War. In Washington, Arnold was one of the staunchest defenders of Lincoln administration policies in the House of Representatives and was a leading proponent of the Thirteenth Amendment, abolishing slavery. He actually had begun work while Lincoln was alive and with the president's blessing on a book about the administration's eradication of slavery. Arnold continued his work after the assassination and in 1866 published his 720-page tome, *The History of Abraham Lincoln and the Overthrow of Slavery,* which examined America's "peculiar institution" from 1788 up to and through the war and contained a brief study of Lincoln's life with the theme that freeing the slaves was Lincoln's lifelong ambition.

Robert, pleased after reading the proofs of the book's introduction that Arnold had sent him, indirectly apologized about not helping more with the research. "I have often wished since you first informed me of the commencement of your book, that you might have access to the papers in my possession," Robert wrote, "but after great reflection and consultation with gentlemen on whose judgment I relied, it seemed best that those papers should remain sealed for a long time to come. The reasons for this cause are doubtless plain to you."[33] Four months later, Hay informed Nicolay that he heard Arnold's next book was going to be a compilation of President Lincoln's writings and speeches. "Bob encourages it, but will not give him the key to the boxes," Hay reported.[34] In later years, Robert did loan Arnold certain items from the Lincoln papers, and he also gave a number of books to Arnold that previously had belonged to Abraham Lincoln.[35]

By the time of his death in 1884, Arnold had written multiple books concerning Abraham Lincoln, and Robert considered Arnold's full Lincoln biography, published in 1885, to be the best one written up to that time.[36] "Many persons write to me asking what life of my father I can commend to them, and I am now glad to be able to refer them to so complete and satisfactory a work as Mr. Arnold's," Robert wrote the book's publisher A. C. McClurg.[37] For the rest of his life, Robert recommended Arnold's biography as the best treatment of his father's religious beliefs.[38]

In 1874, Robert had decided to assist Gideon Welles, President Lincoln's secretary of the navy, in the preparation of his book *Lincoln and Seward.* Welles's book was a defense of Lincoln's leadership in response to Charles Francis Adams's allegations that Lincoln was a lackluster president, intellectually and politically inferior to Secretary of State William H. Seward. Robert long had been intimate friends with the entire Welles family, even staying at their Washington home while he courted Mary Harlan in the mid-1860s. When Robert saw reports of the argument between Welles and Adams, Robert wanted to join the fray. He had asked Nicolay to find in his father's papers, for Welles's use, Secretary Seward's infamous 1861 memorandum to President Lincoln (which suggested he make the decisions and Lincoln be a figurehead) and Lincoln's stolid response. Robert's desire to engage the issue personally was not only because of friendship for Welles but more so to correct Adams's revisionist and incorrect (to Robert) history. But Nicolay resented it. "Your design to let Mr. Welles use the paper in question is the most rash and inconsiderate step two as sensible men as yourself and Judge Davis could possibly devise," Nicolay chafed. "I protest against the injustice you would do to myself and Col. Hay by the course you propose." Nicolay and Hay wanted exclusive access to the papers, and, Nicolay argued, everything should be presented as a whole, and to allow Welles, or anyone else, to publish items piecemeal would divest everything of its overall historical uniqueness and impact. Robert relented.[39]

Separately, Robert read through Allan Pinkerton's manuscript *Spy of the Rebellion*, a memoir of the detective's service as secret-service chief during the war. This young Lincoln did at Pinkerton's request merely to verify that the facts were correct as he knew them, mostly about the inaugural journey and the Baltimore assassination plot. Robert passed Pinkerton's letter and manuscript on to Nicolay for his opinion as well. There is no indication that he gave Pinkerton access to any of President Lincoln's papers.[40]

Journalist Noah Brooks, who had been tapped to become President Lincoln's private secretary during the second term, also benefited from Robert Lincoln's generosity. Brooks put together what became an extensive history of the war and the president through his reporting for the *Sacramento Union* newspaper from 1862 to 1864.[41] These writings and experiences he parlayed into multiple books about the era, his most famous being *Washington in Lincoln's Time*, in 1895. But long before that book was published, Brooks wrote an article about the life and death of Tad Lincoln for the young adult magazine *St. Nicholas*. Robert gave Brooks detailed assistance for his work, including his own reminiscences of Tad, newspaper clippings, and family photos, all of which Brooks made extensive use in his article.[42]

For all the assistance Robert Lincoln gave presidential secretaries Nicolay and Hay, as well as secretary-designate Brooks, no evidence suggests he helped Lincoln's "third" secretary, William O. Stoddard. Stoddard was the most prolific writer of the group, publishing more than one hundred books throughout his life, including six Lincoln-related works between 1884 and 1906.[43] Stoddard's first foray into the Lincoln field was his 1884 *Abraham Lincoln: The True Story of a Great Life*. The book was written as a "strictly personal" life of Lincoln, and one that, as Stoddard explicitly stated in his introduction, would not and could not contend with the definitive work (still in progress at the time) of Nicolay and Hay. Regardless of the disclaimer, the two Johns—especially Hay—were upset by the book, believing it would devalue their own upcoming work. Perhaps their frustration, as well as David Davis's opinion of Stoddard's book as a "humbug" that he considered "throwing in the fire," was the reason Robert politely accepted copies of Stoddard's writings but never offered him any assistance.[44]

Of course, the great elephant in the room of Lincoln historiography is William Herndon. His lectures that so incensed Robert Lincoln in 1867 were not followed up until 1889 with *Herndon's Life of Lincoln*. By then, Robert had no interest or patience with Herndon's statements, and when asked in 1891 if he had read Herndon's *Life*, Robert replied, "No, nor do I wish to see it."[45] In fact, it does not appear that Robert ever read Herndon's book, although he railed against it the rest of his life. Robert believed Herndon's work full of nothing but malicious lies that were written out of revenge against President Lincoln's failure to appoint his former law partner to any sort of lucrative government position.[46] He also thought Herndon was insane. Robert explained to amateur historian L. E. Chittenden in 1890,

> I cannot write with patience about Herndon. Notwithstanding my father's help to him he remained such a man that my father when President simply could not comply with his wishes and since then he has been actuated by a boundless malice in which I think, for the credit of human nature, a lack of mental soundness has had much to do. My own personal experiences with him long ago showed me that he was incapable of distinguishing between truth and his own fancy and that he was either mentally unable to understand or maliciously unwilling to admit the plain meaning of his own written words. If you saw him today he would express the greatest surprise at any offense being taken at his outrages and would amaze you at his view of the meaning of any of his words you might quote. Happily I think my father's memory beyond the reach of such men as Herndon and his follower, Lamon.[47]

Herndon knew of Robert's feelings and often said that Robert hated him "religiously" for "telling naked truths about his noble father."[48] The knowledge of Robert's animosity in turn embittered, even poisoned, Herndon, who belittled Robert Lincoln as a petty, reprehensible person—a Todd and not a Lincoln—at every opportunity. Herndon ultimately was convinced by a rumor in 1889 that Robert, the then-minister to Great Britain, so despised him that Lincoln attempted to purchase and destroy every copy of *Herndon's Life of Lincoln* in England.[49] When Robert heard the accusation—which was untrue—he was "surprised" not only at the absurdity of it but that anyone could believe it.[50]

Part of Robert's disgust at Herndon also related to the negative depiction of Mary Lincoln. There were nowhere near as many writings about Mary Lincoln as there were about Abraham Lincoln during their oldest son's lifetime, but the few there were generally were not complimentary to the former first lady. This stemmed from her volatile reputation during the Springfield and White House years and from her 1875 declaration of insanity by a Chicago jury. This latter issue troubled Robert the most throughout his life. It embarrassed him, but more than that, he considered it an utterly private family affair not fit for public airing. This belief led him to attempt to collect and destroy all of his mother's letters written during what Robert called her "period of mental derangement" and to attempt to block the publication of letters he could not destroy.[51]

One 1887 article on the subject that upset Robert especially was titled "A History of the Insanity of Mrs. President Lincoln," by Adam Badeau. Badeau, a former officer on General Ulysses S. Grant's staff during the Civil War, offered details of his own experiences with Mrs. Lincoln's bizarre behaviors during the war, especially her embarrassing outburst at City Point, Virginia, in 1865. He proclaimed Mary undoubtedly insane but said the proof of that insanity as exhibited during her 1875 insanity trial had "redeemed the unfortunate woman herself from the odium for which she was not responsible." Badeau also praised Robert Lincoln for instituting the trial, calling it an action by a worthy son of a great sire.[52] Robert was "greatly annoyed" by Badeau's article. "Perhaps he thinks that the manner in which he speaks of myself is enough gratification to balance the rest," Robert wrote. "One cannot tell what such fellows think."[53]

Robert previously had helped prevent the publication of a letter by Jane Grey Swisshelm about his mother. Swisshelm, an ardent abolitionist and feminist, had befriended Mary Lincoln at the beginning of the Civil War and mentioned this friendship in her 1880 book, *Half a Century*. She also wrote a eulogy of Mary Lincoln for the *Chicago Tribune* in 1882.[54] In 1884, Swisshelm apparently was seeking to publish an article about Mary Lincoln's 1875 commitment, but an admirer of Robert's named N. P. Reed sought to stop it. Robert appreciated the effort, telling Reed that Swisshelm's writing was "a miserable mess of misstatements, easily shown to be false" and of the type that would annoy him just as it would annoy anyone of his social class "if papers would publish the inventions of discharged chambermaids."[55]

Robert himself tried in later years to prevent the publication of some of his mother's letters by family friend Abram Wakeman Jr. "It is very unpleasant for me to think or to hear of any anticipation of publication of her letters, because, as you know, the shocking circumstances of my father's death completely deranged her, and she spent most of the years afterwards in writing countless letters, which could only have been written in such derangement, and which were a source of great unhappiness to me. I therefore should be very sorry to see the subject opened up again, and I hope that you will avoid doing so," Robert told Wakeman.[56]

The publication about his mother that may have annoyed Robert Lincoln more than any other was Elizabeth Keckly's 1868 memoir, *Behind the Scenes or, Thirty Years a Slave and Four Years in the White House*. Keckly became Mary Lincoln's modiste in 1861, served in that capacity until the end of the war, and remained friends with the former first lady until 1867. *Behind the Scenes* opens with the story of Keckly's life but quickly turns into the telling of witnessed events in the Lincolns' White House during the war and Mary Lincoln's life and actions after the assassination. The book not only includes the complete story of the Old Clothes Scandal in 1867, in which Keckly played a major role as Mary's confidante, but also prints in full a series of private letters from Mary Lincoln to Keckly.

Keckly wrote her book, she claimed, to make Mary more understandable and sympathetic to the American public. She also hoped the book proceeds would help her old friend pay off some debts. The idea backfired. The book was denounced as scandal and trash and lost Keckly many clients and friends. Part of the public outrage was simply because Keckly was black but also concerned the publication of Mary's private letters. Keckly claimed the professional writer who assisted her with her manuscript added the letters to the book without her knowledge or consent. But it didn't matter. Keckly had violated Victorian codes "not only of friendship and privacy, but of race, gender, and class."[57] The *New York Times*, among others, declared, "We cannot but look upon many of the disclosures made in the volume as gross violations of confidence."[58] Mary Lincoln was so angry she never spoke to Keckly again. Robert Lincoln—in his high Victorianism, which included a conscious class separation and bias—was infuriated at what he regarded as a betrayal of trust and an indecent exposure of his family's privacy by a mere servant. Reportedly, he complained to the publisher and had the book suppressed; when he encountered Keckly in Washington years later, he was "so hostile to her that he could not be made to understand her true motive for writing the book."[59]

After organization of his father's papers and the publication of the Nicolay and Hay biography in 1890, Robert Lincoln was more willing to assist certain biographers in their work on both Abraham and Mary Lincoln. He generally limited his assistance to proofreading and occasionally to sharing his own recollections and opinions and referred those seeking actual documents to the Nicolay and Hay works. Robert assisted Frederick Trevor Hill with his 1906 book, *Lincoln the Lawyer*, and was pleased with it.[60] He also aided and encouraged David Homer Bates, a War Department cipher operator during the Civil War, whose 1907 book, *Lincoln in the Telegraph Office*, Robert said, "brings back very vividly the most exciting and interesting days of my life and the reminiscences of my father make him seem to me to be alive again."[61]

One of the most important Lincoln historians during Robert's lifetime whom he assisted was journalist Ida Tarbell. Tarbell had never studied the life of Abraham Lincoln, nor had she intended to, until the publisher of *McClure's* magazine offered her a large sum to undertake the work. Publisher S. S. McClure tasked Tarbell in the early 1890s to seek out unpublished materials about Lincoln as the basis for a series of articles similar to the Nicolay-Hay articles in *Century Magazine*. Tarbell at first thought there could not possibly be anything about Lincoln left unpublished after the mass of books and articles already printed about the man, especially the Nicolay and Hay works. Her research in Kentucky, Indiana, and Illinois, however, ultimately uncovered vast amounts of unpublished materials that she utilized for her series of articles in *McClure's*. This research also led her to continue the project and ultimately write a two-volume *Life of Abraham Lincoln*.[62]

One of Tarbell's first acts for her work was to visit Robert Lincoln in Chicago, a meeting arranged by a mutual friend. Tarbell found Robert—at that time in 1894 or 1895 about sixty years old and special counsel for the Pullman Car Company—a warm and friendly man who was willing to help her but who believed there was nothing unknown left about his father for her to find.[63] The one item he did have was the earliest known daguerreotype of his father, never published, that he had only recently discovered among his mother's possessions. This he allowed Tarbell to copy and publish with her articles in *McClure's*. [64] Robert met with Tarbell multiple times after that first meeting and assisted her with her biographical work as much as he could. "I like her very much," Robert told his father-in-law in 1897. What he also liked was the fact that she was eager to be accurate in her historical writing and not print anything offensive to the Lincoln family.[65] After Tarbell's Lincoln biography was published in 1900, Robert often recommended it and the Nicolay-Hay biography as the two best works about his father.

Along with the Arnold, Nicolay-Hay, and Tarbell works, other books about his father Robert Lincoln thought excellent were L. E. Chittenden's *Recollections of Lincoln and His Administration* (1891), Richard Watson Gilder's *Lincoln the Leader* (1909), and Alonzo Rothschild's *Lincoln, Master of Men* (1906).[66] All of these were highly laudatory paeans to the eminence of Abraham Lincoln—

exactly the type of historical works about his father Robert preferred. Interestingly, the title of Rothschild's subsequent book, *Honest Abe* (1917), so upset Robert that he sent many letters to his old college friend, publisher George Mifflin, in an effort to have it changed from the "temporary and not widely extended vulgarity" of the nickname by which his father was never familiarly addressed. In this, he failed.[67] The fact that a mere book title, as opposed to anything textual and substantive, was so annoying to Robert indicates that as he aged, he became more sensitive to protecting the luster of his father's memory from any sort of tarnish, however minimal.

Robert thought Lord Charnwood's biography of Abraham Lincoln—hailed at the time and still today as one of the best books of its subject—was a horrible book full of lies and mistakes directly inherited from the works of Herndon and Lamon. In 1920, Robert wrote a friend, "They say Charnwood's book is really very good but I have not read it yet. I was made angry by his 'introduction' and lost my temper, but shall of course read it later."[68] The introduction of Robert's copy of the book, still on the shelves at his home in Vermont, contains his angry handwritten comments and corrections in the margins, mostly regarding his father's ancestry and childhood.

One interesting and glaring question that must be asked after examining Robert's dedicated preservation of his father's legacy in print is, Why did Robert himself never write anything? Why no personal memoir, no reminiscences, no historical articles based on family papers? Robert, in fact, was asked more than once to write such pieces, but he had multiple reasons for refusing. One was that being occupied with his profession—legal, political, and business—he did not have the time to undertake the sort of substantial work about his father as was the only kind he would have considered doing. (This sounds a bit like an excuse, but as becomes clearer in subsequent years, Robert was a perfectionist and a micromanager who could not stand doing any activity without giving his full energies.) This, he often said, was why he cooperated and commissioned Nicolay and Hay to undertake their work because they had the necessary expertise and time to accomplish it. He also felt that if he consented to write about his father for one magazine or newspaper, he would then be required, as a man of honor, to give the same consideration to every other request. To do so would take up every moment of every day.

Robert often refused such requests because he self-effacingly claimed he could not contribute anything reliable. He once explained to Alexander K. McClure that he would have no hesitation to write an article about his father "if I could do so to be satisfied with it myself, but it seems impossible. . . . I took no notes [during President Lincoln's administration] and could not trust myself at this late day to put myself in black and white."[69] Robert offered a similar sentiment in regard to writing out his memory of his father's reaction to the aftermath of the Battle of Gettysburg. In 1878, the *Chicago Tribune* was printing articles about General George Gordon Meade's failure to pursue the defeated General Robert E. Lee. Robert remembered that his father instructed Meade to attack, stating that if Meade won, he could take all the glory, but if he lost, the president would take all the blame. This item was not published in the articles, and Robert wanted to write a letter to the *Tribune* recounting the letter and its context. "I remember the contents [of the telegram] because father read it to me before he sent it," Robert later stated. He decided not to write the letter, however, after Nicolay urged him not to but more so because Robert could not corroborate his memory with documents, and he did not want to argue about the event with other writers and historians who would "at once" dispute his memory.[70]

The most important reason for Robert Lincoln's writing and publishing reticence, however, was that he did not feel it proper to impinge himself upon his father's memory. "I have always refrained from making any expression by letter or address in reference to my father's life, and public service, it being my feeling that whatever is to be publicly said or written of him should come from others than myself," Robert told one magazine editor in 1908. "My conviction upon this point is very strong," he replied to another.[71]

One publishing endeavor Robert did contribute his own material to was not about his father or mother but his cousin John Todd Stuart, Abraham Lincoln's first law partner and Mary Lincoln's cousin. had been a generous and sympathetic adviser to Robert from the assassination in 1865 until Stuart's death in 1885. "I have always thought Major Stuart one of the loveliest characters for a very strong man, that I ever knew," Robert said after Stuart died.[72] In 1887, when James Grant Wilson was compiling materials for a book on the presidents of the United States, he asked Robert to proofread the article on Abraham Lincoln written by Hay and to contribute any photographs of his father, mother, and himself that he could. All of this Robert did.[73] Wilson also asked Robert to write his own article on Stuart as an entry in *Appleton's Cyclopedia of American History*, Wilson's next editing project. Robert was delighted to undertake the assignment and after traveling to Springfield, Illinois, for some research, contributed a glowing sketch of Stuart's life and legal reputation.[74]

While articles and books about his father were the more pressing aspects of Abraham Lincoln's legacy that Robert dealt with, they were not the only artistic medium. Robert was constantly approached regarding depictions of his father in photograph, portrait, and sculpture. The most immediate of these concerned President Lincoln's deathbed scene in the Petersen House. Although only a handful of people were actually in the room when Lincoln died, portrayals of the moment included anywhere from ten to nearly fifty witnesses.[75] The largest number of mourners was depicted in Alonzo Chappel's 1868 elaborate oil painting *The Last Hours of Lincoln*. Chappel's work was advertised as the most realistic death scene of the president ever attempted or available, achieved by the principal witnesses' assent to pose for photographs for the artist's use. Standing stark and conspicuous in the foreground of the painting is a mustached Robert Lincoln, head bowed and holding a handkerchief as if in tears. Robert posed for this at Mathew Brady's photographic studio in Washington in about 1868. It was the one and only time Robert participated in such an artistic endeavor concerning his father. No letters or documents exist to explain why the usually private Robert agreed to participate, but he admired the painting so much that he ordered the most expensive engraving of it offered for sale.[76]

Robert's favorite painting of his father was George P. A. Healy's seated portrait, titled simply *Abraham Lincoln*, painted in 1869. "It is in my opinion, the best portrait of my father existing," Robert declared in 1903. "In fact, I do not know of any other that I would care to have."[77] Robert not only owned the original painting, which hung in his house for his entire adult life, but he also played a key part in its creation. In 1866–67, Healy began a painting called *The Peacemakers*, depicting a meeting between President Lincoln and three of his military commanders aboard the steamship *River Queen* at City Point, Virginia, in 1865. Healy painted President Lincoln from photographs and from suggestions made by Robert Lincoln and Leonard Swett, who were present during its creation, and Swett even acted as the model for Lincoln's body. That portrait served as the basis for Healy's seated portrait of Lincoln, which he completed in 1869 and submitted to President Grant, who was at that time selecting a portrait of Lincoln to hang in the White House. Robert wrote to the War Department and recommended the selection of Healy's picture, but Grant chose one by William F. Coggswell instead. The Healy portrait was then "stranded" in Washington, and Robert took the opportunity to purchase it from Healy for a "moderate" price.[78]

Robert Lincoln also greatly admired the work of artist Francis B. Carpenter, who is best known today for his "masterpiece," *The First Reading of the Emancipation Proclamation*, a grouping of Lincoln and his cabinet members that today hangs in the U.S. Capitol. The artist spent six months in the White House in 1864 working on his painting (and later published a book recounting the experience). When it was finished and engraved, Carpenter gave President Lincoln the first copy of the engraving, which Robert kept and had hung in his house.[79] While Robert liked the *First Reading* piece, his preferred Carpenter painting was the 1864 portrait of his father made from life and engraved by

F. Halperin in 1866. Robert told Carpenter in December 1866, after Carpenter sent him a copy of the engraving, that he was not only "perfectly satisfied with it as a portrait" but that his father's friend and his own legal mentor, Samuel W. Fuller, also declared it excellent. One month later, Robert told John Hay it was "the best likeness yet made" of his father.[80]

In photographs, Robert thought the best of his father without a beard was the Alexander Hessler print done in 1860. His favorite photograph of his bearded father was a February 9, 1864, Brady cabinet print, which Robert told Brady he regarded as "by far the best existing portrait of my father."[81] Another Brady print from February 9, 1864, that Robert considered "very good" he allowed the Lincoln National Life Insurance Company of Fort Wayne, Indiana, to use as its masthead and logo in 1905.[82]

In the genre of sculpture, Robert had few favorites. He stated in 1881 that he thought it "impossible" that a bronze heroic statue "can ever be a very faithful likeness of the subject."[83] He similarly told artist Vinnie Ream Hoxie in 1898, "To be perfectly frank with you, I have never seen any statue of my father which gave me a pleasant impression as a portrait."[84] This seems especially discourteous since Ream had made a statue of Lincoln that was placed under the U.S. Capitol dome in 1871—but Robert, as well as his mother Mary, never liked it. Robert also disliked the Gutzon Borglum statue in Newark, New Jersey. "It is a little curious that of all of the statues that have been made of my father, I was asked by the artists in only two instances to look at their work before it was too late to have any suggestions of mine adopted," Robert complained later in life. "These were Mr. [Augustus] Saint-Gaudens, as to both of his statues, and Mr. [Daniel Chester] French, in regard to the statue he is now making for the Lincoln Memorial [in Washington]. In both of these cases I was able to make suggestions which they professed themselves glad to have"[85]

Despite these protestations and criticisms, some statues of his father Robert actually admired. In 1881, Robert expounded at length about depictions of his father in statuary. He stated he always felt the 1860 bust of Abraham Lincoln by Leonard W. Volk was a "most excellent likeness" of his father, but he doubted Volk's overall ability as a sculptor, believing "Mr. Volk possesses no artist sense whatever." Likewise, he criticized Ream as an artist of little talent. He revealed that he had four or five favorite statues of his father existing at that time, but the two he liked best were the Lincoln Tomb statue in Springfield by Larkin Mead and the Lincoln Square statue in Washington, D.C., by Thomas Ball (although the latter he felt represented his father's hair as "too bushy").[86]

Depictions and examinations of Abraham Lincoln in literature and art abounded in the late nineteenth century and increased dramatically with every year. Robert was conscientious in his responsibility as the keeper of his father's legacy; his existing correspondence shows that he responded to every question, every request, and every solicitation he received. He often was gracious, sometimes curt, and occasionally dismissive in his role as gatekeeper and grand opinionator. His letters also show that while he was eager to assist projects that would enhance his father's reputation, he also was not afraid to oppose—directly or indirectly—those that he deemed improper or unworthy. But as the 1909 centennial of his father's birth approached, Robert nearly became overwhelmed in dealing with the business of his father's legacy.

18

"I Don't Want to Be Nobody nor Nothink except a Chicago Shyster"

Ex–Secretary of War Lincoln and his family returned to Chicago in May 1885 to resume the private life that had been put on hiatus in 1881. They did not return to their old house on Wabash Avenue (which Robert continued to lease out) but rented a house at 25 Walton Place while construction began for a new home on the north shore of Lake Michigan. The Lincolns all were pleased to be back in the city they loved, closer to family and friends. Robert was glad to escape public life; Mary and the children—who by 1885 were ages sixteen, thirteen, and ten—especially were happy to be so much nearer to the Harlans in Mount Pleasant, Iowa, whom they visited constantly during the year. Robert stayed in Chicago to work when his family was away but usually went to Mount Pleasant for weekends.

It is a strange circumstance that as Robert, at age forty-one, returned from Washington eager to focus on his law practice, he paralleled his father at the same stage of life. When Abraham Lincoln was forty-one in 1850, he had recently returned from Washington and his one-term stint as congressman and decided to put all his energy into his law practice. While Abraham decided to abandon politics at that point because he felt himself a failure, Robert's similar decision was for completely different reasons. He simply disliked public life. "My short deviation from a purely professional career has shown me the necessity of not again doing anything which does not belong to it," he wrote shortly after his return to Chicago. "And for the future my only appearances will be in professional matters, and not in any public or political character."[1]

Still, Robert Lincoln was continually approached about public-service opportunities. In early 1886, he was offered the presidency of the new American Protective Tariff League, a solidly Republican notion and organization dedicated to protect American labor and products from foreign competition by advocating a high tariff on imports.[2] The group wanted its first president to be a man "possessing a national character" yet not so conspicuous in politics "as to be likely to bring any adverse criticism or jealousy upon the organization."[3] Although Robert agreed with the group's public policy positions, he declined the appointment. He told the head of the invitation committee, "I am exceedingly anxious to 'live down,' if I may use the words, an impression which has been made known to me . . . that I consider my private occupation as subordinate to calls of a public character."[4] As he more whimsically, yet no less seriously, explained to John Hay, "I don't want to be nobody nor nothink except a Chicago Shyster." But more specifically, Robert still, despite having been secretary of war for four years, did not want anything offered that he felt he did not deserve on his own merits.

> I won't attempt to write you as I am going to do to the Committee but for your own private ears here are two good reasons against my accepting. There is no good reason why I should be selected as the formal head of such a League and to anyone who gives it a thought the inquiry is at once suggested what has he done to entitle him to such a place and why does he take it? There is no good answer to either question. I am pretty happy just now. I am let alone in the papers and I don't want my name in them again until I am assured of the regular complimentary notes written by some member of my afflicted family with "no flowers" attached. Like Nanki Pooh, I won't be there to see it, but I don't mind that. God willing I will never again be in the jaws of that damning hyena the public at large and no man of my profession could enter the place suggested without being charged with having his lightning rod up as they say.[5]

Another reason Robert disliked being a public figure was because of the petty annoyances and newspaper-contrived controversies continually manufactured. One such irritation concerned Robert's May 14, 1885, sale of two horses to the quartermaster general's department for $850. This was done as the ex-secretary prepared to leave Washington for Chicago at the end of his cabinet tenure and probably because Lincoln had no more use for the animals. Two years later, a War Department controller disallowed the purchase, stating that even though a board of officers reviewed the sale, it was done without due legal advertisement, as required by law. The newspapers wrote it up as an embarrassing episode to the department.[6] A few months later, a story reported that President Chester A. Arthur had snubbed Frederick D. Grant—and by extension his father, former President Ulysses S. Grant—for an army appointment, which was untrue.[7]

Another minor controversy about Robert's tenure in the War Department occurred in January 1888 when it was reported that then-Secretary Lincoln had ordered captured rebel flags from the Civil War sent back to their home states. "Well what of it? What if the old flags were boxed up?" Robert asked angrily when shown the news dispatch by a reporter.

"The insinuation evidently is that they were boxed up with the intention of returning them to the Southern States from which they were taken," the reporter replied.

"I don't see that there is any reason for such insinuation in that dispatch," Robert replied testily. "It is all poppycock. The thing was never once spoken of, or even thought of, while I was in the department. We had more important matters to think about when I was there than the disposition that should be made of a few rotten old rebel flags."[8]

Robert Lincoln intended to avoid publicity and focus on his law practice, and that is what he did. For the rest of the decade, he and his law partner, Edward Swift Isham, diligently worked to make their firm the most respected in Chicago. In 1886, the founders added a third partner, William G. Beale.

The law firm of Isham, Lincoln, and Beale continued to handle real estate and investment matters and by this period represented numerous large businesses—railroads, banks, insurance companies, and merchants—and wealthy individuals such as Marshall Field, Potter Palmer, and George M. Pullman. One 1887 profile of Robert Lincoln stated, "[H]e is said to be about the most industrious of all the professional men in the city, invariably reaching his office at the unlawyerly-like hour of eight in the morning, and remaining, hard at work all day, until six in the evening. Mr. Lincoln is what is termed a business lawyer. He excels in chancery cases, involving the rights and titles of property, rather than in the miscellaneous or criminal practice."[9]

It was said that in looking up land and property titles, lawyer Lincoln "has no superiors and but half a dozen equals in the city." Due to the damages and burned records from the 1871 Great Fire of Chicago, this talent was an important and lucrative branch of legal work in the city. Robert once spent about four days examining the title of a valuable tract of land in Chicago purchased in 1886 by millionaire businessman Field. For this job, he reportedly received a $5,000 fee, "the largest ever paid for a similar service in the west."[10]

The firm represented the Wabash railroad in numerous legal cases and was reportedly paid $20,000 per year for the job. In 1888, Robert Lincoln was one of the railroad's counsels representing Wabash receiver General John McNulta in a court action to determine his responsibilities, according to the Interstate Commerce Act, in regards to Wabash trains "exchanging traffic" with another railroad (the Chicago, Burlington, and Quincy) whose workers were on strike.[11]

Robert had a reputation not only as a good businessman and keen financier but also as a gifted mathematician. He was the partner who was always called upon to "delve into matters involving intricate financial problems," according to the firm's official historian. (In fact, Robert Lincoln enjoyed numerical problems so much that he often would relax at home by working on complicated mathematical equations in his spare time, as well as undertaking amateur astronomy and surveying—this mechanical inclination was another similarity he shared with his father.)[12] Robert once put his mathematical mind to the test during the estate settlement of Chicago millionaire real-estate investor, banker, and commission merchant Walter L. Newberry. The estate involved around $5 million, multiple heirs, assets and property in multiple states and took six years to settle. Robert's settlement of the estate (which he then personally defended in court when it was contested) was called a "marvel of ingenuity" by one of his peers, was admired by members of the Chicago Bar, and was one of his celebrated legal achievements.[13]

In 1889, the legal journal *Green Bag* praised Robert Lincoln for his "vigorous" and impressive practice of the law since his return to Chicago in 1885 and for the degree of esteem in which his clients, colleagues, and peers held him.[14] Leonard Swett told a reporter how Robert was similar to his presidential father as a lawyer and executive: "[Robert] is rather amiable and obliging and willing to let other people have their own way up to a certain point, but every once in a while he takes the bit in his mouth without saying a word to anybody and goes ahead quite contrary to the wishes of the fellows who think they are driving," Swett stated. "The army people thought for a time that they were running the War Department when he was secretary, but it was not long before they discovered their error."[15]

With the law practice of Isham, Lincoln, and Beale flourishing in the late 1880s, it was reported that the firm's income was $60,000 a year (equal to over $1 million in the twenty-first century)—one of the highest in Chicago.[16]

By this period in his life, Robert Lincoln was becoming a wealthy man. His income came not solely from his work as an attorney but also from his myriad business interests and investments. But his road to affluence was neither easy nor simple. He had tried and failed at numerous investments in land and stocks over the previous twenty years and during the 1870s was so far in debt while waiting for his investments to realize that he had to delay repaying his loans and even take out greater loans. "Of course I don't enjoy losing money more than anyone else," he quipped to one investment partner in 1882, "but it looked to me as if I had found this road to wealth no thoroughfare."[17] Like a savvy businessman, he also put certain of his properties and holdings in his wife's name to prevent a total personal loss in case of bankruptcy.

In 1881, while applying for a $5,000 loan to use in a business opportunity presented to him by "a Pullman friend"—"which is as sure [a thing] as a reasonable man could ask," he stated—Robert estimated he was worth between $50,000 and $75,000 and owed "nothing but a mortgage of $6,000 on one piece of land worth triple the debt, which is not yet due."[18] Much of Robert's worth was actually in land and real estate. He invested in a dozen or more lots in and around Chicago; he owned and leased out lots in Lincoln, Illinois, and Council Bluffs, Iowa, which he had inherited from his father. He also leased his personal houses on Wabash Avenue and West Washington Street (the latter being his mother's former house), as well as multiple rental properties he owned on Morgan Street. In 1886, he considered investing in real estate and cattle in Montana, in cooperation with Russell B. Harrison, son of U.S. Senator (and future president) Benjamin Harrison.[19]

Robert also invested in numerous business ventures, mostly in Chicago. He was a shrewd businessman—surrounded, advised, and partnered with other astute businessmen—who had a prescient eye for becoming involved in endeavors with indispensable future potential, such as telephones, electricity, railroads, and automobiles. He held stocks and bonds in companies such as Carbonate Hill Consolidated Mining Company, North River Construction Company, Chicago Telephone Company, Central Union Telephone Company, Michigan Telephone Company, Midland Telephone Company, Chicago Edison Electric Light Company, American Straw Bond Company, and the Pullman Car Company. His business acumen led him in 1899 to invest in one of the first automobile companies in America, the Illinois Electric Vehicle Transportation Company.

By the late 1880s, Robert Lincoln held multiple executive positions in various business interests. He was a director of Whale Consolidated Gold and Silver Mining Company and the Western Edison Light Company. Robert's public endeavors included being a trustee of Illinois Central Railroad Company, Illinois Boys' Training School, and the Second Presbyterian Church of Chicago; he was one of the original incorporators of the Chicago Bar Association in 1874 and of the Chicago Edison [Electrical] Company in 1887; he was a member and one-time vice president of the Chicago Historical Society and gave them some relics of his father for display. He also was a leading member of a group of Chicago citizens to raise money to present a gift of full dining settings (about $1,500) on behalf of the city's denizens to the steamship *Chicago*.[20]

Personally, as a good man of business and a Victorian gentleman, Robert belonged to numerous clubs and associations throughout his life. He was a member of the Chicago, Chicago Athletic, Union, University, and Chicago Literary Clubs in Chicago, the Harvard Club in New York, the Pelee [fishing]

Club in Sandusky, Ohio, and a founder of the Chicago Golf Club in Wheaton, Illinois. He was a proud and fond alumnus of both Phillips Exeter Academy and Harvard University, attended the annual alumni dinners whenever possible, and even sometimes made brief, innocuous speeches.[21] He shunned public appearances, but he was a man's man and loved spending time with his friends and colleagues in social settings. Robert lunched every day at one of his clubs in Chicago, attended various stag dinners, banquets, and parties at clubs and private homes, was a frequent player of billiards and golf, an astute hand at poker, an inveterate cigar smoker, and a lover of fishing.

The Lincolns as a married couple also were earnestly desired guests at all the top Chicago social functions (although Robert more often than not attended these gatherings and soirees alone since his wife continued to suffer from feeble health). Their friends included all the wealthy and fashionable people of the city, the George Pullmans, the Potter Palmers, the Marshall Fields, the Franklin MacVeaghs, and the Philip Armours, among others. Some of the major social events the Lincolns attended included the golden wedding anniversary of Judge and Mrs. John D. Caton in summer 1885 and a reception given by Mr. And Mrs. George M. Pullman in February 1886.[22] The Lincolns occasionally hosted their own events, as in February 1886 when they acted as manager and patroness of the Second Annual Chicago Charity Ball for the benefit of two city hospitals; Mrs. Lincoln hosted an afternoon reception for Harvard President Charles William Eliot in 1888 to meet the ladies of the city and at times assisted her friends with their own receptions.[23]

Robert's rising income and social prominence were evident when he built his new house on the Gold Coast of Chicago: Lake Shore Drive. The neighborhood was developed by millionaire merchant Potter Palmer in the early 1880s, and lots were sold to his high-standing friends. Robert Lincoln's house at 60 Lake Shore Drive (later renumbered to 1234 North Lake Shore Drive) was completed in 1887 at a total cost of around $50,000.[24] The three-story Lincoln mansion actually looked like a castle, and as such, it harmonized well with the neighboring Germanesque castle of Palmer and the Roman palace of millionaire merchant (and later secretary of the treasury) Franklin MacVeagh. Lincoln's house of red brick with limestone trim and dormer windows on the third floor had twenty rooms, including an oak-paneled reception hall and mahogany-paneled parlor. An architect in the 1950s described the style of the house as "inconspicuous catch as catch can semi-Romanesque of the Gen. Grant period."[25]

The regality of the lake shore was only one of numerous energetic changes to Chicago during the 1880s. The city had grown vibrantly while Robert Lincoln and his family had been in Washington. Electricity, telephone service, and water purification and drainage were introduced in the early part of the decade;

more than a dozen railroad lines ran through Chicago, and augmented by its shipping ports, manufacturing boomed in the city: lumber, steel, iron, furs, machinery, grocery, furniture, clothing, and breweries. Architecture flourished with elegant private homes, luxurious hotels and social clubs, and massive places of business. The city also was a melting pot of cultures, a grand destination for immigrants seeking urban life and work. Between 1880 and 1890, the population of Chicago had increased by half a million people.[26] "The city is a vortex of human activity," one historian wrote. "It is a vortex, into which there is a continual flow of people and of food and other commodities, and out of which there is a flow of people and of goods more or less transformed."[27] Or as poet Carl Sandburg so famously characterized his home city,

> Hog Butcher for the World,
> Tool Maker, Stacker of Wheat,
> Player with Railroads and the Nation's Freight Handler;
> Stormy, husky, brawling,
> City of the Big Shoulders.[28]

Within this blustering and frenetic miasma of activity, not all was storybook happiness and prosperity. Amid the affluence also were poverty and crime; amid the flourishing businesses also were labor strikes and unemployment. The unequal success of the democratic market system led to support for socialism and anarchy. One result was the infamous Haymarket riot in May 1886, during which rallying laborers and anarchists were massacred by police after someone in the crowd threw a pipe bomb that killed a police officer. Chicago was a microcosm of America and indicative of other large cities: expanding and expounding, virulent and virile, suffering the growing pains of industrialization.

President Grover Cleveland, the first Democrat in the White House in a quarter century, was kept busy dealing with the issues of this national industrialization. He signed an act creating the Interstate Commerce Commission in 1887, mainly to regulate the expanding railroads; made railroad companies return to the public land previously obtained by government grant; sought to protect the civil rights of minorities, especially Chinese railroad workers; favored backing American currency with the gold standard, rather than switching to a cheaper silver standard; and favored reducing import tariffs on foreign goods.[29]

While the Democrats were in command of the government, the end of the 1880s witnessed the deaths of numerous Republican luminaries, all of whom were friends or mentors to Robert Lincoln. Former President Grant died in August 1885, and Robert traveled to New York City to attend the funeral. In 1886, ex-President Arthur and former U.S. Senator and U.S. Supreme Court

Justice David Davis—Robert Lincoln's "second father"—also died. These were men Robert Lincoln respected and admired deeply, and their deaths affected him considerably, especially Davis. Robert telegraphed his condolences to both families immediately after hearing of the deaths. To Davis's survivors, Robert wrote, "Please convey to all of Judge Davis's family my sincere sympathy in a loss which affects me closely."[30] Before leaving for Arthur's funeral in Albany, New York, Lincoln issued a statement about his former chief.

> My acquaintance really began with my official connection. Not only did I learn to respect him most highly, but to have a great personal affection for him. It always seemed to me he overcame in an admirable manner the difficulties surrounding him when he became president. While an earnest Republican, he was above all a patriotic citizen, and I know of no act in which he did not have at heart the public interest. I think it is universally conceded that, as far as he was actually responsible, he was able and dignified. His official appointments were always considered with the greatest care, and if any were subject to criticism, it was because of misinformation given him. He was especially earnest in carrying out not only the letter, but the spirit of the Civil Service law, passed during his Administration. In our foreign relations he was as earnest and patriotic as could be desired. There was no need for aggressiveness, but he clearly recognized our situation and repeatedly urged Congress to strengthen his hands. He was a President of whom the country is proud, and for whom it may well mourn.[31]

Lincoln not only attended but served as a pallbearer in both funerals.[32]

In December 1886, former Civil War general, Republican vice-presidential nominee, and current U.S. Senator from Illinois John A. Logan also died. Robert felt "personally greatly grieved" and wrote a lengthy public comment on his feelings for a Chicago newspaper.[33] When Chicago Republican leaders held a memorial gathering to honor Logan, Robert Lincoln was named the presiding officer and principal speaker for the evening.[34] He was asked to be a pallbearer for Logan's funeral but could not travel to Washington due to previously scheduled business. He later served on a committee to supervise the erection of a Logan statue in Illinois.[35]

Logan's death impacted Robert Lincoln publicly as well as privately: it created a vacancy for the Illinois U.S. Senate seat, for which Robert Lincoln's name immediately catapulted to the top tier of possible replacements. Unlike the brief media flirtation with Robert Lincoln for Senate in 1882 merely because of his surname, in 1887 admirers of the ex–secretary of war now pointed to his tenure in the War Department, as 1880 Grant Stalwart and presidential elector, as South Chicago town supervisor, and as respected and successful lawyer and businessman in addition to his name and family resemblance. The *Minneapolis Tribune* declared that the younger Lincoln was "a big enough man" to fill the seat, but "Illinois is infested with great men."[36] The *Chicago Tribune*, always friendly to Robert, declared that he was "a man of vigor, ability and executive capacity, and, like his father, has common sense, and is known for his good judgment and unaffected modesty. Besides, he is energetic and loves to work."[37] Many people and newspapers were suggesting the Senate seat could be his stepping stone to the presidency in 1888.

Just as with mentions of his name previously for Congress, Senate, vice president, and president, Robert Lincoln had absolutely no interest in becoming the new U.S. Senator from Illinois. He publicly declared he was not a candidate, and as one newspaper reported, the "friendly feeling" for Lincoln as Senator would get no traction unless and until he opened a campaign headquarters in the state capital, which he never did.[38] It was suggested by many that Robert would accept the position even if nominated against his will.[39] Chicago businessman and former Republican congressman (and juror during Mary Lincoln's insanity trial) Charles B. Farwell ultimately was elected.

The one national job Robert Lincoln was never promoted for was a seat on the U.S. Supreme Court. It seems odd since by profession he was an attorney, and he hailed from the politically important state of Illinois. This exclusion offers further evidence that despite his hard-earned reputation and self-made successes, Robert Lincoln's public political appeal still lay manifestly in the power of his parentage and surname. Republicans wanted to see his name on an election ballot, not a certificate of appointment. When Supreme Court Chief Justice Morrison Waite died in 1888 and the scuttlebutt was that politics demanded a man from Illinois to be given the place, the son of Abraham Lincoln never was mentioned. Knowing the appointment would favor an Illinoisan, Robert Lincoln, "as a citizen of Illinois and a lawyer," wrote to President Cleveland supporting the nomination of Democrat Chicago attorney Melville Weston Fuller, who received the job.[40]

The year 1887 was a busy one for Robert Lincoln as keeper of the family legacy. During the spring, the bodies of Abraham and Mary Lincoln were moved to a different burial place within the Lincoln Tomb. Since 1882, the Lincolns' bodies had laid undisturbed, secretly buried under a few feet of dirt in the basement to prevent theft attempts. When the tomb monument began to crumble in 1884, a reconstruction was begun, during which the Lincoln Monument Association decided to move the bodies to a newly constructed grave directly beneath the original (and empty) sarcophagus in Memorial Hall—the specious place at which people had been paying their respects to the martyr president.

The new grave pit was six feet deep and surrounded by a brick wall reinforced with cement.[41] Robert Lincoln approved the reconstruction and reburial plans, although he did not attend the official reburial ceremony on April 15, 1887.[42]

In October 1887, a great statue of Abraham Lincoln was officially dedicated before thousands of onlookers in Lincoln Park in downtown Chicago. The bronze effigy of a standing President Lincoln was sculpted by Augustus Saint-Gaudens and cost $40,000 (and was one of Robert Lincoln's favorite statues of his father). Robert and Jack Lincoln attended the ceremony, listened to the music, presentations, and the main oration by Leonard Swett; Robert watched as his fifteen-year-old son, Abraham Lincoln II, raised the veil of American flags to reveal the statue.[43]

The major Lincoln legacy event of 1887, however, was Robert's donation of his father's old home at the corner of Eighth and Jackson Streets in Springfield to the State of Illinois. Robert had administered possession of the home for more than twenty years by that time—first in handling it for his mother and then for himself after he purchased his mother's share of the house from her in April 1874 for $500, making him the sole owner.[44] From his father's death in 1865 until his divestiture of the property in 1887, Robert, through his boyhood friend and empowered agent Clinton Conkling, paid the yearly taxes and insurance and subsidized the maintenance and upkeep of the house. He also rented out his old home to five different men: Lucian Tilton (1861–69), George Harlow (1869–77), Jacob Akard (1877–79), Gustav Wendlandt (1879–83), and Osborn H. Oldroyd (1883–87).

As a real-estate attorney as well as the owner of numerous rental properties in Chicago, Robert's role as landlord of the Old Lincoln Homestead, as it was called, was not a unique situation for him. As with other tenants and other properties, landlord Lincoln had to deal with late rent payments and unresponsive and argumentative tenants. He also had to deal with the house as an unofficial national shrine and the wear and tear of countless tourists every year since he arranged with every tenant to allow "all reasonable visitors" into the house.[45] For this reason, he refused to let any tenant alter the house in any way that would change its appearance from his father's time. It was an aggravating and expensive situation for Robert but one that he endured because of his sentimental attachment to the family home.

Robert kept the house in decent condition but administered the property as cheaply as possible. During his first years as owner, his penuriousness was because he could not afford any but the essential repairs; in later years, as his finances improved, his parsimony seems to have been more a belief that the (by then) extensive renovations necessary would not be worth the cost. He charged Harlow $350 per year (almost $30 per month) in rent, but as he told one friend of his father, "I get just enough rent to pay taxes and necessary expenses."[46] Yet, however aggravated Robert was over Harlow's typically late rent payments, the increasing taxes, and the rising cost of maintenance, when Harlow offered to buy the house outright, Robert refused, saying, "I have concluded to own the house till it ruins me."[47]

Robert's occasional lack of urgency in attending to house maintenance actually lost him Harlow's occupancy. In spring 1877, Harlow requested that his landlord come to Springfield to arrange a contract for long-overdue maintenance on the house. Robert responded that he was extremely busy but would attend to it within about ten days. After an entire month passed with no action by Robert, Harlow terminated the lease and prepared to immediately move out. Robert was shocked at Harlow's (seemingly) abrupt action and tried to explain: "As you were already in occupancy, I did not regard the exact time of going [to Springfield] as exceedingly important and allowed other pressing matters here to delay me."[48] But Harlow left anyway. Robert was angry at what he considered a lack of courtesy but more so at the possibility of a vacant house. He told Conkling to find a new tenant immediately, writing, "I don't want the place torn to pieces" by relic hunters.[49]

By 1878, Robert characterized the house as "getting old and decayed in all parts" and a complete reparation to be extremely expensive. Yet, still he bristled when John Carroll Power, a member of the Lincoln Monument Association and the curator of the Lincoln Tomb, publicly stated that the house had not received any repairs since 1861. "This is a rather careless statement on your part as in fact I have expended nearly $1,100 in repairs on the house in the last ten years," Robert wrote to Power. "While you thought it worth mentioning you could have learned some of the facts from Col. Harlow."[50]

Power was not only the guardian of Abraham Lincoln's tomb but also considered himself somewhat a guardian of Lincoln's life. He was an amateur historian and collector of Lincoln relics, which he displayed at the tomb. In fact, he was so concerned over the poor condition of the Lincoln Homestead that he suggested that the Lincoln Monument Association be allowed to take over and administer the property. After much consideration, Robert decided to offer the house into the care of the association in summer 1879 under condition that it be fully restored and preserved as a memorial; but the group decided the acquisition was not allowed in its charter. Rebuffed, Robert spent considerable money repairing the house, then continued renting it.[51] He had trouble with tenant Akard, who apparently kept the place as a boardinghouse (causing Robert doubled utility bills), refused to clean out the privy vault, and abandoned the property without telling landlord Lincoln.[52] Robert's next tenant, physician Wendlandt, was reliable but stayed only four years.

Robert Lincoln's last renter was the indefatigable Lincoln collector Osborn H. Oldroyd. A failed businessman and author of *The Lincoln Memorial: Album of Immortelles*, Oldroyd began his occupancy of the Lincoln homestead in 1883.[53] He exhibited his collection of nearly two thousand Lincoln-related items in the front and back parlors of the house. Oldroyd allowed visitors into the home, as had his predecessors, but unlike them, he charged admission for entry to see his collection. Robert Lincoln allowed the exhibit and the entry fee and therefore became annoyed when in 1885 Oldroyd began failing to pay his rent—a failure seemingly caused by his proclivity to spend all his money to enlarge his collection. Robert urged his agent Conkling to "keep at him" and get as much money as he could out of Oldroyd but to bring no lawsuits against him, which "may easily cause me more personal annoyance than the loss of ten times the money." He also told Conkling to find a new tenant to replace Oldroyd if possible. "There is no reason that I know of why I should furnish him a house rent free and pay all its expenses," Robert chafed.[54]

In fact, living rent-free in the home of his hero was exactly what Oldroyd wanted to do. Shortly after moving in, he approached a member of the Illinois state legislature about having the state acquire the home and administer it as a historic monument or, as he called it, a "Memorial Hall." Ostensibly, the purpose was to honor Lincoln and create a public shrine, but in reality what he wanted was a place to house his vast collection in which he could live gratis—and draw a salary—as curator.[55] The state legislature passed the resolution in March 1883, but when the governor and later the attorney general of the state made the request from Robert Lincoln, he refused "for reasons not of public interest."[56]

When the state legislature again passed a resolution seeking to purchase the Lincoln homestead in 1887, Robert was more amenable. He told the legislative committee in charge that while he intended to keep the house as his father had it, the "accidents of life" could cause changes, and it was time he took measures to "avoid" such possible events. "If the State will offer to preserve the house as an object of public interest all questions will be avoided and you may say to the chairman that upon such an offer being made I will convey the property to the State without compensation," Robert wrote. The vagaries and aggravations of renting the house, especially Oldroyd's years of neglected rent, persuaded him to finally let go of the property. Robert was tired of dealing with the "dead beat" and "rascal" Oldroyd but correctly reasoned that "the whole proceeding" by the state was undertaken "to provide him a home free of rent, but I do not think that is a matter of any concern to me."[57] Robert officially deeded the house to the State of Illinois on July 21, 1887, under condition that it be kept in good repair and free and open to the public. The house was to be administered by a board of trustees for the state. The first custodian of the home hired was Osborn H. Oldroyd, who received a salary of $1,000 per year and free residence in the house.[58]

Robert was relieved to be free of the responsibility of his father's old home and confident the state would keep it in good condition. Only six years later, however, the state's handling of the Lincoln home caused Robert to inject himself into the administration of it. In 1896, for the first time since the end of the Civil War, a Democrat was elected governor of Illinois. Governor John Peter Altgeld, immediately upon assuming office, fired Oldroyd—who packed up his Lincoln collection and went to Washington, D.C.—and hired a political hack named Herman Hofferkamp as custodian. Robert was deeply disappointed that the job had become a spoil of political office but was especially stung when he learned that Hofferkamp hung a portrait of President Lincoln's assassin, John Wilkes Booth, on the fireplace mantel.

Altgeld proved to be an extremely unpopular governor and was defeated in the next election by Republican John R. Tanner. Just days after the election, Robert Lincoln called on the governor-elect to remove Hofferkamp and make a new appointment "under which, those honoring my father's memory by visiting the house would find themselves in an atmosphere suited to their kind feelings."[59] Robert also requested that the custodian position be made a permanent one and not subject to change with every election. He urged that his cousin Albert S. Edwards, son of Ninian and Elizabeth Edwards, be named to fill the position.[60] Albert was curator of the Lincoln home from 1897 until his death in 1915, after which his wife, Josephine, became curator, and upon her death, the Albert and Josephine's daughter, Mary Edwards Brown, took over. At the time of Robert Lincoln's death in 1926, his cousin Virginia Stuart Brown (great-granddaughter of John Todd Stuart) was curator.

Robert Lincoln's devotion to the Lincoln family legacy was not limited to objects and monuments concerning his parents. He also was involved in honoring the memories of his grandparents. As previously stated, Robert sought to protect the reputation of his grandfather Thomas Lincoln from the barbed—if truthful—pen of John Hay. Before that happened in 1885–86, Robert helped erect a graveside monument in 1881 to Thomas Lincoln in Coles County, Illinois. In fact, despite the distant relationship between Abraham Lincoln and his father during their lifetimes, the president had intended to place a marker at Thomas's grave during the summer of 1865. The assassination thwarted the plan, but Robert and his mother decided to fulfill their patriarch's wishes.[61] Their intention, however, never came to fruition of their own initiatives.

In 1873, a member of the Illinois state legislature introduced a resolution to place a marker on the grave of President Lincoln's father. When Robert and his mother were informed of this effort, they requested that it be abandoned. "I have had for some time an intention of placing monuments on the graves of the father and mother of my father but have been prevented from doing so as yet, by various causes," Robert explained. "Whether I should do that or cause them to be removed to Springfield, I am now of the opinion that I ought to do it myself, and not leave it to others." His mother agreed with this opinion, Robert subsequently stated.[62]

By 1880, there still was no marker on Thomas Lincoln's grave. Residents of Mattoon, Illinois, the town in which the Lincolns were buried, decided as a community that year to erect a monument. Despite his previously stated notions of family duty, Robert Lincoln decided not to inject himself into the town's plan and instead gave his blessing and offered to pay all expenses. In May 1881, when Robert Lincoln was secretary of war, the nine-foot-tall Thomas Lincoln monument, a large Grecian obelisk of Italian marble etched with Thomas Lincoln's biographical information, was dedicated in Mattoon. Secretary Lincoln did not attend the ceremony, but he had contributed $118 for the project.[63]

Twenty years later, a movement and fund drive were initiated to care for the grave of Robert's grandmother Nancy Hanks Lincoln in Spencer County, Indiana. Similar to the 1873 plan for a Thomas Lincoln monument, Robert Lincoln in 1900 considered the erection of a new Nancy Hanks Lincoln monument to be his "individual business" and as such an improper endeavor for anyone else to pay for. Robert told the Indiana governor he felt the current monument on the spot was "not greatly different in character or condition" from what he himself would erect "as an original proposition," and so he decided to leave it there. On the other hand, Robert felt that the part of the Nancy Lincoln project to purchase the public land on which his grandmother's grave stood was a public endeavor, rather than his private family business, and he assented to its undertaking. He donated $1,000 to the fund but required that his donation be anonymous.[64]

By far, the most important and time-consuming event that happened to Robert in the late 1880s was the 1888 presidential election, particularly the vehemence with which Republican leaders and public citizens attempted to draft him into his party's nomination.

After the loss of the White House in 1884, the Republican Party was determined to create a winning ticket in 1888. While many in the party supported the 1884 candidate, James G. Blaine, for another run, the Plumed Knight himself was adamant in his refusal, saying a defeated candidate could only be a burden to his party. So who was the shining light of the Republicans? Who could unite voters in solid support? Party leaders sat down to ruminate, and they asked frankly, What were the most distinguished names in the party that could ensure victory? Answer: Lincoln and Grant. The idea then emerged for a "father's son" ticket made up of Robert T. Lincoln for president and Frederick D. Grant for vice president. Could anyone doubt the invincibility of such a ticket? The magic of the idea disappeared, however, when Grant was defeated for election as secretary of state for New York.[65]

This setback made little difference in the fact that Robert T. Lincoln was a leading presidential possibility. He not only had the name and the endearing connection to his father's memory but also was by this time being seen as his own accomplished man. "This is not the mere stripling of a former Chief Magistrate," famed journalist and novelist George Alfred Townsend declared in a lengthy article declaring Robert Lincoln the best choice of all presidential contenders: "There is a deeper significance to his name than has heretofore been conceded to it."[66]

Despite his continued aversion to the notion, Lincoln's wishes were unheeded by the people and the newspapers. As early as April 1886, the Atlanta, Georgia, *Defiance* was urging the nomination of "Bob" Lincoln for either president or vice president, saying he would undoubtedly bring the southern black vote into the Republican column: "The magic of his talismanic name, the son of 'Abe' Lincoln, the immortal author of the Emancipation Proclamation, will be a tower of strength and the watch-word of victory to the Republican Party."[67] When questioned by a reporter a few days later, Lincoln replied that he was "entirely" out of public office: "I attend strictly to my private business and have no time, nor if I had time any inclination, to discuss public matters."[68]

Unfortunately for Lincoln, it was his complete lack of political ambition in 1884 and his clear statements about it that especially endeared him to voters for the 1888 nomination. One letter to the editor of the *New York Times* quoted Lincoln's 1884 antinomination letter that was published in both the *Times* and *Chicago Tribune* and said that in 1888 the Republican party needed a candidate "of the Lincoln stripe" who "was not forcing his candidacy upon the people."[69]

In May 1887, the Toledo, Ohio, *Blade* took a poll of its readers asking first and second choice for the Republican presidential nomination and first choice for the vice-presidential nomination. Robert Lincoln was "everywhere a good third" in the presidential field but "may almost be said to have had no competitor in the field for the Vice Presidency." The *Chicago Tribune*, following up on this poll, discussed Lincoln's candidacy, acknowledging that although he "has no taste for public life," the American people "are not accustomed to pay much attention to personal likes and dislikes in selecting a President." The Republican party clearly has its eye on Mr. Lincoln, the paper concluded, and "there was never a clearer indication of public sentiment than that if there is to be a dark horse at all it will be the son of Abraham Lincoln."[70]

The boom for Bob Lincoln continued in the pages of the *Chicago Tribune*, and newspapers across the country, through the second half of 1887. In July, the *Tribune* quoted two Massachusetts newspapers that elicited high praise for Lincoln. The Springfield *Republican* called Robert "the honored son of an honored sire," whose nomination would not only capture a large northern vote but also an immense southern black vote. It stated, "In the absence of deep-rooted and exciting issues, such as called forth a master like the elder Lincoln, the son belongs to the class of men who seem best fitted to the office of President in more tranquil times—not men who have been longest identified with the struggles and triumphs of the party in the past, not the giants of past warfare, but younger men of judicial mold, of liberal convictions as to the improvement of public administration and the reform of abuses and sympathetic with every section of a Union truly restored."

The Boston *Herald*, a Democrat paper, called Lincoln a "self-contained, sensible gentlemen" who would make a "sensible and patriotic" president. However, his worth was in his abilities, not simply because of his name, and while he was a dignified man, he was not a great man and not above other potential candidates in value.[71] Even the *Phrenological Journal and Science of Health* (a publication devoted to "ethnology, physiology, phrenology, physiognomy, sociology, psychology, education, mechanical industry, hygiene, and to all those progressive measures which are calculated to reform, elevate, and improve mankind spiritually, intellectually, and socially") made its political contribution. The journal offered comments on the cranial and facial structures—and their concomitant meanings—of Robert T. Lincoln: "The general outline of the head certainly reminds one of General Grant. The eyes show poise of mind, the nose strength of will and executive staunchness, the fullness of the temples taste, practical judgment, and prudence. The fullness of the cheeks shows abundant vital capacity."[72]

A reporter from the *Chicago Tribune* called on Robert Lincoln at his law office in August 1887 to ask him about his potential candidacy. It is one of the longest, most in-depth and revealing interviews with the naturally reticent Lincoln ever published. Lincoln reiterated that he was not a candidate for vice president and would not accept such a nomination if offered: "To take any office at all would be a great sacrifice on my business interests here in Chicago; and the Vice Presidency is not an office of such importance that I could afford to think of such a thing." As for the top job, "[t]he Presidential office is but a gilded prison. The care and worry outweigh, to my mind, the honor which surrounds the position," Robert said. He added that he had had his fill of public life as secretary of war. "I made up my mind at that time that when my official term was completed I should return to Chicago and end my days there in the practice of my profession. . . . I went to Washington, in 1881, with reluctance, and was glad to come away." Lincoln was, however, a man of principle with a Victorian sense of duty. He repeatedly told the reporter that he was not a candidate for president, yet at the end of the interview, he added the caveat, "Well then, I will say this: A duty might be imposed upon a man which he could not honorably avoid."[73]

As February 1888 approached, so, too, the numerous annual observances of Abraham Lincoln's birthday by Lincoln clubs, Republican clubs, and soldiers' groups around the country. Robert received dozens of invitations for these events every year but attended few. When he did attend, he never gave a speech, believing that statements about his father should come from others than him. But in 1888, Robert graciously—yet decidedly—declined every invitation he received in order to prevent further talk of his potential candidacy. As he told the Lincoln Club of Rochester, New York, "I am, in spite of my own efforts, in danger of being drifted by newspaper writers who do not consult me, into the unpleasant position of being an unsuccessful candidate for public office. In order to prevent this . . . I must at least avoid giving such implied assertion as would come from my addressing a public meeting, on any subject not merely local or special."[74]

Lincoln continued voicing his opposition to nomination all the way up to the Republican convention in June 1888. He repeated his opposition to nomination, and his obeisance to duty if nominated, to a *Tribune* reporter in September 1887; he must have been exasperated in October when the *New York Times* reported that his friends were making a strong effort in Chicago to start a boom for his nomination.[75] He told a personal correspondent in January 1888 that any talk of his nomination should be "totally abandoned," and in another letter in March 1888 he said that he was "sorry to see any mention of my name in connection with any political office, and I have said this so often that it is a matter of wonder to me that it does not stop."[76]

Not only did Robert Lincoln not want to be president, he did not feel that he deserved it. Similar to the letter in which he refused the position as head of the Tariff League in 1886, Robert wrote to one admirer,

> I have a repugnance to what is called "public life" that is almost morbid—of course I have what I think are good reasons for my feeling, but good or bad they would on occasion control my action. Aside from this sentiment, I would not be at all proud of a nomination which I could not honestly feel was gained by my own merit as a public man and to such merit I make

> not the slightest pretension. I know perfectly well that what many would consider my availability for one or another place would come in only a very slight degree from anything attributable to myself, a "Campaign" would under such circumstances be to me a Purgatory from which the issue was not possibly to Heaven for in my thinking there are few men in respectable positions in life less to be envied than a President. There is not the faintest glimmer about the place to me.[77]

Lincoln was so adamant about keeping his name out of the contest that he left the country. In June 1888, during the Republican nominating convention, he took his oldest daughter, Mamie, to London for a vacation and also to avoid the bother of politics. "No," he laughed as he told an inquiring British reporter when he arrived, "I am not a dark horse."[78]

Yet, despite his escape across the ocean and his repeated attempts to disassociate himself with a candidacy, Lincoln had strong support; and he again, just as in 1884, took votes at the convention. Blaine's absence and the lack of any other dominant candidate necessitated eight ballots to choose a nominee. Lincoln took votes on five: three on the first, two on the second, two on the third, one on the fourth, and two on the seventh.[79] Robert himself supported federal judge (and postmaster general and treasury secretary in President Arthur's cabinet) Walter Q. Gresham for the nomination, although he expected Blaine to be united on if the convention was deadlocked.[80] Former U.S. Senator Benjamin Harrison finally received the nomination as a compromise candidate, his main virtues being he had no enemies and his grandfather was once president.

It seemed as certain then as it does now that had Robert Lincoln actively sought the Republican presidential nomination in 1888, he would have won it. Likewise, had the convention deadlocked unalterably, Lincoln probably would have become the consensus candidate. Robert's many statements in 1887 and 1888 show that for a while he felt in serious danger of being nominated against his will. Yet, his continuous public repudiation of any ambition or desire for the job, his lack of any active campaigning, and his retreat to London during the convention all ensured his escape from nomination.

When the convention finally ended, Robert Lincoln was relieved. He returned to the United States in August, in good health and high spirits after being abroad with his daughter. "I have only been loafing," he told a reporter, "simply trying to keep in out of the rain during my trip abroad."[81] He returned to Chicago to confront two months of piled-up business, yet eager to campaign for the Republican ticket, which he did in October and November.[82] He was convinced the Republicans would win because the Democrat policies of low tariffs and free trade, coupled with their failure to implement civil-service reform as they promised in 1884, would alienate voters, especially the independents who had abandoned the GOP in 1884.

Harrison recaptured the White House for the Republicans that year, although it was only a half victory: he won the electoral vote but lost the popular vote to President Cleveland. Robert Lincoln, always a dedicated Republican, was pleased his side had prevailed but was more glad that the entire presidential season had ended so he would be left alone by reporters and could get back to work at his law practice. His planned abandonment of public office quickly came to an end, however, when President Harrison, without consulting anyone, offered Robert the most prestigious foreign appointment in the state department. Robert's acceptance would lead directly to his only son's death.

An 1888 "tobacco card" issued by Honest Long Cut Tobacco depicting Robert T. Lincoln of Illinois as a presidential possibility for that year. Lincoln's card was one of twenty-five issued in the series, both Republicans and Democrats, which included politicians such as Grover Cleveland, Benjamin Harrison, and William McKinley. Author's collection.

"Preparing for a Ten Strike," political cartoon from a May 1888 issue of the *Daily Graphic*, showing 1884 Republican presidential candidate James G. Blaine preparing to bowl down his opponents for the 1888 nomination. Robert Lincoln's head is on the pin second from the right. Courtesy of Library of Congress, Prints and Photographs Division.

Robert Lincoln (*back row, second from right*) and his nineteen-year-old daughter Mamie (*bottom row, center, wearing hat*) in Paris, July 14, 1888, during a tour of Europe that father and daughter took partly so Robert could be absent from America during the Republican national nominating convention that June. Courtesy of Hildene, The Lincoln Family Home, Manchester, Vermont.

"The 'Press View' at the Candidate Show," an 1895 political cartoon showing men representing different newspapers, some with magnifying glasses, viewing presidential candidates for the 1896 election. The ultimate winner, William McKinley, sits far right with a sword labeled "protectionism"; former president Benjamin Harrison is front right wearing professorial garb

with a sign stating, "My friends say I am not a candidate"; Robert Lincoln stands in the back row, third from right, below a coat suspended above him (fit for his father), in front of a sign reading, "Bobby Todd Lincoln, there is a good deal in the name." Courtesy of Library of Congress, Prints and Photographs Division.

Robert Lincoln depicted in 1897 during his brief tenure as president of the Chicago Telephone Company. Artist Lloyd Ostendorf was renowned for more than fifty years for his excellent drawings of scenes from the life of Abraham Lincoln. While Ostendorf occasionally included a young Robert in Lincoln family scenes, this is the only drawing by Ostendorf that focuses on Robert as an adult and as the main composition subject. Illustration by Lloyd Ostendorf, author of *Abraham Lincoln: The Boy, the Man*, reproduced courtesy of publisher Phil Wagner, Springfield, Illinois, www.abelincoln.com.

Lincoln "Linc" Isham and his father, Charles, posing on the south porch of Hildene, around 1908. Courtesy of Hildene, The Lincoln Family Home, Manchester, Vermont.

Jessie Harlan Lincoln Beckwith and her children, Peggy (*left*) and Bud, around 1912. At the time of this photo, Jessie was nearing age forty, Peggy was fourteen, and Bud was eight. Courtesy of Hildene, The Lincoln Family Home, Manchester, Vermont.

Robert Lincoln's summer home, Hildene, from a 1909 postcard. Courtesy of Hildene, The Lincoln Family Home, Manchester, Vermont.

Robert T. Lincoln in a studio photograph taken sometime around the turn of the twentieth century, while he served as president of the Pullman Company. In this photograph, Robert looks every inch the self-assured captain of industry that he was. Courtesy of Hildene, The Lincoln Family Home, Manchester, Vermont.

HOO'S HOO TO-DAY.

By JOHN W. CAREY.

Who made his bow in '43 in Springfield, Illinois, when Father Abe gave out the smokes and told 'em; "It's a boy"? Who stuck not to the White House when his dad was president, but went to war like other lads and put up in a tent? Who makes a smashing hit because he's satisfied to be **"just folks"** like us and never flies his **genealogy**? Who's just a plain American and mingles with the mob —a member of the Sons of Toil and always on the job? Who dodges scribes and photo men and all the limelight clan, and, like as not, will shy at this? That Robert Lincoln man.

"Hoo's Hoo To-day" cartoon published across the country by the Associated Newspapers syndicate in 1914 poking fun at Robert Lincoln's well-known aversion to publicity. The artist sent a copy of the cartoon to Robert and told him the drawing and accompanying rhymes "have been written in the spirit of fun, and the author trusts to the good nature of the victims to accept them in that light." Lincoln's reaction, if any, is unknown. Courtesy of Hildene, The Lincoln Family Home, Manchester, Vermont.

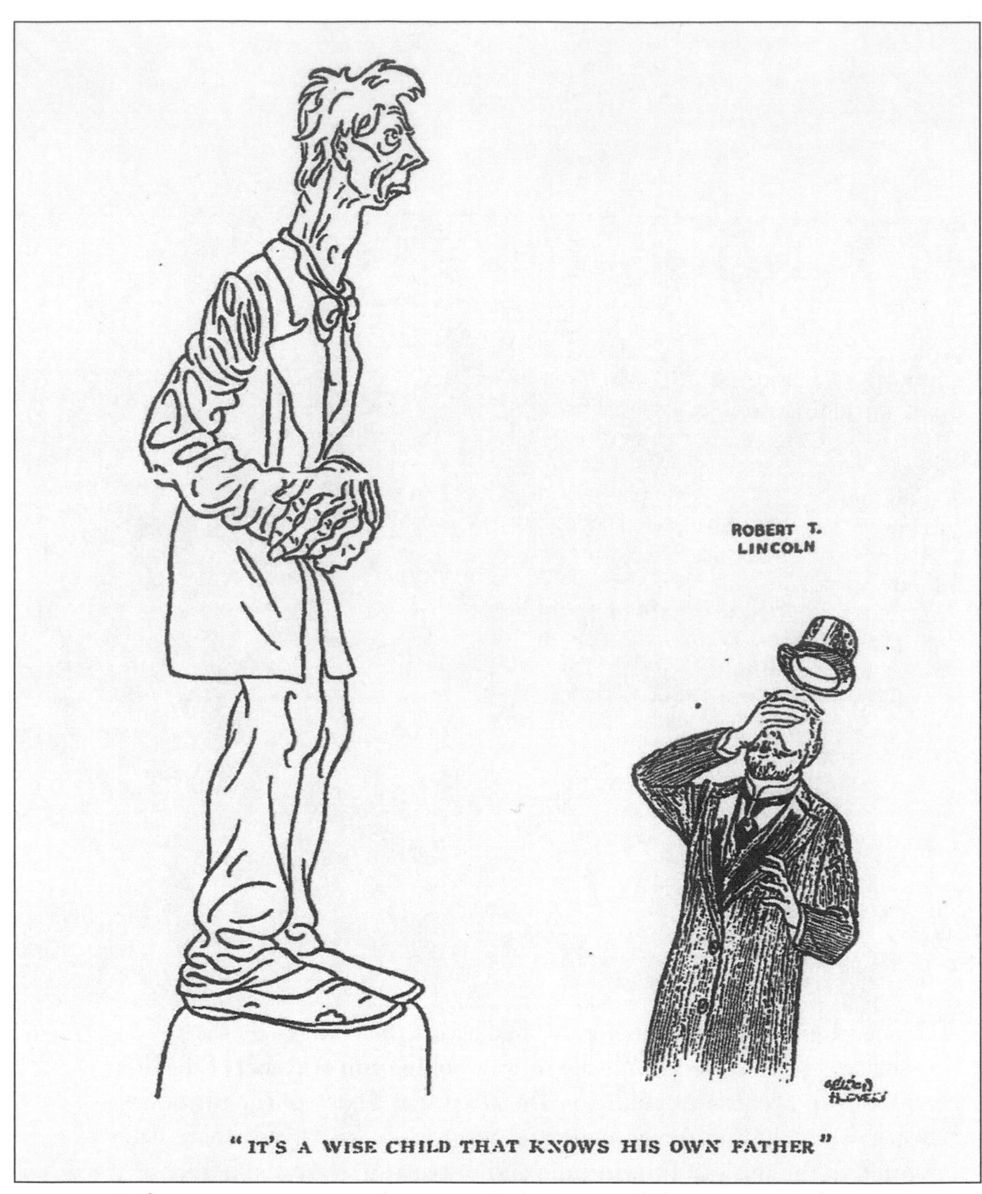

1918 *Life* magazine cartoon depicting Robert Lincoln's angst over the George Gray Barnard statue of Abraham Lincoln that Robert called "a monstrous figure which is grotesque as a likeness of President Lincoln and defamatory as an effigy." Lincoln spent two years publicly denouncing the statue and preventing its placement in London. Author's collection.

Robert Lincoln, age seventy-seven, at the Chevy Chase Golf Club, outside Washington, D.C., sitting with two of his favorite things: a golf club and a cigar. Courtesy of Hildene, The Lincoln Family Home, Manchester, Vermont.

Robert Lincoln posing with his survey equipment on the grounds of Hildene, around 1920. Robert was an amateur, yet adept, surveyor (like his father) who surveyed the grounds, roads, and fences of his Manchester, Vermont, property during the 1903–5 construction. Courtesy of Hildene, The Lincoln Family Home, Manchester, Vermont.

Robert Lincoln's last public appearance, at the Lincoln Memorial dedication, May 30, 1922, in Washington, D.C. He is visible in this photograph on the left, seated behind the two speakers, President Warren Harding and Chief Justice William Howard Taft. Courtesy of Library of Congress, Prints and Photographs Division.

Robert Lincoln's gravesite in section 31, lot 13, of Arlington National Cemetery. Although Robert expected to be buried in the Lincoln Tomb in Springfield, Illinois, his wife decided in the weeks after her husband's death that he was his own great man and deserved "his own place in the sun" separate from his illustrious father. Courtesy of Hildene, The Lincoln Family Home, Manchester, Vermont.

19

"As Much a Man of Destiny as His Lamented Father"

Four months after the presidential election in November 1888, attorney Robert T. Lincoln was busy at work in his law office in the Honoré Building, Dearborn Street, in downtown Chicago. A reporter for the *Chicago Tribune* came calling for an interview.

> As he shoved aside the legal papers which covered his desk, Mr. Robert T. Lincoln's face wore a pleasant smile. It was not a broad smile. But its influence was felt throughout the law offices of Isham, Lincoln & Beale. Even the messenger boy who took the reporter's card had caught its reflection and converted it into a grin.
>
> "You have heard of your appointment as Minister Plenipotentiary and Envoy Extraordinary to the Court of St. James!" asked the reporter, though the answer was in the air.
>
> "That's a high-sounding title for a plain man," answered Mr. Lincoln.
>
> "Will you accept it?"
>
> "I have not had time to give the matter a thought. Until a half hour ago, when I received a telegram from Senator Hale, I did not know that my name had even been contemplated for the place. It is a total surprise. I have no official information of the appointment yet."[1]

Thus was Robert Lincoln informed of his nomination as America's minister to Great Britain, the top foreign appointment in the U.S. State Department. His statement of surprise was not false modesty; he truly had no idea President Benjamin Harrison wanted him for the job. In fact, Harrison told nobody of his decision, not even the two U.S. senators from Illinois, whose advice and consent on such an appointment was not only courtesy but tradition.

Rumors of Lincoln's appointment, however, began circulating in the press at the end of March 1889. It was known that President Harrison intended to give the English mission to someone from Illinois as a political reward to the partisans of that influential state. The proper nouns of "Illinois" and "Lincoln" were as synonymous in 1889 as they are today, and such reflexive pairing appears to be the main reason for the scuttlebutt. Most insiders expected the Illinois appointment to go to respected House member Robert Hitt; Illinois's two U.S. Senators, Shelby M. Cullom and Charles B. Farwell, wanted and recommended eminent Chicago attorney John N. Jewett to the president.

Cullom and Farwell actually were not informed of Lincoln's appointment until a few hours before it was announced on March 28. They had been invited to the White House expecting to hear of Jewett's placement in London but instead heard the president tell them, "I am thinking of sending Robert Lincoln over there. He has had experience in public life, he is well known and well thought of in all parts of the country. I believe his selection would give satisfaction not only in your state but everywhere else."[2] The two senators objected on political grounds: Lincoln was not a factor in Illinois politics and did not even seek the position, they said, and to appoint him was to throw away a juicy plum of patronage for a negligible political benefit. These same objections Harrison had heard from the few western senators he had secretly consulted about nominating Lincoln. He decided to ignore them all and appoint Lincoln anyway.[3]

The announcement of Lincoln's appointment surprised everyone. The consensus by politicians and journalists alike was that Harrison's decision was politically clumsy and valueless yet at the same time was nationally and personally excellent. Robert was lauded as an honest, able, and cultured gentleman; as an eminent and highly successful lawyer, which experience fit well into his upcoming ministerial appointment; and as a reliable administrator, as proven during his successful leadership of the War Department. It was remarked that his surname and parentage also would give him an immediate respect in British politics and society and therefore would make him more effective as a minister. Robert's personal wealth also was mentioned—one newspaper saying he was worth about half a million dollars—as a qualification for the post, since he could afford a job that would probably cost him more money than it paid.

The *Boston Herald* applauded Lincoln's appointment as "the most important and the wisest" appointment yet made by President Harrison.[4] The *New York Herald* opined, "Mr. Lincoln has shown himself equal to every responsibility that has ever been placed upon him, and has done his duty quietly but admirably, in every part of his life."[5] The *New York Sun* declared that Lincoln may likely prove a better minister in England since Charles Francis Adams.[6] Other papers agreed. "The truth is that Robert Lincoln seems to be as much a man of destiny as his lamented father," wrote the Boston *Herald*. "He will almost certainly make a successful minister to England, and it is possible that he may achieve a very remarkable success there."[7]

"Our new minister to London, who is known familiarly here as Bob Lincoln, will, I hope, be liked," commented Henry Adams, scion of the famed Adams family and son of President Lincoln's U.S. minister to England, Charles Francis Adams. "He is a good fellow, rather heavy, but pleasant and sufficiently intelligent. I have known him slightly for some years. [John] Hay has known him since childhood, and is very intimate with him. Unless Hay himself were to have the place, Lincoln was as good a man as was likely to be sent."[8] Hay, a former diplomat whom many people, like Adams, thought would be the man appointed to London, wrote to his friend Robert, "I congratulate you most cordially on the great decoration. It is the most conspicuous compliment in the gift of a president, and I am delighted to see it go to you."[9] Theodore Roosevelt called Lincoln's appointment "admirable" and Lincoln himself, "a very good fellow."[10] Ex–Vice President Hannibal Hamlin also expressed surprise and pleasure at the appointment. "Not so quaint, not so original, not so remarkable a man as his father was in some respects," Hamlin said, "yet I think that, judged fairly, he is, in many respects, very much like him, and in very many respects quite as great a man."[11]

It was reported that Robert's nomination was "well received" throughout England, "where his father's name and memory are held in reverent regard"; British Prime Minister Lord Salisbury called Robert's nomination a "pleasant surprise."[12]

Of course, not every person or newspaper thought so highly of Robert Lincoln or his appointment to London. The *Boston Globe* criticized both, stating, "He is a man of talent, but there is not a spark of fire in him. The last quality that would be sought in him by anybody knowing him is diplomacy and the gift of knowing how to meet men. The popular summing up of Mr. Lincoln is that he is a Todd, or rather the son of his mother instead of the son of his father."[13] Clarence King, former director of United States Geological Survey, had similar feelings to those stated in the *Globe*. "Why did [Harrison] send Lincoln to the one place in all the world where society is above government and where Lincoln's qualities are of least diplomatic value?" King incredulously asked John Hay.[14] Carter Harrison, five times mayor of Chicago, said Robert Lincoln was "a man of mediocre attainments, puffed up with pride almost to the exploding point by the brilliance of his parentage, who, left to his own devices, never would have risen above the ranks of the commonplace."[15]

The U.S. Senate officially confirmed Robert Lincoln for his position on March 30. He immediately traveled to Washington to confer with President

Harrison and the man who would be his direct superior, Secretary of State James G. Blaine.[16] This was Blaine's second time as secretary of state, having briefly filled the post under President James A. Garfield in 1881—at that time being a cabinet colleague of Secretary of War Lincoln. Blaine and Lincoln had always had a cordial relationship, although they did not often agree politically. It was rumored in 1889 that Blaine preferred Jewett over Lincoln for minister, but after Robert's appointment, Blaine expressed his belief that the English mission would be worthily filled by Minister Lincoln.[17]

Once again Robert Lincoln found himself placed in a position of public trust he had not sought. "The news of my confirmation has this moment come to me and I have to face at once the question of breaking up for a time a state of tranquility which I had hoped was not to be disturbed for a good while," he wrote to a friend on March 30.[18] Mary Harlan Lincoln received a note of congratulations from a friend who wrote, "I know your antipathy to public life, therefore you may not consider it a matter of congratulations, still I am glad and will always be happy to hear of your success."[19] Knowing that both Lincolns disliked Robert holding public office and therefore leading a public life, why did he accept the appointment in the U.S. consular service?

Robert never stated his exact reasons, yet clearly the honor and duty of the position were things he felt he could not refuse—just he has had not refused President-elect Garfield in 1881 or the citizens of South Chicago in 1876. Also, being a diplomat is much different than being a cabinet secretary, and not living in Washington removed him from the capital politics and lifestyle he and his wife disdained. But the main reason Robert accepted the appointment appears to have been the chance for his family to live abroad, and for his children—Mamie now nineteen, Jack fifteen, and Jessie thirteen—to be educated in European schools and experience European culture.

Robert especially saw this as an opportunity to better prepare his son for the future. While Robert adored all three of his children, Jack, his only son and the namesake of his revered father, was his pride—and his heir. The Gilded Age still was a culture in America in which boys were educated and prepared for their futures as citizens and business leaders, and girls for their future lives as wives and mothers. Robert already was grooming Jack to follow in his own footsteps: prep at Philips Exeter Academy, college—perhaps also law school—at Harvard, then a desk at Isham, Lincoln, and Beale. Robert saw the family's four years in London as a rare opportunity for Jack, especially for him to study French in Paris. Robert himself was fluent in French and conducted much business in that language, and he believed being multilingual was an important talent for a lawyer to possess.

Robert returned to Chicago from Washington to prepare his family for their trip. It does not seem that he rented out his house this time, as he did in 1881, perhaps because in 1889 he did not need the income but probably because he anticipated his family returning to the United States occasionally for visits. He named Robert S. McCormick—son-in-law of his friend and neighbor *Chicago Tribune* publisher Joseph Medill and nephew of Chicago reaper manufacturer Cyrus McCormick—as his assistant secretary of legation and Charles B. Isham, a distant cousin of Robert's law partner, as his personal secretary.[20] On May 7, the Union League Club of Chicago held a five-hundred-man farewell dinner for its departing member, and the next night, the Chicago Club held a farewell reception of one thousand people for Lincoln, at the time the club's president.[21]

On May 9, Robert and his family, McCormick and his family, and Robert's close friend George M. Pullman all traveled by Pullman car to Washington, where Robert received revised diplomatic instructions from the president and secretary of state.[22] They then traveled to New York City, where they arrived on May 13. On May 14, he was given a dinner at the University Club—where he was a member—by friends and fellow graduates of Harvard University.[23] While in New York, Robert had a long private discussion with former minister to Great Britain (1880–85)—also his former Harvard professor—James Russell Lowell; with Edwards Pierrepont, another former minister to England (1876–77); and with his friend former European diplomat and future ambassador to Great Britain (1897–98) and secretary of state (1898–1905), John Hay.

Minister Lincoln and his party (which included Charles B. Isham, who had joined his new boss in New York) set sail from the port of New York City on the steamship *City of Paris* on May 15, 1889.[24] Among the seven hundred passengers on board was also Allan Thorndike Rice, the newly appointed minister to Vienna, and millionaire industrialist Andrew Carnegie, whom Robert already knew through business ties to the Pullman Company and his friendship with George Pullman. One of the other passengers, Josie Blicq, wrote of the hundreds of people at the docks to see the ship off: "I never [saw] people packed so closely. They cheered us until we were out of hearing." The weather was fine during the entire voyage, and there was singing on board every night, she wrote.[25]

The *City of Paris* arrived in Liverpool, England, on Thursday, May 22, greeted by three thousand spectators and admirers crowding the waterfront. A special tender draped in American flags steamed out to the harbor to bring Minister Lincoln and his party to shore. As they left the ship, all seven hundred passengers "gave three old-fashioned United States cheers for the departing minister" (although they were subsequently annoyed that they were made to wait in the harbor for another hour or so while the diplomat went through customs and met the crowds on shore). The mayor of Liverpool, along with numerous other British dignitaries, greeted Robert at the dock. The party was then driven in a special carriage to the train station and took the express to London. That night, the Lincoln family settled into their temporary apartments at 5 Cadogan Square, Kensington, which had been arranged for them by Henry White, chargé d'affairs of the United States at London, whom Robert retained as his first secretary.[26]

The next day, Minister Lincoln met Prime Minister Lord Salisbury; on Saturday, Lincoln traveled to Windsor Castle to present his credentials to Queen Victoria and officially assume his post. Neither Lincoln nor Victoria made any set speeches but merely exchanged compliments and expressed the hope that the friendly relations existing between the United States and Great Britain would continue.[27] "Never had an American minister . . . evoked greater curiosity," wrote one diplomatic historian of Lincoln's arrival in London. "The Lincoln legend [had] at last reached England."[28]

The position of U.S. envoy extraordinary and minister plenipotentiary to Great Britain was not always as impressive as it sounds. The minister was the personal representative of the president of the United States to the royalty and the government of England, certainly, and was involved in diplomatic issues between the two countries, but within the hierarchy of international relations, a minister was a relatively low personage. Ambassadors were the highest diplomatic post in each country, and ministers were of a lower class. In Britain, ministers also were ranked in order of seniority, and, since the U.S. minister changed every four years or less, the position held a relatively junior rank in London.

The result of this ranking structure was that the U.S. minister to Great Britain, the representative of one of the great powers of the world, was relegated to hours of wasting time sitting in a waiting room while more "important" diplomats, many from countries less internationally important that the United States, preceded him into the halls of government with their business. Once the ambassadors had come and gone through the foreign office each day, and the ministers began being seen, if an ambassador suddenly appeared, the ministers were shunted aside and the ambassador given priority. Minister Lincoln found this situation—as had his predecessors—aggravating as a waste of his time and a farce considering America's high global standing. Minister Lincoln arranged meetings at the foreign minister's private residence as a way to circumvent the rules, but both men found this frequently inconvenient. "No one is more asked out or has a better position here than the United States Minister," wrote Mary

Waddington, wife of the French ambassador the court of St. James—but even importance was subservient to rank in England.[29]

Another degrading aspect of the minister position was the required dress. When the minister went to court or to the foreign office, he donned satin knee breeches, ruffled shirt, and black buckled shoes—an outfit one U.S. Senator dubbed, "a dress which exposes him to be mistaken for a waiter at any festive gathering."[30] How Lincoln felt about his official garb is unknown.

In truth, the ministerial job was as much social and personal as it was diplomatic. Lincoln spent much of his time attending to visiting American politicians and citizens needing his assistance with passport issues, tickets to attend Parliamentary sessions, introductions to British politicians and businessmen, and presentations at court, among other items.[31] When President Harrison's daughter and daughter-in-law visited London in 1891, Minister Lincoln insisted they stay in his home, presented them to the Queen, and escorted them to various destinations such as Westminster Abbey.[32] When former Senator John A. Logan's wife visited London in 1890, Minister Lincoln made introductions for her and secured her invitations to social engagements.[33] But the "typical" incidents at the legation were minor instances, such as when two young American men, on a bicycle tour across Europe and into Asia, needed passports and other paperwork.

> Minister Lincoln was sitting in his private office when we called the next morning at the American legation. He listened to the recital of our plans, got down the huge atlas from his bookcase, and went over with us the route we proposed to follow. He did not regard the undertaking as feasible, and apprehended that, if he should give his official assistance, he would, in a measure, be responsible for the result if it should prove unhappy. When assured of the consent of our parents, and of our determination to make the attempt at all hazards, he picked up his pen and began a letter to the Chinese minister, remarking as he finished reading it to us, "I would much rather not have written it."[34]

And when a young girl from Massachusetts who had run away from home with an English actress found herself alone and penniless in London and called at the legation looking for aid and money. "She seemed to be telling the truth and looked so like a New England girl that I felt sorry for her," Larz Anderson, second assistant at the U.S. legation, wrote in his diary. "I told the Minister and he saw her, too, and promised to advance her a passage home. She seemed grateful and promised to go right away, though of course it all remains doubtful till we hear of her safe return."[35] Of course, Minister Lincoln's famous surname created callers as well, such as an elderly woman who insisted she must see "President Lincoln" and could not be convinced he was long dead, and when a man arrived wishing to see "Lincoln" on something very important, but when he succeeded, he had nothing to say.[36]

Minister and Mrs. Lincoln, accompanied by their oldest daughter, Mamie, who at age nineteen had "come out" in society, also hosted and attended numerous dinners, balls, banquets, exhibitions, and performances as part of their duties.[37] During their first months in London, the Lincolns hosted a grand Fourth of July celebration for resident and visiting Americans in the city; later that month, Robert made his first public appearance at a banquet for American engineers in London, at which he gave a brief speech that was well received.[38] By August, the London *Star* was lauding Minister Lincoln as a superior successor to his worthy New England predecessors. "He is more the typical American. Coming from the West, he brings with him its warm cordiality and heartiness of manner."[39]

One of the first diplomatic issues that confronted Minister Lincoln was the May arrest of Florence Maybrick, a twenty-six-year-old American woman accused of murdering her British husband by arsenic poisoning.[40] In August, she was found guilty of the crime and sentenced to death. The U.S. government gave no official instructions to Minister Lincoln at first, Secretary Blaine believing one country had no right to interfere with another country's justice system. But as public sentiment in America exploded against the "contrived" verdict and Maybrick's "illegal" imprisonment, Blaine began to send directives to London. He sent two petitions for pardon to Lincoln to forward to the British government: one from several hundred citizens of Maine—Mrs. Maybrick's home state—and one from a coalition of three thousand American women. "I was careful to present no request from the Government but simply transmitted the wishes of a very large number of our citizens," Blaine assured President Harrison.[41] Yet, Blaine also instructed Lincoln to use his "unofficial good offices" with the British authorities to have Maybrick's death sentence commuted. Lincoln immediately met with Lord Salisbury and reported back to Blaine that the death sentence "will not be executed."[42] Maybrick's sentence was changed to life imprisonment.[43]

Even though Mrs. Maybrick was not executed, the fact that she was not pardoned caused a general agitation throughout the United States. Politicians, clergymen, and regular citizens demanded her release; their various remonstrances and petitions, as well as those of Mrs. Maybrick herself, inundated the State Department and kept the case an intermittent issue between the United States and the United Kingdom during Minister Lincoln's entire tenure in London—in fact until Maybrick finally was released in 1904. As Lincoln wrote in one eight-page letter about the case in 1892, "I made myself familiar with its details at the time [it occurred] and I have had frequent occasion to refresh my memory."[44]

After the refusal of the British government to pardon Maybrick in 1889, Blaine gave no instructions to Lincoln on the matter until 1891; Lincoln, meanwhile, made no comments on the case in public or private, unwilling to compromise himself in case he received future official instructions.[45] By April 1891, the flood of public comment to Blaine was so large that he wired Minister Lincoln, "Go as far as diplomatic privileges will allow and justify" to seek a pardon.[46] This Lincoln did but to no effect. In 1892, Maybrick petitioned the State Department, through Minister Lincoln, for its intervention on the grounds that she was a U.S. citizen. Blaine replied that her marriage to a British citizen negated her American citizenship, and the United States therefore could not officially interfere.[47] During this period of international correspondence, Lincoln had a lengthy private conversation with British Home Secretary Henry Matthews—who held sole discretion for Maybrick's pardon—on the case. Lincoln suggested that Maybrick's three years in prison by 1892 satisfied the common-law penalty for attempted murder (which many people believed was her actual crime), and her release could be granted while still claiming punishment. Again, Lincoln was rebuffed. It was another twelve years before Maybrick was released.[48]

By September 1889, Minister Lincoln had found a permanent residence at 2 Cromwell Houses, S.W., Kensington. Lincoln moved not only because the place in Cadogan Square was unavailable after August, but the Kensington place also was a "barely decent house" for his family and the social needs of his position. Henry White told John Hay that the new residence was "the best house any U.S. minister here has had since Mr. Motley's time."[49] Lincoln suggested to Blaine that the government should acquire the Cromwell house he was in as a permanent residence for future U.S. ministers to London, even if the position salary had to be reduced as a consequence. The "hustle and embarrassment" of finding a suitable and affordable residence are "very great," he told Blaine.[50]

Still, Minister Lincoln and his family were thoroughly enjoying the foreign assignment. "Our reception here has been in every way most pleasant and hospitable and I am sure those in power are especially solicitous to evince good feeling towards our people," Robert wrote to Blaine in September.[51] It was a position well suited to Lincoln's talents and temperament: professionally he was a diligent, thoughtful, and conscientious worker; socially, he was an excellent conversationalist, a literary and musical man, dignified, and respectable. Although today his reputation is that of a snobbish aristocrat, he had no such reputation at the time; in fact, he was considered a modest gentleman. Ironically, his time in London, where he was lauded as such a genuine and earthy Westerner, most likely created some of his later aristocratic penchants. He became a hardy Anglophile during his years in London and brought some of the social conventions he learned there back home with him to America.

That summer of 1889 "was probably the height of happiness for Robert T. Lincoln," as one historian aptly states.[52] Robert's wife, Mary, described universally as an "invalid" by her contemporaries, was in better health than she had been for years.[53] The children were thriving, and nineteen-year-old Mary had even acquired a beau in Charles Isham, Robert's personal secretary. Unfortunately, the distinguishing event of Minister Lincoln's years in London—in fact, one of the seminal moments in his life—was neither political nor diplomatic. It began in late 1889 and ended with the death of his sixteen-year-old son, Jack, in early 1890.

Abraham Lincoln II was by all accounts an impressive boy. He was mature, honest, intelligent, and generous; he, like his father, never traded on his famous name or became supercilious because of his heritage. He was, as all who knew him testified, "simply Jack Lincoln." Despite statements by newspaper reporters and subsequent historians to the contrary, Jack looked nothing like his namesake, as any photograph of the boy proves. He may have inherited his paternal grandfather's character and intellect, but his looks were all from his mother. Like Mary Harlan, Jack had somewhat-curly blond hair, bright-blue eyes, and a pale complexion one family friend characterized as "pale as a girl's."[54] He was tall but not excessively. At age ten, Jack was measured by his Grandfather Harlan as being an average 4 feet 5 inches.[55] On his fourteenth birthday in 1887, Jack measured 5 feet.[56] Just before the Lincolns sailed for London in 1889, a friend's mother remarked on how tall Jack had grown that year and warned him not to grow as tall as his grandfather. Jack replied, "I would like to be as good, as kind and as wise as he was, but not so tall; he must have bumped his head many times."[57]

It was said that Jack was fascinated by his famous grandfather and had, at an early age, undertaken an examination of President Lincoln's life and character. What he learned he applied to himself to be worthy of his name. C. N. Fessenden, Jack's professor at the University School in Chicago from 1885 to 1889, recalled that young Lincoln was a natural leader and the best student in his school. "Study came easy to him," Fessenden said. "He was the first boy in the school to get through his lessons. Then he was ready to help the others. The result was that he was popular. His schoolmates looked up to him besides." Jack was at college-level proficiency in Latin, Greek, mathematics, and English literature by the time he left for London in 1889, Fessenden said.[58] One of Jack's schoolmates in Chicago recalled Jack reciting the Gettysburg Address to the class, as assigned to him by the teacher: "He did it very simply and soberly, and then sat down."[59]

Both of Robert Lincoln's law partners, Edward S. Isham and William G. Beale, lauded Jack's kind, generous nature and keen intellect. "He was a singularly bright and capable boy, and mastered with facility everything he undertook," Isham said.[60] Beale especially remembered how Jack was fascinated by the history of the American Civil War. "I have seen him lie on the floor in his father's library with war maps spread out before him, a book open, and study a battle by the hour," Beale said. "He was ready to discuss this situation or that in which Gen. Grant and others had found themselves."[61] With such an interest as this, who knows what firsthand stories of the war Robert must have told his eager son, stories the private Robert probably never told anyone else: of life in martial Washington, of President Lincoln's work in the White House, of service in Grant's army, and at the surrender of Appomattox.

Jack came to love anything regarding the military. On one trip to Washington with his father in February 1881, seven-year-old Jack wrote a letter to his Grandfather James Harlan, telling how he and a friend spent an entire day watching soldiers drill, first in front of the Treasury Department and then at the Arlington Hotel. "I followed them a-1–1 over [the city]." Jack wrote.[62] While spending summers with his grandparents in Mount Pleasant, Iowa, Jack loved to play soldiers with his friends. "He would no more than strike his summer home with Senator Harlan than the place was a camp at once," recollected one Mount Pleasant acquaintance. "One summer of which I have knowledge, when not over twelve years of age, he organized a military company immediately after his arrival of thirty or more boys. Tents were put up and the company slept in them the whole summer. Certain hours were for drill, which was taught after the strict rules of the army, and through all that summer these boys kept up the highest state of military discipline, even to the extreme of mounting guard."[63]

Jack loved the navy as well as the army, and while his father was secretary of war in the early 1880s, Jack became a frequent visitor to the Washington Navy Yard (just like President Lincoln). He visited every ship in the service, but his favorite was the president's yacht, the steamer *Despatch*, where he was well known and beloved by the officers and crew.[64] The sailors even chipped in and bought Jack his own seaman's uniform (sewed by the ship's tailor), perfectly regulation from his hat marked "Despatch" to his shined leather shoes. "He is a perfect picture of Gilbert's jolly midshipmité," wrote one admirer; while the *Chicago Tribune*'s Washington correspondent wrote, "[H]e is never so happy as when he has his sailor rig on and is down in the forecastle with the men."[65]

Even Jack's taste in literature bent toward the martial and patriotic. One piece of Jack's schoolwork, dated 1886, that still survives is Jack's handwritten copy of the second stanza of Joseph Rodman Drake's 1819 poem, "The American Flag."[66]

Jack also was an athletic boy who loved being outdoors. Albert T. Ryan, one of Jack's friends in Washington, D.C., vividly recalled their childhood days together riding bicycles and taking photographs.[67] Summers in Mount Pleasant, the townspeople always saw Jack riding around town in his pony cart. He enjoyed hunting for rocks and kept a collection, which he labeled "Collection Illustrating Rounded Pebbles and Sharp Stones; A. Lincoln."[68] Jack also loved to swim. During the summer of 1884 in Mount Pleasant, Jack, along with 150 other boys of the town, became members of the Mount Pleasant Boulder Lake Club. Membership meant the boys could use Cole's Pond—called Boulder Lake because of an immense glacial boulder found when the pond was dig—for swimming, boating, bathing, and skating. To join the club, boys and girls had to sign a document stating they promised to refrain from using intoxicants and alcohol. Jack signed with his full name, Abraham Lincoln II.[69]

Young Lincoln's favorite sports were tennis and baseball. One of the most famous stories about Jack—or as one newspaper called it, "The story which should be known to every boy in the world"—concerned a baseball game and a broken window. Jack and his friends in Chicago loved to play ball in a large field in their neighborhood. One day, a long fly ball shattered the window of a neighboring house, the owner of which was supposedly an unfriendly old man. When he came outside, furious, all the boys ran, except for Jack, who supposedly stayed because he knew his grandfather would never have run away in such a circumstance. He was quickly seized by the angry neighbor.

"What's your name?" the man demanded.

"Abraham Lincoln," answered the boy.

"Don't you lie to me," said the man.

"I didn't lie, sir," Jack responded. The boy then explained in detail that he was the grandson of President Lincoln and that the broken window was an accident. One version of the story claims the man was so astonished at the boy's identity that he turned pale and backed away as though he had seen a ghost. Another version, which painted the man as all but a misanthrope who hated more than anything the sounds of boyish fun, was magically transformed from a "crab" to a "regular fellow" (à la Ebenezer Scrooge) by Jack's admission.[70] The point of the tale is to show Jack's similarity to his namesake in his honestly and sense of responsibility. And while it is a good story, its veracity is questionable. Who, in Jack's own neighborhood, did not know who he was or that the well-known Robert T. Lincoln, son of the former president, had a son named Abraham?

Jack's other favorite pastime was studying the chirography of President Lincoln. The boy's Chicago teacher said Jack's handwriting was identical to the elder Lincoln's, and Jack fervently practiced copying his grandfather's signature. (This he may have done with the assistance of his father, who himself was an accomplished mimic of his own father's signature.)[71] Jack's autograph was so indistinguishable, in fact, that in later years, historians occasionally mistook his signature inside book covers and on scattered papers for the president's. One expert on handwriting forgery stated that had Jack lived to adulthood, "he could certainly have supported himself handsomely by scrawling once or twice a week, in some old books, the most famous name in American history."[72] Not long after arriving in London in 1889, Jack had dinner with friends at the Metropole Hotel. He signed the hotel register with his legal name, "A. Lincoln, USA," in his amazingly similar script. Some British reporters in the hotel noticed the signature and, apparently obtusely unaware that the Civil War president was dead, instituted a search through the hotel for President Lincoln. When they discovered the signature belonged to a sixteen-year-old boy, they were crestfallen.[73]

When Robert Lincoln informed his family of his nomination to London, Jack did not want to go. He did not want to leave the school, the friends, and the home that he loved. Robert decided the call to public service was a duty he could not refuse, and looking on the bright side, he saw it as an educational opportunity for Jack. Robert must have assuaged his son at the time, for on the cross-Atlantic trip, fellow *City of Paris* passenger E. R. Donehoo recalled that Jack enjoyed himself immensely "and frequently spoke to me of the good times he anticipated having in England."[74] At the end of summer 1889, the Lincoln family traveled to Versailles, France, a suburb of Paris, to accompany Jack to Madame Passa's fashionable school, where the boy would study French alongside the sons of U.S. Senator Eugene Hale.[75]

In early November, Jack cut his left arm—possibly the result of martial punishment by his teacher—but the wound apparently was innocuous.[76] His father went to visit him at Versailles on Saturday, November 2, and returned the following Wednesday.[77] Shortly after arriving in London, Minister Lincoln received a telegram that Jack was suddenly and dangerously ill. Robert and his wife immediately went to Versailles, where they found that Jack's cut had become infected. His left shoulder, chest, arm, and hand were so tumescent as to be described by Robert as "elephantine," and a "huge" and "very ferocious" abscess (commonly called a carbuncle at the time) had begun to grow just below the left armpit. The attending French physician, renowned surgeon and gynecologist Jules-Émile Péan, waited until the torso swelling decreased, then cut open the abscess to drain it, after which the boy developed blood poisoning and fever. His condition was critical after the operation, but during the night, he turned a corner and by the morning was doing well. "Indeed, my boy's recovery has been almost as sudden as his illness," Minister Lincoln told a newspaper reporter that day.[78] Lincoln planned to return to London the next day, November 11, but Jack's condition did not improve. The minister and Mrs. Lincoln were worried and decided to stay in Versailles with Jack until he recovered. Minister Lincoln left his first secretary, Henry White, in charge of the legation.

Like all boys before and after him—including his father—Jack Lincoln's life was not free from illness or injury. In late summer 1881, he nearly drowned after he was pulled out to sea by the undertow while the Lincolns (minus father, Robert, who was working in Washington) were on vacation in Rye Beach, New Hampshire. Jack and a rescuer were trapped in the water for more than one hour and were "insensible" when finally brought to the beach. Jack had to be resuscitated by "the electric battery" because his pulse "seemed utterly gone for some time."[79] Jack was down with the chicken pox in March 1882, it appears he had typhoid fever in 1884, and during the summer of 1886 while in Mount Pleasant, he broke his leg.[80]

There is no direct evidence that Robert and Mary were overprotective parents, even though such feelings would certainly be understandable. After all, both Robert and Mary had experienced the deaths of three siblings as children. In a time when childhood mortality still was common, the existence of germs was not universally recognized despite Louis Pasteur's germ theory and pasteurization discoveries, and fatal influenza pandemics were regular, any illness in their children must have been worrisome—but especially so in regards to Jack, who by all accounts was the pride of the family.

In mid-November 1889, Jack's condition became so critical, apparently due to blood poisoning, Robert and Mary thought their son would die. Dr. Péan drained Jack's carbuncle wound again, and the procedure, Robert said, saved the boy's life. "It is doubtful whether another man would have had the nerve to cut as he did for the danger of death from the shock of the operation itself was very great," Robert told John Hay.[81] It was during this scare that the Lincolns sent to London for Mamie and Jessie. Legation secretary Charles Isham escorted the girls across the English Channel to Versailles, and all three stayed in France indefinitely.

Over the next three weeks, Jack improved steadily, although slowly. He was bedridden but courageous and in indomitable high spirits. He read books and newspapers and wrote using his new typewriter. He could feed himself and use the "water closet" on his own. His mother cooked all his meals (apparently

Jack did not take to French food) and had not left his side since first arriving in Versailles in early November. Jack's recovery permitted the minister to return to work in London on December 7; Isham was left in charge of the family in Versailles.[82] One week later, Isham telegraphed Robert to hurry to Versailles, as Jack's condition had worsened. It was not as bad as Lincoln feared—Jack was listless and had contracted pneumonia—but Isham requested Lincoln's presence because Dr. Péan, "always wants to cut something," and Isham "did not want to have him here in my absence," Robert wrote.[83] By the turn of the year, Jack's condition, while continually fluctuating, again seemed to be improving, although his carbuncle wound refused to heal. Minister Lincoln returned to London on December 30 to catch up with work, newspapers in the United States and Britain were reporting the positive news, and Hay even congratulated Robert on his son's recovery.[84]

On Friday, January 10, 1890, Robert and Mary Lincoln had a conference with Dr. Péan and consulting physician Dr. V. Cornil (the third consulting physician, eminent Parisian doctor Alexandre-Emile Vilon, was not present—these men were three of the best doctors in France). Jack was weak and at times feverish and had developed a persistent cough, and his carbuncle wound (which Péan kept cutting open to drain and tear away dead flesh) would not heal; the doctors said the situation was not desperate, yet simultaneously said Jack had between thirty and sixty days before he died of exhaustion.[85] Robert and Mary Lincoln, watching their son slowly fade before their eyes but hearing the French doctors' reassurances, lost confidence in their physicians. At the suggestion of legation secretary Robert McCormick, the Lincolns asked renowned Chicago surgeon H. Webster Jones—McCormick's family physician, who had just arrived in London on a tour—to come to Versailles to consult. "We are desperate here and we must try some change," Lincoln told McCormick.[86]

Dr. Jones arrived in Versailles on January 13 and watched the morning's "manipulations" of Jack by the French doctors, including another session of tearing away the diseased tissue of his carbuncle. The constant operations on Jack's abscess had left an open wound a foot long running along the boy's upper underarm. "He won all my sympathy and admiration," Jones exclaimed later, after watching Jack's heroic behavior during the procedure.[87] But Jack was not getting better, and Dr. Vilon determined not to change the current treatment. As Vilon and Jones consulted that morning, Minister Lincoln overheard the Frenchman say of Jack, "Il est perdu"—*he is lost*.[88]

Jones agreed with Lincoln, however, that hope was not lost and that perhaps a change of scene would improve the boy's health. Robert had considered removing Jack to London back in November, but Jack's weak health prevented the attempt. Mary Lincoln wanted to bring her son back to London in late December, but Robert was too nervous to chance it. By January, everyone agreed it was time to move and risk the consequences. "We all including Jack want no more France," Robert wrote. "I now feel he is sure to die remaining here and . . . we will take the chance and not feel remorse for any direct bad result."[89] Daughter Mamie agreed: "Better run the risk of cold and influenza [crossing the English Channel], than have him lie here and die."[90] Dr. Jones believed the move to be a "grasping at straws" and told McCormick that Mr. and Mrs. Lincoln both "were fully alive to the situation" and therefore somewhat prepared should the worst happen.[91]

On January 17, 1890, Jack was moved from Versailles to London without incident.[92] For the next ten days, staying in his own room with a window facing the garden, attended constantly by his mother, he improved steadily.[93] By early February, the doctors believed Jack's internal problems were all gone and his only trouble now was the open wound on his arm. In addition to Dr. Jones, Minister Lincoln gathered a cadre of the best physicians in London, including medical hygienist Dr. J. Maclagan (brother of Robert's former neighbor in Cadogan Square, General Robert Maclagan), surgeon Dr. Thomas Smith, and even the venerable pathologist and surgeon to Queen Victoria Sir James Paget. Paget himself told Minister Lincoln on February 5 that the doctors all agreed Jack would get well "but for some new unforeseen accident."[94] Yet one week later, Robert revealed to John Hay that Jack was no longer improving.

> We have now been here four weeks and at first our English doctors gave us great encouragement against the desperate opinions of their French colleagues. As time goes on, however, Jack's wound is no better and he has lost his strength and it is difficult to see how he can get well. Two of the most distinguished English surgeons say they never saw or heard of an operation performed in the manner of this and that they are without any experience to guide them in trying to make it heal. The poor boy has now been in bed for nearly fifteen weeks and is wonderfully patient and good. But he is terribly emaciated and we cannot shut our eyes to the indications of the slow exhaustion which seems likely to overcome him.[95]

Edward Isham, Robert's law partner, told a newspaper reporter he had received a letter from Minister Lincoln and found his friend "depressed."[96] By the end of February, the wound on Jack's arm seemed immune to healing, and the boy had developed pleurisy—the same build-up of fluid in the chest that had killed his Uncle Tad in 1871—that was consequently crowding his heart and lungs and made him feel as if a great weight were pressed upon his chest. Jack grew increasingly weaker, his pulse and his breathing became rapid, and his previous high spirits dropped.[97] He underwent more than one painful operation of "tapping" his chest to remove the pleuritic fluid. The end became inevitable; some newspapers prematurely reported that the boy had died.[98]

After seventeen weeks of bed-ridden illness, Jack's body finally gave out on March 5, 1890. He appeared fine when he woke up, but at 11 A.M., when Jack was given a cup of beef broth to drink, the effort of two sips made him fall back against his pillow exhausted. The nurse became alarmed and called for the family. "It's all right," Jack soothed her, seeing the fear on her face. Seven minutes later, he was dead.[99] Henry White, Lincoln's first assistant at the legation, was in the house that morning. "The end came rather suddenly at last," White related to his wife. "I was sitting with Mr. Lincoln as usual latterly before going to the legation when poor Mary rushed in and said to her father, 'Go upstairs quickly!' which of course he did, and returned about ten minutes after to say that all was over."[100] Sixteen-year-old Abraham Lincoln II was dead. It was reported that he died painlessly and with a smile on his lips. A deluge of letters, telegrams, cards, and calling cards were sent to the grieving parents—the archive at the Abraham Lincoln Presidential Library holds more than five hundred such missives.[101] Among the condolences from family, friends, and colleagues also were those from state and local governments, local and national Republican Party organizations, President Benjamin Harrison and numerous U.S. politicians, Queen Victoria, the Prince of Wales, the Duke of Marlborough, Lord Salisbury, members of Parliament, and numerous members of English nobility.[102]

Dr. Maclagan recorded the boy's official cause of death as "Carbuncle under arm 4 months. Pleurisy 4 weeks."[103] Newspaper stories of Jack's death unanimously blamed the actions of the French physicians; so, too, did the boy's English doctors; since he died in London, the French blamed the English.[104] Two American physicians who studied the medical records in the 1930s separately agreed that Jack died of septicemia: Dr. Péan's continued opening of the carbuncle on Jack's arm caused the bacteria it contained to drain into the boy's bloodstream and spread throughout his body.[105]

Regardless of whichever physicians may or may not have been responsible for Jack's death, Robert Lincoln did not care. He blamed himself. Just as he believed in 1865 that had he gone to Ford's Theatre he may have saved his father's life, so in 1890 he felt that had he not accepted the position as minister to Great Britain, if he had stayed in Chicago as Jack wanted, his son might have lived. Knowing this, Robert's law partner William G. Beale wrote to Mary Harlan Lincoln, "How specially sad seems poor Jack's death in the light of his disinclination to go to England! It seems as if he had felt the presentiment of ill. And yet worse might have happened had he, and had you all, remained at home. His preference was natural but it rightly yielded to judgment, for Mr. Lincoln *had* to go. It was right and wise for him to go and there was nothing else to do."[106]

Jack's funeral was held at Minister Lincoln's residence at 2 Cromwell Houses at 3 P.M. on March 7. It was a "strictly private" affair, with only family, intimate friends, and officials at the U.S. legation in London invited. Reverend J. Munro Gibson of St. John's Wood Presbyterian Church in London presided. Strangely, Gibson previously served as the pastor of the Second Presbyterian Church of Chicago, where the Lincolns were parishioners and where he had baptized Jack Lincoln in 1873.[107] Jack's body was interred in Kensal Green Cemetery, until it could be taken back to America.[108]

After the funeral, Henry White convinced the grieving minister to take a walk in Kensington Gardens on the way back to Robert's house. White's biographer states that White was not only an able assistant to Minister Lincoln during the months of Jack's illness but also became "almost another son" in the family's grief over Jack's death. There is no doubt Robert Lincoln had a great affection for White, for he unburdened himself to his assistant as he rarely, if ever, had to anyone else. "He has been telling me how all his interest in the law business was for Jack's sake only, and to keep the place open for him. He also told me a lot about his trouble with his mother, and seemed generally most confidential," White wrote his wife.[109]

The Lincolns were devastated by the death of their only son. Robert McCormick issued a statement to the press that the family was "fatigued and grief-stricken."[110] Robert wrote to Hay, "Jack was to us all that any father or mother could wish and beyond that, he seemed to realize that he had special duties before him as a man, and the thoroughness with which he was getting ready was a source of the greatest pride to me. I did not realize until he was gone how deeply my thoughts of the future were in him."[111] To John Nicolay, Robert wrote, "You can imagine that for more than common reasons our boy's life was very precious to us and as his character and ability became year by year more unusual, I had good reason for setting no limit in our hopes for him. Now that there is nothing left but a memory, the loss is very hard to bear."[112]

Newspapers were filled with words of sympathy for the minister, not only for the death of his boy but also for the loss of a second Abraham Lincoln who had promised to be as great and good as the first. "The courage and sweetness of temper with which he bore exhaustive pain, and the wonderful strength of nerve and constitution which he displayed, has filled the nation with admiration and revived a love which is part a memory," the Waterbury, Connecticut, *American* newspaper stated.[113] The *Washington Post* lamented in a sentiment repeated across the country, "We are moved, indeed, by a sense of national loss."[114]

Robert Lincoln, who so long had lived in his father's shadow, was not obtuse to the popular connection between his father and his son. For him, it was also personal. "I have had many reasons for knowing in what regard my father's memory is held and the burden of our loss is made greater if possible by the extinction of an earthly hope of a son who promised in every way morally and intellectually to be in time a worthy representation of his grandfather in fact as well as in name," he stated one month after Jack's death.[115]

In the wake of the Lincoln family's great personal tragedy, newspapers and politicians across the country waited for the minister's resignation.

20

"Minister Lincoln Was Quietness Personified"

John Hay once wrote of his friend Robert Lincoln, "He is not a man to give way to misfortune, however sorely tried."[1] Robert had proven that statement correct time and again in his forty-six years, such as during the deaths of his brothers and father, his broken engagement to Mary Harlan, his mother's commitment to an asylum, and the ups and downs of his personal investments. The death of his only son in March 1890, however, was unlike any ordeal Robert Lincoln had ever had to endure. Lincoln's longtime friend and law partner, Edward Isham, feared the effect the boy's death would have on his parents. "The whole family seemed to center around him," Isham said, but Minister Lincoln, especially, was "devoted to the boy."[2] Reverend E. R. Donehoo, who crossed the Atlantic with the Lincolns in 1889, recalled that while Robert and Mary were clearly devoted to all three of their children, "it was plain to be seen that the hope of the parents was centered in Jack."[3]

Robert's law partner William G. Beale gave an interview indicating his hope that Minister Lincoln would resign and return to Chicago to be near friends in his bereavement, a statement that newspapers transmuted into a rumor that the minister planned to resign.[4] Upon Secretary of State James G. Blaine's friendly inquiry on the matter, Robert immediately denied the story via telegram, then explained further with a letter: "I have not myself spoken of [resignation] except to my wife when in our stunned feeling which needs no description to you it seems as though we must do something for relief and go away. It took but a moment for us to reflect that no mere change of place or occupation could mitigate our distress and that to yield to such an impulse would be useless and unwise and, for me, unmanly."[5]

Ironically, Lincoln had decided to resign *before* Jack died—possibly even before Jack became ill—so the family could return to America and be together while Jack finished his education in the United States. Robert had intended to leave London as soon as affairs would allow. Jack's illness prevented the plan; Jack's death changed it. Robert now had no reason to leave. In fact, he told Blaine he would rather stay and keep occupied. "The most important considerations are [now] obliterated and I am as contented personally here as I could be anywhere," Lincoln wrote. "I do not forget that the important place I hold is not a personal vocation concerning only myself and my family and that if there were good reasons for my being asked to assume my present public duties they are not removed by what has come. . . . I therefore have no intention except to go on with the work before me."[6]

Robert's wife, Mary, perpetually sick and physically delicate, surprised the entire family by not completely breaking down after Jack's death. "I would not have believed that any human could have stood the strain of months as she did with apparent cheerfulness, even when she had no hope," Robert wrote.[7] But Mary was too distraught to continue public functions, and she did not attend the Queen's next drawing-room function in May.[8] In early August, Mary fled the lugubrious London memories and took Mamie and Jessie on their annual summer pilgrimage to the Harlan home in Mount Pleasant, Iowa—more a place of sanctuary in 1890 than ever before.[9] They stayed there for the next six months. Robert stayed in London, alone. Such a separation was not unusual for the Lincolns during their marriage—nor for many upper-class Victorian-era couples where the husband was hard-working and successful—but clearly Mary was running away from her grief, while Robert needed to stay for his job. He began to reenter society in July, which Henry White thought would be good for him, but Robert's grief was deep.[10] "I would find life in London very agreeable but for the cloud that is in my house—it shadows everything," Robert wrote not long after his son's death.[11]

During their immediate grief, the Lincolns began planning for artistic likenesses to be made of Jack. The parents had had a death mask of their son created, which they intended to use as the basis for a sculpture.[12] The work was awarded to famous Washington, D.C., sculptor Theophilus Fisk Mills, who created a head-and-shoulders bust of Jack as a virile young man.[13] The Lincolns also wanted to commission a portrait of their lamented son, and Robert wrote to his friend Hay seeking a reference.[14]

The ultimate monument to and for Jack, however, was his burial in the Lincoln tomb in Springfield, Illinois. The National Lincoln Monument Association, the group in charge of maintaining the tomb, passed a resolution in early April 1890 to correspond with Minister Lincoln about interring Jack in the tomb. Association Secretary Ozias M. Hatch followed with a letter in July to the same effect. Robert replied in September to Hatch—and also wrote to his longtime friend and association member Clinton Conkling to press the point—that he wanted to bury his son in the tomb only if there could be a "family arrangement" that Robert and his wife, and his daughters if unmarried, would be interred there as well. If the association agreed, Robert would pay whatever the expense; if the association did not feel such an arrangement would fit within its charter or within the purpose of the tomb, Robert would, without any ill feeling, build his own family tomb.[15] The association agreed.

On Wednesday, November 5, 1890, Minister Robert T. Lincoln, looking older and careworn after a stormy, six-day steamship journey across the Atlantic Ocean, arrived at the port of New York bearing the remains of his son. "It was easy to see that the death of his son still weighed heavily on Mr. Lincoln's mind," the *Chicago Tribune* reported. "The lines of his face had deepened, and he was not the same cheery, happy-looking man who stepped so briskly up the gangway some months ago."[16] Robert was met at the docks by his longtime friend Edgar T. Welles, as well as a score of other men. He spent the night at Welles's house in the city, and the two friends set out the next morning for Chicago, a brief stop on their way to Springfield.

Robert previously had written to Clinton Conkling that in regards to his son's reburial, he wanted to "end this unhappy chapter of my life as quietly as possible and without any ceremonial whatever."[17] On Saturday, November 8, at nine o'clock in the morning, the Lincoln Guard of Honor escorted the body of Abraham Lincoln II from the Springfield train depot to Oak Ridge Cemetery. The body then was interred in the Lincoln Tomb without ceremony—fourteen years and one day after the attempt to steal the remains of President Abraham Lincoln from the crypt. Along with Robert Lincoln and Edgar Welles, the dozen or so men gathered that morning included members of the Lincoln Guard of Honor, the monument association, U.S. Senator Shelby M. Cullom, former Governor Richard J. Oglesby, and current Governor Joseph W. Fifer. Mrs. Lincoln, Mamie, and Jessie were not present. After his son's body was placed in the crypt, Minister Lincoln turned to the men with him and said simply, "Gentlemen, I thank you for this kindness," and the group dispersed.[18]

Robert returned to his home in Chicago that same night. He stayed in America on his annual leave of absence for the next two months, dividing his time between his family in Mount Pleasant and attending to business in Chicago. In January, Minister Lincoln traveled to Washington to confer with Secretary Blaine on diplomatic issues before his return to London. It was reported widely that Blaine had instructions for Lincoln regarding the troublesome disagreement over international hunting of fur-bearing seals—

and concomitantly of national sovereignty—in the Bering Sea, over which the United States and Great Britain had been arguing for some years. By January 1891, newspapers were reporting that if the issue was not settled, the seizure of Canadian ships in the area by U.S. revenue cutters could lead to war. All eyes were on the diplomacy Minister Lincoln would bring to London upon his return. "They expect me to turn things upside down," Lincoln wryly said to a reporter shortly before sailing for London.[19]

Lincoln's four years in Great Britain from 1889–93 were a relatively quiet time in American-British relations. Minister Lincoln's diplomatic job in London was basically the continuation of previous policies and the discussing of ongoing issues. These he handled with the tact and dignity befitting a gentleman and American minister, while showing the respect expected from the British government. "Peace and goodwill are often the product of quiet, and Minister Lincoln was quietness personified," one historian states. "His manner and his methods were particularly genial to the British Foreign Secretary, Lord Salisbury."[20]

State Department annual reports to Congress show that the general issues confronted by Minister Lincoln related mainly to issuing passports and handling extradition cases.[21] In 1889–90, Lincoln negotiated with Lord Salisbury for revisions to the U.S.-British extradition treaty.[22] From August 1891 through October 1892, Lincoln had a significant role in organizing an International Monetary Conference desired by President Benjamin Harrison. The U.S. goal in calling for the conference—the fourth such in twenty-five years—specifically was to gain international agreement to allow free coinage and greater usage of silver as currency throughout the world or, at least, to stabilize the ratio value of silver to gold.[23] This issue of "bimetallism" was a hotly debated topic in America and a serious economic issue considering that the value of silver—which America had in large supplies—was depreciating rapidly.[24] Harrison and Blaine knew that such a conference could not occur without the participation of Great Britain, and so in August 1890, Blaine directed Minister Lincoln to assess the British feeling about such a gathering. Lincoln's approach to carrying out his instructions gives an insight into his diplomatic style. He explained to Blaine:

> After some waiting and reflecting as to the best means of carrying out the instruction, it seemed to me that I was not going beyond its terms to take advantage a short time ago of the silver question generally having been broached by an American gentleman at a dinner table in answer to a question of Mr. Goschen, the Chancellor of the Exchequer, as to present party divisions in the United States. Mr. Goschen and myself being a few moments later apart from others, I continued the conversation and brought it around

to the subject of an international ratio. Mr. Goschen at once spoke as freely and fully on the subject that it would be impossible to give more than the mere substance of his remarks.[25]

For many months, Lincoln did not think the British would be interested in compromising the gold standard for silver, since they used the former. "We are a queer people" to expect the British to cooperate, Robert privately wrote to a friend. "Just now for us to expect the English bankers to join us in absorbing silver would be I fear like a Jew, who had burned his shop and had been paid more insurance money than his debts, to ask his creditors to compromise with him on the ground of his general unhappiness."[26]

By the end of January 1892, however, Lincoln had convinced Lord Salisbury to be "inclined" to participate in the conference and by May had received a definite acceptance.[27] Lincoln spent the ten months from January to October solidifying British participation and acting as point man for Blaine in the organization of the conference, dealing with issues such as whether the United States or Britain would request and lead the conference, how many delegates each country could appoint, and where it would be held.[28] "I had some share in arranging for that," Lincoln modestly told reporters shortly before the meeting of twenty nations commenced in Brussels, Belgium, that November.[29]

The two major diplomatic issues between the United States and Great Britain during this time, however, related to seal hunting in the Bering Sea and a disputed boundary between Venezuela and British Guiana.

The Bering Sea question was "one of the most important diplomatic controversies during the Blaine period," according to the preeminent historian of Blaine's foreign policy.[30] The disagreement centered on the hunting of fur-bearing seals at the sealing grounds off the Alaskan Pribilof Islands and in the Bering Sea. America had regulated hunting in the area since the purchase of Alaska from Russia in 1867. Continuing the previous Russian policy, the United States had limited seal hunting on the islands to certain times of the year, certain gender of seals (males only), and a certain number of pelts. In the 1880s, Canadian hunters began sealing in open water, called pelagic sealing, in the Bering Sea to avoid the U.S. limitations and regulations. By 1885, seal numbers were found to have decreased so sharply as to have caused a severe diminution of American profits in the fur industry and even to endanger the seals' very existence.

Under President Grover Cleveland's administration in the late 1880s, American revenue cutters began to seize Canadian vessels hunting in the Bering Sea, arrest the crews, and sell off the skins for damages. The British government, which oversaw the foreign policy of its Canadian dominion, protested the seizures, demanded the release of the Canadian ships and sailors, compensation for the lost revenue, and the immediate end to U.S. patrols in the area. The British challenged the American claim that its jurisdiction extended beyond the internationally recognized three-nautical-mile limit from its Alaskan coast. Diplomacy of the issue began during Cleveland's administration but remained unsettled when Harrison, Blaine, and Lincoln entered office in 1889.[31]

Harrison continued his predecessor's seizure policy during his first year in office. Secretary Blaine saw this as an important international issue: defending the sovereignty of the United States and protecting not only the industrial and pecuniary interests involved but also the conservation of the seal herds. By May 1890, Lord Salisbury issued a formal protest of the American policy, adding a warning that further "unlawful interference" of Canadian ships in the area would come with consequences. He then ordered four British ironclad warships to prepare to sail to the Bering Sea. With both countries convinced of their positions and failing to back down, a real threat of war existed. "If both sides push their pretensions to the extreme, a collision is inevitable," Salisbury wrote to his American minister, Sir Julian Pauncefote.[32] Blaine refused to publicly declare an end to seizures, but privately he backed down and ordered all U.S. revenue cutters not to arrest Canadian sealers for the remainder of the year.

By January 1891, no agreement on the sealing issue had been reached, and the new hunting season was approaching. In Washington that month, Lincoln had detailed discussions with the secretary of state; he returned to London on January 16, 1891, and the next week met for three hours with Lord Salisbury on the Bering Sea question.[33] Lincoln acted as intermediary and facilitator of negotiations between Blaine and Salisbury as the two men exchanged detailed arguments about the issue, specifically the various points of international law, previous Russian territorial boundaries, and current U.S. sovereignty beyond the traditional three-mile coastal limits. Minister Lincoln had assisted in a direct role with Blaine to formulate his arguments. Generally, the minister was the secretary's eyes and ears in London and sent numerous British news clippings and political updates. In August 1890, Blaine asked Lincoln to search British libraries for early maps of the Bering Sea showing previous Russian boundaries. Blaine wanted to argue that the Russians had exercised the same territorial prerogatives and restrictions that the United States was then enforcing. Lincoln, assisted by his private secretary Charles Isham, worked "discreetly" in the British Museum and the Royal Geographical Society Library on the task. By September, Lincoln had transmitted several pages of notes to Blaine, but the minister was amazed and disappointed to find that early British maps of the Bering Sea showed no Russian possessions at all.[34]

After further months of discussions, debates, and political posturing—during which Minister Lincoln continually telegrammed Blaine updates and news clippings on the British actions—all parties finally agreed to an international arbitration that, in 1895, decided against the United States on all counts.[35]

The second major diplomatic issue during Minister Lincoln's tenure, the Venezuela boundary dispute, was, like the Bering Sea controversy, an issue of long-standing history inherited by the Harrison administration. Venezuela and Great Britain had been in disagreement since 1841 over the boundary between Venezuela and Guiana, a British colony. Numerous attempts at mediation and arbitration had been attempted, but all had failed. Meanwhile, British subjects were increasingly encroaching into Venezuelan territory. In 1887, Secretary of State Thomas F. Bayard offered U.S. assistance to mend the dispute, but Salisbury demurred. With the advent of the Harrison administration in 1889, the Venezuelan government sought U.S. mediation that year, appealing with the claim that the British extensions into the disputed territory were a violation of America's Monroe Doctrine.[36]

Secretary of State Blaine is considered by historians one of the great American diplomats of the Gilded Age, especially during his second tenure at the State Department from 1889–92. He is credited as a reinterpreter of the Monroe Doctrine and the architect of American imperialism as later carried out under Presidents William McKinley and Theodore Roosevelt. Blaine's grand diplomatic vision, dubbed his "Pan Americanism," was focused on Latin and South America, increasing U.S. influence there and reducing European presence. He wanted the lower American countries to look to the United States for social, economic, and military cooperation or assistance rather than looking to Europe. Blaine's outstanding diplomacy toward England was mostly as it affected this Pan American ideal. The Venezuela boundary dispute gave Blaine an opportunity to implement this vision.

In December 1889, Blaine cabled First Secretary Henry White (Minister Lincoln was in Versailles tending to his ill son), authorizing him to confer with Lord Salisbury on reestablishing diplomatic relations between Great Britain and Venezuela.[37] This offer apparently went nowhere, and in May 1890, Blaine instructed Minister Lincoln to "use his good offices with Lord Salisbury" and with "an attitude of impartial friendliness" induce a resumption of relations between the arguing countries.[38] Specifically, he told Lincoln to suggest a tripartite conference to be held in Washington or London. Salisbury received Lincoln's approach favorably but had numerous concerns and conditions about any actual negotiations. Lincoln followed this up in late June 1890 by presenting the Venezuelan envoy to England, Senor Pulido, to Lord Salisbury, at which time the two men made an acquaintance and iterated a mutual hope of finding a solution to the conflict.[39]

Finger-pointing and disagreements caused another break in the negotiations, which Minister Lincoln again restored through his "good offices" in September 1892.[40] Another breach came in 1893, and continuing disagreements and conflicts caused the dispute to linger through the second Cleveland administration (which began in 1893) and was only concluded in 1897.[41]

As America's diplomat to Great Britain, a relatively wealthy man, and the son of the revered Abraham Lincoln, Minister Lincoln lived a life of high society. In early 1891, he and his family reentered the London social scene, which they had more or less forsaken due to Jack's illness and death. Robert made his reappearance at the London opera in early February.[42] Mary and the girls returned to London from Mount Pleasant in early March, and the next week Mrs. Lincoln, dressed in black mourning, attended the Queen's drawing room and "presented" numerous American women to the court; she then held a drawing-room tea for all the American women after the ceremony.[43] In June, the Lincolns attended a concert at Buckingham Palace and held a dinner at their house.[44] They held their annual Fourth of July reception in 1891—which held about seven hundred people and was hailed as "the most brilliantly successful in the history of the legation"—and later that month the Lincolns were the only Americans invited to a grand ball given by Henry and Mrs. White, at which the "leaders of aristocratic society" were present.[45]

As famous and important as Robert Lincoln was, his life was not free from the mundane or the bizarre. From May to June 1890, he had a short period of administrative and political drama when Second Secretary of Legation Robert S. McCormick resigned his post after Lincoln refused to promote him to first secretary. Apparently, Secretary Blaine had promised McCormick the promotion when he was first assigned to London in September 1889 but had not consulted Lincoln about it. When McCormick demanded action, Blaine deferred to Minister Lincoln, as was customary in hiring and firing legation staff, but Lincoln had no intention of removing White. So McCormick resigned.[46] Lincoln filled the vacancy in June with twenty-five-year-old Larz Anderson, a recent Harvard graduate and the son of Robert's longtime friend General Nicholas Longworth Anderson.[47]

As for the bizarre, at one dinner the Lincolns hosted in summer 1891, a valuable diamond necklace was stolen from guest Mrs. Bradley Martin. Scotland Yard detectives were called to investigate, a reward of five hundred pounds was offered, but the jewelry never was recovered. A few months later, Lincoln's butler, John Thompson, turned himself in to the police and claimed to be the thief. He was held at Scotland Yard for one day, but his story was incoherent. He was determined to be insane and was released. Minister Lincoln fired Thompson shortly thereafter for drunkenness, although the butler's role in the theft—either as thief, claimant of the theft, or possible delusional and insane person—certainly must have contributed to his dismissal. A few weeks later, Thompson killed himself by cutting his own throat.[48]

Robert often attended social engagements both professional and personal and spent much time outside of the legation with Henry White, who had become a trusted companion. Lincoln entertained numerous American friends, acquaintances, and associates who were in London on vacations, such as his law partner Edward Isham; his close friends Nicholas Anderson, Marshall Field, John Hay, Potter Palmer, Edgar T. Welles, and Norman Williams; writers Henry Adams, Bret Harte, Henry James, and Bram Stoker; millionaires William Astor, Andrew Carnegie, and Cornelius Vanderbilt; and U.S. politicians John Bigelow, Shelby Cullom, Chauncey M. Depew, George Hoar, and John Sherman.[49] Robert also was an inveterate traveler, and he did not let his time across the ocean go to waste. He traveled extensively—sometimes with his family and sometimes alone or with male friends—around Britain, Scotland, and Ireland, across the European continent, and into the Orient. He visited Paris, Homburg, Rome, Athens, and Constantinople. He also returned to America every year during his annual two-month vacation.

Professionally, Lincoln often was required to attend dinners and give brief speeches at events of international significance. In May 1891, he spoke before the British and Foreign Sailors' Society and proposed the resolution that the society cooperate with other such charities in other countries, especially the American Seaman's Friend Society.[50] When a new American copyright law was passed in June 1891, Minister Lincoln attended and spoke at a celebratory dinner of British writers, among whom were Arthur Conan Doyle, Thomas Hardy, Bret Harte, and Oscar Wilde. The law reciprocated U.S. with British copyright law, ensuring both rights and royalties to British authors for American editions of their works, and vice versa.[51] "A new stimulus to study and literary effort is given that will be long felt on both sides of the Atlantic," said Lincoln, himself a voracious reader and lover of literature.[52] In early 1893, Lincoln attended a luncheon on board the steamship *New York* in Southampton, at which 250 people—including distinguished diplomats and politicians from Britain, Canada, and the United States—celebrated the new ship and the British-American commercial relationship. "The sight of one's flag in a foreign port is thrilling," Lincoln said in a brief speech and then offered a toast to the Stars and Stripes.[53]

Despite Lincoln's busy social schedule, legation secretary Larz Anderson confided to his diary that the minister was unusually solemn. He did not begin to emotionally recover from Jack's death until the end of 1891. That Christmas, with his family in America, Lincoln spent the holidays with Henry White's family at their country estate in Bracknell, about thirty miles west of London. "The minister was regaining his spirits, and his sunny disposition began to show itself again," Anderson, also a guest, wrote. "It was very enjoyable to see him happy and talking at a tremendous rate. He insisted on sitting up till all hours."[54]

Other than the death of his son, Jack, perhaps the most memorable moment of Robert Lincoln's time in London for him was the marriage of his oldest daughter, Mary, to his former private secretary Charles B. Isham. Ironically, the latter event appears to have been caused by the former.

Isham was hired in April 1889 to be Minister Lincoln's private secretary in London, probably through the auspices of Edward Isham, a distant cousin and Lincoln's law partner. Charles Isham, born in 1853, was raised in New York City, where his father was president of the Metropolitan Bank. He graduated from Harvard University in 1876, later achieved law degrees from Harvard and the University of Berlin, and was admitted to the New York State Bar in 1881. He was at various times librarian, secretary, and member of the committee on publications for the New York Historical Society, a member of the Geographical Society, and secretary of the Bar Association of the City of New York. But he was foremost a historian. His major work was a five-volume biography of Silas Deane, America's first foreign diplomat. Isham was fluent in both German and French and had a reputation as a learned scholar and brilliant intellectual.[55]

Isham first met Mamie in spring 1889 when Minister Lincoln and his party sailed to England aboard the *City of Paris* ocean liner. The two apparently became acquainted during the eight-day journey and maintained a friendship in London. When Jack Lincoln first became seriously ill in France during November 1889, Isham escorted Mamie and Jessie to Versailles from London. He stayed with the Lincolns at the Hotel Vatel for the next nine weeks and often was left in charge by Robert, who had to make occasional trips back to London for legation business. Charles and Mamie's daily contact in Versailles, no doubt enhanced by Isham's sensitivity and strength during the entire ordeal, caused their friendship to blossom into love. Even though Charles was sixteen years older than Mamie, "[i]t was a natural match," according to Mamie's sole biographer. "The two were alike in temperament and enjoyed the same cultural entertainments."[56]

After the Lincoln women left for Mount Pleasant in August 1890, Isham stayed in London. He traveled to America with Minister Lincoln that November but stayed home in New York City when the minister went to Springfield to bury Jack. Isham's diary shows that he and Mamie corresponded regularly while she was in Iowa. When Robert Lincoln returned to New York in early January 1891 on his way back to London, he and Isham had a meeting.[57] It is unknown what the two men discussed, possibly legation business, but it seems more likely that Isham asked Robert Lincoln either for permission to court his daughter or for his daughter's hand in marriage. Lincoln liked and respected his secretary—who also was a fellow Harvard alumni, fellow lawyer, and member of the same social clubs in New York as Robert—and obviously gave his permission. When Mary, Mamie, and Jessie traveled east on their return to London a few weeks later, Isham met them at the Washington, D.C., train station. While in the capital, Charles and Mamie took a walking tour. Two days later, Charles took Mamie to have dinner with his parents—the announcement of an amorous understanding, perhaps?

The official engagement of Charles Isham, of New York City, and Mary Lincoln, of Chicago, Illinois, was publicly announced in July 1891.[58] The event was duly reported in newspapers around the world, some stating that Americans were pleased that Abraham Lincoln's granddaughter was "a refreshing exception to the almost universal practice of American ladies abroad of mating with members of English or continental aristocratic families."[59] One newspaper opined that Isham must be "pure and brave as Sir Galahad himself to be worthy of such a maiden's heart."[60] Legation secretary Larz Anderson wrote in his diary that London reporters were hounding him incessantly for information about the match, looking for every detail, including who would make the bride's bouquet and who would provide refreshments. "Reportorial cheek is as great here as it is in America," he declared.[61]

The Lincolns held a prenuptial feast at their Cromwell Road house for the two families. The marriage took place at 2:30 P.M. the next day, on September 2, 1891, at Brompton Parish Church, a large, ivy-covered, Gothic structure with stained-glass windows and surrounded by an ancient graveyard. Inside, the church was decorated with palms, ferns, and flowers, with Easter lilies draping the lectern and filling the church with their pungent aromas. Less than one hundred people attended the ceremony, including the families of the bride and groom, members of the U.S. legation staff, U.S. diplomatic and military officials, foreign dignitaries, and Minister Lincoln's friends from Chicago Mr. and Mrs. Edward Isham and Mr. and Mrs. Marshal Field. "A remarkable thing was the absence of pages, bridesmaids, ushers and the usual pomp of the weddings in diplomatic circles," wrote one reporter.[62] But such modesty was typical of the reserved Lincoln family and may have been influenced by the still-painful absence of Jack.

Minister Lincoln escorted his daughter out of her carriage, down the tree-canopied lane through the graveyard, and to the church entrance. Mamie wore a white satin gown with a full court train, a lace veil caught up with diamonds and pearls that hung down her back to the ground, a wreath of fresh orange flowers in her hair, and a sparkling diamond necklace given her by her fiancé. Instead of a bouquet, she carried an ivory prayer book. Robert walked his daughter up to the altar, gave her away to Charles Isham, then stood beside her during the ceremony. Mary and Jessie sat in the front pew. The wedding ceremony was simple and unostentatious, accompanied by organ music and a boys' choir singing hymns, and ended with the bride and groom kneeling in prayer before the altar. "It was such a wedding as would have delighted old Abraham Lincoln," the *New York Herald* reported. "Mr. and Mrs. Lincoln seemed to be overcome at the thought of parting with their daughter."[63]

After the ceremony, the new couple, members of the wedding party, and intimate family friends were conducted to the church vestry to sign the wedding register.[64] They all then drove to the Lincoln residence on Cromwell Road and enjoyed an informal reception of about fifty people. Minister Lincoln gave his daughter a silver service set as a wedding gift. At 5 P.M., Mr. and Mrs. Charles B. Isham left London for a monthlong wedding tour of the European continent before returning to America and their new home in New York City.

For the next two years, Mary Harlan Lincoln and Jessie were not often in London. Mary preferred to spend time in the United States visiting either her father in Mount Pleasant or Mamie and Charles in New York City. The Lincoln marriage does not appear to have been strained during this period, but after Jack's death, Mary just could not endure the painful reminders of her boy surrounding her in London. She especially wanted to be in America after she learned that Mamie was expecting a baby.

The boy, born on June 8, 1892, had black hair and brown eyes. "It is a very big baby they say," Jessie wrote to her Grandfather Harlan the next day, shortly after she and her mother had arrived in New York. "I must confess it does not look gigantic to me!" The boy weighed eleven pounds.[65] The newest addition to the Lincoln family line was named Abraham Lincoln Isham.[66] Robert was thrilled by the boy's birth and relieved that the delivery occurred without any complications for his daughter.[67] Robert was not able to meet the new arrival until five months later during a visit to Mount Pleasant, Iowa. "Mrs. Lincoln and I have a very creditable grandson," he wrote at the time. "For a first attempt in that direction, it is a very great success."[68] Being placed in "another category" as a grandfather, however, did make him feel the weight of years. When "Linc," as the boy was called, got his first tooth in January 1893, Robert confided to a friend that it made him feel "about 900 years old."[69]

Even though Robert Lincoln was an ocean away from American politics, his name continued to be broached as a desired possibility for higher public offices. In January 1891, upon the death of Secretary of the Treasury William Windom, Lincoln was mentioned as his likely replacement; in March 1891, he was touted for mayor of Chicago; in June 1891, an expected cabinet reshuffling upon the rumored resignation of Interior Secretary John W. Noble caused rumors that Lincoln would be made secretary of the Interior Department or even returned to the War Department; when James G. Blaine resigned as secretary of state in June 1892 due to ill health, it was reported President Harrison was eager to elevate Lincoln to the cabinet.[70]

Of course, the elephant in the room (or in the country, as it were) was the 1892 presidential election. "There is one quiet man, not now much talked of, whom all the Presidential aspirants want to keep their eyes on, and that man is Robert T. Lincoln," one Republican insider told the *Washington Post*. "His name in connection with the Presidential nomination . . . is like a motion to adjourn—it is always in order."[71] Just as in the past two presidential elections, Lincoln abhorred the notion of himself in the White House. When Mary Alsop King Waddington, the wife of the French foreign minister in London, began teasing Minister Lincoln about his presidential prospects at a dinner party, she said, "He assured us there was no possible chance of it, and no one would be as a sorry as he himself if ever the thing came to pass. It certainly would be difficult to be a second President Lincoln."[72]

Lincoln's distaste for the gilded prison, as he called it, did not stop the speculation. *Harper's Weekly* ran a column on "presidential speculations" in January 1891 and declared Robert T. Lincoln as "the most promising Republican candidate."[73] In April 1892, in the *Washington Post* printed excerpts from various newspapers around the country that declared Lincoln "the only man in sight" on the Republican ticket who could defeat the Democrat nominee, former President Cleveland, because of Lincoln's illustrious name, his ability to win the black southern vote, and his impressive public record as secretary of war and ambassador to England.[74] The *New York Times* printed articles for the first six months of 1892 continually mentioning Lincoln as a potential candidate, including one item in which Lincoln "expressed his earnest wish" that his name not be used for political speculation.[75] But it was *Harper's Weekly* that showed its acumen in May 1892 when it concluded that Harrison would surely be renominated, although Lincoln was "always" the clearly defined dark horse who could unite a fractured delegation. "It is the irony of the Republican situation that there is a candidate upon whom the party could unite at once, and joyfully, but who declines the nomination."[76]

Robert repeatedly announced his support for Harrison's renomination and declared himself overjoyed when it was accomplished at the Republican convention on June 11. While Lincoln's support at the convention was not as strong as it was in 1884 and 1888, he did receive one vote for president on the first ballot.[77] Robert was relieved when the presidential danger had passed. He wrote to his son-in-law, Charles Isham, that after Mamie's safe delivery three days previous "and with the nominating convention a thing of the past," he was "about as easy in my mind as I can be."[78]

In September, the Republican National Committee told Minister Lincoln they wanted him—and his famous name—to travel to the United States and participate in the campaign. Lincoln found the request strange and after doing some research discovered that none of his predecessors in London for the past seventy years had ever gone home to campaign during a presidential election. Lincoln explained this to President Harrison in a letter, adding, "I do not feel justified in breaking the line of precedent . . . without your sanction."[79] Harrison told him to come.

Lincoln arrived in New York on October 16.[80] He told reporters his visit was simply his annual two-month leave of absence rather than politics, but after receiving multiple Republican politicians at his hotel and visiting the Harrison campaign headquarters, it was obvious he was there for politics as well.[81] On October 24, Minister Lincoln served as chairman of a four-thousand-person Republican rally in Chicago. He gave a brief speech extolling his party's policies and excoriating those of the Democrats, specifically in regard to the tariff and sound money questions. "We do not want what the Democrats promise us and threaten us with—free trade and a wildcat currency," Lincoln said.[82] The next day in Quincy, Illinois, Lincoln addressed a five-thousand-person Republican rally and continued his attack on the Democrats, calling them "the party of obstruction, destruction, and calamity, and of nothing else."[83] On November 3, Lincoln spoke to crowds of thousands of people in both Brazil and Sullivan, Indiana, repeating the same campaign themes.[84]

The rematch of Cleveland versus Harrison for the presidency was little contest this time around. The former president won with a large margin of victory in both popular votes and Electoral College votes. Robert Lincoln, at home in Chicago, was as disappointed as any Republican in the results. At the end of December, he traveled to Washington to consult with the president and with Blaine's successor, Secretary of State John W. Foster, and returned to London at the beginning of the new year.[85]

Due to the change in presidential administration—especially the change in political party—Minister Lincoln resumed his post knowing that he soon would be replaced. He submitted his letter of resignation to the State Department on February 25, 1893, one week before president-elect Cleveland took his oath of office.[86] Although some Democrats—particularly those in Illinois—lobbied to keep Lincoln at the London legation, nobody truly expected Cleveland to allow a Republican to have the top foreign post in the State Department. On March 30, Secretary of State Walter Q. Gresham informed Lincoln that the president had accepted his resignation.[87]

The next day, former Secretary of State Bayard was nominated and confirmed as America's first ambassador plenipotentiary to Great Britain. On March 1,

Congress finally had made the change in diplomatic designation that countless U.S. senators and American foreign ministers had been lobbying for for years. Robert T. Lincoln, therefore, was the last U.S. Minister Plenipotentiary and Envoy Extraordinary to the Court of St. James. "It is a change which has long been needed, and, aside from adding to the dignity of the United States representatives abroad, it will be of great practical value in the transaction of business," Lincoln declared.[88]

Lincoln had performed his ministerial duties in a manner that further polished his high reputation as his own man and as his father's son. He followed his directives responsibly and professionally and never overstepped his bounds; he made no mistakes and caused no embarrassments to his president or his country. "All of our envoys to London have been pro-British except Bob Lincoln," Theodore Roosevelt is quoted as saying.[89] The *Hartford Courant* opined that Minister Lincoln "has acquitted himself with dignity and credit, and he leaves nothing but respect and good will behind him."[90] It honestly must be noted, however, that Lincoln's tenure in London was not extraordinary. He blazed no trails and had no overwhelming effect on U.S.-British relations. Other men of similar education, intellect, experience, and ability could have performed the work just as well as Lincoln did. He simply did his duty to his best abilities, which was, in fact, all he wanted to do.

As he prepared to return to America, Robert and his wife made their final social calls around London, including dinner with Queen Victoria at Windsor Castle.[91] On May 5, Minister Lincoln for the last time donned his satin knee breeches, ruffled short, and buckled shoes to present his letter of recall to the Queen.[92] "I am not especially sorry to put off the 'robes of office,'" Lincoln wrote to a friend that evening, "but it is with the greatest regret that I am severing by so great a distance the delightful relations of my social life in England."[93]

On May 6, 1893, ex-Minister Lincoln sailed for America. He traveled alone since Mary and Jessie had left the previous month for Mount Pleasant. It was a bittersweet return for Robert, for although he was happy to be back, it was an empty joy without his son. Without Jack preparing for entry into the Isham, Lincoln, and Beale law firm, Robert lost interest in his profession. But what else would he do? The possibilities for the respected and accomplished Robert T. Lincoln, son of President Abraham Lincoln, were endless. Robert had in mind to take an active interest in some of the businesses with which he was associated. But it was a job offer from his old friend and client George M. Pullman, founder and president of the Pullman Palace Car Company, that changed the course of Robert Lincoln's life.

21

"What Would His Father Say?"

When forty-nine-year-old Robert returned to America from Great Britain in May 1893, he did not return to any type of work immediately but allowed himself a lengthy vacation. He did this not only for a rest after his diplomatic work but he also was reluctant to return to the city and the job that reminded him so painfully of his son. (He and his family also could not return to their home until 1894 because it was being leased out.) So Robert spent some time in New York City visiting his daughter Mamie and her family and also spending time with his good friend Edgar Welles. He went fishing with friends at Pelee Island, Lake Erie, in mid-May, made a brief trip home to Chicago in early June during which he visited the World's Fair, attended a lavish ball in honor of Princess Eulalie of Spain, and participated in the unveiling of the Fort Dearborn Massacre Memorial at the Chicago Historical Society.[1] Robert returned east to attend the Harvard graduation ceremony on June 28, at which he was given an honorary Doctorate of Laws (LLD). At the alumni dinner that night, Robert gave a brief speech in which he attacked the Illinois governor, Democrat John Peter Altgeld, for his pardon of two of the anarchists convicted during the 1886 Haymarket riot. "This act of a demagogic Governor with a little temporary power, this slander upon justice, I must denounce, and if I did not I would consider myself an apostate to my own State of Illinois," Lincoln said.[2]

From Boston, Robert traveled up to the tiny seacoast village of Little Boar's Head, New Hampshire, for a summer vacation with his family. The Lincolns had been vacationing in the area—which Robert discovered during his days as a student at Phillips Exeter Academy—since the 1870s. It was a place of peace and comfort for Robert, and he especially enjoyed it in 1893 because his entire family, including Mamie and her family, was there with him. "I am so far from care and worry this summer that it seems one of the happiest of my life," Robert wrote to a friend that July.[3] The Lincolns stayed at Little Boar's Head until mid-September before going home to Chicago. In October, he again went fishing at Pelee Island. In November, Robert left home to spend a week visiting friends in New Orleans and Baton Rouge, Louisiana, while Mary and Jessie went to Mount Pleasant, Iowa.

It was not until January 1894 that Robert finally settled down to return to work in Chicago, but he found himself unhappy. "I am trying to get to work again but the shop has ceased to interest me I am sorry to say," he told his friend John Nicolay, who was at that time preparing an edition of Abraham Lincoln's collected works for publication at Robert's behest. But the ex-minister was unsettled, and in February 1894, he traveled to California for a month's holiday. Robert Lincoln was not a man prone to depression, but the absence of Jack clearly was something with which he struggled. By the end of the year, Robert was telling his friend Nicolay, "I wonder if you are getting to feel so miserably old as I do. My daughter and the baby live a thousand miles away and the whole future seems merely so many days to be passed."[4]

Robert knew he had to get back to work in early 1894, however, because he also needed to replenish his bank account. In his four years as minister to Great Britain, Lincoln in fact spent more than twice as much money as he made. This was not due to Lincoln being irresponsible or a spendthrift but necessary to fulfill the duties of his position. On a salary of $17,500 per year, the minister was required to hire and pay rent on a house, supply his own furniture, and be a leading participant and host in British society. These latter duties Robert did as modestly and infrequently as possible, yet it still was so expensive he had to regularly draw funds from his income from the Isham, Lincoln, and Beale law firm. Shortly after his return to the United States in 1893, Lincoln told a friend that he spent $35,000 per year as minister, and the $17,500 difference between his income and expenditures he supplied himself.[5]

Still, Robert Lincoln was a wealthy man at this point in his life. He had a continuing income from his law firm, which he received as a founding partner whether he practiced actively or not, and he had his numerous business investments. His Chicago bank account alone had a balance of a little more than $13,000 in 1893—equivalent to more than $200,000 today—and he had other bank accounts in New York and Washington as well.[6] His account shows continuous income from dividend checks from his stock holdings in Chicago, Central Union, and Michigan Telephone companies, the Chicago Edison electric company, and the Pullman Palace Car Company.[7]

Although all of Robert Lincoln's financial records are not available today, it is clear that by this time, he was a millionaire. He was in fact not only a member but the anointed leader of the "Chicago 300"—a phalanx of the city's most socially prominent (and therefore wealthy) people. The group was created ostensibly for the purpose of organizing a succession of winter balls in the city, but as the *New York Times* stated, the three hundred were "the most exclusive set any American city, not even excepting that from which the idea was borrowed [New York], has ever known."[8] The founders and members included Lincoln's two law partners, Edward Isham and William G. Beale, as well as the Potter Palmers, the Cyrus McCormicks, and the George Pullmans.

As the newly appointed "society leader" and "practical dictator" of high-society membership, Robert Lincoln approved the guest list for each ball given. "What would his father say to this new distinction of the son?" the *Springfield (MA) Republican* newspaper critically inquired about the news. "Moreover, what chance would 'Old Abe' stand of being admitted to the 300?"[9] A damning question on its face but, in reality, rhetorical and sensationalist nonsense. At the height of his career in the late 1850s, Abraham Lincoln was a leader in Springfield society; as an ex-president, Abraham Lincoln, had he lived, would have been included in any and every social group in America he wanted, as was Ulysses S. Grant after his presidency. The question is evidence not only of Abraham Lincoln's growing everyman mythos and general apotheosis by the end of the nineteenth century but also the beginnings of negative attitudes towards Robert Lincoln for his wealth and his high social standing, so antithetical to his father's roots.

Robert's reputation as a cold, calculating, aristocratic businessman became further entrenched when he was hired as George Pullman's personal legal adviser in the spring of 1894. Robert Lincoln had a long history of association with Pullman and with the Pullman Palace Car Company. The two men had been friends since the 1870s, and Lincoln, through his law firm, had been a company attorney for decades. Robert was a longtime stockholder in Pullman; in 1880, he became a company director, although he resigned in 1881 after being appointed secretary of war.[10] Although he was officially designated as a "special counsel" for the Pullman Palace Car Company in 1894, Lincoln's job was to advise president George Pullman, not the company. The company's other special counsel, John S. Runnels, who had been with Pullman since 1888, was focused on corporate legalities.

Not long after Pullman hired Lincoln, thousands of his employees walked off their jobs, an action that culminated in the historically infamous Pullman Strike of 1894. The initial cause of the strike was the panic of 1893—the U.S.'s worst economic depression of the nineteenth century. Foreign-market downturns, agricultural failures, high federal deficits, collapsing stocks, railroad overbuilding, and shallow financing and a rush on American gold reserves caused a financial panic. Major banks and railroads around the country began to fail, prices soared, businesses closed, and millions of people lost their jobs and their homes.[11]

In Chicago, the Midwestern hub of the railroad industry, the corporate giant Pullman Palace Car Company was not immune to the depression. The company had been founded in 1867 by George Mortimer Pullman, a cabinet maker and inventor who revolutionized railway travel with his new sleeping cars. Instead of making cars and selling them, Pullman retained ownership and leased his cars to the railroads, asking also a percentage of the increased ticket sales. Pullman cars were so revolutionary the public's desire to ride in them became universal.

From his initial success of the "Pioneer" car in 1865, Pullman continued to improve and modify his creations. Prior to Pullman cars, railroad travel was ascetic: cold, drafty, and uncomfortable; overnight journeys generally were made either tossing and turning in wooden bunks or staying awake and sitting up in wooden seats. Pullman's creations already were more luxurious than ever thought possible with soft, comfortable seats, bedding changed daily, thick carpets and curtains, gilded mirrors and chandeliers, and patent heating and ventilation systems. Pullman next developed the hotel car, which had a kitchen built at one end for complete culinary service. Next, he built the dining car, devoted entirely to restaurant purposes; this was followed by the parlor car, a lush, comfortable place to sit and socialize during a long journey. Pullman's following revolution was to develop and patent a connecting vestibule between cars to allow for passage while the train was in motion. Pullman's railroad cars were so successful that from $1 million starting capital in 1867, the company's capital stock was worth $15.9 million with assets over $29 million in less than twenty years.[12]

In 1880, amid the necessity to build new shops, George Pullman decided to build his own model town in the southern outskirts of Chicago to house his employees. Pullman believed that a well-planned community with attractive homes, beautiful parks and landscaping, and plentiful amenities would create stability in his workforce. It would eliminate discontent caused by the typical crowded and unhealthy housing conditions for workers so prevalent in other major cities across the United States. "I believe that men who have pleasant surroundings will be better men than those whose surroundings are bad, and that, this being the case, the employer will derive a benefit," he said.[13]

The model town of Pullman, Illinois, became a wonder of community planning and was thoroughly praised by all who visited for its beauty, its healthy charm, and its modern advancements, such as complete water and sewer service. It was enthusiastically described by one writer as "a town where the homes, even to the most modest, are bright and wholesome and filled with pure air and light; a town, in a word, where all that is ugly, and discordant, and demoralizing, is eliminated, and all that inspires to self-respect, to thrift and to cleanliness of person and of thought is generously provided."[14]

As generous as the creation of the town sounds, Pullman built it to help himself, not his workers. "The building of Pullman was undertaken simply as a matter of business," he said. "I have little of the sentimental in my nature. I abhor abstruse problems. I can see nothing in this enterprise which is not a matter of finance, pure and simple."[15] He wanted residency in the town to stabilize his workforce and help attract highly skilled mechanics; he believed content workers created less likelihood of labor disputes. To this end, the Pullman company, in fact, regulated every aspect of life in the town, even to the circulation of company informants amid the inhabitants. A later federal commission declared that as beautiful as the town was, the "air of business" of the place prevented any sort of "grateful acceptance" of it by the Pullman employees. "Men, as a rule, even when employees, prefer independence to paternalism in such matters," the commission stated.[16]

When the 1893 depression began to deepen, Pullman, like every other employer, was forced to take steps to keep his company solvent. He canceled building contracts, closed his Detroit plant, laid off more than one thousand workers throughout the company, and reduced the wages of the remaining employees an average of 25 percent. These actions were typical business maneuvers in such economic times, but as the months of these conditions stretched on, Pullman employees began to become disgruntled. One reason was the unfairness that Pullman managers and executives had retained their full salaries, and Pullman stockholders continued to receive 2 percent dividend payments. But the major issue was that after cutting wages, Pullman refused to reduce rents, fees, or prices on anything in the town of Pullman, declaring that the corporation and the town were two separate business endeavors. As an employer, wage reductions were necessary actions, but as a landlord, it was legitimate to keep rents up regardless of the wages of the tenants, the company claimed.[17]

By 1894, the Pullman Palace Car Company had capital value of $36 million, with forty-two hundred stockholders, about ten thousand total employees, and the ownership and operation of the town of Pullman, Illinois. It also had more than 2,500 cars operating on 125,000 miles of railroad, being about three-fourths of the entire railway mileage of the United States. Despite this success, Pullman employees were suffering and restive, so in April thousands of them joined the American Railway Union (ARU), a national group representing 465 local unions and more than 150,000 members. In early May, a delegation of employees met with Pullman company managers to request a restoration of wages to the previous year's rates. The company refused, stating that current business conditions did not justify such a restoration. The next day, three of the delegates were fired for "lack of work." The Pullman company in actuality detested any sort of labor groups or unions, and the dismissals were a warning to employees not to make waves. That evening, the local unions met and voted to strike immediately.

On May 11, 1894, about twenty-five hundred workers at the Chicago plant walked off their jobs. The Pullman company executives were utterly surprised by the action, believing the employees were satisfied with current conditions. Pullman, however, immediately fired the remaining six hundred nonunion employees and locked up the shops, intent to wait out the unions. Thus began the infamous Pullman Strike of 1894.[18]

Throughout most of June, the ARU convened for its annual meeting in Chicago. On June 15, the union voted to seek arbitration with the Pullman company over the strike and the issue of employee wages. Pullman refused. On June 21, the ARU voted to boycott the Pullman Company beginning July 26 by refusing to haul or handle Pullman cars on every railroad throughout the country unless Pullman agreed to arbitrate. Pullman refused, saying there was nothing to arbitrate. "The question, to my mind, has resolved itself into this: Shall the railroads be permitted to manage their own business or shall they turn it over into the hands of [the labor unions]?" Pullman said.[19] And so the Chicago strike became a national boycott that paralyzed the nation's railways.

On July 2, a U.S. Circuit Court issued an injunction against the ARU to stop its boycott, which was declared to be an interference with interstate commerce and U.S. mail delivery. On July 3, President Cleveland ordered U.S. troops to Chicago to enforce the injunction and prevent the strikers from impeding rail traffic. The arrival of the army led to riots, which continued for five days. By the time order was restored, thousands of dollars in property damage had occurred, at least a dozen people had been killed, and dozens more seriously wounded. The executives of the ARU were arrested on July 7 and indicted for conspiracy against the United States.

Shortly after the boycott began, George Pullman decided to distance himself from the scene and traveled to his summer home in Long Branch, New Jersey. He did not make an official company statement about the strike or the boycott until after the army had broken the strike. When he appeared in New York City on July 13 to speak to reporters, he did so accompanied by his personal attorney, ex-minister to Great Britain Robert T. Lincoln.

One of the most pervasive and conspicuous questions concerning Robert Lincoln's professional association with the Pullman Company always has been,

How much was he involved in the 1894 Pullman Strike? The answer, actually, is, very little. Pullman records show that it was John Runnels who handled the day-to-day issues involved in the strike.[20] During February and most of March 1894, Robert was on a trip to California and in the beginning of May was fishing at Pelee Island in Lake Erie. Robert took his wife and daughter to Europe in June, and on their return in July, the Lincolns went straight to Rye Beach, New Hampshire, for their summer vacation.[21]

It was not until mid-July 1894 that Robert Lincoln became actively engaged in the strike. He left his family in New Hampshire for a week to help George Pullman prepare a press statement. Lincoln met with Pullman at Castle Rest, the Pullman family's Thousand Island, New York, island estate, and then accompanied the railroad magnate to New York City. Pullman vice president Horace Porter and special counsel Runnels joined Pullman and Lincoln at the Pullman offices there, where the four spent the day conferring. On July 13, Pullman outlined the history of the strike and pronounced that arbitration was impossible. "Can I, as a business man, knowing the truth of the facts which I have stated, bind myself that I will, in any contingency, open and operate the Pullman car shops at whatever loss, if it should happen to be the opinion of some third party [not concerned with the interest of the company's shareholders] that I should do so? The answer seems to be plain," Pullman declared.[22]

The strike was broken, and the union leaders were arrested in mid-July, and on August 2, the ARU officially ended the boycott. Management reopened the Pullman works in Chicago on company terms: one thousand strikers were fired, those who returned to work did so at their previous wage, rents in the town of Pullman remained the same, and all employees were required to sign a pledge abdicating all present and future union membership. In a word, the Pullman company had won. With all the unpleasantness of the strike over, George Pullman returned to Chicago in late August accompanied by his attorney, Robert T. Lincoln.[23]

The strike was over, but its magnitude was so pervasive that President Cleveland created a federal commission to investigate its causes. Hearings began on August 15 in the Federal Building in downtown Chicago. George Pullman testified on August 27, during which he defended the actions of his company.[24] Lincoln, as Pullman's attorney, accompanied him to the hearing and afterward edited Pullman's testimony for publication. When the commission asked the Pullman Company for additional information and exhibits, Lincoln prepared them.[25]

The final report of the U.S. Strike Commission was issued in November 1894. It sought to convey an objective tone but was critical of the Pullman Company's actions, empathetic to the employees, and offered general support to the formation and rights of labor unions. Pullman's secretary, Charles Sweet (formerly Secretary of War Lincoln's secretary in the 1880s), told him that company counsel Lincoln and Runnels found the report "inimical" to the company. "It all rather seemed like the work of an advocate wishing to avoid wild and extravagant statements, but not unwilling to leave unnoticed arguments not helping his side," Sweet wrote.[26]

In early February 1895, the final public act of the Pullman Strike drama occurred in the conspiracy trial of union leader Eugene V. Debs. The circuit court judge wanted George Pullman to testify, but the U.S. marshal could not locate him. Pullman had, in fact, purposely evaded the marshal and fled to New York City, apparently unwilling to submit under oath to questions from Debs's attorney. Pullman left Chicago either on the advice or with the aid of his attorney, Robert T. Lincoln, who was with him the morning he left. Pullman later claimed that as soon as he learned he was sought by court authorities, he contacted Lincoln and then arranged to return to Chicago. As blatantly false as the story was, since no official subpoena had been delivered to him, and he claimed he did not know he was being sought, the judge did not cite Pullman for contempt of court.[27]

These events are all that is known of Robert Lincoln's role in the infamous Pullman Strike and Boycott of 1894.[28] The reasons for Lincoln's relatively diminutive role are unclear, although they can be speculated. First and most simple, the strike was a corporate issue, not one personal to George Pullman, so the legalities fell to Runnels, not to Lincoln. Robert's participation, as currently known, clearly was limited to assisting George Pullman personally. Of course, Lincoln could easily have participated or been asked to assist in handling the corporation aspect of the strike by Runnels or even by Pullman himself. If so, Robert declined. The logical reason for that would be that Robert Lincoln was smart enough to know to avoid involving himself in a national labor-management dispute—avoid it from damaging his personal reputation, the reputation and business of his law firm, and, most important, the legacy and reputation of his father as perceived through the actions of the son. Robert always was conscious of how his actions affected his father's legacy, and he never consciously did anything that could possibly cause damage.

Not everyone believed Robert Lincoln's role during the strike was as limited as is now known. The *Detroit Free-Press*, in an editorial attacking the Republican Party for reportedly desiring Lincoln to run for U.S. Senate from Illinois, declared that Lincoln was not only the "legal advisor and defender" of George Pullman but also "framed the cold refusals with which his wealthy client met all proffers of arbitration or mediation looking to a peaceful settlement. Mr. Lincoln was the brains and generalship of the Pullman side of the controversy.

He managed the entire campaign and was the instigator of everything."[29] One Chicago Democratic newspaper called Lincoln George Pullman's "personal private bodyguard attorney."[30] The *Chicago Herald* claimed that Lincoln was George Pullman's "constant and inseparable" companion, as well as the author of every statement issued by the company president. "I wonder what Abraham [Lincoln] would say if he were still in the flesh and could speak to his son who has been advising Mr. Pullman how to starve his employees into subjection," the paper quoted one of President Lincoln's "admirers" as saying.[31]

Many have said then and now that Abraham Lincoln would have been ashamed of his son for siding with the Pullman Company. It is forgotten that attorney Abraham Lincoln did much the same thing. He worked for the people who hired him. He more than once defended slave owners in suits to recover runaway slaves, just as he defended runaway slaves from reclamation by their owners. By the end of the 1850s, Abraham Lincoln himself was a corporate railroad lawyer, who once made an exorbitant $5,000 fee for defending the Illinois Central Railway Company. Like his father, Robert Lincoln was an attorney working for his client.

This is not to say that Robert disagreed with Pullman's opinions or actions concerning his workers and the interference from their unions. His later actions and declarations prove he mostly did not. While Abraham Lincoln clearly was a champion of labor, Robert Lincoln clearly was a champion of big business. Part of this disparity between father and son was the changed generational nature of the Republican political philosophy in which Robert believed and that likewise changed its support from labor to business in the decades since the Civil War. But more than that, it was Robert's inherent nature gained from his life experiences. While his father had been a poor wage earning youth with great faith in the abilities if the common worker, Robert was a Harvard man, an entrepreneur, an investor, a stockholder, and a corporate executive. He believed in the superiority of the educated management, the essential ignorance in administrative affairs of the lower-class wage workers, and the seditious and undemocratic influences of the meddling labor unions.

With the end of the strike, business in Chicago returned to normal. Lincoln continued as Pullman special counsel and as attorney with his own firm, but he took few legal cases. For the rest of the decade, Robert turned away from the law and more towards business. Among Robert's multiple roles during these years, he was a director of Commerce National Bank of Chicago, Commonwealth Electric Company, Chicago Edison Electric Company, Chicago Telephone Company, and the Equitable Life Assurance Society. He also helped underwrite, invested in, and took an active interest in the Glucose Sugar Refining Company of Illinois. From 1895 to 1897, Robert was president of the Chicago

Gas, Light, and Coke Company, a part of the Chicago Gas Trust owned by John D. Rockefeller's Standard Oil Company.[32] Lincoln also was president of the Chicago Telephone Company for six months in 1897. "I am pegging away at a little law and little business," Robert wrote tongue-in-cheek to John Hay during this time, "but am trying to keep myself fairly free from what is real toil."[33]

Robert's extensive and varied business career in Chicago inevitably caused commentary and comparison with his father. One magazine article declared Robert Lincoln the most successful and impressive living son of a past president, although he was nothing like his father. "The son is a hard, matter-of-fact man in the extreme. . . . His eyes are dark and piercing. He looks like a typical Chicago board of trade man."[34] A Chicago newspaper, commenting on the same topic, said that instead of a man of the people like his father, Robert Lincoln was "clubman, university man, corporation lawyer, corporation president, representative of centralization of power in the hands of accumulated wealth."[35]

With the approach of the 1896 presidential election, Robert Lincoln was, again, mentioned as an ideal candidate. (In November 1894, Robert had been mentioned as a possible candidate for U.S. senator from Illinois. The *St Louis Globe Democrat* newspaper wryly commented on the rumor by stating, "One of the purposes for which Mr. Lincoln exists, by the way, is that of being spoken of for places that other people get.")[36] An old family friend, William Lincoln Shearer, wrote Robert numerous letters urging him to run for president. Shearer was a journalist and enthusiastic Republican Party worker who for two years asked if he could advance Robert's candidacy. "In the absence of any accident we ought to have either Harrison or McKinley," Robert told Shearer in 1894. "There never was a better president than Mr. Harrison and if he wants it, the country owes him a second term."[37] In 1895, Lincoln responded to Shearer's badgering by stating, "I am simply not in the running and will not be and I have never for a moment felt otherwise."[38]

While Lincoln continued to have his political admirers, talk of his possible nomination diminished with each passing electoral cycle. By 1896, the number of articles about his candidacy was scant. The *New York Times* reported that Thomas L. James, former postmaster general, said Lincoln was the strongest candidate possible, having the name and the popularity among black southern voters.[39] The *Washington Post* also mentioned Lincoln's name as a possible candidate a few times but acknowledged that he was "the only man who has declined the Republican nomination."[40]

At the Republican National Convention in St. Louis, Ohio Governor and former Congressman William McKinley was nominated on the first ballot. The Democrats nominated William Jennings Bryan, former Nebraska congressman, as their candidate. The 1896 campaign is well known for various reasons. It has been dubbed the "Front Porch Campaign" because McKinley did no traveling but literally sat on his front porch in Canton, Ohio, and let people come to him. Bryan's tactic, equally original at the time, was to relentlessly traverse the country and speak out on his own behalf, rather than let his supporters and subordinates do the talking. The primary issue in 1896 was economic: Would America remain on the gold standard, as supported by McKinley and the Republicans, or would the United States switch to the free silver policies espoused by Bryan and the Populists?

Robert Lincoln, being the loyal Republican that he was, as well as a fervent gold standard–supporting businessman, campaigned extensively for the McKinley ticket. Before he hit the campaign trail, however, Lincoln traveled to Galesburg, Illinois, to participate in two massive celebrations. The first was the dedication of a Civil War soldiers' monument in Hope Cemetery. Lincoln gave an extensive speech concerning the reasons and the beginnings of the civil war—"The gloom of those threatening days can never be forgotten by those who had passed the age of childhood," he said—and the meaning of the conflict and the sacrifice of those who fought for liberty. "For this we come today to the graves of these dead soldiers, who were of the men willing to give their lives that their country might live," Lincoln said in a statement evocative of his father's hallowed Gettysburg Address. "We should never cease our thanks to God that their offered gift was not in vain. . . . One great lesson to be learned from the lives of these men and their comrades is that there is no danger to the Republic so great that it may not be overcome by the union of patriots. . . . No one lives under its flag who does not at heart rejoice that the rock of Disunion was exploded from its path and the canker of human slavery torn from its framework."[41]

The second event the day was at Knox College for the celebration of the thirty-eighth anniversary of the Lincoln-Douglas debate held on that campus in 1858. The Galesburg debate was the fifth of the famous debates between Abraham Lincoln and Stephen A. Douglas in the senatorial contest of 1858. It is seen as the turning point in the campaign in which Abraham Lincoln began to stress the moral issue of slavery as one of right versus wrong, rather than mere politics.[42]

The day of the 1896 commemorative event celebration, October 7, broke crisp, warm, and cloudless in Galesburg. More than twenty thousand people thronged the town and the college campus. The main speaker of the day was Chauncey M. Depew—a renowned orator, New York State politician, and railroad executive—who paid an eloquent tribute to Abraham Lincoln. U.S. Senator John M. Palmer, who knew both Lincoln and Douglas, also gave a long tribute to both men; Frank Hamlin, son of Lincoln's first vice president, Hannibal Hamlin, also gave a brief address.[43] But the one speaker who drew thousands of people to the crowd was ex-minister to Great Britain Robert T. Lincoln.

Robert's speech that day was one of the rare times in his life in which he publicly spoke about his father. His participation is evidence of his deep reverence not only for his father but also for the historic importance of the debates themselves and the part his father played in eradicating slavery. Standing on the platform facing twenty thousand people, with a bust of his father on the platform beside him, Robert Lincoln, portly, bearded, and impeccably dressed—looking, in fact, nothing like Abraham Lincoln—said:

> On an occasion of this peculiar significance it would suit me far better to be a listener or to give you hearty assurance of the grateful emotions that overcome me on witnessing this demonstration of respect for my father. He knew that here he had many sympathizing friends, but what would have been his feelings could he have known that after nearly forty years, after his work was done over thirty years, there would come together such a multitude as this to do him honor! It is for others and not for me to say, I will give expression to but a few thoughts. . . .
>
> The issues of 1858 have long been settled. My father called the struggle one between right and wrong. In spite of the great odds against him he battled on, sustained by conscience and supported by the idea that when the fogs cleared away the people would be found on the side of right. . . .
>
> He was right, and today not a man could be found who would not resist the evil against which he protested. This should give us confidence in our battle against the evils of our own times. Now, as then, there can be but one supreme issue, that between right and wrong. In our country there are no ruling classes. The right to direct public affairs according to his might and influence and conscience belongs to the humblest as well as to the greatest. The elections represent the judgments of individual voters. Perhaps in times one vote can destroy or make the country's prosperity for thirty years. The power of the people, by their judgments expressed through the ballot box, to shape their own destinies, sometimes makes one tremble. But it is times of danger, critical moments, which bring into action the high moral quality of the citizenship of America. The people are always true. They are always right, and I have an abiding faith they will remain so.[44]

The event was intended as a commemoration of the debate, but, as one newspaper reported, it "could not help becoming a Republican rally in this stronghold of Republicanism."[45]

One week later, Robert Lincoln began campaigning on behalf of the Republican presidential ticket. His first event was to preside on October 25 over the

American Republican College League meeting in Chicago, where Theodore Roosevelt was the featured speaker.[46] The next week, Lincoln began a whirlwind speaking tour around the Midwest. He gave three speeches in Minnesota, four in Illinois, and two in Indiana, each time appearing before crowds of tens of thousands of people.[47] In his speeches, Lincoln supported McKinley, the Republican Party, and the continuance of the gold standard, and he railed against the Democrats for wanting to kill American businesses and destroy the American economy. After returning home to Chicago on November 1, Robert wrote to John Hay, "There is nothing I hate as much as speech making, but I started out two weeks ago and have been at it ever since."[48]

Robert did find one pleasing diversion while out on the campaign trail when he discovered that his childhood nurse and cook, Mariah Vance, was living in Danville, Illinois.[49] According to U.S. Representative Joseph G. "Uncle Joe" Cannon, who was from Danville and accompanied Robert Lincoln during the campaign event there, Robert disappeared from his hotel room prior to his speech. He was found in Vance's house, where he had evidently been for several hours, "enjoying one of the finest meals of corn pone and bacon you ever tasted." Cannon and the other politicians quickly hustled Lincoln away to the rally. As soon as the event was over, however, Robert eschewed the politicians seeking his company and instead went straight back to Vance's house, where he stayed for several more hours until he had to catch his train. "From that day until her death, 'Mammy' Vance received a substantial check each month from [Robert in] Chicago," Cannon stated.[50]

On election day, McKinley handily defeated Bryan to become the twenty-fifth president of the United States. When asked by a friend if he would hold any appointed position under McKinley, Lincoln responded, "There is not the remotest possibility of my being in office under the new administration."[51] Whether this was decision or design by Robert is unclear; he did meet with McKinley when the president-elect was in Chicago in December.[52] Robert's only political hope after the canvass was that his longtime friend John Hay would be appointed ambassador to Great Britain, which he was. Robert was "more delighted than I can express" about the appointment, he told Hay in a letter of congratulation.[53]

The year 1897 was for Robert T. Lincoln a life-changing time due to two major events. The first occurred in October when his friend and employer, George Mortimer Pullman, died. Under the terms of the will, attorneys Robert Lincoln and Norman Ream were named executors. It was a vast and complicated estate worth nearly $8 million in personal property, dealing with numerous heirs, multiple assets and real-estate properties, stocks and bonds, debts and collections, and multiple charitable bequests.[54] This was nothing Lincoln had not faced before as an attorney, specifically, as the executor of the Walter Newberry estate during the 1880s. Perhaps this was the reason that Lincoln was the primary executor and attended to the majority of the settlement work.[55] Lincoln and Ream settled the Pullman estate in two years, during which time the principal was increased from about $8 million to nearly $14 million. For their work, the executors were paid $425,000—said to be the largest amount ever allowed any executors of any estate handled in the Chicago probate courts.[56]

The pressing issue after Pullman's death, however, was not his estate but the presidency of his company. Unlike most corporations in which a board of directors made the important decisions, George Pullman ran his business himself, and his board merely rubber-stamped his actions. As one newspaper wrote, "George Pullman was the Pullman Palace Car Company."[57] Who could and would replace such a man at the head of such a company? Speculation began immediately in the national newspapers, and much like with each U.S. presidential election, Robert T. Lincoln was a leading contender for the place. The *Chicago Tribune* stated that Lincoln was the likely man because his close relationship with Pullman and the company for so many years made him intimately familiar with all the details of running the company.[58] Papers in New York and Boston reported the rumor that Pullman, anticipating his death, had specifically selected Robert Lincoln to succeed him.[59]

For once, media rumors proved correct. When the Pullman Company board of directors met on November 11, 1897, Lincoln was named acting president until a permanent president could be chosen.[60] "The directors decided the choice of a president be delayed until careful consideration could be given to the subject," reported the *Chicago Tribune.* "It is possible that some railroad man may finally be elected to the position."[61] Lincoln actually was one member of a three-man executive committee chosen by the board of directors and authorized to exercise general supervision and control of the company. The other two members of the executive committee, Marshall Field and H. C. Hulbert, voted to make Lincoln chairman and thereby the acting company president because he was the only one of the three who had sufficient time to devote to company affairs.

The national media was strangely dispassionate in reporting Robert's new position, stating the fact of it and nothing else. One politician did retort what was perhaps on many minds at the time: "It seems strange to me that he should consider the presidency of a private corporation, above the Presidency of the greatest of all Republics. How unlike his father!"[62] Responding to congratulations about his new position, Lincoln more than once wrote half-jokingly that his new responsibilities were so onerous "that the work thrown upon me makes me the subject of anything but congratulations."[63] It soon became apparent to everyone that Robert Lincoln was an extraordinary businessman and, whether he knew it at the time or not, had found his destiny.

Only the day before succeeding to the head of one of America's largest and wealthiest corporations, Robert was confronted with another life-changing event. This one was personal rather than professional, was immeasurably distressing to Robert and his wife, and created newspaper headlines around the country. On November 10, 1897, in direct disregard of her parents' objections, the Lincolns' youngest daughter, Jessie, eloped with a football player.

Jessie Lincoln was not only the youngest of Robert's three children but also the wild child. Perhaps this was inevitable considering that the first two children, Mary and Abraham, named after Robert's illustrious parents, were perfect, petted, and admired offspring. Jessie, named after Mary Harlan's grandmother, was just Jessie. There is no evidence that she was disregarded or unloved in her family, but it seems obvious she was overshadowed by her two older siblings.

Jessie was an intelligent, pretty, and vivacious girl. She grew up wanting for nothing, the granddaughter of a president and the daughter of an esteemed businessman and public servant, exposed to the highest social circles in Chicago, Washington, and London. In personal correspondence, Robert Lincoln generally wrote of all his children as a group, rarely singling any out. He did name a boat after Jessie at his Pelee Island fishing club; and when he was secretary of war, nine-year-old Jessie was selected to christen a new American steamer (although she thought the bottle of wine decorated with red, white, and blue ribbons was too pretty to break against the prow, so she hugged it tightly instead).[64] In 1890, at age fifteen, Jessie followed her mother's and her sister's paths into school at Iowa Wesleyan University, where she took the classical courses but focused her studies on music. Jessie loved spending time at her grandparents' house in Mount Pleasant, and it was during a visit there that she became acquainted with a dashing young athlete named Warren Beckwith and with whom she fell rapturously in love.

Beckwith was the son of a longtime friend of the Harlan family in Mount Pleasant. Two years older than Jessie, Beckwith was described by one newspaper as "a harum-scarum young fellow, devoted to athletics, belonging to the local college football and basketball teams, a good horseman, bicyclist, boxer, and shot, but with a decided aversion to educational matters and the confining requirements of a business career."[65] Another newspaper reported that his friends called him "the Dude" and "the Lady Killer," that he would never pitch a baseball game without first combing and brushing his hair faultlessly, and that he always carried a mirror in his pocket to check himself before stepping onto the baseball diamond.[66] He was just such a virile, rebellious young man to attract a romantically inclined girl. Robert and Mary Lincoln immediately opposed the match, believing Beckwith was all brawn and no brains, was not serious about his future, and therefore was not good enough for their daughter. (The Lincolns had, in fact, previously secured Beckwith a job with the Chicago Gas, Light and Coke Company, of which Robert Lincoln was president, but Warren quickly quit to return to baseball.) When Jessie and Warren became engaged in 1896, the Lincolns broke the couple up and forbid any contact or communication between the two. As far as they knew, their daughter obeyed them.[67]

On the morning of November 10, 1897—four days after her twenty-second birthday—Jessie left her parents' home on Lake Shore Drive ostensibly to go shopping downtown. She actually drove to the train station, where Warren was waiting for her, and the two took the first train to Milwaukee. There, they registered at a hotel and then immediately went to the home of a Methodist Episcopal minister, who married them. The newlyweds returned to Chicago that same night and separated. Warren went to a hotel, and Jessie went back to her parents' home as if nothing had happened.[68]

According to newspaper reports, Robert and Mary Lincoln were informed of their daughter's marriage not by her but by a reporter who telephoned to ask for a comment on the wedding. Thinking it was a joke, Mary went up to her daughter's room to inquire and was told the truth.[69] The Lincolns were shocked and distraught, but Robert also was furious at what his daughter had done. "I have not seen Mr. Beckwith, and what is more, I have no desire to see him. If I continue in my present mind I shall never forgive him," Robert said the next morning to the reporters swarming outside his house. "I cannot say what [the newlyweds'] plans are, but I know what mine will be. Miss Lincoln will remain here, and I shall devote a portion of my time to disposing of Mr. Beckwith."[70] That same day, Robert was named interim president of the Pullman Company.

Robert kept his daughter sequestered in her room for the next two days, while Warren waited first in Chicago and then in Aurora, Illinois, for an invitation to the Lincoln home that did not come. "I shall not extend my pardon to him," Robert Lincoln said when asked about a reconciliation.[71] For his part, Warren, after reading the newspaper stories, promised Jessie in a letter that he would make a successful and happy life for them, and added, "I care nothing for what your father may personally think of me."[72]

On the twelfth, Warren traveled to Mount Pleasant to practice for the upcoming Iowa Wesleyan football game, which he had promised to play in, but declared he would return to Chicago and bring his bride back with him with or without her parents' consent.[73] Jessie was just as determined to rejoin her husband as he was to reclaim her. The discussions and arguments in the Lincoln house during those days were likely long, loud, and turbulent, especially when Robert got home at the end of each day. At some point, the parents reached an understanding that their daughter was married and was determined to remain so, so they released her to join her husband in Iowa. Mary Lincoln accompanied her daughter to the train station but did not travel with her.[74] Robert Lincoln stayed home.

At Mount Pleasant, the newlyweds lunched with Jessie's Grandfather Harlan. Warren then donned his uniform and played in the football game between the Iowa Wesleyan and the Keokuk Medicals, in which he dominated the other team "inspired by the presence of his bride."[75] The couple told the milling reporters that they intended to settle down in Mount Pleasant just as any other married couple. Beckwith said he planned to go into business with his father, who worked in railroads, and would neither seek nor accept a position at the Pullman Company to please or appease his new father-in-law.[76]

As the new century approached, Robert T. Lincoln, nearing age sixty, already had achieved an extraordinary life. He was now president of one of the largest corporations in America, after having been a leading Chicago attorney, secretary of war, and minister to Great Britain. He was, in fact, exactly the type of man his father had hoped he would become: successful, respected, wealthy, and with a happy and loving family. What's more, the son had earned it all on his own initiative and notwithstanding his illustrious parentage. Robert Lincoln, born and raised in a time of privies and candlelight, now lived with electricity, telephones, and indoor plumbing, among the myriad other inventions and advancements of the Gilded Age.

Robert had lived to see the reverence for his father's memory continue to grow to unparalleled heights and had assisted as best he could to protect and enhance that legacy. With the opening of the twentieth century, Robert would find that dealing with his father's legacy would grow to nearly overwhelming proportions. But before confronting the national celebration of the centennial of his father's birth in 1909, Robert had to face numerous other items and events. Perhaps the most dramatic was the assassination of a third U.S. president in less than four decades—an event to which Robert Lincoln would be connected, making him the only person in American history associated with all three murders.

22

"I Am Now a Vermont Farmer!"

On the evening of February 15, 1898, the USS *Maine*, a second-class naval battleship stationed in Havana harbor, suddenly exploded, killing nearly three-quarters of the three-hundred-man crew. The ship had been sent to Cuba only three weeks previous to protect American interests during a revolt of the Cubans against the Spanish government. It was determined that the *Maine*'s forward gunpowder magazines had ignited and caused the explosion, although whether by accident or intent was unclear. The world was shocked at the news of the tragedy; politicians were on edge for the possibility of military repercussions. Speculation was rampant about exactly what had happened. It quickly was determined that the Spanish had not attacked the ship. So the questions were, Was it the action of a terrorist person or group unaffiliated with the Spanish government? Was it an accidental external explosion caused by a submerged harbor mine? Or was it some sort of accidental internal explosion? Both governments instituted boards of inquiry.

The general feeling in America was that it was not an internal accident; angry citizens clamored for military retaliation against Spain, which they considered responsible. President William McKinley and many members of Congress counseled patience, desiring to wait for the decision from the board of inquiry. McKinley, a Civil War veteran, said he had seen enough war to ever want to see another one. One week after the explosion, within the tumult of the anger and the argument, former secretary of war and minister to Great Britain Robert T. Lincoln went on record stating that Spain was not at fault for the explosion if it was an accident or the action of a lone fanatic. "In neither case would the slightest liability attach to Spain," Lincoln said. "It is an elementary principle of international law that a government is in no way responsible for the acts of private citizens. . . . It is another primary principle that no nation is responsible for accidents."[1] In the anti-Spanish fervor of the moment, Lincoln's statements shocked and even disgusted many people. The *Mt. Pleasant News* in Iowa declared, "It would be difficult to imagine an opinion more out of harmony and of all sympathy with the prevailing sentiment than this." The *Chicago Times Herald* added that Lincoln's opinion was "not endorsed by men who are classed as authorities [in international law]."[2]

The results of the two boards of inquiry, released simultaneously on March 25, differed in their conclusions. The Spanish board "emphatically" declared the explosion came from inside the ship. The U.S. board decided the explosion came from a submarine mine outside the ship, the explosion of which ignited the forward gunpowder magazines.[3] The findings only intensified American anger, which the Congress followed to support Cuba in its revolution against Spain and to declare the island an independent country. On April 25, Spain declared war on the United States; the next day, the United States declared war on Spain. The explosion of the *Maine* was the specific catalyst for the war, and cries of "Remember the *Maine*!" became the American war cry.

President McKinley immediately issued a call for 125,000 military volunteers. One of the eager young men to join the American army was Robert Lincoln's son-in-law, Warren Beckwith. Since his elopement with Jessie Lincoln in November 1897, Beckwith had tried to settle down into a business career with his father in Mount Pleasant, Iowa, but failed. He then attempted to return to the life he loved as a baseball player, signing with a team in Ottumwa, Iowa, only to be released two weeks later at the insistence of his mother.[4] Beckwith's parents, just like his in-laws, wanted him to go into some form of steady business pursuit, not waste his time playing games. After his baseball plan was thwarted, he went to work in Creston, Iowa, either ranching on his father's farm or working as a brakeman on the Burlington railroad. Shortly after the wedding, Jessie discovered she was pregnant.

Soon after America declared war on Spain in late April 1898, the state of Iowa began enlisting volunteers. On May 3, 1898, Beckwith was the first man in Creston to present himself for physical examination to join the army. According to one news story, the Beckwiths hoped that Warren's enlistment would help his father-in-law to recognize him "as something more than a 'baseball buffoon,' as Robert Lincoln has contemptuously described him."[5] Warren passed the physical and on May 16 was officially enlisted as a private in Company F, Fiftieth Regiment, Iowa National Guard.[6]

The Spanish-American War ended nearly as quickly as it started. After American victories in Cuba, Puerto Rico, and the Philippines, a peace protocol for a ceasefire between Spain and the United States was signed on August 12, less than four months after the war had begun. A peace conference convened in

Paris on October 1, and a final treaty of peace was signed on December 10. The war gained for the United States the territories of Puerto Rico and Guam and catapulted it from a parochial North American country to a world power. U.S. Ambassador to Great Britain John Hay famously called the Spanish-American conflict "a splendid little war."[7]

Warren Beckwith was at an army training camp in Jacksonville, Florida, when the ceasefire was signed in mid-August. Barely two weeks later, on August 22, 1898, Warren and Jessie Beckwith's first child was born. Warren was granted a furlough and hurried home to Mount Pleasant, where Jessie had given birth to a nine-pound baby girl.[8] They named her Mary Lincoln Beckwith, although the family called her Peggy. One local Mount Pleasant story states that when Peggy was a newborn, her father went galloping around town telling anyone listening that he was taking a bottle of milk to Abraham Lincoln's great-granddaughter.[9]

Aside from Beckwith's lack of ambition or any sort of business success, stories like this added even more reason to the distinguished Robert Lincoln's dislike of his flamboyant son-in-law. Warren's enlistment did nothing to endear Robert to him nor did the birth of his first granddaughter. As Robert wrote to one friend in late 1899, "Jessie is with us and has a darling little girl. My affection for the little creature is mixed with dread for I cannot foresee what trouble may come from the scamp of a father."[10] Beckwith did not disappoint such low expectations. After his discharge from the army on November 30, 1898, he left Jessie alone in Mount Pleasant (although she soon went to her parents' house in Chicago) while he traveled the west, bouncing from job to job. Beckwith, still uncertain about his future, went back to baseball, playing on teams in Missouri, Colorado, and California; he also tried his hand at cattle and sheep ranching in Indian Territory, Oklahoma, and apparently went back to the Burlington railroad in Creston, Iowa.[11]

This was a busy time for Robert Lincoln, particularly in his new role as president of the Pullman Company. Sometime around March 1898, Robert suffered the onset of severe health issues. He called it "nervous prostration," and it appears to have been acute anxiety, coupled with occasional bouts of mild depression. It caused him to suffer physically from dizziness when in large crowds, exhaustion, and daily attacks of gout.[12] His troubles probably were the result of the combination of job-related stress, Jessie's disheartening defiance and elopement, the distance separating him from Mamie and her family (about which he previously had lamented), his own innate anxiety issues (inherited from the Todd family), and a lingering depression over Jack's death.

Robert took a number of days off work at the direction of his doctor, who told him that after a few days of "absolute rest," he would feel better.[13] But by mid-April, he did not feel better, so his doctor sent him east "to get away," but he actually felt worse away from his "home comforts," and so he returned to Chicago. "My trouble comes on in without a moment's warning," he told a friend while explaining why he could not attend the Harvard alumni annual dinner in June. "If I am not then far better than now I must not only give up my Harvard Dinner and engagements but arrange to give up for a good while my business. I must not butt my head against a wall much longer."[14]

Robert's health improved slowly but was good enough so that in July he accepted a position as first vice president on the U.S. Sanitary Commission, an organization to care for the sick and wounded of the Spanish-American War, and in October he accepted reappointment as interim president of the Pullman Company.[15] By the end of the year, Robert had a relapse, and on the advice of his doctor, he spent two months in California.[16] This nervous prostration, along with numerous other physical ailments, would affect Robert for the rest of his life; his surviving letters are filled with mentions of his suffering, doctor visits, and physician-suggested vacations.

Interestingly, for all of Robert's reliance on medical professionals, his wife, forever sickly, had lost her faith in doctors. In early 1898, Mary Harlan Lincoln left the Presbyterian Church that she had been associated with for decades and joined the Christian Science Church; her oldest daughter, Mary Isham, had become a Christian Scientist in 1897.[17] Stated simply, Christian Scientists do not believe in the consultation with doctors or the use of medicines but instead proscribe to healing through Christian prayer. The religion was founded by Mary Baker Eddy in 1867 and explained in her 1875 book, *Science and Health with Key to the Scriptures*. Eddy established the First Church of Christ, Scientist in 1879 in Boston and published a major revision of her book in 1891.

Exactly why Mary Lincoln and Mary Isham underwent such religious conversions is unknown. One plausible reason was the death of Jack Lincoln in 1890. Both mother and sister had watched as Jack painfully fought his illness for four months, as his arm carbuncle was continually cut open and drained, as he was given various medications, finally succumbing to what most people believed to be death caused by the physicians' medical maltreatment. It is easy to see how the two Marys could have lost all faith in medicine and turned instead to a faith in the power of religion. Perhaps in the midst of their bereavement, the two discovered and were convinced by the 1891 revision of Eddy's *Science and Health*. It was not long after Jack's death that the Lincoln women became acquainted with Mrs. Eddy.[18]

By the final year of the nineteenth century, Robert Lincoln, at age fifty-six, was not only suffering physical setbacks but emotional ones as well. In March 1899, James C. Conkling, father of Robert's lifelong friend Clinton Conkling, and a close friend of Abraham Lincoln, died in Springfield. Robert sent his friend a letter of condolence, and in it he somewhat sadly realized, "You and I are far more advanced in age than was your father when I knew him best [in Springfield], and indeed we are nearly as old as my father was at the time of his death."[19] In June 1899, one of his closest friends, Norman Williams, died from Bright's disease. Robert attended the funeral in Woodstock, Vermont, and was greatly distressed at the loss of his friend of more than thirty years.[20]

Four months later, Robert's father-in-law, James Harlan, suddenly died at age seventy-nine. On October 1, Harlan had collapsed in his home. He passed away five days later from what was reported as congestion of the lungs complicated with liver and kidney trouble.[21] His daughter Mary Harlan Lincoln, who was visiting Mamie's family in New York City, was called immediately to her father's side in Mount Pleasant and was present when he died. "It was quite sudden to us for he had concealed from her a trouble of the liver and heart, when she thought he only suffered from asthma," Robert, who was in Chicago, wrote to a friend.

Mary stayed in Mount Pleasant alone to go through her father's possessions and burn his letters and papers and had a "dismal time" doing so, Robert wrote. He met his wife there a few days after his father-in-law's death and attended the funeral, along with his daughter Jessie Beckwith, on October 9.[22] Despite James Harlan's own impressive accomplishments—rising from poverty to become a lawyer, college president, U.S. Senator, and presidential cabinet member—his death was heralded primarily as the passing of the last member of President Lincoln's Civil War cabinet. It "severs the last link that connected the administration of Abraham Lincoln with the living of today," wrote the *Philadelphia Times*.[23] Of course, the presence of the Great Emancipator's son at the funeral was not ignored. Mary was named executrix of her father's estate, which was valued at less than $50,000, and inherited all his possessions, including the Harlan homestead.[24]

Despite Robert's continuing health problems and family drama, his first two years at the head of the Pullman Palace Car Company, from October 1897 to October 1899, were hugely successful. In that time, the Pullman Company's capital (total) value more than doubled from $36 million to $74 million. A large part of this increase was from the Pullman takeover of the Wagner Palace Car Company in 1899—a consolidation negotiated on the Pullman side mainly by President Robert Lincoln. Wagner was Pullman's last great rival in the sleeping-car business, and its absorption marked a basic monopoly in the industry by Pullman. The deal also added Wagner board members William K. Vanderbilt and Frederick W. Vanderbilt (grandchildren of "the Commodore" Cornelius Vanderbilt) and banker J. P. Morgan to the board of Pullman directors. It also was after this deal that the Pullman Palace Car Company changed its name to simply the Pullman Company. "All this was work and not fun," Robert told a friend while also explaining his health problems. "I have dragged through my work and it has been heavy. . . . I thought I was nearly well last spring but as I am now, I see that I was still in my bad condition."[25]

Robert's corporate success was no accident, nor was his appointment to the head of the Pullman Company a blind reverence to his surname. All of the company directors who voted him in had known him personally and professionally for decades. They knew him as an indefatigable worker, a successful attorney and businessman, a self-made man of wealth, and a company insider in whom George Pullman had held the utmost confidence. Robert's remarkable two years as interim president of Pullman rewarded the directors' decision, and at the annual board meeting in 1899, Robert Lincoln was named the permanent president of the Pullman Company, a position he would hold for the next twelve years. Although his ascension as interim president oddly had caused minimal newspaper comment in 1897, Robert's permanent appointment in 1899 was mentioned only in passing as a reappointment, one action of many during the annual directors' meeting.[26]

By the turn of the twentieth century, America had come out of the financial panic and depression of the 1890s to find prosperity again; it had become a world power after routing the Spanish in a brief war; it had taken over previous Spanish colonies in the Pacific and Caribbean and annexed Hawaii, all of which had, according to many, inaugurated an age of American Empire; the United States also was at the forefront of scientific invention and cultural advancement in the world. Little wonder, then, that the Republican Party renominated President McKinley to run for a second term in office. He had a different running mate, New York Governor Theodore Roosevelt, but the same opponent from 1896, William Jennings Bryan, whom he resoundingly defeated.

Six months after McKinley's second inauguration, in September 1901, Robert Lincoln took his family to Buffalo, New York, to visit the Pan-American Exposition. The Lincolns had spent the entire summer on vacation in Deal, New Jersey, and decided to experience the exposition the weekend of September 6 on their way home to Chicago.[27] The exposition was a world's fair designed to promote trade and friendship among the United States, Canada, and Latin America. It was laid out as a huge city with buildings and exhibits representing all the Latin-American countries, demonstrating the latest products, technologies, and industrial accomplishments of the hemisphere. The entire exposition was lit by Nikola Tesla's new alternating current, using power generated by nearby Niagara Falls. Such sights were a wonder for Americans at the time, adults and children alike, and while Robert was eager for his children and grandchildren to witness these things, he, too, was excited. Robert, like his own father, had a penchant for science and math; he was an avid amateur surveyor and astronomer who also was fascinated by new technologies such as automobiles and telephones.

When the Lincolns arrived at the Buffalo train station the night of Friday, September 6, the superintendent of the Buffalo Pullman car repair shop, J. K. Bennett, was waiting for his boss on the platform. He handed Robert a telegram from his secretary in Chicago: "President McKinley was shot down by anarchist in Buffalo this afternoon. He was hit twice in the abdomen. Condition serious."[28] Robert arranged for his family to go to their hotel and then immediately drove to the home of John G. Milburn, president of the exposition, where McKinley had been taken to recover after an operation at the exposition hospital.[29]

Robert quickly learned that while holding a brief public reception in the exposition's Temple of Music, President McKinley had been shot twice by a .32 caliber revolver wrapped in a white handkerchief in the assassin's right hand.[30] Surgeons determined that one bullet caused only a superficial wound, but the second hit McKinley in the abdomen, passed through his stomach, injured the kidney, and lodged somewhere in the muscles of his back. They were able to repair the internal damage but could not find the bullet, so they left it in the president's body.[31] McKinley came through the surgery well with no signs of infection, and his physicians expected a full recovery.

Robert and his family stayed in Buffalo for the weekend and since the president was declared out of danger, probably felt free to enjoy themselves at the exposition on Saturday. On Sunday, September 8, Robert again went to the Milburn home to see the president and was pleased that the injured chief executive appeared hearty and ably recuperating. "My visit has given me great encouragement," Robert told milling reporters as he exited the Milburn house. "I feel more hopeful now than I have at any time." Lincoln's visit occurred at the same time as that of Vice President Roosevelt, and the two men had a few minutes' chat together.[32]

That Robert Lincoln was once again near the scene of a presidential assassination has become one of the hallmark facts of his life. He is the only known person in American history to be directly associated with all three. He was not in Ford's Theatre when his father was shot, but he was in the Petersen house when his father died; he was not with Garfield when he was shot, but he was only yards away, having just arrived at the Baltimore and Potomac Railroad Depot; he was not with McKinley when he was shot, but he was on his way to the Pan-American Exposition.[33] Such coincidences are the stuff of legends, and Robert Lincoln's proximity to so many presidential assassinations spawned the folklore not only that he was jinxed but also that *he believed* he was cursed. Numerous stories have been told—particularly in obituaries and stories after his own death—that Robert Lincoln never again attended any presidential events. "If only they knew, they wouldn't want me there," he supposedly said in response to one future invitation. "There is a certain fatality about presidential functions when I am present."[34] There is no direct proof that Robert ever said this or that he believed it, and he actually did attend at least two more presidential functions, but it certainly is a good story.[35]

But still, being so near to all three presidential assassinations—and the first two so personal to him—Robert could not but have been affected by McKinley's shooting. He and his family left Buffalo relieved, however, that McKinley was expected to survive. Less than one week later, however, the president died of infection. Vice President Roosevelt, who had traveled to the Adirondacks for vacation, rushed back to Buffalo, where he was sworn in to office on September 14.

Robert Lincoln, working from the New York City offices of the Pullman Company, followed the news reports of President McKinley's health and death along with all Americans. Shortly after Theodore Roosevelt was sworn in as the twenty-sixth president of the United States, Robert Lincoln sent him a personal letter:

> When I had the pleasure of seeing you at Buffalo, neither of us I think supposed that the great burden of care which is now yours was so soon to fall upon you. I do not congratulate you, for I have seen too much of the seamy side of the Presidential Robe to think of it as an enviable garment, but I do hope that you will have the strength and courage to carry you through a successful administration. You have the deserved confidence of all and the knowledge of this must be a help to you in the many troubles you must meet. No one can wish you a happy triumph more sincerely than I do.[36]

Roosevelt, who had an abiding love and respect for Abraham Lincoln, cherished the letter and responded to it with an invitation for Robert to visit the White House for a talk in the near future.[37] The two men's cordial relationship would not last.

After the onset of his health issues in 1897, which continued for the rest of his life, Robert Lincoln decided to build a summer estate in the east. He desired a place where he could do his Pullman work in a relatively stress-free environment, with plenty of rest and relaxation, and where he could indulge himself in his beloved game of golf, which he played as often as possible and credited with keeping him in decent health. He decided to purchase land and build his summer estate in Manchester, Vermont.

Robert had known Manchester since he accompanied his mother there and stayed in the famed Equinox House Hotel in summer 1864.[38] He became reacquainted with the area in the 1890s after visits to his law partner, Edward S. Isham, who owned a grand estate known as Ormsby Hill outside the town.[39] During the handful of visits he made to Isham at Manchester between 1895 and 1901, Robert became enamored of the beauty of the Green Mountains, the New England attractiveness of the village of Manchester, and the proximity and superlative quality of the Ekwanok Country Club golf course.[40]

Robert Lincoln's relationship to Manchester, Vermont, changed in February 1902 after Isham's death. It was "a great shock and grief to me, as you can imagine," Robert wrote shortly after returning from the funeral in New York City, where he acted as an honorary pallbearer.[41] It is unknown if Lincoln attended Isham's Manchester funeral a few days later, but he did return to the village six months later with his wife, accompanied by daughter Mamie and grandson, Linc, where they all stayed at the Equinox House for two weeks.[42] Apparently, sometime after Isham's death, the Lincolns decided to purchase land in Manchester on which to build "a modest summer place," and their August 1902 visit was done to scout real estate.

The Lincolns found their ideal site just a few miles south of the village, comprising more than one hundred acres covered in woods and valleys, open meadows and river wetlands, and capped with a perfect place to build a house on an impressive bluff with a gorgeous view. The land was adjacent to Ormsby Hill and included about forty acres of the Isham property, which Robert bought from the Isham heirs for $30 an acre. He then purchased eighty-five additional acres from two other landowners at about the same price, and within a year he had purchased two adjoining farms to own a total of five hundred acres of land.[43] "I think I have found that the summer climate of Vermont is better for me than that of the seashore," Robert wrote a friend in December 1903, "and I have become so convinced of it that I have bought quite a farm near Manchester, Vermont, which overlooks one of the best golf courses in the country."[44]

Robert was almost childishly giddy at the prospect of his purchase and the beginning of a new hobby in the Vermont mountains. "My main business . . . is as a dairy farmer in which I hope to gain a reputation, probably an unprofitable one," he lightheartedly told one friend. while to another he boasted, "I bought a 320 acre farm at Manchester, and own 40 cows. The farmer makes about 100 pounds of butter a week. . . . Mrs. Lincoln is delighted."[45] One year after the farmland purchases, Robert reveled to another friend, "I am now a Vermont farmer! and beginning to enjoy life."[46]

Once Robert acquired all the acreage he desired in 1903, he hired the highly respected Boston architectural firm of Sheply, Rutan, and Coolidge to design what he would come to call his "ancestral home." Constructed by the Boston builder Ira G. Hersey, the twenty-four-room Georgian revival mansion contained a grand entryway, parlor, dining room, library/den, office, eight bedrooms for family and guests, and an open-air porch. The servants' quarters in the main house included the kitchen, butler's and maid's pantries, servants' dining room, six servants' bedrooms, and a bath. A frame building next to the house held additional servants' rooms, and an apartment sat over the carriage barn. The Lincolns also installed a modern annunciator system as a way to summon servants to one of several stations in the house.[47] The house and outbuildings cost a total of $63,500 to design and $77,984 to construct—more than $3 million today.[48] Construction began on April 18, 1904, and the Lincolns moved in to their new summer home, named Hildene, on June 20, 1905.[49]

In later years, the Lincolns continued to improve upon their property. In 1907, Jessie Beckwith, an avid gardener, designed an elaborate formal garden resembling a stained-glass Gothic window behind the house. In 1908, the open-air patio was enclosed, an office for Robert's secretary was added, and a new self-playing, electric pneumatic Aeolian pipe organ was installed in the house. The organ, a gift from Robert to his wife, cost $11,500, or about one-sixth of the cost of designing the house.[50] Also that year, Robert added an observatory to the grounds.

Robert had been interested in astronomy since he was a young man in Chicago, probably introduced to it by his mentor Jonathan Young Scammon, an avid amateur astronomer. In Chicago in the 1870s, Robert often used the large Dearborn Observatory telescope at Chicago University (now at Northwestern University), in company with his friend and later renowned astronomer Shelbourne Wesley Burnham. Later in life, Robert was a voracious reader of books on the subject as well as a practitioner.[51] "I belong to the class of old-young amateurs in astronomy, but I enjoy my study of it very much," he once wrote to the director of the Lick Observatory in California.[52] Before constructing the observatory, Robert used his telescope on a tripod. Every day, he went into the Manchester telegraph office with a stopwatch to make an exact notation of noon, because precise time is an important part of astronomical calculations. In 1907, he installed a box sounding relay in Hildene so he could get exact noontime readings directly via telegraph without going into town.[53]

For the observatory in 1908, Robert selected and surveyed the site himself, locating it on a high point of land eighty yards from the main house that offered a clear and unobstructed view of the sky. The original telescope Lincoln had installed, a four-inch Bardon, soon proved inadequate for his needs, and in 1909, he commissioned the construction of a six-inch refracting telescope as a replacement.[54] Robert not only loved using his observatory but also was quite proud of it. He once wrote to his friend Nicholas Murray Butler, "Your train is due (R.R. time) to pass a small station at Sunderland, at 9:05 A.M. Not far beyond it, if you will look to the left in the valley, you can see on a hillside a bright spot in the trees which is my observatory. From it I look nightly into a universe wherein there is no Referendum or Recall and only one body which is at once powerful and incalculably erratic and though still influential upon the tides, it is said to be dead. I refer only to the Moon."[55]

During his years in London as U.S. minister, Robert had learned to love the English way of life and had become quite an Anglophile. Not surprisingly then, the summer estate and summer life that he ultimately created for himself in Manchester were akin to those of a member of British landed gentry: he was a gentleman farmer with hundreds of acres of land worked by hired help that he administered; the mansion, staffed by servants who lived in quarters in the house, would be familiar in any British countryside; the 1907 gardens were fashioned directly after British styles. Here Robert not only accomplished Pullman business but also indulged his pastimes of golf, astronomy, mathematics, surveying, and leisurely study.

During the summers of 1903–4, the Lincoln family spent their summers in Manchester, Vermont, staying at either the Equinox House hotel or a nearby house named the Gables, while Robert oversaw Hildene's construction. He was, in fact, an indefatigable micromanager when it came to the construction and maintenance of all his houses throughout his life; one can only speculate how the architects and builders felt about his detailed interest in every aspect of the project. One of Robert's great joys during those summers, in fact, was personally surveying his entire acreage, including all the routes for building fencing and roads for the property.[56]

In July 1904, as the house and grounds were in the middle of construction, Robert and his wife were informed that Jessie had given birth to her second child (after a stillborn birth in 1901) and their third grandchild. She named the boy Robert Todd Lincoln Beckwith, in honor of her father. Bud, as the family called the boy, was born in Riverside, Illinois, a suburb of Chicago, where Jessie and Warren Beckwith were living at that time.[57] Less than one month after the birth, Jessie packed up the baby and six-year-old Peggy and traveled the nearly nine hundred miles to Manchester, Vermont, to be with her parents. "He really is a fine little chap and is very serious in examining me and sizing me up," Robert joyfully wrote his son-in-law Charles Isham about his first meeting with his namesake.[58] Whether Jessie's trip was simply to introduce the newest family member to his grandparents or the result of marital discord between her and Warren is unclear. It is clear, however, that the Beckwith marriage was a tumultuous and ultimately unhappy one.

Less than four years earlier, in December 1900, newspapers across the country had printed stories stating that the Beckwiths secretly had gotten divorced. The news came out during a probate court hearing in Mount Pleasant, Iowa, between Mary Harlan Lincoln, as executrix of her father's estate, and her cousin James C. Whitford, who was suing for money from the estate.[59] Mary Harlan Lincoln was called to testify at the hearing but did not appear because she was in New York City caring for Jessie and Peggy, the latter having scarlet fever, and the family therefore being quarantined. It was during the hearing that the statement of a divorce, supposedly preceded by two years of separation, was made. The *Associated Press* reported that although court records could not be found in Mount Pleasant about the split, Warren Beckwith verified that a divorce was granted to Jessie on the grounds of abandonment and nonsupport.[60] Another story said, "When and where this alleged divorce was secured is not known."[61] No records of this supposed divorce ever have been found, and the story appears to have been incorrect. It seems more likely that Jessie and Warren were separated, and the newspapers wrote it up as divorced.

But the Beckwiths certainly were not happy, and shortly after Bud was born, they separated (again). Jessie and her two children went to visit Robert and Mary in Chicago in January 1905. By March, after numerous arguments with her husband over the telephone, Jessie moved out of their Riverside house, stored her belongings in the Harlan house in Mount Pleasant, and with the children moved in with her parents on Lake Shore Drive in Chicago.[62] Warren Beckwith later said the end of the marriage came in 1906 when Mary Harlan Lincoln decided to take Jessie and the children to Europe. Beckwith not only objected but also threatened divorce on grounds of desertion. "Mrs. Lincoln said I couldn't get one, but I showed her," he later said. "Mrs. Lincoln was always interfering in our marriage. She kept taking Jessie and the children away from me. Mrs. Lincoln said she was lonely since the death of her son, Abraham Lincoln II."[63]

On January 31, 1907, Warren Beckwith filed suit in district court in Mount Pleasant for a divorce from Jessie on grounds of desertion. Jessie was with her father in Augusta, Georgia, intending to wait until the Iowa courts finished the case and hopeful "that Mr. Beckwith would win."[64] A few days later, however, Jessie was called to appear at court in Mount Pleasant to finalize the case. The final proceedings occurred on February 12, 1907 (Abraham Lincoln's ninety-eighth birthday). The divorce was granted under the charged grounds of desertion, and Jessie was given custody of the children.[65] Warren never saw Peggy or Bud again. He later said that in 1917, while passing through Washington, he telephoned Jessie and asked to see the children. "She said there was no point to it, to let the past be, and that was the end of that," Beckwith said.[66]

Family letters show that Mary Harlan Lincoln, Lincoln family friend and Mount Pleasant attorney W. I. Babb, and Robert's former law partner William G. Beale handled most details of the divorce.[67] Robert, of course, knew what was happening, and he had opinions. His main belief was that the issue should be settled quickly.[68] Interestingly, despite Robert's well-known dislike of Warren Beckwith and anger over his daughter's elopement ten years previously, Beckwith later denied that he did not get along with his father-in-law: "I was a frequent visitor at his home and he was always very nice to me."[69] True or not, Robert certainly was relieved to get rid of the "scamp" he had objected to from the beginning.

As a businessman during these early years of the twentieth century, Robert Lincoln was leading the Pullman Company through some of its most successful times. During his first full year as the permanent company president, 1899–1900, the company grossed $3.3 million in increased revenue, prompting the *Chicago Tribune* to print an entire story about the "Good Year for the Pullman Company."[70] Robert told a Pullman director about the successful year, writing, "Our general business is keeping up exceedingly well. Our own earnings run in excess of the previous fiscal year," and "Our car building business has been the best we have ever had, and quite satisfactory as to profits."[71] By 1906, business was so fruitful that the company paid out $45 million in stock dividends (36 percent) to its shareholders, which was, according to Wall Street, probably the "largest distribution ever made to the stockholders of an industrial company."[72] The last big dividend dispersal of the company had been in 1898 (50 percent), and in the eight years between then and 1906, stock dividends had paid about 8 percent annually.

The 1899 Wagner deal and the 1906 dividend were two of the major events during Robert's tenure as Pullman president. Another was the introduction of the all-steel passenger car in 1907, which led to a complete change in car construction and ensured better safety and durability. Everything else was routine business for President Lincoln. He dealt with labor relations, finances, business contracts, dismantling the town of Pullman (per a previous Illinois court decision), and generally protecting and expanding the Pullman business.

Robert's correspondence and papers show that while he was a good and decent man who cared about the health and well-being of his employees, he still was upper management and a man of business. His primary concerns were the company's bottom line, its stock dividends, and its overall success. For example, the Pullman Company under President Lincoln despised labor unions and did everything in its power to prevent and destroy them, including spying on, blacklisting, and firing agitating employees. To the Pullman administrators, unionization led to grievances and endless negotiations, work stoppages, higher wages, higher costs, and reduced revenues. It was seen as undemocratic in that it allowed the employees to dictate to the company owners how to run their own business. Union busting was a policy created by George Pullman in the wake of the 1894 strike and one that Robert Lincoln supported and continued.

Pullman management quashed numerous unionization attempts after the strike, the most famous being that of the black car porters. George Pullman began hiring freed slaves as soon as the Civil War ended, recognizing a huge and available labor pool and believing that ex-slaves, due to their previous roles as servants, would make excellent car porters. Black porters assisted in the care and comfort of the passengers. They took care of luggage, shined shoes, brushed coats, turned down beds, and looked to any need or request of a Pullman passenger. For former slaves, it was a prestigious job that filled them with pride, paid them more money than they had ever seen, and allowed them the opportunity to travel the country. The porters' friendly, smiling, conscientious service was a hallmark of the Pullman Company and one that George Pullman often said he could not be successful without.

By the end of the nineteenth century, Pullman porters still were all black, but they no longer were humble ex-slaves, often meek and easily grateful for the chance to work for any sort of payment. They were now the children of slaves, free blacks who had grown up in a different world: in a more educated and self-reliant black society, in a market-based economic environment. This new generation of African Americans now saw themselves as citizens and their labor as a commodity no longer to be taken for granted or given away for a pittance.

Here and there throughout the Pullman Company, porters, after decades of witnessing white railroad workers conduct labor strikes, began to ask for higher wages and less hours. Porters were paid small salaries—between $25 and $50 per month by the turn of the century—that were supplemented with tips from the passengers. Like food-service employees today who also rely on tips to make a decent living, porters had to silently endure all sorts of degrading treatment from white passengers in order to receive their tips, a necessity for them to feed their families. Porters also often worked shifts of anywhere from twelve to thirty-six hours without a break, and any porter who fell asleep, lagged in his work, or was not fresh and crisp in appearance and demeanor would often find himself dismissed from service for failing to uphold the Pullman standard. Porters also had to purchase their own work supplies, such as shoeshine equipment, which cut into their monthly pay.

The porters' plight first received something like national attention in 1904, after the publication of a forty-six-page pamphlet titled, "Freemen Yet Slaves under 'Abe' Lincoln's Son, or Service and Wages of Pullman Porters." The booklet, circulated around the country at a cost of twenty-five cents, was written by a former Pullman porter who had been dismissed ostensibly for poor performance but apparently for unionizing. The author, C. F. Anderson, had circulated a letter to porters around the country, asking to support the creation of a committee to ask for higher wages and lower hours for porters.

"Freemen Yet Slaves" detailed the wages and working conditions of Pullman porters and contrasted them with the pay and hours of the white Pullman employees (conductors, managers, superintendents). "The Pullman Company regards the six thousand or more porters now in the service as so many slaves to be used in whatever way they can be made to bring the company the most money," Anderson said.[73] He also printed in full his attempts to redress his dismissal, particularly his correspondence to Pullman President Robert T. Lincoln, the man who was, ironically, the son of the Great Emancipator.

Anderson denied attempting to form a union but admitted writing the circular that asked for a reasonable increase in wages, less hours, better treatment, and fair hearings against dismissals—all of which the enormously rich and successful company could well afford. He also called out President Lincoln for taking his "blood money" salary of $50,000 a year while not lifting a finger to improve the lives or redress the grievances of the porters, who would have to work 150 years to accumulate what Lincoln made in one year. "The situation that confronted your father was chattel slavery," Anderson admonished. "The thing that confronts you now is industrial slavery, which is even worse in some respects than was the former."[74]

The pamphlet shows that Anderson's first letter to Lincoln seeking redress was answered by Lincoln's secretary, Charles Sweet. Sweet replied that Lincoln had personally examined the papers of Anderson's case, where he saw that the termination was made after supervisors wrote up multiple instances of Anderson's unsatisfactory performance. "Inasmuch as the operating officials do not feel that they can consistently recommend a reemployment, and as their conclusion seems to be justified by the record, it would not be practicable for Mr. Lincoln to interfere and direct a reinstatement," Sweet wrote. Anderson noted in his pamphlet that Lincoln "did not so much as sign his name to the above letter."[75]

Robert's actions here are difficult to assess without knowledge of him as a person and as an administrator. On its face, it looks like simple racism. Yet, his volumes of existing letters show that as head of the Pullman Company, and as secretary of war in the 1880s, Lincoln replied to every letter seeking a job, a raise, a promotion, a transfer, or a redress from dismissal, whether from a white man or a black man, in exactly the same way: he reviewed the documentation of each case and relied upon the determinations and recommendations of the immediate supervisor in charge of the applicant. He never, as far as his existing letters show, contradicted or acted against his subordinates' decisions if they were supported by solid reasoning and documentation.

It is interesting to note, however, that Robert did not sign the letter himself but had his secretary sign it. Robert typically did this when he was too busy to deal with matters he considered mundane or if, especially when dealing with correspondence regarding his father's legacy, he felt the letter or the writer to be particularly offensive, ignorant, or otherwise not worth his time. What category Anderson was considered is unclear. But after making the dig about comparing Robert's actions to his father's actions—something Robert always reviled and found insufferable—Robert, if he even read the pamphlet, certainly never would have given Anderson another consideration.

"Freemen Yet Slaves" was published not long after another controversy concerning African Americans and the Pullman Company. Beginning in 1900 but hitting a crescendo in 1903, a number of southern states passed "Jim Crow" laws segregating Pullman cars to prevent blacks from entering cars for whites. The famous black leader Booker T. Washington and his associates earnestly worked to overturn or prevent such laws from taking effect. Washington wrote multiple letters to Robert Lincoln seeking his support to protest such laws, but Lincoln refused all efforts, saying it might do more harm than good for him to meet with black leaders.[76] In 1904, Washington wrote that he considered Lincoln largely to blame for the segregation of sleeping cars, saying, "if he would just stand up straight there would be little trouble . . . George Pullman let the world understand that no discrimination was to be tolerated, consequently there was practically no trouble while he lived."[77]

The Pullman Company's troubles with its African American employees did not end there. But it did take ten years before the efforts of the porters to improve their situation and unionize bore greater fruit. In 1915, the issue of Pullman porters receiving less than livable wages, being dependent on tips, being, in effect, industrial slaves, was not only taken up in newspapers across the country but also by Congress. The Federal Commission on Industrial Relations called extensive hearings on the subject and called as a witness chairman of the Pullman board, Robert T. Lincoln, who testified that he thought wages should be increased, although he also defended the Pullman policy.[78]

Robert's racial travails within the Pullman Company, as well as the vociferous, public, anti-Lincoln protests and accusations of black leaders such as Booker T. Washington, Asa Philip Randolph (president of the Brotherhood of

Sleeping Car Porters Union), and Harlem Congressman Adam Clayton Powell, have led directly to subsequent charges that Robert Lincoln was a racist. Although untrue, they remain stuck to Robert's name.[79] While Lincoln clearly did not actively campaign for civil rights or racial equality as these leaders desired, neither did he actively practice racism as a man or an executive. His management style and policy both in the War Department and at the Pullman Company show he was a delegator. He relied upon the recommendations and actions of his supervisory subordinates and upon the written records related to a given case and acted or refused to act accordingly.[80]

During the fourteen years of Lincoln's presidency, Pullman business flourished. The company achieved increased revenues by an average of $1 million to $5 million every year except one. The one down year, 1908, was a loss of $500,000 and necessitated a layoff of about five thousand employees—the result of the financial panic of 1907.[81]

While in charge of Pullman, Robert also continued his other business endeavors. He remained on the board of directors for the Commonwealth Electric and Edison Electric (later consolidated into Commonwealth Edison) companies, Michigan Telephone, Chicago Telephone, Central Union Telephone Company, Commercial National Bank of Chicago, and the Pullman Savings and Loan Bank. He augmented also his investment portfolio by purchasing thousands of shares of stock in the National Biscuit Company, founded in Chicago in 1898 (now Nabisco), from which he earned large dividends.

Robert also was on the board of directors for the Equitable Life Assurance Society, one of the biggest insurance companies in the country.[82] During an internecine management battle for control of the company in 1905, Robert's respected reputation as a businessman caused him to be one of the leading names mentioned to become the new chairman of the board of directors. "He has been considered an independent in the factional fight. He is a man of national reputation, and many of the directors think he would be the man to bring peace to the society," commented one newspaper.[83] Due to his current position as president of Pullman, as well as his poor health, Robert immediately announced that "under no circumstances" would he accept such a position.[84] Two days later, he joined with a group of other directors and resigned his position on the board in objection to multiple issues created by the factional dispute. "I do not intend to have anything more to do with [the Equitable's] affairs," he wrote.[85]

Due to his numerous business endeavors and successes, Robert Lincoln increasingly became identified during these years as a "captain of industry" and was labeled as such in the newspapers. For example, when Prince Henry of Prussia—brother of the German Emperor—visited America in February

1902, he was hosted by the one hundred American captains of industry. Among the guests were men named Morgan, Rockefeller, Vanderbilt, Field, Armour, Edison, Tesla, Havemeyer, Westinghouse, Schwab, and Robert T. Lincoln. Robert, along with Mamie and Linc, also accompanied the prince to the Lincoln monument in Lincoln Park in Chicago, where Henry laid a wreath at the foot of the statue to honor the Great Emancipator.[86]

Robert's self-made reputation as a businessman still did not diminish his popularity as a potential politician. He did not participate in the presidential election of 1900, although he was mentioned as a possible running mate for President McKinley. Of course, Lincoln wanted none of it and told one supporter, "I do not know anything that would make me more unhappy than the nomination for a public office."[87]

Lincoln still and always was an ardent Republican, not just personally but professionally. In his capacity as president of the Pullman Company, he oversaw corporate contributions to support the work of the Republican National Committee and assisted prominent party members in their travel needs to yearly nominating conventions. He appears to have especially disliked the Democrat Party under the leadership of its 1896 and 1900 presidential nominee, William Jennings Bryan. "There is more Bryanism out here than is comfortable," Lincoln wrote from Chicago shortly before the 1900 election. "It would be appalling if, by any inertness [by the Republicans], the country was turned over to Bryan and his friends."[88]

In 1904, Robert did make a few political appearances but not many. President Roosevelt that year was nominated to run in his own right, and Lincoln's name was mentioned as a potential nominee for the second place on the ticket. During the Republican National Convention in June 1904, Robert's secretary told him in a letter that Pullman special counsel John S. Runnels "had saved you at least a dozen times since Saturday afternoon from being nominated vice president."[89]

As every year of the new century advanced, Robert's health continued to fluctuate but did not readily improve. Throughout his entire adult life, Robert took his family for a vacation every summer out east, typically to the New Hampshire or New Jersey seashore, and then beginning in 1903 to Manchester, Vermont. After his health turned, Robert began to leave Chicago every winter—generally for one month from mid-February to mid-March—either west to California or south to Augusta, Georgia, in order to recoup his health through warm weather, avoidance of work, and the physical activity of golf. He also traveled to various locations around the country whenever his doctor told him he needed to get away.

In May 1900, Robert declared that his health had been "restored" after suffering for years from his 1897 attack of nervous dyspepsia.[90] In January 1901, however, he suffered a relapse, and in October of that year, he was complaining of digestive trouble and rheumatism in his back in addition to his previous symptoms.[91] A string of deaths of people close to Robert also hindered his progress and contributed to his occasional bouts of mild depression. In February 1902, his friend Edward Isham died. In October 1902, his longtime friend John A. Dillon, whom Robert had known since college, died. Robert was "deeply grieved" by the news. He attended the funeral in St. Louis and gave complimentary Pullman car passes to Dillon's entire family to travel from Maine to Boston and then to St. Louis.[92]

In 1905, Thomas Wickes, Pullman Company vice president, also died, which not only grieved Robert but also increased his nervousness and stress by increasing his workload.[93] The entire year of 1905 was one of worsening nerves for Robert, but it reached a culmination with the death of Robert's longtime friend and golfing partner Marshall Field at the turn of the new year. Robert called it "a great affliction" and was so affected that his doctor ordered him to take a vacation. Robert went to Augusta, Georgia, where he was "neglecting all business," but depressed at the loss of his golfing partner, he also "attempted no recreation," apparently giving in to a bout of depression.[94] The effects of the death may have been worsened by feelings of guilt because Robert had gone golfing with Field in the snow; later Field contracted pneumonia, which at the time people believed was due to exposure to cold and wet.[95]

In spring 1908, Robert wrote to an old acquaintance, "I hope you are standing your seventy-three years better than I am standing my sixty-five. I have not yet been able to get out of the business harness entirely, but do get away as much as I can from work and play golf and make the acquaintance of my grandchildren."[96] That fall, he suffered from a "bilious attack," which was "very disagreeable to me, and makes me disagreeable to everyone."[97]

One of the major cares on Robert's mind and affecting his health during these years was his responsibility as steward and guardian of his father's legacy. Every year, a flood of letters and requests for some piece of the Lincoln legacy, some information or assistance, some attendance or contribution in his father's honor, deluged Robert. His private secretary, Charles Sweet, assisted him in his responses, but it was a daunting task because Robert made a conscientious effort to answer every piece of correspondence concerning his father.

As the years passed, as the books, the articles, the statues, and the paintings about his father multiplied, as President Lincoln's reputation and legend soared to unparalleled heights, Robert was always painfully aware of the inexorable approach of the centennial of his father's birth in 1909. Robert admitted in 1908 to his father's old White House secretary, William O. Stoddard, that he was "dreading" the upcoming year: "I am not by any means as well as I should like to be, and I am already beginning to receive a good many letters asking information which it takes a good deal of trouble to give sometimes, and making a good many requests with which it is very difficult to comply."[98]

Robert turned down scores of invitations to speak or attend various centennial celebrations, continuing his lifelong policy. But he also knew that 1909 was a landmark year that he could not ignore. So Robert Lincoln decided to make two exceptions to his long-held rule about not appearing at events in honor of his father. He agreed to attend the centennial celebration at his father's family home in Springfield, Illinois, and the dedication of a monument at his father's birthplace in Hodgenville, Kentucky. Both events impressed and affected him tremendously.

23

"My Filial Gratitude Cannot Find Adequate Expression"

Today, Abraham Lincoln generally is considered by laypeople and scholars alike to be the greatest president in American history. But this was not always so. George Washington, the "father of the country," was universally held to be the greatest for more than one hundred years after his death in 1799. The reputation and esteem of the martyred Lincoln continually ascended with each passing year after his assassination, but he rarely topped Washington in respect or popularity. This all changed in 1909, after the celebration of the centennial of Lincoln's birth. Just as Lincoln's death brought the country together in a shared grief, so his centennial again united America in a national pride. "Lincoln's centennial intensified his memory by encasing it in ritual activities of unprecedented scale," sociologist Barry Schwartz writes. "This ritual process established Lincoln's reputation after his assassination and revitalized it forty-four years later."[1] Or as one commentator of the day more simply remarked, "The nation hasn't felt this deeply since Lincoln's death."[2]

Although the Congress failed to create a commission to organize a national celebration of Lincoln's one hundredth birthday, local, regional, and state governments across America organized their own. Schools and businesses closed, and ceremonies, banquets, and parades were held in what became an unofficial national holiday that year. The biggest celebrations were naturally held in the largest cities, including Washington, D.C., Boston, New York, Cincinnati, Denver, and Philadelphia. There were fifty public meetings in Chicago alone, including a speech by Princeton University President (and future U.S. president) Woodrow Wilson. Vice President Charles W. Fairbanks spoke in Pittsburgh, Vice President–elect James S. Sherman spoke in Harrisburg, President-elect William Howard Taft spoke in New Orleans, and President Theodore Roosevelt spoke and laid the cornerstone to the new Lincoln memorial in Hodgenville, Kentucky, Abraham Lincoln's birthplace.

The eyes of the nation, of course, were centered on the celebrations scheduled in Lincoln's hometown of Springfield, Illinois. Preparations for the event had begun in October 1907, when the Illinois House and Senate passed resolutions to appoint a commission to make the arrangements.[3] It was to be a daylong celebration with multiple happenings around the city. The major events were to be lunch and dinner meetings with panegyrics to Lincoln given by the great orator William Jennings Bryan, English Ambassador James Bryce, French Ambassador Jean Jules Jusserand, and U.S. Senator Jonathan P. Dolliver. Religious services were to be held at Lincoln's old church; a memorial tablet was to be placed at Lincoln's old law office; a reception was to be held at Lincoln's old home; and a reverent visit paid to Lincoln's tomb.[4] For many people, the most impressive arrangement of the entire day was the fact that Abraham Lincoln's only surviving son, Robert T. Lincoln, a man who, for forty-four years, consistently avoided such events, would be present.

Every day of his life, Robert Lincoln received letters, inquiries, invitations, books, poems, articles, or something regarding his father. The closer 1909 approached, the more the interest in Abraham Lincoln's legend and legacy increased—and the bulkier Robert's incoming mail became. Some of the most common letters came from elementary-school principals, teachers, classrooms, students, and parents. They asked Robert to visit, to speak, to share stories, or, most frequently, to share lessons offered by his father's life. That his father had become an interest and an inspiration to children filled Robert Lincoln with a joy and a pride that he often responded was "not possible for me to adequately express."[5] Robert never visited or spoke at schools (again because if he went to one, he felt obligated to go to them all), but he always responded and typically offered the children one lesson from his father's life that Robert felt was the most important: "the possibility of advancement from the most obscure beginning to even the highest place for a citizen of our country who is faithful to the principles on which the institutions are founded."[6]

Robert also received numerous letters by schoolchildren concerning his father's Gettysburg Address, which was one of the main facets of his life they studied. Robert took great pleasure in responding to their inquiries by sending them a copy of John G. Nicolay's 1894 article titled "Lincoln's Gettysburg Address," which Robert felt to be the definitive explanation of the speech's composition and delivery and which he therefore had reprinted as a pamphlet in 1908 at his own expense for his personal use.[7] In fact, the increased general interest in the Gettysburg Address starting in 1908, as well as Robert

Lincoln's admiration for it, caused Robert to contribute to two endeavors that significantly affected the way both historians and everyday Americans viewed the speech.

In preparation for the 1909 anniversary, Robert loaned a number of his father's original manuscripts to Columbia University and to the Chicago Historical Society for their respective centennial exhibits.[8] One item that had been mentioned, and Robert himself had considered as "extraordinarily interesting" to possibly loan to the Columbia exhibit or to be published in *Century* magazine, was the original delivery copy of the Gettysburg Address. The only problem was that Robert did not have it in his father's papers in his possession. He thought Helen Nicolay, John Nicolay's daughter, owned it, but she could not find it either. After extensive searching by both Robert and Helen throughout November 1908, they decided it either was lost or stolen from her possession. Then in December, John Hay's widow, Clara, discovered a copy in her husband's papers that she had no idea was there.

What turned out to be a shock to everyone was that the Hay copy was not the "original" copy of the address that John Nicolay had owned but was something completely unknown. It was determined to be a draft of a revision that Lincoln had made in Washington after delivering the speech in Gettysburg. Despite the excitement of this discovery, the Nicolay copy still was missing, and Mrs. Hay said it was not in her possession. It was nearly seven years later, after Mrs. Hay had died, when Robert was informed by a friend that John Hay's daughter, Alice Hay Longworth, was telling people she owned the original (Nicolay) manuscript. One month later, her brother Clarence said his family owned "two copies" of the Gettysburg Address.

Robert decided to investigate and scheduled a meeting with Alice Longworth. No record of the meeting is known to exist, but shortly thereafter, Mrs. Longworth suddenly "discovered" the Nicolay copy in her family's possession and claimed she had no idea it was there. This manuscript technically belonged to Helen Nicolay, but rather than argue about ownership of Lincoln manuscripts, the Hay and Nicolay heirs donated both copies to the Library of Congress in 1916. As Martin P. Johnson, who wrote a definitive account of these events, correctly states, "Robert Todd Lincoln's search for the Gettysburg Address had resulted not only in the recovery of the 'original manuscript,' but the re-discovery of the Hay draft, which no one in 1908 . . . even knew existed."[9] It also could be said that by ferreting out the embarrassing truth about who owned which copy of the Gettysburg Address, which resulted in a desire by both the Hay and Nicolay families to avoid a battle over ownership, Robert Lincoln (however inadvertently) secured both copies' donation to the Library of Congress.

Robert's second historical impact regarding the Gettysburg Address concerned which draft of the speech would be considered the official version used by the U.S. government—in effect, which draft would be read by millions of Americans. There were at that time, as today, five copies of the speech in Lincoln's own handwriting known to exist: the Nicolay and Hay copies, a copy written out for the 1863 Gettysburg ceremony's main orator, Edward Everett, and two copies written for historian George Bancroft to be included in his book *Autograph Leaves of Our Country's Authors* (the first was unusable, and a second was requested), which was sold at the 1864 Baltimore Sanitary Fair for soldier relief. The final Bancroft copy, which today is called the Bliss copy and hangs in the White House, is the most commonly reproduced version of the speech.

In early 1909, the War Department had determined to erect at Gettysburg National Cemetery—and eventually in every national military park and national cemetery in the country—a bronze tablet containing the text of Lincoln's address. When Robert Lincoln learned of this in April 1909, he was informed that it was the Hay copy that was to be used. Robert, at age sixty-six more than ever the hagiographer intent to portray the purest version of his father, immediately telegraphed the quartermaster general of the army, asking him to delay work on the tablet, then wrote him a lengthy letter stating that the Hay copy, while authentic, was a mere draft and should not be used.[10] He urged instead that the second Bancroft copy be substituted: "The Baltimore Fair version represents my father's last and best thought as to the address, and the corrections in it were legitimate for the author, and I think there is no doubt they improve the version written out for Col. Hay."[11]

It turns out that the quartermaster general had intended all along to use the Baltimore Fair version, but his staff mistakenly called it the Hay copy. A draft of the proposed tablet was sent to Robert, which he noticed was his preferred version but which contained a punctuation error. He suggested that it be fixed.[12]

In a similar vein and during the same period, Robert also contributed his opinions and efforts to the location of the original 1864 letter from his father to Lydia Bixby. The Bixby letter, a message of condolence to a widow whose five sons supposedly died fighting for the Union during the war, is considered one of Abraham Lincoln's greatest literary legacies.[13] While copies of the Bixby letter were prevalent in 1909, the location of the original was unknown. It is now known that Mrs. Bixby was a Southern sympathizer, and upon receiving President Lincoln's letter, she tore it up and threw it in the trash.[14] During the centennial, the Lincoln exhibit at Columbia University contained a copy of the letter. Robert wrote to the Columbia librarian, James Canfield, and asked if it was the original and if so, who owned it. "I have long been desirous of what has become of the original 'Bixby' letter, which I regard very highly," Robert wrote.[15]

Robert actually had begun looking for the original Bixby letter sometime between September 1901 and January 1902, after he received lithograph copies from two different sources.[16] During that time, he looked at various copies of the letter in museums, was approached by a man (who turned out to be a charlatan) trying to sell the "original," and consulted John Hay about the letter's origins. Robert's efforts come up empty; and in 1909, Canfield said he could shed no light on the mystery.[17]

Robert's efforts here sound rather innocuous, but in the context of what has become a heated debate over the authenticity of the Bixby letter, his actions and opinions turn out to be revelatory. Starting in the 1920s, rumors began swirling that Abraham Lincoln did not write the Bixby letter at all, but that his secretary Hay actually was the author. In 1999, historian Michael Burlingame published what appeared to be definitive evidence that Hay was indeed the author.[18] A recent uncovering of numerous letters by Robert Lincoln about the Bixby letter, however, not only shows that Robert knew his father wrote it but proves that John Hay did not.[19]

The correspondence occurred in 1917 between Robert Lincoln and historian Isaac Markens, when Markens wrote to Lincoln to inquire about the original Bixby letter. Robert explained his previous efforts to locate the original near the turn of the century. Amid the half-dozen letters to Markens that Robert wrote on the subject, the "smoking gun" was Robert's statement that Hay had told him he did not write the letter:

> Your suggestion that neither Nicolay nor Hay probably had any special knowledge of the letter at the time is correct. *Hay himself told me so*; when I took the matter up Nicolay had died and it was he who had compiled the collection of papers. It is entirely possible that neither of them knew of the letter at all; my father had no letter books and copies of his letters and documents were only made in special cases, many such copies being in the papers I now have, mostly drafts in his own hand; it is entirely possible that my father wrote this letter at his desk, folded it, addressed it and gave it to General [William] Shouler [adjutant general of the Commonwealth of Massachusetts, who delivered it to Mrs. Bixby] without anybody else about him knowing about it.[20]

When the issue of the location of the original Bixby letter came up again in a *New York Times* article in 1925, instituting a worldwide search for the document, Robert, age eighty-two, made clear his belief who the author was. In response to multiple letters asking for his comments or assistance, Robert refused to get involved in the issue, but he did state, through his personal secretary, "there can be no question but that his father wrote [the Bixby letter]."[21]

Of course, Robert dealt with numerous other issues regarding his father's life and legacy due to the approach of the centennial year. Temperance advocates often asked him his father's position on alcohol, to which Robert always replied that his father did not imbibe. "I never saw him use spirituous liquors, and I do not think that he ever did so," he once explained in detail. "I have seen him take a taste of wine at his own dinner table in Washington, but only once or twice, and I am sure it was no pleasure to him. He never gave me any paternal teaching upon the subject other than by his example."[22] Another common question was whether or not his father was a Spiritualist, claims of which started at the end of the nineteenth century.[23] Robert, who believed Spiritualism a sham, vehemently denied the idea, both to the press and, later, to the famous magician and psychic investigator Harry Houdini.[24] In 1909, Robert replied to an inquiry about southern Reconstruction after the Civil War, by stating it would have been "very different and more happy" had his father lived:

> Of course I myself think this is true, because I know, as you know, that his first wish was a complete and friendly restoration of the Union, and that in his work he would have brought no animosities of his own, for he had none, and that on some of the questions which gave the greatest trouble in the south during the reconstruction period, and are still doing so, his personal views were not of the radical nature which perhaps gave the most trouble. He would have found it at the best a most difficult task, and no one can tell how great his success would have been.[25]

One of Robert's more famous actions during this time was to allow the Lincoln National Life Insurance Company of Fort Wayne, Indiana, to use a portrait of Abraham Lincoln as its emblem. Robert—a probusiness Republican to his core—not only had "no objection" to the idea but also sent the company one of his favorite photos of his father for its use.[26]

A few years earlier, he had presented a portrait of his father to the state of Mississippi to be hung in the new state capitol building—an action that not only caused controversy but also significantly increased the number of portrait requests in Robert's incoming mail.[27] The deluge of requests became so great—from libraries, historical societies, colleges, soldiers' homes, cities, state capitals, and Lincoln clubs—that he had to refuse nearly every one. "Such things are naturally progressive," Robert explained to one correspondent, "and my experience has shown that whenever I have felt justified in sending a picture, publicity has very soon followed, the result being a new grist of requests, and the list has gone far beyond my power of supply."[28] One of the few exceptions he made was to his old alma mater, Phillips Exeter Academy, to which he presented a portrait of his father and two autograph letters in 1909.[29]

Among the hundreds—perhaps thousands—of various requests Robert received every year, his greatest and most sought after contribution was his personal presence. "I am having an almost endless correspondence on the subject from all parts of the United States," he wrote to one such invitation in January 1909.[30] In the years leading up to 1909, Robert consistently refused to attend celebrations honoring his father, especially ones held on February 12.[31] He had decided shortly after his father's death that it would be more appropriate and honorable to leave public expressions about his father to other people. He also generally disliked the notion of accepting some invitations but refusing others, and as the years passed, he realized that every accepted invitation would lead to dozens, perhaps hundreds, more. His sense of duty, respect, and egalitarianism prompted his belief that he should either accept every invitation he received or none. His desire to live his own life and not consume himself with his father's legacy made the final decision relatively simple. He could not be everywhere and please everyone.

But Robert knew that 1909 would be different. "It really does seem that the general estimation of [my father] and his work grows in value every year," he had commented in 1905.[32] Robert recognized that his father's memory had reached a national apotheosis by the centennial, so the last Lincoln son decided that year to make two exceptions to his long-standing rule of avoiding public celebrations.

Robert had determined that he would spend his father's one hundredth birthday, February 12, 1909, in his old hometown of Springfield, Illinois. The Lincoln Centennial Association of Illinois had invited him in early January to participate in the celebration. Robert accepted on the condition that he would not be expected to speak or take any part in the day's activities, "that my part in them shall be absolutely limited to my personal presence."[33] This condition was not only in keeping with Robert's policy of not publicly speaking about his father but also because of his poor physical health at age sixty-five and the anxiety he felt in large crowds.

It was arranged, therefore, that Robert, his wife, and a group of people he personally invited to travel with him would journey from Chicago to Springfield the night of February 11, in Lincoln's private Pullman car.[34] The Lincolns would spend the night in their car and have breakfast there as well before attending the day's events. "He does not always feel well early in the morning, and of course the day will be a peculiarly trying one for him," his secretary explained about the morning plans. It was arranged that Robert would attend the official luncheon at the Illini Country Club in the afternoon, the public meeting at the Tabernacle, and the formal banquet at the Springfield Armory in the evening. He asked that he be permitted to visit his father's tomb and his old home at Eighth and Jackson Streets by himself and not as part of the official ceremonies at each location, which was agreed by the committee.[35]

While such limitations may seem as though Robert Lincoln was unhappy, wary, or even reluctant about the event, such was not the case. He actually contributed to the planning in multiple ways. When the chairman of the centennial association's transportation committee asked for reduced Pullman rates for the international visitors to travel to and from Washington D.C., the Pullman Company refused because it was against policy. Robert could not grant an exception, so instead he personally paid for the transportation costs in question, "supposing that there will be plenty of need for all the funds of the Association at Springfield." He requested anonymity, however, in his donation.[36] English Ambassador Bryce was to be in Chicago prior to attending the centennial celebration, and Robert arranged and rearranged his own plans in order for Bryce and him to travel to Springfield together.[37] Finally, when the main orator for the celebration, William Jennings Bryan, sent Robert an advance copy of his speech, Robert read it over and offered comment.[38]

February 12, 1909, was a windy, chilly, overcast day in Springfield, but the celebratory spirits in the town were not dampened. The city effloresced with flags and bunting and pictures of Abraham Lincoln everywhere. Tens of thousands of people thronged the streets that the Great Emancipator once walked. Amid the myriad events occurring that day, the official celebration began with a pilgrimage to the old Lincoln Home, then from there past his old church, past his law office, past the courthouse where he practiced law, and finally ended at the Lincoln tomb, where wizened Civil War soldiers stood guard with bayonets. At every associated Lincoln site were various presentations, speeches, meetings, tree plantings, and plaque dedications.

The two main events of the celebration were the mass public meeting at the city Tabernacle in the afternoon and the dinner banquet in the evening. The Tabernacle was crammed with eight thousand people—with thousands more turned away—who listened to addresses by Bryan and U.S. Senator Dolliver, and informal remarks by French Ambassador Jusserand and English Ambassador Bryce. More than seven hundred men attended the evening banquet at the State Armory, including the governor, state officers, and politicians and distinguished guests from across the country. Visitor galleries on the second level were thronged with fifteen hundred spectators. (Ironically, blacks were neither invited nor allowed to attend and so held their own celebration ceremony at the St. Paul's church.) Ambassadors Jusserand and Bryce gave the main addresses of the evening, with informal remarks made by Bryan and

Dolliver. Although only three months earlier Robert had commented, "So much has been written and spoken of my father, that it seems to me an almost hopeless task for anybody to try to say anything new, or to say the old things over again in a better way than has already been done," he actually was quite impressed by the originality of Bryan's speech on "Lincoln as an Orator."[39]

Robert Lincoln's presence that day was, of course, noticed by all the spectators and newspaper reporters in attendance, although no one commented on the fact that he did not speak or play any public role in the day's events. It was widely reported, however, that the most impressive moment of the entire day was when Robert paid his respects at the Lincoln tomb. He "stood beside the sarcophagus in which the body of his father rests, and bowed his head with tear-dimmed eyes in silent meditation," according to newspapers.[40] *Outlook* magazine stated that the scene of Robert at his father's grave "gave the day a touch of that intimate affection in which Lincoln is held."[41]

Another touching and impressive moment was Robert's visit to his old home at the corner of Eighth and Jackson Streets. He greeted his cousins Albert Edwards and Josephine Edwards, who were the state-appointed caretakers, and asked to be shown the room he slept in as a boy. "In the sacred presence of memory he was left alone in the room and remained there some time," noted the local newspaper, "friends keeping intruders from venturing inside to disturb whatever thought the visit recalled to his mind."[42] Imagine the swirl of images and memories and feelings the sixty-five-year-old Robert must have felt as he walked through the old house he had not seen in more than twenty years. It must have been with a dampened—perhaps even forlorn—pleasure that he recalled his carefree childhood days when his father and brothers were alive and his mother was young and happy.

Even though Robert found himself "pretty well worn out" by the centennial and the weeks leading up to it, he was forever glad that he had attended the Springfield celebration. "Nothing could have been more splendid or more perfect than the arrangements at Springfield on the 12th," he wrote one week after the event. "It was a beautiful tribute to my father and I am very grateful for it."[43]

Of course, Springfield was only one among hundreds of Lincoln celebrations that day in 1909, and Robert was overwhelmed with emotion at the thought of them all. He told one friend, "They were, of course, most deeply gratifying to me, and I think, have been of real public use throughout the country."[44] This use, Robert believed, was in helping to bring the country more fully together even though the Civil War was more than forty years in the past. He was particularly moved by Lincoln birthday celebrations in the south, of which there were many, which showed "how completely the great wish of my father's heart, and the object of his last years have been reached, and it is very affecting to me."[45]

Robert said that of all the southern services on February 12, the most poignant to him was at Trinity Church in Atlanta, Georgia. "None of the occurrences of last week have affected me so much as this meeting, as an indication of the realization of the hopes which I think guided every act of [my father] while President," Robert wrote to that day's speaker, Reverend James W. Lee. "It is dramatic that this proof should come from a City destroyed by one of the armies under his supreme command and be presented by Confederate soldiers listening with approval to the address of such eloquence and patriotic feeling as yours. As his son I am very gratified for the meeting and more than gratified for your distinguished part in it."[46] Similarly, Robert wrote to a group of former Confederates in Augusta, Georgia, after a southern Lincoln celebration there in February 1904, "I take this as proof most grateful to myself that whatever may have been the differences of long ago times, you now believe that [my father] had at heart only the good of our nation; that he wished equally the prosperity of the South and the North, making as he always phrased it, our Common Country. I wish he could see, as I do, how well realized are his ardent hopes for the oblivion of the old animosities."[47]

Four months after the Springfield centennial celebration, Robert again eschewed his typical nonparticipation in Lincoln events and attended a ceremony in Hodgenville, Kentucky, to dedicate a statue to the memory of his father. Hodgenville was, of course, Abraham Lincoln's birthplace; and on February 12, 1909, President Roosevelt had spoken at the Lincoln Farm there and laid the cornerstone for a monument. On May 31, 1909, Robert attended the ceremony in the town square of Hodgenville, about two miles distant from the Lincoln farm, for the unveiling. His Aunt Emily Todd Helm was to pull the cord to unveil the statue.

Robert had accepted the invitation for the event in mid-May, on the condition, just like the Springfield celebration in February, that he not be expected to participate in the program in any way other than his presence.[48] He planned to travel in his private Pullman car, first to Louisville, to pick up his Aunt Emily and assorted cousins, a few Kentucky friends, and the speaker of the day, Henry Watterson, a former Confederate newspaper editor, and from there on to Hodgenville.[49] Robert was to sit on the speaker's platform and listen to the perorations of the afternoon, then travel to the Lincoln farm to see for the first time his father's birthplace.

The day was so hot and sunny, and the crowd of thousands so large, that once Watterson ended his speech around noon, Robert Lincoln nearly collapsed. According to newspaper reports, Robert felt weak and distressed, and Watterson caught him and assisted him off the platform and to Robert's private car. It was reported that Lincoln said his left side went numb, and he feared paralysis. After resting for a few hours, during which Robert missed the pilgrimage to the Lincoln farm, he and his party left Hodgenville for Louisville, and upon their arrival, Robert felt entirely recuperated.[50]

The newspaper reports of Robert Lincoln being "overcome" by the heat during the ceremony have led historians to wonder whether the not-always-healthy sixty-five-year-old Lincoln suffered some sort of severe illness or even stroke that day. He did not. The issue was not only the heat but also the chronic anxiety he suffered when surrounded by large crowds, which, as he said many times, often made him dizzy.[51] The nationwide reports of his "collapse" annoyed him as evidence that, as always, the media could not be trusted to report events accurately. "Disregard newspaper report my illness Kentucky yesterday," Robert telegraphed his wife at Hildene. "Great heat and crowd made me unpleasantly dizzy for a few moments but I recovered in the car, and am as well as ever this morning."[52] He told another correspondent that his "little mishap" at Hodgenville was only temporary, and "perhaps not unnatural in view of the impressiveness of the occasion, the great crowd, and the intense heat."[53] Despite his need to retreat out of the heat and his inability to see the Lincoln farm that day, Robert found the event a most impressive and memorable occasion.[54]

Once the major events of the Lincoln centennial year were accomplished, Robert Lincoln was relieved. He often mentioned how overwhelming was the amount of correspondence and invitations he received that year; and he hoped, and rather somewhat believed, that, other than the disposition of his father's papers still in his possession, his public participation in events regarding his father would be over from then on. And for a while they were. But then, eight years later, in 1917, Robert found himself so incensed over one artist's portrayal of his father that he, for the first and only time in his life, personally unleashed a vociferous public campaign against it.

At issue was a statue of Abraham Lincoln by sculptor George Gray Barnard. Barnard, a former student of August Rodin, widely was considered America's greatest living sculptor. He had been commissioned in 1910 by Charles P. Taft, the brother of former President Taft, to create a Lincoln statue for a public park in Cincinnati, Ohio. The unveiling of the statue occurred on March 31, 1917, but once the statue was completed in late 1916, it was exhibited in New York City.

Barnard's bronze sculpture was twice the size of life. It depicted a full-body Lincoln from about 1858, standing straight, wearing worn, wrinkled, ill-fitting clothing, with knobby, coarse, veined hands folded over its stomach; the face was unbearded, the hair tussled, the neck elongated, and the feet overly large.

Barnard wanted to depict Lincoln not as a great statesman but as a common man of clay, as "the mighty man who grew from out the soil and the hardships of earth," as he later declared.[55] He believed the "imaginary," purified Lincoln (such as Robert espoused) was an insult to America and to democracy. Barnard therefore used as his model a forty-year-old Kentuckian who had lived on a farm and split rails his entire life.

Barnard's sculptured Lincoln—similar to William H. Herndon's literary Lincoln—was as completely rural and coarse, even feral, as the creator intended. Its uniqueness and distinctiveness in this way caused it to be both lauded and criticized in its representation of the man who had by then transcended humanity and become a secular godhead of Democracy. In his dedicatory address at the unveiling ceremony, former President Taft declared that Barnard had successfully captured in his sculpture "the contrast between the pure soul and the commanding intellect of one who belongs to the ages, and the habit, and the garb of his origin and his life among the plain people—a profound lesson in democracy and its highest possibility."[56] Former President Roosevelt also praised Barnard's creation as a "unique" statue, "full of life," that finally revealed the true Lincoln to the world.[57]

Only nine days before he gave his address in Cincinnati, President Taft had received a letter from his friend Robert T. Lincoln expressing "great concern" about the statue and asking for Taft's assistance. Robert had viewed photographs of the Barnard statue that winter and was horrified by what he saw. He considered it "a monstrous figure which is grotesque as a likeness of President Lincoln and defamatory as an effigy." Robert had nothing to say about the statue being placed in Cincinnati, but, he told Taft, he had recently learned of a proposition to place copies of it in London and Paris as gifts from Charles P. Taft. Robert had never met the president's brother, and he therefore wrote to his friend "to beg you on my account to intercede with him" and convince him to abandon the project. "That my father should be represented in those two great cities by such a work as that of which I am writing to you, would be a cause of sorrow to me personally, the greatness of which I will not attempt to describe," Robert wrote.[58] Taft responded that he was "greatly distressed" by his friend's letter, but he disagreed with Robert's opinion and the project was too far advanced to be stopped.[59]

Had the Barnard statue not been chosen to be placed in London and Paris, the controversy over its artistic vision probably never would have occurred. Originally, a replica of the Augustus Saint-Gaudens statue in Lincoln Park, Chicago, was to be placed in those cities. This had been decided by an international commission formed to celebrate one hundred years of peace between the United States and Great Britain. The outbreak of World War I had suspended the commemorative effort, and when the issue came up again after 1914, no money was available to purchase a Saint-Gaudens replica. When Charles Taft was informed of the situation, he offered to donate replicas of the Barnard statue to be used instead, which both the American and British committees accepted.[60] When news of this substitution became public, the controversy began.

Robert Lincoln's letter to President Taft was only the opening salvo in his effort to stop the Barnard statue from being placed in London and Paris. He began contacting all the important people he knew in politics, art, and publishing to enlist them in his cause. One of his most effective allies became F. Wellington Ruckstuhl, editor of *Art World* magazine. Ruckstuhl had jumped into the fray on his own in his June issue with a detailed critique and condemnation of the statue and a suggestion that Barnard take it down and start over.[61] In August, he again attacked the statue, calling it, among other things, "a libel on Lincoln against which the whole nation should enter a protest."[62] Numerous other publications made similar statements. The *New York Times*, for example, called the Barnard statue "not only plain, but grotesque." It editorialized that Barnard's Lincoln was "a long-suffering peasant, crushed by adversity. His pose is ungainly, the figure lacks dignity, and the huge hands crossed over the stomach suggest that all is not well with his digestion. The largeness of both hands and feet is unduly exaggerated."[63]

Ruckstuhl sent a copy of his June and August editorials to Robert Lincoln and enclosed a letter asking Robert's personal feelings on the matter. Robert responded enthusiastically and included a copy of his letter to President Taft, and letters of condemnation of the statue by his childhood friend Clinton Conkling (also endorsed by Springfield, Illinois, banker John W. Bunn) and former U.S. Ambassador to Great Britain Joseph Choate, all of whom had known Abraham Lincoln. Ruckstuhl printed these letters, along with numerous other letters against the statue and his own call to his readers to "follow the lead of Mr. Robert Lincoln" and protest against the statue, in his October issue of *Art World*.[64]

Part of Robert Lincoln's fight against the Barnard statue was in printing and distributing a package of anti-Barnard papers he prepared. The entire contents of his package are unclear, but it is known that it included Robert's letter to President Taft, a letter from Conkling to Robert Lincoln (separate from the letter mentioned above) in which Conkling explained the opposition in Springfield, Illinois, to the Barnard statue and named six specific men who knew Abraham Lincoln and why they disapproved.[65] The package probably also included other testimonies against the statue from people who knew Abraham Lincoln or were great students of his image and life, such as the great collector of Lincolniana and Lincoln photographs Frederick Hill Meserve, and various supporting newspaper and magazine clippings.[66] Existing correspondence proves that Robert sent this package to the London Board of Works, the entity responsible for accepting the statue and having it erected; to the highly influential Alfred Lord Northcliffe, publisher of the London *Times* and the London *Daily Mail*; and to U.S. Ambassador to London Walter Hines Page, who then forwarded it to the British Foreign Office. Robert undoubtedly also sent the package to various artists, politicians, magazines, and newspapers around the country. Unlike Robert's lifelong public reticence to speak out about his father, in his fight against the Barnard statue, as he told Ruckstuhl, "I am making no secret of my efforts."[67]

These efforts were highly successful, and his opinions on the statue and his letter to President Taft were reported on and reprinted in news publications across the country. Multiple people, organizations, and newspapers felt that whatever anyone's personal opinion of the statue, the fact that Abraham Lincoln's son opposed it was enough reason to prevent its erection overseas. In addition to *Art World*, the *Washington Post* and London *Times* mentioned Robert's opposition, the *American Magazine of Art* said Robert's right to criticize and object to the statue was "undisputed," and respected art critic George L. Raymond called it a "strange inconsiderateness" and "discourtesy" to Robert Lincoln to erect the Barnard statue against his opposition.[68]

Many who supported and admired the Barnard statue believed the adverse criticism came from those who had not seen the actual bronze in person, or, as the *American Review of Reviews* editorialized, their judgments were "based upon the exceedingly faulty photographs which distort the surface planes of the figure."[69] When historian Isaac Markens made a similar intimation to Robert Lincoln and asked if the son had seen the statue, Lincoln replied, "I am glad to tell you that I have never seen the beastly thing and I hope I may never do so. I am quite satisfied that the photographs I have seen do not lie in depicting its various atrocities. Photographs could not show them if they did not exist."[70]

Some people criticized Robert Lincoln. John A. Stewart, member of the American Peace Centenary Committee and the man who was most responsible for trying to send the Barnard statue to London and Paris, stated that Robert was too young in the 1850s to remember what his father looked like then; similarly, George Gray Barnard wrote to Robert and suggested that the seventy-four-year-old son was too old to remember what his father looked like as a beardless man.[71] *Outlook* magazine rather condescendingly lamented the fact that Lincoln's son lacked the imagination to see the "intangible, mysterious, inexplicable power and beauty" of the statue that "appeals to the spirit rather than to the eyes of men."[72]

During that entire winter of 1917–18, Robert Lincoln was relentless in his efforts to prevent Barnard's statue from being erected in Europe. He wrote more than one hundred letters concerning the affair, voicing his opposition, seeking other people's opinions and support, and urging opponents to go public with their outrage. To this end, he supplied Ruckstuhl with the names of people who knew his father and who opposed the statue and even with testimonial letters of their opinions, which Ruckstuhl printed in his magazine. Lincoln even considered writing his own editorial to be published in *Art World* but in the end decided simply to disburse his letter to Taft, which he felt explained his feelings exactly.[73]

By the end of 1917, the furor about the statue was undeniable and had become embarrassing to both the American and the British Peace Centenary Committees. In addition to opposition from newspapers, politicians, artists, and Robert Lincoln, the New York Chapter of the American Institute of Architects, the National Academy of Design, and the Washington, D.C., Art Association all came out in opposition of the Barnard statue. But the real nail in the coffin came on January 1, 1918, when a poll of the American Peace Centenary Committee resulted in a nearly unanimous opposition to the Barnard statue.[74]

A select council of the American Peace Centenary Committee was then tasked to investigate the controversy. It was composed entirely of Robert Lincoln's friends and supporters: Columbia University President Nicholas Murray Butler, former Senator and Secretary of State Elihu Root, banker J. P. Morgan, diplomat Henry White, and famed artist Howard Russell Butler. The group found that a majority of American and British artists, public officials, and citizens opposed the Barnard statue and favored sending the Saint-Gaudens statue instead.

Robert had maintained all along, whenever questioned by friends or supporters, that his fight was to *prevent* the Barnard statue, not to *establish* a monument to his father. Such activism was against his lifelong policy. Eventually, however, Robert began to realize that in order to thoroughly "kill" the Barnard, it would be necessary to support the erection of some other statue in its place. For this, Robert declared his preference for the Saint-Gaudens in Lincoln Park, which he always had admired. Since a replica of that statue had been the originally intended monument overseas before the financial difficulties arose, Robert believed that to introduce a new statue would create new difficulties.[75]

By February 1918, Robert was convinced that he had won the battle: that there was so much popular hostility to the Barnard statue that neither the American nor the British centenary committees would dare erect it in London or Paris.[76] He was correct, although the British Peace Centenary Committee did not officially accept the substitution until December 1918, which ended the public controversy.[77] The idea of a statue in Paris was dropped. There is no doubt that Robert Lincoln's opposition and efforts beginning in March 1917 played a large role in the final outcome, as a survey of the correspondence and published reports of the controversy proves. *Art and Archeology* specifically credited Robert's letter to President Taft, which was reprinted in newspapers and magazines around the country, as "an important factor in the final choice."[78]

To cement his victory, however, and to prevent the possibility of another financial shortfall such as had created the issue in the first place, Robert secretly had offered to pay for the monument himself. In mid-1918, he had deposited around $50,000 with J. P. Morgan's bank as a guarantee on the expenses of the replication, transportation, and erection of the Saint-Gaudens statue in London. This was arranged through his friend Nicholas Murray Butler, whom Robert had enlisted to his cause in September 1917.[79] In the end, however, Robert did not pay any money for the project, even though he wanted to. Butler apparently misunderstood Robert's feelings and intentions and arranged the entire cost to be covered by what he called "other sources," which apparently was the Carnegie Endowment for International Peace. "While I had a feeling that it was better that the memorial should be essentially not a simple filial act of my own, I hoped and expected that I should have some private practical part in it," Robert wrote to Butler. "I should be very glad if it is not really too late, that this might be arranged."[80] Butler, still misunderstanding, responded to Robert that he would call upon the bank and make sure Robert's money would in no way be drawn upon for any expenses.[81]

Once the battle was won, and the Saint-Gaudens statue was being prepared, Robert declared, "From being a very great trouble and anxiety to me, the London statue affair has been transformed into a pleasure by the work of friends inspired by feelings for which my filial gratitude cannot find adequate expression."[82] The depth and genuineness of Robert's feelings over the entire episode is evident in his reaction after the Saint-Gaudens statue was placed and dedicated in Westminster in London in July 1920. "I am simply overwhelmed by my emotions in trying to express my gratitude to you for the result of your great work in placing in Westminster the St. Gaudens statue as an American public gift, and so excluding the proposed Monstrosity," Robert wrote to Butler. "I am more than ever proud of a father for whom friends came so nobly to the rescue of his memory from an enduring outrage."[83]

Two years later, while entertaining an author at his house in Manchester, Vermont, Robert's rancor toward the Barnard statue episode still was evident. The author recorded the interview in her memoir.

> Nearby [in the library] were the casts of [Abraham] Lincoln's hands also by [Leonard] Volk and mention of these brought out the most interesting part of the interview. I said as I looked at the casts, "Your hands are like your father's I think." He smiled, replying, "Yes they are, and they are not unusually large are they." He then placed the casts on the desk, closed his right hand over a small piece of wood and put it beside the right-hand cast of his father's hand. They were remarkably alike. I then said, "Why did George Gray Barnard make those abnormal hands on the statue he made of your father?" His eyes flashed and he spoke with great vehemence, "George Gray Barnard was crazy when he modeled that statue, and I have just discovered this summer that the man he used for his model had a well-known disease which caused enlargement of the hands and feet. Think of having a diseased man as a model for my father!" Well I said, "You must be happy to think that you prevented that statue from being placed in front of Westminster Abbey in London." He turned to me with great seriousness and said, "Mrs. Thayer I gave the best of two years to accomplish this. I pulled every wire. I wrote. I spoke publicly and privately. I did everything I could to keep it out of London, and I consider that the last public service I shall ever render."[84]

Perhaps to Robert Lincoln, that was his last public service. To history, however, it was not. Before his death, Robert would make two last great offerings to the nation in memory of his father, both in Washington, D.C., and both of which forever changed the perception and legacy of Abraham Lincoln.

24

"I Am Now Enjoying Life"

The 1909 centennial events took a physical as well as emotional toll on Robert Lincoln, as his dizzy spell at Hodgenville showed. But in general, and not unusual for his age, Robert's health declined with every passing year. His major issue was anxiety—what doctors then called nervous dyspepsia—but he also suffered from high blood pressure, digestive trouble (biliousness), rheumatism, gout, and occasional bouts of mild depression. Robert's poor health had caused him to take some time off from Pullman in early 1906.[1] Newspapers reported that Pullman President Lincoln actually had tendered his resignation at the time, but the board of directors refused to accept it and instead gave him a six-month leave of absence. Lincoln later told the Associated Press that rumors of his resignation were "entirely without foundation."[2]

By 1911, however, Robert's health at age sixty-eight was worsening, and he spent much of the beginning months of that year away from the office on physician-ordered rest. In April, Lincoln concluded that he was too permanently unwell to continue in his job, so he resigned his position as president of the Pullman Company. His successor was his friend and Pullman Vice President and Special Counsel John S. Runnells, who had been with the company since 1887 and vice president since 1905.[3] Robert later explained his resignation to a friend, "I . . . was no longer able to stand up under the strain of the regularly recurring problems which only a few years ago it was a positive pleasure to tackle. If I had tried to keep on, I should now, I am sure, be dead."[4]

Robert T. Lincoln had been president of the Pullman Company for thirteen years when he retired in 1911. During his leadership, the company's success and value had skyrocketed. Total revenue during Robert's first full year as president in 1897 was $10.6 million; revenue for his last full year in 1911 was about $40 million.[5] The statistics of the company, such as revenue, dividends, cars built, contracts made, miles of track covered, and number of passengers carried, all steadily increased during Lincoln's tenure; the company was valued at $120 million in 1911.[6]

Although Robert retired, he did not walk away from Pullman. He remained on the board of directors and was elected its chairman in 1911, the year he retired. In this position, he earned $25,000 per year, a halving of his $50,000 salary as president.[7] His main duty as chairman of the board was to attend the yearly directors' meeting—and any other meetings—and to contribute to the decisions about the operations of the company as a member of the board of directors.

Lincoln remained chairman of the board until 1922. During these years, he also retained his leadership roles in other businesses as well. He was vice president and a director of Commonwealth Edison (resigned in 1914)[8] and a director of the Continental and Commercial National Bank, the Chicago Telephone Company, the Pullman Trust and Savings Bank, and the John Crerar Library in Chicago.[9] He also was a trustee of Knox College and the Mark Skinner Library in Manchester, Vermont. These positions, as well as his numerous other investments, sustained Lincoln's million-dollar fortune.

His retirement from Pullman in May 1911 was followed in October that year by the sale of his Chicago home on Lake Shore Drive and the purchase of a house at 1775 N Street NW (later renumbered 3014 N Street NW) in the Georgetown section of Washington, D.C.[10] The move was done because Mary, Jessie, and her children (who had lived with Robert and Mary since Jessie's divorce in 1907) all preferred winters in Washington to Chicago, and "Mrs. Lincoln has become so devoted to her country place [in Manchester] that it is unlikely that she would care hereafter to spend much time in the Chicago house," Robert explained.[11] He did not mind the relocation but was a bit saddened to leave the city he had lived in for nearly fifty years and the home he had built that he always said suited him perfectly. But he was comfortable in the new house—a three-story, red-brick colonial mansion originally built in 1790 by tobacco merchant John Laird—and was fascinated by its rich history.[12]

The Lincolns always had enjoyed Washington, especially Robert's wife, who had lived there for many years as a young girl while her father was a senator; and Washington society was abuzz at the news that Abraham Lincoln's son was returning to the capital. "The advent of the Lincoln family [in Washington] will be a matter of much importance and more than local interest," one society columnist declared.[13] Another newspaper wondered why Robert would return to a city so filled with tragedy for him: "His life has had more sadness than sunshine in it, and one may imagine how the most depressing of memories will surge through his mind as he again takes up life at the national capital."[14] Yet,

Washington also held memories more pleasant than unpleasant for Robert, such as when his father and brothers were alive and his mother was happy, when he was visiting and courting Mary Harlan, and his years as secretary of war when his children were young and Jack was alive.

After 1911, Robert and Mary, along with Jessie and her children, spent their winters in Washington. The majority of their time, however—typically from April until October—they lived at their beloved Hildene. "We are simply killing time until we can get back to our farm," Robert wrote in early 1916.[15] Robert liked to call Hildene his ancestral home, and it truly was his personal sanctuary. In the mornings, he would attend to his correspondence and any Pullman or other business; every day, he took a drive in his car and always stopped in town for his mail; often, he would get out his equipment and survey the grounds of Hildene or the nearby Ekwanok Country Club; evenings, he would spend reading literature or history or solving complicated mathematical problems; at night, he would go out to his observatory, look at the stars, and practice his astronomy.[16]

Robert's greatest personal passion, however, was golf. He was introduced to the game in July 1893 by Charles B. Macdonald, one of the founders of American golf and golf course architecture, when Macdonald was organizing the Chicago Golf Club. The club, a nine-hole course originally located in Belmont, Illinois, became so popular that it was moved to Wheaton, Illinois, in 1894 and extended to eighteen holes. Its membership was limited to 250 men and was familiarly known as "the millionaire's club." Robert Lincoln became one of the founding members and took lessons from Macdonald and professional golfer Jim Foulis Jr. to learn and improve his game.[17]

Once Robert was exposed to golf, he became a dedicated and passionate player. He played at the Chicago Golf Club as often as he could all year-round (including in the snow), usually with his close friend Marshall Field. In May 1900, Lincoln said Field and he were playing golf three times a week at Wheaton.[18] Field's nephew Stanley sometimes accompanied the pair to the club and once related how around this time the three of them "matched coins" to see who would pay for the bus and train fare between Chicago and Wheaton. Stanley lost and was obliged to pay the cost out of the $15 or so per week he earned as an employee at Marshall Field & Company. "Both Robert Lincoln and Marshall Field seemed to get amusement out of Stanley's poor luck," the story went.[19]

As a golfer, Lincoln was popular, enthusiastic, and frequently invited to play with top golfers and professionals.[20] In 1900, he played a pairs match in Deal, New Jersey, with Macdonald as his partner, opposed by British Open champion J. H. Taylor and his partner, Judge Morgan J. O'Brien. Macdonald later described the end of the match in which, coming down the final hole, it was Lincoln's turn to drive the ball: "I cautioned my partner to take an iron, with which he was extremely good, and not his driver, with which he had been playing erratically. Nothing daunted, he exclaimed, 'I shall take my driver,' with the determination, so far as I could see, of reaching the green off the tee. Taking a mighty swipe at the ball, he sliced badly to the right onto a tennis court. . . . Robert Lincoln was most depressed." They were playing alternate shots, and Macdonald then miraculously drove the ball onto the green, and Lincoln made the putt to tie the match. "That did not pacify Robert Lincoln," Macdonald recalled. "He turned to his caddy and said, 'Caddy, take these clubs and throw them into the lake, and if you don't do that I will make you a present of them.'"[21]

As the story shows, Robert Lincoln loved golf, but he was not terribly good at it. In 1901, he entered the Ekwanok President's Cup tournament, where he finished second to last.[22] But at least Lincoln knew he was not a great golfer, and true to his excellent sense of humor, he liked to joke about it. When he was notified of his nomination for president of the Chicago Golf Club in 1905, Robert responded, "I duly appreciate this compliment which I understand generally to mean that I am supposed to be the worst player in the club. I am president of another club in Vermont on that basis."[23] The other club was the Ekwanok Golf Club, only two miles from Hildene, of which Robert was elected president in 1904. He held the Ekwanok presidency, as well as the position of chairman of the club's finance committee, for the next twenty-two years.[24]

Robert's friendship with Charles Macdonald also led him to support Macdonald's founding of another world-class golf course at Shinnecock Hills (Southampton), Long Island, in 1908. Lincoln wrote a $1,000 check as a founder and incorporator of the National Golf Club of America and sat on the board of directors.[25] "Of course I'll give you $1,000," Lincoln wrote to Macdonald at the time. "The golf that you have taught me has saved me that much a year in doctors' bills, and I am perfectly confident it will add years to my life."[26]

Due to his well-known love of golf and to the upcoming centennial of his father's birth, in 1908 Robert Lincoln was offered the presidency of the United States Golf Association for the year 1909. He declined due to his poor health and his lack of time to devote to the duties of such a position. His refusal was characteristically humorous: "I am, as you know, a very enthusiastic golfer, although unhappily not a very good one; but I believe the Presidents of the Association and Presidents of Golf Clubs are not expected to be good golfers. At one time I held the presidency of two golf clubs, I think my selection being made on the ground of my duffer status."[27]

In addition to his home courses in Chicago and Manchester, Robert joined the Chevy Chase Club outside Washington, D.C., after his move to Georgetown in 1911. After picking up the game, Robert played golf anywhere and everywhere he could. During his summer vacations in Little Boar's Head, New Hampshire, Long Branch, New Jersey, and eventually Manchester, Vermont, Lincoln tried to play golf every day, his health permitting. He regularly traveled every winter to warm destinations, usually Coronado Beach, California, or Augusta, Georgia, and occasionally to Hot Springs, Virginia, specifically to indulge his love of the game.

At Augusta, Lincoln was a member of an informal group of important men known as the "Little Mothers," a name given in jest by a woman who insisted that when the group came together, "it was for the purpose of rocking the cradle of the universe." The Little Mothers met every March at the Hotel Bon Air, where they would play golf during the day and sit and talk—mostly politics—at night. In addition to Lincoln, members of this group included governors, congressmen, senators, and President Warren G. Harding. Robert Lincoln was "very much at home" in this group and often told interesting and amusing stories to the group of his experiences as secretary of war and minister to Great Britain.[28]

Robert's favorite home course was the Ekwanok in Manchester, and he was a regular player whenever he was in residence at Hildene. It was said that his daily eighteen-hole game was "as much a part of his day as was his dinner."[29] His regular companions on the links were his friends and fellow Ekwanok board members Robert Janney of Philadelphia and George H. Thacher and Horace G. Young of Albany. They were known as the "Lincoln Foursome," and they played together for multiple years until Janney's death in 1920. Robert was always the scorekeeper.

As president of the Ekwanok, Lincoln did not play in the club's annual tournaments, but he tried always to be present to watch the notable golfers who came to compete and to award the cup to the winner. He enjoyed setting up his telescope on the clubhouse porch so he could follow the golfers as they played, reporting on the progress of the matches to his friends sitting nearby.[30] One of the numerous champion golfers Robert Lincoln met and entertained at the Ekwanok was sixteen-year-old (and later world-famous) Bobby Jones, who played in a three-day wartime benefit for the Manchester Red Cross in August 1918.[31]

Probably the most famous golfing partner Robert ever had was President William Howard Taft. Taft was the first American president to play golf. He commonly espoused its benefits as excellent outdoor exercise and sought to widen its popular appeal by insisting it was not "a rich man's game," as many believed.[32] Lincoln and Taft previously had golfed together at Augusta, Georgia, in March 1911.[33] Taft, while president, first visited Lincoln at Hildene in

October 1912 for an overnight visit. The two former secretaries of war went to the Equinox Hotel, where the president gave a speech, and then back to Hildene, where they dined and were entertained by singers.[34]

Ex-president Taft returned to Hildene in September 1913 for a weekend during which he declared to Lincoln it would give him an opportunity to "golf with you on Saturday, to worship on Sunday, and then to take a stirrup cup with you on Monday."[35] Actually, the two men golfed four times in the three days of the visit. The Tafts arrived in Manchester the afternoon of Friday, September 5, and within an hour, Taft and Lincoln were out on the Ekwanok links. That night and the next, the Lincolns held large dinner parties in honor of their guests, after which the assembled group was entertained by dancing, vocalists, and violinists. Twice on Saturday and once Monday morning, the two men golfed at the Ekwanok Country Club with three of the four members of the Lincoln Foursome, and Robert told Taft he was now an "honorary member" of the group "and must come to meetings."[36]

Taft was impressed by the beauty and the comfort of Hildene, and Robert always was keen to show off his beloved estate. The place was not only Lincoln's personal sanctuary but also the summer home in which he indulged his love of his family. Although Jessie Beckwith and her two children lived with Robert and Mary for many years after her 1907 divorce, Jessie ultimately began renting apartments in New York City. At some point, Robert bought Jessie a house neighboring his own on N Street in Washington. But no matter where they were, the Beckwiths spent at least a part of every summer at Hildene.

The Ishams, who lived in New York City, not only visited the Lincolns often but also had bought their own house in Manchester village in 1905, the same year that Hildene was completed.[37] On his sixty-second birthday that August, Robert wrote a friend, "I celebrated an unpleasantly high figured birthday yesterday but it was made as pleasant as possible by the presence of all my family—children and grandchildren included—all very happy and well."[38] With his children and grandchildren so close to him every summer thereafter, Robert was personally content and liked to say he was "comfortably and happily situated."[39]

Robert's grandchildren loved spending time at Hildene with "gran" and "gramps." They had a playhouse and an Indian tepee out in the woods and enjoyed playing with boats on the pond by the garden and just generally romping around the hundreds of acres of grounds. Robert made for them an ornamental bedtime story screen on which he pasted pages of illustrated children's books containing stories such as Little Red Riding Hood, Sleeping Beauty, Puss N Boots, and the Three Bears. The grandchildren could select a favorite story to have gramps read to them before bed at night.[40]

Granddaughter Peggy loved animals, and Robert bought her a pony named Aricula in 1907 for her ninth birthday. Even though the animal was a little small for Peggy, Robert decided to keep it because he had "a very much smaller grandson who will, before long, wish to amuse himself" with his sister's pony.[41] Both Peggy and Linc played golf, most likely inspired or even taught by their grandfather on the Hildene grounds. Peggy often played at the Ekwanok Country Club, where her grandfather was a member; and in 1925, Robert bought Peggy a lifetime membership to the Equinox Links golf course.[42] Grandfather Lincoln probably also enjoyed showing his grandchildren the wonders of the night sky through his telescope in the observatory.

The Lincolns, of course, loved having their grandchildren with them and had many dances and birthday parties for the grandkids at Hildene. In 1909, Mary Harlan Lincoln gave a dance at Hildene for seventeen-year-old Lincoln Isham.[43] In 1911, the Lincolns gave a grand birthday party for Bud when he turned seven. One of the local children who attended later remembered the highlight of the party being the kids lying down, hugging their arms to their sides, and rolling down the big hill on the west terrace. Their clothes became covered in grass stains, and the next day, Mrs. Lincoln sent her chauffeur around to collect every child's clothing for cleaning by her laundress.[44]

The grandchildren could get into trouble as well. Perhaps the most infamous incident occurred in July 1907, when Robert's chauffeur, who later revealed he had a penchant for whiskey and unseemly companionship, let fifteen-year-old Lincoln Isham drive Robert's 1905 Thomas Flyer automobile around the Hildene grounds. Robert explained, "[H]e unwisely let my young grandson handle the machine at a dangerous place near the stable, and it was run over a sloping bank, and was so badly injured that I had to send it to Albany to have one axle straightened and some other repairs made."[45] Linc later remembered that his usually staid and placid grandfather was extremely angry over the incident, and, according to one of his friends, the boy felt himself "in disgrace" about it.[46] The coachman soon was fired.

During these years, Robert was not only a grandfather but also still a father. While Mamie had an independent family and life of her own, Jessie was a constant presence in her parents' lives. On June 22, 1915, Robert's youngest daughter was married for the second time, in a ceremony at Hildene.[47] Her new husband was an artist and archeologist named Frank Edward Johnson. Robert described his new son-in-law as "a Connecticut man of good family whom she met in Washington. Mary and I think well of him and are glad there will be somebody of good sense to look out for her and her children when we are out of the ring."[48] Johnson, unlike the eloper Warren Beckwith, not only asked for the Lincolns' permission to wed Jessie but also sent a note of thanks for their assent and told them not to worry about the future, "for we have our lives before us and it would be unworthy of us to do anything that would cause you anxiety."[49]

Unfortunately, such was not the case. In 1919, Jessie was having a rather open affair with a man named Robert J. Randolph, and by early 1920, the Johnsons had separated. Jessie's estranged husband wrote a letter to Robert Lincoln one year later and explained the circumstances; he felt the only solution to the situation was a divorce, and he asked his father-in-law to draw up the divorce papers under the cause of desertion.[50] "What a damned fool the man is to think I will do this business for him!" Robert declared.[51] When Jessie later married Randolph, an electrical engineer from New York City, she did so after her father was dead—perhaps to avoid his censure on her third marriage.[52]

Besides her personal problems, Jessie also caused Robert numerous financial headaches. She was constantly writing to her parents, asking for loans and handouts, even after Robert had established a trust account for her from which she could draw an annual allowance of $15,000.[53] In 1920, she asked her father to finance the purchase of a farm in Virginia, at a cost of about $200,000, saying it was not only a good investment but that she was tired of living like a hobo in various apartments. Robert answered her, "I find it difficult to [respond] without straying from the affectionate terms which are usually appropriate to a daughter of your age." He admonished her for wanting to spend more than two-thirds of the value of her entire trust fund on a "scheme" that, even if legitimate, would be "a folly" to expect her to give the detailed and close management it would necessitate to be successful. As to her complaints about apartment living, he rejected that as ridiculous because of her own "caprice" in selling the house in Washington he had bought for her without consulting him, her husband, or anybody. "The allowance which I settled upon you thirty months ago is greater than the salary of the Commanding General of the Army or of a Justice of the Supreme Court," he continued. In the end, he refused to help her buy the place, although he did increase the amount of her annual income from her trust by $10,000 to help with the rising cost of living.[54]

Despite his retirement from Pullman, Robert Lincoln still was a public figure of sorts; and regardless of his great aversion to any sort of attention, he never could vanish completely from the public eye. During the presidential election year of 1912, Lincoln's name was often in the news—first in a war of words with Theodore Roosevelt and later as a possible candidate.

When President Roosevelt finished his second term of office in 1908, he handpicked his secretary of war, William Howard Taft, to be his successor. Taft won the presidency that year, but his conservative administration was not what the progressive Roosevelt had expected. Their philosophical differences turned into a severe political rift that led ex-President Roosevelt to seek the Republican presidential nomination in 1912 and oust his former protégé.

Roosevelt began his campaign for the nomination in the spring and in April was speaking across Illinois. He not only was orating in the land of Lincoln, visiting Lincoln's tomb and house and church pew in Springfield, but also declaring his progressive "New Nationalism" ideas of a larger, more paternalistic, antibusiness government, to be those identical to Abraham Lincoln's political philosophy. Robert Lincoln, himself a conservative Republican previously disenchanted by Roosevelt's presidency, was outraged at the comparison and issued a public rebuke. "My personal feelings are unimportant," Robert wrote, "but I am not only impatient but indignant that President Lincoln's words and plain views should be perverted and misapplied before trusting people into support of doctrines which I believe he would abhor if living."[55] Robert's letter induced supportive newspaper editorials and numerous letters to the editors promoting not only Robert's statements but also his name for president in the upcoming election.[56]

Of course, the idea of Robert Lincoln for president had been a popular notion for the past twenty-eight years, but in 1912, conditions were different. In the past, the party had had disagreements about the best candidate; in 1912, the Republicans were in the midst of a civil war between supporters of Taft and supporters of Roosevelt. Many Republicans feared that a party split would lead to an election loss, and they believed the only solution was to find a compromise candidate on whom both sides could unify. Many people thought Robert Lincoln was that man. Even Lincoln's friend and golfing partner George H. Thacher, a member of the Lincoln Foursome, wrote to Lincoln suggesting him as a candidate. The sixty-eight-year-old Robert replied that such a situation "cannot possibly come about" due to his advanced age and his poor health, which had forced his retirement from Pullman. "For me to drop into such an idea as you present, if it was presented by supreme authority, would be fixing the date of my actual physical funeral at a date not more than 30 days off," Lincoln wrote. "There is no possible doubt about it and I can simply say that I am now enjoying life and should positively and quickly decline to commit suicide. A man ought not to shirk public duties, but equally he ought not to undertake them if he knows he has become unfit to do them."[57]

Robert himself was in Chicago just days before the beginning of the Republican convention in mid-June, and he declared, "I never saw such a mess in all my experience."[58] The Taft-Roosevelt split divided the entire party as expected and made any consensus on one single candidate doubtful. People began whispering about a planned "stampede" to a compromise candidate that would unite the party. That man, unsurprisingly, was Robert T. Lincoln.[59] There was even a rumor that Taft and Roosevelt both agreed to accept Lincoln as the candidate if the convention was unalterably deadlocked.[60] In the end, Taft's men controlled the political machinery at the convention, and their candidate triumphed. Roosevelt, crying foul about "stolen" delegates, angrily bolted from the Republicans and formed the Progressive Party (also called the Bull Moose Party) to run as a third-party candidate.

Interestingly, a story surfaced twelve years later contending that a failed movement in Chicago to swing delegates to Robert Lincoln almost gave the Republican nomination to Roosevelt. According to Grosvenor B. Clarkson, the convention fight between Taft and Roosevelt for delegates was so tightly drawn that few people realized that the sixty-six black delegates actually held the balance of power. Clarkson's father, General James S. Clarkson, a Roosevelt supporter, conceived the idea to convince the black delegation to vote for Robert T. Lincoln after the leader of that delegation, Henry Lincoln Johnson, approached him asking for advice on how they should vote.

Clarkson wrote to Johnson that in commemoration of the semi-centennial of the emancipation of black Americans, the delegation should vote for the Great Emancipator's son. He wrote that the Republican Party had "betrayed Lincoln's promises" to them, allowed political and civil rights for black southerners to disappear, and stopped appointing black Americans to southern political offices. Clarkson stated that the delegation could use its votes to "arouse the Republican Party from its indifference to your rights" and "compel attention." He urged the delegation to vote for Lincoln for president and continue voting for him on successive ballots either until he was nominated or the convention agreed to recognize their rights. Clarkson's real intention was to prevent Taft from receiving the black vote.

The younger Clarkson took the letter to Roosevelt on the day Taft's name was to be called up. Roosevelt reportedly said, "This is an inspiration. Go to it as fast as you can." Clarkson ran to the convention to deliver his father's letter to Johnson but found all entrances blocked by Taft supporters. He could not gain entrance, and Johnson, hobbled by a previously broken leg, could not exit through the throng. The letter was never delivered. "Had it been," Clarkson said in 1924, "I firmly believe it would have diverted enough negro votes to have swung the convention to Roosevelt."[61]

Robert Lincoln, always a loyal Republican, was disappointed in the party split and the Roosevelt apostasy and believed it likely that the Democratic candidate, New Jersey Governor Woodrow Wilson, would win the White House. "I used to think highly of him but the twists and turns he has taken have very much altered my opinion," Lincoln wrote. "However, he is an educated gentleman and if he is elected the responsibility will, no doubt, as it always has done to everybody except the Colonel [Roosevelt], have a sobering affect upon him."[62]

During the canvas, Lincoln supported Taft for president and donated $1,000 to his friend's campaign.[63] He also introduced him before a campaign speech in Manchester, Vermont, that October.[64] But the divided party, as always the way in elections, caused a divided vote, which allowed Wilson to win a resounding victory. Roosevelt actually placed second, while President Taft won only eight electoral votes—the worst defeat for an incumbent president in American history.

During President Wilson's first term in office, Robert Lincoln grew to despise the man and his policies. He opposed Wilson's reelection in 1916 and supported Republican candidate Charles Evans Hughes. Lincoln's stalwart Republicanism was not surprising, but he was so dissatisfied with Wilson that he uncharacteristically joined with a group called "the National Hughes Alliance" and signed his name to its national political advertisement, which stated, among other things, "We have no faith in Woodrow Wilson because he has evinced no faith in himself. We are not sure what he stands for nor how long he will stand by any principle he claims to stand for."[65] As war between Germany, France, and England raged in Europe, Wilson was reelected by a narrow margin, using as his main slogan, "He kept us out of war." In a personal letter, Lincoln commented, "[I]f it had not been for the horrible election, I should have thought myself over the worst of my griefs."[66]

The United States joined the war against Germany in April 1917 in response to the unlimited German naval warfare that was sinking American merchant ships. Lincoln's opinion on the United States joining the war is unknown, but in 1915, he joined a syndicate of more than two hundred individuals and business interests, headed by J. P. Morgan & Company, that agreed to underwrite a loan of $500,000,000 to the anti-German allies of Great Britain and France. Lincoln did this not only out of his innate sense of patriotism but also because it was good business for the Pullman Company.[67]

The war had a minor impact on the Lincoln family. Robert's oldest grandchild, twenty-five-year-old Lincoln Isham, was too fragile of health with poor eyesight and weak nerves (because of which he had previously dropped out of college at Harvard) to be drafted.[68] He eventually volunteered to drive ambulances for the Red Cross.[69] Nineteen-year-old Peggy Beckwith, who was living at that time with her mother and stepfather Johnson in Cuba, declared she would return to America to "engage in useful and patriotic work." She moved to Hildene to support U.S. agriculture by helping plow the farm fields since there were not enough men to do the job. "I could not sit on a veranda in Cuba and knit when there was a man's place to be filled here," she said.[70] Peggy also declared her intention to enroll at Cornell University to study agriculture and to organize a unit of young women to aid farmers in harvesting, as she was doing. "Mrs. Beckwith is a trump!" admired one newspaper.[71]

It is unknown how Robert Lincoln felt about the war itself, but he was vehemently opposed to President Wilson's postwar policies. "The Lord only knows where Wilson is going to land us and I am scared for my descendants," Robert wrote in May 1919.[72] In June, while commenting on his health, he wrote, "My only serious trouble is the annoyance made by our pestiferous president. In that I have many fellow sufferers."[73] In July, Lincoln commented, "I am, as is everybody except Mr. Wilson, greatly disturbed by the general condition of our public affairs, both from the political and the business points of view."[74]

As the twentieth century neared the end of its second decade, Robert Lincoln knew he was entering his twilight years. He had lived a long life, achieved great successes in law and business, and retired a respected and wealthy man. His children were grown and married, and his grandchildren even were entering their own adult years. There remained for Robert, however, one last great piece of unfinished business—the disposition of his father's papers. "I am getting old," the seventy-four-year-old Robert wrote in 1917, "and feel the necessity of getting my affairs in rather better order than they have been for some time."[75]

After John Nicolay and John Hay completed their biography and subsequent collected works of Abraham Lincoln, the Lincoln papers remained in Nicolay's possession, where they had been since Robert entrusted him with their use and stewardship in 1874. After Nicolay died in 1901, the papers were transferred to the temporary stewardship of then–Secretary of State John Hay, who stored them in the vaults of the U.S. State Department.[76] As he had done from 1865 to 1874, Robert again procrastinated the job of reacquiring and ordering the papers. "I ought not to delay doing this much longer for it is very clear to myself that I am not as young as I used to be," he wrote to Hay in 1904, but still he did nothing.[77] After Hay died in July 1905, Robert knew he could no longer postpone the work.[78]

In October 1905, Robert traveled to Washington and personally took possession of his father's papers, which filled seven steamer trunks.[79] He took them to Chicago and stored them in his office safe, where they remained for the next seven years. During that time, Robert himself did not look through the papers but had his Chicago secretary, Charles Sweet, whom Robert had known, worked with, and trusted incomparably since the 1870s, examine, organize, and "overhaul" them. During these years, Sweet was the only person who knew what exactly was in the Lincoln papers.[80] He would continually update

Robert on what he had discovered, and Robert often would give pieces of his father's writings or correspondence to the people (or their family) to whom it was related.[81]

After Charles Sweet died in 1912, Robert began keeping his father's papers in his personal possession, either at his house in Georgetown or at Hildene. He had a special railroad car in which to transport the papers between his two houses whenever he changed his residence. But the final disposition—as well as the safety—of the collection was constantly on Robert's mind. As he wrote in 1902, "If my son were still alive, I should probably leave the papers in his hands, but as it is, I think it is my duty to select some depository for them, just what it will be I am not yet prepared to say."[82] The Chicago Historical Society, of which Robert had previously been vice president, had asked him for the papers in 1882, but he declined because Nicolay and Hay still were composing their biography.[83] But it was Herbert Putnam, the indefatigable Librarian of Congress, who ultimately triumphed.

Putnam approached Robert Lincoln about the Lincoln papers after Nicolay's death in 1901 and again after Hay's death in 1905. Robert was unprepared to make any decisions either time but agreed to meet with Putnam in Washington in winter 1905. The two men had more correspondence in July 1906, at which time Robert explained that he wanted his secretary to examine and organize the Lincoln papers before entrusting them to any institution. "It is a subject which is constantly presenting my mind, and I do not intend to let it drag along much longer," Robert wrote.[84] But he actually did let it drag on for the next thirteen years, although it appears that by 1910, Robert had told Putnam he had decided to eventually deposit the papers in the Library of Congress.[85]

It was not until nine years later, however, that Robert finally was ready to let his father's papers out of his hands. On May 7, 1919, a government wagon called at Lincoln's house at 3014 N Street NW to collect eight trunks of papers to be delivered unopened to the Manuscripts Division of the Library of Congress.[86] This disposition was made only for the "safekeeping" of the papers; Robert retained ownership of them.[87] The deposit was made under the conditions that it be kept from the public, that a library official examine and arrange the papers under Robert's direction, and that the papers could only be consulted after gaining Robert's permission.[88] More than ten thousand manuscripts are in the collection.

It was nearly four years later, on January 23, 1923, before Robert Lincoln formally donated the papers, now known as the Robert Todd Lincoln Collection of the Papers of Abraham Lincoln, to the United States of America, "to be deposited in the Library of Congress for the benefit of all the People."[89] It was, quite simply, the single greatest gift of historical materials to the library in

American history. Librarian Putnam, who had sought the acquisition of these papers for twenty-two years, accepted the gift "with profound satisfaction at the definiteness of this action."[90]

Included in the terms of Robert's deed of gift was a condition that the papers be sealed from public view until twenty-one years after his death. This caveat has—strangely and needlessly—been the cause of immense curiosity, consternation, accusation, and conjecture ever since. The perpetual questions have been, Why? Why would Robert Lincoln do this? What was he hiding and from whom? To this day, people, including lifelong Lincoln scholars, still ask these questions. Rumors have been rampant: he was hiding letters about his father's love affair with Ann Rutledge, about his mother's insanity, or about Edwin M. Stanton's alleged complicity in Abraham Lincoln's assassination; he was hiding the entire lot because he simply was embarrassed by his father's humble beginnings.

The most prevalent accusation (for there really is no other word for it, with the appropriate pejorative meaning) was that Robert petulantly wanted to prevent Lincoln scholar Albert Beveridge from using the papers. Beveridge had been pestering Robert Lincoln over access for years, first on his own and then under the auspices of Robert's friend Nicholas Murray Butler.[91] Robert quite simply and straightforwardly denied Beveridge's request, as he had denied countless others, because he felt Nicolay and Hay's great biography was definitive, and there was no need for another.[92] Also, Robert felt that if he gave access to Beveridge, he would have to give access to everyone, which he was not prepared to do.

Robert Lincoln's enduring reticence over the public opening of his father's papers always stemmed from one single reason. The papers contained references to people that were not always flattering, and, to Robert's Victorian-era belief system, to expose such statements about people still living or their immediate descendants was utterly improper. Robert gave this reason dozens, perhaps even hundreds, of times to inquirers beginning in May 1865. He had previously counseled his friend Edgar Welles not to publish the diary of his father, Secretary of the Navy Gideon Welles, for the same reason. In fact, in Robert's 1923 deed of gift, he explicitly stated, "This condition is imposed by me because said papers contain many references of a private nature to the immediate ancestors of persons now living, which, in my judgment, should not be made public, and also much information and matter of a historical character which I have heretofore authorized and permitted John G. Nicolay and John Hay to use in the preparation of their Life of my father."[93]

In January 1926, Robert amended his deed of gift to allow his wife access to the papers and the authority to permit their examination by anyone she chose. This power was hers until her own death or until his original twenty-one-year embargo elapsed.[94] Mrs. Lincoln later gave access permission to her daughter Mary Lincoln Isham—but not to Jessie Lincoln Beckwith Johnson Randolph—and although she did not grant personal access to Robert's cousin Katherine Helm, who wrote the family-authorized biography of Mary Todd Lincoln, she did have a search of the collection for anything about Mary Todd Lincoln made by her attorneys for Helm's benefit.[95] Mary Harlan Lincoln also refused permission for personal access to historians James G. Randall and W. A. Evans (and probably to Beveridge and William E. Barton) and the request of David Davis, a descendent of Abraham Lincoln's friend of the same name, to open the papers up to the public in general.[96]

Perhaps the greatest myth concerning the Abraham Lincoln papers—and certainly the most enduring—is that Robert Lincoln, before giving them up, purposely burned countless of his father's manuscripts in order to purge and purify the family legacy. The primary source for this belief was Robert's friend Nicholas Murray Butler, who wrote a fantastic story in his memoirs declaring that Robert had decided to burn *all* of his father's papers, but Butler, arriving at Hildene in the nick of time just as Robert was bending over the fire with the first batch of manuscripts, shrieked at his friend—"[T]hose papers do not belong to you. Your father has been the property of the nation for fifty years, and those papers belong to the nation!"—and convinced him to donate the entire collection to the Library of Congress.[97] It is an exciting and emotional story; the only problem, however, is that it is not true.

Butler was adamant that it occurred and that it happened in 1923. Of course, at that time, the collection had been out of Robert's hands and already at the Library of Congress for four years.[98] However, what Butler may have witnessed was Robert burning *his own* papers, which he not only did frequently but also often even kept a record of what he had destroyed.[99] Similar stories have been told that Robert's servants at Hildene or his attorney, Frederic Towers, also saw Lincoln burn bundles of papers. Again, they all were almost certainly Robert's own correspondence.[100]

Robert Lincoln knew full well his father's iconic place in American history, and he never consciously destroyed anything important. Throughout his life, whenever he talked of "purging" or "overhauling" his father's papers, what he meant was removing not only useless items—such as receipts or one-line notes—but also items "purely private" to the Lincoln family.[101] Robert never made any secret of his inflexible belief in personal privacy and of his insistence on being the arbiter of what was or was not appropriate for release. For example, when William H. Herndon gave his famous Abraham Lincoln–Ann Rutledge love-story lecture in 1866, Robert believed it mattered little whether the story was true or not (and he thought not), but he felt the disclosure of his father's intimate feelings was completely inappropriate.[102]

One excellent example of Robert's notions of family privacy concerns the letters of his mother, Mary Todd Lincoln. Robert at one time in his life attempted to collect and destroy all the letters written by his mother during what he called her "period of mental derangement." But there were other letters he most likely destroyed as well. In July 1865, Mary Lincoln told a friend that she had been reading through a "large package" of "loving" letters from her husband, "many of them written to me, in the 'long ago,' and quite yellow with age, others, more recent."[103] Those letters have never been found; and they are *exactly* the type of materials that Robert would abhor becoming public knowledge and therefore certainly would have destroyed.

During these years that Robert dealt with the arrangement and disposition of his father's papers, another unprecedented tribute to his father's life and legacy was simultaneously occurring and in which he took part. On the grounds of what was then called Potomac Park in Washington, D.C. (now called the National Mall), a grandiose monument to Abraham Lincoln was being erected. Robert would live to see his father apotheosized as a nineteen-feet-high marble statue in a one-hundred-feet-high Greek temple in the nation's capital. His attendance at the Lincoln Memorial dedication ceremony would be his last public appearance.

25

"He Simply Went to Sleep"

May 30, 1922, was a warm and sunny spring day in Washington as fifty thousand people crowded the National Mall from the steps of the Lincoln memorial to the mile-distant base of the Washington Monument. This throng of citizens represented an incalculable array of age, race, gender, financial status, political affiliation, and nationality, all of them present to pay tribute to the memory of Abraham Lincoln.

The few remaining wizened veterans, both Union and Confederate, of the Civil War stood at the front of the crowd at the base of the Lincoln Memorial steps. Distinguished attendees seated at various tiers along the steps included members of Congress, justices of the Supreme Court, governors, military officials, and foreign diplomats. In the Memorial Hall itself, where the speaker's rostrum stood, sat the members of the Lincoln Memorial Commission, the architect and the sculptor, the day's orators, the Chief Justice of the U.S. Supreme Court, members of the president's cabinet and their wives, President and Mrs. Harding, and distinguished guests.

As the attendees assembled that afternoon, one in particular stood out to many in the crowd. He was an elderly man with a white beard, carrying a cane, and wearing a black suit and a familiar black stovepipe hat.[1] He was escorted and assisted by a two-man military honor guard up the fifty-seven steps from the road to the top. The old man was seventy-nine-year-old Robert T. Lincoln, only surviving son of the president, who was accompanied by his wife, Mary (and his personal physician).[2] When they reached their seats on the top tier of the memorial, they were given a loud ovation from the crowd.[3] For Robert, this day would be one of the most moving of his life.

Of all the monuments to Abraham Lincoln since his death in 1865, the Lincoln Memorial was to be the most impressive, and the most national, in nature. Planning began at the turn of the twentieth century, with the location in Potomac Park selected in 1901 and the political machinery started in 1902. A Lincoln Memorial Commission, chaired by President Taft and tasked with the job of bringing the project to fruition, was created in 1911, and construction begun in 1912.[4]

Architect Henry Bacon designed the memorial building in the form of an ancient Greek temple standing 190 feet long, 119 feet wide, and almost 100 feet high. In the central hall, flanked by two of his greatest speeches carved into the walls, sits a nineteen-feet-high, white-marble statue of President Abraham Lincoln seated in a flag-draped chair, the creation of renowned American artist Daniel Chester French.[5]

During the decade-long process of creating the Lincoln Memorial, Robert Lincoln kept himself informed of the political debates, the artistic considerations, and the construction progress. During 1913 and 1914, he held a correspondence with commission chair Taft concerning the political arguments over construction materials that threatened to derail the entire project.[6] In 1915, Robert participated in the laying of the memorial's cornerstone by contributing a history of his father that he, the son, had signed, to be placed in the copper box in the keystone.[7] In 1916, Robert visited French's studio to view the sculptor's model of the Lincoln Memorial statue, at which meeting he offered suggestions on its likeness that French professed to be most helpful.[8] In 1920, Robert requested and received permission from the U.S. Corps of Engineers to visit the memorial and show it to a group of friends while it was still under construction.[9]

Because he admired the memorial so much, Robert was deeply appreciative of all the politicians who helped make it a reality. He was particularly grateful to U.S. Representative John W. Dwight of New York, Republican majority whip, who played a key role in marshalling the necessary support to pass the final appropriation bill on the House of Representatives—for without the funding, the memorial never would have been built.[10] In 1916, Robert wrote a note of thanks to Dwight for his work. He also sent him a gift of the original handwritten manuscript of the speech President Lincoln gave from the White House immediately after the 1864 election. "I wish you to have something tangible as a testimonial of my feeling and which may be associated by you in your memory of that part of your public work," Robert wrote.[11]

Once the Lincoln Memorial was completed and plans were made for the dedication ceremony, Taft, supported by President Warren G. Harding, invited Robert Lincoln to attend as the guest of honor.[12] With his typical modesty and reticence, Robert agreed to be present only if there was no special fuss made over his appearance. "We of course shall attend, but only on par with the general public," Robert responded. "We prefer that no notice whatever be taken of us."[13]

During the dedication ceremony, which was broadcast across the grounds through loudspeakers and throughout the nation via radio, Chief Justice Taft presented the Lincoln Memorial to the government, and President Harding accepted it. Both men gave eloquent eulogies to the memory of the Great Emancipator. Robert R. Moton, president of the Tuskegee Institute, gave an address on the feeling of black Americans toward president Lincoln, although, ironically, blacks were segregated from the majority white crowd that day (as they had been at the 1909 centennial of Lincoln's birthday in Springfield, Illinois). Edwin Markham read his poem "Lincoln, the Man of the People."

At the end of the ceremony, Taft and Harding shook hands with Robert Lincoln, at which time the crowd shouted out another loud ovation for the son of the Great Emancipator. Lincoln then held an "informal reception" near the speaker's podium, where numerous government dignitaries approached him to congratulate him on the completion of nation's memorial to his father.[14] The Associated Press account of the day called the Lincoln Memorial "[t]his new shrine of democratic liberty" and commented that the great figure must have seemed familiar to Lincoln's son: "Often he must have seen [his father] in life when he sank back in his heavy chair at his desk in the White House and brooded over the havoc that civil war would make."[15]

It is difficult to imagine what must have been Robert Lincoln's thoughts and feelings that day as he looked upon the colossal white-marble memorial. Even before it was complete, he called it "magnificent" and declared, "I think [it] surpasses anything that has ever been erected of the kind."[16] After nearly sixty years of protecting and preserving his father's memory, Robert had lived to see his father become a national secular godhead, to become the worldwide avatar of liberty and democracy. How can his pride and his burden be described? Perhaps the best indicator of Robert's feelings was stated by a business colleague who wrote to Robert in 1925, "I well remember your remark that you 'did not remember Abraham Lincoln as President of the United States but as your father.'"[17]

Supposedly, for the rest of his life, whenever Robert Lincoln took a drive in his car in Washington, no matter where he rode, his itinerary always took a turn around the Lincoln Memorial. As the car approached the steps, he would call to the chauffeur, "Stop the carriage, stop the carriage!" and looking up at the colossal marble effigy of his father, he would exclaim, "Isn't it beautiful?"[18] Methodist Bishop Joseph C. Hartzell also recalled a visit to the Lincoln Memorial in which he witnessed Robert Lincoln in "deep reverence" before his father's statue, "as if he were at worship." He then "waved a last adieu to the cold stone face and departed."[19]

Robert's attendance at the Lincoln Memorial dedication was the last public appearance of his life. It also was the final, and greatest, monument to his father in which he took part. As a zealous, yet judicious, steward of his father's legacy during the fifty-seven years since the assassination, Robert Lincoln actively had assisted with an impressive list of memorials and tributes to President Lincoln's memory. In addition to the various writings and works of art to which Robert offered advice or assistance, he also maintained the Lincoln home in Springfield and then donated it to State of Illinois; he continuously monitored and kept informed of the condition and upkeep of the Lincoln tomb in Springfield, including the major part he played in foiling the attempt to steal his father's body in 1876; he sponsored the Nicolay and Hay biography of his father and solicited their edition of Lincoln's collected works, both of which were considered definitive and unsurpassed for decades; he spoke at Knox College in 1896 about the Lincoln-Douglas debates; he gave $1,000 to help sustain the Lincoln birthplace site in Hodgenville, Kentucky; he gave $1,000 to aid in the creation of the Abraham Lincoln School in Lexington, Kentucky; he loaned some of his father's manuscripts to the centennial exhibits at the Chicago Historical Society and Columbia University Library in 1909; he attended centennial celebration events in Springfield and Hodgenville in 1909; he successfully prevented the attempt to place the Barnard Lincoln statue in London and Paris; and he kept, organized, and preserved his father's papers before donating them to the Library of Congress in 1923. Additionally, Robert contributed to monuments for his paternal grandparents (which were reflections of their son's fame). He helped pay for the grave monument for Thomas Lincoln, in Coles County, Illinois, in 1881; he contributed $1,000 to the Nancy Hanks Lincoln memorial park project in Spencer County, Indiana, in 1900.

Robert also contributed to the legacy of his mother. Her posterity was far inferior to her husband's, of course, but by the 1920s, she was becoming her own object of historical study. Robert's primary contribution to his mother's memory was his destruction of countless letters written during her "period of mental derangement," which the son felt reflected badly on his mother and the entire family. When a portrait of Mary Todd Lincoln was requested by President and Mrs. Calvin Coolidge to hang in the White House in the early 1920s, Robert and Mary Harlan Lincoln commissioned Robert's cousin Katherine Helm to do the work. Helm's painting of her Aunt Mary was hung in the White House in 1925; none of the Lincolns attended the ceremony.[20] Robert also encouraged and assisted Helm with her biography of Mary Lincoln, which was published in 1928 and was the first full-length book published about Mary in her own right.[21]

Once the Lincoln Memorial was dedicated in 1922, Robert Lincoln lived the remaining few years of his life as quietly as possible. His only real business commitment was to attend, if his health permitted, the annual board of directors meeting for the Pullman Company in Chicago. He and his wife spent winter at their Georgetown home and spring, summer, and fall at Hildene. Robert liked to take a drive in his car every day if the weather was decent, take walks, visit friends, follow current events, and do a great deal of reading.[22] Every August 1 for his birthday, Robert played a few holes of golf at the Ekwanok with George Thacher and Horace G. Young, followed by a birthday dinner with his family at Hildene.[23] By 1924, at age eighty-one, Robert was forced to give up his beloved pastime on the advice of his physician, who thought there was a danger of his patient falling on the golf course and breaking a limb.[24]

Robert continued to have health issues, especially his attacks of nervous dyspepsia, which, by 1923, were so bad he was unable to write letters, and his wife and secretary did not allow him to read any incoming mail they felt would worry him and worsen his condition.[25] He developed chronic conjunctivitis, which his physician checked and treated every day and for which Robert underwent minor surgery in 1925.[26] He and his wife both had major dental issues, with the two of them having a combined total of nineteen teeth removed by the dentist in 1920, to be replaced by dental plates.[27] But still, Robert could joke about his poor health. In October 1921, he wrote, "[T]he Demon, old age, who sits astride my shoulders, only says to me, 'Cheer up! The worst is yet to come!'"[28]

In these sunset years, it often was wondered by the public and the press why and how Robert Lincoln, this living tangible connection to America's greatest president and himself an accomplished man, always kept his name out of the limelight. *Leslie's Weekly* declared in a 1922 story titled, "Lincoln's Silent Son," that despite a decade-long residence in Washington, Robert was rarely recognized on the street: "It is doubtful if more than a hundred residents of Washington know him by sight."[29] Robert, of course, preferred this anonymity, to the point of refusing all requests by newspapers for his photograph. It was said by news photographers in Washington that the most desired—and most difficult—photograph of a public personality to attain was of Robert Lincoln. Whenever he played golf at the Chevy Chase Club, cameras were banned from the course.[30]

When a reporter asked Lincoln for a statement in 1921, Robert responded that he did not believe he had anything to say that the people would care to hear.

The paper commented that Lincoln's self-effacement "springs from a feeling that the name of Lincoln came to him in trust to be preserved as his immortal father left it, without change or addition by any other man."[31] And despite the perpetual public fascination over Robert's reticence, a survey of articles about him shows that his modesty was generally understood and accepted. "He is a plain citizen, natural and democratic," editorialized one newspaper. "He loves nothing so much as the sanctity of his home and of a charming family to whom he is thoroughly devoted."[32]

Robert allowed one small moment of publicity in his later years when he met Great Britain's former Prime Minister David Lloyd George at the Manchester, Vermont, train station in October 1923. George had been traveling from New York City to Montreal, Canada, and at every stop he gave a speech in which he referred to Abraham Lincoln as the "man among all men in history" who most influenced him. Even though Robert's health was poor at the time and his physician urged him not to leave the house, Lincoln wanted to meet the man who held his father in such high esteem. "This is Abraham Lincoln's son," George told his wife and daughter as he introduced them to Robert, an old man in a heavy overcoat buttoned up to his chin. "You two know how I worship his father."[33]

The ex-premier, who had guided Great Britain through World War I, asked Robert what he remembered of the Civil War, to which Robert replied, "It is not much, except that I saw my father grow older and sadder as the struggle went on." When asked about the assassination, Robert said he heard first that his father had been shot only in the arm, and he flippantly remarked, "Oh, father will get over that all right." When the brief meeting was over and George resumed his journey, he was full of his talk with Robert Lincoln and said the meeting would be one of his most treasured memories.[34]

During the final two years of his life, 1924–26, Robert was, according to his family, "very methodical" in his daily habits. He took breakfast in bed and remained there until after his physician's visit between 10 and 11 A.M.; he then attended to his mail and correspondence in his library (with his attorney and secretary, Frederic N. Towers) until lunch at 1:30. After a half-hour rest after lunch, he went for a drive and visited friends either at a social club or at their homes. Returning home, he either rested or read until dinner, dined with his family, joined them in the library until 10 P.M., and then went to bed. Ordinarily he read until eleven or twelve o'clock before turning out his light.[35]

By early 1926, after years of poor health and grumblings of feeling old, Robert apparently felt that his long life finally was nearing its conclusion. In March, he gave his wife 5,063 shares of Commonwealth Edison stock and 5,000 shares of National Biscuit Company stock; in April, he gave her $100,000 worth of

Norfolk and Western Pocahontas Coal and Coke Company bonds. Combined, these stocks were worth about $1.2 million—a tax-free gift to his spouse as a way to avoid government estate taxes after his death.[36]

In mid-May, as Robert approached his eighty-third birthday, he wrote to his longtime friend and golfing partner Thacher, "I think I am feeling about as well as a man of eighty-three can expect to feel. . . . I am a little afraid, however, that I have played my last game of golf."[37] In June, Robert heard of the death of David Homer Bates, a War Department telegraph officer during the Civil War and author of the book *Lincoln in the Telegraph Office*. After Bates's death, Robert was morbidly informed that he and banker Henry B. Rankin of Springfield, Illinois, were the last two people left alive with any intimate connection with Abraham Lincoln.[38] Robert also was the last living witness to the Confederate surrender at Appomattox in 1865.

On July 25, 1926, Robert Lincoln took his usual Sunday afternoon drive in his 1925 Rolls Royce, which his wife had bought him for his eighty-second birthday. That evening, he dined with his wife and his grandchildren Peggy Beckwith and Bud Beckwith, who were visiting while their mother was in Washington. Robert went to bed as usual. The next morning, when the butler went into Robert's bedroom at the usual 9 A.M. to call for breakfast, he found his employer dead. "Mr. Lincoln's passing was quiet and peaceful: he simply went to sleep to wake no more," wrote Towers.[39] Robert was six days away from his eighty-third birthday.

Robert's Manchester physician, Dr. Claude M. Campbell, was called immediately. He determined that Lincoln had been dead for about four hours, the cause being cerebral hemorrhage resulting from arterial sclerosis. Dr. Campbell, Mary Lincoln, and Towers all later said Robert's death was completely unexpected. When Robert had arrived in Manchester two months earlier, his physician found Robert's health better than it had been for several years; when Robert went to bed the previous night, he was in "good spirits."[40] Later that afternoon, Mary Lincoln telegraphed the news to Helm: "Mr. Robert Lincoln passed away about ten this morning. A great loss to his friends who loved him. This country which treasured him as a fine man and splendid citizen. My dearest love to your mother [Emily Todd Helm] in the loss of a beloved nephew and friend."[41] Telegrams also were sent to Katherine's brother, Ben Hardin Helm Jr., and Robert's cousin Mrs. Edward D. Keys, in Springfield, Illinois: "Services here on Wednesday. Deferring interment at Springfield until Autumn."[42]

The death of Robert T. Lincoln, last surviving son of Abraham Lincoln, secretary of war, minister to Great Britain, and president of the Pullman Company, was a nationally and internationally recognized event. President Coolidge praised him as "a man of remarkable attainments who, while under tremendous handicap by constant comparison with his father, had a remarkable career and left behind him a most creditable record; one of which any American citizen should be proud."[43] Secretary of State Frank B. Kellogg declared, "The nation will look back with gratitude and affection upon his great services as a statesman and publicist. His death is the nation's loss."[44] Former Speaker of the House of Representatives "Uncle" Joe Cannon, who had known Lincoln for more than fifty years, said of his friend, "Mr. Lincoln's death removes one of the most misunderstood citizens of the country. The public I do not suppose, ever will come to regard the man at his true worth."[45]

The U.S. War Department honored its past secretary by calling him one of America's "most able and useful citizens" and by ordering flags at all military posts across the country to be displayed at half-mast on July 28, the day of his funeral.[46] Flags in Springfield, Illinois, were placed at half-mast at the Lincoln Tomb and Lincoln Home immediately on receiving news of Robert's death.[47]

Across the country, numerous resolutions, statements, and memorials were issued in Lincoln's honor by businesses and organizations in which he had been involved, such as the Mark Skinner Library and Ekwanok Country Club in Manchester, Vermont, and the John Crerar Library, Chicago Bar Association, Chicago Historical Society, Commercial Club, and Illinois Bell Telephone (the modern incarnation of the Chicago Telephone Company), in Chicago.[48] Officials at the Pullman Company extolled their former president and chairman of the board succinctly by declaring, "He was a Pullman man to the last." The company newsletter described Robert's dedication to the company by explaining that just a few weeks before his death, he had volunteered to attend a directors' meeting in New York to assure a quorum, despite his advanced age and poor health: "It was not necessary but it showed the Pullman spirit."[49]

News reports of Robert Lincoln's death typically told of his personal and family history, his business and political accomplishments, his stewardship of his father's papers and legacy, the fact that he was connected to three presidential assassinations, and that he would be buried in his father's tomb in Springfield. Every report talked of Robert primarily as the son of Abraham Lincoln, and yet fair space was given to explain that Robert had distinguished himself as his own man without trading on his family name while also remaining cognizant of his responsibility to the family legacy.

The *New York Herald Tribune* praised him as a "modest, conscientious, capable and successful American, absorbed in his work and standing on his own feet."[50] The *New York Times* stated, "Although Mr. Lincoln played a great part in public life in his earlier years, he always was of a retiring disposition and shunned politics for a career in corporation law and business, where he could succeed on his own merits."[51] The widely reprinted Associated Press story said, "[H]is retiring nature sometimes made it appear to many that he was taciturn, but his close friends described him as a 'warm-hearted, lovable, charming gentlemen.' He was a delightful conversationalist, a great raconteur, and if he knew his companions well, he would talk without reserve."[52] The *Chicago Tribune*, in its coverage of Lincoln's death, printed one of Robert's favorite stories about his father during the war, as recalled by a fellow member of the Chicago Club, F. Willis Rice.

> One day, seven or eight years ago, I was talking with Mr. Lincoln inside one of the big windows of the Chicago Club on Michigan Avenue, when a military parade passed by. For some reason they stopped within our view for several minutes, and as we watched them, Mr. Lincoln laughed softly, and he told me a story that has been often related.
>
> "This reminds me of father," he said. "He always was eager, when he saw marching troops, to know what state they came from. Once as we were driving in Washington, our carriage was stopped by a body of troops crossing a corner. In his eagerness to know from where they hailed, father opened the door and stepping halfway out, shouted to a group of workmen standing close by, 'What is it, boys,' meaning where did they come from. One short little red-haired man, with a typical Irish face, affixed him with a withering glance and retorted, 'It's a regiment, you damned old fool.'
>
> "In a fit of laughter, father closed the door, and when his mirth had somewhat subsided, turned to me and said, 'Bob, it does a man good sometimes to hear the truth.'"[53]

The *Philadelphia Ledger* called Robert "one of the few sons of Presidents who achieved a national reputation."[54] Across the ocean, the London *Times* said of the former U.S. minister to Great Britain, "Seldom do sons of the great achieve the distinction and the glory of their fathers. . . . Yet in his way Lincoln served his country well in more than one high position, and in old age he had won the respect and esteem of all who knew him."[55]

Of all the eulogies and editorials printed throughout the United States, journalist and Lincoln scholar F. Lauriston Bullard summed up better than anyone else the quintessence of Robert Lincoln's relationship to his father's legacy.

> To be known always and everywhere as the son of Abraham Lincoln in itself was a heavy responsibility. Easily Robert Lincoln might have hindered the development of his father's fame. Had he seized upon every opportunity to 'tell stories' of his father; had he leaped into print at the slightest provocation with interpretations and explanations, affirmations and denials, of events

> and letters through all these years in which the Lincoln accumulations have grown to astounding dimensions; had he striven to capitalize his father's name in his own interest, he might well have made himself a bore and a nuisance, doing himself no good and doing his father's reputation real harm.
>
> Robert Lincoln chose to play a far better part. He did not strive for public notice. He went about his business quietly, with dignity, keeping in the shadows. . . . He considered reticence the wise course and he was right. . . . With awe he knew when he reached three-score-and-ten that his father already had become as universal a figure as Shakespeare. What a responsibility to live a worthy life as the son of such a man.[56]

Mary Harlan Lincoln handled her husband's death well, causing family attorney Towers to declare, "My respect for and high regard for her wonderful Faith and strong character increases as I know her better."[57] Her daughter Mary Lincoln Isham was at her own Manchester home when her father died and so helped her mother make the funeral arrangements.[58] Jessie Lincoln Johnson came to Manchester from Washington, and Lincoln Isham came from Brielle, New Jersey, where he was spending the summer.

Robert T. Lincoln's funeral was held at Hildene two days after his death, on Wednesday, July 28. Only his immediate family and his two remaining golfing partners, Thacher and Young, along with their wives, were present. The Reverend D. Cunningham-Graham, pastor of the Congregationalist Church of Manchester, officiated. He offered no eulogy—which was fitting to Robert's nonreligious nature—but read Psalm 23 and selections from I Corinthians and Revelations. Alfred Tennyson's poem "Crossing the Bar" also was read by request of the family.[59]

Robert's casket was borne from the house by seven pallbearers, among whom were his grandsons Lincoln Isham and Robert Beckwith and his two Washington attorneys Towers and Norman Frost. The hearse traveled only one mile down the Lincolns' private road to Dellwood Cemetery. The body was placed in the Maxwell vault, where it would rest temporarily until its removal to the Lincoln Tomb in Springfield, Illinois, in the fall. The Reverend Graham offered a prayer and a benediction, and the funeral was over. "Everything [was] as simple as Mr. Lincoln himself would have wished," the Reverend Graham told his congregation the following Sunday; the Associated Press reported, "Extreme simplicity marked the brief services."[60]

There were no public demonstrations in Manchester that day or even bystanders around the cemetery—the village residents chose instead to respect the Lincoln family's desire for privacy. The silent symbol of the community's grief was its lowered flags.

When Robert Lincoln's will was filed for probate, it was revealed that his personal estate of stocks, bonds, and cash in the bank was valued at approximately $1 million (about $11 million today), and his summer home, Hildene, was assessed at $125,000. He bequeathed everything to his wife.[61] His children and grandchildren were not mentioned in the will because he previously had opened trust funds for his daughters (which were worth nearly $1 million each by 1926) and had arranged monetary gifts for his grandchildren.[62]

The general public, however, was not so much interested in Robert's wealth as in the disposition of his family heirlooms—particularly, his father's papers. Robert's will revealed his previously secret donation of the papers to the Library of Congress with a twenty-one-year seal attached.[63] Reactions to the news were mixed. The *Indianapolis News* said Robert's action "serves no good purpose" and harms the cause of history, while the *Independent* called him "[k]ind but misguided" and said, "Historical truth is so bright a gem that it should be hidden in archives no longer than is necessary."[64] On the other hand, the New York *Evening World* found Robert's reticence "refreshing in view of the tendency in recent years for living men to rush into print with the private letters of historical personages."[65]

As the country buzzed over the news concerning the Lincoln papers, state officials in Illinois were preparing for what they considered the final local chapter in the Lincoln family legacy. It had been announced at Robert's death that he would be buried in Springfield later in the fall, there to rejoin his parents, his brothers, and his only son and to fill the penultimate empty crypt in the Lincoln Tomb (the final vacancy was for Mary Harlan Lincoln). Initial telegrams to family members said the same, and Mary Lincoln Isham reiterated the intention to Robert's cousin Keys, in September.[66] The Illinois director of public works and buildings wrote to Mary Harlan Lincoln to begin planning the burial.[67] Officials and organizations in Chicago, Robert's hometown for more than fifty years, were considering celebrations in honor of their native son in hopes his funeral train would pass through the city, as his father's had more than sixty years earlier.[68] It was, therefore, a shock to the nation—and to some in Springfield, an outrage—when Robert's widow, Mary Harlan Lincoln, suddenly changed her mind and decided not to bury her husband in Illinois after all.

Epilogue: "His Own Place in the Sun"

For Robert Lincoln's entire adult life, he intended his final resting place to be with his family in the Lincoln Tomb at Oak Ridge Cemetery in Springfield. As he wrote to the head of the National Lincoln Monument Association in 1890, while arranging for burial of his son, Jack, in the tomb:

> Upon the death of my son, I foresaw the extinction upon my own death, of my father's descendant's bearing his name, [and] the desire came upon me that, if it met the views of every member of the Monument Association, arrangements might be made for the burial in the monument, of my son and thereafter of myself and my wife and of my two daughters, *unless they should marry*. It is the arrangement I would make, under the peculiar circumstances, if the tomb of my father were, as would usually be the case, in my care.[1]

In a separate letter of the same day, Robert told his friend Clinton Conkling, "You will understand that I wish to make a *family* arrangement [in the tomb], under the circumstances, but if what I wish is not entirely satisfactory to any member, I would not press it for a moment, but would build my own family tomb somewhere and bury my son in it."[2] As previously stated, the association accepted Robert's arrangement, and he, therefore, did not build his own family tomb. As late as 1922, Robert told his friend Nicholas Murray Butler that he had "arranged that my wife and myself shall be entombed" in Springfield.[3]

When Robert died, Mary Harlan Lincoln notified the family that her husband's final interment would be in Springfield. But two weeks later, the widow was struck with what she called "inspiration": she would bury her husband in Arlington National Cemetery in Washington, D.C. Not in Springfield. As a former secretary of war, as well as a captain on General Grant's staff during the Civil War, Robert was entitled to such a burial. "You know, our darling was a personage, made his own history, *independently* of his great father, and should have his own place 'in the sun!'" Mary wrote her cousin-in-law Katherine Helm. "After prayerful thought over this, for many weeks I knew I was right, so I began to set the wheels in motion."[4]

When Mary left Manchester in 1926 to spend her winter in Washington, she brought her husband's body with her. It was placed in a temporary vault in Arlington while plans for a final interment and monument were made.[5] Mary selected for the burial site a "beautiful wooded knoll" directly in line and with a full view of the Lincoln Memorial. She personally went to the War Department to get the secretary's approval of her lot choice and then worked with Charles Moore, chairman of the Committee of Fine Arts, on the design and aesthetics of what they called the Robert Lincoln Monument.[6]

Robert's body was permanently interred in section 31, lot 13, of the cemetery on March 14, 1928.[7] Four months later, Mary Harlan Lincoln contracted with sculptor James Earle Fraser, a former student of Augustus Saint-Gaudens, to design a sarcophagus for her husband's burial site at a cost of $25,000.[8] The final creation was a "warm low-colored granite" sarcophagus six feet high, ten feet long, and five feet across, with two benches at the end and backed by evergreen trees. The *Washington Star* newspaper reported that friends of Robert Lincoln considered the "simple yet impressive" monument "eminently fitting" in its appearance and location.[9] It was placed atop Robert's grave in late fall 1929.

Ironically, while Robert Lincoln was connected with the first three presidential assassinations during his life, in death he lies within sight of the grave of the fourth murdered chief executive, John F. Kennedy.

While construction of her husband's monument was underway, Mary Lincoln began the process to transfer the body of her son, Jack, to Arlington from Springfield, where it had been in the Lincoln Tomb since 1890. This was a move that had been expected in Springfield since Robert's Arlington burial was announced in 1926, although when Mary's request finally came in 1929, state officials checked with the attorney general for his legal position on Mrs. Lincoln's application. He said her wishes should be respected.[10]

True to the Lincoln family character, Mary did not want publicity for the event. So when she heard that the Lincoln Tomb was to be remodeled in 1930 and that the bodies of everyone inside—except President Lincoln under his ten feet of concrete and steel—would be temporarily removed during the work, she used the opportunity to retrieve her son's body. On the evening of May 22, 1930, a group of men secretly met at the Lincoln Tomb to remove the remains of President Lincoln's grandson. Five days later, Jack Lincoln was at rest beside his father in Arlington National Cemetery.[11]

Due to cemetery regulations at the time, Jack's name could not appear on his father's monument because he was a minor and a dependent. Instead, a small footstone, flush with the ground, was placed beside the monument and reads simply, "A. L. II." When the regulation was changed half a century later, seventy-nine-year-old Robert Todd Lincoln Beckwith requested and paid for his uncle's name to be added to the Robert Lincoln Monument.[12]

Mary Harlan Lincoln outlived her husband by eleven years. During that time, she continued to live between her winter home in Georgetown and her summer home in Manchester. In 1929, she built an addition onto her Washington house, into which moved her daughter Mamie, who herself had been widowed in 1919.[13] Mary further honored her husband's memory by donating his golf bag and clubs (and a glass display case) to the Ekwanok Country Club and established the annual Robert T. Lincoln Memorial golf tournament.[14] Mary also augmented the Lincoln family collection in the Library of Congress with more donations and continued to deny public access to the materials until the end of her husband's previously imposed deadline.[15]

Mary Harlan Lincoln died in her Georgetown home on March 31, 1937. She was ninety years old. Her will, which was valued at more than $1 million, established a trust fund with income for her children and grandchildren and that if and when the family line ended, the estate be divided equally between the First Church of Christ, Scientist, in Boston, the American Red Cross, and Iowa Wesleyan College. She also bequeathed to her oldest daughter, Mary Lincoln Isham, the George P. A. Healy portrait of Abraham Lincoln, which Robert considered the best likeness of his father ever painted, and her summer home, Hildene.[16] Both of these last two bequests had conditions. Upon Mamie's death, the Healy portrait would go to the U.S. government to be hung in the White House, and Hildene would go to Peggy Beckwith.

Unfortunately, Mamie's death would come sooner than anyone expected. After her mother's death, Mamie continued to live at the N Street house in Washington and began to refurbish Hildene. In May 1938, she was diagnosed with cancer, and five months later her right kidney was removed at the New York Presbyterian Hospital. She appeared to be recovering well, but in November, she died suddenly at the age of sixty-nine from a pulmonary embolism.[17]

Jessie Lincoln Beckwith Johnson Randolph was divorced for the third time in 1946. Her rebellious and irresponsible nature throughout her life no doubt was the cause of her parents' decision to disinherit her from ownership of Hildene. But when Peggy took possession of her grandfather's old summer home in 1938, she invited her mother to come live with her there. Jessie divided her time between Hildene and a Virginia estate she inherited from her third husband. She died on January 4, 1948, at age seventy-two.[18]

Robert Lincoln's grandchildren, Lincoln Isham, Mary Beckwith, and Robert Beckwith, the last direct descendants of Abraham Lincoln, all lived quiet, retired lives and shunned any sort of publicity. Linc married a New York socialite named Leahalma Correa in 1919 and helped raise her daughter, Frances Mantley.[19] The Ishams had no children of their own. They lived between their New York City apartment and their small estate in Dorset, Vermont, and liked to travel in Europe and North Africa. Linc was an avid golfer, art collector, musician, and songwriter. During his life, he donated numerous family items to the Smithsonian Institution and the Library of Congress.[20] He died on September 1, 1971.

Peggy Beckwith lived at Hildene for the rest of her life. She was a liberated woman who refused to conform to the social expectations of her time. She preferred pants and men's shirts to wearing dresses. She enjoyed pursuits considered then to be more masculine than feminine, such as farming, hunting and fishing, golfing, photography, painting and sculpting, and car collecting. She also was an avid aviator who bought her own plane and built a landing strip on the Hildene grounds. One of Peggy's friends said of her, "She should have been a man."[21]

Peggy disliked being related to Abraham Lincoln. "I don't care much about ancestors" was a statement she often made. "It always provokes me when people stare at me and say, 'That's Lincoln's great-granddaughter.' For heaven's sake! It was just luck that A. L. happened to be a relative!"[22] When Peggy commented in 1963 that she disagreed with government-forced desegregation, a reporter asked how her great-grandfather would feel about her position. She replied, "I can't say. I'm as far away from him as anyone."[23]

Peggy did at least once attend an event honoring her famous ancestor. On May 14, 1960, the new ballistic-missile, nuclear-powered submarine USS *Abraham Lincoln* was launched from Portsmouth, New Hampshire. Mary Lincoln Beckwith, dressed uncharacteristically in a blue and white polka-dot dress, white gloves, white hat, and a pearl necklace, broke a bottle of champagne on the bow and christened the ship.[24] How impressed she was by the occasion is found in her diary, in which she recorded that night: "Cloudy A.M. Sun out P.M. Broke bottle on boat. So home to bed."[25] Mary Lincoln Beckwith died July 10, 1975, in Rutland, Vermont, from colon cancer at the age of seventy-seven.[26] She never married or had any children. She deeded Robert Lincoln's beloved Hildene to the Christian Science Church.[27]

Robert Todd Lincoln Beckwith received a law degree from Georgetown University but never practiced law. He lived off his family fortune and spent most of his time at his farm in Hartfield, Virginia, although for a time he also had a home in Washington, D.C. Beckwith was rather indifferent to his lineage. He once said that he never asked his grandfather Robert T. Lincoln for stories about President Lincoln, life in the White House, or events of the Civil War because he was "not especially interested." Rather than familial comparisons, Beckwith often said, "I just want to live my own life."[28] Occasionally, he participated in Lincoln-related events, such as when he went to Gettysburg for the seventieth anniversary of President Lincoln's address and when he traveled to New York to celebrate Illinois Day at the 1964 World's Fair.[29] He donated numerous family items to the Illinois State Historical Society.[30]

People always were surprised to discover that Beckwith was a Lincoln descendant. As one Lincoln authority said after meeting Bud, "Lincoln was tall, strong, outspoken; Beckwith is short, fragile, and shy."[31] He also had a severe speech impediment, hearing difficulties, and later in life suffered from Parkinson's disease. People who knew Beckwith said that although he did not look like the Great Emancipator, he inherited the family humor and wit. He once described himself as "a spoiled brat," and one of his longtime friends said, "He had three great passions in life—cars . . . boats and a beautiful woman."[32] Beckwith was married three times but had no children.

Robert Todd Lincoln Beckwith, the last direct descendant of Abraham Lincoln, died at his Virginia home on December 24, 1985. He was eighty-one years old.[33]

Although the Lincoln lineage died, the family legacy has lived on. Abraham Lincoln is the most written-about figure in American history. Mary Lincoln is one of the most studied first ladies, and her legacy currently is undergoing its own renaissance. Robert Lincoln, on the other hand, is at best a mere side character and at worst a mustache-twirling, heartless villain. Robert's negative reputation has certain specific origins. Because he was a millionaire and a captain of industry in his work at the Pullman Company, the quick conclusion is that he was a selfish and avaricious CEO. Because he was reticent to speak about his father or about himself (as a reflection of his father), both to the press and to the public, he has been dubbed a snobbish aristocrat who scorned the average person. But the one event that damaged Robert's reputation more than anything else was his decision to commit his mother to a sanitarium in 1875. During Robert's lifetime, his action was understood and generally respected, but later historical revisionism damned him. His motives since have been declared duplicitous, illegal, and downright evil: he bribed the judge and jury, he instituted a kangaroo court, he shut her away because she was an embarrassment and so he could steal her money.[34] As the historical record proves, all of these accusations are false, yet, they have become so ingrained in the Lincoln mythology that they are cited as "fact" whether or not they are "truth."

The truth is that had Robert Lincoln not been the son of Abraham Lincoln, his achievements today would be studied by schoolchildren along with other captains of industry such as Carnegie, Rockefeller, Morgan, and Pullman. Robert Lincoln was born in a rented room in a boardinghouse lit with candles and having no running water and died in a twenty-four-room mansion with electricity, indoor plumbing, and an automobile in the garage. He rose from the unpaved streets of a small Midwestern city to graduate from Harvard College and become one of the premier attorneys in Chicago. He served ably as secretary of war and minister to Great Britain. He worked as a president or director of numerous businesses, utilities, and banks, among which was the million-dollar Pullman Company. In the midst of all this, Robert also was the steward of his father's papers and legacy. He walked an incredibly difficult tightrope in which he preserved and protected his father's memory yet never himself traded on the family name. His great responsibility burdened him as well as sustained him, and he died as he lived: both as his father's son and as his own man.

Robert's golfing partner Horace G. Young wrote a tribute in the *Manchester (VT) Journal*, in which he declared of his longtime friend, "[T]he secret of his life was character."[35] In addition to Robert's lifetime achievements and successes, he also was a genuinely good man. He was kind and generous to a fault, scrupulously honest and hardworking, a great friend and mentor, and a loving family man. In short, between his personal and professional lives, Robert Lincoln was exactly the man his father wanted him to be.

Robert once refused a journalist's photo request by saying, "My father was a great man, but I am not."[36] It is fair to say that many people, both during and after his long and impressive life, would respectfully disagree.

Notes
Bibliography
Index

Notes

The following abbreviations are used in some citations.

ACPL	Lincoln Financial Foundation Collection at Allen County Public Library, Fort Wayne, Indiana
ALPL	Abraham Lincoln Presidential Library, Springfield, Illinois
CHM	Chicago History Museum
DDFP	David Davis Family Papers, Manuscripts Division, Abraham Lincoln Presidential Library, Springfield, Illinois
H-W	Herndon-Weik Collection of Lincolniana, Manuscripts Division, Library of Congress
Hildene Archives	Hildene, The Lincoln Family Home, Friends of Hildene Inc., Manchester, Vermont
IF	Mary Todd Lincoln Insanity File, Lincoln Financial Foundation Collection at Allen County Public Library, Fort Wayne, Indiana
LB	Robert Todd Lincoln Letterpress Books, Abraham Lincoln Presidential Library, Springfield, Illinois. Citations are in the form LB, followed by volume, microfilm reel, and page numbers separated by colons, for example, Robert Lincoln to Frank Ashbury Johnson, July 5, 1898, LB, 33:54:247.
LOC	Library of Congress
NARA	National Archives and Records Administration, Washington, DC
OR	*The War of the Rebellion: A Compilation of the Official Records of the Union and Confederate Armies.* Edited by Robert N. Scott. Series 1, vol. 46. Washington, DC: GPO, 1895. 127 vols.
RTL	Robert T. Lincoln
RTLFP	Robert Todd Lincoln Family Papers, Manuscripts Division, Library of Congress

Introduction

1. "The Feeling for Lincoln," *Chicago Tribune*, August 31, 1887, 1.
2. RTL to H. H. Warner, May 8, 1884, folder 1, RTL Collection, CHM.
3. "Gossip from the Capitol," *Chicago Tribune*, August 9, 1890, 7.
4. RTL to John S. Phillips, October 14, 1908, LB, 41:71:361.
5. RTL to Mary Lincoln, Dec. 2, 1860, RTL Collection, Phillips Exeter Academy.

1. "I Was Born in the Globe Tavern"

1. Springfield is two hundred miles southwest of Chicago and about one hundred miles north-northwest of St. Louis.
2. Wallace, *Past and Present*, 1:5; Peck, *Traveler's Directory for Illinois*, 164–65; Federal Land Surveyors' Field Notes.

3. Angle, *Here I Have Lived*, 6.

4. *Western Tourist and Immigrant's Guide*, (1840), 133; *Western Tourist and Immigrant's Guide*, (1845); Peck, *Traveler's Directory*, 166–67. Population numbers are an average of conflicting estimates.

5. Wallace, *Past and Present*, 6; Peck, *Traveler's Directory*, 165, 167. On November 4, 1840, the *Morning Courier* (Springfield, Illinois) newspaper stated, "Springfield has improved more than twice as much this season as in any former one. . . . The small enclosures, near the city, that have been in cultivation for several years, are giving way, and buildings are stretching into the prairies in every direction." 2.

6. Wallace, *Past and Present*, 6; Peck, *Traveler's Directory*.

7. Elizabeth Edwards, interview with William Herndon, January 10, 1866, Lamon Papers. See also Wilson and Davis, *Herndon's Informants*, 443.

8. William Herndon to Jesse Weik, January 16, 1886, in Hertz, *Hidden Lincoln*, 136–37; Herndon and Weik, *Herndon's Life of Lincoln*, 134.

9. James C. Conkling to Mercy Ann Levering, September 21, 1840, folder 1, box 1, Conkling Family Papers; Ninian Edwards quoted in K. Helm, *True Story of Mary*, 81.

10. K. Helm, *True Story of Mary*, 73–74.

11. Abraham was nine when his mother died of milk sickness; Mary was six when her mother died due to complications from childbirth.

12. Elizabeth Edwards, interview with William Herndon, January 10, 1866, 2:220–26, LN 2408, Lamon Papers; Herndon and Weik, *Herndon's Life of Lincoln*, 166–67. See also Mrs. B. S. Edwards, interview with *Chicago Tribune*, February 12, 1900, Nicolay Papers.

13. Abraham Lincoln to Joshua Speed, Springfield, March 27, 1842, in Basler et al., *Collected Works*, 1:282; Elizabeth Edwards, interview with William Herndon, January 10, 1866, in Wilson and Davis, *Herndon's Informants*, 443; D. L. Wilson, "Abraham Lincoln and 'That Fatal First of January,'" 99–132. This broken engagement is usually referred to as "that fatal first of January" 1841, although even the accuracy of this reference is debatable.

14. For a good examination of the Lincoln-Todd courtship, see D. L. Wilson, *Honor's Voice*, 220–64.

15. Abraham Lincoln to Joshua Speed, May 18, 1843, in Basler et al., *Collected Works*, 1:325; Hickey *Collected Writings of James T. Hickey*, 59. The tavern was located at 315 East Adams Street between Third and Fourth Streets.

16. Hickey, *Collected Writings of James T. Hickey*, 58; Frances Todd Wallace, interview by William Herndon, 1865–66, in D. L. Wilson and Davis, *Herndon's Informants*, 485.

17. Abraham Lincoln to Samuel D. Marshall, Springfield, November 11, 1842, in Basler et al., *Collected Works*, 1:305.

18. Abraham Lincoln to Joshua Speed, March 26, 1843, ibid., 1:319.

19. Abraham Lincoln to Joshua Speed, May 18, 1843, ibid., 1:325.

20. Abraham Lincoln to Joshua Speed, July 26, 1843, ibid., 1:328.

21. Mary Lincoln to Mary Harlan Lincoln, Frankfurt a [*sic*] Main, October 16, 1869, folder 1, box 1, IF. It is unknown who attended Mary during the birth, although it seems logical that her brother-in-law Dr. William Wallace was there.

22. Mary Lincoln to Mary Harlan Lincoln, Kronberg, Germany, September 4, 1869, folder 1, box 1, IF. See also Mary Lincoln to Rhoda White, December 20, 1869, in Turner and Turner, *Mary Todd Lincoln*, 536.

23. K. Helm, *True Story of Mary*, 98; W. H. Townsend, *Lincoln and His Wife's Home Town*, 89.

24. Edward Thayer, statement in the *Kansas City (MO) Star*, quoted in Hertz, *Lincoln Talks*, 112.

25. RTL to John Hay, November 3, 1886, microfilm reel 8, John Hay Papers, John Hay Library.

26. Sophie Bledsoe Herrick, "The First Lincoln Baby and a Friend's Sound Advice," in R. R. Wilson, *Intimate Memories of Lincoln*, 61. For decades after Abraham Lincoln's death and during his apotheosis, old relatives, friends, and neighbors (like Sophie Bledsoe) continually sought to write themselves into his legend. Bledsoe, in creating a small importance for herself and her mother, omits that Mary's sisters may have helped the new mother as well. By August 1843, Mary had three sisters living in Springfield, two with children and one a doctor's wife. On the other hand, Mary still resented her family's failure to fully accept Abraham as a suitable husband for a Todd. Mary's refusal to have the baby at the home of one of her sisters rather than the Globe Tavern is suggestive of Mary's resentment. This is not to discount Sophie or her mother's aid, but that Mary had no help from family and that a six year-old girl was allowed to take Robert out alone seem implausible. Randall, *Mary Lincoln*, 82.

27. Statement by Emily Huntington Stuart, quoted in Beulah Gordon, untitled unpublished essay, p. 7, Mary Todd Lincoln Vertical File. *Summer complaint* was a popular term for any diarrheal disorder occurring in summer, especially when produced by heat and indigestion. The tradition at the time was that sick children were helped to get well by being in motion.

28. Temple, *By Square and Compass*, 31–34; Pratt, *Personal Finances*, 64–65. The cash plus the lot made the total price $1,500.

29. The Eighth Judicial Circuit covered fourteen counties in central Illinois, comprising eleven thousand square miles. The typical circuit term was three months in the spring and three months in the fall. Lincoln was the only lawyer who rode the entire circuit. Weik, *Real Lincoln*, 188–89.

30. Pratt, *Personal Finances*, 84.

31. Bayne, *Tad Lincoln's Father*, 47.

32. Mary Lincoln, interview by William H. Herndon, September 1866, 2:228, LN 2408, Lamon Papers.

33. Mary Lincoln to Alexander Williamson, Hyde Park Hotel, [Chicago], June 15, 1865, in Turner and Turner, *Mary Todd Lincoln*, 251.

34. Harriet A. Chapman to William Herndon, Charleston, Illinois, November 21, 1866, frames 1069–70, microfilm reel 8, series 4, H-W. See also Wilson and Davis, *Herndon's Informants*, 407; Weik, *Real Lincoln*, 54–55.

35. Herndon and Weik, *Herndon's Life of Lincoln*, 257.

36. Ibid., 257–58; Hertz, *Hidden Lincoln*, 177.

37. Hertz, *Hidden Lincoln*, 177.

38. John Hay, "Tad Lincoln," *New York Tribune*, July 17, 1871, reprinted in *Chicago Tribune*, July 19, 1871, 1.

39. Frances Todd Wallace, interview by William H. Herndon, 1865–66, in Wilson and Davis, *Herndon's Informants*, 485; RTL to Josiah G. Holland, June 6, 1865, RTLFP.

40. Baker, *Mary Todd Lincoln*, 120.

41. Lincoln's absence from home upset Mary a great deal. She once told a neighbor that if her husband stayed home "as he ought to," she could "love him better." James Gourley, interview by William Herndon, February 9, 1866, LN 2408, 2:124–30, Lamon Papers.

42. Harriet A. Chapman to William H. Herndon, Charleston, Illinois, November 21,

1866, and December 10, 1866, frames 1069–70 and 1270–71, microfilm reel 8, series 4, H-W. See also Wilson and Davis, *Herndon's Informants*, 407, 512; Weik, *Real Lincoln*, 55.

43. James Gourley interview by William Herndon, 2:124–30, LN 2408, Lamon Papers. See also Wilson and Davis, *Herndon's Informants*, 453; Hertz, *Hidden Lincoln*, 384.

44. Harriet A. Chapman, interview by Jesse Weik, 1886–87, in Wilson and Davis, *Herndon's Informants*, 646.

45. Harris, "My Recollections of Abraham Lincoln," 11.

46. Abraham Lincoln to Joshua Speed, October 22, 1846, in Basler et al., *Collected Works*, 1:391.

47. This recollection may be suspect as the interview states that Ryan "lived at Lincoln's House till Feby 1860." Robert was then away at Harvard, and, even if Ryan had been at the house for multiple years, Robert probably hadn't been whipped since the mid-1850s, at the latest. However, I include this recollection simply to put all the facts into evidence. Margaret Ryan, interview by Jesse Weik, October 27, 1886, in Wilson and Davis, *Herndon's Informants*, 597.

48. Mary Lincoln to Alexander Williamson, Hyde Park Hotel, [Chicago], June 15, 1865, in Turner and Turner, *Mary Todd Lincoln*, 251.

49. Abraham Lincoln to Joshua Speed, October 22, 1846, in Basler et al., *Collected Works*, 1:391.

50. Abraham Lincoln to Buckner S. Morris and John J. Brown, Springfield, Illinois, October 19, 1847, in Basler et al., *Collected Works*, 1:405; Helm, *True Story of Mary*, 99; *(Springfield) Illinois Journal*, October 28, 1847, extract in Paul Angle to William H. Townsend, September 14, 1927, folder 5, box 6, 1998 MS 005, W. H. Townsend Collection. Lincoln wrote an associate, "I start for Washington, by way of Kentucky, tomorrow."

51. Lease contract between Abraham Lincoln and Cornelius Ludlum, October 23, 1847, in Basler et al., *Collected Works*, 1:406–7; Pratt, *Personal Finances*, 85; Temple, *By Square and Compass*, 61–62; Miers, *Lincoln Day by Day*, 1:295.

52. At this time in American history, the typical modes of transportation in the Midwest were horseback, carriages, boats, and railroads. C. B. Johnson, *Illinois in the Fifties*, 138; Miers, *Lincoln Day by Day*, 1:295; W. H. Townsend, *Lincoln and His Wife's Home Town*, 140–41; "Horrid Murder," *Lexington (KY) Observer and Reporter*, November 3, 1847, 3.

53. K. Helm, *True Story of Mary*, 101–2. Mary Lincoln's brother-in-law Clement B. White, husband of Mattie Todd, later claimed that he was the family member on the train with the Lincolns and their children, who were "the crossest brats I have seen." White's "recollections" are suspect, however, and should not eclipse Helm's. "Lincoln's Brother-in-Law," *Boston Globe*, February 13, 1899, 4.

Emily Todd Helm's reminiscences are some of the only reliable, remaining sources describing Robert as a child. The book by Emily's daughter, Katherine Helm, therefore, contains a gold mine of materials that, in many cases, no longer exist. Katherine Helm wrote using her mother's letters and personal diary—which the family destroyed after allowing historian William H. Townsend to look at it. The book also was written with Robert and Mary Harlan Lincoln's knowledge, approval, and aid, and, in fact, contains some of their personal letters that no longer exist. Frederic N. Towers to Mrs. Edgar Witt, February 12, 1926, and Towers to Katherine Helm, April 1, 1927, folder "Correspondence 1926–1927," F box 2, and Emily Todd Helm pencil response on Thomas M. Galey to Emily Helm, April 26, 1928, folder "Letters to Emilie Todd Helm and Kate Helm," F box 2, and William H. Townsend to Ida Tarbell, September 16, 1927, folder 5, B box 6, Helm and Todd Family Items, W. H. Townsend Collection.

54. K. Helm, *True Story of Mary*, 100–101.

55. Statement of Emily Todd Helm to William H. Townsend, June 15, 1927, in W. H. Townsend, *Lincoln and His Wife's Home Town*, 194.

56. For a detailed account of the Lincolns' Lexington visit, see W. H. Townsend, *Lincoln and His Wife's Home Town*.

57. Autobiographical essay of Robert T. Lincoln, *Harvard Class Book*, HUD 264.714F, Records of Harvard College Class of 1864.

58. Bryan, *History of the National Capital*, 2:357.

59. Busey, *Personal Reminiscences and Recollections*, 64. Bus drivers physically struggled to obtain fares, which resulted in fast and reckless driving, collisions and profanity, and overall obnoxious and dangerous conditions. Bryan, *History of the National Capital*, 2:360.

60. Gouverneur, *As I Remember*, 170.

61. Busey, *Personal Reminiscences*, 64–65; Gouverneur, *As I Remember*, 173; R. R. Wilson, *Washington*, 2:66.

62. Busey, *Personal Reminiscences*, 64.

63. Bryan, *History of the National Capital*, 2:368.

64. Busey, *Personal Reminiscences*, 87, 91.

65. Nelson, "Old Letter," 28.

66. Miers, *Lincoln Day by Day*, 1:296; Abraham Lincoln to David A. Smith, December 3, 1847, in Basler et al., *Collected Works*, 1:416; Mary Lincoln to Caleb B. Smith, May 31, 1861, in Turner and Turner, *Mary Todd Lincoln*, 87.

67. The Library of Congress now occupies the site.

68. Busey, *Personal Reminiscences*, 25–28.

69. Abraham Lincoln to Mary Lincoln, Washington, April 16, 1848, in Basler et al., *Collected Works*, 1:465.

70. Abraham Lincoln to Mary Lincoln, Washington, July 2, 1848, in ibid., 1:495.

71. Busey, *Personal Reminiscences*, 28.

72. V. Miller, "Dr. Thomas Miller and His Times," 3:307; Busey, *Personal Reminiscences*, 87.

73. Mearns, *Lincoln Papers*, 1:4–5; Dobyns, *Patent Office Pony*, 150.

74. The Patent Office, 410 feet by 275 feet, stretched from Seventh to Ninth and F to G Streets. Ames, *Ten Years in Washington*, 437–38; Dobyns, *Patent Office Pony*, 185–87.

75. Mearns, *Lincoln Papers*, 1:4–5.

76. Lincoln invented a "device to buoy vessels over shoals." Abraham Lincoln, 1849, Buoying Vessels over Shoals, U.S. Patent 6469, filed March 10, 1849, and issued May 22, 1849, in Basler et al., *Collected Works*, 2:32–36. See also Emerson, *Lincoln the Inventor*.

77. Busey, *Personal Reminiscences*, 65.

78. Abraham Lincoln "Spot" Resolutions in the U.S. House of Representatives, December 22, 1847, and Speech in United States House of Representatives: The War with Mexico, January 12, 1848, U.S. Congress, *Congressional Globe*, 30th Cong., 1st sess., new series no. 1, 1847–48, 1:64, 154–56, and also in Basler et al., *Collected Works*, 1:420–22 and 431–42; *Speech of Mr. Lincoln*. This speech angered his constituents, who saw it as disrespectful and unsupportive of the troops, and gained him the epithet "Spotty Lincoln."

79. James K. Polk, diary entry, January 23, 1848, in Nevins, *Polk*, 308.

80. Lincoln had long admired George Washington and just a few months prior to the ceremony had made his first visit to Washington's home. Temple, "Lincoln's Admiration of Washington and His Visit to Mount Vernon," 62–67.

81. W. H. Townsend, *Lincoln and His Wife's Home Town*, 164.

82. "Howes & Cos Great American Circus," advertisement, *Lexington (KY) Observer and Reporter*, August 5, 9, 16, 1848, 1; "Stickney's Circus" and "Stickney's Grand National

Circus," advertisement, *Lexington (KY) Observer and Reporter*, August 30, 1848, 3; W. H. Townsend, *Lincoln and His Wife's Home Town*, 174.

83. Untitled articles and "$5,000 Reward," advertisement, *Lexington (KY) Observer and Reporter*, August 9, 12, and 19, 1848, 3; August 20, 1848, 46M79, 1:283, William Moody Pratt Diaries; W. H. Townsend, *Lincoln and the Bluegrass*, 154–55.

84. Mary Lincoln to Mary Jane Welles, Near Chicago, July 11, 1865, in Turner and Turner, *Mary Todd Lincoln*, 257. Mary Lincoln had a package of her correspondence with her husband. It has never been found. Robert admitted burning family papers he considered too private for public viewing, and, presumably, most of Abraham and Mary's correspondence suffered this fate. This is discussed in later chapters.

85. Abraham Lincoln to Mary Lincoln, Washington, July 2, 1848, in Basler et al., *Collected Works*, 1:496.

86. Abraham Lincoln to Mary Lincoln, Washington, April 16, 1848, in ibid., 1:465.

87. Ibid., 1:465–66. Lincoln had a profound belief in the prophetic power of his dreams, especially during the Civil War.

88. Mary Lincoln to Abraham Lincoln, Lexington, May 1848, in Turner and Turner, *Mary Todd Lincoln*, 37–38 (emphasis in original).

89. Abraham Lincoln to Mary Lincoln, Washington, June 12, 1848, in Basler et al., *Collected Works*, 1:478 (emphasis in original).

90. Abraham Lincoln to William Schouler, Washington, August 8, 1848, in ibid., 1:516; Riddle, *Congressman Abraham Lincoln*, 132.

91. Abraham Lincoln to Junius Hall, Washington, September 3, 1848, in Basler, *Collected Works of Abraham Lincoln Supplement*, 11–12; Abraham Lincoln, "Speech at Worcester, Massachusetts," September 12, 1848, in Basler et al., *Collected Works*, 2:1; Schouler, "Lincoln at Tremont Temple," 81–82. That Mary and the boys accompanied Lincoln to New England is proven in Mary's own letter and a statement of William Herndon. Mary Lincoln to Henry C. Deming, Chicago, December 16, 1867, in Turner and Turner, *Mary Todd Lincoln*, 463; William Herndon, "Lincoln's Boat," monograph, in Hertz, *Hidden Lincoln*, 396. Junius Hall, a Whig attorney from Boston, invited Lincoln.

92. Basler, *Collected Works of Abraham Lincoln Supplement*, 11; Temple, *Lincoln's Connection with the Illinois & Michigan Canal*, 31.

93. Mary Lincoln to Henry C. Deming, Chicago, December 16, 1867, in Turner and Turner, *Mary Todd Lincoln*, 463.

94. Weed, *Autobiography of Thurlow Weed*, 602–3; Van Deusen, *Thurlow Weed*, 164. The journey across the Great Lakes usually took seven days, but this one was three days overdue because of severe weather. The Lincolns arrived in Chicago on October 6, 1848. *Chicago Daily Journal*, October 6, 1848, 2. For a detailed examination of the Lincolns' journey from Washington to Springfield, see Temple, *Lincoln's Connection with the Illinois & Michigan Canal*, 32–54. See also Roy Johnson, "Lincoln Spoke 21 Times in New England," *Boston Sunday Globe*, February 7, 1965, A-5.

95. The Lincolns traveled by land through Illinois, Missouri, Kentucky, Virginia, Maryland, Pennsylvania, New York, and Massachusetts and by water through Lakes Ontario, Erie, Huron, and Michigan. Also, Robert later said that when he was a young boy, his mother took him to Columbia, Missouri, to visit her relatives there (as she had previously done in 1840). RTL to North Todd Gentry, June 12, 1907, LB, 40:68:141½; North Todd Gentry to Ben Hardin Helm, August 13, 1927, folder 3, box 3, Emily Todd Helm Papers.

96. Hickey, *Collected Writings of James T. Hickey*, 62.

97. Temple, *By Square and Compass*, 68–73.

98. This trip has gone unnoticed by previous historians. Robert wrote in 1864, "The

following winter [1848–49] I lived with my grandfather in Lexington, Ky." That could only be true if Robert traveled with his father in November 1848. There is no other year in which Robert could have spent the winter in Lexington. It is known through correspondence that Robert was with his family in Washington the winter of 1847, and Robert S. Todd died in July 1849. Robert would not have spent the winter of 1846 in Lexington, at age three, nor would he have remembered it, most likely. Robert's previous visit was during the spring and summer of 1848. While it is conceivable for a person to state a year incorrectly, it is highly unlikely Robert could mistake summer for winter. It is also known that Abraham Lincoln was late for the start of the congressional session in fall 1848. It is logical that his tardiness was caused by stopping in Lexington to drop his son off with the Todds. Autobiographical essay of Robert T. Lincoln, *Harvard College Class of 1864 Class Book*, Harvard University Archives; Abraham Lincoln to Charles R. Welles, Washington, February 20, 1849, in Basler et al., *Collected Works*, 2:29; Temple, "Lincoln's Route to Washington from Springfield in 1848," 7–8; Miers, *Lincoln Day by Day*, 1:324.

99. Randall, *Lincoln's Sons*, 26. The notion that Robert as an adult was a snobby, aristocratic prig has long held sway in Lincoln circles, with little foundation to sustain it. Robert was a different person from his father, was certainly more of a dandy as a dresser, and was a successful industrialist in later years, but these "proper" traits were acquired during his college years at Northeastern Ivy League schools. To attribute Robert's later character to a few months of experiences as a five-year-old is too simplistic, but, unfortunately, it is an easy way for historians who dislike Robert to peg him as the snob they have unjustly determined him to be.

100. Most of these letters are now in the Chicago History Museum.

101. "The Cholera," *(Springfield) Illinois State Register*, April 4, 1849, 2; *(Springfield) Illinois Journal*, April 2, 1849, 2; A. G. Henry, W. A. Wallace, and J. Richardson, "To the Honorable City Council of Springfield," *(Springfield) Illinois Journal*, April 3, 1849, 3.

102. Abraham Lincoln to William B. Warren and Others, Springfield, April 7, 1849, to Elisha Embree, Springfield, May 25, 1849, to John Addison, Springfield, September 27, 1849, to John M. Clayton, Springfield, September 27, 1849, and to Thomas Ewing, Springfield, September 27, 1849, in Basler et al., *Collected Works*, 2:41, 51, 65; William Herndon to Jesse Weik, Springfield, January 8, 1886, in Hertz, *Hidden Lincoln*, 127–28; K. Helm, *True Story of Mary*, 107; Herndon and Weik, *Herndon's Life of Lincoln*, 189–90, 192–93. For a full-length discussion of this event, see Riddle, *Congressman Abraham Lincoln*, 198–235. Some historians claim Lincoln refused the Oregon offers because Mary refused to live and raise the children in such a wilderness, while others say it was simply his decision alone to avoid political suicide, as would have been any post in the overwhelmingly Democrat territory.

2. "Is Bicarb a Swear Word?"

1. C. B. Johnson, *Illinois in the Fifties*, 18–19.

2. *Springfield City Directory for 1857–1858*, 17; "Businessmen of Springfield," *(Springfield) Illinois Journal*, 1849, TS, call no. G896.2 S76, ALPL.

3. Wallace, *Past and Present*, 18–27.

4. John Hay wrote of the Springfield streets, "The richness of the soil was seen in the mud of the streets, black as ink, and of an unfathomable depth in time of thaw. There were, of course, no pavement or sidewalks; any attempt at crossing was made by laying down large chunks of wood." Nicolay and Hay, *Abraham Lincoln*, 1:156. See also Elizabeth Lushbaugh Capps, "Early Recollections of Abraham Lincoln," n.d., Reminiscences folder, A. Lincoln Collection, ALPL.

5. Angle, *Here I Have Lived*, 138.

6. "A Lincoln Nurse," *(Springfield) Illinois State Journal*, February 12, 1895, 3; Diary of Elizabeth (Mrs. William M.) Black, SC 126, ALPL; Temple, *Abraham Lincoln*, 33.

7. "A Lincoln Nurse," *(Springfield) Illinois State Journal*, February 12, 1895, 3.

8. Weik, *Real Lincoln*, 100; Elizabeth Edwards, interview by William Herndon, 1865–66, and Margaret Ryan, interview by William Herndon, October 27, 1886, Wilson and Davis, *Herndon's Informants*, 445, 597; Herndon and Weik, *Herndon's Life of Lincoln*, 258–59.

9. "Recollections of Lincoln," Gibson William Harris, box 1, Jesse Weik Papers; Harriet A. Chapman to William Herndon, Charleston, Illinois, December 10, 1866, in Wilson and Davis, *Herndon's Informants*, 512.

10. Josiah P. Kent to R. B. Van Cleave, secretary, Lincoln Centennial Association, Lanesville, Illinois, January 23, 1909, folder "Lincoln Reminiscences J–K," box 1, Lincoln Centennial Association Papers.

11. Mary Lincoln to Mary Harlan Lincoln, Leamington, England, September 16, 1870, folder 1, box 1, IF.

12. A notation in the Todd Family Bible states Robert S. Todd died "on July 17th 1849 at 10 o'clock A.M. at his farm in Franklin County, Ky. in his 59th year." This contradicts the Lexington newspaper obituary, which states he died on July 16. Photocopy of Levi Todd Family Bible (privately owned). "Death of Robert S. Todd," *Lexington (KY) Observer & Reporter*, July 18, 1849, 3; *(Springfield) Illinois Daily Journal*, July 23 and 25, 1849. I am indebted to Wayne C. Temple for sharing his photocopy of the family history pages of the Todd Family Bible with me.

13. *(Springfield) Illinois Weekly Journal*, November 21, 1849, extract quoted in Paul M. Angle to William H. Townsend, September 14, 1927, folder 5, B box 6, W. H. Townsend Collection; W. H. Townsend, *Lincoln and His Wife's Home Town*, 206–24. There is no definite indication in any primary or secondary sources whether Robert and Eddie accompanied their parents on this trip, although in a 1920 letter to his aunt, Robert, age seventy-six, recollected a visit to Lexington: "I remember being there as a very small boy but cannot recall my grandfather. No doubt because he was no longer living." RTL to Emily Helm, Washington, March 19, 1920, folder 8, RTL Papers, CHM.

14. A notation in the Todd Family Bible states Elizabeth R. Parker died "on the 22nd of January 1850 at her residence on Short Street at 5 minutes of 11 o'clock P.M. aged about 80 and supposed to be in her 81 first year from September following." This contradicts the Lexington newspaper obituary, which states she died on January 21. Levi Todd Family Bible, photocopy, courtesy of Wayne C. Temple; *Lexington Observer & Reporter*, January 26, 1850, 3.

15. U.S. Census Bureau, *Mortality Schedule for Springfield, Sangamon Co., Illinois*, MS, U.S. Census 1850, 787, Illinois State Archives; *(Springfield) Illinois Daily Journal*, February 2, 1850; Abraham Lincoln to John D. Johnston, February 23, 1850, in Basler et al., *Collected Works*, 2:76–77. The pain of the Lincolns' loss can be seen and felt in the anonymous poem "Little Eddie" that was published two days after the boy's death. Emerson, "'Of Such Is the Kingdom of Heaven.'"

16. Mrs. John Todd Stuart, interview, *Chicago Tribune*, February 12, 1900, Nicolay Papers; Roberts, *Lincoln in Illinois*, 67.

17. Mrs. John Todd Stuart, interview, *Chicago Tribune*, February 12, 1900, Nicolay Papers.

18. Abraham Lincoln to John D. Johnston, Springfield, February 23, 1850, in Basler et al., *Collected Works*, 1:76.

19. I am grateful to Jason Meyers, curator of the Museum of Funeral Customs, in Springfield, Illinois, for explaining 1850s funeral customs to me.

20. K. Helm, *True Story of Mary*, 117.

21. W. H. Townsend, *Lincoln and His Wife's Home Town*, 226–30.

22. Ibid., 230.

23. Katherine Helm states that Robert, with his mother and brother Willie, also visited Lexington in summer 1851, but the facts indicate she confused the year and miscast Eddie from 1847 as Willie in 1851. *True Story of Mary*, 102–3.

24. Ibid., 106.

25. For the best examinations of the Lincoln family's religion, see Temple, *Abraham Lincoln*.

26. Barton, *Soul of Abraham Lincoln*, 162.

27. James Smith to William Herndon, January 24, 1867, in Wilson and Davis, *Herndon's Informants*, 550; Mary Lincoln to John Todd Stuart, Chicago, December 15, 1873, in Turner and Turner, *Mary Todd Lincoln*, 604; Harris, "My Recollections of Abraham Lincoln," 11. "From the time of the death of our little Edward, I believe my husband's heart, was directed towards religion," Mary later professed. Two of Lincoln's in-law relatives, John Todd Stuart and Ninian Edwards, and acquaintance Thomas Lewis also stated a change in Lincoln's religious beliefs. Mary Lincoln to Dr. James Smith, Marienbad, Germany, June 8, 1870, in Turner and Turner, *Mary Todd Lincoln*, 567; T. Lewis, "New Light on Lincoln's Life," 134; statements of Stuart, Edwards, and Lewis quoted in Barton, *Soul of Abraham Lincoln*, 163–64; Pratt, *Personal Finances*, 93.

28. A more specific examination of Robert's religion is in chapter 15.

29. "A Lincoln Nurse," *(Springfield) Illinois State Journal*, February 12, 1895, 3; Black, "Reminiscences of the First Presbyterian Church Sabbath School," 19, 30; T. Lewis, "New Light on Lincoln's Life," 134–35.

30. "A Lincoln Nurse," *(Springfield) Illinois State Journal*, February 12, 1895, 3; Lizzie D. Black to Dr. Thomas D. Logan, March 8, 1909, quoted in Temple, *Abraham Lincoln*, 46–47.

31. RTL to John F. Dillon, January 5, 1905, RTL Papers, ALPL; RTL to Isaac Markens, Manchester, Vermont, November 4, 1917, folder 5, RTL Papers, CHM.

32. Jayne, "Personal Reminiscences of Abraham Lincoln," 10–11.

33. Evans, *Mrs. Abraham Lincoln*, 138.

34. Miers, *Lincoln Day by Day*, 31–32.

35. The surviving lists of Lincoln family accounts at local stores have many notations stating the purchases were made "by son," "by Bob," or "by Robert." Lincoln family purchases from John Williams & Co., Springfield, Illinois, 1851–60, and from Corneau and Diller, Springfield, Illinois, 1855–60, and from C. M. & S. Smith, Springfield, Illinois, account for Abraham Lincoln for 1859, Pratt, *Personal Finances*, appendix, 145–61.

36. Isaac R. Diller, interview by Beulah Gordon, untitled essay, p. 9, Mary Todd Lincoln Vertical File.

37. "From Illinois," *(New York) Commercial Advertiser*, October 29, 1867; "Mr. Lincoln's Sons," *(Keene) New-Hampshire Sentinel*, November 14, 1867, 2.

38. "Lincoln as a Father," *Leslie's Monthly*, reprinted in *Brooklyn (NY) Eagle*, August 3, 1901, 15.

39. C. H. Graves to Amelia DeMotte, Mound City, Missouri, September 3, September 15, and October 3, 1926, copies, enclosures in Amelia DeMotte to Roy P. Basler, Jacksonville, Illinois, n.d., Reminiscences Folder, A. Lincoln Collection, ALPL; Walter Graves to Ida Tarbell, Salina, Kansas, August 18, 1929, Tarbell-Lincoln Collection.

40. Reminiscences of W. C. Atkinson, *Davenport (IA) Democrat and Leader*, July 3, 1927, clipping in "Reminiscences of Springfield Area Residents" folder, A. Lincoln Collection, ALPL.

41. Reverend C. O. Hultgren, "L. P. Esbjorn," notes to unpublished manuscript, box 1, MS 13, Esbjorn Papers.

42. K. Helm, *True Story of Mary*, 108. The term *Chesterfield* most likely comes from the book *Letters to His Son* (1774), by Philip Dormer Stanhope, Fourth Earl of Chesterfield, who portrays the ideal eighteenth-century gentleman.

43. Capps, "Early Recollections of Abraham Lincoln." See note 4.

44. Frances Todd Wallace, interview by William Herndon, 1865–66, Wilson and Davis, *Herndon's Informants*, 485; Herndon and Weik, *Herndon's Life of Lincoln*, 264; Mary Edwards Brown, interview by Dorothy Kunhardt, in Kunhardt, "An Old Lady's Lincoln Memories," 57, 59–60; J. Gillespie to William Herndon, Edwardsville, Illinois, January 31, 1866, in Hertz, *Hidden Lincoln*, 289. The madstone soaked in a liquid, usually milk and then placed against the bite, or on the inside of the wrist; the stone would draw out the poison. Until Louis Pasteur's remedy for hydrophobia in 1885, there really was no medical treatment for the disease except the mad-stone. Cansler, "Madstones and Hydrophobia," 95–105; Brewster, "Specimens of Folklore from Southern Indiana," 363; "Madstones," 292–93; Shutes, *Lincoln and the Doctors*, 61.

45. Ward Hill Lamon, "About Robert Lincoln," May 1883, p. 2, LN 2415, Lamon Papers.

46. Robert Lincoln's grandson Lincoln Isham suffered a severe case of crossed eyes that was surgically fixed sometime around the turn of the twentieth century.

47. C. H. Graves to Amelia DeMotte, *At Home* (Mound City, MO), October 3, 1926, copy, enclosure in Amelia DeMotte to Roy P. Basler, Jacksonville, Illinois, n.d., and "Local Footprints of Abraham Lincoln . . . Friend of H. M. Powel, Who Tells of Their Relations," *(Taylorville, IL) Semi Weekly Breeze*, February 12, 1909, and reminiscences of W. C. Atkinson in "Tells of Standing Three Hours in Rain to Hear Talk Given by Abraham Lincoln," *(Davenport, IA) Democrat and Leader*, July 2, 1927, clipping, "Reminiscences of Springfield Area Citizens" folder, Lincoln Collection, ALPL; "Peddlers Dogged Son of Lincoln, Friend Says," *Associated Press*, n.d., clipping, "Correspondence" box, RTL Papers, ALPL.

48. "Local Footprints of Abraham Lincoln . . . Friend of H. M. Powel, Who Tells of Their Relations," *(Taylorville, IL) Semi Weekly Breeze*, February 12, 1909; W. C. Atkinson, reminiscence, "Tells of Standing Three Hours in Rain," *(Davenport, IA) Democrat and Leader*, July 2, 1927, clipping, "Reminiscences of Springfield Area Citizens" folder, Lincoln Collection, ALPL; DeWitt Smith interview, "Body of Son of Martyred President to Rest in Tomb," *(Springfield) Illinois State Journal*, July 27, 1926, 9; Harry J. Dunbaugh, "Robert Todd Lincoln: Lawyer, Executive, and Public Servant," speech before the Fortnightly, May 2, 1962, folder 2, RTL Papers, CHM; Temple, *Abraham Lincoln*, 45–46. Three of Robert's boyhood friends stated only that he had his eye corrected, while one member of Lincoln's law firm in Chicago stated that Robert went blind in one eye due to "an imperfect operation as a boy." Historian Wayne C. Temple postulates that Dr. J. Drake Harper straightened Robert's eye with an operation, based on an old newspaper advertisement that shows Abraham Lincoln vouching for the surgical skills of Harper, who claimed to fix crossed eyes. Ibid., all.

49. For a more detailed description of squint operations, see Revell, *Strabismus*, 4. See also Langworthy, "Eye Examination, Treatment and Operation," 804; DeWitt, "Concerning Eyes," 893–98.

50. It is difficult to draw conclusions about possible recovery from a surgical operation from the Lincolns' known drug purchases. Accounts from Corneau & Diller drugstore show the Lincolns purchased "1 box pain Extractor" on October 24, 1849, bottles of pain

extractor and quinine in October and November 1851, opium and pain extractors in spring 1852, and opium and pain extractor in early 1853. Hickey, *Collected Writings of James T. Hickey*, 224–25.

51. Having the patient look at a stereoscopes several times a day was also a common remedy, and the Lincolns did have a stereoscope in their home. G. C. Harlan, *Eyesight, and How to Care for It*, 87–88; Revell, *Strabismus*, 5, 14–16, 46, 49; Lancaster, "Crossed Eyes in Children," 535; McLean, "Eye Surgery," 492; Rosner, "Newer Concepts of Strabismus," 921–25.

52. Randall, *Lincoln's Sons*, 33.

53. RTL to John Nicolay, Chicago, December 23, 1894, box 5, Nicolay Papers; RTL to Colonel Joseph H. Acklen, March 25, 1904, LB, 37:63:257; Harry J. Dunbaugh, "Robert Todd Lincoln," RTL Papers, CHM.

54. Gemeroy, "Strabismus in Children," 516–17. See also G. C. Harlan, *Eyesight, and How to Care for It*, 87.

55. Dunbaugh, "Robert Todd Lincoln," RTL Papers, CHM.

56. RTL to Colonel Joseph H. Acklen, March 25, 1904, LB, 37:63:257.

57. RTL to John Nicolay, December 23, 1894, Nicolay Papers; Horace Young to RTL, March 18, 1925, RTL Collection, Hildene Archives.

58. For a full examination of Mary Lincoln's mental illness and later insanity, see Emerson, *Madness of Mary Lincoln*.

59. Orville Hickman Browning, interview with John G. Nicolay, Springfield, June 17, 1875, in Burlingame, *Oral History of Abraham Lincoln*, 1.

60. Fred T. Dubois, "Another Boy's Memories of the Lincolns," in R. R. Wilson, *Lincoln among His Friends*, 99.

61. Capps, "Early Recollections of Abraham Lincoln." See note 4.

62. "Recollections of Lincoln," Gibson William Harris, box 1, Weik Papers; Harris, "My Recollections of Abraham Lincoln," 11.

63. William Herndon to Jesse Weik, Springfield, January 9, 1886, in Hertz, *Hidden Lincoln*, 130–31; Milton Hay statement to Jesse Weik, and "a lady relative" to Jesse Weik, in Weik, *Real Lincoln*, 91, 94.

64. Margaret Ryan, interview by Jesse Weik, October 27, 1886, in Wilson and Davis, *Herndon's Informants*, 596–97. For the best examination of Mary's bad behavior, see Burlingame, "Lincolns' Marriage."

65. "Practical Habits and Manners of Lincoln," *(Belvedere, IL) Standard*, April 14, 1868, 1, clipping, "Reminiscences of Springfield Area Citizens" folder, A. Lincoln Collection, ALPL.

66. William Herndon to Jesse Weik, Springfield, January 11, 1886, in Hertz, *Hidden Lincoln*, 133–34. A similar version of the story, without mentioning Robert, is also in Herndon and Weik, *Herndon's Life of Lincoln*, 261–62.

67. Dubois, "Another Boy's Memories of the Lincolns," in R. R. Wilson, *Lincoln among His Friends*, 97.

68. RTL to Thomas Lowry, Augusta, Georgia, December 31, 1907, LB, 40:69:466. Carl Sandburg relates this story in his Lincoln biography, although his wording was slightly different, and he characterizes Robert as a small child, although Robert said he was about fifteen. Since there is no evidence he ever spoke to Robert Lincoln, and the book does not cite the source of the story, Sandburg probably got it from Lowry. *Abraham Lincoln*, 2:249.

69. "The First Stop," *Chicago Tribune*, October 26, 1884, 11.

70. Stringer, *History of Logan County, Illinois*, 1:567–69.

71. Robert Lincoln's statement seems to prove that he was the "youngest American" who shared with his father. Another man, however, John S. Stevens, who was thirteen in 1853, claimed he was the "youngest American" who shared the watermelon with Lincoln, although there is nothing to corroborate his statement. John S. Stevens to Lawrence B. Stringer, St. Louis, April 30, 1926, and affidavit of Blanche Martin, "Concerning the Events Surrounding the Christening of the City of Lincoln," Lincoln, Illinois, May 20, 1970, Lincoln Collection, Lincoln College Museum.

72. G. T. M. Davis, *Autobiography of the Late Col. George T. M. Davis*, 362–64; Walter B. Stevens, *Reporter's Lincoln*, 102–3. A slightly different version of this story was published in an untitled article in the *Hartford (CT) Courant*, April 16, 1861, 2.

73. Recollections of Ardelia Wheelock, in Ayres, "Lincoln as a Neighbor," 183–85.

74. James Gourley, interview by William Herndon, February 9, 1866, Lamon Papers; also in Wilson and Davis, *Herndon's Informants*, 452. A slightly different version of the story can be found in "Mrs. Lincoln Buildeth," *Sterling [IL?] Republican and Gazette*, April 26, 1862, 1.

75. Mary Lincoln to Emily Todd Helm, Springfield, February 16, 1857, in Turner and Turner, *Mary Todd Lincoln*, 48 (emphasis in original).

76. William Herndon to Jesse Weik, January 8, 1886, in Hertz, *Hidden Lincoln*, 128.

77. T. D. Vredenburgh to R. B. Van Cleave, Springfield, July 7, 1908, folder "Letters T–V," box 1, Lincoln Centennial Association Papers.

78. John T. Stuart to Elizabeth J. Stuart, Springfield, February 11, 1855, quoted in Pratt, *Personal Finances*, 97.

79. Untitled article, *(Springfield) Illinois State Journal*, June 29, 1858, 3.

80. Ibid., January 7, 1859, 3.

81. *(Springfield) Illinois State Journal*, October 16, 1858, 3; untitled article, *Alton (IL) Courier*, reprinted in *(Springfield) Illinois State Journal*, October 20, 1858, 3; RTL to Judd Stewart, October 18, 1917, HM 8430, RTL Collection, Huntington Library.

82. Autobiographical essay of Robert T. Lincoln, *Harvard College Class of 1864 Class Book*, Harvard University Archives; Page, *Abraham Lincoln in New Hampshire*, 5–6. Robert supposedly told Frederick W. Lehmann that his father "very much desired that Robert should go to Harvard." Stevens, *Reporter's Lincoln*, 72.

83. There is a tradition that Robert conceived of attending Harvard from John Hay, although an early Hay biographer discredited this rumor. Thayer, *Life and Letters of John Hay*, 1:23.

84. Abraham Lincoln had only a few terms of formal schooling, long enough mainly to learn to read and write and do basic mathematics; thereafter, he taught himself. As a girl, Mary Todd spent six years at Dr. John Ward's Academy, four years at Madame Victorie Charlotte Leclere Mentelle's boarding school, where French was the only language allowed spoken, and, after a brief visit to Springfield, Illinois, Mary returned to Dr. Ward's tutelage for two years of "a sort of post-graduate work." E. T. Helm, "Mary Todd Lincoln," 476–80; Randall, *Mary Lincoln*, 23–28.

3. "The Most Profitable [Year] of My Life"

1. RTL to John F. Dillon, January 5, 1905, folder "Robert Todd Lincoln Letters," RTL Papers, ALPL.

2. K. Helm, *True Story of Mary*, 108; Mrs. R. F. Donaldson (granddaughter of Elizabeth Grimsley Brown, Mary's cousin), statement to Beulah Gordon, untitled, undated essay, p. 14, Mary Todd Lincoln Vertical File.

3. James H. Methany, interview by William Herndon, 1865–66, in Wilson and Davis, *Herndon's Informants*, 470. For Lincoln's poetry, see Emerson, "Poetic Lincoln," 4–12.

4. Emerson, *Lincoln the Inventor.*

5. Elizabeth Humphreys Norris to Emily Todd Helm, Garden City, Kansas, September 28, 1895, quoted in E. T. Helm, "Mary Todd Lincoln, 477–78.

6. K. Helm, *True Story of Mary*, 108. An 1847 copy of Scott's book *Lady of the Lake*, inscribed by Mary Lincoln to her cousin Helen M. Morse—and perhaps even the very same book Mary read to Robert—is part of the Lincoln archival collection (call number PR 5308.A11847) at the Abraham Lincoln Library and Museum, Harrogate, Tennessee.

7. Herndon and Weik, *Herndon's Lincoln*, 207.

8. Harriet A. Chapman to William Herndon, Charleston, Illinois, December 10, 1866, frames 1270–71, reel 8, series 4, H-W; Wilson and Davis, *Herndon's Informants*, 512. See also Elizabeth Lushbaugh Capps, "Early Recollections of Abraham Lincoln," n.d., Reminiscences folder, A. Lincoln Collection, ALPL.

9. Kaine, "Lincoln as a Boy Knew Him," 557.

10. Both Robert Lincoln and Herndon recalled seeing Lincoln studying Euclid's geometry, which Abraham later boasted he "nearly mastered." Friend and colleague Leonard Swett remembered Lincoln on the circuit "with 'a geometry,' or 'an astronomy,' or some book of that kind, working out propositions in moments of leisure." One 1867 newspaper article listed all the books on the Lincoln & Herndon law office bookshelf, which includes the topics of grammar, morality, history, physics, philosophy, and zoology. Abraham Lincoln, autobiography written for John L. Scripps, June 1860, in Basler et al., *Collected Works*, 4:62; RTL to Isaac Markens, Manchester, Vermont, November 4, 1917, folder 5, RTL Papers, CHM; William Herndon to Jesse Weik, Springfield, February 11, 1887, in Hertz, *Hidden Lincoln*, 172; Weik, *Real Lincoln*, 239; Leonard Swett, "Mr. Lincoln's Story of His Own Life," in A. T. Rice, *Reminiscences of Abraham Lincoln by Distinguished Men of His Time*, 467; V. H., "Abraham Lincoln: His Office, His House, and His Tomb, as They Are: Interesting Reminiscences," *Cincinnati Commercial*, July 25, 1867, 2 (also reprinted in Temple, "Herndon on Lincoln," 34–50); Joseph Gillespie to William Herndon, Edwardsville, Illinois, December 8, 1866, and John T. Stuart, interview by William Herndon, December 20, 1866, in Wilson and Davis, *Herndon's Informants*, 505–6, 519; Whitney, *Life on the Circuit with Lincoln*, 49; "Lincoln, Miss Roby, and Astronomy."

11. Autobiographical essay of Robert T. Lincoln, *Harvard College Class of 1864 Class Book*, Harvard University Archives.

12. Hart, *Lincoln's Springfield: Springfield's Early Schools*, 37; Hart, *Lincoln's Springfield: Abel W. Estabrook*, 17; Wallace, *Past and Present of the City of Springfield*, 18; Pulliam, "Changing Attitudes toward Free Public Schools in Illinois 1825–1860," 193–94; Walker, "Development of the Free Public High School in Ill. during the Nineteenth Century," 268–69, 271. The academy charged between $2 and $5 per quarter in tuition, depending on the department enrolled in and the classes taken.

13. "From Ill.," *Commercial Advertiser* (New York City), October 29, 1867; "Local Footprints of Abraham Lincoln . . . Friend of H. M. Powel, Who Tells of Their Relations," *Taylorville (IL) Semi Weekly Breeze*, February 12, 1909, typed copy, folder "Reminiscences of Springfield Area Citizens," Lincoln Collection, ALPL.

14. Pulliam, "Changing Attitudes toward Free Public Schools in Illinois 1825–1860," 195.

15. Ibid., 202–3; Walker, "Development of the Free Public High School in Illinois during the Nineteenth Century," 268–69.

16. Mary Lincoln to Margaret W. Preston, Springfield, Illinois, July 23, 1853, 63M349, box 48, Wickliffe-Preston Papers; *History of Sangamon County, Ill.*, 914. Mary Lincoln boasted to a friend in 1853 that ten-year-old Robert was studying Latin and Greek.

17. Estabrook eventually became principal of Springfield's Third Ward free school, where the students learned reading, spelling, history, geography, and English grammar. "Examination of the Free Schools," *(Springfield) Illinois State Journal*, July 15, 1858, 3; Hart, *Lincoln's Springfield: Springfield's Early Schools*, 66.

18. *History of Sangamon County, Ill.*, 479–80; Evjen, "Illinois State University, 1852–1868," 54–56. For a complete history of the school, see Lentz, *Miracle of Carthage: History of Carthage College, 1847–1974*.

19. Illinois State University, first annual announcement, quoted in *History of Sangamon County, Ill.*, 480.

20. Ibid.; Evjen, "Illinois State University," 56.

21. Evjen, "Illinois State University," 58–59; Lentz, *Miracle of Carthage*, 39. Lincoln purchased the scholarship from Springfield druggist P. C. Canedy and paid the required yearly interest of $19.50 on the fund until April 27, 1860. Lincoln canceled his scholarship on November 26, 1864, by paying fifty dollars to the Board of Trustees. Benjamin C. Suesserott to RTL, Springfield, Illinois, November 18, 1864, RTL Papers, ALPL.

22. *Annual Catalogue of the Officers and Students of Ill. State University, Springfield, Ill., 1858–1859*, 12; *Springfield City Directory for 1857–1858*, 7.

23. Autobiographical essay of Robert T. Lincoln, *Harvard College Class of 1864 Class Book*, Harvard University Archives.

24. RTL to Reverend C. M. Esbjorn, December 16, 1897, LB, 33:54:46.

25. Evjen, "Ill. State University," 62.

26. George H. Schnur to RTL, Erie, Pennsylvania, December 11, 1925, RTL Collection, Hildene Archives.

27. Leonard Swett, "Mr. Lincoln's Story of His Own Life," in A. T. Rice, *Reminiscences of Abraham Lincoln by Distinguished Men of His Time*, 79. One neighbor said Lincoln would study Latin with Robert, often "declining Latin words out loud while engaged in doing his chores around the house." "Local Footprints of Abraham Lincoln," *Taylorville (IL) Semi Weekly Breeze*, February 12, 1909, ALPL.

28. Evjen, "Illinois State University," 61–64.

29. Lentz, *Miracle of Carthage*, 42.

30. Conkling's daughter later characterized her father as "a friend of Robert Lincoln all his life." Katherine Conkling McCormick, cover letter to Clinton Conkling Papers, folder 297, box 16, series 2, group 352, Miscellaneous Manuscript Collection.

31. Chapman, "Boyhood of John Hay," 445–46.

32. Thayer, *Life and Letters of John Hay*, 1:21.

33. Dennett, *John Hay*, 25; F. J. Williams, "Robert Todd Lincoln and John Hay, Fellow Travelers," 4; Goff, "Education of Robert Todd Lincoln," 343.

34. RTL to William Roscoe Thayer, Manchester, Vermont, August 6, 1914, bMS Am 1081 (1060), William Roscoe Thayer Papers.

35. Ibid.

36. Dennett, *John Hay*, 59.

37. "Lincoln Kin Gives Books to Library," *Washington Post*, May 31, 1960, B1.

38. Secretary of State, *Illinois State Library: Register of Books Loaned to Members of the Legislature, Officers and Members of the Illinois State Library*, Illinois State Archives (also, transcript in Sutton, "Lincoln and Son Borrow Books," and in Sutton-Kellerstrass, "Lincoln and Son Borrow Books"); Sorenson, "Ill. State Library: 1818–1870." One family friend

later recalled that Robert was "very fond of books; he would pay no attention to anyone or anything. . . . [H]e was a great student." Julia Sprigg, interview by Carlos W. Goltz, January 8, 1928, in Goltz, *Incidents in the Life of Mary Todd Lincoln*, 47–54.

39. RTL to Isaac Markens, Manchester, Vermont, November 4, 1917, folder 5, RTL Papers, CHM; Secretary of State, *Illinois State Library*.

40. Sutton-Kellerstrass, "Lincoln and Son Borrow Books," 13–16. Some of these books he certainly borrowed to help with his schoolwork. For example, he borrowed Homer's *Iliad* in June 1858, which was during the second session of his sophomore year at Illinois State University, and for which the book was required reading. *Annual Catalogue of the Officers and Students of Ill. State University*, 11.

41. Autobiographical essay of Robert T. Lincoln, *Harvard College Class of 1864 Class Book*, Harvard University Archives.

42. RTL to Robert S. Rantoul, February 20, 1909, original in RTL Papers, ALPL, and copy in LB, 42:72:186. Robert and George also traveled with Charles Chase. Charles W. McLellan, who moved to Springfield in 1856 and knew the Lincoln family, said good-bye to the three boys at the train station. "The mothers, I believe it was Mrs. Lincoln alone, had cooked a whole ham and carried it with their other lunch in a coffee sack," McLellan later wrote. "I remember Charlie telling afterwards of his taking Bob's watch, and he thought a good part of the trip that it had been stolen." Abraham Lincoln did not accompany his son. Unpublished memoirs of Charles W. McLellan, private collection.

43. Mary Lincoln to Hannah Shearer, Springfield, August 28, 1859, in Turner and Turner, *Mary Todd Lincoln*, 58.

44. Hale, "James Russell Lowell and His Friends," 62–63; Hale, *James Russell Lowell and His Friends*, 200–201.

45. RTL to Hale, March 19, 1909, LB, 42:73:299–300. This should not be construed that Robert was upset about the incorrect story. In his first letter to Hale, he wrote, "It is a good story, and its accuracy is, of course, not necessary for the illustration of the point which you make." RTL to Edward Everett Hale, Chicago, May 29, 1899, folder 21, box 36, Hale Family Papers.

46. RTL to Edward Everett Hale, Chicago, May 29, 1899, Hale Family Papers. Robert made similar statements to a different correspondent one month before he wrote to Hale. In that letter he postulated that perhaps it was the bond with cover letter by Julius Rockwell that Robert gave Harvard President Walker—in which Rockwell probably mentioned the Lincoln-Douglas debates—that confused Hale. RTL to William Roscoe Thayer, Chicago, April 24, 1899, bMS Am 1081 (1060), William Roscoe Thayer Papers.

47. RTL to Edward Everett Hale, March 19, 1909, LB, 42:73:299–300.

48. Harvard University Entrance Examinations, 1836–1925, box 1, HUC 7000.2, Harvard University Archives. The incomplete archives of 1859 entrance exams has examples from June, July 13, July 14, July 18, and September, but there is no way to tell how many other examinations, and on what dates, there were. It seems that Robert took his in August.

49. Barton, *Life of Abraham Lincoln*, 1:409. Barton does not cite his source for this, and the Harvard University Archives does not contain any record of Robert's 1859 failure. Barton's writing sounds as though he interviewed Robert Lincoln for the book, which is impossible, as Robert refused to aid him in his Lincoln work. While subsequent historians cite this fifteen-of-sixteen number, none have citation for it, and it seems to have all come from Barton's book. The incomplete Harvard University Archives records of the 1859 entrance examinations show only ten subjects.

50. In 1850, the Harvard entrance exams took eight hours to administer; by 1865, they

took three days. Robert's friend and Illinois State University classmate George C. Latham also failed to enter Harvard; and John Hay, a student at Brown University, later criticized his own education in Springfield. Story, "Harvard Students, the Boston Elite, and the New England Preparatory System, 1800–1876," 285.

51. Abraham Lincoln to George C. Latham, Springfield, Illinois, July 22, 1860, in Basler et al., *Collected Works*, 4:87 (emphasis in original).

52. Autobiographical essay of Robert T. Lincoln, *Harvard College Class of 1864 Class Book*, Harvard University Archives; RTL to Edward Everett Hale, Chicago, May 29, 1899, folder 21, box 36, Hale Family Papers; RTL to Hale, March 19, 1909, LB, 42:73:299–300.

53. Crosbie, *Phillips Exeter Academy*, 32–33.

54. After 1850, Phillips Exeter supplied one half of all academy boys at Harvard, an average of perhaps fifteen per year. Story, "Harvard Students," 289. See also Crosbie, *Phillips Exeter Academy*, 275.

55. Batchelder, *Bits of Harvard History*, 308.

56. Carol Walker Aten, "Exeter Is a Seaport," in Bolster, *Cross-Grained and Wiley Waters*, accessed on the Exeter Historical Society web page, http://exeterhistory.org/; C. H. Bell, *History of the Town of Exeter*, 317–34.

57. M. R. Williams, *Story of Phillips Exeter*, 209.

58. Cunningham, *Familiar Sketches of the Phillips Exeter Academy and Surroundings*, 240–43.

59. Page, *Abraham Lincoln in New Hampshire*, 98.

60. Hoyt, *Phillips Family and Phillips Exeter Academy*, 24–25; catalogue, Phillips Exeter Academy, 1859–60, RTL Collection, Phillips Exeter Academy Archives; Cox, "Abraham Lincoln in Exeter, Feb. 29–Mar. 5, 1860," 2; Crosbie, *Phillips Exeter Academy*, 95. Robert gave an autographed photo portrait of himself to Mrs. Clarke as a Christmas gift in 1905, signing it, "to Mrs. S. B. Clarke, with my affectionate remembrance of her kindness to me as a boy in 1859." Original photograph in RTL Collection, Phillips Exeter Academy Archives. Students of indigent circumstances were offered free or discounted boarding in Abbott Hall on campus. The academy also offered extensive financial aid for students of less-prosperous families.

61. Autobiographical essay of Robert T. Lincoln, *Harvard College Class of 1864 Class Book*, Harvard University Archives. *Subfreshman* means Robert was considered a senior at Phillips Academy and would enter Harvard as a freshman. Hoyt, *Phillips Family*, 25.

62. RTL to Reverend J. B. L. Soule, April 11, 1881, LB, 4:6:112. For other statements of his affection for the school, see RTL to Albert C. Perkins, June 12, 1882, RTL to B. L. S. Harman, November 16, 1908, and RTL to Frank Hamlin, May 8, 1909, LB 7:9:23, 41:71:405, and 42:73:422. Robert continued his connection with his alma mater throughout his life also by attending graduation ceremonies, being a member of the alumni association, donating money to the alumni endowment fund, and agreeing to submit a portrait of himself to Alumni Hall. See RTL to Albert C. Perkins, June 12, 1882, LB, 7:9:23, and to S. H. Dana, clerk, Phillips Exeter Academy, March 3, 1921, folder 11, box 5, RTLFP; RTL Lincoln to B. F. Prescott, Chicago, January 26, 1894, Rauner Manuscript 894126, Rauner Special Collections Library; "Alumni of Phillips Exeter Academy," *New York Times*, March 29, 1885, 7; "Phillips Exeter Academy," *New York Times*, June 18, 1903, 5; "To Direct $2,000,000 Drive," *New York Times*, July 21, 1919, 24; "News of the School," 23.

63. C. H. Bell, *History of the Town of Exeter, New Hampshire*, 295.

64. Crosbie, *Phillips Exeter Academy*, 95; Cunningham, *Familiar Sketches*, 51.

65. Cunningham, *Familiar Sketches*, 51.

66. Crosbie, *Phillips Exeter Academy*, 100.

67. M. S. Snow, "Abraham Lincoln—A Personal Reminiscence," 30; "Reminiscences of Robert Lincoln and Abraham Lincoln," 8–9.

68. Class of 1860 Grade Book, Phillips Exeter Academy Archives. Robert's grades improved every term with one exception. In the term beginning August 31, 1859, Robert scored 9 on his average of Recitations, 8.8 on his average of Compositions, and 8.5 on his average of Declamation. In the term beginning December 14, 1859, Robert scored 9.2 on his average of Recitations, 8.6 on his average of Compositions, and 8.6 on his average of Declamation. In the term beginning April 4, 1860, Robert scored a 9.3 on his average of Recitations, 9 on his average of Compositions, and 8.9 on his average of Declamation.

69. Cunningham, *Familiar Sketches*, 57–58, 149.

70. Ibid., 149.

71. "Robert Lincoln Better Athlete Than Student While at Exeter," *Boston Sunday Globe*, n.d., clipping in RTL Collection, Phillips Exeter Academy.

72. Autobiographical essay of Robert T. Lincoln, *Harvard College Class of 1864 Class Book*, Harvard University Archives.

73. Untitled article, *New York Tribune*, June 10, 1878, 4; statement of Gideon Lane Soule, quoted in unnamed, undated newspaper clipping in Goff Papers. A third account states that the boys were not caught by the law but merely guilted into replacement, repair, and monetary remuneration after a speech by Principal Soule to the student body, in which he reminded them of the honor of appropriate conduct and that "a gentleman owes it to himself to repair as soon as possible any injury that he has done to another." Statement of Reverend John H. Morison, quoted in Cunningham, *Familiar Sketches*, 52–53.

74. Autobiographical essay of Robert T. Lincoln, *Harvard College Class of 1864 Class Book*, Harvard University Archives.

75. Abraham Lincoln to Norman B. Judd, Springfield, November 16, 1858, in Basler et al., *Collected Works*, 3:337. This was a constant cycle for Abraham Lincoln; while neglecting business for politics in nearly every election cycle, the close of the contests inevitably led him back to business. Pratt, *Personal Finances*, 99–114.

76. Account books for John Williams & Co., Corneau & Diller, and C. M. & S. Smith, Springfield, Illinois, 1859, in Pratt, *Personal Finances*, 149, 152, 157–58, 160.

77. This number does not include whatever cash Abraham Lincoln could and probably did give Robert during the former's visit in February 1860. Abraham Lincoln bank account, Springfield Marine and Fire Insurance Company, withdrawals, 1859, in Pratt, *Personal Finances*, 167–79.

78. Mary Lincoln to Hannah Shearer, Springfield, October 2, 1859, in Turner and Turner, *Mary Todd Lincoln*, 59.

79. Abraham Lincoln to James A. Briggs, Danville, Illinois, November 13, 1859, in Basler et al., *Collected Works*, 3:494. For the latest examination of Lincoln's trip to New York City to deliver his Cooper Union speech, see Holzer, *Lincoln at Cooper Union*.

80. Whether Lincoln wanted to visit his son and so accepted the invitation or accepted the invitation and then decided to visit his son has been debated by previous historians. George Haven Putnam's version is the most cited source of the former view, in which he wrote in 1922 that Robert Lincoln told him his father had planned in January 1859 to visit Exeter, using funds from a client's fee. When the fee was not forthcoming, Lincoln had to cancel the trip. One week later, Lincoln was invited to speak in New York, and the men "have sent me money for the trip. I can manage the rest of the way." This story, although repeated by subsequent historians, appears to be a fiction. Putnam's first version of the

story, printed in a book in 1909, does not include it, and the 1909 letter from Robert to Putnam about Abraham Lincoln's visit included in the book gives no indication of the elder Lincoln's motivations for agreeing to the speech. The letter simply states, "After the Cooper Institute address, my father came to Exeter to see how I was getting along." It also has been subsequently proven that Lincoln originally was invited to speak in New York in October 1859, not February 1860. Ostensibly, the dissection of Lincoln's primary motive goes toward the closeness or estrangement between father and son. Such a Manichaean view does injustice to both Lincolns. It is most likely no more complicated than that Lincoln wanted both to visit Robert and to speak in the East, and he was able to accomplish both desires, as well as earn a fee, in the process. Putnam, "Speech That Won the East for Lincoln," 220–21; Page, *Abraham Lincoln in New Hampshire*, 5–6; Goff, *Robert Todd Lincoln*, 30; Putnam, *Abraham Lincoln*; RTL to George Haven Putnam, Manchester, Vermont, July 27, 1909, in Putnam, *Abraham Lincoln*, 209; Abraham Lincoln to James A. Briggs, Danville, Illinois, November 13, 1859, 3:494; Holzer, *Lincoln at Cooper Union*, 22.

81. Holzer, *Lincoln at Cooper Union*, 8.

82. Abraham Lincoln, speech at Springfield, Illinois, June 26, 1857, in Basler et al., *Collected Works*, 2:403.

83. William B. Morrill to Abraham Lincoln, February 28, 1860, Abraham Lincoln Papers, LOC.

84. George W. Benn to "son of A. Lincoln," Dover, New Hampshire, February 27, 1860, and RTL to George W. Benn, Exeter, New Hampshire, February 28, 1860, in Page, *Abraham Lincoln in New Hampshire*, 26–27.

85. This assumption is logical but unknowable. In fact, a letter from Tuck written in May 1860 refutes this possibility. While traveling from Chicago to St. Louis, Tuck was "urged" to visit Lincoln while in Springfield. "I was acquainted with him, as you know, on Cong., and hence consented," Tuck wrote. It is interesting that Tuck did not mention anything about previously visiting with Lincoln in Exeter or offering him a room. Amos Tuck to "Abby and Ellen," Springfield, Illinois, May 20, 1860, folder 10, box 19, Benjamin B. French Family Papers. The story that Tuck hosted Lincoln is in Harlan Trott, "Exeter Still Cherishes Visit of A. Lincoln," *Christian Science Monitor*, November 19, 1931, clipping, RTL Papers, Phillips Exeter Academy Archives, and "Exeter Still Cherishes the Visit of Abraham Lincoln," *(Dover, NH) Foster's Daily Democrat*, February 11, 1932, clipping, RTL Papers, Phillips Exeter Academy Archives.

86. Abraham Lincoln to Mary Lincoln, Exeter, New Hampshire, March 4, 1860, Abraham Lincoln Papers, LOC; RTL to James Schouler, Augusta, Georgia, December 27, 1907, RTL Papers, ALPL. Lincoln's letter to Schouler, as well as two other letters on the same topic, are reprinted in Schouler, "Lincoln at Tremont Temple," 81–82. See also Page, *Abraham Lincoln in New Hampshire*, 28, 46.

87. The only full account of Lincoln's speech that night is in the *American Ballot, and Rockingham County Intelligencer* (Exeter and Portsmouth, NH), March 8, 1860, 3.

88. Snow, "Abraham Lincoln," 31–32; also reprinted in Crosbie, *Phillips Exeter Academy*, 257–58, and in "Reminiscences of Robert Lincoln and Abraham Lincoln," 8–9. See also A. Blair, "Abraham Lincoln Visit to Exeter in 1860," 4–5; Warren Prescott interview in Edgar Warren, "Did Lincoln's Visit to Exeter in 1860 Make Him President?" *Boston Evening Transcript*, October 29, 1927, 3; Prescott interview also in "Whitfield Farmer Impressed by Abraham Lincoln's Talk in 1860," unnamed clipping, February 1968, Abraham Lincoln Collection, Phillips Exeter Academy Archives.

89. Snow, "Abraham Lincoln," 31–32.

90. Cox, "Abraham Lincoln in Exeter," 4.

91. Abraham Lincoln to Mary Lincoln, Exeter, New Hampshire, March 4, 1860, Abraham Lincoln Papers, LOC.

92. Page, *Abraham Lincoln in New Hampshire*, 112–13.

93. Blair, "Abraham Lincoln Visit to Exeter in 1860," 4–5; "Reminiscences of Robert Lincoln and Abraham Lincoln," 7–8. Robert may actually have gotten one, or at least tried to play one, for when reminiscing years later about a visit to Vermont in 1864, he wrote to a friend, "I don't know what musical instrument he then handled. My efforts were devoted to the banjo!" RTL to Mrs. Munson, Manchester, Vermont, August 29, 1912, RTL Collection, Hildene Archives.

94. RTL to George Haven Putnam, Manchester, Vermont, July 27, 1909, reproduced in Putnam, *Abraham Lincoln*, 209; RTL to James Schouler, Augusta, Georgia, December 27, 1907, RTL Papers, ALPL; "Mr. Lincoln in New England," *(Springfield) Illinois State Journal*, March 16, 1860, 2; Roy Johnson, "Lincoln Spoke 21 Times in New England," *Boston Sunday Globe*, February 7, 1965, A5.

95. Abraham Lincoln to Mary Lincoln, Exeter, New Hampshire, March 4, 1860, Abraham Lincoln Papers, LOC.

96. RTL to James Schouler, January 29, 1908, RTL Papers, ALPL.

97. Blair, "Abraham Lincoln Visit to Exeter in 1860," 4–5; "Reminiscences of Robert Lincoln and Abraham Lincoln," 7–8. J. H. Littlefield, a student in the Lincoln & Herndon law office in 1860, recalled Lincoln telling his partner, "Billie, that boy Bob says he must have some money, as he has got to entertain his class in consequence of my having been nominated for the presidency." "Memories of Lincoln, by a Brooklynite Who Was a Student in His Law Office," *Brooklyn (NY) Eagle*, October 16, 1887, 7.

98. "Reminiscences of Robert Lincoln and Abraham Lincoln," 7. Phillips Exeter Academy's official school historian, Myron R. Williams, also called it "a cherished bit of Exeter tradition" that Lincoln's visit there is what made him president. M. R. Williams, *Story of Phillips Exeter*, 57.

99. Untitled article, *New York Times*, July 18, 1860, 2; untitled article, *(Springfield) Illinois State Journal*, July 26, 1860, 2; Cunningham, *Familiar Sketches*, 115; John Langdon Sibley's diary (known as Sibley's private journal), entry for July 16, 1860, HUG 1791.72.10, Harvard University Archives, available at http://hul.harvard.edu/huarc/refshelf/Sibley.htm#1860. Robert took the exams at Phillips Exeter. Ibid., all.

100. Autobiographical essay of Robert T. Lincoln, *Harvard College Class of 1864 Class Book*, Harvard University Archives.

101. Abraham Lincoln to Anson G. Henry, Springfield, Illinois, July 4, 1860, in Basler et al., *Collected Works*, 4:82.

102. Amos Tuck to David Davis, Exeter, New Hampshire, August 24, 1860, folder 51, box 8, David Davis Papers, CHM. Tuck no doubt expressed a similar sentiment to Lincoln himself during a visit to the newly named presidential candidate at Springfield in May 1860. Amos Tuck to "Abby and Ellen," Springfield, Illinois, May 20, 1869, folder 10, box19, Benjamin B. French Family Papers, LOC.

4. "Robert Lincoln Has Been Dubbed the Prince of Rails!"

1. Mary Lincoln to Adeline Judd, Springfield, June 13, 1860, in Turner and Turner, *Mary Todd Lincoln*, 64 (emphasis in original).

2. "Celebration of Independence" and "The Fourth at Stratham," *Portsmouth (NH) Journal of Literature and Politics*, June 30, July 3 and 7, 1860, 2; *(Springfield) Illinois State*

Journal, July 7, 1860, 3; untitled article, *Hartford (CT) Daily Courant*, July 10, 1860, 2; "Portsmouth Items," *Boston Globe*, August 11, 1874, 1.

3. "Utah's War Governor Talks of Many Famous Men," *New York Times*, October 1, 1911, SM 10.

4. Harvard University Admission Records, box 1, HUC 860, Harvard University Archives. Such a bond, "executed by two bondsmen, one of whom, at least, is a resident of Massachusetts," was a standard admission policy at Harvard. Ibid.

5. Lincoln also wrote his longtime friend David Davis—who, through Davis's wife's brother, was Rockwell's brother-in-law—and asked that he write to Rockwell to endorse the request. Davis forwarded Lincoln's letter to Rockwell and wrote on it, "I need not assure you that *there will be no danger* of signing this bond." Rockwell's response to Davis has not been found. Abraham Lincoln to Julius Rockwell, Springfield, July 27, 1860, and Abraham Lincoln to David Davis, Springfield, July 27, 1860 (endorsed with note by Davis to Julius Rockwell, Bloomington, Illinois, July 29, 1860), folder 50, box 8, David Davis Papers, CHM; also in Basler, *Collected Works Supplement*, 57 (full text of both letters also in *Rail Splitter*, 12, nos. 1–2 [Fall–Winter 2007]: 28]. Robert Lincoln later wrote that his father thought over the matter of whom to ask as a surety and said he had "very good relations" with Rockwell. RTL to Edward Everett Hale, Chicago, May 29, 1899, RTL Papers, ALPL. (Emphasis in original.)

6. Abraham Lincoln's bank account at Springfield Marine and Fire Insurance Company shows a $150 draft to Robert "to enroll at Harvard College." Pratt, *Personal Finances*, 172.

7. Lyon, "College Recollections and Stories," 183.

8. "Recollections of Charles S. Fairchild about the hazing of Robert Lincoln at Harvard," miscellaneous file #816, Vermont Historical Society. The Harvard faculty tried to stop the hazing custom in 1860, going so far in November 1860 as to suspend eight sophomores for one year for being caught in the practice. Sibley's private journal, entry for November 20, 1860, Harvard University Archives; see also S. E. Morison, *Three Centuries at Harvard: 1636–1936*, 311–12.

9. Robert T. Lincoln list of classes and list of grades, Archives Biographical File, HUG 300, Harvard University Archives.

10. Autobiographical essay of Robert T. Lincoln, *Harvard College Class of 1864 Class Book*, Harvard University Archives.

11. Latham was severely distraught at the rejection. As his friend's father David McConkey wrote to Harvard President Cornelius Fulton, "The poor fellow, I understand, wants very much to be at Cambridge, with his friend and neighbor Lincoln who was to have roomed with him." Despite this personal plea for another immediate test for Latham, he never made it to Harvard and instead attended Yale University. He withdrew one year later, however, after the death of his brother. David McConkey to Cornelius Fulton, West Chester, Pennsylvania, September 3, 1860, 27:272, 1860, second series, Harvard College Papers, Harvard University Archives 1, 5.125; *Account of the Triennial and Sexennial Meetings of the Class of 1865 (Yale College)*, 115.

12. Autobiographical essay of Robert T. Lincoln, *Harvard College Class of 1864 Class Book*, Harvard University Archives; RTL to Clement A. Griscom, January 14, 1903, LB, 36:61:271.

13. Lyon, "College Recollections and Stories," 183.

14. Cornelius Felton to Abraham Lincoln, Cambridge, January 20, 1862, Papers of Cornelius Felton, College Letters, 1860–62, 1, 15.890.3, 5:316, Harvard University Archives.

15. Harvard Faculty Meeting, October 1, 1860, Faculty Records, 16:3, 5.5.2, Harvard University Archives.

16. Lyon, "College Recollections and Stories," 183.

17. "Minor Topics," *New York Times*, June 23, 1860, 4.

18. "The Prince's Tour in the States," *New York Times*, September 19, 1860, 4. The prince also visited Harvard on October 19, 1860, where he was introduced to each college class and perhaps even met Robert Lincoln personally. "Prince in Boston," *New York Times*, October 20, 1860 1; "Prince of Wales' Visit to Cambridge," *Cambridge (MA) Chronicle*, October 20, 1860, 2.

19. Untitled article, *(Springfield) Illinois State Journal*, October 12, 1860, 2.

20. Mercy Conkling to Clinton Conkling, Springfield, Illinois, October 20, 1860, folder 14, box 1, Conkling Family Papers; also in Pratt, *Concerning Mr. Lincoln*, 24–25.

21. Harry Gourley to RTL, Springfield, February 22, 1861, frame 7453, reel 17, series 1, Abraham Lincoln Papers, LOC.

22. *(Springfield) Illinois State Journal*, August 4–9, 1860; see also Mansch, *Abraham Lincoln, President-Elect*, 3–13.

23. Lincoln Club, advertisement, *Cambridge (MA) Chronicle*, August 11, 1860, 3; untitled article, *Cambridge (MA) Chronicle*, September 29, 1860, 2.

24. Sibley's private journal, entry for October 16, 1860, Harvard University Archives.

25. Lyon, "College Recollections and Stories," 183.

26. Untitled article, *Hartford (CT) Daily Courant*, November 12, 1860, 2; "The Son of Abe Lincoln and the Harvard College Students," *(Springfield) Illinois State Journal*, November 16, 1860, 2.

27. "Policy of the Lincoln Party," *Weekly Mississippian* (Jackson, MS), November 14, 1860, 1.

28. "Correspondence of the Courier," *Charleston (SC) Courier*, November 15, 1861, 1.

29. James Conkling to Clinton Conkling, Springfield, Illinois, January 1, 1861, folder 297, box 16, Series 2, Group 352, Clinton Conkling Papers.

30. Villard, *Memoirs*, 145.

31. John Langdon Sibley's private journal, entry for April 29, 1861, Harvard University Archives; "Seventeen Southern Law Students Have Left the Cambridge Law School on Account of the Election of Lincoln," *Semi-Weekly Mississippian* (Jackson, MS), November 23, 1860, 1; Morison, *Three Centuries of Harvard*, 302.

32. "Harvard University," *Boston Daily Advertiser*, April 27, 1861, 1; Robert T. Lincoln Alumni File, HUG 300, Harvard University Archives. The exact number of freshmen for the 1860–61 year is difficult to state exactly because many left school due to the war.

33. RTL to Mary Lincoln, Exeter, December 2, 1860, RTL Collection, Phillips Exeter Academy Archives. The phrase "phancy my phelinks," slang for "fancy my feelings," was a common figure of speech in 1860 and later. For instances of its use, see J. G. Baldwin, *Flush Times of Alabama and Mississippi*, 316; "The Overland Diary of 'Nonsensical Nellie' Phelps," *Mountain Democrat* (Placerville, NV), 1860, available online at http://www.nevadaobserver.com/Nellie.htm; Hughes, *Letters and Recollections of John Murray Forbes*, 1:295; Peavy and Smith, *Gold Rush Widows of Little Falls*, 79.

34. *Harvard College Course Catalog*, 1860–61, Harvard University Archives.

35. "Personal," *Chicago Tribune*, January 17, 1861, 2.

36. Mercy Levering Conkling to Clinton Conkling, Springfield, Illinois, January 19, 1861, and Clinton Conkling to Mercy Levering Conkling, New Haven, Connecticut, January 20, 1861, and James Conkling to Clinton Conkling, Springfield, Illinois, January 30, 1861, folder 15, box 1, Conkling Family Papers; Julia Jayne Trumbull to Walter Trumbull, Washington, DC, January 30, 1861, Walter Trumbull Papers; "Personal," *Chicago Tribune*, January 17, 1861, 2; "From New York," *Hartford (CT) Daily Courant*, January 23, 1861, 3;

"Return of Mrs. Lincoln," *(Springfield) Illinois Journal*, January 28, 1861, 1; "The Incoming Administration," *New York Herald*, Springfield, February 1, 1861, 5.

37. "The Incoming Administration," *New York Herald*, Springfield, February 1, 1861, 5; also in Villard, *Lincoln on the Eve of '61*, 55.

38. Ibid.

39. Mercy Levering Conkling to Clinton Conkling, Springfield, Illinois, February 12 and March 13, 1861, folder 15, box 1, Conkling Family Papers.

40. John W. Bunn, interview by Jesse W. Weik, n.d., in Weik, *Real Lincoln*, 282–85.

41. Mercy Levering Conkling to Clinton Conkling, Springfield, November 12, 1860, folder 14, box 1, Conkling Family Papers (emphasis added).

42. Abraham Lincoln to Alexander Stephens, Springfield, Illinois, December 22, 1860, in Basler et al., *Collected Works*, 4:160.

43. It was known throughout the country that Trumbull's statements were those of the president-elect. "Passage Written for Lyman Trumbull's Speech in Springfield, Illinois," November 20, 1860, and Lincoln to Henry J. Raymond, Springfield, Illinois, November 28, 1860, in Basler et al., *Collected Works*, 4:141–42, 145–46; "'Honest Abe Lincoln' and His Henchman, Senator Trumbull, on the Crisis," *New York Herald*, November 22, 1860, 6.

44. Villard, *Lincoln on the Eve of '61*, 16.

45. "Important from Springfield," *New York Herald*, January 25, 1861, 5; "Personal," *New York Times*, January 31, 1861, 3; Villard, *Lincoln on the Eve of '61*, 53.

46. "Important from Springfield," *New York Herald*, January 25, 1861, 5; Mercy Levering Conkling to Clinton Conkling, Springfield, Illinois, February 12, 1861, and James Conkling to Clinton Conkling, Springfield, Illinois, February 12, 1861, folder 15, box 1, Conkling Family Papers; "The Journey of the President Elect," *New York Herald*, February 13, 1861, 4; Samuel H. Melvin, affidavit, "Memorandum of Certain Facts for Information of Those Who Follow After," in Howell, *Discoveries and Inventions*, 13–17.

47. Mercy Levering Conkling to Clinton Conkling, Springfield, Illinois, February 12, 1861, folder 15, box 1, Conkling Family Papers.

48. "Effect of Horace Greeley's Visit," *New York Herald*, February 16, 1861, 2; in Villard, *Lincoln on the Eve of '61*, 63. See also K. Helm, *True Story of Mary*, 155–56.

49. Mercy Levering Conkling to Clinton Conkling, Springfield, Illinois, February 12, 1861, folder 15, box 1, Conkling Family Papers.

50. Lincoln rented his house to Lucian Tilton, president of the Great Western Railroad, on February 8, 1861, for $350 per year. After Lincoln's assassination, ownership of the house reverted to Mary. Temple, *By Square and Compass*, 139–40, 184.

51. Nicolay and Hay, *Abraham Lincoln*, 3:290n1; H. Nicolay, *Lincoln's Secretary*, 62; Villard, *Memoirs*, 1:149.

52. Abraham Lincoln, "Farewell Address at Springfield, Illinois," in Basler et al., *Collected Works*, 4:190–91. Lincoln's departure from Springfield has been written about numerous times. For the original, contemporary news report of the event, see "Mr. Lincoln Off for Washington," *New York World*, February 12, 1861, 4, which was reprinted nationally through the Associated Press.

53. James Conkling to Clinton Conkling, Springfield, Illinois, February 12, 1861, folder 15, box 1, Conkling Family Papers.

54. Nicolay, "Some Incidents in Lincoln's Journey," Nicolay Papers; "The New Regime," *New York Herald*, February 10, 1861, 4; Villard, *Lincoln on the Eve of '61*, 68–69.

55. Lamon, *Recollections of Abraham Lincoln*, 36.

56. Robert Lincoln later wrote, "I have good cause to remember the printed inaugural. It was set up in confidence by Mr. Bailhache, a practical printer, one of the editors & pro-

prietors of the Illinois State Journal and a small number of the corrected proofs, which my father took with him on leaving Springfield, was the sole evidence of the proposed address. He put them in a small black hand-bag and gave it to me. The story of how near it came to being lost at Indianapolis was long ago printed." RTL to Judd Stewart, Washington, January 8, 1920, HM 8480, RTL Collection, Huntington Library.

57. John Nicolay to Therena Bates, Indianapolis, February 11, 1861, box 2, Nicolay Papers.

58. H. Nicolay, *Lincoln's Secretary*, 64.

59. John Nicolay, unpublished essay, "Some Incidents in Lincoln's Journey from Springfield to Washington," item 53, box 12, Nicolay Papers; also in Burlingame, *Oral History of Abraham Lincoln*, 109–10.

60. H. Nicolay, *Lincoln's Secretary*, 65. Ward Hill Lamon had a different recollection of the event: "I had never seen Mr. Lincoln so much annoyed, so much perplexed, and for the time so angry." Lincoln, he said, "seldom manifested a spirit of anger toward his children,—this was the nearest approach to it I had ever witnessed." Lamon, *Recollections of Abraham Lincoln*, 36. I give prominence to the Helen Nicolay–Robert Lincoln version of events over Lamon's because Lamon's reminiscences involving Robert Lincoln must be used warily, as Lamon despised the younger Lincoln for sabotaging his appointment to a federal job in 1883. Also, Lamon not only glorifies his own role in the incident but also incorrectly stated the episode as occurring in Harrisburg, Pennsylvania, rather than Indianapolis, Indiana. Interestingly, both John Nicolay and Lamon differ in their statements from Robert Lincoln's recollection in that they stated Abraham Lincoln kept the bag for the rest of the journey to Washington rather than returning it to his son. Nicolay, "Some Incidents in Lincoln's Journey," Nicolay Papers; H. Nicolay, *Personal Traits of Abraham Lincoln*, 162–65. For other versions of the event, see also Poore, *Reminiscences of Sixty Years in the National Metropolis*, 1:65–67; Sterling, "How Lincoln 'Lost' His Inaugural Address," 23–25.

61. Statement of George C. Latham, January 1918, enclosed in Clinton Conkling to Jesse W. Weik, January 22, 1918, folder 28, box 2, Conkling Family Papers; Mercy Levering Conkling to Clinton Conkling, Springfield, Illinois, February 12, 1861, and James Conkling to Clinton Conkling, Springfield, Illinois, February 12, 1861, folder 15, box 1, Conkling Family Papers.

62. Nicolay and Hay, *Abraham Lincoln*, 3:291–92. Henry Villard has a similar recollection in *Memoirs*, 151.

63. "Movements of the President Elect," *Baltimore Sun*, February 15, 1861, 1.

64. "The Presidential Progress: The Journey of Mr. Lincoln and Suite from Buffalo to Albany," *New York Herald*, February 19, 1861, 1.

65. "The Heads of the Nation: The Lincoln Family at Barnum's," *New York Herald*, February 21, 1861, 8.

66. Diary entry, February 10, 1861, January 6, 1861–July 27, 1862, p. 12, Anna Ridgely (Hudson) journal, ALPL.

67. "The Progress of the President-Elect," *New York Herald*, February 15, 1861, 5; *Dover (NH) Gazette*, March 9, 1861, quoted in Scott, "Press Opposition to Lincoln in New Hampshire," 334.

68. "From Illinois," *New York Commercial Advertiser*, October 29, 1867; "Mr. Lincoln's Sons," *(Keene) New-Hampshire Sentinel*, November 14, 1867, 2; *New York World*, February 26, 1861, 3, in Burlingame, *Lincoln's Journalist*, 47.

69. "Mr. Lincoln Off for Washington, *New York Herald*, February 10, 1861, 4.

70. "Mr. Lincoln's Journey to Washington," *New York Herald*, February 14, 1861, 5.

71. "The Presidential Progress: Ovations and Speeches en Route from Albany to New York," *New York Herald*, February 20, 1861, 1.

72. Untitled article, *New York Tribune*, February 22, 1861, 5.

73. *New York Herald*, February 13, 1861, 4, clipping, in binder 1, box 128, Mearns Papers; Villard, *Lincoln on the Eve of '61*, 79.

74. *New York World*, February 15, 1861, 4, in Burlingame, *Lincoln's Journalist*, 28–29.

75. John Nicolay to Therena Bates, Cleveland, Ohio, February 15, 1861, box 2, Nicolay Papers.

76. John Nicolay to Therena Bates, Buffalo, New York, February 17, 1861, and Nicolay, "Some Incidents in Lincoln's Journey from Springfield to Washington," boxes 2 and 53, Nicolay Papers; "The Presidential Progress: Ovations and Speeches en Route from Albany to New York," *New York Herald*, February 20, 1861, 1.

77. Seward, arriving at the hotel of the presidential party in Philadelphia, found Lincoln surrounded by well-wishers. "Clearly, this was no time for the delivery of a confidential message," he concluded, and he sought out Robert Lincoln instead. Robert, "surrounded by a group of young friends," greeted Seward "with courteous warmth," and introduced Seward to Ward Lamon, who then took him to see the president-elect. Seward, *Reminiscences of a War-Time Statesman and Diplomat*, 135. For details on the plot, see "The Plot to Assassinate Mr. Lincoln," *Boston Daily Advertiser*, April 12, 1861, and "Mr. Lincoln's Extraordinary Midnight March," *Baltimore Sun*, February 26, 1861, 1.

78. For the most complete account from primary recollections about that night, see Pinkerton, *History and Evidence of the Passage of Abraham Lincoln*. Many of Pinkerton's papers relating to the plot can be found in folders 4–8, box 23, and folders 1–2, box 24, Pinkerton National Detective Agency Records. See also Nicolay and Hay, *Abraham Lincoln*, 3:302–16; Lamon, *Life of Abraham Lincoln*, 512–27; Lamon, *Recollections of Abraham Lincoln*, 38–47.

79. Allan Pinkerton to William Herndon, Philadelphia, August 23, 1866, copy, folder 4, box 23, Pinkerton National Detective Agency Records; also in Cuthbert, *Lincoln and the Baltimore Plot*, 13.

80. Statement of George C. Latham, January 1918, Conkling Family Papers.

81. "The Trip of the Presidential Suite," *New York Herald*, February 24, 1861, 1; "Trip of the Presidential Party," *New York Times*, February 25, 1861, 1; "The President Elect at Washington," *Philadelphia Inquirer*, February 25, 1861, 1.

82. "The Trip of the Presidential Suite," *New York Herald*, February 24, 1861, 1.

83. Cuthbert, *Lincoln and the Baltimore Plot*, 17.

84. "Movements of the President Elect," *Baltimore Sun*, February 25, 1861, 1.

85. "The Incoming Administration: All about the Change of Program," *New York Times*, February 26, 1861, 8.

86. Margaret D. Williams, "A Brief Reminiscence of the First Inauguration of Abraham Lincoln as President," January 4, 1921, Williams Collection; copy in letter file A, RTL Papers, ALPL.

87. "Movements of the President Elect," *Baltimore Sun*, February 25, 1861, 1; "Mr. Lincoln in Washington," *New York Times*, February 25, 1861, 1; "The Incoming Administration: All about the Change of Program," *New York Times*, February 26, 1861, 8.

88. RTL to Isaac Markens, Chicago, June 14, 1910, RTL Papers, ALPL.

89. John Nicolay to Therena Bates, Washington, February 24, 1861, box 2, Nicolay Papers; diary entry, Saturday, February 23, 1861, in Lomax, *Leaves from an Old Washington Diary*, 144.

90. Julia Jayne Trumbull to Walter Trumbull, Washington, January 30, 1861, Walter Trumbull Papers.

91. "Progress of Events: The Features in Washington," *Philadelphia Inquirer*, February

27, 1861, 1. By 1861, twelve years after receiving his patent for a device to buoy vessels over shoals, Abraham Lincoln's patent model had long been lost to obscurity on the shelves of the Patent Office. Shortly after his inauguration—possibly due to Robert's visit to the Patent Office and failure to find his father's handiwork—the president directed a Patent Office employee to find his model for him. "President Lincoln's Model," *Boston Daily Advertiser*, May 15, 1865, 2; "President Lincoln as an Inventor," 340; Ames, *Ten Years in Washington*, 443; Dobyns, *Patent Office Pony*, 188.

92. John Nicolay to Therena Bates, March 5, 1861, box 2, Nicolay Papers.

93. Williams, "A Brief Reminiscence of the First Inauguration," Williams Collection.

94. "Affairs of the Nation: Important News From Washington," *New York Times*, February 27, 1861, 1.

95. The *New York Times* incorrectly reported that the night before the inauguration, Robert handwrote a copy of the inaugural address to give to the Associated Press the next day and also helped his father put the "finishing touches" on the speech the next morning. Lincoln's secretary Nicolay actually wrote and delivered the text; however, knowing that Robert was there to assist his father and that the newspapers mentioned him helping, it is not outlandish to assume that Robert was at least present while Lincoln and Nicolay worked. "The New Administration," *New York Times*, March 5, 1861, 1; "The Change of Administrations Today," *New York Times*, March 4, 1861, 1; "First Inaugural Address—First Edition and Revisions," March 4, 1861, in Basler et al., *Collected Works*, 4:249n1; John G. Nicolay to Ben Perley Poore, November 5, 1881, folder January–December 1881, Box 4, Nicolay Papers.

96. McCoy, *Inauguration Day, March 4, 1861*, 3.

97. "First Inaugural Address—Final Text," March 4, 1861, in Basler et al., *Collected Works*, 4:271.

98. McCoy, *Inauguration Day, March 4, 1861*, 3.

99. "The Inauguration," *Chicago Tribune*, March 8, 1861, 2.

100. John Nicolay to Therena Bates, Washington, March 5, 1861, box 2, Nicolay Papers; Bayne, *Tad Lincoln's Father*, 7.

101. Andrew D. White, diary entry, Friday, September 27, 1889, in Ogden, *Diaries of Andrew D. White*, 293; Anna Chittenden Thayer, "My Interview with Robert Lincoln, September 1922," Anna Gansevoort Chittenden Thayer Memoirs.

102. John Hay, "The Heroic Age in Washington," lectured delivered in Buffalo, New York, and other cities in 1871 and 1872, in Burlingame, *At Lincoln's Side*, 188–19.

103. John Nicolay to Therena Bates, Washington, March 5, 1861, box 2, Nicolay Papers; "The Inauguration," *Chicago Tribune*, March 8, 1861, 2. See also Margaret D. Williams, "A Brief Reminiscence of the First Inauguration," Williams Collection.

104. "Personal," *Boston Daily Journal*, March 7, 1861, 2; *Harvard College Course Catalog, 1860–1861*, Harvard University Archives.

105. "The New Government," *New York Herald*, March 5, 1861, 1. The *Boston Daily Journal* also reported that Robert "expressed himself glad to escape the high life in Washington." "Personal," *Boston Daily Journal*, March 7, 1861, 2.

106. Bayne, *Tad Lincoln's Father*, 3.

5. "He Is Only Mr. Robert Lincoln, of Cambridge"

1. Robert T. Lincoln list of classes and list of grades, Archives Biographical File, HUG 300, Harvard University Archives.

2. RTL to John Hay, Cambridge, March 21, 1861, reel 8, Hay Papers, Brown University.

3. "The New War Secretary," *New York Times*, March 10, 1881, 2.

4. Curiosity about Robert led at least one person to inquire about him in a letter to the Harvard College president, to which the writer received a simple reply that Robert was a student there, "pursuing his studies regularly and faithfully." Cornelius C. Felton to Thomas F. Scott, Cambridge, September 30, 1861, College Letters, 1860–1862, 5:237, UA I 15.890.3, Felton Papers.

5. Huidekoper, *Personal Notes and Reminiscences of Lincoln*, 5. The actual letter from father to son has not been found. Robert remained friends with Huidekoper for more than twenty years after college graduation. RTL to Frank Hatton, December 27, 1884, LB, 12:18:193.

6. In early 1861, Robert recommended his roommate's brother for an appointment to West Point but was told by his father that he could "make no promise" about it. In October 1862, Robert did succeed in getting an appointment as an assistant paymaster in the navy for his Cambridge friend Henry Munroe Rogers. RTL to James H. Elliot, Long Branch, New Jersey, August 21, 1861, RTL Papers, ALPL; Abraham Lincoln to Gideon Welles, October 27, 1862, in Basler et al., *Collected Works*, 5:480; Rogers, *Memories of Ninety Years*, 69–70; "Harvard Alumnus Is 98," *New York Times*, March 1 and 30, 1937, 14, 23.

7. "The New War Secretary," *New York Times*, March 10, 1881, 2.

8. Huidekoper, *Personal Notes and Reminiscences of Lincoln*, 5; "The New War Secretary," *New York Times*, March 10, 1881, 2.

9. "Robert T. Lincoln," *St. Louis Globe-Democrat*, reprinted in *Chicago Inter Ocean*, April 20, 1880, 1.

10. Sibley's private journal, n.d. [January 1?], 1861, Harvard University Archives.

11. "Effect of the War News," *Boston Daily Journal*, April 13, 1861, 2.

12. Sibley's private journal, entry for April 13, 1861, Harvard University Archives. For a solid book about the episode at Fort Sumter, see Detzer, *Allegiance*.

13. Batchelder, *Bits of Harvard History*, 73.

14. Sibley's private journal, entry for April 16, 1861, Sibley Diary; Batchelder, *Bits of Harvard History*, 73. Several Harvard graduates joined the Cambridge volunteers but no undergraduates. One Boston newspaper reported that more than one hundred men had enlisted in the army and navy between April 8 and April 12. "Effect of the War News Upon the Recruiting Offices," *Boston Daily Journal*, April 12, 1861, 4.

15. Sibley's private journal, entry for April 20, 1861, Sibley Diary.

16. Huidekoper, *Personal Notes and Reminiscences of Lincoln*, 600; Sibley's private journal, entries for April 29 and May 1, 1861, Sibley Diary.

17. From *Harvard Magazine*, quoted in Batchelder, *Bits of Harvard History*, 74.

18. Sibley's private journal, entries for April 29 and May 1, 1861, Sibley Diary.

19. For a great book about Harvard men in the war, see R. F. Miller, *Harvard's Civil War*; "Harvard Graduates in the Field," *Boston Daily Advertiser*, June 11, 1861, 1.

20. Batchelder, *Bits of Harvard History*, 75.

21. C. F. Adams, *Theodore Lyman and Robert Charles Winthrop, Jr.*, 160.

22. RTL to William Roscoe Thayer, Manchester, Vermont, August 6, 1914, bMS Am 1081 (1060), William Roscoe Thayer Papers.

23. Keckley, *Behind the Scenes*, 121; K. Helm, *True Story of Mary*, 227.

24. Keckley, *Behind the Scenes*, 182.

25. W. O. Stoddard, *Inside the White House in War Times*, 33.

26. Keckley, *Behind the Scenes*, 121–22. By 1863, after the death of numerous of Mary's family members in the war and her son Willie in 1862, Emily Todd Helm, Mary's sister, told the president that Mary's mental state seemed so precarious that she felt "if anything

should happen to you or Robert or Tad it would kill her." K. Helm, *True Story of Mary*, 225–26, 229–30.

27. For Lincoln as a father figure, see Emerson, *Madness of Mary Lincoln*, 11; Burlingame, *Inner World of Abraham Lincoln*, 280, 295–96.

28. Abraham Lincoln to George D. Prentice, Springfield, Illinois, October 29, 1860, in Basler et al., *Collected Works*, 4:134–35.

29. RTL to Winfield M. Thompson, Washington, March 2, 1915, in "Robert Lincoln Letter, His First Published, Recounts Father's Opinion on Law as Profession," *New York Herald Tribune*, August 1, 1926, 3:1, and reprinted in *Magazine of History*, 34, no. 1, extra no. 133, Lincoln no. 31, Tarrytown, New York, 1927, 57; "Captain Lincoln Episode." *Lincoln Lore*, no. 1410, April 16, 1956.

30. "Robert Lincoln," *Atlantic Democrat and Cape May County (NJ) Register*, December 26, 1863, 3; *Indianapolis Sentinel*, December 3, 1864, quoted in Harper, *Lincoln and the Press*, 331; K. Helm, *True Story of Mary*, 229–30.

31. The May recess for 1861 began Tuesday evening, May 28, and ended Sunday evening, June 2. Robert left Cambridge for Washington that Tuesday evening and returned to school on Tuesday, June 4. *Harvard College Course Catalog, 1860–61*, Harvard University Archives; RTL to Mr. Norris, Cambridge, June 4, 1861, RTL MS, Abraham Lincoln Collection, Hay Library.

32. John Nicolay to Therena Bates, April 27 and May 1, 1861, box 2, Nicolay Papers.

33. Historians continually transpose Ellsworth's first two names and call him Elmer E., but historian Wayne C. Temple has proven that "Elmer" was in fact the colonel's middle name. "Will the Real E. E. Ellsworth Step Forward?" 23.

34. "Assassination of Colonel Ellsworth—Details of the Tragedy—Grief of the President," *Chicago Tribune*, May 28, 1861, 1. Lincoln met Ellsworth in Springfield in 1859 and took him into his law office as a clerk. "Our affliction here, is scarcely less than your own," Lincoln wrote in a letter of condolence to Ellsworth's parents. Abraham Lincoln to Ephraim D. and Phoebe Ellsworth, Washington, May 25, 1861, in Basler et al., *Collected Works*, 4:385–86.

35. John Nicolay to Therena Bates, May 31, 1861, box 2, Nicolay Papers.

36. Grimsley, "Six Months in the White House," 58–59. Mary arrived in Cambridge on the evening of Saturday, May 18, and left on the afternoon of Monday, May 20. "Movements of Mrs. Lincoln," *New York Herald*, May 16, 1861, 4 and May 18, 1861, 5; "Departure of Mrs. Lincoln," *New York Tribune*, May 18, 1861, 8; Turner and Turner, *Mary Todd Lincoln*, 87–89.

37. Mary shopped at stores such as Brewster's, A. T. Stewart, Lord & Taylor, and Arnold & Constable and spent thousands of dollars to purchase clothing, carpets, wallpaper, curtains, furniture, china, glassware, and a new carriage. *New York Tribune*, May 10–18, 1861, and *New York Herald*, May 16–18.

38. Turner and Turner, *Mary Todd Lincoln*, 89.

39. C. F. Adams, *Charles Francis Adams 1835–1915*, 103. For an impressive examination of Mary's bad behavior, see Burlingame, "Mary Todd Lincoln's Unethical Conduct as First Lady."

40. Grimsley, "Six Months in the White House," 67.

41. Abraham Lincoln to Cambridge Telegraph Office, July —, 1861, RTL Papers, ALPL.

42. RTL to Abraham Lincoln, Cambridge, July 17, 1861, RTL Papers, ALPL. Harvard commencement occurred on July 17. 1861, so Robert most likely had intended to return to Washington that night, until the mumps made him postpone his trip a few days. On July 22, he was in Philadelphia, where he telegraphed presidential secretary John Nicolay

and asked him to send ten dollars to the Continental Hotel. RTL to John Nicolay, Philadelphia, July 22, 1861, box 128, Nicolay Papers; *Harvard College Course Catalog, 1860–1861*, Harvard University Archives.

43. "The Great Rebellion," *New York Times*, August 4, 1861, 1; "Dinner at the White House," *(Concord) New-Hampshire Statesman*, reprinted from the *New York World*, August 17, 1861, 1; Grimsley, "Six Months in the White House," 33. A seating chart of the dinner given for Prince Napoleon shows that Robert was seated next to John Hay, three seats from the prince, who sat next to Mary Lincoln and across from President Lincoln. Seating chart, box 9, Nicolay Papers.

44. "Great Rebellion," *New York Times*, August 5, 1861, 1.

45. The *New York Herald* had an embedded reporter in Long Branch who followed and detailed every move of the first family. "Movements of Mrs. Lincoln," *New York Herald*, August 16 and 17, 1861, 1.

46. For day-by-day reporting of the entire trip to Long Branch, see "Movements of Mrs. Lincoln," *New York Herald*, August 16–24, 1861, 1. See also "Movements of Mrs. Lincoln," *Philadelphia Inquirer*, August 20, 1861, 2.

47. "Movements of Mrs. Lincoln," *New York Herald*, August 18, 1861.

48. John Hay to Mrs. Fanny Campbell Eames, Washington, August 21, 1861, frames 0009–0015, reel 3, Hay Papers, LOC.

49. Miers, *Lincoln Day by Day*, 3:62; "Dispatch to the Associated Press" and "News of the Day," *New York Times*, August 26, 1861, 1, 4. John Hay wrote in a letter that Robert had come to the White House "bringing positive orders from his mother for me to join her at New York for an extension of her trip. I don't know where. Of course I can't go—as things look." John Hay to John G. Nicolay, Washington, August 24, 1861, in Dennett, *Lincoln and the Civil War in the Diaries and Letters of John Hay*, 26.

50. Robert T. Lincoln alumni files, list of classes (TS) and list of classes with grades (handwritten), HUG 300, Harvard University Archives.

51. H. Adams, *Education of Henry Adams*, 55.

52. S. E. Morison, *Three Centuries at Harvard*, 312; Harvard University admission records, box 1, HUG 860, Harvard University Archives.

53. S. E. Morison, *Three Centuries at Harvard*, 315–17, 313.

54. Lyon, "College Recollections and Stories," 183.

55. W. L. Richardson, "Robert Todd Lincoln," 378.

56. "Movements of Mrs. Lincoln," *New York Herald*, August 18, 1.

57. The Delta was a triangle of land defined by Cambridge, Kirkland, and Quincy Streets and the present location of Memorial Hall. Rogers et al., *Photographic History of Cambridge*.

58. Robert T. Lincoln, autobiographical essay, class book, records of Harvard College class of 1864, Harvard University Archives; also in RTL Papers, ALPL.

59. Records, October 1, 1860, January 15, 1862, and June 22, 1863, 16:16, 146, 304, UA 3, 5.5.2, Harvard Faculty Records, Harvard University Archives.

60. Thomas Hill, president of Harvard College, to Abraham Lincoln, Cambridge, Massachusetts, December 9, 1862, in Holzer, *Dear Mr. Lincoln*, 314–15; Records, September 22, 1862, and December 8, 1862, 16:221, 249–50, UA 3, 5.5.2, Harvard Faculty Records, Harvard University Archives. Transgression of school rules at Harvard were three grades of admonition, suspension and expulsion, which was the same system used at Phillips Exeter Academy. Cunningham, *Familiar Sketches of Phillips Exeter Academy*, 125.

61. Cornelius C. Felton to Abraham Lincoln, Cambridge, Massachusetts, January 20, 1862, college letters, vol. 5, 1860–62, 316, UA 3, 15.890.3, Felton Papers.

62. "Arrivals in the City," *New York Times*, January 17, 1862, 8; Horatio Nelson Taft, *Washington during the Civil War: The Diary of Horatio Nelson Taft, 1861–1865*, John Sellers, ed., January 18, 1862, vol. 1, Manuscripts Division, LOC. Also available online at http://memory.loc.gov/ammem/tafthtml/tafthome.html.

63. Bayne, *Tad Lincoln's Father*, 3. Julia's father, Horatio Nelson Taft, called Willie "an amiable good hearted boy," who "had more judgment and foresight than any boy of his age that I have ever known"; while editor and Lincoln family friend N. P. Willis wrote, "He was so bravely and beautifully himself . . . unalterably pure and simple, till he died." Taft, *Washington during the Civil War*, February 20, 1862, vol. 2, and December 14, 1864, vol. 3, Manuscripts Division, LOC; Willis, "President's Son," 154.

64. Baker was killed at the Battle of Ball's Bluff in October 1861. The poem was published in the Washington *National Republican*, November 4, 1861, 1, and also reprinted in Keckley, *Behind the Scenes*, 99–100.

65. John Nicolay to Therena Bates, Washington, February 11 and 21, 1861, box 2, Nicolay Papers.

66. "I never saw a man so bowed down with grief," Elizabeth Keckly recorded. "His grief unnerved him and made him a weak, passive child." Keckley, *Behind the Scenes*, 103.

67. Bayne, *Tad Lincoln's Father*, 82; Benjamin B. French diary, March 2, 1862, 304, frame P000359, reel 2, vol. 8, French Family Papers.

68. Spiritualism was the belief in the continuity of life into the afterlife. Contact with spirits was achieved through séances with the communication often consisting of rapping and knocking, table tipping, automatic speech, and automatic writing. Spiritualists often consisted of the grieved and the gullible, seeking connections to lost loved ones. Spiritualism began in 1848 but burgeoned during the vast death and loss of the Civil War. By the 1890s, the movement claimed eleven million followers. Mary Lincoln participated in numerous séances while first lady and even held some in the White House. For a good summary of Mary's spiritualist beliefs, see Temple, *Abraham Lincoln*, 196–203. See also Anson G. Henry to his wife, Washington, May 8, 1865, SC 683, Anson G. Henry Papers; Taylor, *Shadow Culture*, 137; Braude, *Radical Spirits*, 5–6, 140; "A Plea for Spiritualism," *Chicago Tribune*, January 13, 1868, 2; "Spiritualism," *New York Times*, January 26, 1873, 2; "A Decline in Spiritualism," *New York Times*, February 23, 1875, 4; "Done with the Big Toe: Margaret Fox Kane Shows How Spirit Rapping Is Produced," *New York Times*, October 22, 1888, 5; "Spiritualism or Insanity?" *New York Times*, February 3, 1892, 8.

69. Keckley, *Behind the* Scenes, 104–5, 181–82.

70. Elizabeth Edwards to Julia Edwards (Baker), Washington, March 2, 1862, SC 445, Elizabeth Parker Todd Edwards Letters; Bayne, *Tad Lincoln's Father*, 83.

71. Poore, *Reminiscences of Sixty Years*, 1:115–16; Steell, "Mrs. Abraham Lincoln and Her Friends," 621. There are no known documents written by Robert revealing his feelings about Willie's death. One week after the funeral, John Hay forwarded a letter from Robert to a doctor "over the water," although who this was or what the letter said is unknown. John Hay to "My dear Doctor," Washington, March 2, 1862, microfilm reel 5, Hay Collection, Brown University.

72. Mercy Levering Conkling to Clinton Conkling, Springfield, February 24, 1862, folder 18, box 2, Conkling Family Papers; Elizabeth Edwards to Julia Edwards (Baker), Washington, March 2 and 12, 1862, SC 445, Edwards Family Papers, ALPL.

73. Elizabeth Edwards to Julia Edwards (Baker), Washington, March 2 and 12, 1862, SC 445, Edwards Family Papers.

74. Benjamin B. French diary, March 2, 1862, frame P000359, reel 2, Vol. 8:304, French Family Papers.

75. Ibid.; "Funeral of Willie Lincoln," *Washington National Intelligencer*, February 24, 1862, 1; Pease and Randall, *Diary of Orville Hickman Browning*, 1:531.

76. This book with Robert's signature is in the Lincoln collection of the Allen County Public Library, Fort Wayne, Indiana. "Captain Lincoln Episode."

77. Mary Lincoln to Julia Sprigg, May 29, 1862, first published in Goltz, *Incidents in the Life of Mary Todd Lincoln*, 35. Goltz also printed his interview with Mrs. Sprigg from January 1928, when she was seventy-six years old. *Incidents in the Life of Mary Todd Lincoln*, 47–54. See also Turner and Turner, *Mary Todd Lincoln*, 127–28.

78. "Excursion of Mrs. Lincoln in New-York Harbor," *New York Times*, July 15, 1862, 5; Temple, "Mary Todd Lincoln's Travels," 185.

79. Mary Lincoln to Mrs. Charles Eames, Soldiers' Home, July 26, 1862, in Turner and Turner, *Mary Todd Lincoln*, 131.

80. Mary Lincoln to Abraham Lincoln, New York, November 2, 1862, in Turner and Turner, *Mary Todd Lincoln*, 139; Abraham Lincoln to Mary Lincoln, Washington, November 9, 1862, in Basler et al., *Collected Works*, 5:492; Temple, "Mary Todd Lincoln's Travels," 185.

81. Some of Robert's college textbooks from 1861–63 are in the archives at his Vermont house, Hildene, and include titles by James Parton, Isaac Disraeli, and Samuel Warren. G. G. Benedict, Harvard archivist, to Ida Tarbell, Cambridge, June 8, 1928, Robert T. Lincoln autobiographical file, HUG 300, Harvard University Archives.

82. In his annual report to the college overseers for the academic year 1864–65, President Thomas Hill lamented the deficiencies of the undergraduate education. He stated that the student numbers were so high that teaching by recitation alone was insufficient, and more lecturing and an increase in tutors needed to be undertaken. "By the ordinary mode of recitation, when the classes become large, neither the poorer scholars receive the aid from the instructor they require, nor the better scholars the opportunity and stimulus to do well." *Thirty-Ninth Annual Report of the President of Harvard College to the Overseers*, 18–24, and *Fortieth Annual Report of the President of Harvard College to the Overseers*, 7, 10–16, online at http://pds.lib.harvard.edu/pds/view/2574320?n=1625&s=4.

83. Robert T. Lincoln alumni files, list of classes (printed) and list of classes with grades (handwritten), HUG 300, Harvard University Archives; Kimball C. Elkins, assistant, Harvard University Archives, to Ruth Painter Randall, Cambridge, June 29, 1954, box 72, Randall Family Papers.

84. S. E. Morison, *Three Centuries at Harvard*, 308.

85. RTL to Edward Everett Hale, Chicago, October 7, 1895, folder 21, box 36, Hale Family Papers; Hale, *James Russell Lowell*, 142–43; Hale, "James Russell Lowell and His Friends," 325; RTL to Charles Eliot Norton, Legation of U.S., London, October 29, 1891, bMS Am 765 (38), Lowell Papers.

86. Hale, *James Russell Lowell*, 139; RTL to James Green, November 21, 1910, LB, 44:76:385.

87. James Russell Lowell to Henry White, October 11, 1890, quoted in Nevins, *Henry White*, 69.

88. Palfrey also served as professor of biblical literature in the Harvard Divinity School (1831–39), editor of *North American Review* (1835–43), member of the Massachusetts State Legislature (1842–43), and secretary of the Commonwealth of Massachusetts (1844–48). He was an ardent abolitionist. His principal literary endeavor was his multivolume *History of New England*, published between 1858 and 1890. One scholar wrote that as a historian, Palfrey's style was "clear, graphic, and vigorous, precise in statement, often pictorial, and

especially lifelike [in his] descriptions of characters." He died in Cambridge on April 26, 1881. Eliot, *Heralds of a Liberal Faith*, 2:150–53; Cunningham, *Familiar Sketches of Phillips Exeter Academy*, 60–61. See also Gattell, *John Gorham Palfrey and the New England Conscience*.

89. C. F. Adams, *Charles Francis Adams*, 100–102.

90. In one June 1861 letter to Palfrey, Robert apologized for not calling sooner, but he had had his "pocket picked of everything it contained" while at the gymnasium and was awaiting a letter from Washington, presumably for money. RTL to John G. Palfrey, June 6, 1861, November 11, 1862, December 4, 1862, and November 24, 1863, bMS Am 1704 (543), Palfrey Family Papers, Houghton Library. A search through the Palfrey Family Papers at Louisiana State University discovered no correspondence with Robert Lincoln.

91. RTL to Edward Everett Hale, Chicago, May 29, 1899, RTL Papers, ALPL.

92. In October 1860, Palfrey wrote to Abraham Lincoln, "taking it for granted that you are about to be President of the United States," to recommend Charles Francis Adams for a position in the cabinet. In March 1861, he again wrote to Lincoln to request a government job for himself. No other letters are known to exist between the two men. Robert Lincoln stated that he did not think Palfrey and his father "ever had any correspondence regarding me at any time." John G. Palfrey to Abraham Lincoln, Cambridge, October 25, 1860, and March 6, 1861, bMS Am 1704.1 (192), Palfrey Family Papers, Houghton Library; RTL to Edward Everett Hale, Chicago, May 29, 1899, RTL Papers, ALPL.

93. The DKE founding constitution declares the group's objects to be "the cultivation of general literature and social culture, the advancement and encouragement of intellectual excellence, the promotion of honorable friendship and useful citizenship, the development of a spirit of tolerance and respect for the rights and views of others, the maintenance of gentlemanly dignity, self-respect, and morality in all circumstances, and the union of stout hearts and kindred interests to secure to merit its due reward." More fraternal than its rival societies, DKE recruited men who combined "in equal proportions the gentleman, the scholar, and the jolly good fellow." "DKE Heritage"; Robert T. Lincoln, autobiographical essay, *Class of 1864 Class Book*, HUD 264.714F, Harvard University Archives, copy in RTL Papers, ALPL.

94. "Prominent Alumni from Yesterday"; "College Fraternities Have 600,000 Members," *New York Times*, February 8, 1925, 19. The DKE international organization in Ann Arbor, Michigan, does not have this letter, nor has it ever been found.

95. RTL to John Hay, Chicago, January 14, 1874, reel 8, Hay Papers, Brown University.

96. Robert T. Lincoln, autobiographical essay, *Class of 1864 Class Book*, HUD 264.714F, Harvard University Archives, a copy is also in RTL Papers, ALPL; Kimball C. Elkins, assistant, Harvard University Archives, to Ruth Painter Randall, July 8, 1954, RTL folder, box 72, Randall Family Papers.

97. For an amusing history of the club, see Calnek, *Hasty Pudding Theatre*.

98. "The New War Secretary," *New York Times*, March 10, 1881, 2. One of Robert's classmates remembered how on stage Robert "made an excellent father, of the grocery sort." Garrison, "HPC Theatre."

99. Hasty Pudding Club, *Illustrated History*. Strange, this book has no page numbers, but all playbills are printed in chronological order.

100. RTL to Edward Freiberger, Augusta, Georgia, March 10, 1910, RTL Papers, ALPL.

101. "Edwin Booth and Robert Lincoln," *Chicago Tribune* [reprint of *New York Times*], April 25, 1865, 2; for an examination of the episode, its facts and fabrications, see Emerson, "How Booth Saved Lincoln's Life."

102. RTL to Richard Watson Gilder, Chicago, February 6, 1909, RTL Papers, ALPL; RTL to Emily Todd Helm, Washington, May 6, 1919, folder 8, box 235, RTL Papers, CHM. Dr. Charles A. Moore, head of the Manuscript Division at the Library of Congress, recounted in 1926 that Robert told him of the incident and even commented, "It certainly was a strange coincidence in view of later events." "Simple Rites Mark Lincoln Funeral Today," *Albany Evening News*, July 28, 1926, clipping in folder 2, box 234, RTL Papers, CHM.

103. RTL to E. C. Benedict, Washington, February 17, 1918, in E. C. Benedict, "Edwin Booth," 182.

104. Ibid., 183. Booth himself also remembered the incident with nostalgia, especially after he, an ardent Unionist, learned that his brother had murdered the president. One friend recalled that in the days of his grief after the assassination, one of the two things that maintained Edwin Booth's sanity was the knowledge that he had saved Robert Lincoln that day in Jersey City. Edwin Booth to Adam Badeau, April 16, 1865, folder 6, box 1, Gen. MSS 257, Series 1, Abraham Lincoln Collection, General Collection, Beinecke Rare Book and Manuscript Library; Bispham, "Memories and Letters of Edwin Booth," 133.

105. "President Lincoln Is Coming to New England," *Lowell (MA) Daily Citizen and News*, August 1, 1863, 2; Untitled article, *Manchester (VT) Journal*, August 30, 1864; John Hay to John Nicolay, Washington, August 7, 1863, reel 5, Hay Papers, Brown University; RTL to Mrs. Munson, Manchester, Vermont, n.d., Hildene Archives.

106. W. O. Stoddard, *Inside the White House in War Times*, 150.

107. RTL to J. E. Holland, June 6, 1865, cont. 1, part 1, RTLFP.

108. Coddington, *Gettysburg Campaign*, 540.

109. Abraham Lincoln, "Announcement of News from Gettysburg," in Basler et al., *Collected Works*, 6:314.

110. Abraham Lincoln to Henry H. Halleck, July 7, 1863, in ibid., 6:319.

111. Abraham Lincoln to George G. Meade, Washington, July 14, 1863, in ibid., 6:327–28.

112. Robert T. Lincoln, "Reminiscence of Abraham Lincoln after Gettysburg," in RTL to John Nicolay, January 2, 1885, reel 10, Hay Papers, LOC; Haupt, *Reminiscences of General Herman Haupt*, 224; Thacher, "Lincoln and Meade after Gettysburg," 282–83 (Thacher was a personal friend of Robert Lincoln's and had transcribed the story as Robert told it to him); statement of James Harlan, quoted in Bullard, "The Magnanimity of Abraham Lincoln," 296–97. Navy Secretary Gideon Welles also recorded in his diary Lincoln's reaction: "On only one or two occasions have I ever seen the President so troubled, so dejected and discouraged." Diary entry, July 14, 1863, Welles, *Diary of Gideon Welles*, 1:371.

113. Abraham Lincoln to RTL, Washington, July 3, 1863, in Basler et al., *Collected Works*, 6:314. Mary in fact suffered a bleeding wound on the back of her head caused by a sharp stone; doctors at the nearby hospital quickly stitched the cut up. "Serious Accident to Mrs. Lincoln," *Washington Evening Star*, July 2, 1863, 2; "Accident to Mrs. Lincoln," *(Washington) Daily National Intelligencer*, July 3, 1863, 3; "News From Washington: Accident to Mrs. Lincoln," *New York Times*, July 3, 1863, 5; Boyden, *War Reminiscences*, 143–44.

114. Abraham Lincoln to RTL, Washington, July 11 and 14, 1863, in Basler, *Collected Works*, 6:323, 327.

115. John Hay, diary entry, July 15, 1863, in Dennett, *Lincoln and the Civil War*, 67.

116. Abraham Lincoln to Henry W. Halleck, Washington, October 16, 1863, in Basler, *Collected Works*, 6:518; diary of Theodore Lyman, October 17, 1863, in Lowe, *Meade's Army*, 53; "The War in Virginia," *Chicago Tribune*, October 23, 1863, 1.

117. Robert called his recollection of this event "clear" and "perfectly distinct." For Robert to have been at the White House on that day, Friday, October 16, 1863, he must

have gone to Washington to visit for the weekend. RTL to John Nicolay, Chicago, June 14, 1878, box 4, Nicolay papers; RTL to Isaac Arnold, Washington, November 11, 1883, folder 1, RTL Papers, CHM; RTL to Charles A. Tinker, July 20, 1907, LB, 40:68:198–99; Robert T. Lincoln, "Reminiscence of Abraham Lincoln after Gettysburg," reel 10, Hay Papers, LOC; Thacher, "Lincoln and Meade after Gettysburg," 282–83; Bullard, "Magnanimity of Abraham Lincoln," 296; Joseph Medill, "Recollections of Lincoln," *Chicago Tribune*, April 28, 1895, 44; Joseph Medill, "Memories of Lincoln," *Portland Oregonian*, April 28, 1895, 16.

118. John Nicolay to John Hay, Washington, February 17, 1864, box 3, Nicolay Papers.

119. Helen Nicolay, John Nicolay's daughter, wrote that Robert told her the story of the denouement of the Cabinet crisis "as his father had told it to him." H. Nicolay, *Lincoln's Secretary*, 159.

120. RTL to John Nicolay, January 2, 1885, box 11, Nicolay Papers, LOC.

121. RTL to David Homer Bates, June 22, 1907, RTL Papers, ALPL.

122. Abraham Lincoln to the House of Representatives, February 10, 1865, in Basler et al., *Collected Works*, 8:274–85; Nicolay and Hay, "Abraham Lincoln," 846–52; Bates, *Lincoln in the Telegraph Office*, 322–42; Temple, *Lincoln's Travels on the River Queen*, 15–22.

123. RTL to David Homer Bates, June 22, 1907, RTL Papers, ALPL.

124. Carpenter, *Six Months at the White House*, 300; Brooks, "Boy in the White House," 61.

125. Carpenter, *Six Months at the White House*, 45; John Nicolay to John Hay, Washington, February 10, 1864, and John Nicolay to Therena Bates, Washington, February 12, 1864, box 3, Nicolay Papers; Sarah Davis to George Davis, Washington, February 24, 1864, folder 79, box 13, Davis Papers, CHM. Carpenter mistakenly wrote that Robert was talking with John Hay about the loss of greenbacks, but, as a letter from Nicolay to Hay that same evening—discussing Cooper's loss of money—shows, Hay was not in Washington at the time.

126. John Hay to John Nicolay, July 18, 1863, reel 5, Hay Papers, Brown University.

127. Diary entry, July 25, 1863, diary of John Hay, in Dennett, *Lincoln and the Civil War*, 72; Basler et al., *Collected Works*, 6:353.

128. RTL to Judd Stewart, September 14, 1919, HM 8476, RTL Collection, Huntington Library; Boyden, *War Reminiscences*, 98–99.

129. "From Illinois," *Commercial Advertiser* (New York), October 29, 1867; "Mr. Lincoln's Sons," *(Keene) New-Hampshire Sentinel*, November 14, 1867, 2.

130. Frances (Fanny) Seward diary, February 12, 1863, reel 198, no. 6662, p. 177, Papers of William H. Seward.

131. Frances (Fanny) Seward diary, February 11, 1864, reel 198, no. 6666, p. 146, Seward Papers.

132. RTL to Alice M. Huntington, October 8, 1861, and January 11, 1862, SC 669, Huntington Family Papers; RTL to Alice M. Huntington, undated invitation to Harvard Class Day, RTL Papers, ALPL.

133. John Hay to John Nicolay, Washington, August 7, 1863, reel 5, Hay Papers, Brown University.

134. "Booth and Bob Lincoln," *Chicago Inter Ocean*, June 18 and 19, 1878. Robert Lincoln's wife, Mary Harlan Lincoln, also denied the story when it was reprinted in 1926. "Living Dead Man," *Time* 7, no. 10, March 8, 1926, 38–39; Frederic Towers, writing for Mary Harlan Lincoln, to Katherine Helm, May 7, 1926, RTL Collection, Hildene Archives; Houmes, "Lincoln & Booth," 5–11. For an outlandish telling of the tale, see also Babcock, *Booth and the Spirit of Lincoln*.

135. This was, in fact, exactly how Minnie characterized Mary. In the girls' correspon-

dence, Minnie Chandler asks Mary about her beaux and names half a dozen men, including Robert and Robert's good friend Edgar Welles. Minnie Chandler to Mary Harlan, January 15, March 2, and August 4, 1866, Chandler Papers.

136. K. Helm, *True Story of Mary*, 274–75. One of the first lady's friends later reminisced that Mary Lincoln first saw Mary Harlan at an opera and said, "I should like Robert to marry just such a girl as that," to which her husband observed to Senator Charles Sumner, "My wife is a great match-maker. She will make a match between Harlan's daughter and Bob; see if she don't." Reminiscence of Mrs. William Preston, printed in "Mrs. Lincoln's Ambition," untitled, undated newspaper clipping, box 74, Randall Family papers. See also Miriam Elkins to James Gordon Bennett, February 23, 1865, Bennett Papers.

137. W. L. Richardson, "Robert Todd Lincoln," 378; "Local Matters," *Boston Daily Advertiser*, January 18, 1864, 1; RTL to John Nicolay, Cambridge, March 10, 1864, box 3, Nicolay Papers.

138. "Local Matters," *Boston Daily Advertiser*, June 25, 1864, 1; Clark A. Elliott, assistant curator, Harvard University Archives, to R. Gerald McMurtry, October 21, 1971, RTL Collection, ACPL.

139. "Mrs. Lincoln Visits Cambridge," *Baltimore Sun*, June 21, 1864, 4; RTL to H. P. Sprague, Washington, July 18, 1864, RTL Papers, ALPL.

140. RTL to John Nicolay, Cambridge, March 10, 1864, box 3, Nicolay Papers. Whether she was invited and subsequently attended is unknown.

141. Robert T. Lincoln, autobiographical essay, *Harvard Class of 1864 Class Book*, HUD 264.714F, Harvard University Archives; also in RTL Papers, ALPL.

142. RTL to William Roscoe Thayer, Manchester, Vermont, August 6, 1914, bMS Am 1081 (1060), William Roscoe Thayer Papers.

143. "Lincoln's Son Going into the Army," reprint from *Boston Post*, in *San Francisco Bulletin*, July 29, 1864, 3.

144. RTL to Winfield M. Thompson, Washington, March 2, 1915, published in "Robert Lincoln Letter, His First Published, Recounts Father's Opinion on Law as Profession," *New York Herald Tribune*, August 1, 1926, 3:1; also in *Magazine of History*, 34, no. 1, extra no. 133, Lincoln no. 31, 1927, 57.

6. "A Very Dreadful Night"

1. *Harvard Class of 1864 Class Book*, HUD 264.714F, p. 483, and Robert T. Lincoln attendance card, Robert T. Lincoln autobiographical file, HUG 300, Harvard University Archives; *Fortieth Annual Report of the President of Harvard College to the Overseers*, 17–18; *Centennial History of the Harvard Law School*, 23–25. Harvard Law School did not issue grades to its students until 1870; examinations prior to that were oral quizzes and not recorded. David Warrington, Librarian for Special Collections, Harvard Law School Library, e-mail to author, February 1, 2007.

2. Abraham Lincoln, "Memorandum Concerning His Probable Failure of Re-election," Washington, August 23, 1864, frame 35496, reel 79, series 1, Abraham Lincoln Papers, LOC; also in Basler et al., *Collected Works*, 7:514; John Hay diary entry, November 11, 1864, in Dennett, *Lincoln and the Civil War*, 237–38.

3. Putnam, *Memories of My Youth*, 394–96.

4. RTL to David Homer Bates, June 22, 1907, RTL Papers, ALPL; "News from Washington," *New York Times*, January 3, 1865, 4. From January 4 to 6, Robert was sent by his father to accompany Secretary of State Seward and presidential secretary Nicolay to the funerals in Philadelphia and Trenton of George M. Dallas, former minister to Great

Britain, and William L. Dayton, former minister to France, respectively. The president sent his emissaries as a "mark of respect" for the "eminent worth and high public service" of the deceased. This is yet another indication of the trust and value Abraham Lincoln placed in his son. John Nicolay to Therena Bates, Washington, July 6, 1865, Nicolay Papers, LOC; "Washington Items," *Baltimore Sun*, January 4, 1865, 1; "The Latest News," *Hartford (CT) Daily Courant*, January 4, 1865, 3.

5. Abraham Lincoln to Lieutenant General Ulysses S. Grant, Washington, January 19, 1865, frame 43220, reel 97, series 2, Abraham Lincoln Papers, LOC; also in Basler et al., *Collected Works*, 8:223.

6. Nuhrah, "Commission for Robert," 143.

7. Ulysses S. Grant to Abraham Lincoln, Annapolis Junction, Maryland, January 21, 1865, in Simon, *Papers of Ulysses S. Grant*, 13:281; RTL to James H. Canfield, February 23, 1909, LB, 42:72:198. Someone must have leaked President Lincoln's original intent to the press, however, for on February 3, it was reported that Robert would join the army as a volunteer without pay. "General News," *Hartford (CT) Daily Courant*, February 3, 1865, 2.

8. RTL to Ulysses S. Grant, January 22, 1865, quoted in Simon, *Papers of Ulysses S. Grant*, 13:282. This letter is cited as being in the holdings of the Western Reserve Historical Society, Cleveland, Ohio, but a thorough search by this author and several Western Reserve staff members could not find it there.

9. Miriam Elkins to James Gordon Bennett, February 23, 1865, Bennett Papers.

10. Robert T. Lincoln military commission as assistant adjutant general of volunteers, War Department, February 12, 1865, frame 118, reel 182, M1064, record group 94, Letters Received by the Commission Branch of the Adjutant General's Office, 1863–70, L34 (C.B.) 1865, NARA; Robert's military commission also in OV 2, cont. 1, part 1, RTLFP; "Death of Senator Hicks," *Baltimore Sun*, February 14, 1865, 4; "General News," *New York Times*, February 15, 1865, 4; "Robert Lincoln in the Army," *Boston Transcript*, February 15, 1865, clipping, Lincoln Children Vertical File.

11. RTL to Alice James, October 18, 1921, RTL Collection, Phillips Exeter Academy; Bullock, "President Lincoln's Visiting Card," 567, also in R. R. Wilson, *Lincoln among His Friends*, 357–58.

12. RTL to Major S. F. Chalfin, Washington, February 20, 1865 and Oath of Office, February 20, 1865, frames 120 and 122, reel 182, M1064, record group 94, Letters Received by the Commission Branch of the Adjutant General's Office, 1863–70, L34 (C.B.) 1865, NARA; Special Orders No. 83, War Department, Adjutant General's Office, Washington, February 20, 1865, in *OR*, 2:602.

13. Catton, *Stillness at Appomattox*, 321.

14. The description of City Point is taken from Catton, *Stillness at Appomattox*, 321. See also Crook, *Through Five Administrations*, 41–42.

15. Abraham Lincoln to Ulysses S. Grant, Washington, February 24, 1865, in Basler et al., *Collected Works*, 8:314; Ulysses S. Grant to Abraham Lincoln, City Point, Virginia, February 24, 1865, in Simon, *Papers of Ulysses S. Grant*, 14:32; Lincoln to Grant and Grant to Lincoln, February 24, 1865, also both in *OR*, 2:668; untitled article, *Hartford (CT) Daily Courant*, February 25, 1865, 3; "Son Robert Reports for Duty," *Daily Ohio Statesman* (Columbus), March 2, 1865; Ulysses S. Grant, report of officers on staff, City Point, Virginia, March 1, 1865, in *OR*, 2:770.

16. H. Porter, "Campaigning with Grant: Preparing for the Last Campaign," 592; also in H. Porter, *Campaigning with Grant*, 388–89.

17. "Second Inauguration of President Lincoln," *New York Herald*, March 5, 1865, 1.

18. Welles, *Diary of Gideon Welles*, 2:252. For a description of Johnson's entire inaugural scene, see Trefousse, *Andrew Johnson*, 189–91.

19. Brooks, *Washington in Lincoln's Time*, 212–13.

20. Basler et al., *Collected Works*, 8:332–33.

21. Robert later recalled being present in the Senate chamber during the vice presidential inauguration. RTL to Isaac Markens, Washington, January 19, 1921, folder 6, RTL Collection, CHM.

22. John Nicolay to Therena Bates, March 5, 1865, box 3, Nicolay Papers; Brooks, *Washington in Lincoln's Time*, 213.

23. Brooks, *Washington in Lincoln's Time*, 215.

24. "Our Special Account," *New York Times*, March 6, 1865, 1.

25. Recollection of F. Willis Rice, in "Chicago Friend Relates Anecdotes of Robert Lincoln," *Chicago Tribune*, July 27, 1926, 6.

26. "The Inaugural Ball," *New York Times*, March 8, 1865, 1; "Items about the Inaugural Ball," *Daily Ohio Statesman* (Columbus), March 15, 1865, 1.

27. "The Inaugural Ball," *Washington Evening Star*, March 7, 1865, 2; Brigham, *James Harlan*, 196.

28. Mrs. Ann Eliza Harlan to John Hay, January 11, 1865, reel 5, Hay Papers, Brown University; John Nicolay to Therena Bates, January 13, 1865, Nicolay Papers.

29. RTL to Woodward Emery, March 1, 1865, telegram endorsed by Abraham Lincoln, in Basler et al., *Collected Works*, 8:326.

30. "Capt. Robert Lincoln," *Baltimore Sun*, March 7, 1865, 1; E. T. Helm, "President Lincoln and the Widow of General Helm," 318; RTL to Emily Helm, Washington, April 14, 1924, in K. Helm, *True Story of Mary*, 250–51.

31. RTL to John Hay, City Point, Virginia, March 14, 1865, reel 8, Hay Papers, Brown University.

32. Brigadier-General James W. Forsythe to Brigadier-General J. A. Rawlins, March 21, 1865, in *OR*, 3:67–68.

33. J. D. Grant, *Personal Memoirs of Julia Dent Grant*, 142.

34. Ulysses S. Grant to Abraham Lincoln, City Point, Virginia, March 20, 1865, and Lincoln to Grant, Washington, March 20, 1865, in *OR*, 3:50; RTL to Abraham Lincoln, Fortress Monroe, Virginia, March 21, 1865, RTL Papers, ALPL. Mary Lincoln also mentioned this trip in a letter on that day. Mary Lincoln to Abram Wakeman, March 20, 1865, in Turner and Turner, *Mary Todd Lincoln*, 205–6.

35. Gustavus V. Fox to Abraham Lincoln, Norfolk, Virginia, March 21, 1865, in *OR*, 3:62; Barnes, "With Lincoln from Washington to Richmond in 1865," 37–56.

36. Abraham Lincoln to RTL, Washington, March 21, 1865, in Basler et al., *Collected Works*, 8:369; Abraham Lincoln to Ulysses S. Grant, March 23, 1865, in *OR*, 3:86. See also Mary Lincoln to Charles Sumner, March 23, 1865, in Turner and Turner, *Mary Todd Lincoln*, 209. For an excellent study of Lincoln's time at City Point in 1865, see Temple, *Lincoln's Travels on the River Queen*.

37. J. D. Grant, *Personal Memoirs*, 142.

38. Cadwallader, *Three Years with Grant*, 281.

39. Abraham Lincoln to Edwin Stanton, City Point, Virginia, March 25, 1865, in *OR*, 3:109, and Basler et al., *Collected Works*, 8:373; Barnes, "With Lincoln from Washington to Richmond," 41.

40. Edwin Stanton to Abraham Lincoln, Washington, March 25, 1865, in *OR*, 3:109. In his diary, John Hay mentions Lincoln under fire at Fort Stevens; see Dennett, *Lincoln and the Civil War*, 208–9.

41. Sherman, *Memoirs of William Tecumseh Sherman*, 2:324–31; D. D. Porter, *Incidents and Anecdotes of the Civil War*, 313–16; Barnes, "With Lincoln from Washington to Richmond," 49–51.

42. Cadwallader, *Three Years with Grant*, 282.

43. Badeau, *Grant in Peace from Appomattox to Mount McGregor*, 356–60; Cadwallader, *Three Years with Grant*, 282; J. D. Grant, *Personal Memoirs*, 146–47; Sherman, *Memoirs of William Tecumseh Sherman*, 2:332; H. Porter, "Campaigning with Grant," 600, 602; Barnes, "With Lincoln from Washington to Richmond," 46–47. Mrs. Grant, however, while admitting Mary's annoyance at Mrs. Ord, disputed the story as hyperbole in her memoirs.

44. Mary Lincoln to Abraham Lincoln, Washington, April 2, 1865, and Mary Lincoln to Abram Wakeman, Washington, April 4, 1865, in Turner and Turner, *Mary Todd Lincoln*, 211, 212.

45. Crook, *Through Five Administrations*, 47–48; D. D. Porter, *Incidents and Anecdotes of the Civil War*, 290; Abraham Lincoln to Ulysses S. Grant, City Point, Virginia, April 2, 1865, in Basler et al., *Collected Works*, 8:383. Robert later wrote, "I myself with a squad of cavalry escorted [my father] to Petersburg and back to City Point." RTL to A.K. McClure, May 10, 1879, LB, 3:5:699.

46. Abraham Lincoln to Mary Lincoln, City Point, Virginia, April 3, 1865, in Basler, *Collected Works Supplement*, 285.

47. RTL to [U.S. Supreme Court Associate] Justice [John Marshall] Harlan, May 7 and May 15, 1908, LB, 41:70:156–65; RTL to Judd Stewart, October 18, 1917, and June 1, 1918, and May 14, 1919, HM8430, HM 8471, and HM 8475, RTL Collection, Huntington Library. See also Charles Marshal, aide-de-camp and military secretary to R. E. Lee, "The Last Days of Lee's Army," and Gibbon, "Personal Recollections of Appomattox."

48. "Lee's Surrender at Appomattox," *Washington Post*, April 10, 1881, 3.

49. U. S. Grant, *Personal Memoirs of U. S. Grant and Selected Letters 1839–1865*, 750.

50. J. D. Grant, *Personal Memoirs*, 153.

51. Mary Lincoln to Francis Bicknell Carpenter, November 15, 1865, and to Mary Jane Welles, July 11, 1865, in Turner and Turner, *Mary Todd Lincoln*, 257, 284–85.

52. Keckley, *Behind the Scenes*, 137.

53. RTL to Judd Stewart, Washington, May 14, 1919, HM 8475, RTL Collection, Huntington Library.

54. J. D. Grant, *Personal Memoirs*, 154; Abraham Lincoln to Ulysses S. Grant, Washington, April 14, 1865, in Basler et al., *Collected Works*, 8:411. Julia Grant states in her memoirs that in his note to General Grant that morning, Lincoln made the comment about wanting to see Robert that morning. But the letter simply says, "Please come at 11 A.M. today instead of 9, as agreed last evening." Her statement that Lincoln postponed the meeting in order to see his son may have been something Lincoln *said* to General Grant that morning, the general then said it to his wife, but she remembered it as being in the note. Robert Lincoln himself may have told this to Mrs. Grant—which is possible. Ibid., all.

55. George Alfred Townsend, "The Empty White House," *Louisville Daily Journal*, June 5, 1865, 4.

56. Mary Lincoln, interview by William Herndon, September 1866, 2:227–28, LN 2408, Lamon Papers; Mary Lincoln, interview by William Herndon, 1866, in "Lincoln's Religion: Answer of William H. Herndon, Esq., to Mrs. Lincoln," Springfield, Illinois, January 12, 1874, TS, frame 1728, reel 9, group 4, H-W; Mary Lincoln to Mary Jane Welles, October 14, 1865, and Mary Lincoln to James Smith, December 17, 1866, in Turner and Turner, *Mary Todd Lincoln*, 276–78 and 399–400; Mary Lincoln to Myra Bradwell, Sor-

rento, Italy, April 22, 1878, in Emerson, *Madness of Mary Lincoln*, 174–75; "Mrs. Lincoln's Presentiment," *New York Times*, May 1, 1865, 5.

57. Mary Lincoln said they had decided to move to Chicago, but others have said Lincoln was determined to return to Springfield. Mary Lincoln, interview by William H. Herndon, September 1866, 2:227–28, LN 2408, Lamon Papers; John Todd Stuart, interview with John G. Nicolay, June 24, 1875, in Burlingame, *Oral History of Abraham Lincoln*, 14; Mrs. John Todd Stuart, interview by *Chicago Tribune*, in "His Early Social Life and Marriage," *Chicago Tribune*, Patriotic Supplement no. 4, Abraham Lincoln, February 12, 1900, 14, located in Memoranda/Clippings Folder, Research Material, 1860–1942, box 8, Nicolay Papers; Chambrun, *Impressions of Lincoln and the Civil War*, 33–34; Brooks, "Personal Reminiscences of Lincoln," 681.

58. Mary Lincoln to Francis Bicknell Carpenter, November 15, 1865, in Turner and Turner, *Mary Todd Lincoln*, 284–85 (emphasis in original). While the accuracy of anyone quoting another's words is always suspect, Mary, in the next sentence, unwittingly offers credibility for the historian: "Every word, then uttered, is deeply engraven, on my poor broken heart." Lincoln's playfulness is also mentioned in Mary Lincoln to Mary Jane Welles, July 11, 1865, ibid., 257.

59. Mary Harlan and family did accompany Mary Lincoln to City Point after the fall of Richmond in early April, but she did not see Robert during the trip. Robert was with Grant at the front, and so, despite what previous historians have stated, he could not have been at City Point during Mary Harlan's visit.

60. RTL to Judd Stewart, Washington, May 14, 1919, HM 8475, RTL Collection, Huntington Library.

61. Welles, *Diary of Gideon Welles*, 2:280; untitled article, *Daily Central City (CO) Register*, July 10, 1870, 1.

62. Hollister, *Life of Schuyler Colfax*, 253; Bates, *Lincoln in the Telegraph Office*, 366–67.

63. RTL, interview by George A. Dondero, March 5, 1923, in "My First Interview with Robert Todd Lincoln," unpublished MS, Hildene Archives.

64. Nicolay and Hay, *Abraham Lincoln*, 10:301. One biographer of John Hay suggests that Robert and Hay may have been studying Spanish, which seems most unlikely. Dennett, *John Hay*, 36.

65. Abraham Lincoln, "Card of Admission for George Ashmun," April 14, 1865, in Basler et al., *Collected Works*, 8:413; Pendel, *Thirty-Six Years in the White House*, 39–40.

66. "I remember distinctly the shock of surprise and the impression, at the time, that he had never said it before," Crook later wrote. *Through Five Administrations*, 68. See also L. Lewis, *Myths after Lincoln*, 297.

67. RTL, interview by George A. Dondero, March 5, 1923, in "My First Interview with Robert Todd Lincoln," unpublished MS, Hildene Archives.

68. Nicolay and Hay, *Abraham Lincoln*, 10:301.

69. Alexander Williamson, "Reminiscences of Lincoln," *Weekly Leader*, April 15, 1869, 4, clipping, folder "Reminiscences," Lincoln Collection, ALPL; "Was at Lincoln's Death," *New York Tribune*, June 4, 1903, 16. See also Alexander Williamson, "Reminiscences of Lincoln," *(Washington, DC) Sunday Chronicle*, March 7, 1869, and "He Taught Tad Lincoln," *New York Press*, April 14, 1889, both reproduced in Temple, *Alexander Williamson*, 29–33, 36–41. Williamson spent much of the night at the Petersen House and was later included in one of the many paintings of Lincoln's death, "The Last Moments of Lincoln," published in 1866 by Philip & Solomons, Washington, D.C. After the assassination, Mary Lincoln wrote to President Johnson and asked that he fulfill a promise made by her husband to

give Williamson a federal job appointment. Mary Lincoln to Andrew Johnson, April 29, 1865, frame 3097–98, reel 14, series 1, Abraham Lincoln Papers, LOC, also in Turner and Turner, *Mary Todd Lincoln*, 226.

70. Pendel, *Thirty-Six Years in the White House*, 42–43; Thomas Pendel, undated, untitled newspaper clipping, reminiscences folder, Lincoln Collection, ALPL; "Years in the White House: An Old Employee Talks about the Presidents since Lincoln's Time," *New York Times*, October 10, 1886, 6. Mary Lincoln actually asked President Johnson to keep Pendel as the principal White House doorkeeper. Mary Lincoln to Andrew Johnson, May 1865, in Turner and Turner, *Mary Todd Lincoln*, 229.

71. C. C. Bangs, "News of Booth's Shot," *Washington Post*, April 12, 1896, 20. Bangs also states he received a letter from Robert Lincoln "vouching for the facts (in part) above named." This letter has not been located. C. C. Bangs, "News of Booth's Shot," *Washington Post*, April 12, 1896, 20.

72. A. B. Johnson, "Recollections of Charles Sumner," 224. See also Pierce, *Memoirs and Letters of Charles Sumner*, 4:237, and "Memories of Lincoln," *New York Times*, January 20, 1901, 2.

73. Chaplin and Chaplin, *Life of Charles Sumner*, 414–16; "Reminiscences of Mr. Sumner," *New York Times*, March 17, 1874, 5.

74. RTL to George H. Haynes, March 10, 1909, LB, 42:73:267.

75. Ibid. (emphasis added).

76. Nicolay and Hay, *Abraham Lincoln*, 10:301. As one writer imagines the scene, "When the driver tried to turn off G Street into Tenth—a block and a half from the theater—a mass of humanity blocked the road and Robert Lincoln put his head in his hands and moaned. When soldiers tried to turn the carriage away, Lincoln, in anguish, said: 'It's my father! I'm Robert Lincoln! I'm Robert Lincoln!'" Bishop, *Day Lincoln Was Shot*, 224–25.

77. Nicolay and Hay, *Abraham Lincoln*, 10:301.

78. For a fascinating treatise on exactly who was in the death room and when that night and how those numbers swelled in subsequent legend, see Holzer and Williams, *Lincoln's Deathbed in Art and Memory*.

79. Robert Lincoln sent for Mrs. Dixon to come to his mother. Elizabeth Dixon to "My dear Louisa," May 1, 1865, reproduced in *Surratt Society News* 7, no. 3 (March 1982): 3–4; letter also excerpted and discussed in Sanka Knox, "Woman Describes Death of Lincoln," *New York Times*, February 12, 1950, 42.

80. RTL to Mrs. Henry C. Hall, February 20, 1909, LB, 42:72:180.

81. Gilder honored Robert's request. RTL to Richard Watson Gilder, February 5 and 20, 1909, LB, 42:72:114, 190.

82. "The Scene at the President's Death-Bed," *(Cleveland) Ohio Farmer*, April 22, 1865, 124.

83. Welles, *Diary of Gideon Welles*, 2:287.

84. For accounts of the night by surgeons who were present, see Dr. Charles A. Leale to Major General Benjamin F. Butler, chair of House Assassination Investigation Committee, official statement regarding assassination of President Abraham Lincoln, New York, July 20, 1867, box 43, General Correspondence, Benjamin F. Butler Papers; "Closing Scenes," *New York Times*, April 16, 1865, 1; Charles S. Taft, "Lincoln's Last Hours," *New York Times*, October 14, 1900, A2. For a newspaper account, see "Our Great Loss—Death of President Lincoln," *New York Times*, April 16–17, 1865, 1. Willie Clark, in whose room and on whose bed Lincoln died, wrote his sister a few days later that he intended to give Robert Lincoln the pillow on which the president died. Willie Clark to "Dear Sister Ida," Washington, April 19, 1865, in Borreson, *When Lincoln Died*, 49.

85. Field, *Memories of Many Men and of Some Women*, 325.
86. Welles, *Diary of Gideon Welles*, 2:288.
87. K. Helm, *True Story of Mary*, 260.

7. "I Feel Utterly without Spirit or Courage"

1. Crook, *Through Five Administrations*, 69.
2. RTL telegraph to David Davis, Washington, April 15, 1865, RTL Papers, ALPL.
3. Sarah Davis to her children, Chicago, April 16, 1865, folder 84, box 13, Davis Papers, CHM.
4. Welles, *Diary of Gideon Welles*, 2:290; Taft, *Washington during the Civil War*, April 30, 1865, vol. 3, LOC; Thomas Pendel, undated, untitled newspaper clipping, "Reminiscences" folder, Lincoln Collection, ALPL.
5. Keckley, *Behind the Scenes*, 191.
6. Elizabeth Dixon to "My dear Louisa," May 1, 1865, reproduced in *Surratt Society News* 7, no. 3 (March 1982): 3–4; letter also excerpted and discussed in Sanka Knox, "Woman Describes Death of Lincoln," *New York Times*, February 12, 1950, 42; Welles, *Diary of Gideon Welles*, 2:290; Benjamin B. French diary, April 15, 1865, frame P000666, reel 2, vol. 9, French Family Papers.
7. C. M. Smith to RTL, New York, April 15, 1865, Emily Todd Helm to RTL, April 15, 1865, and Clinton Conkling to RTL, Springfield, Illinois, April 17, 1865, Telegrams Collected by the Office of the Secretary of War, 1861–82, reel 224, Telegrams Received by Government Officials, Mainly of the War and Navy Departments, April 7–18, 1865, 463:267, 281, 477, NARA.
8. Mrs. N. W. Edwards to Mary Lincoln, Springfield, Illinois, April 18, 1865, Telegrams Collected by the Office of the Secretary of War, 1861–82, roll 225, Telegrams Received by Government Officials, Mainly of the War and Navy Departments, April 17–May 1, 1865, 464:57, NARA.
9. John B. S. Todd to John Todd Stuart, Washington, April 15, 1865, SC 913–2, John B. S. Todd Papers. Grimsley did not come.
10. Keckley, *Behind the Scenes*, 195.
11. RTL to F. J. Child, Washington, April 27, 1865, RTL Collection, Phillips Exeter Academy.
12. Butler, *Across the Busy Years*, 379.
13. John Nicolay to Therena Bates, Executive Mansion, April 18, 1865, box 3, Nicolay Papers.
14. "Our Great Loss," *New York Times*, April 16, 1865, 1.
15. "The Funeral: A Solemn Day," *Washington Star*, April 20, 1865, 1; "The Obsequies," *New York Times*, April 20, 1865, 1.
16. Henry Ames Blood to "My Dear Mother [Livinia Fletcher]," Washington, April 18, 1865, Hildene Archives. See also Emerson, "Aftermath of an Assassination."
17. Major General John J. Peck to Edwin M. Stanton, New York, April 15, 1865, *OR*, 782.
18. Robert E. Lee to Count Joannes, September 4, 1865, in Jones, *Personal Reminiscences, Anecdotes, and Letters of Gen. Robert E. Lee*, 204.
19. RTL to Samuel Bishop, January 29, 1900, LB, 34:56:148. None of the contemporary newspaper accounts of the train tell whether Robert was on board or not.
20. "Presentation to Mrs. Lincoln," *Washington National Intelligencer*, May 23, 1865, 1; "Presentation to Mrs. Lincoln," *New York Times*, May 24, 1865, 8; Gerry, *Through Five Administrations*, 69–70; RTL to Andrew Johnson, April 25, 1865, frames 2957–58, reel 13, series 1, Andrew Johnson Papers.

21. Mary Lincoln to Mrs. Kasson, Chicago, January 20, 1866, Lincoln Collection, ALPL, quoted in Schwartz and Bauer, "Unpublished Mary Todd Lincoln," 1–21.

22. "Mr. Seward's Opinion of the Assassination—Mrs. Lincoln and Her Family," *Washington National Intelligencer*, April 24, 1865, 1; Gerry, *Through Five Administrations*, 70.

23. RTL to Lorenzo Thomas, Adjutant General of the U.S., Washington, April 21, 1865, Lincoln Collection, ALPL; E. D. Townsend, assistant adjutant general, Special Orders No. 229 (May 15, 1865) and 294 (June 10, 1865), box 38, entry 158, record group 94, Staff Papers, Records of the Adjutant General's Office, War Department, NARA; Return of the Subsistence Department, U.S. vols., March, April, and May, 1865, folder 57, box 62, entry 518, record group 94, Union staff officer files, 1861–66, Records of the Adjutant General's Office, War Department, NARA. On April 30, 1865, Lieutenant General Ulysses S. Grant endorsed Robert's April 21 resignation letter with this note: "In approving the resignation of Capt. Lincoln it affords me pleasure to testify to the uniform good conduct of this young officer and to say that by his course in the performance of his duties, and in his social intercourse, he has won the esteem and lasting friendship of all with whom he has come in contact."

24. RTL and Mary Lincoln to Judge of County Court, Sangamon County, Illinois, Washington, April 24, 1865, folder 84, box 13, Davis Papers.

25. John Nicolay to Therena Bates, Executive Mansion, April 24, 1865, box 3, Nicolay Papers; RTL to F. J. Child, Washington, April 27, 1865, RTL Collection, Phillips Exeter Academy; Mary Lincoln to Senator Howard, Chicago, February 27, 1866, Mary Todd Lincoln Papers, ACPL; David Davis to Jeremiah Black, August 19, 1870, frame 60074, reel 26, vol. 52, Jeremiah S. Black Papers; copy of Davis letter also in box 128, Mearns Papers. For an example of Robert's possible involvement in reviewing his father's papers for storage, see Basler et al., *Collected Works*, 6:373n1.

26. David Davis to Jeremiah Black, August 19, 1870, frames 60073–74, reel 26, vol. 52, Jeremiah S. Black Papers; Mary Lincoln to Senator Howard, Chicago, February 27, 1866, Mary Todd Lincoln Papers, ACPL.

27. RTL to F. J. Child, Washington, April 27, 1865, RTL Collection, Phillips Exeter Academy. Journalist Noah Brooks similarly reported on May 17 that Robert had sealed up the president's papers and "intends to publish them after a considerable lapse of time shall have passed—not before three or four years. Then he will merely spread before the world the letters of his father, arranged in some order, with brief annotations, leaving the material to future historians or biographers to arrange at their own convenience." "The Lincoln Family," *Sacramento Daily Union*, June 14, 1865, transcript in Reminiscences Funeral folder, Lincoln Collection, ALPL; also reproduced in Burlingame, *Lincoln Observed*, 197.

28. James Parton was one of the most popular writers of American biographies of his day. By 1865, his major works included lives of Aaron Burr (1857), Andrew Jackson (1859–60, 3 vols.), and Benjamin Franklin (1864, 2 vols.). Robert had in college read Parton's life of Andrew Jackson; his copy is still at his Vermont house, Hildene. RTL to James Parton, Washington, May 10, 1865, RTLFP.

29. RTL to Josiah G. Holland, Chicago, June 6, 1865, RTLFP; also found in folder 37, box 6, Lincoln Collection, Miscellaneous Manuscripts.

30. RTL to Thomas Dent, September 12, 1919, quoted in W. L. King, *Lincoln's Manager*, 244.

31. The most prominent proponent of the Stanton theory is Otto Eisenschiml, who details his beliefs in two books, *Why Was Lincoln Murdered?* 432–36, and *In the Shadow of Lincoln's Death*, 191–234.

32. RTL to David H. Bates, October 2, 1911, LB, 45:79:276. Robert also wrote to Stan-

ton's son, "[W]hen I recall the kindness of your father to me, when my father was lying dead and I felt utterly desperate, hardly able to realize the truth, I am as little able to keep my eyes from filling with tears as he was then. I can never forget his kindness then and since." RTL to Edwin L. Stanton, December 24, 1869, in unpublished manuscript, "Edwin M. Stanton: A Personal Portrait," Gideon Townsend Stanton, ed., Edwin L. Stanton Papers.

33. Mary Lincoln, interview by William Herndon, September 1866, 2:227–28, LN 2408, Lamon Papers; Mary Lincoln, interview by William Herndon, 1866, in "Lincoln's Religion: Answer of William H. Herndon, Esq., to Mrs. Lincoln," Springfield, Illinois, January 12, 1874, TS, frame 1728, microfilm reel 9, group 4, H-W; Mary Lincoln to Mary Jane Welles, October 14, 1865 and to James Smith, December 17, 1866, in Turner and Turner, *Mary Todd Lincoln*, 276–78 and 399–400; Mary Lincoln to Myra Bradwell, Sorrento, Italy, April 22, 1878, in Emerson, *Madness of Mary Lincoln*, 174–75; "Mrs. Lincoln's Presentiment," *New York Times*, May 1, 1865, 5.

34. Pease and Randall, *Diary of Orville Hickman Browning*, April 20, 1865, 2:23–24.

35. "Mr. Lincoln's Remains," *(Springfield) Illinois State Journal*, April 17, 1865, 2; Power, *Abraham Lincoln*, 106.

36. The current Illinois State Capitol sits on the spot.

37. "From Springfield," *Chicago Tribune*, April 18, 1865, 1.

38. Pease and Randall, *Diary of Orville Hickman Browning*, April 15 and 17, 1865, 2:20, 22; "The President's Obsequies," *New York Times*, May 3, 1865, 1. See also "The Burial: President Lincoln Again at His Western Home," *New York Times*, May 5, 1865, 1.

39. Arnold, *Life of Abraham Lincoln*, 435.

40. Oak Ridge was designed in 1855 to replace Hutchinson's cemetery—burial place of four-year-old Eddie Lincoln in 1850—as the principal burial place for Springfield citizens. *Oak Ridge Cemetery*, 8.

41. "An Infected District," *Chicago Tribune*, April 24, 1865, 2; "From Springfield," *Chicago Tribune*, April 26, 1865, 1; "The Last Resting Place of President Lincoln's Remains," *Lowell (MA) Daily Citizen and News*, April 29, 1865; "From Springfield," *Chicago Tribune*, May 2, 1865, 1; Anson G. Henry, "From Washington," *Chicago Tribune*, May 9, 1865, 2. See also "National Monument to President Lincoln," *New York Times*, April 20, 1865, 4.

42. Anson G. Henry, "From Washington," *Chicago Tribune*, May 9, 1865, 2. After reading Henry's letter in the newspaper, Julia Trumbull, wife of U.S. Senator Lyman Trumbull from Illinois, wrote to her husband, "Whatever may be said of the propriety of provoking ill feelings at such a time, it cannot be denied that the closing paragraph shows some ability to be severe, and being truthful may not be wholly undeserved. I do not doubt that some of the individuals named felt themselves as fit as Mr. L for the presidency." Julia Trumbull to Lyman Trumbull, May 9, 1865, folder 15, box 1, Lyman Trumbull Papers.

43. John B. S. Todd to John Todd Stuart, Washington, April 28, 1865, SC 913–2, John B. S. Todd Papers; Edwin Stanton to John Todd Stuart, April 28, 1865, Telegrams Collected by the Office of the Secretary of War (Bound), 1861–1882, microcopy 473, roll 89, and Telegrams Sent by the Secretary of War, RG107, Records of the Office of the Secretary of War, 187:152–53, NARA; "The Funeral of Abraham Lincoln," *Chicago Tribune*, May 6, 1865, 2; Anson G. Henry, "From Washington," *Chicago Tribune*, May 9, 1865, 2.

44. John B. S. Todd to John Todd Stuart, Washington, April 31, 1865, John B. S. Todd Papers; Anson G. Henry, "From Washington," *Chicago Tribune*, May 9, 1865, 2.

45. RTL to Hon. R. J. Oglesby, Washington, May 1, 1865, RTL Papers, ALPL; "The President's Obsequies," *New York Times*, May 3, 1865, 1.

46. John B. S. Todd to Clark M. Smith, Washington, May 1, 1865, SC 913–2, John B.

S. Todd Papers; Anson G. Henry to John Williams, White House, May 1, 1865, SC 683, Anson G. Henry Papers.

47. S. P. V. Arnold to Danforth, Springfield, Illinois, December 26, [1899?], item 1, Lincoln Collection, Houghton Library. One citizen of Jacksonville, Illinois, later wrote that to her it was "strange that Mrs. Lincoln should act the way she has after all they [the burial committee] have done." John Todd Stuart later wrote to Mary that the citizens of Springfield yielded to her decision "cheerfully but still reluctantly, and with many regrets." One reason for some of the regrets may have been, as the *Chicago Tribune* reported on May 6, that numerous land speculators had bought up every lot surrounding the Mather estate in an effort to profit from the assured tourism to Lincoln's tomb. Julia D. Kirby to Joseph Duncan, Jacksonville, Illinois, May 7, 1865, in Pratt, *Concerning Mr. Lincoln*, 133; John Todd Stuart to Mary Lincoln, Springfield, Illinois, July 14, 1865, box 1, Stuart-Hay Family Papers; "From Springfield," *Chicago Tribune*, May 6, 1865, 1. See also Beall, "Recollections of the Assassination and Funeral of Abraham Lincoln."

48. "President Lincoln's Residence," *(Springfield) Illinois State Journal*, May 6, 1865, 3; "The Funeral of Abraham Lincoln," *Chicago Tribune*, May 6, 1865, 2. For a more detailed account of the feelings and reactions of the Springfield, Illinois, populace on the news of Lincoln's death, see Power, *Abraham Lincoln*, 104–7, 116–19.

49. RTL to Elizabeth Grimsley, Washington, May 1, 1865, RTL Papers, ALPL; John B. S. Todd to Clark M. Smith, Washington, May 1, 1865, John B. S. Todd Papers; "From Washington," *Chicago Tribune*, May 3, 1865, 1; "Arrival of Robert Lincoln," *(Springfield) Illinois State Journal*, May 4, 1865, 2; Julia D. Kirby to Joseph Duncan, Jacksonville, Illinois, May 7, 1865, in Pratt, *Concerning Mr. Lincoln*, 133. Robert had originally arranged to stay with his mother's cousin Elizabeth Todd Grimsley, but her house was so full of boarders she had no room. RTL to Elizabeth Grimsley, Washington, May 1, 1865, RTL Papers, ALPL.

50. "An Illinois Farmer during the Civil War," 131. See also Elbridge Atwood to Alice Atwood, Springfield, May 7, 1865, in "Lincolniana," 142.

51. E. D. Townsend, assistant adjutant-general, to Hon. Edwin M. Stanton, secretary of war, Springfield, May 4, 1865, in *OR*, 1:46:3:1090.

52. "Final Depository of Mr. Lincoln's Remains at Springfield," *Milwaukee (WI) Sentinel*, May 6, 1865, 1.

53. "From Springfield," *Chicago Tribune*, May 6, 1865, 1.

54. Julia D. Kirby to Joseph Duncan, Jacksonville, Illinois, May 7, 1865, in Pratt, *Concerning Mr. Lincoln*, 132.

55. RTL to J. B. S. Todd, Springfield, Illinois, May 1865, Telegrams Collected by the Office of the Secretary of War, 1861–82, roll 226, Telegrams Received by Government Officials, Mainly of the War and Navy Departments, April 30–May 13, 1865, 466:333, NARA.

56. "From Springfield—Mr. Lincoln's Final Resting Place," *Chicago Tribune*, May 6, 1865, 1.

57. RTL to John Todd Stuart, Washington, May 8, 1865, Stuart-Hay Family Papers.

58. Mary Lincoln to Charles Sumner, May 9 and 14, 1865, and to Mrs. Off and Mrs. Baker, May 16, 1865, in Turner and Turner, *Mary Todd Lincoln*, 227–29.

59. "Postscript, 4 o'clock A.M.," *Chicago Tribune*, May 23, 1865, 1.

60. Mary Lincoln to Charles Sumner, May 9, 1865, in Turner and Turner, *Mary Todd Lincoln*, 227–28.

61. Robert's anxiety was a condition inherited from both his mother and maternal grandfather. Although mild in his early adulthood, it became more prevalent in his later life and was labeled by both him and his physicians as "nervous dyspepsia."

62. Mary Lincoln to Anson G. Henry, July 26, 1865, in Turner and Turner, *Mary Todd Lincoln*, 263.

63. White House seamstress Elizabeth Keckly stated the president told his son on the morning of April 14 that he wanted him to resign from the army, return to college, and read law for three years, "and at the end of that time I hope we will be able to tell whether you will make a lawyer or not." The speculation that Robert would apprentice in Washington is a logical surmise knowing that Robert's family, closest friends, and the girl he was courting all lived in the capital. Keckley, *Behind the Scenes*, 138.

64. For a description of these social mores, see Rotundo, *American Manhood*, 12–13.

65. Keckley, *Behind the Scenes*, 122–24.

66. Rotundo, *American Manhood*, 13–14.

67. Mary Lincoln to Oliver S. Halstead Jr., Chicago, May 29, 1865, and Mary Lincoln to Harriet Howe Wilson, near Chicago, June 8, 1865, in Turner and Turner, *Mary Todd Lincoln*, 236, 243; "From Chicago . . . Mrs. Lincoln Again," *New York Times*, June 25, 1865, 3; Stronks, "Mary Todd Lincoln's Sad Summer in Hyde Park."

68. Keckley, *Behind the Scenes*, 212–13.

69. Browning, diary, July 3, 1873, ALPL. Davis reportedly stated there were too many proofs against Mary Lincoln "to admit of doubt" of her looting the White House, that she was "a natural born thief; that stealing was a sort of insanity with her," and she had taken numerous items of no value "only in obedience to her irresistible propensity to steal." Ibid.

70. Mary Lincoln to Sally Orne, January 13, 1866, to Alexander Williamson, January 17 and 26, 1866, to Oliver S. Halstead Jr., January 17, 1866, in Turner and Turner, *Mary Todd Lincoln*, 326–30; "The West," *New York Times*, June 4, 1865, 3; "Remonstrance against Free Trade . . . Brutal Charges against Mrs. Lincoln," *Chicago Tribune*, January 16, 1866, 1. Keckly explains that the boxes contained mostly presents given to the entire first family during their four-year stay. Keckley, *Behind the Scenes*, 206–7.

71. Mary Lincoln to Alexander Williamson, August 17, 1865, and Mary Lincoln to David Davis, September 12, 1865, in Turner and Turner, *Mary Todd Lincoln*, 264–65, 274.

72. Pratt, *Personal Finances*, 131–41.

73. RTL to David Davis, Chicago, June 24, 1865, folder A-109, box 7, Davis Family Papers.

74. Mary Lincoln to Anson G. Henry, July 17, 1865, in Turner and Turner, *Mary Todd Lincoln*, 261 (emphasis in original).

75. Hall, "My Impressions of America," 157. Hall visited Robert Lincoln at his law office in Chicago in September 1867.

76. Abraham Lincoln to J. M. Brockman, Springfield, Illinois, September 25, 1860, in Basler et al., *Collected Works*, 4:121.

77. Untitled article, *Chicago Tribune*, November 21, 1865, 2; "Robert T. Lincoln as a Law Student," 21; Busby, "A Coming Man," 1; Elizabeth V. Benyon, assistant law librarian, University of Chicago, to John Goff, March 7, 1960, Goff Papers. A personal visit to the (new) University of Chicago archives and consultation with assistant archivists and the curator failed to unearth any records concerning Robert Lincoln's 1865–66 activities, classes, or grades at the "old" university law school.

78. Palmer, *Bench and Bar of Illinois*, 1:73–74.

79. Andreas, *History of Chicago*, 1:551; Palmer, *Bench and Bar of Illinois*, 1:73–74; Bateman, Selby, and Shonkwiler, *Historical Encyclopedia of Illinois*, 1:467.

80. Wilkie, *Sketches and Notices of the Chicago Bar*, 16–18; Goodspeed and Healy, *History of Cook County, Illinois*, 2:205.

81. Wilkie, *Sketches and Notices of the Chicago Bar*, 16–18.

82. Mary Lincoln to Oliver S. Halstead Jr., Chicago, May 29, 1865, and to Harriet Howe Wilson, near Chicago, June 8, 1865, in Turner and Turner, *Mary Todd Lincoln*, 236, 243; Stronks, "Mary Todd Lincoln's Sad Summer in Hyde Park."

83. "Robert T. Lincoln as a Law Student," 21.

84. Turner and Turner, *Mary Todd Lincoln*, 237.

85. One such solicitation declared the monument should be "of a character corresponding with the fame, wealth, and power of this nation—should be, architecturally, of the grandest scale, combining evidences for succeeding generations, in marble, stone, iron, brass, bronze and glass." J. T. D., "Proposed National Monument to Abraham Lincoln at Springfield, Ill.," 357.

86. Mary Lincoln to Richard J. Oglesby, June 5, 10, and 11, 1865, and "Request for Agreement," June 1865, in Turner and Turner, *Mary Todd Lincoln*, 241–45; untitled article, *Daily Cleveland (OH) Herald*, June 15, 1865, 1.

87. Mary Lincoln to Richard J. Oglesby, near Chicago, June 10, 1865, in Turner and Turner, *Mary Todd Lincoln*, 243–44; Richard J. Oglesby and Ozias M. Hatch to Mary Lincoln, Tremont House, Chicago, June 12, 1865, and Richard J. Oglesby and Ozias M. Hatch, "Report to National Lincoln Monument Committee," n.d. [probably either June 13 or 14, 1865], "Correspondence to Mrs. Lincoln" folder, box 7, Hatch Papers; "From Springfield," *Chicago Tribune*, June 13, 1865, 1; "The Lincoln Monument," *Chicago Tribune*, June 14, 1865, 4.

88. Richard J. Oglesby to Mary Lincoln, Springfield, Illinois, June 14, 1865, "Correspondence to Mrs. Lincoln" folder, box 7, Hatch Papers; "From Springfield," *Chicago Tribune*, June 16, 1865, 1.

89. Turner and Turner, *Mary Todd Lincoln*, 243n2; Powers, *Abraham Lincoln*, 229; untitled article, *Daily Cleveland (OH) Herald*, June 15, 1865, 1.

90. RTL to Edgar Welles, Chicago, October 16, 1865, RTL Papers, ACPL.

91. Mary Todd Lincoln to Mary Jane Welles, October 14, 1864, in Turner and Turner, *Mary Todd Lincoln*, 277.

92. Ibid., December 6, 1865, 294 (emphasis in original).

93. Edwin M. Stanton to RTL, Washington, July 6, 1865, Telegrams Collected by the Office of the Secretary of War, 1861–82, roll 89, Telegrams Sent by the Secretary of War, April 21–October 3, 1865, 188:259, NARA.

94. In the first year alone, nearly five hundred books and pamphlets on Lincoln were published, most of which were memorial-type addresses. See Monaghan, *Lincoln Bibliography*, 1:91–210.

95. RTL to David Davis, Chicago, August 8, 1865, folder A-109, box 7, DDFP.

96. Ibid., December 22, 1865; Powers, *Abraham Lincoln*, 229.

97. Mary Lincoln to Sally Orne, Chicago, December 24, 1865, and Mary Lincoln to Mary Jane Welles, Chicago, December 29, 1865, in Turner and Turner, *Mary Todd Lincoln*, 311, 315.

98. RTL to David Davis, Chicago, December 22, 1865, and January 3, 1866, folder A-109, box 7, Davis Family Papers.

8. "One of the Most Promising Young Men of the West"

1. Mary Eunice Harlan records, *Iowa Wesleyan University Catalog*, Harlan-Lincoln House Collection; Haselmayer, *Harlan-Lincoln Tradition at Iowa Wesleyan College*, Harlan-Lincoln House Collection, 7. Mary took the typical female courses of "preparatory" but

focused her studies on music. In Washington, she attended Madame Smith's French School. Ibid., both.

2. Snively, "James M. Davidson," 187; Bayne, *Tad Lincoln's Father*, 26; Temple, "Alexander Williamson—Tutor to the Lincoln Boys," 16; "Robert Todd Lincoln Could Tickle the Keys," 4.

3. "Robert Lincoln—Gossip in High Life," *Memphis (TN) Daily Avalanche*, April 7, 1866, 4; "Robert Lincoln's Love Affair," *Milwaukee (WI) Daily Sentinel*, April 9, 1866, 1; "Robert Lincoln—Gossip in High Life," *Daily Miners' Register* (Central City, CO), April 19, 1866, 1.

4. "Robert Lincoln's Love Affair," *Milwaukee (WI) Daily Sentinel*, April 9, 1866, 1. After their marriage, another newspaper recalled the broken engagement: "Rumor says marriage was interdicted by the old people. Scandal says the young lady thought she could do better." "Bob Lincoln's Marriage," *New Orleans Times*, September 30, 1868, 1.

5. Mary Harlan to Minnie Chandler, March 2 and August 4, 1866, Chandler Papers.

6. Ibid., January 15, 1866.

7. Ibid., March 2, 1866.

8. Ibid., August 4, 1866.

9. Ibid., December 16, 1866.

10. Ibid., October 3, 1866, February 10, March 17, and April 28, 1867.

11. RTL to David Davis, Chicago, January 19, 1867, folder A-109, box 7, DDFP; Mary Lincoln to David Davis, Chicago, January 9, 1867, in Turner and Turner, *Mary Todd Lincoln*, 405.

12. RTL to John Hay, January 28, 1867, reel 8, Hay Collection, Brown University.

13. RTL to Frank Ashbury Johnson, July 5, 1898, LB, 33:54:247. Johnson wrote to Robert that he could not find the latter's name on the Chicago Bar Association Roll of Attorneys admitted to practice in the state of Illinois. Robert responded that he still had his original "parchment" that consisted of three parts: the license, oath, and certificate. Ibid.

14. "From Cincinnati," *Chicago Tribune*, March 12, 1867, 1.

15. RTL to John Hay, January 28, 1867, reel 8, Hay Collection, Brown University; Mary Lincoln to Alexander Williamson, Chicago, October 17, 1866, in Turner and Turner, *Mary Todd Lincoln*, 393.

16. *Edwards' New Chicago Directory*, 485; untitled 1883 newspaper clipping, Robert T. Lincoln alumni folder, HUG 300, Harvard University Archives. Many records from the firm can be found in Robert Lincoln's Letterpress Books, reels 2–4, Lincoln Collection, ALPL.

17. Robert, of course, did not read law under a Judge Logan but under Scammon, McCagg, and Fuller. The journalist either got the name wrong or the relationship. Leonidas L. Logan was a judge in Chicago in the 1880s and perhaps is the Logan referred to in the story. Most likely, one of Robert's three mentors gave him the advice about fees.

18. "Bob Lincoln's First Fee," 1889, unidentified clipping, Goff Papers.

19. Carpenter, *Six Months in the White House*, 252.

20. W. L. King, *Lincoln's Manager*, 233.

21. Pratt, *Personal Finances*, 25.

22. Abraham Lincoln, "Fragment: Notes for a Law Lecture," in Basler et al., *Collected Works*, 2:82.

23. Ibid.

24. "Robert T. Lincoln as a Law Student," 21.

25. Hall, "My Impressions of America," 157.

26. Mentor, "Robert Todd Lincoln," *Los Angeles Times*, May 21, 1887, 10.

27. "Robert T. Lincoln," *Chicago Tribune*, October 21, 1867, 4; untitled article, *Daily Cleveland (OH) Herald*, October 21, 1867, 1.

28. "Robert T. Lincoln as a Law Student," 21.

29. Wilkie, *Sketches and Notices of the Chicago Bar*, 73.

30. Woldman, *Lawyer Lincoln*, 350. It appears that Abraham encouraged his son to study the law even before Robert went to Harvard. In 1858, Abraham had Robert assist him in acting as a pension attorney, collecting and disbursing money for Thomas Threlkeld, a War of 1812 veteran. Robert even ventured on his own and did the same for Sabra VanDike, a Revolutionary War widow. See Lupton, "Abraham Lincoln: Pension Attorney," 1, 7–8.

31. Mary Lincoln to David Davis, Chicago, August 12, 1866, in Turner and Turner, *Mary Todd Lincoln*, 381. RTL to David Davis, Chicago, October 30, 1866, folder A-109, box 7, DDFP; RTL to John Hay, Chicago, November 1, 1866, reel 8, Hay Papers, Brown University; RTL to Francis B. Hart, February 9, 1903, LB 36:61:305. In the August 12, 1866, letter, Mary wrote that Robert went to "Mackinaw" but did not specify the state. There is a Mackinaw, Illinois, outside Peoria, and a Mackinaw City at the northern tip of Michigan, right on the shore of Lake Huron. As a lakeshore city seems more appealing for a summer vacation than a land-bound town, I presume Robert journeyed to the Michigan city.

32. For a full account of the trip and its background, see Seymour, *Incidents of a Trip through the Great Platte Valley*. See also Perkins, *Trails, Rails, and War*, 205–6; Hirshson, *Grenville M. Dodge*, 141.

33. RTL to John Hay, Chicago, November 1, 1866, reel 8, Hay Papers, Brown University.

34. RTL to George M. Pullman, January 29, 1881, 7:355–58, Records of Isham, Lincoln, and Beale Law Firm, CHM.

35. RTL to Edgar Welles, Chicago, May 30, 1867, RTL Papers, ACPL.

36. John Hay to RTL, Paris, July 17, 1866, frames 158–59, reel 1, Hay Papers, Brown University.

37. Mary Lincoln to David Davis, Racine, Wisconsin, June 30, 1867, and to Elizabeth Emerson Atwater, Racine, Wisconsin, June 30, 1867, in Turner and Turner, *Mary Todd Lincoln*, 424–25; RTL to William Herndon, July 29, 1867, LB, 1:1:45; "The Surratt Trial," *Chicago Tribune*, July 6, 1867, 1. For the full court transcripts, see *Trial of John H. Surratt*. Tad was called to testify about a man he had seen—John Surratt, according to the prosecution—trying to gain access to the president on the *River Queen* in March 1865. For Tad's testimony, see *Trial of John H. Surratt*, 1:525–26.

38. "Arrivals in the City," *New York Times*, July 17, 1867, 5; RTL to David Davis, Chicago, July 29, 1867, folder A-109, box 7, DDFP; RTL to Mary Jane Welles, August 25, 1868, frames 31907–8, reel 35, Miscellany, Welles Papers, LOC.

39. Sadly, no letters by either Robert or Mary recounting this momentous event survive. The engagement ring is now in the Hildene collections.

40. RTL to James Harlan, Chicago, July 30, 1867, Mary G. Townsend Collection. Robert sent a copy of this letter to his Aunt Emily Helm. A transcript of the Helm copy was made at Helm Place in the late 1990s by historian Donna McCreary, who kindly shared it with me. McCreary had befriended Mrs. Mary Murphy, daughter of Lincoln historian and collector William Townsend and owner of Helm Place, and was allowed to look through the family papers there. Unfortunately, after Mrs. Murphy died in 2000, the whereabouts of this letter has been unknown.

41. "The City," *Burlington (IA) Hawk-Eye*, September 15, 1867, clipping, Harlan-Lincoln Collection.

42. RTL to James Harlan, Chicago, August 5, 1867, Mary G. Townsend Collection.

43. RTL to David Davis, July 29 and August 1, 1867, folder A-109, box 7, DDFP.

44. Ibid., January 17, 1868.

45. For a full examination of Lincoln's estate and Davis's handling of it, see Pratt, *Personal Finances*, 131–41. For Davis's financial report of his administration of the estate, see 140–41.

46. David Davis to Norman B. Judd, Bloomington, Illinois, July 17, 1866, David Davis MS, Lincoln Collection, Hay Library, Brown University.

47. RTL to David Davis, Chicago, November 18, 1867, folder A-109, box 7, DDFP.

48. Mary Lincoln to David Davis, Chicago, November 18, 1867, in Turner and Turner, *Mary Todd Lincoln*, 458.

49. King, *Lincoln's Manager*, 242. Indeed, after reading through all of Robert's letters to Davis, I agree with King's assessment.

50. RTL to David Davis, July 29, 1867, folder A-109, box 7, DDFP. In late 1867, as Davis was finalizing the settlement of the Lincoln estate, Robert wrote to him, "If I can be of any service to you at Bloomington or Springfield in settling up our affairs, please let me know and I will go down at any time." In November 1868, Robert made out for Davis the final administrator's report for the estate and also a full guardian's report regarding Tad. He did this "[i]n order to save you as much trouble as possible," he told Davis. Lincoln to Davis, September 2, 1867, and November 11 and 16, 1868, ibid.

51. Mary Lincoln to Elizabeth Emerson Atwater, Racine, Wisconsin, June 30, 1867, in Turner and Turner, *Mary Todd Lincoln*, 425; RTL to F. Lauristan Bullard, Hildene, October 15, 1915, Lincoln Collection, Howard Gotlieb Archival Research Center.

52. Keckley, *Behind the Scenes*, 197.

53. Mary Lincoln to Sally Orne, December 12, 1869, in Turner and Turner, *Mary Todd Lincoln*, 534 (emphasis in original).

54. Mary Lincoln to Francis Bicknell Carpenter, Chicago, November 15, 1865, in ibid., 284.

55. Keckley, *Behind the Scenes*, 215–16.

56. RTL to Mrs. Corall Davis, September 10, 1866, folder 1, RTL Papers, CHM.

57. John Hay, "Tad Lincoln," *Chicago Tribune*, July 19, 1871, 1; "Thomas Lincoln," *Frank Leslie's Illustrated Newspaper*, August 12, 1871, 359; RTL to Noah Brooks, Washington, April 5, 1882, folder 1, RTL Papers, CHM; Brooks, "Boy in the White House," 65.

58. RTL to David Davis, Chicago, January 17, 1868, folder A-109, box 7, DDFP.

59. For an impressive medical consideration of Tad's speech, teeth, voice, and palate, see Sotos, *Physical Lincoln Sourcebook*, 356–57, 365–67, 368. See also Hutchinson, "What Was Tad Lincoln's Speech Problem?" 35–51.

60. RTL to David Davis, Chicago, January 17, 1868, folder A-109, box 7, DDFP.

61. Ibid., February 21, 1866.

62. Mary Lincoln to David Davis, Chicago, June 17 and November 9, 1867, in Turner and Turner, *Mary Todd Lincoln*, 423, 451; RTL to David Davis, Chicago, June 25, 1866, and July 29 and August 1, 1867, folder A-109, box 7, DDFP. Robert drew up the guardianship paperwork.

63. For the definitive examination of this period, see Foner, *Reconstruction*.

64. For a well-done account, see M. L. Benedict, *Impeachment and Trial of Andrew Johnson*.

65. Goodspeed and Healy, *History of Cook County, Illinois*, 2:388–90.

66. RTL to David Davis, Chicago, February 3, February 21, and September 4, 1866, folder A-109, box 7, DDFP.

67. Ibid., September 4, 1867.

68. John Hay to RTL, Paris, France, July 17, 1866, 158–59, reel 1, Hay Papers, Brown University.

69. "Personal and Political," *Hartford (CT) Daily Courant*, September 22, 1868, 2.

70. Norman Williams to Charles W. Willard, Chicago, August 17, 1868, doc. 29, #5063, Willard Papers.

71. "Political Items," *Milwaukee (WI) Daily Sentinel*, September 14, 1868, 1.

72. RTL to A. Reece, September 17, 1867, LB, 1:1:47–48.

9. "I Am Likely to Have a Good Deal of Trouble"

1. RTL to David Davis, December 22, 1865, folder A-109, box 7, DDFP.

2. King, *Lincoln's Manager*, 235–36.

3. Turner and Turner, *Mary Todd Lincoln*, 247. Jean H. Baker, Mary's most cited biographer, offers the figure of $10,000 debt, although she has no evidence to support it. *Mary Todd Lincoln*, 258. Elizabeth Keckly states a $70,000 debt. Keckley, *Behind the Scenes*, 204. See also W. L. King, *Lincoln's Manager*, 235–37. Supposedly, just one of Mary's debts was $27,000 owed to A. T. Stewart's fabulous Marble Dry Goods Palace in New York City. Hendrickson, *Grand Emporiums*, 36.

4. Mary Lincoln to James H. Orne, Marienbad, Bohemia, May 28, 1870, in Turner and Turner, *Mary Todd Lincoln*, 562; RTL to Lyman Trumbull, Chicago, April 7, 1870, Trumbull Family Papers; Burlingame, "Mary Todd Lincoln's Unethical Conduct as First Lady," in Burlingame, *At Lincoln's Side*, 185–203.

5. Mary Lincoln to Alexander Williamson, May 11, 1866, to Simon Cameron, May 19, 1866, and to David Davis, April 6 and June 30, 1867, in Turner and Turner, *Mary Todd Lincoln*, 364, 366, 424.

6. "Mrs. Lincoln's Wardrobe," *Chicago Tribune*, October 8, 1867, 2; "Articles of Dress and Jewelry, the Property of Mrs. Lincoln, on Exhibition and Offered for Sale," *Frank Leslie's Illustrated Newspaper*, October 26, 1867, 88; Keckley, *Behind the Scenes*, 267–331.

7. Mary Lincoln to Elizabeth Keckley, October 6, 8, and 9, 1867, in Turner and Turner, *Mary Todd Lincoln*, 440–44.

8. Untitled article, *Lowell (MA) Daily Citizen and News*, October 24, 1867, 1.

9. "Mrs. Lincoln," *(Springfield) Illinois Daily State Journal*, October 10, 1867, 1. See also "Mrs. Lincoln: A Woman's Appeal," *Chicago Tribune*, October 9, 1867, 2; editorial, *Chicago Tribune*, May 20, 1875, 4; editorial, *Chicago Inter Ocean*, May 20, 1875, 4.

10. Davis to Miss Addie Burr, July 19, 1882, Green Papers.

11. Robert T. Lincoln to Mary Harlan, October 16, 1867, quoted in K. Helm, *True Story of Mary*, 267–77. This letter no longer exists and can be found only in Helm's book. It is known to be reliable, however, because Robert and Mary Harlan Lincoln assisted Helm as she wrote.

12. Pratt, *Personal Finances*, 141; "Settlement of the Lincoln Estate," *Chicago Tribune*, November 16, 1867, 1.

13. Mary Lincoln to Elizabeth Keckly, November 9, 1867, in Turner and Turner, *Mary Todd Lincoln*, 449.

14. Mary Lincoln to David Davis, Chicago, November 18, 1867, and Mary Lincoln to Elizabeth Keckly, November 21, 1867, in Turner and Turner, *Mary Todd Lincoln*, 458–59; RTL to David Davis, Chicago, November 18 and December 6, 1867, folder A-109, box 7, DDFP.

15. Mary Lincoln to Elizabeth Keckly, January 12, 1868, in Turner and Turner, *Mary Todd Lincoln*, 468.

16. Mary Lincoln to Elizabeth Keckly, October 13, 1867, in ibid., 443.

17. RTL to Mary Lincoln, December 18, 1867, LB, 1:1:50–51. Mary apparently borrowed money from Robert often, so much so that she had to make herself a pledge to stop. Mary Lincoln to David Davis, Chicago, December 1866, in Turner and Turner, *Mary Todd Lincoln*, 402.

18. RTL to Mary Lincoln, January 4, 1868, LB, 1:1:52–53.

19. RTL to Mary Lincoln, December 18, 1867, and January 4, 1868, and RTL to Dennis Wall, January 13, 1868, LB, 1:1:50–53, 55.

20. Mary did, however, immediately move out of Cole's house and return to her former lodgings at the Clifton House. See Mary Lincoln to Elizabeth Keckly, Clifton House, January 12, 1868, in Turner and Turner, *Mary Todd Lincoln*, 468.

21. RTL to Clinton Conkling, December 17, 1917, RTL Papers, ALPL.

22. RTL to David Davis, Chicago, August 8 and December 22, 1865, folder A-109, box 7, DDFP; Power, *Abraham Lincoln*, 229.

23. RTL to David Davis, Chicago, February 11, 1866, folder A-109, box 7, DDFP; RTL to William Herndon, May 24, 1867, reel 8, group 4, H-W; RTL to Herndon, July 29, 1867, LB, 1:1:45; RTL to Frederic Geiger, January 16, 1919, RTL Papers, ALPL.

24. Herndon's handwritten lectures are now in the Huntington Library in California. For a complete publication of the lectures, see *Abraham Lincoln Quarterly* 1, no. 7 (September 1941): 343–83, and 1, no. 8 (December 1941): 403–41. An abstract can be found in Carpenter, *Six Months at the White House*, 323–50.

25. William Herndon to Charles H. Hart, Springfield, Illinois, January 8, 1866, in Hertz, *Hidden Lincoln*, 29.

26. RTL to William Herndon, Chicago, January 8, 1866, frames 493–94, reel 8, group 4, H-W.

27. RTL to David Davis, Chicago, January 25, 1866, item 1, Lincoln Estate Papers, Lincoln Collection, ALPL.

28. RTL to David Davis, Chicago, August 21, 1866, folder A-109, box 7, DDFP; Mary Lincoln to William Herndon, Chicago, August 28, 1866, and RTL to William Herndon, Chicago, October 17, 1866, reel 8, group 4, H-W.

29. For a good examination of Herndon's relationship with Mary Lincoln and the foundations of his Ann Rutledge lecture, see "Herndon and Mrs. Lincoln," in Donald, *Lincoln Reconsidered*, 37–56.

30. Herndon honestly believed he was doing Mary Lincoln a favor by revealing the "truth" behind her marriage. "The world does not know her, Mrs. L's, sufferings, her trials, and the cause of things. Sympathize with her. I shall never rob Mrs. Lincoln of her justice—justice due her," he wrote to Isaac Arnold. For Herndon's reasoning behind his lecture, see Herndon to Charles H. Hart, Springfield, Illinois, November 1 and 26, 1866, and to Isaac Arnold, November 20, 1866, in Hertz, *Hidden Lincoln*, 35–41.

31. Mary Lincoln to David Davis, Chicago, March 4 and 6, 1867, in Turner and Turner, *Mary Todd Lincoln*, 414–15.

32. RTL to David Davis, Chicago, November 16, 1866, folder A-109, box 7, DDFP.

33. Ibid., December 8, 1866.

34. "Herndon's Statement—Memoranda," in Hertz, *Hidden Lincoln*, 439.

35. RTL to William Herndon, Chicago, December 13, 1866, LB, 1:1:23 (emphasis in original); also in frame 1292, reel 8, group 4, H-W.

36. RTL to William Herndon, Chicago, December 27, 1866, LB, 1:1:28; William Herndon to Isaac Arnold, Springfield, Illinois, November 20, 1866, in Hertz, *Hidden Lincoln*, 38.

37. William Herndon to Truman H. Bartlett, Springfield, Illinois, November 10, 1888,

in Hertz, *Hidden Lincoln*, 222; William Herndon to Jesse Weik, n.d., [probably 1888], quoted in Donald, *Lincoln's Herndon*, 230. Donald states the letter is in the Herndon-Weik Collection, LOC, but I was unable to locate it.

38. William Herndon to Jesse Weik, Springfield, Illinois, January 5, 1889, William Herndon to Truman H. Bartlett, Springfield, Illinois, November 10, 1888, and William Herndon to Jesse Weik, Springfield, Illinois, March 7, 1890, in Hertz, *Hidden Lincoln*, 222, 238, 249.

39. William Herndon to Truman H. Bartlett, Springfield, Illinois, November 10, 1888, in ibid., 222.

40. "Herndon's Statement—Memoranda," in Hertz, *Hidden Lincoln*, 438. As Herndon wrote in the preface to his Lincoln biography, "Some persons will doubtless object to the narration of certain facts which appear here for the first time, and which they contend should have been consigned to the tomb. Their pretense is that no good can come from such ghastly exposures. To such over-sensitive souls, if any such exist, my answer is that these facts are indispensable to a full knowledge of Mr. Lincoln in all the walks of life." Herndon and Weik, *Herndon's Lincoln*, 4.

41. Jesse W. Weik to Lyon Gardiner Tyler, Greencastle, Indiana, March 20, 1917, reel 2, series 2, Tyler Papers.

42. RTL to William Herndon, Chicago, December 24, 1866, LB, 1:1:26 (emphasis in original); also in frames 1326–27, reel 8, group 4, H-W.

43. RTL to William Herndon, Chicago, January 4, January 11, and July 29, 1867, LB, 1:1:30, 32, 45. Herndon's eventual collaborator, Jesse Weik, later explained the rift: "The difficulty between [Robert] and Herndon grew out of a lecture which Herndon prepared between '66 and '67 in which he gave the public some idea of Lincoln's domestic life and his wife's extraordinary temper, etc., which it would have been better at the time to have left unsaid." Weik to Lyon Gardiner Tyler, Greencastle, Indiana, March 20, 1917, reel 2, series 2, Tyler Papers.

44. Mary Lincoln to David Davis, Chicago, March 4 and 6, 1867, in Turner and Turner, *Mary Todd Lincoln*, 414–16.

45. Mary Lincoln to Rhoda White, Chicago, May 2, 1868, ibid., 475–76. Mary had other reasons for going to Europe as well. Besides her emotional pain at the public criticism, she loved to travel, and she and her husband had planned a European tour at the end of his second term, which she wanted to fulfill. She also believed that Tad would receive a better education in Europe than in Chicago.

46. "The Wedding of Mr. R. T. Lincoln," *(Springfield) Illinois State Journal*, October 3, 1868, 2, in Brigham, *James Harlan*, 237.

47. Mary Lincoln seems to have spoken precipitately when she told her friend Rhoda White about the wedding on August 19, for she wrote back a week later asking her to keep the information to herself. Mary Harlan did not tell—or even invite—her good friend Minnie Chandler to the wedding. It is unclear why, and even Chandler did not understand it in her angry letter of chastisement to Mary, but perhaps Minnie was a gossiper. Whatever the reason, it ended their friendship for the next thirteen years. Mary Lincoln to Rhoda White, Altoona, Illinois, August 19 and 27, 1868, in Turner and Turner, *Mary Todd Lincoln*, 481–82; Minnie Chandler to Mary Harlan, September 1868, Chandler Papers.

48. I have been unable to discover exactly who Miss Caleb was (or her first name), but the position of her names in the various newspapers' lists of guests—after Robert's friends, which were after the parents' friends and other distinguished political guests—logically suggests she was Mary's friend.

49. Welles, *Diary of Gideon Welles*, September 25, 1868, 3:444; Mary Lincoln to Rhoda

White, Altoona, Illinois, August 19 and 27, 1868, in Turner and Turner, *Mary Todd Lincoln*, 481–82.

50. Marriage license of Robert T. Lincoln and Mary E. Harlan, September 24, 1868, T1868.09.24, RTL Papers, Lincoln Collection, ALPL; details of the wedding found in "Washington News and Gossip," *Washington Star*, September 24–26, 1868, 1,1,1; "Marriage of Captain Robert Lincoln," *New York Times*, September 25, 1868, 4; untitled article, *Washington National Intelligencer*, September 25, 1868, 1; "Bob Lincoln," *Chicago Tribune*, September 30 and October 3, 1868, 2, 2; "Bob Lincoln's Marriage," *New Orleans Times*, September 30, 1868, 1; untitled article, *New York Observer and Chronicle*, October 1, 1868, 318; "Personal Items," *Christian Advocate*, 43, no. 40, October 1, 1868, 317; "Bob Lincoln's Marriage," *Chicago Times*, October 2 and 3, 1868, 6, 6; "The Wedding of Mr. R. T. Lincoln," *(Springfield) Illinois State Journal*, October 3, 1868, 2.

51. Untitled article, *Washington Star*, October 3, 1868, 1.

52. The house cost Robert $18,500, which amounts to roughly $240,000 in today's money. RTL to Mark Skinner, Chicago, May 11, 1877, LB, 3:5:542.

53. Mary Lincoln to Eliza Slataper, Baltimore, September 25, 1868, in Turner and Turner, *Mary Todd Lincoln*, 484. Mary wrote that Mrs. Scammon was taken sick on her way to the wedding but sent her gifts ahead. No mention is made about Mr. Scammon.

54. Abraham Lincoln received 40 acres of land in Tama County, Iowa, and 120 acres of land in Crawford County, Iowa, through government grants for his military service in the Black Hawk War; he was deeded lots in Lincoln, Illinois, and Council Bluffs, Iowa, as payment for debts. Upon his death, ownership was transferred to his wife and children. Mary Lincoln seemed to have had no interest, and took no part, in administration of this land and eventually gave it to Robert and Tad to share. Pratt, *Personal Finances*, 54, 58–70, 78–79; Petersen, "Lincoln and Iowa," 87–89; Hickey, "Abraham Lincoln's Lot in Lincoln, Illinois," in Hickey, *Collected Writings of James T. Hickey*, 1–4 (reprint from Spring 1953 *Journal of the Illinois State Historical Society*); Temple, "Thomas and Abraham Lincoln as Farmers," 33–36; "To Sell 150 Acres Owned by Lincoln," and "Bluffs Lots Part of Lincoln Estate," *Council Bluffs (IA) Nonpareil*, April 29, 1927, and February 12, 1933, clippings, Council Bluffs Iowa Public Library; Robert Lincoln, "Account of Real Estate Owned by Robert T. Lincoln and Thomas Lincoln in Common," 1868–69, LB, 1:1:78. For other letters by Robert concerning the Iowa and Illinois lands, see LB, 1:1:14, and 3:4:28–29, 45, 62, 242, 247, 278, 314, 317, and 3:5:494, 513, 529–30, 540–41, 617, 630–31, 653, 729, 992; RTL to Frank Fisk, London, May 8, 1889, RTL MS, Lincoln Collection, John Milton Hay Library, Brown University.

55. RTL to James C. Conkling, June 18, 1869, LB, 2:3:436. Some of Robert's personal account figures for 1869–70 can be found in LB, 1:1:76–81.

56. Eleven letters from RTL to Gideon Welles concern Mrs. Grand's loan spanning 1870–77, folder 8, box 3, Welles Papers, Connecticut Historical Society; see also RTL to Gideon Welles, December 7, 1869 and May 16, 1870, LB, 2:3:561, 656; RTL to Edgar Welles, Chicago, November 20, 1869, RTL Papers, ACPL.

57. Walling and Rupp, *Diary of Bishop Frederic Baraga*, 63n114.

58. Robert and Carrey were acquaintances, if not friends, moving in the same social circles and both being founding members of the Chicago Club in 1869. E. T. Blair, *History of the Chicago Club*, 80.

59. Royce actually had laid out the original survey boundaries of Escanaba in 1864 and during his life held the offices of postmaster, judge of probate, member of the council, mayor, and city engineer. Sawyer, *History of the Northern Peninsula of Michigan and Its People*, 3:1394–95.

60. The full story of the Duroc matter is related by Robert Lincoln in a letter to W. H. Wellsteed, vice president, Delta County Historical Society, Manchester, Vermont, October 21, 1916, RTL Papers, ALPL. See also W. H. Wellsteed to RTL, Escanaba, Michigan, October 7 and 16, 1916, and RTL to E. P. Royce, Chicago, June 27, 1870, ibid.; RTL to Charles Lapalu, May 31, 1869, LB, 2:3:417–18.

61. W. H. Wellsteed to RTL, Escanaba, Michigan, October 16, 1916, RTL Papers, ALPL.

62. RTL to W. H. Wellsteed, vice president, Delta County Historical Society, Manchester, Vermont, October 21, 1916, RTL Papers, ALPL.

63. Mary Lincoln to Rhoda White, Altoona, Illinois, August 27, 1868, in Turner and Turner, *Mary Todd Lincoln*, 482. Mary Harlan Lincoln thereafter began all her letters to her mother-in-law with "Dear Mother." Mary Lincoln to Eliza Slataper, Germany, December 13, 1868, ibid., 495.

64. Mary Lincoln to Eliza Slataper, Germany, December 13, 1868, and Mary Lincoln to Rhoda White, Cronberg, Germany, August 30, 1869, in Turner and Turner, *Mary Todd Lincoln*, 495, 517.

65. Mary Lincoln to Mary Harlan Lincoln, Frankfurt, Germany, March 22, 1869, in Turner and Turner, *Mary Todd Lincoln*, 504–6.

66. Mary Lincoln to Sally Orne, Frankfurt, Germany, October 23, 1869, in ibid., 520.

67. Mary Todd Lincoln in fact speculated on what the baby's name would be, hoping it would be Mary but thinking it would be "rather too much" to have grandmother, mother, and child all sharing a name. She was wrong. Mary Lincoln to Sally Orne, Frankfurt, Germany, November 7, 1869, ibid., 522; K. Helm, *True Story of Mary*, 275.

68. RTL to David Davis, Chicago, November 4, 1869, folder A-109, box 7, DDFP. Fuller must have traveled to Washington shortly after the birth.

69. RTL to Edgar Welles, Chicago, November 10, 1869, RTL Collection, ACPL.

70. K. Helm, *True Story of Mary*, 277. For Helm's portrayal of the family relationship and transcripts of the correspondence, see 277–91. See also Mary Todd Lincoln to Mary Harlan Lincoln, March 22 and August 20, 1869, May 19, September 10, November [n.d.] 1870, January 26 and February 12, 1871, Mary Todd Lincoln to Rhoda White, August 30 and December 20, 1869, Mary Todd Lincoln to Sally Orne, September 10, October 23, November 7, 1869, and Mary Todd Lincoln to Eliza Stuart Steele, May 23, 1871, all in Turner and Turner, *Mary Todd Lincoln*, 504–6, 511, 515–16, 517–22, 536, 559, 577–78, 580–84, 588. Transcripts of Mary Todd Lincoln letters to Mary Harlan Lincoln also in Neely and McMurtry, *Insanity File*, 147–82.

10. "I Am in Better Shape Than Most"

1. RTL to Noah Brooks, Washington, April 5, 1882, folder 1, RTL Papers, CHM. See also Brooks, "Boy in the White House," 57–65.

2. "News of the Week," *Independent* (New York), 23, no 1173, May 25, 1871, 5.

3. Edwin L. Stanton to John Hay, May 22, 1871, reel 11, Hay Papers, Brown University; Mary Lincoln to Eliza Stuart Steele, Chicago, May 23, 1871, and Mary Lincoln to Rhoda White, Chicago, May 23, 1871, in Turner and Turner, *Mary Todd Lincoln*, 588–89. "I am very solicitous to have Mary with her Mother as much as possible while I am compelled to be absent: it is almost a necessity that this should be so," James Harlan wrote to Robert. "I would not remain away from Mrs. Harlan unless assured that she is both well taken care of and satisfied. When Mary is with her I know everything will be all right." James Harlan to RTL, Mount Pleasant, Iowa, July 3, 1871, reproduced in K. Helm, *True Story of Mary*, 291–92.

4. Mary Lincoln to Eliza Stuart Steele, Chicago, May 23, 1871, in Turner and Turner, *Mary Todd Lincoln*, 588.

5. RTL to F. Lauristan Bullard, Vermont, November 25, 1914, Lincoln Collection, Howard Gotlieb Archival Research Center. Newspapers reported that Tad "got up in the night, wandered around lightly clad, on returning to his room swooned, and grew steadily worse from that moment." The owner of the Clifton House, where Tad died, later recalled that Tad "contracted a severe cold on the ocean trip home, that I have always thought had its effect on the fatal termination of his sickness." W. A. Jenkins to J. R. Van Cleave, Chicago, January 23, 1909, folder J–K, box 1, Lincoln Centennial Association Papers; "Obituary: Death of Thomas Lincoln," *Chicago Tribune*, July 16, 1871, 3; "Thomas Lincoln," *Frank Leslie's Illustrated Newspaper* 828, August 12, 1871, 359.

6. RTL to Heinrich Best, July 24, 1871, LB, 3:4:11; RTL to Noah Brooks, Washington, April 5, 1882, folder 1, RTL Papers, CHM.

7. RTL to Noah Brooks, Washington, April 5, 1882, folder 1, RTL Papers, CHM.

8. RTL to Henry Draper & Co., July 10, 1871, LB, 3:4:3; unknown writer, on behalf of RTL, to A. L. Fish, August 13, 1871, LB, 3:4:14.

9. RTL to Mary Harlan Lincoln, n.d., reproduced in K. Helm *True Story of Mary*, 294–95; "Obituary: Death of Thomas Lincoln, Youngest Son of the Late President," *Chicago Tribune*, July 16, 1871, 3; "Death of Tad Lincoln," *New York Times*, July 16, 1871, 1; John Hay, "Tad Lincoln," *Chicago Tribune*, July 19, 1871, 1. Dr. Milton H. Shutes more specifically explains Tad's death: "With serious effusion compressing the lungs and crowding the nearby heart, there was not enough oxygen to maintain the life centers of the brain." Dr. W. A. Evans reasoned in 1932 that Tad's fatal pleurisy could have been tubercular in origin. Shutes, "Mortality of the Five Lincoln Boys," 7; Evans, *Mrs. Abraham Lincoln*, 340. For an excellent and exhaustive medical survey of Tad's final illness and death, see Sotos, *Physical Lincoln Sourcebook*, 344–49.

10. RTL to Mary Harlan Lincoln, n.d., reproduced in K. Helm, *True Story of Mary*, 294–95; "The Late Thomas Lincoln," *Chicago Tribune*, July 17, 1871, 4; W. A. Jenkins to J. R. B. Van Cleave, Chicago, January 23, 1909, box 1, Lincoln Centennial Association Papers.

11. W. A. Wilson to J. R. B. Van Cleave, Springfield, Illinois, February 3, 1908, Lincoln Centennial Association Papers.

12. "Funeral of Tad Lincoln," *Chicago Tribune*, July 17, 1871, 1; "Illinois," *Chicago Tribune*, July 18, 1871, 1; RTL to Mary Harlan Lincoln, n.d., in K. Helm *True Story of Mary*, 294–95.

13. "Death of Tad Lincoln," *New York Times*, July 16, 1871, 1; "Obituary: Death of Thomas Lincoln," *Chicago Tribune*, July 16, 1871, 3.

14. RTL to David Davis, Chicago, July 18, 1871, folder A-109, box 7, DDFP; RTL to Mary Harlan Lincoln, n.d., in K. Helm, *True Story of Mary*, 294–95.

15. RTL to Mary Harlan Lincoln, n.d., in K. Helm *True Story of Mary*, 294.

16. RTL to Noah Brooks, Washington, April 5, 1882, folder 1, RTL Papers, CHM.

17. Mary Lincoln to Eliza Slataper, July 27, 1871, and August 13, 1871, in Turner and Turner, *Mary Todd Lincoln*, 591–92. "I was compelled to bar my office for as long a period as possible and I only returned in time to commence regular fall work," Robert wrote to Hackett. RTL to James H. Hackett, Chicago, September 28, 1871, RTLFP.

18. Mary Lincoln to Eliza Slataper, July 27 and August 13, 1871, in Turner and Turner, *Mary Todd Lincoln*, 591.

19. RTL to David Davis, Chicago, August 24, 1871, folder 101, box 16, Davis Papers, CHM.

20. "Removal of the Remains of President Lincoln," *Hartford (CT) Daily Courant*, September 20, 1871, 3; "Lincoln," *Chicago Tribune*, September 22, 1871, 2; "The Martyred President," *New York Times*, September 23, 1871, 5.

21. Tad's estate consisted of $1,315.16 in cash and $35,750 in bonds. RTL to David Davis, Chicago, September 2, 1871, and receipt for $1,323.81 received from Davis, dated September 20, 1871, folder 101, box 16, Davis Papers, CHM; RTL to David Davis, September 21 and November 9, 1871, folder A-109, box 7, DDFP; Mary Lincoln to David Davis, November 9, 1871, in Turner and Turner, *Mary Todd Lincoln*, 597; Pratt, *Personal Finances*, 184.

22. Cromie, *Great Chicago Fire*; Sawislak, *Smoldering City*; Bales, *Great Chicago Fire and the Myth of Mrs. O'Leary's Cow*.

23. Untitled, undated article, *Boston Transcript*, clipping, John Goff Papers; "Incidents," *Chicago Tribune*, January 5, 1879, 3.

24. J. H. [John Hay], "Burned Chicago," *New York Tribune*, October 14, 1871, 1. See also E. J. Goodspeed, *History of the Great Fires in Chicago and the West*, 378–79; Colbert and Chamberlin, *Chicago and the Great Conflagration*, 354.

25. RTL to A. G. Randall, Chicago, December 1871, LB, 3:4:54; RTL to P. S. Wynkoop, February 29, 1876, LB, 3:4:396.

26. Robert also lost in the fire a number of letters written to him by his friend John Hay. RTL to unknown recipient, Chicago, December 11, 1871, Robert T. Lincoln Autograph File; RTL to O. S. Mahon, February 19, 1903, LB, 36:61:333; RTL to William Roscoe Thayer, Manchester, Vermont, August 6, 1914, bMS Am 1081 (1060), William Roscoe Thayer Papers.

27. RTL to David Davis, Chicago, October 30, 1871, folder A-109, box 7, DDFP. Robert did lose his home mortgage records, which were in J. Y. Scammon's safe. RTL to Isaac H. Burch, May 18, 1877, LB, 3:5:545.

28. RTL to David Davis, Chicago, October 30, 1871, folder A-109, box 7, DDFP.

29. "Personal," 787.

30. Palmer, *Bench and Bar of Illinois*, 1:389–93; *Report of the Twenty-Sixth Annual Meeting of the American Bar Association*, 712–13.

31. Isham and Lincoln both were founding members of the Chicago Club in 1869. E. T. Blair, *History of the Chicago Club*, 80.

32. Interview with Edward S. Isham, "Gath's Gossip," *Boston Daily Globe*, December 2, 1883, 16.

33. RTL to Mark Skinner, April 10, 1875, 2:201, Isham, Lincoln, & Beale Letterpress Books, Records, Isham, Lincoln, and Beale Law Firm.

34. RTL to Elizabeth Edwards, August 7, 1875, LB, 1:1:133–139; "Clouded Reason: Trial of Mrs. Abraham Lincoln for Insanity," *Chicago Tribune*, May 20, 1875, 1; "Mrs. Lincoln: The Widow of the Martyr President Adjudged Insane in County Court," *Chicago Inter Ocean*, May 20, 1875, 1; "A Mind Diseased: The Evidence of Mrs. Lincoln's Mental Aberration," *Chicago Journal*, reprinted in *(Springfield) Illinois State Journal*, May 22, 1875, 2.

35. Mary Lincoln to James H. Knowlton, Waukesha, Wisconsin, August 3, 1872, Mary Lincoln to Norman Williams, Waukesha, Wisconsin, August 8, 1872, and Mary Lincoln to John Todd Stuart, Chicago, December 15, 1873, in Turner and Turner, *Mary Todd Lincoln*, 598, 599, 603; Wendt, "Mary Todd Lincoln," 14–19; Krueger, "Mary Todd Lincoln Summers in Wisconsin," 249–52.

36. Mrs. Ellen Fitzgerald was the mother of the famous vaudeville actor Eddie Foy. See Foy and Harlow, "Clowning through Life," 30.

37. Robert's passport application from May 28, 1872, describes him as 5 feet, 9½ inches tall with gray eyes and brown hair; he had a "medium" complexion, an "ordinary" nose,

and a "dimpled" chin. R. B. Shipley, director, U.S. Department of State Passport Office, to David C. Mearns, May 27, 1954, box 85, Mearns Papers.

38. "English Notes," *Albany Law Journal*, July 20, 1872, reprinted in Thompson, *Albany Law Journal*, 6:51; RTL to Antonio Barabe, Chicago, December 4, 1872, and RTL to A. L. Fish, Chicago, December 10, 1872, LB, 3:4:73, 76.

39. Notes on Mary Harlan Lincoln visits to Mount Pleasant, Harlan-Lincoln House Collection.

40. This explanation was given by both Robert's law partners, Edward Isham and William Beale, and by Jack's teacher C. N. Fessenden. The more romantic, popular, and apocryphal story of Jack's nickname is that Robert told his son the name "Abraham Lincoln" was too reverential a name to be bestowed until the boy had earned the right to wear it, which his father would decide at age twenty-one. "'Jack's' Bright Career," *Chicago Tribune*, February 27, 1890, 1; "'Jack' Lincoln Is Dead," *Chicago Tribune*, March 6, 1890, 5; "'Jack' Lincoln Dead," *Boston Globe*, March 6, 1890, 8; "Interesting Story Brought to Light," *Springfield Republican*, n.d., Lincoln Collection, ACPL.

41. RTL to David Davis, Chicago, August 13, 1867, folder A-109, box 7, DDFP.

42. RTL to James H. Hackett, Chicago, September 28, 1871, RTLFP.

43. RTL to William Herndon, Chicago, December 24, 1866, LB, 1:1:26; also in frames 1326–27, reel 8, group 4, H-W.

44. RTL to David Davis, November 26 and December 8, 1869, folder A-109, box 7, DDFP; RTL to Ward Hill Lamon, Chicago, December 30, 1869, LN 1159, RTL Letters, LN 1159, Huntington Library.

45. For the story of Lamon's biography and his purchase of the Herndon materials, see Thomas, *Portrait for Posterity*, 26–90; Donald, *Lincoln's Herndon*, 250–55.

46. "President Lincoln," *Chicago Tribune*, December 14, 1873, 2.

47. Mary Lincoln to John Todd Stuart, Chicago, December 15 and 16, 1873, and January 20 and 21, 1874, in Turner and Turner, *Mary Todd Lincoln*, 603–6; RTL to John Nicolay, December 16, 1873, LB, 1:1:111; RTL to Isaac Markens, April 16, 1908, RTLFP.

48. RTL to Isaac Markens, April 16, 1908, RTLFP. Nearly every one of Robert's letters after 1873 concerning Herndon makes this same argument. Herndon claimed President Lincoln did, in fact, offer him a federal job, but he refused it. This is true, but it was a nominal job, of only one month's duration and paying only five dollars a day. Herndon and Weik, *Herndon's Life of Lincoln*, 299n.

49. RTL to David Davis, Washington, November 28, 1872, folder A-109, box 7, DDFP.

50. RTL to John Nicolay, December 16, 1873, box 4, Nicolay Papers; also in LB, 1:1:111–12.

51. Ibid., December 18, 1873, and January 10, 1874.

52. Undated clipping enclosed in RTL to John Nicolay, January 10, 1874, box 4, Nicolay Papers.

53. "Springfield: A Correction—Mrs. Lincoln on Herndon's Lecture," *Chicago Tribune*, December 19, 1873, 4. Mary met Herndon at the St. Nicolas Hotel in Springfield in September 1866. For Herndon's interview notes, see Wilson and Davis, *Herndon's Informants*, 357–61.

54. W. H. Herndon, "Lincoln's Religion: Answer of William H. Herndon, Esq., to Mrs. Lincoln," Springfield, Illinois, January 12, 1874, published in *(Springfield) Illinois State Register*, January 14, 1874, TS in frames 1726–36, reel 9, group 4, H-W; W. H. Herndon, "Mr. Lincoln," *Chicago Tribune*, January 16, 1874, 2.

55. Chauncey Black to William Herndon, York, Christmas morning, 1873, and January 18, 1874, and William Jayne to William Herndon, Springfield, Illinois, January 19, 1874, frames 1657, 1677, 1681–83, reel 9, group 4, H-W.

56. Her hallucinations included persecution by an Indian spirit and conversations with imagined voices coming from the walls and floors. Dr. Willis Danforth, insanity-trial testimony, published in "Clouded Reason," *Chicago Tribune*, May 20, 1875, 1; "Mrs. Lincoln," *Chicago Inter Ocean*, May 20, 1875, 1; "A Sad Revelation: Mrs. Mary Lincoln, the Widow of the Late President, Adjudged Insane," *Chicago Times*, May 20, 1875, 2; "A Mind Diseased," *(Springfield) Illinois State Journal*, May 22, 1875, 2; "Mrs. Lincoln Insane," *Chicago Post and Mail*, reprinted in *(Springfield) Illinois State Journal*, May 21, 1875, 2; "Current Events," *New York Evangelist*, May 27, 1875, 8.

57. Foy, "Clowning through Life," 30.

58. Arnold, *Life of Abraham Lincoln*, 439.

59. Mary Lincoln to Edward Isham, Jacksonville, Florida, March 12, 1875, and March 12, 1875, folder 3, box 1, IF; "Clouded Reason," *Chicago Tribune*, May 20, 1875, 1; "Mrs. Lincoln," *Chicago Inter Ocean*, May 20, 1875, 1.

60. J. J. S. Wilson, superintendent, to station manager, Jacksonville, Florida, undated, John Coyne, manager, to J. J. S. Wilson, for RTL, Jacksonville, Florida, March 12, 1875, and John Coyne, manager, to J. S. S. Wilson, superintendent, Jacksonville, Florida, March 13 1875, folder 3, box 1, IF.

61. "A Sad Revelation," *Chicago Times*, May 20, 1875, 2.

62. Exactly how long Robert slept nights in the room next to Mary's is unknown. As the trial testimony shows, it was at least until April 1, but it may have been all the way up to the May 19 trial.

63. "Clouded Reason," *Chicago Tribune*, May 20, 1875, 1; "Mrs. Lincoln," *Chicago Inter Ocean*, May 20, 1875, 1; "A Sad Revelation," *Chicago Times*, May 20, 1875, 2.

64. In the more than ten weeks between her arrival in March and the day of the hearing in mid-May, she bought $600 worth (forty pairs) of lace curtains, three watches costing $450, $700 worth of jewelry, $200 worth of soaps and perfumes, and a whole piece of silk. "Clouded Reason," *Chicago Tribune*, May 20, 1875, 1; "Mrs. Lincoln," *Chicago Inter Ocean*, May 20, 1875, 1; "A Sad Revelation," *Chicago Times*, May 20, 1875, 2; "Insanity's Freaks," *Chicago Times*, May 21, 1875, clipping in folder 31, box 2, IF.

65. RTL to Leonard Swett, May 25, 1884, folder 3, box 2, IF.

66. The newspapers stated only that Robert had "a man" watching her, but Swett identified him as "Pinkerton's man." Leonard Swett to David Davis, Chicago, May 24, 1875, folder A-73, box 5, DDFP; "Clouded Reason," *Chicago Tribune*, May 20, 1875, 1; "Mrs. Lincoln," *Chicago Inter Ocean*, May 20, 1875, 1.

67. Some historians claim Robert's sole rapacious concern at this time was to prevent his mother from frittering away his inheritance. For example, see Baker, *Mary Todd Lincoln*, 323.

68. Robert's letter has not been found, but Brown's response quotes from it. Elizabeth J. Todd Grimsley Brown to RTL, March 16, 1875, folder 10, box 2, IF.

69. RTL to Ninian Edwards, November 15, 1875, folder 2, box 2, IF.

70. Neely and McMurtry, *Insanity File*, 8. I was unable to find the primary source for this statement in the Insanity File, which Neely and McMurtry cite as miscellaneous expense accounts.

71. RTL to Elizabeth Edwards, August 7, 1875, LB, 1:1:133–39.

72. David Davis to RTL, May 23, 1875, folder 15, box 2, IF.

73. RTL to Ninian Edwards, November 15, 1875, folder 2, box 2, IF.

74. David Davis to Leonard Swett, Indianapolis, May 19, 1875, folder 15, box 2, IF; John Todd Stuart to RTL, May 10 and May 21, 1875, and John Todd Stuart to Leonard Swett, May 21, 1875, folder 26, box 2, IF.

75. Leonard Swett to David Davis, Chicago, May 24, 1875, folder A-73, box 5, DDFP.

76. Dr. Willis Danforth, Mary's previous physician, did not attend the meeting but probably shared his experiences either in writing or through Robert Lincoln, and he did testify at Mary's insanity trial in agreement with the conclusion of the other six doctors. David Davis to Leonard Swett, May 19, 1875, folder 15, box 2, IF; Leonard Swett to David Davis, Chicago, May 24, 1875, folder A-73, box 5, DDFP; RTL to Leonard Swett, June 2, 1884, folder 3, box 2, IF.

77. One family friend said Mary "was laboring under the impression that fire menaced her from all directions." Lincoln Dubois, "Personal Reminiscences of Lincoln," folder "Miscellaneous," box 74, Randall Family Papers; "Clouded Reason," *Chicago Tribune*, May 20, 1875, 1; "Mrs. Lincoln," *Chicago Inter Ocean*, May 20, 1875, 1; "A Sad Revelation," *Chicago Times*, May 20, 1875, 2; "Mrs. Lincoln Insane," *Chicago Post and Mail*, reprinted in the *(Springfield) Illinois State Journal*, May 21, 1875, 2.

78. RTL to Leonard Swett, June 2, 1884, folder 3, box 2, IF.

79. RTL to Mrs. James H. (Sally) Orne, June 1, 1875, folder 2, RTL Papers, CHM; RTL to John Hay, June 6, 1875, reel 8, Hay Papers, Brown University.

80. Renton, "Comparative Lunacy Law," 266–67. The Illinois statute was one of the most liberal mental-health laws in the entire country in 1875. Previously—and still in other states—a woman could be declared insane for no other reason than a man's accusation. *Laws of the State of Illinois, Passed by the Sixteenth General Assembly*, 98; Ray, "American Legislation on Insanity," 21–56. For a full examination of the Illinois jury trial statute and its effects on Mary Lincoln's commitment, see Emerson, *Madness of Mary Lincoln*, 54–57.

81. Statement of Dr. Ralph N. Isham, May 18, 1875, petition of Robert Lincoln to have Mary Lincoln declared insane, May 19, 1875, and order to arrest Mary Lincoln, May 19, 1875, Documents folder 33, box 2, Cook County Court, IF.

82. "The Case of Mrs. Lincoln," *Chicago Tribune*, May 21, 1875, 4.

83. David Davis to Leonard Swett, Indianapolis, May 19, 1875, folder 15, box 2, IF; Leonard Swett to David Davis, Chicago, May 24, 1875, folder A-73, box 5, DDFP.

84. Leonard Swett to David Davis, Chicago, May 24, 1875, folder A-73, box 5, DDFP.

85. "Mrs. Lincoln," *Chicago Inter Ocean*, May 20, 1875, 1; "Clouded Reason," *Chicago Tribune*, May 20, 1875, 1.

86. Ibid.

87. "A Sad Revelation," *Chicago Times*, May 20, 1875, 2; "Mrs. Lincoln's Insanity," *Chicago Times*, May 23, 1875, 6.

88. "Mrs. Abraham Lincoln," *Atlanta Constitution*, May 22, 1875, 1.

89. RTL to Elizabeth Edwards, August 7, 1875, LB, 1:1:133–39; Leonard Swett to David Davis, Chicago, May 24, 1875, folder A-73, box 5, DDFP.

90. Robert T. Lincoln to LeGrand Van Valkenburgh, May 26, 1913, RTL Papers, ALPL; RTL to Emily Helm, June 15, 1913, folder 8, RTL Papers, CHM. A more detailed examination of Robert Lincoln and his family papers—including stories of possible letter burning—is discussed in later chapters, especially chapter 24.

91. RTL to Elizabeth Edwards, August 7, 1875, LB, 1:1:133–39.

92. RTL to Lyman Trumbull, Chicago, April 7, 1870, unprocessed collection, Trumbull Family Papers.

93. Verdict of Jury Declaring Mary Lincoln Insane, May 19, 1875, Documents folder 33, box 2, Cook County Court. IF. The *Inter Ocean* of Chicago reported the jury deliberating for "ten minutes," while the *Tribune* reported "but a few minutes." The *Times* did not give a time.

94. "Mrs. Lincoln," *Chicago Inter Ocean*, May 20, 1875, 1; "Mrs. Lincoln Insane,"

(Springfield) Illinois State Journal, May 21, 1875. This fact about state hospital placement and Robert's decision to send her to a private one was stated during the trial.

95. Letters of Conservatorship, Estate of Mary Lincoln, June 14, 1875, folder 30, box 2, County Court of Cook County, IF. Photostats of these and all other legal documents on Mary Lincoln's case are also found in "The Insanity of Mary Lincoln," William E. Barton Scrapbook, Lincoln Collection, University of Chicago Library.

96. Inventory of Real and Personal Estate of Mary Lincoln, May 19, 1875, folder 33, box 2, IF.

97. Leonard Swett to David Davis, Chicago, May 24, 1875, folder A-73, box 5, DDFP.

98. Mary Lincoln's suicide attempt is explained in detail in Leonard Swett to David Davis, Chicago, May 24, 1875, folder A-73, box 5, DDFP, and also reported by the Chicago press in "Mrs. Lincoln: Attempt at Suicide," *Chicago Tribune,* May 21, 1875, 8; "Insanity's Freaks," *Chicago Times,* May 21, 1875, clipping in folder 31, box 2, IF; untitled article, *Chicago Inter Ocean,* May 21, 1875, 4; "Crime: Mrs. Lincoln Makes Persistent Effort to Commit Suicide," *(Springfield) Illinois State Journal,* May 21, 1875, 1; "Mrs. Lincoln Attempts Suicide," *Atlanta Constitution,* May 22, 1875, 1. See also Hirschhorn, "Mary Lincoln's Suicide Attempt."

99. Leonard Swett to David Davis, Chicago, May 24, 1875, folder A-73, box 5, DDFP.

100. "President Lincoln's Widow," *New York Tribune,* May 22, 1875, 6; RTL to John Hay, June 6, 1875, reel 8, Hay Papers, Brown University.

101. Leonard Swett to David Davis, Chicago, May 24, 1875, folder A-73, box 5, DDFP; "Insanity's Freaks," *Chicago Times,* May 21, 1875, clipping, folder 31, box 2, IF.

102. RTL to John Hay, June 6, 1875, reel 8, Hay Papers, Brown University.

103. David Davis to RTL, May 23, 1875, folder 15, box 2, IF.

11. "I Have Done My Duty as I Best Know"

1. RTL to Elizabeth Edwards, April 18, 1879, RTL Collection, ACPL. For a complete examination of Mary Lincoln's insanity case and commitment, see Emerson, *Madness of Mary Lincoln.*

2. "Patient Progress Reports," 26, transcribed in Ross, "Mary Todd Lincoln," 26. The Bellevue Place daily records of the doctors and nurses, called the Patient Progress Reports, are privately owned. All entries pertaining to Mary Lincoln are printed in Ross, "Mary Todd Lincoln," 5–34. In all citations of these reports, first listed is the page number of the report and then the page number of Ross's article on which the report appears.

3. Ross, "Mary Todd Lincoln," 10.

4. Descriptions based on Bellevue Place Sanitarium Advertising Brochures, n.d., 2 pages, and 1895, 15 pages, Batavia Historical Society; "Mrs. Lincoln: A Visit to Her by 'the Post and Mail' Correspondent: How She Passes the Time at Dr. Patterson's Retreat," *Chicago Post and Mail,* July 13, 1875, clipping, Pritchard Family Papers.

5. Ibid., all.

6. "Mrs. Lincoln," *Chicago Post and Mail,* July 13, 1875; Ross, "Mary Todd Lincoln," 10. For one nurse's recollections of Mary Lincoln at Bellevue, see Lutz White, "Now and Then: Before the Tardy Bell Rings," *Aurora (IL) Beacon-News,* December 25, 1932, 6.

7. "Mrs. Lincoln," *Chicago Post and Mail,* July 13, 1875; RTL to Mason B. Loomis, n.d., folder 37, box 2, IF.

8. RTL to John Hay, June 6, 1875, reel 8, Hay Papers, Brown University; "Patient Progress Reports," 26, transcribed in Ross, "Mary Todd Lincoln," 26–28. A brief description of her first month can also be found in an article "Mrs. Lincoln," *Chicago Post and Mail,* July 13, 1875.

9. Untitled editorial, *Chicago Tribune*, May 20, 1875, 4; "The Case of Mrs. Lincoln," *Chicago Tribune*, May 21, 1875, 4.

10. Robert kept at least three examples of such correspondence: J. M. Gibson to RTL, May 21, 1875, folder 18, box 2, L. M. McGinnis to RTL, May 22, 1875, folder 21, box 2, and L. M. McGinnis Samuels (?) to RTL, April 25, 1876, folder 25, box 2, IF.

11. RTL to John Hay, June 6, 1875, reel 8, Hay Papers, Brown University.

12. Ibid.

13. Editorial, *New York Tribune*, June 14, 1875, 6. This article is a verbatim reprint of RTL to Mason B. Loomis, n.d., folder 37, box 2, IF. Loomis was a county judge and member of the Chicago City Council. No connection between him and the *Tribune* could be found.

14. RTL to Mrs. James H. (Sally) Orne, June 1, 1875, folder 2, RTL papers, CHM. This letter is also printed in full in K. Helm, *True Story of Mary*, 295–96.

15. Orne to Lincoln, August 8, 1875, folder 2, RTL papers, CHM. This letter is also printed in full in K. Helm, *True Story of Mary*, 297–98.

16. "Insanity's Freaks," *Chicago Times*, May 21, 1875, clipping, folder 31, box 2, IF; "Mrs. Lincoln's Sad Condition," *Boston Globe*, May 25, 1875, 2; "Mrs. Lincoln and Her Friends," *(Springfield) Illinois State Journal*, May 28, 1875, 2.

17. "Mrs. Lincoln," *Chicago Post and Mail*, July 13, 1875.

18. *Myra Bradwell v. State of Illinois*, 83 U.S. 130 (1872); Friedman, *America's First Woman Lawyer*, 18; Gilliam, "Professional Pioneer," 105–13. Both the Illinois Supreme Court and the U.S. Supreme Court upheld the denial.

19. "Mrs. Lincoln," *Chicago Post and Mail*, July 13, 1875; "Patient Progress Reports," 40, transcribed in Ross, "Mary Todd Lincoln," 28; "The Condition of Mrs. Lincoln: She Is Not Improving," *Boston Globe*, July 14, 1875, 5; Myra Helmer Pritchard, "The Dark Days of Abraham Lincoln's Widow, as Revealed by Her Own Letters," unpublished manuscript, 1927, 1:14, part 2, container 8, folder 5, RTLFP.

20. "Patient Progress Reports," 43, transcribed in Ross, "Mary Todd Lincoln," 29. On Mary's attitude toward her sister, see RTL to Elizabeth Edwards, August 7, 1875, LB, 1:1:133.

21. Mary Lincoln to James Bradwell, Batavia, Illinois, July 28, 1875, part 2, cont. 8, folder 1, RTLFP (emphasis in original).

22. "Patient Progress Reports," 47, transcribed in Ross, "Mary Todd Lincoln," 30–31 (emphasis in original).

23. James Bradwell to John Todd Stuart, Chicago, July 30, 1875, and Myra Bradwell to Elizabeth Edwards, Chicago, July 30, 1875, in Pritchard, "Dark Days of Abraham Lincoln's Widow," 3:12–13, part 2, cont. 8, folder 5, RTLFP.

24. Elizabeth Edwards to Myra Bradwell, Springfield, August 3, 1875, part 2, cont. 8, folder 1, RTLFP (emphasis in original). Mary's cousin Elizabeth Grimsley Brown also told Robert she believed Mary insane but objected to the idea of an asylum. Elizabeth J. Todd Grimsley Brown to RTL, May 19, 1875, folder 10, box 2, IF.

25. RTL to Elizabeth Edwards, August 7, 1875, LB, 1:1:133–39.

26. Ibid.

27. Ibid.; K. Helm, *True Story of Mary*, 295–96. Such acquiescence to duty is a theme Robert would refer to numerous times during the year in which he dealt with his mother's commitment. He had previously told his mother's friend Sally Orne, "The responsibility that has been and is now on me is one that I would gladly share if it was possible to do so, but being alone as I am, I can only do my duty as it is given me to see it, trusting that I am guided for the best." RTL to Mrs. James H. (Sally) Orne, June 1, 1875, folder 2, RTL papers, CHM. This letter is also printed in full in K. Helm, *True Story of Mary*, 295–96.

28. Elizabeth Edwards to RTL, Springfield, Illinois, August 11 and 12, 1875, folder 16, box 2, IF (emphasis in original).

29. Mary Lincoln to Myra Bradwell, Batavia, Illinois, August 2, 1875, in Pritchard, "The Dark Days of Abraham Lincoln's Widow," 4:2–4, part 2, cont. 8, folder 5, RTLFP.

30. Mary Lincoln to Myra Bradwell, Friday, August [13,] 1875, part 2, cont. 8, folder 1, RTLFP (emphasis in original).

31. Dr. R. J. Patterson to Myra Bradwell, Batavia, Illinois, August 9, 1875, folder 23, box 2, IF.

32. RTL to Elizabeth Edwards, August 10, 1875, LB, 1:1:141–42 (emphasis in original).

33. "Patient Progress Reports," 55, transcribed in Ross, "Mary Todd Lincoln," 33. Wilkie was described in 1868 as a man of large imagination, who wrote with ease and rapidity, preferred sentiment to dry logic, and hesitated at no subject. "Franc B. Wilkie," 580–81.

34. "Patient Progress Reports," 55, transcribed in Ross, "Mary Todd Lincoln," 33; Dr. R. J. Patterson to Myra Bradwell, Batavia, Illinois, August 9, 1875, folder 23, box 2, IF.

35. RTL to Myra Bradwell, Chicago, August 14, 1875, part 2, cont. 8, folder 1, RTLFP, and folder 1, box 2, IF, and LB, 1:1:143–44.

36. RTL to Mary Lincoln, Chicago, August 15, 1875, folder 1, box 2, IF.

37. Dr. R. J. Patterson to RTL, Batavia, Illinois, August 9, 1875, folder 23, box 2, IF.

38. Elizabeth Edwards to RTL, Springfield, Illinois, August 17, 1875, folder 16, box 2, IF (emphasis in original).

39. Dr. R. J. Patterson to RTL, Batavia, Illinois, August 17, 1875, folder 23, box 2, IF.

40. RTL to Dr. Richard J. Patterson (telegram), Rye Beach, New Hampshire, n.d., folder 37, box 2, IF. Based upon the other evidence in the Insanity File, the logical date for this telegram is August 17—the same day Robert received Dr. Patterson's letter asking if he should release Mary Lincoln, and the day before, Patterson wrote to Judge Bradwell that Bradwell was no longer allowed to visit. Robert did write to his aunt and told her to "do nothing whatever about proposed visit until you receive my letter of today." RTL to Mrs. N. W. Edwards, Rye Beach, New Hampshire, August 23, 1875, telegram, folder 17, box 2, IF.

41. Dr. R. J. Patterson to James Bradwell, Batavia, Illinois, August 18, 1875, folder 23, box 2, IF, and part 2, cont. 8, folder 1, RTLFP.

42. James B. Bradwell to Dr. R. J. Patterson, Chicago, August 19, 1875, in "Mrs. Abraham Lincoln: Correspondence of Dr. Patterson and Judge Bradwell," *Chicago Tribune*, August 31, 1875, 8. The original letter has not been found.

43. "Reason Restored: Mrs. Lincoln Will Soon Return from Her Brief Visit to the Insane Asylum," *Chicago Times*, August 24, 1875, 4.

44. Ibid.

45. RTL to Dr. R. J. Patterson, September 2, 1875, folder 3, box 2, IF, and LB, 3:4:349.

46. Dr. R. J. Patterson to RTL, Batavia, Illinois, September 7, 1875, folder 23, box 2, IF.

47. Andrew McFarland was superintendent of the Jacksonville, Illinois, State Hospital for the Insane; Alexander McDill was superintendent of the Madison, Wisconsin, State Hospital for the Insane. RTL to Dr. Andrew McFarland, September 4, 1875, LB, 1:1:145–46, and photocopy in folder 3, box 2, IF. This letter is annotated at the top, "Letter exactly the same as this written to A. J. McDill, supt. State asylum for the insane, Madison, Wisconsin."

48. Dr. A. J. McDill to RTL, September 6, 1875, folder 19, box 2, IF; RTL to Dr. A. J. McDill, September 9, 1875, folder 3, box 2, IF, and LB, 1:1:149.

49. Dr. Andrew McFarland to RTL, September 8, 1875, folder 20, box 2, IF.

50. RTL to Dr. R. J. Patterson, Chicago, September 9, 1875, LB, 1:1:147–48, and photocopy in folder 3, box 2, IF.

51. Dr. Andrew McFarland to RTL, September 10 and September 11, 1875, folder 20, box 2, IF.

52. RTL to Elizabeth Edwards, August 7, 1875, LB, 1:1:138.

53. Elizabeth Edwards to RTL, Springfield, September 15, 1875 (two separate letters, both with same date), folder 16, box 2, IF.

54. Ibid., separate enclosure labeled "private."

55. Mary's grandfather Levi Owen Todd, brother Levi, niece Mattie Todd, and grandniece Georgie Edwards all died in insane asylums; fourteen members of the Canfield family (cousins) were in various asylums; Mary's brother George suffered depression, and her grandniece Nellie Canfield committed suicide. Evans, *Mrs. Abraham Lincoln*, 44–50; Temple, *Abraham Lincoln*, 421, 384; RTL to Ben [Helm], Chicago, January 11, 1909, RTL Papers, CHM; Elizabeth Edwards to Emily Todd Helm, Springfield, June 22, [no year indicated], Emily Todd Helm Papers.

56. Dr. R. J. Patterson to RTL, Batavia, Illinois, September 21, 1875, folder 23, box 2, IF.

57. Ninian Edwards to RTL, Springfield, November 17 and December 1, 1875, folder 17, box 2, IF; Elizabeth Edwards to RTL, Springfield, November 12 and December 1, 1875, folder 16, box 2, IF.

58. Elizabeth Edwards to RTL, Springfield, November 12, 1875, folder 16, box 2, IF.

59. RTL to David Davis, Chicago, November 16, 1875, folder 2, box 2, IF, and folder A-109, box 7, DDFP.

60. RTL to Ninian Edwards, November 15, 1875, folder 2, box 2, IF.

61. RTL to Ninian Edwards, Chicago, December 21, 1875, folder 2, box 2, IF.

62. RTL to Elizabeth Edwards, May 17, 1876, LB, 1:1:168–69, and folder 3, box 2, IF.

63. RTL to John Todd Stuart, Chicago, November 15, 1875, folder 2, box 2, IF.

64. RTL to David Davis, Chicago, November 16, 1875, folder 2, box 2, IF, and folder A-109, box 7, DDFP.

65. Elizabeth Edwards to RTL, Springfield, November 12, 1875, folder 16, box 2, IF; RTL to David Davis, Chicago, November 16, 1875, folder 2, box 2, IF, and folder A-109, box 7, DDFP.

66. David Davis to RTL, Washington, DC, November 20, 1875, folder 15, box 2, IF.

67. Ninian Edwards to RTL, Springfield, December 18, 1875, folder 17, box 2, IF; RTL to Judge M. R. M. Wallace, December 10 and December 15, 1875, folder 33, box 2, IF.

68. Ninian Edwards to RTL, Springfield, December 22, 1875, folder 17, box 2, IF.

69. Ninian Edwards to RTL, Springfield, December 18, December 22, 1875, and January 15, 1876, folder 17, box 2, IF; Elizabeth Edwards to RTL, Springfield, December 1, 1875, folder 16, box 2, IF.

70. RTL to David Davis, Chicago, November 16, 1875, folder 2, box 2, IF, and folder A-109, box 7, DDFP. In this letter, Robert also alluded to a similar remark he made to his aunt in a previous letter. That letter appears to no longer exist.

71. RTL to Ninian Edwards, Chicago, December 21, 1875, folder 2, box 2, IF.

72. RTL to Elizabeth Edwards, May 17, 1876, LB, 1:1:168–69, and folder 3, box 2, IF.

73. RTL to Ninian Edwards, Chicago, December 21, 1875, folder 2, box 2, IF.

74. Ninian Edwards to RTL, Springfield, December 18 and December 28, 1875, folder 17, box 2, IF.

75. RTL to J. M. Palmer, Chicago, December 23, 1875, folder 2, box 2, IF.

76. Ninian Edwards to RTL, Springfield, January 14, 1876, folder 17, box 2, IF. Where

Mary got the pistol has never been definitely proven, but it seems likely it was Tad's old revolver, which Mary and Abraham had given him in 1863. Bayne, *Tad Lincoln's Father*, 56–57; Randall, *Lincoln's Sons*, 160–61; see also Abraham Lincoln to Mary Lincoln, Washington, June 9, 1863, in Basler et al., *Collected Works*, 6:256.

77. RTL to Ninian Edwards, Chicago, January 17, 1876, LB, 3:4:379–81.

78. These merchants were not legally allowed to incur debts from Mary Lincoln, only from her conservator, Robert, who informed them that he legally could not recognize or pay any such debts. See RTL to "My dear Kimble," November 29, 1875, LB, 3:4:363.

79. Ibid.

80. RTL to Elizabeth Edwards, Chicago, January 17, 1876, folder 1, box 2, IF, and LB, 3:4:382–83.

81. David Davis to RTL, Bloomington, Illinois, May 22, 1876, folder 15, box 2, IF.

82. RTL to Ninian Edwards, May 24, 1876, LB, 1:1:170.

83. RTL waiver, June 15, 1875, folder 33, box 2, IF; RTL to Ninian Edwards, May 24, 1876, LB, 1:1:170; Ninian Edwards to David Davis, June 8, 1876, folder 17, box 2, IF.

84. Mary Lincoln petition to Cook County Court, June 1876, Ninian Edwards's testimony, and Verdict of the jury in the case of Mary Lincoln, June 15, 1876, folder 33, box 2, IF; "A Happy Denouement," *Chicago Times*, June 16, 1876, 3; "Mrs. President Lincoln," *Chicago Tribune*, June 16, 1876, 8. No one knows why Mary was declared "restored to reason"; probably it was because the Illinois laws would not allow the control of property to be returned to some *not* restored to reason.

85. Conservator of Mary Lincoln, Account of Receipts and Disbursements, June 15, 1876, folders 30 and 33, box 2, IF. This increase was due in part to Robert's investment in additional government bonds and in part to the accumulated interest on her total bonds.

86. Mary Lincoln to Myra Bradwell, Springfield, Illinois, June 18, 1876, part 2, cont. 8, folder 2, RTLFP.

87. Mary Lincoln to RTL, June 19, 1876, in Turner and Turner, *Mary Todd Lincoln*, 615–16 (emphasis in original).

88. Ninian Edwards to Leonard Swett, Springfield, Illinois, June 22 and 24, 1876, and Ninian Edwards to RTL, Springfield, Illinois, June 26, 1876, folder 17, box 2, IF; Leonard Swett to Ninian Edwards, June 20, 1876, folder 27, box 2, IF, and July 1, 1876, LB, 1:1:172–79.

89. Leonard Swett to Ninian Edwards, July 1, 1876, LB, 1:1:172–79.

90. Ibid.

91. Ninian Edwards to Leonard Swett, Springfield, June 22, 1876, folder 17, box 2, IF.

92. Elizabeth Edwards to RTL, Springfield, October 29, 1876, folder 16, box 2, IF.

93. Ibid.; Mary Lincoln to Edward Lewis Baker, Pau, France, June 22, 1879, in Turner and Turner, *Mary Todd Lincoln*, 682.

94. RTL to Elizabeth Edwards, April 18, 1879, RTL Collection, ACPL.

95. RTL to Reverend Henry Darling, November 15, 1877, folder 38, box 6, Lincoln Collection, Miscellaneous Manuscripts.

96. RTL to Elizabeth Edwards, April 18, 1879, RTL Collection, ACPL.

97. RTL to Gideon Welles, December 29, 1877, folder 9, box 3, Welles Papers, Connecticut Historical Society.

98. Ibid.

99. RTL to Edgar Welles, Chicago, April 28, 1870, RTL Collection, ACPL.

100. Quit-claim deed between Mary Lincoln and RTL, April 16, 1874, Lincoln Collection, ALPL; reproduction of deed in Temple, *By Square and Compass*, 176. Robert's ownership of his father's house is explored in chapter 18.

101. "Abraham Lincoln," *New York Times*, October 16, 1874, 1.
102. Lutz White, "Now and Then: Before the Tardy Bell Rings," *Aurora (IL) Beacon-News*, February 13, 1927, 6.
103. RTL to Schuyler Colfax, December 18, 1874, LB, 3:4:318–19.
104. Harry J. Dunbaugh to John S. Goff, Chicago, June 5, 1958, Goff Papers.
105. "Personal," *Harper's Bazaar* 4, no. 27, July 8, 1871, 419.
106. "Robert T. Lincoln," *Chicago Inter Ocean*, March 8, 1880, 4.
107. Busbey, "Coming Man," 1.
108. Dunlevy, "Robert Todd Lincoln," 322.
109. Dunlevy, "Robert Todd Lincoln," 322; *Arthur W. Windett v. the Connecticut Mutual Life Insurance Co.*; *Arthur W. Windett v. the Connecticut Mutual Life Insurance Co., Mark Skinner, Anson Sperry, and Henry P. Isham*, partial abstract of record, Supreme Court of Illinois, Northern Grand Division, September term 1888, appeal from Appellate Court (Chicago: Barnard & Gunthorp, 1888), in Hildene Archives; "*Windett v. Connecticut*," 1887.1. A letter describing the Windett trial, although extremely difficult to read because of faded ink, can be found in RTL to Colonel J. L. Green, February 3, 1887, LB, 3:5:916. The original Windett case appears to have been from 1879 to 1880, and the appeals took place in 1887.
110. Mary Lincoln to David Davis, Germany, December 15, 1868, in Turner and Turner, *Mary Todd Lincoln*, 497; land patent from the United States to Abraham Lincoln, September 28, 1850, patent record no. 165, Tama County, Iowa, patent book 165:483, and deed of Mary Lincoln to Robert T. Lincoln, April 16, 1874, patent book 43:162, and deed of Robert T. Lincoln to Adam Brecht, February 18, 1875, patent book 44:392, Office of the Tama County Recorder, Toledo, Iowa. I am indebted to T. J. Heronimus for sharing with me this information.
111. "Washington," *Chicago Tribune*, April 18, 1872, 2.
112. RTL to Edgar Welles, Chicago, April 2, 1870, RTL Collection, ACPL.
113. RTL to Joseph Ennis, Chicago, September 17, 1873, RTL Papers, CHM.
114. RTL to W. H. Banks, May 21, 1874, and RTL to Louis Gorstein, November 21, 1874, LB, 3:4:285–86, 313.
115. RTL to J. W. Edgerly, May 13, 1874, LB, 3:4:281.
116. RTL to H. Simonton, December 5, 1876, RTL to A. J. Areneck, June 22, 1877, RTL to James Harlan, June 22, 1877, RTL to Thomas G. Robinson, September 15, 1878, and RTL to Henry Lee, November 1, 1878, LB, 3:5:462, 563–64, 632, 641.
117. "Jubilee Notes," *Chicago Tribune*, May 11, 1873, 16.
118. E. T. Blair, *History of the Chicago Club*, 52, 80; Andrews, *Battle for Chicago*, 57, 81.
119. "Bar Association," *Chicago Tribune*, January 12, 1879, 13; Currey, *Chicago*, 2:319–20; Gookin, *Chicago Literary Club*, 38, 224; Andreas, *History of Chicago*, 3:413, 797; "On Their Way to Boston," *New York Times*, June 13, 1879, 3; Register [of members], 1842–1942, 286–87, MS, Archives, Second Presbyterian Church.
120. "Feet," *Chicago Tribune*, December 14, 1879, 12.
121. RTL to Gideon Welles, Chicago, November 24, 1874, folder 8, box 3, Welles Papers, Connecticut Historical Society.
122. "The Campaign of 1876," *New York Times*, September 27, 1876, 1; Busbey, "Coming Man," 1.
123. "Col. Robert Lincoln's Position," *New York Times*, July 27, 1876, 5; untitled article, *Milwaukee (WI) Sentinel*, July 28, 1876, 1.
124. RTL to John Hay, Chicago, January 14, 1874, reel 8, Hay Papers, Brown University.

12. "I Could Have Stopped This Scheme with Little Trouble"

1. Records of the U.S. Secret Service, Daily Reports of Operative Patrick D. Tyrrell (hereafter labeled "Tyrrell Daily Report"), November 21 and 23, 1875, frames 517–18, 521–22, 527–28, roll 283, U.S. Secret Service; "The Lincoln Tomb Robbers," *Chicago Inter Ocean*, March 15, 1877, 2; "An Expert Coneyman," *St. Louis Globe-Democrat*, December 28, 1885, 1; Tyrrell, "Lincoln Tomb Robbers—Part 2," 581; Power, *History of an Attempt to Steal the Body of Abraham Lincoln*, 14–17.

2. "The State Capital," *Chicago Inter Ocean*, August 11, 1876, 1; "Lincoln's Tomb," *(Springfield) Illinois State Journal*, November 20, 1876, 4; "The Lincoln Tomb Robbers," *Chicago Inter Ocean*, March 15, 1877, 2.

3. F. J. Wilson, "Plotting Ghouls of the Catacombs," 85; "The Vandals," *Chicago Tribune*, November 9, 1875, 5. See also Tyrrell, daily report, Daily Reports of Operatives, October 27, 1876, frame 436, roll 283, Records of the U.S. Secret Service.

4. See Fanebust, *Missing Corpse*.

5. Papers of Harrison H. Dodge, Collection of Mount Vernon Library, quoted in Craughwell, *Stealing Lincoln's Body*, 78–79.

6. Bowen and Neal, *United States Secret Service*, 12–17. See also Glaser, *Counterfeiting in America*; Unger, *Greenback Era*; D. R. Johnson, *Illegal Tender*.

7. Tyrrell, "Boscobel Coniackers," 238.

8. Ibid., 236.

9. "Patrick D. Tyrrell," 892–93; "A Detective's Story," *St. Louis Globe-Democrat*, January 2, 1882, 3. Tyrrell actually wrote about a number of his cases, more than a dozen of which were published posthumously in *Flynn's* detective magazine in 1925 and 1926. The Winnetka murder case he wrote about is "A Chain of Circumstances," *Flynn's* 12, no. 5 (January 23, 1926): 706–14.

10. Tyrrell, "Lincoln Tomb Robbers—Part 1," 349.

11. Tyrrell relates the entire saga of the arrest in his "Lincoln Tomb Robbers—Part 1," 348–57; see also Tyrrell, daily report, Daily Reports of Operatives, October 21, 1875, RG 87, T-915, roll 282, frames 371–75, and U.S. Secret Service, General Register of the U.S. Secret Service, Description and Information of Criminals, RG 87, 10:331–33, National Archives II. See also "Notes from the Capital," *New York Times*, October 23, 1875, 2; "Hunted Down," *St. Louis Globe-Democrat*, October 26, 1875, 1; "The Boss Counterfeiter," *Chicago Times*, in the *Georgia Weekly Telegraph*, November 9, 1875, 1; "Counterfeiters Caught," *New York Times*, January 16, 1876, 10; "Sinuous Sinners," *Chicago Inter Ocean*, January 20, 1876, 1; "By Mail and Telegraph," *New York Times*, February 13, 1876, 7; untitled article, *Boston Daily Advertiser*, February 17, 1876, 1.

12. Tyrrell, "More Queer Than Genuine," 109.

13. Tyrrell, "Lincoln Tomb Robbers—Part 2," 579.

14. U.S. Secret Service, General Register of the U.S. Secret Service, Description and Information of Criminals, RG 87, 5:388, National Archives II.

15. Power, *History of an Attempt to Steal the Body of Abraham Lincoln*, 13.

16. U.S. Secret Service, General Register of the U.S. Secret Service, Description and Information of Criminals, RG 87, 5:387, National Archives II.

17. Ibid., 6:79.

18. "Lincoln's Tomb," *(Springfield) Illinois State Journal*, November 20, 1876, 4; L. Lewis, *Myths after Lincoln*, 273.

19. Tyrrell explained his second informant in a later article: "McClaughrey had frequented the place till he had become a recognized member of the informal club at 294

[the Hub], and he was cunning enough to keep in close touch with the operations and plans of his associates, even in matters in which he did not intend to participate actively himself. It does not matter how I first enlisted the good offices of McClaughrey; suffice it to say that he had given me valuable information on more than one occasion. He knew every step made by the criminals in the Lincoln tomb robbing plot, although he was not active in the affair, and in my dealings with him he had always told me the exact truth, as demonstrated by subsequent events." Tyrrell, "At A. T. Stewart's Tomb," 425, 427.

20. Tyrrell, daily reports, October 26 and 30, 1876, roll 283, frames 432–34, 444–45, National Archives II.

21. In the few books published since 1890 that have examined the plot to steal Abraham Lincoln's body, all of them have either overlooked or completely misconstrued Robert's role in the affair. The typical—and incorrect—story line has been that Robert learned of the plot (somehow), asked for help from the Secret Service, and then more or less washed his hands of the affair. The most recent book on the subject, *Stealing Lincoln's Body*, by Thomas J. Craughwell, although otherwise excellent, both miswrites the facts concerning Robert's role and mischaracterizes Robert's entire reaction. Craughwell states that Robert "appears to have been exquisitely detached" when told of the plan and "express[ed] nothing" but a bland assurance to help Tyrrell if he could. "How can a man be indifferent while the desecration of his family tomb was under discussion?" Craughwell shockingly wonders. 98–99. The only other histories of the plot are Power, *History of an Attempt to Steal the Body of Abraham Lincoln* (1890), L. Lewis, *Myths after Lincoln* (1929), and Speer, *Great Abraham Lincoln Hijack* (1997).

22. Leonard Swett, letter to the editor, "Lincoln Monument 'Sensation,'" *Chicago Inter Ocean*, November 23, 1876, 6; RTL to John Hay, June 6, 1875, reel 8, Hay Papers, Brown University.

23. Tyrrell, daily report, October 29, 1876, roll 283, frame 436, National Archives II; RTL to Charles F. Conant, March 13, 1877, and RTL to James J. Brooks, chief of the Secret Service, May 10, 1877, LB, 3:5:501–4; 535–39; Leonard Swett, letter to the editor, "Lincoln Monument 'Sensation,'" *Chicago Inter Ocean*, November 23, 1876, 6; Tyrrell, "Lincoln Tomb Robbers—Part 2," 582–83.

24. Pinkerton performed multiple services for President Lincoln, and Pinkerton detectives had worked for Robert in 1875 following and protecting his mother. F. J. Wilson, "Plotting Ghouls of the Catacombs," 86.

25. For entire events of November 6, see Tyrrell, daily report, November 6, 1876, frames 463–69, roll 283, National Archives II.

26. Ibid., November 7, 1876, frame 479.

27. Tyrrell, "Lincoln Tomb Robbers—Part 2," 584.

28. Ibid.

29. Tomb custodian Power wrote in his book about the affair, "Each party [of officers] came so near being shot, as to feel the wind from the balls fired by the other side as they whistled by their faces." Power, *History of an Attempt*, 61. Tyrrell, daily report, November 7, 1876, frame 479, roll 283, National Archives II. Tyrrell's nine-page report for November 7, 1876, gives full details of the events at the tomb that night.

30. Power, *History of an Attempt*, 60. The most recent retelling can be found in Craughwell, *Stealing Lincoln's Body*, 109.

31. Tyrrell, "Lincoln Tomb Robbers—Part 2," 585.

32. Tyrrell, daily report, November 8 and 17, 1876, frames 483–84, 503–6, roll 283, National Archives II.

33. "Horrible: Dastardly Attempt to Despoil the Lincoln Monument," *Chicago Tribune*,

November 8, 1876, 5; "Sacrilege," *Chicago Inter Ocean*, November 9, 1876, 2; "Atrocious Vandalism," *(Springfield) Illinois State Journal*, November 8, 1876, 1; "A Dastardly Desecration," *St. Louis Globe-Democrat*, November 8, 1876, 5.

34. "The Lincoln Tomb Robbery—Is It a Plant?" *Chicago Inter Ocean*, November 20, 1876, 4; "Was Washburn Guyed?" *Chicago Inter Ocean*, November 22, 1876, 5; "Lincoln Tomb Robbery," *(Springfield) Illinois State Journal*, November 23, 1876, 4; "The Lincoln Monument 'Plant,'" *Chicago Inter Ocean*, November 28, 1876, 8; Tyrrell, daily report, December 3, 1876, frames 563–64, roll 283, National Archives II.

35. Tyrrell, daily report, November 17, 1876, frames 503–6, roll 283, National Archives II; Leonard Swett to John T. Stuart, Chicago, November 28, 1876, folder "1875–1876," box 3, National Lincoln Monument Association Papers.

36. Tyrrell, daily reports, November 21 and 23, 1876, frames 521–22, 528–29, roll 283, National Archives II.

37. U.S Secret Service, General Register of the U.S. Secret Service, Description and Information of Criminals, RG 87, 5:388, National Archives II; "Crime and Criminals," *Chicago Inter Ocean*, May 31, 1877, 3. Straw bail was a common problem at the time. Tyrrell called it "one of the greatest hindrances to effective police work"; that detectives always had two tasks in each case: first to capture his man, second to prevent his immediate release on a worthless bond. Tyrrell, "More Queer Than Genuine," 114; Tyrrell, "Thieves' Syndicate," 846.

38. The only historian to write anything about this aspect of the Lincoln Tomb plot was James T. Hickey, Illinois State Historian, in "Robert Todd Lincoln and His Father's Grave Robbers; or, Left in the Lurch by the Secret Service," originally published in the *Illinois Historical Journal* (Winter 1984) and republished in Hickey, *Collected Writings*, 227–32.

39. Leonard Swett, letter to the editor, "Lincoln Monument Sensation,'" *Chicago Inter Ocean*, November 23, 1876, 6; RTL to David Davis, March 13, 1877, LB, 3:5:497–500.

40. Leonard Swett to William Coolbaugh and Leonard Swett to John Todd Stuart, November 28, 1876, folder "1875–1876," box 3, National Lincoln Monument Association Papers.

41. RTL to Charles H. Reed (two telegrams) and RTL to Charles F. Conant (two telegrams), March 9, 1877, LB, 3:5:492–93.

42. RTL to David Davis, March 13, 1877, LB, 3:5:500.

43. RTL to Charles F. Conant, March 13, 1877, LB, 3:5:501–4.

44. Robert's entire correspondence for this period can be found in LB, 3:5:492–570; see also Tyrrell, daily report, May 3–June 26, 1877, frames 389–602, roll 283, National Archives II.

45. RTL to James J. Brooks, May 10, 1877, LB, 3:5:535–39.

46. RTL to James J. Brooks, May 3 and June 12, 1877, LB, 3:5:527, 556.

47. RTL to James J. Brooks, June 26, 1877, LB, 3:5:568–70; Tyrrell, daily report, June 26, 1877, frames 595–602, roll 283, National Archives II.

48. Tyrrell, daily report, June 21, 1877, frames 585–86, roll 283, National Archives II; RTL to Lyman J. Gage, Secretary of the Treasury, November 17, 1897, LB, 33:54:13. The portrait is still owned by the Tyrrell family. It is engraved with a plaque that reads, "Presented to P. D. Tyrrell, U.S.S.S. by Robert T. Lincoln, April 14, 1887, For Loyalty and Service to His Father Abraham Lincoln." The ten-year discrepancy appears to have been because Tyrrell was not allowed to accept the gift while a member of the Secret Service and so had to wait to receive it until he left the agency.

49. Tyrrell, "At A. T. Stewart's Tomb," 424–33. See also Fanebust, *Missing Corpse*.

50. "Tried to Steal Lincoln's Body," *Milwaukee (WI) Sentinel*, November 5, 1887, 4;

"Tried to Steal Lincoln's Body," *(San Francisco) Daily Evening Bulletin*, November 14, 1887, 3; "Stole Lincoln's Body," *Phoenix (AZ) Weekly Herald*, April 22, 1897, 1.

51. RTL to Governor John R. Tanner, June 12, 1899, LB, 33:55:455. For interesting stories and photographs about the 1901 reburial, see "Strange History Brought to Light: Rare Photos of Lincoln's Exhumation," *Life*, February 15, 1963, 85–88; "Postscript to the Life Magazine Article 'What Happened to Lincoln's Body,'" *Lincoln Lore*, no. 1502 (April 1963): 4, and no. 1503 (May 1963): 3.

52. Robert hired the Pullman burial architect, S. S. Beman of Chicago, to construct the vault for his father's tomb. See correspondence between RTL and Illinois Governor Richard Yates, May 1901–October 1901, Governors' Files.

53. For a detailed list of the viewing of Lincoln's remains from 1865–1901, see "Plot to Steal the Lincoln Corpse"; "Report Unfounded," *(Springfield) Illinois State Journal*, October 1901, and "Opened Casket Despite Protest," September 1901, clippings in folder "Newspaper Clippings," box 4, National Lincoln Monument Association Papers.

54. "Violated an Agreement," *(Springfield) Illinois State Journal*, October 1901, "Bayliss Makes Statement," *Bloomington (IL) Pantagraph*, October 9, 1901, and "Can Never Be Forgiven: Mr. Bayliss Says Casket Opening Was a Ghoulish Act," October 18, 1901, folder "Newspaper Clippings," box 4, National Lincoln Monument Association Papers. Robert's correspondence at this time does not show this latter belief.

13. "I Don't Want to Be Minister to England or Anywhere Else"

1. "A New York Editor Spends an Evening with Old Abe," *Danville (IL) Vermilion County Press*, July 7, 1860, 2.

2. "Political," *Chicago Tribune*, April 4, 1876, 1.

3. "Deliverance: At Last the Hordes of Town Bummers and Tax Thieves Have Been Routed," *Chicago Times*, April 5, 1876, 1.

4. "Political: Result of the Chicago Town Elections Today," *Chicago Tribune*, April 5, 1876, 1; "Deliverance: At Last the Hordes of Town Bummers and Tax Thieves Have Been Routed," *Chicago Times*, April 5, 1876, 1.

5. "Political: Thornton and His Bummers Do Their Work," *Chicago Tribune*, April 8, 1876, 1; "After This, What?" *Chicago Times*, April 8, 1876, 1; "The Rogue's March," *Chicago Times*, April 16, 1876, 2.

6. "Hang 'Em!" *Chicago Times*, April 9, 1876, 6.

7. "We, the People," *Chicago Times*, April 12, 1876, 1.

8. Ibid.

9. "The Rogue's March," *Chicago Times*, April 16, 1876, 2; "Chicago's Citizens Still After the Political Bummers," *Boston Globe*, April 17, 1876, 1.

10. RTL to Leonard Swett, December 27, 1879, LB, 3:5:722–24. Justice of the Peace Calvin De Wolf nominated Robert Lincoln to fill the vacant post of town supervisor immediately after the board accepted Ryan's resignation. "Mr. Lincoln, being asked if he would accept it, said he would if appointed. This answer was received with applause," the *Chicago Times* reported. "Mr. Lincoln was approved by acclamation, and he came forward, was applauded, sworn, and given a seat on the board." "The Rogue's March," *Chicago Times*, April 16, 1876, 2; "Bounced," *Chicago Tribune*, April 16, 1876, 1.

11. Untitled editorial, *Chicago Tribune*, April 17, 1876, 4.

12. RTL to H. Lieb, Cook County Clerk, December 21, 1876, and RTL to Michael Evans, Chicago, January 5, 30, and 31, 1877, LB, 3:5:463, 466–67, 473, 474–76. Robert fixed the necessary bond after consulting with the county clerk.

13. "The Collectorship," *Chicago Tribune*, January 30, 1877, 3; "Exit Mike," *Chicago Tribune*, February 13, 1877, 3.

14. "Mike Evans: An Effort to Dissolve the Injunction," *Chicago Tribune*, February 16, 1877, 3; "Beaten Again: Judge Farwell Sits Down on Mike Evans," *Chicago Tribune*, February 27, 1877, 3. Related articles were in the *Tribune* on February 17, 18, 24, and 25, 1877.

15. "Evans and His Bond," *Chicago Tribune*, February 2, 1877, 4.

16. RTL to C. S. Easton, February 10, 1877, LB, 3:5:479–82.

17. "The Town Boards," *Chicago Tribune*, March 28, 1877, 8; "The Town Elections," *Chicago Tribune*, April 2, 1877, 8; "The South Town," *Chicago Tribune*, April 4, 1877, 1; RTL to Leonard Swett, March 28, 1879, LB, 3:5:681–84. Robert also was paid $116 in expenses and $200 in legal expenses.

18. Untitled editorial, *Chicago Tribune*, April 5, 1877, 4.

19. "The Town Elections," *Chicago Tribune*, April 2, 1877, 8.

20. Untitled editorial, *Chicago Tribune*, March 28, 1877, clipping in scrapbook "newspaper cuttings," RTL Papers, ALPL.

21. "The South Town," *Chicago Tribune*, April 11, 1877, 3.

22. Busbey, "Coming Man," 1.

23. Dunlevy, "Robert Todd Lincoln," 321.

24. The notebook is part of the Lincoln Collection, ALPL.

25. RTL to Leonard Swett, March 28, 1879, LB, 3:5:681–84; RTL to H. M. Jackson, April 11, 1881, LB, 4:6:110.

26. *Laws of the State of Illinois Passed by the Thirtieth General Assembly*, 11–12; "The Douglas Monument," *Chicago Journal*, reprinted in *New York Times*, July 6, 1877, 2; "The City," *Chicago Tribune*, August 10, 1879, 8; RTL to D. N. Bash, May 16, 1879, LB, 3:5:703–5; RTL to Melville Weston Fuller, September 29 and December 17, 1902, RTL to J. S. McCullough, October 4 and 11, and December 18, 1902, LB, 36:60:92–94, 104–5, 194–95, 199; Eisendrath, "Illinois' Oldest Memorial," 127–48. The monument commissioners received no compensation for their work.

27. Temple, *Stephen A. Douglas*, 64–69.

28. RTL to President Rutherford B. Hayes, Chicago, October 10, 1877, LB, 3:5:583, and in Hayes Papers. Hayes wrote on the back of Robert's letter, "From a son worthy of his illustrious father, Abraham Lincoln." See also "Personal," *Harper's Weekly*, December 1, 1877, 939.

29. RTL to William M. Evarts, Secretary of State, Chicago, October 10, 1877, LB, 3:5:585–86.

30. Ibid. (emphasis added).

31. "Personal," *Washington Post*, August 21, 1878, 2; "Personals," *Hartford (CT) Courant*, August 21, 1878, 2; RTL to Charles W. Thomas, Chicago, June 20, 1878, LB, 3:5:618.

32. RTL to John Hay, December 12, 1879, reel 8, Hay Papers, Brown University.

33. Badeau, *Grant in Peace*, 321.

34. "At Potter Palmer's: An Elaborate Affair," *Chicago Tribune*, November 16, 1879, 2.

35. "The Grant Boom," *Chicago Tribune*, April 11, 1880, 2.

36. "Robert T. Lincoln," *Chicago Inter Ocean* and *Chicago Tribune*, April 16, 1880, 1. The law Robert referred to was an attempt in 1879 by the Democrats in Congress to eliminate funding in the 1880 legislative and judicial bills for appropriations for law-enforcement deputies to guard election polling places and ballot boxes during elections. The Republicans vociferously opposed this—and President Hayes vetoed the bill—charging that its purpose was to allow fraud and intimidation on election day to elect a Democrat president

in 1880. "Why the Democrats Dislike the Election Law," *New York Times*, April 19, 1879, 1; *Republican Campaign Text Book for 1880*, 48–55.

37. "Robert T. Lincoln," *St. Louis Globe Democrat*, reprinted in *Chicago Inter Ocean*, April 20, 1880, 1.

38. H. L. Stoddard, *As I Knew Them*, 102.

39. E. Davis, *Proceedings of the Republican National Convention*; Curtis, *Republican Party*, 2:82–83.

40. RTL to George W. Curtiss, August 17, 1880, LB, 3:5:753.

41. RTL to William K. Ackerman, president of the Illinois Central Railroad, Chicago, October 26, 1880, and RTL to Shelby M. Cullom, Governor of Illinois, Chicago, October 26, 1880, LB, 3:5:763–65; "Robert Todd Lincoln," *Harvard College Class of 1864 Secretary's Report*, 95.

42. "Illinois: Getting the Returns," *Chicago Tribune*, November 26, 1880, 2; Andreas, *History of Chicago*, 3:852.

43. RTL to John Hay, November 30, 1880, microfilm reel 8, Hay Papers, Brown University.

44. "Personals," *Hartford (CT) Courant*, August 19, 1880, 2; RTL to Mrs. Gideon [Mary Hale] Welles, Chicago, August 13, 1880, frames 32880–81, microfilm reel 35, Miscellany, Welles Papers, LOC. The *Hartford Courant* stated that Robert was on a car of the Pittsburgh, Fort Wayne, & Chicago Railway. A story in the *New York Times* stated that a railway collision "disaster" occurred at May's Landing, near Camden, New Jersey, involving the West Jersey and Atlantic Railroad in which at least three people died. "The May's Landing Collision," *New York Times*, August 20, 1880, 2, and "The Collision at May's Landing," *New York Times*, August 25 1880, 2.

45. RTL to John Hay, November 30, 1880, microfilm reel 8, Hay Papers, Brown University.

46. Peskin, *Garfield*, 514.

47. Logan, *Reminiscences of a Soldier's Wife*, 413.

48. "Long talk with Cameron. He inclines to be pleased with the suggestion of MacVeagh for atty genl and suggested Robert Lincoln for Cabinet." Entry for Wednesday, December 29, 1880, in Brown and Williams, *Diary of James A. Garfield*, 4:517.

49. RTL to John A. Logan, Chicago, January 10, 1881, LB, 3:5:769–70, and in folder January–May 1881, box 3, Logan Family Papers.

50. Ulysses S. Grant to John A. Logan, January 10, February 15, and February 28, 1881, folder January–May 1881, box 3, Logan Family Papers. In February 1881, a newspaper article stated that Grant objected to Lincoln being part of the cabinet, which was untrue. Grant's friend Adam Badeau—who served with Lincoln on Grant's staff in 1865—wrote to Lincoln to assure him the story was false. Robert replied that he thought too highly of Grant to believe the article. Badeau, *Grant in Peace*, 327; RTL to "My dear General," February 27, 1881, HM 4662, RTL Papers, Huntington Library.

51. Joseph Medill to John A. Logan, Chicago, January 27, 1881, folder January–May 1881, box 3, Logan Family Papers.

52. J. D. Harvey to John A. Logan, Chicago, March 3, 1881, folder January–May 1881, box 3, Logan Family Papers.

53. Petition to President-elect James A. Garfield, January 14, 1881, reel 85, vol. 123, series 4, J. A. Garfield Papers.

54. Entry for Sunday, January 16, 1881, in Brown and Williams, *Diary of James A. Garfield*, 4:527.

55. James A. Garfield to John Hay, Mentor, Ohio, January 25, 1881, reel 119, series 6A, J. A. Garfield Papers. Longtime Washington insider Ben Perley Poore recalled, "The name of Robert Lincoln was talked over [in 1881], and General Garfield indicated an intention to give him some fitting recognition in his Administration, not only because he considered Mr. Lincoln a bright young man, but because he should take pleasure in making so graceful a tribute to the memory of his father. He did not intimate, however, that it would be by offering the son a seat in the Cabinet, nor did he say it would not be done in that way." Poore, *Reminiscences of Sixty Years*, 2:387.

56. James A. Garfield to John A. Logan, Mentor, Ohio, January 31 and February 21, 1881, folder January–May 1881, box 3, Logan Family Papers, and reel 119, series 6A, J. A. Garfield Papers; entry for Sunday, February 11, 1881, in Brown and Williams, *Diary of James A. Garfield*, 4:543.

57. James A. Garfield to David Davis, Mentor, Ohio, February 17, 1881, and David Davis to James A. Garfield, Washington, D.C., February 20, 1881, reel 91, series 4, and reel 119, series 6A, J. A. Garfield Papers. Both letters also in folder 123, box 20, Davis Papers, CHM.

58. RTL to John Hay, Chicago, February 7, 1881, reel 8, Hay Papers, Brown University.

59. RTL to John Hay, Chicago, February 27, 1881, reel 8, Hay Papers, Brown University.

60. James A. Garfield to RTL, February 28, 1881, reel 119, series 6A, J. A. Garfield Papers; entry for Mon., February 28, 1881, in Brown and Williams, *Diary of James A. Garfield*, 4:550.

61. Edward S. Isham to Robert Lincoln, telegram, March 1, 1881, 7:432–33, Records of Isham, Lincoln, and Beale Law Firm; RTL to James. A. Garfield, Springfield, Illinois, March 2, 1881, reel 92, series 4, J. A. Garfield Papers; Cullom, *Fifty Years of Public Service*, 124–27. Cullom also took credit in his memoir for broaching Robert's cabinet appointment with Garfield, although the historical evidence proves this wishful thinking.

62. Robert T. Lincoln, appointment as Secretary of War, March 5, 1881, OV 3, cont. 1, part 1, RTLFP; President James A. Garfield, notice of appointment of Robert T. Lincoln as Secretary of War, March 5, 1881, frame 384 (pp. 187–88), vol. 92, reel 82, M6, RG 107, Records of the Office of Secretary of War.

63. RTL to W. H. Bridges, March 8, 1881, LB, 4:6:774.

64. "Secretary Lincoln," *Chicago Tribune*, March 8 and 9, 1881, 8; "The Secretary of War," *Chicago Inter Ocean*, March 9, 1881, 4.

65. "Prominent Hotel Arrival," *Washington Post*, March 11, 1881, 4; RTL to Colonel A. Webster, March 8, 1881, LB, 3:5:776; RTL to John Hay, Chicago, February 27, 1881, reel 8, Hay Papers, Brown University; RTL telegram to James A. Garfield, March 7, 1881, reel 93, series 4, J. A. Garfield Papers; "General Garfield's Cabinet," *Boston Transcript*, March 7, 1881, 1.

66. Crook, *Through Five Administrations*, 259; entry for Thursday, March 10, 1881, in Brown and Williams, *Diary of James A. Garfield*, 4:555; "Secretary Lincoln Sworn In," *Washington Post*, March 11, 1881, 1. Crook also wrote that Robert had "always shown me much of his father's pleasant kindness"; and after taking his oath of office, he told President Garfield of Crook's faithful service to President Lincoln and asked that he be retained under Garfield's administration.

67. "Robert Lincoln and the Cabinet," *Chicago Inter Ocean*, March 7, 1881, 4.

68. Ibid.; "The Cabinet: Brief Biographies of President Garfield's Advisors," *Boston Transcript*, March 7, 1881, 2; "The New War Secretary," *New York Times*, March 10, 1881, 2; "The Son of Lincoln," *Washington Post*, March 12, 1881, 4.

69. Untitled newspaper clipping, *New York Evening Mail*, March 7, 1881, reel 93, series 4, J. A. Garfield Papers; George Alfred Townsend, "President Garfield and His Cabinet," 4.

14. "How Many Hours of Sorrow I Have Passed in This Town"

1. "The Son of Lincoln," *Washington Post,* March 12, 1881, 4; William H. Busbey, "Coming Man," 1. Robert's first day as secretary of war was March 11, 1881.

2. For letters requesting autographs, see RTL to unknown, RTL to Judson P. Etheridge, RTL to B. H. Beardsley, RTL to J. M. Gitterman, and RTL to F. J. Stewart, March 12, 1881, LB, 4:6:1–5.

3. Robert, in fact, denied a request of David Davis to promote Charles D. Clay, the grandson of the legendary U.S. Senator Henry Clay, to a second lieutenant, citing the opposition of existing law. RTL to David Davis, April 27, 1881, LB, 4:6:162–63.

4. Ella Canfield to RTL, November 11, 1880, and RTL to John Hay, November 15, 1880, MS Lincoln 1880 November 15, Hay Collection, Brown University.

5. Emily Helm was Robert's beloved playmate and companion in the 1840s and 1850s during his visits to the Todd home in Lexington, Kentucky, and her visits to the Lincoln home in Springfield. Robert and Emily remained close their entire lives and kept up a constant correspondence from the end of the Civil War until the early twentieth century.

6. RTL to Miss Margaret Todd, May 19, 1881, LB, 4:6:335–39. See also RTL to President Rutherford B. Hayes, Chicago, November 19, 1878, LB, 3:5:645–46; RTL to J. Ward, November 10, 1878, LB, 3:5:647–48; RTL to Mrs. Ninian Edwards, March 24, 1881, LB, 4:6:29; RTL to J. Proctor Knott, May 1, 1881, LB, 4:6:231–33; RTL to John P. Baker, May 22, 1881, LB, 4:6:330–31; RTL to Mrs. General J. B. S. Todd, May 23, 1881, LB, 4:6:332–33.

7. RTL to Mrs. E. L. Danenhower, April 11, 1881, LB, 4:6:120.

8. RTL to Harry W. Gourley, March 30, 1909, LB, 42:73:327.

9. Charles Sweet to Edward S. Isham, March 18, 1881, LB, 4:6:7.

10. RTL to James H. Eliot, April 7, 1881, LB, 4:6:95.

11. RTL to E. L. Baker, May 23, 1881, LB, 4:6:334–35.

12. "Secretary Lincoln," *Chicago Inter Ocean,* April 15, 1881, 8. Robert rented his house at 1330 Wabash Avenue partly furnished for $1,350 per year. RTL to Mark Skinner, June 7, 1882, LB, 7:9:9.

13. T. C. Crawford, "Robert Lincoln," *Chicago Tribune,* May 31, 1884, 13; "Social Notes," *Washington Post,* April 3, 1881, 2.

14. Marian (Hooper) Adams to her father, Robert William Hooper, Washington, February 20, March 27 and April 3, 1881, in Thoron, *Letters of Mrs. Henry Adams,* 269.

15. Letter of March 3, 1881 (incorrectly dated as 1880), in Dodge, *Gail Hamilton's Life in Letters,* 2:814.

16. RTL to C. E. Weston, December 17, 1883, LB, 10:14:106; Abram Garfield letter to John S. Goff, June 14, 1958, quoted in Goff, *Robert Todd Lincoln,* 118.

17. Minnie Chandler to Mary Harlan Lincoln, Washington, November 8, 1881, Chandler Papers.

18. "Abraham Lincoln's Grandson," New *York Times,* July 23, 1882, 7.

19. "Phil Sheridan's Visit," *Washington Post,* May 3, 1881, 1.

20. RTL to George B. Loring, Commissioner of Agriculture, June 16, 1881, LB, 4:6:422; "The Yorktown Commission," *Washington Post,* July 24, 1881, 1; RTL letter to unnamed correspondent, August 24, 1881, printed in "Yorktown Celebration," *Chicago Inter Ocean,* August 29, 1881, 4; *Report of the Commission Created in Accordance with a Joint Resolution of Congress,* 3–5.

21. RTL to Elizabeth Edwards, April 18, 1879, RTL Papers, ACPL.

22. RTL to Frances Wallace, April 25, 1881, LB, 4:6:145.

23. Fannie died of "brain fever" on May 10 and was buried three days later in Oak Ridge Cemetery. "Local Notes and Personals," *(Springfield) Illinois State Journal,* May 11, 12, and

13, 1881, 6; "Mortuary Matters," *(Springfield) Illinois State Register*, May 13, 1881, 4; RTL to John P. Baker, May 22, 1881, LB, 4:6:332–33; Burial Records, Oak Ridge Cemetery, Springfield, Illinois. Thanks to Wayne Temple for assisting me with the newspaper citations.

24. RTL to Brigadier General John Pope, May 7, 1881, LB, 4:6:220; RTL to George C. Clark, May 23, 1881, LB, 4:6:344–45; RTL to General O. O. Howard, June 2, 1881, LB, 4:6:365; RTL to John D. Defrees, June 4, 1881, LB, 4:6:379; RTL to John G. Nicolay, June 14, 1881, LB, 4:6:412.

25. Untitled article, *(Springfield) Illinois State Journal*, May 27, 1881, 6, and May 28, 1881, 4, 6; RTL to Sally Orne, Washington, DC, June 2, 1881, RTL Papers, ALPL. Tradition erroneously holds that Robert was in the city on a personal visit and brought his daughter Mamie with him—Mary Lincoln's little namesake whom she adored—as a way to help smooth the peace. This is a case of historical hearsay, and primary evidence proves it a myth. Historians W. A. Evans and Carl Sandburg began the Mamie story in separate 1932 biographies, both without citation. Sandburg's account is especially egregious, however, as he claims Robert's entire family went to Springfield to see Mary. The newspaper accounts and Robert's letters prove this untrue. In 1953, Ruth Painter Randall, who cites Evans, repeats the Mamie story, and subsequent historians have considered the story authentic. Evans, *Mrs. Abraham Lincoln*, 53; Sandburg and Angle, *Mary Lincoln, Wife and Widow*, 158; Randall, *Mary Lincoln*, 440.

26. Indications of her burgeoning love and forgiveness of her son occurred in 1879 and 1881: the former when she declared herself "elated" by a newspaper article proclaiming Robert T. Lincoln's inevitable candidacy for president of the United States; the latter when she became terrified (even paranoid) that Robert as secretary of war would be assassinated just like his father. Mary Lincoln to Edward Lewis Baker, Pau, France, June 22, 1879, in Turner and Turner, *Mary Todd Lincoln*, 682; J. C. A., "Mrs. Abraham Lincoln," *Chicago Tribune*, August 6, 1881, 6.

27. RTL to Sally Orne, Washington, June 2, 1881, RTL Papers, ALPL; RTL to Benjamin Richardson, June 3, 1881, LB, 4:6:376.

28. For the best book-length study of the expedition, see Todd, *Abandoned*. Facts about the expedition also can be found in the annual reports for the War Department, 1881–84, and in Greely's memoir, *Three Years of Arctic Service*. The most recent book on the subject is Guttridge, *Ghosts of Cape Sabine*.

29. Robinson, *Coldest Crucible*, 92.

30. "A New Scientific Expedition," *Washington Post*, March 13, 1881, 2; "Army and Navy News," *New York Times*, March 22, 1881, 2; "Science at the Pole," *Washington Post*, March 26, 1881, 4; "Bound for Arctic Seas," *Washington Post*, April 3, 1881, 1.

31. Greely, *Three Years of Arctic Service*, 1:36; General Orders No. 35, Headquarters of the Army, Adjutant General's Office, April 12, 1881, in *Annual Report of the Secretary of War*, 1:438; Robert T. Lincoln, memorandum upon charges preferred by the chief signal officer against First Lieutenant E. A. Garlington, January 9, 1885, in "Garlington Letter," 1881.1.10, Hildene Archives, and also in "Hazen and Garlington," *New York Times*, January 13, 1885, 3.

32. RTL to Norman Williams, Washington, April 14, 1885, RTLFP.

33. G. A. Townsend, "President Garfield and His Cabinet," 6.

34. "Robert Lincoln and the Cabinet," *Chicago Inter Ocean*, March 7, 1881, 4.

35. "Personal," *Washington Post*, April 9, 1881, 2; RTL to General J. K. Barnes, May 9, 1881, LB, 4:6:223; RTL to James Harlan, July 7, 1881, LB, 5:7:42.

36. Briggs, *Olivia Letters*, 424–26; E. E. Brown, *Life and Public Services of James A. Garfield*, 215–16.

37. In a 1923 interview, Robert recalled the event by saying, "I was within forty feet of

Garfield when he was shot and called Dr. Bliss." George A. Dondero, "My First Interview with Robert Todd Lincoln," March 5, 1923, Hildene Archives.

38. RTL to Norman Williams, July 28, 1881, RTLFP. Bliss corroborated Robert's statement about his initial call to the station in his article "The Story of President Garfield's Illness."

39. An array of telegrams to U.S. Senator John A. Logan in Chicago from Lincoln can be read in folder "June–Dec 1881," box 3, Logan Family Papers. Numerous other telegrams and letters on Garfield's condition can be found in LB, 5:7. See also Gerry, *Through Five Administrations*, 271; J. B. McClure, *Gen. Garfield*, 168–69.

40. RTL to Norman Williams, July 28, 1881, RTLFP.

41. For example, see "The Vice President Justified," *Washington Post*, July 7, 1881, 1; "Mr. Arthur's Friends," *Washington Post*, August 20, 1881, 1; "Contingency of 'Inability,'" 144–45. For the best Arthur biography, which explains his actions at this time in detail, see Reeves, *Gentleman Boss*.

42. Blaine and Lincoln to John Hay, 1881, reel 2, Hay Papers, Brown University. One of Guiteau's letters to President Garfield (March 8, 1881) expecting an appointment as counsel general at Paris is in the J. A. Garfield Papers in the Library of Congress, series 4, microfilm reel 93, frame 75890.

43. Charles Guiteau to the White House, July 2, 1881, and Charles Guiteau to General W. T. Sherman, July 2, 1881, both in Hayes and Hayes, *Complete History of the Life and Trial of Charles Julius Guiteau*, 145, 146. See also "A Great Nation in Grief," *New York Times*, July 3, 1881, 1.

44. RTL to Norman Williams, July 28, 1881, RTLFP.

45. "A Great Nation in Grief," *New York Times*, July 3, 1881, 1; McClure, *Gen. Garfield*, 173; "In the Darkest Hours," *Washington Post*, September 27, 1881, 3. White House employee Thomas Pendel, who worked in the Lincoln White House but whose reminiscences are not always reliable, claimed that Secretary Lincoln, when he saw him later that day, exclaimed, "Pendel, isn't this awful!" recalling the night of his father's murder. Thomas F. Pendel interview, *Philadelphia Press*, October 7, 1886, reprinted in "Years in the White House," *New York Times*, October 10, 1886, 6.

46. Ironically, for all of the historical interest in Robert Lincoln's association with his second assassination—and it would not be his last—his actual *role* in the event and aftermath has never been examined. Only Robert's presence at the train depot is ever mentioned, if at all. Not only have Robert's decisive actions as Secretary of War been ignored, as has his continual presence in the White House while Garfield lay wounded, but also none of his personal and public documents concerning the event ever have been examined or cited. The reason seems to be that historians have considered Robert Lincoln a small man with a big name who could not possibly contribute anything to the historical record—just as Lincoln scholars have believed Robert disliked his father and so knew nothing about his patriarch's life or presidency—both notions egregiously false. Minnie Chandler to Mary Harlan Lincoln, July 15, 1881, Chandler Papers.

47. RTL to James Harlan, July 7, 1881, LB, 5:7:42–43.

48. RTL to Edward Isham, July 7, 1881, LB, 5:7:26–30. In May 1882, Robert wrote a six-page letter to Dr. Bliss, recounting, at Bliss's request, his recollections of how Bliss was called to the train depot and ultimately put in charge of the president's care. This letter includes how the cabinet deliberated about which of the myriad doctors immediately in attendance on Garfield in the White House would be kept and which sent away. RTL to D. W. Bliss, May 23, 1882, LB, 6:8:466–71.

49. RTL to Lieutenant General Phillip Sheridan, July 8, 1881, LB, 5:7:45–48. See also RTL to J. E. Stuart and A. B. Spaulding, July 16, 1881, LB, 5:7:103–6.

50. RTL to John Hay, July 18, 1881, reel 8, Hay Papers, Brown University.

51. RTL to Norman Williams, July 28, 1881, RTLFP.

52. RTL to Major A. F. Stevenson, July 8, 1881, and RTL to S. Millett Thompson, July 8, 1881, LB, 5:7:57–59.

53. RTL to John Hay, August 16, 1881, reel 8, Hay Papers, Brown University; "Intense Anxiety in the City," *New York Times*, August 16, 1881, 1; RTL to Colonel T. F. Barr, August 20, 1881, LB, 5:7:238–40; RTL to J. M. Dalzell, August 29, 1881, RTLFP.

54. RTL and William Hunt to William Windom, S. J. Kirkwood, T. L. James, and Wayne MacVeagh, telegram, 3 P.M., August 16, 1881, LB, 5:7:209.

55. The daily press releases concerning Garfield's medical condition can be found in reel 166, Subseries 17J, Series 17, J. A. Garfield Papers.

56. Robert wrote on July 7 to a physician from Chicago, "It is not known with any adequate degree of certainty where the ball is now lodged. The president might be cut to pieces before it is actually found. The president's condition indicates that the presence of the ball itself is not doing any harm." RTL to J. H. Jordan, July 7, 1881, LB, 5:7:40.

57. For a detailed description, based on government documents, of the assassination and aftermath, see Doyle and Swaney, *Lives of James A. Garfield and Chester A. Arthur*, 60–160. See also "Scenes in the Sick Room," *Washington Post*, July 7, 1881, 1.

58. RTL to George M. Pullman, September 2 and September 5, 1881, LB, 5:7:285–88, 292.

59. Medical Bulletin, Elberon, New Jersey, September 20, 1881, reel 166, subseries 17J, series 17, J. A. Garfield Papers; also published in Doyle and Swaney, *Lives of James A. Garfield*, 159–60.

60. Garfield's autopsy shows the bullet did not strike any major organs, arteries, or veins and came to rest just below his pancreas. It pierced his vertebra but missed his spinal cord. The vertebrae and other items relating to the assassination today are held in the National Museum of Health and Medicine in Washington, D.C. Amanda Schaffer, "Assassin's Bullet Had 'Help' Killing President Garfield," *New York Times*, July 25, 2006.

61. "In the Darkest Hours," *Washington Post*, September 27, 1881, 3.

62. For the full trial transcripts, see Hayes, *Complete History*.

63. General Orders No. 71 and 72, Washington, September 20, 1881, in "Military and Naval Honors: The President's Death Formally Announced to the Army and Navy," *New York Times*, September 21, 1881, 5.

15. "The Best Secretary of War since Jefferson Davis"

1. Karabell, *Chester Alan Arthur*, 68.

2. "The Retiring Cabinet," *Washington Post*, October 2, 1881, 1; "Washington Affairs—The President Desires Robert Lincoln to Remain," *Brooklyn (NY) Eagle*, April 9, 1882, 6. Robert's official salary was listed in, among other publications, *J. Babeuf's Directory of Springfield, Illinois, and Business Mirror for 1881–1882*, 1.

3. Newspapers reported that former President Grant and Illinois U.S. Senator Logan both lobbied Arthur to retain Lincoln in the War Department. "Mr. Arthur's Cabinet," *Washington Post*, October 19, 1881, 1.

4. RTL to D. W. Lusk, Washington, January 7, 1884, LB, 10:14:205–6.

5. RTL to John Hay, Washington, March 23, 1882, reel 8, Hay Papers, Brown University.

6. President Arthur was in favor of assimilating the Native Americans into American

culture by creating schools, allowing land ownership, and extending state and territorial laws to the reservations. See Reeves, *Gentleman Boss*, 362–63. For general U.S. policy toward Native Americans, see Prucha, *Great Father*. Volume 2 of Prucha's work focuses on the policy of the 1880s including Indian education and citizenship. See also Hays, *Editorializing the "Indian Problem."*

7. RTL to John Conness, December 18, 1882, LB, 8:10:82–83.

8. Mary Lincoln to Edward Lewis Baker, Pau, France, January 19 and June 12, 1880, in Turner and Turner, *Mary Todd Lincoln*, 695, 699; "Mrs. Lincoln's Illness," *New York Times*, October 31, 1880, 5; "Mrs. Lincoln in Want," *New York Times*, November 23, 1881, 5; K. Helm, *True Story of Mary, Wife of Lincoln*, 298–99.

9. "Mrs. Lincoln's Illness," *New York Times*, October 31, 1880, 5.

10. "Mrs. Lincoln's Health Improving," *New York Times*, July 15, 1881, 8; J. C. A., "Mrs. Abraham Lincoln," *Chicago Tribune*, August 6, 1881, 6; "Mrs. Lincoln's Distress," *Chicago Tribune*, October 2, 1881, 2; "Mrs. Lincoln Going to Canada," *Chicago Inter Ocean*, reprinted in *New York Times*, October 10, 1881, 4.

11. The list of subscribers to the "Garfield Fund" and amounts given can be found in reel 168, subseries 17N, series 17, J. A. Garfield Papers. See also "The Fund for Mrs. Garfield" and "The Garfield Fund," *New York Times*, July 9, 1881, 8, and September 28, 1881, 8; "What Congress Did for Mrs. Lincoln," *New York Times*, September 26, 1881, 5; "News in Brief," *Chicago Tribune*, November 24, 1881, 1.

12. Mary Lincoln to Josephine Remann Edwards, October 23, 1881, and Mary Lincoln to Noyes W. Miner, February 21, 1882, in Turner and Turner, *Mary Todd Lincoln*, 708–9, 714. In late 1881, she spent six weeks in New York City consulting world-renowned orthopedic physician and childhood friend Dr. Louis A. Sayre and receiving electric and message treatment at Dr. E. P. Miller's hotel and medical baths establishment, which cost $60 per day. "Mrs. Lincoln in Want," *New York Times*, November 23, 1881, 5; "President Lincoln's Widow," *Boston Globe*, November 29, 1881, 1.

13. The *Chicago News* also believed Mary's illnesses were mostly imaginary, stating, "Since coming to Springfield it has been Mrs. Lincoln's pleasure to consider herself hopelessly ill—a confirmed invalid, without the slightest chance of recovery. . . . The burden of her conversation was about her sufferings. No one could live a week and suffer the pains which she described as afflicting her." RTL to Sally Orne, Washington, June 2, 1881, RTL Papers, ALPL; "Mrs. Lincoln's Health," *Chicago News*, reprinted in *New York Times*, July 22, 1881, 3.

14. "Mrs. Lincoln in Want," *New York Times*, November 22, 1881, 5. See also "Mrs. Lincoln's Pecuniary Condition," *(Springfield) Illinois State Journal*, November 26, 1881, 4.

15. Mary Lincoln to Noyes W. Miner, January 3, 1882, in Turner and Turner, *Mary Todd Lincoln*, 711–12 (emphasis in original).

16. "Mrs. Lincoln: Broad Denial of the Stories Set Afloat by Dr. Sayre," *Chicago Tribune*, November 24, 1881, 3; "News in Brief," *Chicago Tribune*, November 24, 1881, 1. The *(Springfield) Illinois State Journal* editorialized, "[W]hile Mrs. Lincoln is, undoubtedly, physically and mentally ill, she is a hypochondriac as to her health and a monomaniac on the subject of money." "Mrs. Lincoln's Pecuniary Condition," *(Springfield) Illinois State Journal*, November 26, 1881, 4.

17. "Mrs. Lincoln: Broad Denial of the Stories Set Afloat by Dr. Sayre," *Chicago Tribune*, November 24, 1881, 3; "Mrs. Lincoln: She Corrects Some Reports Concerning Her Financial Condition," *(Springfield) Illinois State Journal*, November 29, 1881, 1.

18. Robert probably was not the one to talk to Field, because it would be unseemly in his position as secretary of war. One newspaper article, purporting to be based on an

interview with "a member of the family of Mrs. Lincoln," stated that Robert "has done all he could quietly do" to actually *defeat* her 1881 pension bill, just as he tried to defeat her 1870 pension. In both cases, the article stated, Robert thought the pension unnecessary because his mother had plenty of money on which to live, and her beliefs in her poverty were just a symptom of her insanity. "Mrs. Lincoln in Want," *New York Times*, November 23, 1881, 5; "Mrs. Lincoln," *Chicago Tribune*, November 24, 1881, 3; "Mrs. Lincoln's Whims," *Chicago Tribune*, February 7, 1882, 11.

19. U.S. House member William M. Springer, a Democrat from Springfield, Illinois, also furthered Mary's cause when he requested Sayre and three other eminent physicians—experts in ophthalmology, neurology, and kidney diseases—examine the widow's case and give a report of her physical condition to Congress. The physicians declared she suffered from chronic inflammation of the spinal cord, chronic disease of the kidneys, and commencing cataract of both eyes; the effects of her maladies would be ultimate paralysis of her lower limbs and loss of eyesight. They declared her condition would never improve considering its nature and her age. Mary Lincoln to Noyes W. Miner, January 3, 1882, in Turner and Turner, *Mary Todd Lincoln*, 711; "New York: The Health of Mrs. Abraham Lincoln Not Improving," *Chicago Tribune*, January 15, 1882, 6; U.S. Congress, *Congressional Record*, 47th Cong. 1st sess., 1882, 13:402.

20. U.S. Congress, *Congressional Record*, 47th Cong. 1st sess., 1882, 13:578, 652, 705–6, 882; "Mrs. Lincoln's Needs," *New York Times*, January 25, 1882, 3; "Coke's Bill," *Chicago Tribune*, February 3, 1882, 2; "Notes from Washington," *New York Times*, February 3, 1882, 1; "Mrs. Lincoln's Pension," *New York Times*, March 17, 1882, 5. President Arthur signed the bill on February 2, 1882.

21. Mary Lincoln to Noyes W. Miner, February 5, 21, and 24, 1882, in Turner and Turner, *Mary Todd Lincoln*, 712–15; "Mrs. Lincoln," *Chicago Tribune*, November 24, 1881, 3; "Mrs. Lincoln's Pension," *New York Times*, March 17, 1882, 5.

22. Florence Snow to Rosemary Ketchum, July 1939, in Snow, *Pictures on My Wall*, 71–72, reprinted in "Some Intimate Glimpses into the Private Lives of the Members of the Robert Lincoln Family." See also Juhl, *James Harlan and Robert Todd Lincoln Families' Mount Pleasant Memories*, 27–35.

23. Robert wrote a friend on June 26 that his wife was "trying to regain her health in Colorado. She has not been at all well for a number of months." RTL to Charles C. Goddard, June 26, 1882, LB, 7:9:86.

24. "Obituary: Death at Springfield, Illinois, of the Widow of Abraham Lincoln," *Chicago Tribune*, July 17, 1882, 2; "Mary Todd Lincoln," *(Springfield) Illinois State Journal*, July 17, 1882, 6; Affidavit of Decease, Mary Lincoln Estate File.

25. "The Funeral," *(Springfield) Illinois State Journal*, July 19, 1882, 6. It is typically claimed that Mary Harlan's absence at her mother-in-law's funeral was the final slight of a long-insulted daughter-in-law. The evidence is clear, however, that Mary Harlan was too ill and worn out from travel to attend. Robert's law partner, Edward Isham, characterized Mary Harlan as "for years an invalid." "Isham and Lincoln," *Chicago Tribune*, November 24, 1883, 8.

26. "Mrs. Lincoln's Health," *New York Times*, July 16, 1882, 7; "Death of Mrs. Lincoln," *New York Times*, July 17, 1882, 1; "Secretary Lincoln," *(Springfield) Illinois State Journal*, July 18, 1882, 4; "Awaiting the Burial," *(Springfield) Illinois State Journal*, July 18, 1882, 6.

27. Mary Lincoln to RTL, August 1874, Lincoln Collection, ALPL; Extract of letter from Mary L. D. Putnam to her sons St. Clair and Clement Putnam, December 8, 1882, sent from Paul M. Angle to William E. Barton, January 10, 1927, William Barton scrapbook, vol. 63, Lincoln Collection, University of Chicago Library; "Awaiting the Burial," *(Spring-*

field) Illinois State Journal, July 18, 1882, 6; "Mrs. Lincoln's Funeral," *New York Times*, July 18, 1882, 1; "Dust to Dust: The Body of Mrs. Abraham Lincoln Consigned to the Tomb," *Chicago Tribune*, July 20, 1882, 7; Kunhardt, "An Old Lady's Lincoln Memories," 59–60.

28. "Laid to Rest: The Last Sad Rites Paid to the Remains of Mary Todd Lincoln," *(Springfield) Illinois State Journal*, July 20, 1882, 1; editorial, *(Springfield) Illinois State Journal*, July 20, 1882, 4; "Burial of Mrs. Lincoln," *Boston Globe*, July 20, 1882, 1; "Funeral of Mrs. Lincoln," *New York Times*, July 20, 1882, 1. For a detailed account of Mary's funeral, including a full transcript of Reed's eulogy, see Temple, *Abraham Lincoln*, 395–411.

29. Both a photograph and sketch of the funeral scene inside the church were made at the time and now are in the Lincoln Collection, ALPL.

30. James A. Reed, eulogy, TS, frames 297–302, reel 5, group 5, H-W; "Laid to Rest," *(Springfield) Illinois State Journal*, July 20, 1882, 1; "Dust to Dust," *Chicago Tribune*, July 20, 1882, 7.

31. "Consigned to the Tomb," *St. Louis Globe-Democrat*, July 20, 1882, 4.

32. In Chicago, he served as an elected trustee of the Second Presbyterian Church but was not a member. Two respected scholars who studied Robert Lincoln's life, Ruth Painter Randall and David C. Mearns, discussed his possible religious affiliations in a 1955 correspondence. They both agreed that he had none, and religion did not seem to figure largely in his life. RTL to George C. Clarke, February 9, 1885, LB, 12:18:324; Andreas, *History of Chicago*, 3:797; Temple, *Abraham Lincoln*, 413–14; Randall to Mearns, January 11 and 23, 1955, and Mearns to Randall, January 19, 1955, Ruth Painter Randall correspondence folder, box 38, Mearns Papers.

33. Power, *History of an Attempt*, 86.

34. RTL to Clinton L. Conkling, Washington, July 26, 1882, in Power, *History of an Attempt*, 87; RTL to John T. Stuart, Washington, July 26, 1882, box 1, Stuart-Hay Family Papers; for Power's description of Mary's reburial, see *History of an Attempt*, 86–87. Mary's secret reburial was unknown to the public until the remains were again moved in 1887. "Illinois' Hallowed Spot," *Chicago Inter Ocean*, April 15, 1887, 1; "Lincoln's Body," *Morning Oregonian* (Portland), April 15, 1887, 1.

35. Myra Pritchard, "The Dark Days of Abraham Lincoln's Widow," 7:4, folder 5, cont. 8, part 2, RTLFP. To read the existing parts of the will and a discussion of its contents, see Emerson, *Madness of Mary Lincoln*, 135–38, 177–78.

36. Mary's estate consisted of $72,000 in bonds, $555 in currency, $5,000 in personal effects, and $6,480 in bond interest. Robert Lincoln, Deposition on Personal Estate of Mary Lincoln, and Petition for Letters of Administration, and Bond of Administration, and Inventory of Real Estate, and Final Report of Administrator, Sangamon County Court, September 1882, part 2, cont. 8, RTLFP, also located in Mary Lincoln Estate File; "Mrs. Lincoln's Estate," *Washington Post*, September 29, 1882, 1; "Estate of Mrs. Lincoln," *New York Times*, September 29, 1882, 2.

37. Florence Snow to Rosemary Ketchum, July 1939, in F. Snow, *Pictures on My Wall*, 71. Mary sent numerous items, filling nearly a dozen trunks, to Elizabeth Edwards and the other Todd sisters in Springfield that October. The next summer the Lincolns had the remaining fifty or so trunks shipped to Mount Pleasant, where Mary Harlan spent weeks examining the contents. Charles Sweet (for Robert T. Lincoln) to Mrs. Ninian Edwards, October 26, 1882, and Charles Sweet (for Robert T. Lincoln) to Mrs. John Baker, October 26, 1882, folder 34, box 2, IF; Elizabeth Edwards to RTL, Springfield, November 9, 1882, folder 16, box 2, IF.

38. RTL to General W. S. Hancock, September 7, 1882, LB, 7:9:301–2; RTL to James

Harlan, September 9, 1882, LB, 7:9:314; RTL to Sherburne House, Atlantic City, New Jersey, telegram, September 9, 1882, LB, 7:9:316–17.

39. RTL to John A. Dillon, October 22, 1882, LB, 7:9:442.

40. John Nicolay to John Hay, Washington, February 18, 1883, reel 9, Hay Papers, Brown University.

41. "Robert T. Lincoln: Personal Characteristics of the Secretary of War," unknown newspaper, June 1, 1883, clipping in Robert T. Lincoln Alumni Folder, HUG 300, Harvard University Archives. See also "Lincoln and the Presidency," *New York Times*, December 29, 1883, 1; "Robert T. Lincoln's Growth," *New York Times*, April 6, 1884, 4.

42. RTL to Walter B. Phillips, March 20, 1882, and to J. Floyd King, March 31, 1882, and to John H. Hamilton, March 21, 1883, LB, 6:8:250, 289, and 8:11:499–501; E. W. Gould, *Fifty Years on the Mississippi*, 261–64.

43. The federal government confiscated Arlington during the Civil War and held it until the U.S. Supreme Court declared in December 1882 that it had been confiscated without due process. The court ordered the land returned to Custis Lee, eldest son of General and Mrs. Lee. Congress purchased the property from Lee for $150,000 on March 3, 1883. RTL to Senator George Edmunds, January 15, 1883, LB, 8:10:170.

44. RTL to Frederick W. Tompkins, July 7, 1883, LB, 9:12:267–68; "Secretary Lincoln Condemned," *New York Times*, May 3, 1883, 1; "Government Reservations: Why Secretary Lincoln Refused a Permit to Build a Church," *San Francisco Bulletin*, reprinted in *New York Times*, August 3, 1883, 4; "The Montana Grazing Grounds," *New York Times*, August 21, 1883, 2.

45. RTL to John Hay, March 23, 1882, reel 8, Hay Papers, Brown University. The two most pressing cases involved men named Whittaker and Flipper. For Lincoln on race relations, see "Color in the Signal Service," *Christian Recorder*, July 3, 1884; "Secretary Lincoln and the Color Line," *Frank Leslie's Illustrated Newspaper*, October 11, 1884; Marszalek, *Assault at West Point*. For Lincoln's general opinion on discharging West Point cadets based on performance and statute, see RTL to General Wesley Merritt, February 3, 1883, LB, 8:10:291–94.

46. RTL to Major Asa Bird Gardner, October 22, 1882, LB, 7:9:440; RTL to Schuyler Colfax, January 28, 1883, LB, 8:10:259–60; RTL to President Chester A. Arthur, April 3, 1883, archival item 1881.1.10, Hildene Archives. Mason's story was almost daily news across the country after his arrest and during his 1882 trial. For examples, see "Gunning for Guiteau," *Washington Post*, September 12, 1881, 1; "An Attempt to Kill Guiteau," *New York Times*, September 12, 1881, 1; "Sergt. Mason's Case," *New York Times*, October 18, 1881, 4; "Sergt. Mason's Sentence," *New York Times*, March 11, 1882, 8; "Pardoned at Last," *Boston Globe*, November 25, 1883, 1.

47. "The Elizabethtown Postmistress," *Washington Post*, March 22, 1883, 2; "A Post Office Fight Ended," *New York Times*, April 9, 1895, 9.

48. RTL to George B. Loring, March 17, 1883, LB, 8:11:484.

49. Ward Lamon to RTL, Denver, May 3, 1883, reel 12, group 5, H-W.

50. Robert here refers to the assertion that Thomas Lincoln and Nancy Hanks were never officially married, and therefore their son Abraham was illegitimate. Lamon wrote, "It is admitted by all the old residents of the place that they were honestly married, but precisely when or how no one can tell. Diligent and thorough searches by the most competent persons have failed to discover any trace of the fact in the public records." Lamon, *Life of Abraham Lincoln*, 10.

51. Robert wrote to his father's cousin Dennis F. Hanks in Charleston, Illinois, and

with little effort Robert found his grandparents' marriage certificate. RTL to Dennis F. Hanks, Chicago, December 4, 1872, LB, 3:4:69–72, and January 17, 1873, LB, 3:4:131–32. See also RTL to Henry Whitney Cleveland, August 20 and September 18, 1886, AAA 466 and 472, HM 23444 and 23428, RTL Letters, RTL Collection, Huntington Library.

52. RTL to Ward Lamon, May 10, 1883, LB, 8:11:672–75; also in reel 12, group 5, H-W.

53. Ward Lamon to RTL, May 30, 1883, reel 12, group 5, H-W. See also Lamon's nine-page excoriation of Robert, "About Robert Lincoln," May 1883, p. 2, LN 2415, Lamon Papers, Huntington Library.

54. RTL to H. M. Teller, Washington, June 22, 1883, LB, 9:12:183–86.

55. For example, see David Davis to John P. Usher, July 8, 1885, Ward Lamon to Leonard Swett, July 23, 1885, and Ward Lamon to David Davis, July 25, 1885, folder 131, box 21, Davis Papers, CHM.

56. For a more thorough examination of the trip, see Haynes, "Expedition of President Chester A. Arthur to Yellowstone National Park in 1883"; Reeves, "President Arthur in Yellowstone National Park"; Hartley, *Saving Yellowstone.*

57. Philip Sheridan to RTL, Chicago, July 26 and 27, 1883, Philip Sheridan to H. A. Preston, *New York Herald*, July 27, 1883, and Philip Sheridan to E. J. Gibson, *New York Tribune*, 638–40, 712–13, reel 63, Sheridan Papers; RTL to Philip H. Sheridan, July 27, 1883, LB, 9:13:351.

58. The party first had a stopover in Lexington, Kentucky, where after brief remarks by the president at the train depot, the party visited Ashland, the home of Henry Clay. Secretary Lincoln also visited personally with his cousin Dr. L. B. Todd and other members of the Todd family and told a reporter that "he always had a soft place in his heart for Kentucky and Kentuckians." "The President in Lexington," *Lexington (KY) Weekly Press*, August 1, 1883, 1.

59. "The President," *Chicago Tribune*, August 3, 1883, 1, and August 4, 1883, 1.

60. "Among the Indians," *New York Times*, August 10, 1883, 4; "The Official Report," *Chicago Tribune*, August 10, 1883, 1.

61. "Still Catching Trout," *New York Times*, August 25, 1883, 1.

62. "President Arthur's Trip," *New York Times*, August 27, 1883, 5.

63. James B. Williams, assistant to the president, Northern Pacific Railroad Company, to President Chester Arthur, New York, July 26, 1883, reel 2, series 1, Arthur Papers; RTL to Henry Villard, Yellowstone Lake, telegram, August 28, 1883, reel 2, series 1, Arthur Papers; "Mr. Villard's Party," *New York Times*, September 5, 1883, 4; Villard, *Memoirs of Henry Villard*, 2:309–10; McCormack, *Memoirs of Gustave Koerner*, 2:678; *Grand Opening of the Northern Pacific Railway*, 41–47.

64. "Booming Arthur in Chicago" and "The President in Chicago," *New York Times*, September 4, 1883, 1, and September 5, 1883, 4.

65. *Mt. Pleasant (IA) News*, September 13, 1883, Iowa Wesleyan University Archives.

66. *Journey through the Yellowstone National Park and North-Western Wyoming, 1883*; Lieutenant General Philip Sheridan to RTL, October 20, 1883, and to Brigadier General R. C. Drum, October 20, 1883, 755–57, reel 25, Sheridan Papers; RTL to F. Jay Haynes, January 28, 1884, RTL Papers, ALPL; RTL to J. H. Roberts, March 15, 1884, LB, 10:15:574; RTL to Governor J. Schuyler Crosby, March 16, 1884, LB, 10:15:577–78. Only twelve copies of the book were made, and only three are known to exist. Robert's copy is in the Lincoln Collection of the ALPL.

67. *Annual Report of the Secretary of War for the Year 1882*, 1:xxi; *Annual Report of the Chief Signal Officer, United States Army, to the Secretary of War for the Fiscal Year Ending June 30, 1882*, 1:65–68.

68. *Annual Report of the Secretary of War for the Year 1883*, 1:19–20.

69. *Report of the Secretary of War . . . Second Session of the Forty-Eighth Congress*, (1884), 1:22–25.

70. *Annual Report of the Secretary of War for the Year 1883*, 1:19–20, and "Memorandum," 1:22–23; *Report of the Secretary of War; Being a Part of the Message and Documents Communicated to the Two Houses of Congress*, (1882), 1:22–26.

71. RTL to Norman Williams, Washington, April 14, 1885, part 1, cont. 1, RTLFP.

72. "The Proteus and the Yantic," *New York Times*, November 1, 1883, 2. Garlington was found to have made bad decisions but was exonerated from blame due to the difficult and unusual circumstances he faced at the time. Secretary Lincoln and the board instead blamed Chief Signal Officer General Hazen's insufficient and confusing orders for the failure. "Gen. Hazen's Mistake," *New York Times*, February 14, 1884, 3. See also "Story of the Expedition," *New York Times*, July 18, 1884, 1; "A Horrible Discovery," *New York Times*, August 12, 1884, 1.

73. *Report of Board of Officers to Consider an Expedition for the Relief of Lt. Greely and Party*, copy in Greely Relief folder, 1881.1.16, Hildene Archives; RTL to William Kislingbury, January 28, 1884, LB, 10:15:304; RTL to G. T. Lanigan, March 3, 1884, LB, 10:15:491–94; RTL to Marius de Lazare, April 7, 1884, LB, 11:16:20; "For the Rescue of Greely," *New York Times*, January 3, 1884, 3; Schley and Soley, *Rescue of Greely*.

74. Greely later stated the "turning point" in the fortunes of the expedition was when Congress offered the bounty to whalers to be the first to find the survivors: "No relief or expeditionary vessels ever ventured at so early a date the dangers of Melville Bay." *Three Years of Arctic Service*, 2:334–35.

75. For the full story of their rescue, see Schley and Soley, *Rescue of Greely*. See also Harlow, "Greely at Cape Sabine."

76. *Annual Report of the Chief Signal Officer of the Army to the Secretary of War for the Year 1884*, 18. For Hazen's full report on the Greely expedition, see pages 14–21.

77. *Report of the Secretary of War . . . Second Session of the Forty-Eighth Congress*, (1884), 1:25–26; Schley and Soley, *Rescue of Greely*, 99–100.

78. *Report of the Secretary of War . . . Second Session of the Forty-Eighth Congress*, 1:25.

79. Ibid. See also "Hazen and Secretary Lincoln," *New York Times*, November 29, 1884, 4.

80. General W. B. Hazen to RTL, February 17, 1885, and Lincoln to Hazen, February 27, 1885, RTL Papers, ALPL.

81. General Court-Martial Orders No. 37, Washington, April 17, 1885, copy in Greely/Hazen file, 1881.2.2, Hildene Archives. The charges against Hazen also were published in "Gen. Hazen's Trial Begun," *New York Times*, March 12, 1885, 3, and his sentence published in "Gen. Hazen Reprimanded," *New York Times*, April 18, 1885, 4. The *Times* published daily reports on the progress of the court-martial from March 12 to March 21.

82. Greely, *Three Years of Arctic Service*, 2:194, 336.

16. "I Am Not a Candidate"

1. Gordon, *Massa Linkum's Boy*.

2. Untitled editorial, *Washington Post*, February 9, 1882, 2; "The Republican Leaders," *New York Times*, April 16, 1882, 1; "Secretary Lincoln's Hopes," *New York Times*, September 6, 1882, 1; RTL to H. S. Clark, Washington, December 4, 1882, LB, 8:10:39; RTL to S. M. Cullom, January 16, 1883, LB, 8:10:173.

3. RTL to S. Newton Pettis, November 26, 1882, LB, 8:10:7.

4. Senator Preston B. Plumb interview, "Senator Plumb," *Chicago Tribune*, January 21, 1883, 8.

5. RTL to S. Newton Pettis, February 4, 1883, LB, 8:10:297–98.

6. RTL to Stanford Newell, May 30, 1884, LB, 11:17:319–21; RTL to Colonel Abner Taylor, May 30, 1884, LB, 11:17:324–25; RTL to General Martin Beem, June 30, 1884, LB, 11:17:422.

7. "Lincoln for the People: The Masses Solid for Old Abe's Son," *New York Times*, June 4, 1884, 8.

8. "In Lighter Vein," 512.

9. A. Cowles to Horace White, May 7, 1884, folder 3, box 1, Horace White Papers.

10. "Lincoln to Be Selected," *Boston Globe*, April 16, 1884, 1. This unnamed observer could have been Henry Cabot Lodge, a native of Boston and a delegate-at-large to the 1884 Republican convention. His biographer John A. Garraty stated that Lodge was actively working to unite all anti-Blaine elements behind Robert Lincoln at the convention. Garraty, *Henry Cabot Lodge*, 76.

11. John Hay to Levi Parsons Morton, January 19, 1884, in McElroy, *Levi Parsons Morton*, 155.

12. Rothacker to John A. Logan, May 20, 1884, folder "January–June 1884," cont. 4, Logan Family Papers.

13. Schuyler Colfax to Richard J. Oglesby, May 21, 1884, folder 1, box 13, Oglesby Papers.

14. "Men Who May Be Chosen," *New York Times*, April 14, 1884, 5.

15. Carl Schurz to John A. Logan, February 29, 1884, in Bancroft, *Speeches, Correspondence and Political Papers of Carl Schurz*, 4:195.

16. "Blaine and Conkling and the Republican Convention of 1880," 282.

17. T. C. Crawford, "Robert T. Lincoln," *Chicago Tribune*, May 31, 1884, 13.

18. "Robert T. Lincoln," *Chicago Times*, June 1, 1884.

19. "Mr. Lincoln's Candidacy," *Chicago Tribune*, April 17, 1884, 4; "A Letter from Mr. Lincoln," *New York Times*, April 17, 1884, 5.

20. Lincoln to H. H. Warner, May 8, 1884, folder 1, RTL Papers, CHM.

21. "Mr. Lincoln's Candidacy," *Chicago Tribune*, April 17, 1884, 4.

22. Philip Sydney Post to Richard J. Oglesby, January 7, 1887, folder 9, box 13, Oglesby Papers.

23. "The Convention's Choice," *New York Times*, June 7, 1884, 1.

24. Ibid.; "Logan for Vice President," *Boston Globe*, June 7, 1884, 2; "Secretary Lincoln," *New York Times*, June 13, 1884, 3.

25. RTL to James R. Doolittle, Washington, June 9, 1884, in Mowry, "Robert T. Lincoln and James R. Doolittle," 474.

26. Reeves, *Gentleman Boss*, 370.

27. RTL to S. M. Cullom and RTL to Norman Williams, War Department, June 5, 1884, LB, 11:17:342–43.

28. "Robert T. Lincoln: An Eloquent Address by the Secretary of War," *Chicago Tribune*, October 25, 1884, 2.

29. "The Political Prize: Secretary Lincoln's Welcome to Illinois," *Chicago Tribune*, October 23, 1884, 3.

30. "A Monster Meeting," *(Springfield) Illinois State Register*, October 26, 1884, 1.

31. "Northwest News," *Chicago Tribune*, November 7, 1884, 7.

32. "Dedicated! The Act Which Completes the Washington Monument," *Washington Post*, February 22, 1885, 1.

33. For the best examination of Arthur's presidential accomplishments, see Reeves, *Gentlemen Boss*, 251–419.

34. McClure, *Recollections of Half a Century*, 115.

35. RTL to William E. Chandler, June 7, 1886, quoted in Chandler, *President Chester A. Arthur*, 42.

36. RTL to Daniel Huntington, December 27, 1884, LB, 12:18:185. The portrait now hangs in the Pentagon.

37. William T. Sherman to RTL, Washington, October 8, 1884, RTL Lincoln to Sherman, Washington, October 10, 1883, William T. Sherman, General Orders No. 77, November 1, 1883, and Phillip H. Sheridan, General Orders No. 78, November 1, 1883, in Sherman, *Memoirs of Gen. W. T. Sherman*, 2:461–64.

38. Lieutenant General P. H. Sheridan to RTL, September 25 and October 7, 1883, 723–26, 741–42, reel 25, Sheridan Papers; RTL to Lieutenant General P. H. Sheridan, September 29, 1883, LB, 9:13:508–9.

39. RTL to Lieutenant General P. H. Sheridan, Washington, December 9, 1884, and January 17, 1885, RTL notebook, 1881.1.10, RTL Collection, Hildene Archives.

40. "Defining His Authority," *New York Times*, August 29, 1885, 3; "How Robert T. Lincoln Checkmated Sheridan," *Brooklyn (NY) Eagle*, October 3, 1898, 7; RTL to John C. Pearson, January 31, 1902, RTL Papers, ALPL; RTL to John B. Randolph, January 4, 1909, LB, 41:71:490.

41. "Gen. Grant's Retirement," "The Retirement of Gen. Grant" and "Last Hours in the House," *New York Times*, March 5, 1885, 1, 4, 5. See also A. D. Richardson, *Personal History of Ulysses S. Grant*, 596–601.

42. RTL to Stilson Hutchins, Washington, March 8, 1885, RTL Papers, ACPL.

43. Ibid.; RTL to W. E. Mead, Chicago, June 1, 1886, LB, 3:5:843–44; "Gen. Grant's Commission," *New York Times*, March 8, 1885, 1.

44. For an excellent overview of Robert's accomplishments in office, see T. C. Crawford, "Robert T. Lincoln," *Chicago Tribune*, May 31, 1884, 13. See also W. G. Bell, *Secretaries of War and Secretaries of the Army*, 88–89.

45. "How Robert T. Lincoln Checkmated Sheridan," *Brooklyn (NY) Eagle*, October 3, 1898, 7.

46. RTL to unknown recipient, May 5, 1884, LB, 11:16:174.

47. RTL to Thomas Evert and Charles Mooney, Committee, November 29, 1884, and RTL to Darwin C. Pavey, editor, *Eagle* (Pittsfield, MA), December 1, 1884, LB, 12:18:88–89, 102–3.

17. "I Expect Only the Greatest Satisfaction"

1. Herndon and Weik, *Herndon's Lincoln*, 264–65n; William Herndon to Jesse Weik, January 2 and 22, 1887, in Hertz, *Hidden Lincoln*, 152.

2. David Davis to Jeremiah Black, Bloomington, Illinois, August 19, 1870, frames 60073–76, reel 26, vol. 52, Jeremiah S. Black Papers. It is unknown who "some persons" specifically were.

3. RTL to F. J. Child, Washington, April 27, 1865, RTL Collection, Phillips Exeter Academy; "The Lincoln Family," *Sacramento (CA) Daily Union*, June 14, 1865, transcript in Reminiscences Funeral folder, Lincoln Collection, ALPL.

4. RTL to David Davis, Chicago, August 24, 1871, folder A-109, box 7, DDFP; RTL to John Nicolay, June 16, 1873, box 4, Nicolay Papers.

5. RTL to James H. Hackett, Chicago, March 17, 1871, RTLFP; John Nicolay to RTL,

Springfield, Illinois, May 31, 1873, box 4, Nicolay Papers; RTL to David Davis, Chicago, June 24, 1873, folder A-109, box 7, DDFP.

6. RTL to David Davis, Chicago, February 18, 1874, folder A-109, box 7, DDFP.

7. John Nicolay to RTL, Washington, March 3, 1874, box 4, Nicolay Papers (emphasis in original).

8. Stories of Robert Lincoln arbitrarily burning multitudes of his father's papers have been overblown and in some cases fabricated, especially the well-known statement by Nicholas Murray Butler. These are examined and explained in later chapters, especially chapter 24.

9. RTL to John Nicolay, Washington, January 5, 1885, and Robert T. Lincoln, "Reminiscence of Abraham Lincoln after Gettysburg," vol. 16, reel 10, Hay Papers, LOC; RTL to John Nicolay, January 2, 1885, box 11, Nicolay papers. Both are published in Burlingame, *Oral History of Abraham Lincoln*, 88–89. Robert's personal reminiscences regarded his father's reactions to the aftermath of the Battle of Gettysburg and the issuance of the Pomeroy Circular.

10. John Hay to RTL, February 14, 1878, in Thayer, *Life and Letters of John Hay*, 2:20–21; RTL to John Hay, April 15, 1878, January 2, 1880, and January 10, 1886, reel 8, Hay Papers, Brown University; Edgar T. Welles to John Nicolay, Hartford, October 18, 1878, box 4, Nicolay Papers; RTL to Edgar T. Welles, November 23, 1908, LB, 41:71:423–24; RTL to Elihu B. Washburne, June 24, 1883, LB, 9:12:203–4.

11. RTL to John Hay, Chicago, April 15, 1878, and December 7, 1886, reel 8, Hay Papers, Brown University.

12. Robert also wrote of the ten-volume work, "I do not know a more splendid American publication. As I said to Nicolay I shall never cease to congratulate myself that the making up of my father's record in its enduring form fell into the hands of you and him." RTL to John Hay, April 14, 1888, copy of letter pasted in Memory Book, box 1, Symington Collection, and December 27, 1890, reel 8, Hay Papers, Brown University.

13. William Herndon to Jesse Weik, January 2 and 22, 1887, in Hertz, *Hidden Lincoln*, 152, 158.

14. RTL to Messrs. G. P. Putnam's Sons, December 28, 1885, LB, 3:5:791–92. See also RTL to Houghton, Mifflin & Co., March 29, 1887, folder 1, bMS Am 1925 (1903), Houghton Mifflin Company Papers; John Nicolay to Isaac Arnold, Greenland, New Hampshire, September 17, 1874, box 4, Nicolay Papers.

15. Mearns, *Lincoln Papers*, 1:70.

16. The only Lincoln scholar to understand this is Burlingame, *Abraham Lincoln*, 6.

17. John Hay to RTL, January 27, 1885, in Thayer, *Life and Letters of John Hay*, 2:24–25.

18. RTL to John Hay, February 4, 1885, reel 8, Hay Papers, Brown University.

19. Lamon had previously published the hog story in his 1872 biography, and Herndon used it in his 1889 biography. Lamon, *Life of Abraham Lincoln*, 82; Herndon and Weik, *Herndon's Life of Lincoln*, 59–60.

20. For examples of Hay's original manuscript and Robert's editing of it, see Thomas, *Portrait for Posterity*, 111–18, and Burlingame, *Abraham Lincoln*, 7–8.

21. RTL to John Hay, April 17, 1885, and January 10, 1886, reel 8, Hay Papers, Brown University.

22. John Hay to RTL, April 20, 1885, in Mearns, *Lincoln Papers*, 1:75.

23. John Hay to RTL, January 6, 1886, in ibid.

24. RTL to John Hay, January 10, 1886, reel 8, Hay Papers, Brown University. This response has been excluded from all previous studies of the subject due to the unstudied and uncollected nature of Robert's life and letters.

25. RTL to John Hay, September 7, 1886, reel 8, Hay Papers, Brown University.

26. Historian Benjamin Thomas declared that while Robert's tinkering actually improved the manuscript, "to a modern historian such truckling to the whims of Robert Lincoln [by Nicolay and Hay] would seem intolerable." Thomas added, however, "[I]t is not without a feeling of sympathy that we see Robert striving to maintain his forebears' status." *Portrait for Posterity*, 118.

27. John Hay to John Nicolay, Cleveland, Ohio, August 10, 1885, in Thayer, *Life and Letters of John Hay*, 2:33.

28. John Hay to RTL, January 6, 1886, in Mearns, *Lincoln Papers*, 1:75.

29. John Hay to William H. Herndon, September 5, 1866, reel 8, group 4, H-W.

30. RTL to John Nicolay, May 30, 1893, box 5, Nicolay Papers.

31. Dennett, *John Hay*, 134.

32. Monaghan, *Lincoln Bibliography*, 1:211–82.

33. RTL to Isaac Arnold, Chicago, November 9, 1866, LB, 1:1:16–17. These reasons, as always in Robert's mind, reflected his desire not to reveal his father's personal feelings or criticisms of persons still living.

34. John Hay to John Nicolay, Warsaw, Illinois, March 18, 1867, reel 6, Hay Papers, Brown University.

35. Most of these items, unfortunately, burned during the Great Fire of Chicago in 1871. Isaac Arnold to RTL, August 1871, folder 1, box 11, Arnold Collection, CHM; RTL to John Nicolay, December 18, 1887, box 4, Nicolay Papers; RTL to Katherine Arnold, Chicago, May 3, 1888, folder 1, RTL Papers, CHM.

36. Robert's personal and inscribed copy of Arnold's 1885 biography still resides on the bookshelves of Robert's home, Hildene, in Manchester, Vermont.

37. RTL to General A. C. McClurg, January 5, 1885, LB, 18:12:218.

38. RTL to Judd Stewart, Chicago, March 12, 1889, HM 20103, RTL Collection, Huntington Library; RTL to John W. Starr, November 10, 1908, LB, 41:71:397. See also Starr, *Abraham Lincoln's Religion in His Eldest Son's Estimation*.

39. RTL to John Nicolay, Chicago, July 10, 1874, and John Nicolay to RTL, July 17, 1874, box 4, Nicolay Papers.

40. RTL to John Nicolay, May 14, 1881, and RTL to Allan Pinkerton, May 14, 1881, LB, 4:6:262, 267–68.

41. See Burlingame, *Lincoln Observed*.

42. RTL to Noah Brooks, Washington, April 5, 1882, folder 1, RTL Papers, CHM; Brooks, "Boy in the White House," 57–65. In 1914, Robert also wrote a reminiscence of his youngest brother for historian F. Lauriston Bullard. Bullard's subsequent book, *Tad and His Father*, Robert declared to be "a most delightful reminder to me of a time which is far gone by, but which had many pleasures, as well as troubles." He told Bullard, "You have given to me an affecting sketch of the mischievous, charmingly affectionate little boy who was such a comfort to my father." RTL to F. Lauriston Bullard, November 25, 1914 and October 15, 1915, Lincoln Collection, Howard Gotlieb Archival Research Center; Bullard, *Tad and His Father*.

43. Holzer, *Lincoln's White House Secretary*, 12–13.

44. RTL to John Hay, April 7, 1884, and RTL to William O. Stoddard, April 16, 1884, LB, 11:16:14, 63; David Davis to John P. Usher, July 8, 1885, folder 131, box 21, Davis Papers, CHM.

45. William Herndon to Jesse Weik, February 5, 1891, in Hertz, *Hidden Lincoln*, 261.

46. Robert repeated this belief numerous times throughout his existing correspondence. For examples, see RTL to Robert T. Hubard, April 29, 1903, LB, 36:61:373; RTL

to Clinton Conkling, Washington, December 17, 1917, Conkling Family Papers; RTL to Isaac Markens, September 3, 1920, RTLFP.

47. RTL to L. E. Chittenden, Chicago, November 21, 1890, LB, 13:19:128–30.

48. William Herndon to Jesse Weik, January 22, 1887, and William Herndon to Truman H. Bartlett, November 10, 1888, in Hertz, *Hidden Lincoln*, 154–55, 222.

49. William Herndon to Jesse Weik, January 15 and December 20, 1889, and March 7, 1890, in ibid., 238, 244, 249.

50. I have found no evidence that Robert Lincoln suppressed the book. Herndon's biographer, David Herbert Donald, likewise stated he found no evidence to support Herndon's claim but believed the rarity of the book was because of its small press run of fifteen hundred sets and the poor marketing of the publisher. RTL to Charles L. Hammond, Chicago, February 11, 1903, RTL Papers, ALPL; Donald, *Lincoln's Herndon*, 335.

51. RTL to Abram Wakeman, November 28, 1908, LB, 41:71:430; RTL to Le Grand Van Valkenburgh, May 26, 1913, RTL Papers, ALPL; RTL to Emily Todd Helm, June 15, 1913, RTL Papers, CHM.

52. Adam Badeau, "Adam Badeau's Letter: A History of the Insanity of Mrs. President Lincoln," *Chicago Tribune*, January 17, 1887, 10.

53. RTL to Colonel Frederick D. Grant, Chicago, February 4, 1887, RTL Collection, Hildene Archives. Grant had written to Robert apparently on behalf of his mother, Julia Grant, to absolve her of any connection with the article, since she is mentioned and even quoted numerous times. Mrs. Grant actually wrote her own memoir, begun around the time of Badeau's article, in which she mentions the City Point episode but contradicts Badeau's most outrageous accusations concerning the behavior of Mary Lincoln. J. D. Grant, *Personal Memoirs*, 142–47.

54. Swisshelm, *Half a Century*; Jane Grey Swisshelm, "Tribute to the Dead from Mrs. Jane Grey Swisshelm," *Chicago Tribune*, July 20, 1882, 7.

55. RTL to William H. Reed, May 5, 1884, folder 34, box 2, and RTL to Leonard Swett, May 25, 1884, folder 3, box 2, IF. I did not find Swisshelm's article and cannot account for its contents.

56. RTL to Abram Wakeman, November 28, 1908, LB, 41:71:430.

57. Fleischner, *Mrs. Lincoln and Mrs. Keckly*, 316–17.

58. "New Publications," *New York Times*, April 19, 1868, 10.

59. Anna Eliza Williams to John E. Washington, June 1938, in Washington, *They Knew Lincoln*, 221–22; Parker, in Keckley, *Behind the Scenes*; Fleischner, *Mrs. Lincoln and Mrs. Keckly*, 318.

60. "Lincoln Again," 158; F. T. Hill, *Lincoln the Lawyer*, xvii.

61. RTL to David Homer Bates, August 26, 1907, reel 1, Bates Papers, Alfred Whital Stern Collection of Lincolniana. There are in total eleven letters between Robert Lincoln and David Homer Bates in the Bates Papers, ranging from 1907–10, all about the book. See also RTL to David Homer Bates, June 22, 1907, RTL Papers, ALPL.

62. Tarbell, *Life of Abraham Lincoln*. See also Rice, "Ida M. Tarbell."

63. Ida Tarbell to Jesse Weik, New York, January 14, 1896, folder "1896–1899," box 1, Weik Papers; Tarbell, *All in the Day's Work*, 166.

64. Robert later apologized to John Hay for giving the picture to Tarbell and not to him and Nicolay. He had only just discovered the photo, he explained, because he had "dreaded" going through his mother's papers and had not done so since her death in 1882. But, more than that, he also wanted to put Tarbell "under a little obligation to me." RTL to John Hay, Chicago, November 19, 1895, reel 8, Hay Papers, Brown University.

65. RTL to James Harlan, November 13, 1897, LB, 33:54:2.

66. Robert wrote to Chittenden, "I am none the less glad that you have supplemented the excellent work of Mr. Arnold and the splendid views of the labors of Mrrs Nicolay & Hay, by your sympathetic, appreciative and exhaustive 'Study' which will no doubt be read by many who would in this busy land, hesitate to attack the longer books." RTL to L. E. Chittenden, Chicago, November 21, 1890, LB, 13:19:128–30. Robert praised Gilder's article by saying, "I really cannot recall any article upon my father which has pleased me as much as yours, and it is in reality an astonishing article in its fullness and yet comprehension." RTL to Richard Watson Gilder, January 25, 1909, LB, 42:72:70–72; also in Gilder, *Letters of Richard Watson Gilder*, 479–81.

67. RTL to J. T. Harahan, May 12, 1909, LB, 42:73:425; RTL to Isaac Markens, November 17, 1916, and RTL to George H. Mifflin, November 22, 1916, folder 1, bMS Am 1925 (1903), Houghton Mifflin Company Papers.

68. RTL to Alice James, Manchester, Vermont, October 3, 1920, bMS Am 1928 (197), William James Papers; RTL to Colonel Hopkins, August 2, 1917, RTL Collection, Hildene Archives.

69. RTL to A. K. McClure, May 10, 1879, LB, 3:5:697–700.

70. RTL to John Nicolay, Chicago, June 14, 1878, and Nicolay to RTL, June 25, 1878, and September 5, 1881, box 4, Nicolay Papers; RTL to Isaac Arnold, Washington, November 11, 1883, and March 27, 1884, folder 1, RTL Papers, CHM.

71. RTL to William Griffith, November 2, 1908, LB, 41:71:379; RTL to Charles M. Fays, January 7, 1909, LB, 42:72:24. See also RTL to Lionel Stagge, editor, *Illustrated American Magazine*, May 29, 1899, LB, 33:55:442.

72. RTL to C. C. Brown, February 17, 1903, LB, 36:61:326; RTL to David Davis, Chicago, February 6, 1886, Green Papers.

73. RTL to James Grant Wilson, June 21, 1887, LB, 3:5:964–65; J. G. Wilson, *Presidents of the United States*, 300–335.

74. RTL to James Grant Wilson, March 27, 1888, LB, 13:19:52; "John Todd Stuart," in Wilson and Fiske, *Appleton's Cyclopedia of American History*, 5:731.

75. Depictions of this moment have been aptly dubbed the "Rubber Room" Phenomenon, due to the ever-increasing number of witnesses at Lincoln's bedside. Holzer and Williams, *Lincoln's Deathbed*.

76. Robert signed for a $100 artist's proof. See Holzer and Williams, *Lincoln's Deathbed*, 29–33.

77. RTL to W. D. Washburn, January 30, 1903, LB, 36:61:291. Robert also wrote in 1902, "I have never seen a portrait of my father which is to be compared with it in any way"; his wife, Mary Harlan Lincoln, wrote in 1920, "[W]e think it the best likeness in existence." RTL to W. D. Washburn, December 26, 1902, RTL Collection, Hildene Archives; Mary Harlan Lincoln to Miss Jackson, Manchester, Vermont, September 30, 1920, RTL Collection, ACPL.

78. RTL to W. D. Washburn, December 26, 1902, RTL Collection, Hildene Archives; RTL to Richard Watson Gilder, February 24, 1908, RTL Papers, ALPL; "Open Letters—The Healy Portrait," 959. In her will, Mary Harlan Lincoln bequeathed the Healy portrait first to her daughter Mary Lincoln Isham and, upon her death to the U.S. government, provided that the painting would be hung in the White House. It was given to the government in 1939, and President Franklin D. Roosevelt hung it above the fireplace mantel in the State Dining Room. "Lincoln Portrait by Healy Slated for White House," *Christian Science Monitor*, April 10, 1937, 7; Frost, Myers, & Towers, attorneys and counselors at

law, to President Franklin D. Roosevelt, Washington, December 28, 1938, RTL Papers, ALPL; E. B. Helm, *Captains and the Kings*, 284–85.

79. RTL to J. J. Egan, September 17, 1877, LB, 3:5:580. The print still hangs in Hildene, Robert's home in Manchester, Vermont.

80. RTL to Francis B. Carpenter, Chicago, December 24, 1866, LB, 1:1:24–25, also in folder 1, RTL Papers, CHM; RTL to John Hay, Chicago, January 28, 1867, reel 8, Hay Papers, Brown University.

81. RTL to Matthew Brady, August 10, 1882, LB, 7:9:195; RTL to Ewing Hill, Chicago, July 2, 1887, LB, 3:5:983; Hickey, "Robert Lincoln on Artists and Sculptors of President Lincoln," 1–3.

82. RTL to Arthur F. Hall, secretary, the Lincoln National Life Insurance Company of Fort Wayne, Indiana, August 3, 1905, RTL Collection, ACPL.

83. RTL to George Payson, June 25, 1881, LB, 4:6:464–68.

84. RTL to Vinnie Ream Hoxie, February 21, 1898, LB, 33:54:127.

85. RTL to Clinton Conkling, Washington, DC, November 24, 1917, folder 10, box 2, Conkling Family Papers.

86. RTL to George Payson, June 25, 1881, LB, 4:6:464. See also RTL to Louis J. Keller, April 22, 1909, LB, 42:73:376.

18. "I Don't Want to Be Nobody nor Nothink except a Chicago Shyster"

1. RTL to Edmund H. Shepard, Chicago, February 3, 1886, LB, 3:5:812.

2. See Reitano, *Tariff Question in the Gilded Age*; L. L. Gould, *Grand Old Party*, 90–93.

3. "Presentation of a Testimonial to President Ammidown," *American Economist*, January 23, 1891, clipping, RTL Collection, Hildene Archives.

4. RTL to Cornelius N. Bliss, Chicago, March 20, 1886, LB, 3:5:820–22. For Robert's views on the tariff, see also RTL to Thomas H. Dudley, May 22, 1888, RTL File, Harlan-Lincoln House Collection.

5. RTL to John Hay, Chicago, March 14, 1886, reel 8, Hay Papers, Brown University.

6. U.S. War Department, form no. 9, voucher no. 22, abstract A, R. N. Batchelder, deputy quartermaster general, receipt to Robert T. Lincoln, June 30, 1885, RTL Collection, Phillips Exeter Academy; "Robert Lincoln's Sale of Horses," *Chicago Tribune*, August 11, 1887, 5.

7. "Fred Grant," *Chicago Tribune*, October 13, 1885, 8.

8. "Those Rebel Flags," *New York Times*, January 13, 1888, 2.

9. Mentor, "Robert Todd Lincoln," *Los Angeles Times*, May 21, 1887, 10.

10. Ibid.

11. "Wabash Repairs," *New York Times*, March 11, 1887, 2; "The Burlington Beaten," *New York Times*, March 13, 1888, 3; Onstot, *Pioneers of Menard and Mason Counties*, 176; Gresham, *Life of Walter Q. Gresham*, 1:409–14.

12. Harry J. Dunbaugh, "Robert Todd Lincoln: Lawyer, Executive, Public Servant," paper read before the Fortnightly, May 2, 1962, folder 2, RTL Papers, CHM. For Abraham Lincoln's mechanical inclinations and talents, see Emerson, *Lincoln the Inventor*.

13. Dunlevy, "Robert Todd Lincoln," 322.

14. Ibid., 321–22.

15. Mentor, "Robert Todd Lincoln," *Los Angeles Times*, May 21, 1887, 10.

16. Ibid.

17. RTL to Horace Porter, April 19, 1882, LB, 6:8:372.

18. RTL to H. F. Eames, June 23 and 27, 1881, and RTL to Horace Porter, July 1, 1881,

LB, 4:6:448–49, 486, 493. See also Robert's statement of real-estate accounts, year ending June 30, 1881, LB, 5:7:98–100.

19. Robert's personal real estate figures and transactions—many of which have been cited in previous chapters—fill voluminous pages in his letterpress books. For Robert's interest in Montana investments, see RTL to James Harlan, January 23, 1886, and RTL to Russell B. Harrison, Chicago, January 23, 1886, LB, 3:5:804–5, 806.

20. For letters on the "Chicago" endeavor, see RTL to Commodore John G. Walker, Chicago, June 4, 1887, LB, 3:5:950–51, and to George E. Adams, member of Congress, January 14, 1889, LB, 13:19:102.

21. For example, see "Sons of Harvard," *Chicago Inter Ocean*, February 25, 1887, 4.

22. "Half a Century," *Chicago Tribune*, July 29, 1885, 2; "Society," *Chicago Tribune*, February 3, 1886, 1.

23. "Events in Society," *Chicago Tribune*, June 9, 1886, 3; "The Week in Chicago," *Chicago Tribune*, February 12, 1888, 3.

24. Mentor, "Robert Todd Lincoln," *Los Angeles Times*, May 21, 1887, 10.

25. "Seeks to Raze Chicago Home of R. T. Lincoln," *Chicago Tribune*, April 15, 1957, 10; "Lincoln Son's Home Facing Wreckers," *New York Times*, January 18, 1959, 44; "Haffa Buys Lincoln Home and Saves It from Wrecker," *Chicago Tribune*, January 31, 1959, 1.

26. Of the many books on Chicago history, see specifically Harper, *Chicago*, 45–51.

27. Goode, *Geographic Background of Chicago*, 1.

28. Sandburg, *Chicago Poems*, 3.

29. For excellent biographies of Cleveland and his presidential policies, see McElroy, *Grover Cleveland*; Jeffers, *Honest President*.

30. "The Great Dead," *Chicago Tribune*, June 28, 1886, 1. Robert also participated in presenting a bust of David Davis—made from a death mask created by sculptor Leonard Volk—to the State of Illinois. "A Valuable Gift to Illinois," *Chicago Tribune*, December 25, 1888, 1.

31. "Chester A. Arthur Dead," *Chicago Tribune*, November 19, 1886, 1; "Messages of Condolence," *New York Times*, November 19, 1886, 2; "Expressing Their Sorrow," *New York Times*, November 20, 1886, 3. Robert Lincoln also made a similar speech extolling his dead chief at a monument-dedication ceremony in 1903 in Chester Arthur's birthplace, Fairfield, Vermont. RTL to William E. Chandler, January 23, 1903, and RTL to Governor William Stickney, June 16, 1903, LB, 36:61:284–85, 422; "Memorial to Arthur," *New York Tribune*, August 21, 1903, 5; Chandler, *President Chester A. Arthur*, 42.

32. "Bloomington in Morning," *New York Times*, June 29, 1886, 5; "Among the Dead," *Chicago Inter Ocean*, June 30, 1886, 6; W. L. King, *Lincoln's Manager*, 307; "Ready for the Funeral: How General Arthur Will Be Buried," *New York Tribune*, November 22, 1886, 1.

33. "A True, Warm Friend," *Chicago Tribune*, December 27, 1886, 5.

34. "The Meeting Last Night" and "The Lost Leader," *Chicago Tribune*, December 30, 1886, 1, 4.

35. RTL to R. S. Tuthill, Chicago, December 29, 1886, and RTL to John Sherman, December 29, 1886, LB, 3:5:883, 884; "Gen. Logan's Last Resting Place," *Chicago Tribune*, February 26, 1887, 1; Logan, *Reminiscences of a Soldier's Wife*, 432.

36. "Can Lincoln Get There?" *Chicago Tribune*, January 6, 1887, 3.

37. "Robert T. Lincoln's Candidacy," *Chicago Tribune*, January 11, 1887, 3.

38. "Lincoln Not Seeking the Office" and "A Friendly Feeling for Lincoln," *Chicago Tribune*, January 8, 1887, 3, and January 10, 1887, 2.

39. For example, see "Lincoln Not Seeking the Office," *Chicago Tribune*, January 8, 1887, 3.

40. RTL to President Grover Cleveland, Chicago, April 12, 1888, LB, 13:19:57–58; "Illinois Gets the Prize," *New York Times*, May 1, 1888, 5.

41. Power, *History of an Attempt*, 88–91; N. Hill, "Transformation of the Lincoln Tomb," 46–47.

42. "President Lincoln's Remains," *Chicago Inter Ocean*, April 14, 1887, 3; "Illinois' Hallowed Spot," *Chicago Inter Ocean*, April 15, 1887, 1; "Abraham Lincoln's Body," *Chicago Tribune*, April 15, 1887, 1; "Lincoln's Secret Burial," *Chicago Inter Ocean*, April 16, 1887, 2.

43. Martha Freeman Esmond to Julia Boyd, Chicago, October 23, 1887, in Herma Clark, "When Chicago Was Young," *Chicago Tribune*, September 6, 1936, E4; "Chicago's Lincoln Statue," *New York Times*, October 20, 1887, 1; "The Lincoln Statue," *Chicago Tribune*, October 22, 1887, 4; "Lincoln in Bronze," *New York Times*, October 23, 1887, 3; "The Martyr President," *Chicago Tribune*, October 23, 1887, 9.

44. Quit-claim deed between Mary Lincoln and RTL, April 16, 1874, Lincoln Collection, ALPL. For a complete study of the Lincoln Home, see Temple, *By Square and Compass*. For an interesting study of Robert as owner, see Hickey, "'Own the House Till It Ruins Me.'"

45. RTL to Lyman Trumbull, Chicago, April 17, 1870, unprocessed collection, Trumbull Family Papers.

46. RTL to David Davis, Chicago, January 21, 1868, folder A-109, box 7, DDFP; RTL to Lyman Trumbull, Chicago, April 17, 1870, unprocessed collection, Trumbull Family Papers; RTL to George Harlow, February 26, 1875, LB, 3:4:333.

47. RTL to George Harlow, May 3, 1873, LB, 3:4:238. Robert responded to another offer by a private citizen in 1882 by stating he had no "intention of parting with" the house. RTL to Benjamin Richardson, March 20, 1883, LB, 8:11:518.

48. RTL to George Harlow, March 31, April 28, and May 2, 1877, LB, 3:5:508–9, 515–16, 519–20.

49. RTL to Clinton Conkling, April 30, 1877, LB, 3:5:517–18.

50. RTL to J. C. Power, May 18, 1878, LB, 3:5:613.

51. RTL to Clinton Conkling, July 30, August 12, and 25, 1879, LB, 3:5:713, 715, 716; RTL to O. M. Hatch, August 25, 1879, LB, 3:5:717; and RTL to J. C. Power, February 28, 1880, LB, 3:5:728; "The Lincoln Monument," *New York Times*, August 1, 1879, 2.

52. RTL to Clinton Conkling, July 26 and November 27, 1878, LB, 3:5:628, 649–50. See also Temple, *By Square and Compass*, 168–70.

53. Osborn H. Oldroyd's book *Lincoln Memorial* is a compilation of reminiscences about Abraham Lincoln by his friends and acquaintances. It was then and remains today a significant historical contribution to Lincoln scholarship.

54. RTL to Clinton Conkling, January 31 and March 3, 1887, LB, 3:5:914, 926.

55. *Journal of the Senate of the Thirty-Third General Assembly of the State of Illinois*, 422, 426; Oldroyd, *Lincoln Memorial*, viii; Hickey, "'Own the House Till It Ruins Me,'" 292–94.

56. RTL to Governor John M. Hamilton, Washington, April 9, 1883, LB, 8:11:569–70, and RTL to James McCartney, June 9, 1884, LB, 11:17:348–49.

57. RTL to Clinton Conkling, April 30, April 30 (separate letter of same date), and June 21, 1887, and January 11, 1888, LB, 3:5:940–41; 942, 962; 13:19:27.

58. RTL to Governor Richard J. Oglesby, Chicago, July 21, 1887, LB, 3:5:978; RTL to Clinton Conkling, July 21, 1887, LB, 3:5:979–80; "Lincoln Homestead," chapter 82a, in Hurb, *Revised Statutes of the State of Illinois, 1887*, 854.

59. RTL to Samuel Inglis, superintendent of public instruction, Chicago, February 8, 1897, SC 923, Albert S. Edwards Papers.

60. Albert Edwards to Samuel Inglis, Springfield, November 23, 1896 and February 20, 1897, RTL to Samuel Inglis, superintendent of public instruction, Chicago, February 8, 1897, and RTL to Lincoln Homestead Trustees endorsing appointment of Albert S. Edwards, February 1897, SC 923, Albert S. Edwards Papers. See also RTL to Governor Richard Yates, December 5, 1900, LB, 34:57:365–66; RTL to Alfred Bayliss, January 13, 1901, LB, 34:57:483; RTL to Charles S. Deneen, December 17, 1904, LB, 37:63:508–10.

61. Mary Lincoln to Sarah Bush Lincoln, Chicago, December 19, 1867, in Turner and Turner, *Mary Todd Lincoln*, 464–65.

62. RTL to A. M. Jones, Springfield, Illinois, March 4 and 8, 1873, pp. 11 and 21, letterpress 1:11, 21, Records of Isham, Lincoln, and Beale law firm.

63. The entire project cost about $300, but the town had already raised money and so asked Robert to pay only the difference. Senator Horace Clark to RTL, February 8, 1881, Joseph C. Glenn to RTL, Mattoon, Illinois, February 16, 1881, and "Thomas and Sarah Lincoln," undated clipping, *Pullman Journal*, file 2, cont. 1, part 2, RTLFP; "A Monument for Lincoln's Father," *Chicago Inter Ocean*, February 24, 1881, 3; RTL to W. B. Dunlap, May 7, 1881, LB, 4:6:215; "The Thomas Lincoln Monument," *Chicago Inter Ocean*, May 13, 1881, 3; "Appreciation of Robert Todd Lincoln."

64. RTL to Governor James A. Mount, March 9 and April 19, 1900, LB, 34:56:192, 207; "Appreciation of Robert Todd Lincoln."

65. H. L. Stoddard, *As I Knew Them*, 157. Grant's son Ulysses S. Grant III told Robert Lincoln's first biographer, John S. Goff, that he did not think the "father's son ticket" was under serious consideration at the time or else he would have remembered it, which he did not. Grant to Goff, June 25, 1958, in Goff, *Robert Todd Lincoln*, 168.

66. "Robert T. Lincoln," *Chicago Inter Ocean*, March 13, 1888, 6.

67. "Booming for Bob," *Chicago Tribune*, April 13, 1886, 9.

68. Untitled article, *Chicago Tribune*, April 28, 1886, 3.

69. "The Lincoln Movement," *New York Times*, March 9, 1887, 10.

70. "Robert T. Lincoln," *Chicago Tribune*, July 16, 1887, 2.

71. "High Praise for Lincoln," *Chicago Tribune*, July 23, 1887, 12.

72. "Notable People of the Day," 305.

73. "The Feeling for Lincoln," *Chicago Tribune*, August 31, 1887, 1.

74. RTL to Committee, Lincoln Club of Rochester, New York, January 13, 1888, LB, 13:19:28–29. Robert gave a similar refusal to a Columbus, Ohio, meeting a week later. RTL to J. B. Foraker, January 27, 1888, copy, Goff Papers, Hildene Archives, original in Historical and Philosophical Society of Ohio.

75. "A Talk with Robert Lincoln," *Chicago Tribune*, September 25, 1887, 9; "Starting a Lincoln Boom," *New York Times*, October 25, 1887, 2.

76. Lincoln to A. K. Rodgers, January 31, 1888, folder 1, RTL Papers, CHM; "Mr. Lincoln Again Declines," *Chicago Tribune*, March 12, 1888, 2.

77. RTL to Edwards Pierrepont, Chicago, June 28, 1887, RTL Papers, ACPL.

78. RTL to John Wannamaker, May 20, 1888, RTL Papers, ACPL; "Robert Lincoln Talks," *Chicago Tribune*, June 22, 1888, 5.

79. "Ending the Long Fight," *New York Times*, June 26, 1888, 2.

80. "Robert Lincoln Talks," *Chicago Tribune*, June 22, 1888, 5.

81. "Ex-Secretary Lincoln Returns," *New York Times*, August 20, 1888, 8.

82. "To Enter the Fight," *Los Angeles Times*, August 20, 1888, 5; RTL to J. S. Clarkson,

vice chairman, Republican National Committee, August 27, 1888, LB, 13:19:72; RTL to William Walter Phelps, September 8, 1888, LB, 13:19:78; "Republican Rallies in Illinois," *Chicago Tribune*, October 1, 1888, 2; "The Enthusiasm Damped," *New York Times*, October 19, 1888, 5; "Just Outside the City," *Chicago Tribune*, November 4, 1888, 6.

19. "As Much a Man of Destiny as His Lamented Father"

1. "Minister to England," *Chicago Tribune*, March 28, 1889, 5. A similar story was published in the *Omaha (NE) Bee* of the same day, although the reporter claimed to have informed Lincoln of the appointment himself, to which Robert replied, "How the appointment came to me is beyond my knowledge or belief." "Taken by Surprise," *Omaha (NE) Bee*, March 28, 1889, 1.

2. "Minister to England," *Chicago Tribune*, March 28, 1889, 5. The citizens and politicians of Illinois were indeed pleased at the nomination. On the day it was announced, members of the Illinois state Senate and House of Representatives unanimously endorsed Lincoln's nomination as a "wise and able selection." Joint Resolution, "Robert T. Lincoln, Minister to England," adopted in the senate and concurred by the house, March 28, 1889, *Laws of the State of Illinois, Passed by the Thirty-Sixth General Assembly*, 369–70.

3. Cullom, *Fifty Years of Public Service*, 126; Hoar, *Autobiography of Seventy Years*, 2:216–17; "Senator Farwell Angry," *New York Times*, April 7, 1889, 1; "Not a Snub to Farwell," *Chicago Tribune*, December 29, 1890, 1; "Senator Farwell's Quarrel," *Chicago Tribune*, December 31, 1890, 4.

4. "His Own Selection: President Surprises the Politicians," *Boston Herald*, March 28, 1889, clipping, Goff Papers.

5. "The Diplomatic Appointments," March 28, 1889, clipping, Goff Papers. See also "Abraham Lincoln's Son," *Hartford (CT) Courant*, March 29, 1889, 4.

6. "The Diplomatic Appointments," March 28, 1889, clipping, Goff Papers.

7. "His Own Selection: President Surprises the Politicians," *Boston Herald*, March 28, 1889, clipping, Goff Papers.

8. Henry Adams to Charles Milnes Gaskell, Washington, April 21, 1889, in Ford, *Letters of Henry Adams*, 398.

9. John Hay to RTL, March 27, 1889, Hay, *Letters of John Hay and Extracts from Diary*, 2:163.

10. Theodore Roosevelt to Henry Cabot Lodge, March 27, 1889, and Theodore Roosevelt to Cecil Arthur Spring Rice, New York, April 14, 1889, in E. E. Morison, *Letters of Theodore Roosevelt*, 1:155, 157.

11. Hamlin interview, "Our Minister to England," *Boston Globe*, May 31, 1889, 12.

12. "Ministers Lincoln and Egan," *New York Times*, March 29, 1889, 5; "The New American Minister to England," *Graphic* (London), April 20, 1889; "Letters from England," *Christian Advocate* (New York), 64, no. 17, April 25, 1889, 270.

13. "Lincoln a Man of Talent," *Boston Globe*, March 28, 1889, 4.

14. Clarence King to John Hay, New York, April 17, 1889, reel 8, Hay Papers, Brown University.

15. Harrison, *Stormy Years*, 276.

16. Robert T. Lincoln, appointment as envoy extraordinary and minister plenipotentiary to Great Britain, March 30, 1889, OV 3, cont. 1, part 1, RTLFP; "These Passed Muster," *St. Paul (MN) Globe*, March 31, 1889, 5.

17. "Our Envoy to England," *Chicago Tribune*, April 5, 1889, 2.

18. RTL to Edwards Pierrepont, Chicago, March 30, 1889, RTL papers, CHM.

19. Mrs. M. L. Brown to Mary Harlan Lincoln, Washington, March 28, 1889, letter file A, RTL Papers, ALPL.

20. RTL to Frank R. Thompson, April 18, 1889, LB, 13:19:120; "Robert T. Lincoln in Town," *New York Times*, May 14, 1889, 8.

21. "Dinner to Mr. Lincoln," *Hartford (CT) Courant*, May 8, 1889, 1; "The Minister to England," *New York Times*, May 10, 1889, 1; Blair, *History of the Chicago Club*, 34, 49.

22. RTL to E. H. Halford, May 11, 1889, reel 20, series 1, Harrison Papers; "Ready to Sail for England," *Chicago Tribune*, May 14, 1889, 2.

23. Richard Derby to John Hay, New York, April 25, 1889, reel 4, Hay Papers, Brown University; "Dinner to Robert T. Lincoln," *New York Times*, May 15, 1889, 2; "Minister Lincoln Given a Dinner," *Chicago Tribune*, May 15, 1889, 3.

24. Inman & International Steamship Company, list of salon passengers, *City of Paris*, Wednesday, May 15, 1889, letter file A, RTL Papers, ALPL; "Starting for Europe," *New York Times*, May 15, 1889, 8.

25. Josie Blicq to "My dear friend Nellie," May 29, 1889, Josie A. Blicq MSS, Lincoln Collection, Hay Library, Brown University.

26. "Affairs in Foreign Lands," *New York Times*, May 19, 1889, 5; "Honors for Mr. Lincoln," *Chicago Tribune*, May 23, 1889, 1; "Mr. Lincoln in London," *New York Times*, May 23, 1889, 5; "The New American Minister," *London Times*, May 23, 1889, 9.

27. "Mr. Lincoln at His Post," *New York Times*, May 24, 1889, 1; "To Visit the Queen Today," *Chicago Tribune*, May 25, 1889, 5; untitled article, *Penny Illustrated Paper* (London), June 1, 1889, 6.

28. Willson, *America's Ambassadors to England, 1785–1928*, 398.

29. Waddington, *Letters of a Diplomat's Wife, 1883–1900*, 380–81.

30. Hoar, *Autobiography of Seventy Years*, 2:226; Smith, *Colonel*, 43.

31. RTL to John Hay, London, May 27, 1889, reel 8, Hay Papers, Brown University; Norton, "Four Men Whom I Saw in London," 1292; Dingley, *Life and Times of Nelson Dingley, Jr.*, 361.

32. I. Anderson, *Larz Anderson*, 73–75; "White House Ladies to Visit Europe," *Chicago Tribune*, March 24, 1891, 1; "For a Summer in Europe" and "Latest News From Europe," *Sun* (New York), June 2 and 21, 1891, 1, 1.

33. Logan, *Reminiscences*, 438.

34. Allen and Sachtleben, "Across Asia on Bicycle," 84.

35. I. Anderson, *Larz Anderson*, 76–77.

36. Ibid., 75.

37. The RTL Papers at the Abraham Lincoln Presidential Library in Springfield, Illinois, has two boxes containing thousands of calling cards and invitations to and from Minister and Mrs. Lincoln for such events.

38. RTL to "my dear Colonel," London, June 17, 1889, RTL papers, ACPL; "Americans Abroad Celebrate," *Chicago Tribune*, July 5, 1889, 5; "Dining the Engineers," *Chicago Tribune*, June 14, 1889, 1; "Russia and the Balkans," *New York Times*, July 16, 1889, 1.

39. *Star* (London), quoted in untitled article, *St. Paul (MN) Globe*, August 12, 1889, 4.

40. Maybrick's case, famous in itself, has gained renewed interest in recent years after it was claimed her husband, cotton merchant James Maybrick, was in fact Jack the Ripper, and his murder caused the end of the Ripper's killing spree. Numerous books have been published on the Florence Maybrick murder case, including her memoir, *Mrs. Maybrick's Own Story*. A few of the more recent titles include: Blake, *Mrs. Maybrick*; Graham, Emmas, and Skinner, *Last Victim*; Ryan, *Poisoned Life of Mrs. Maybrick*.

41. James G, Blaine to Benjamin Harrison, Bar Harbor, Maine, August 23, 1889, in Volwiler, *Correspondence between Benjamin Harrison and James G. Blaine*, 77.

42. James G. Blaine to RTL, Bar Harbor, Maine, August 21, 1889, and RTL Lincoln to Blaine, London, August 22, 1889, reel 22, series 1, Harrison Papers.

43. "Mrs. Maybrick Guilty," *New York Times*, August 8, 1889, 5; "Flora Maybrick Saved," *New York Times*, August 23, 1889, 2.

44. RTL to Mary A. Dodge, London, February 29, 1892, RTL Collection, Hildene Archives.

45. RTL to James G. Blaine, September 19, 1889, LB, 14:20:55.

46. James G. Blaine to RTL, April 18, 1891, in Clark Bell, "American Government," 588.

47. James G. Blaine to RTL, March 7, 1892, in ibid., 592–93, and in Maybrick, *Mrs. Maybrick's Own Story*, 249–51. See also Clark Bell, "Rights of American Girls Who Marry Foreigners," 74.

48. For an excellent compilation of the multiple diplomatic dispatches between Blaine and Lincoln in the Maybrick case, see C. Bell, "American Government," 585–95. The Maybrick case is not mentioned in Blaine's official papers relating to foreign relations submitted yearly to the president and to Congress.

49. Henry White to John Hay, September 4, 1889, reel 2, Hay Papers, Brown University.

50. RTL to James G. Blaine, September 19, 1889, LB, 14:20:57–58.

51. Ibid., LB, 14:20:56.

52. Goff, *Robert Todd Lincoln*, 194.

53. RTL to James G. Blaine, n.d. [September 19, 1889?], LB, 14:20:58.

54. Ellen H. Simpson to Robert and Mary Lincoln, Philadelphia, March 7, 1890, letter file K, RTL Papers, ALPL.

55. The height measurements of Jack, Mamie, and Jessie still are marked on the door in the Harlan house in Mount Pleasant, Iowa. McMurtry, "Harlan-Lincoln Tradition at Iowa Wesleyan College," 4.

56. Entry for August 14, 1887, Jack Lincoln notebook, item 1887.2, RTL Collection, Hildene Archives.

57. J. Allen Boteler to Jessie Lincoln Randolph, April 2, 1934, Lincoln Collection, ALPL.

58. C. N. Fessenden interview, "Jack's Bright Career," *Chicago Tribune*, February 27, 1890, 1.

59. Baldwin, "Personal Experience with Jack Lincoln," 97. See also Poole, *Bridge*, 15–16, 188.

60. Isham interview, "Young Abraham Lincoln," *New York Times*, February 28, 1890, 3; Edward S. Isham interview, "Jack Lincoln Is Dead," *Chicago Tribune*, March 6, 1890, 5; William G. Beale interview, "Jack's Bright Career," *Chicago Tribune*, February 27, 1890, 1.

61. Beale interview, "Jack's Bright Career," *Chicago Tribune*, February 27, 1890, 1.

62. Abraham "Jack" Lincoln to James Harlan, Washington, D.C., February 23, 1881, photocopy, Hickey File.

63. Harriet G. Walker, "Young Abraham Lincoln," *New York Times*, March 9, 1890, 2.

64. William E. Chandler, memoriam to Jack Lincoln, April 14, 1891, unnamed clipping, letter file K, RTL Papers, ALPL, and in RTL Collection, Hildene Archives.

65. "The War Secretary's Sailor Boy," *New York Times*, May 12, 1884, 2; "Robert Lincoln," *Chicago Tribune*, May 31, 1884, 13. The reference is to W. S. Gilbert's ballad "The Yarn of the 'Nancy Bell.'"

66. "School Work by Jack Lincoln," December 8, 1886, photocopy, Hickey File.

67. Albert T. Ryan to Mary Harlan Lincoln, Washington, March 7, 1890, letter file K, RTL Papers, ALPL. See also "The Death of Young Abraham Lincoln," *Frank Leslie's*

Illustrated Newspaper, March 22, 1890, 148. Ryan especially remembered that he and Jack opened their own card-printing business of "Ryan and Lincoln."

68. Jack's rock collection is located in the Harlan-Lincoln Home Collection, as is his tennis net, which he gave to a friend to borrow in 1889 until Jack returned from London. McMurtry, "Harlan-Lincoln Tradition," 7.

69. *Mt. Pleasant (IA) Journal*, August 28, 1884, quoted in Juhl, *James Harlan and Robert Todd Lincoln Families' Mount Pleasant Memories*, 30.

70. "Interesting Story Brought to Light," n.d., clipping, Lincoln Collection, ACPL; "Few Descendants of Lincoln Live," *(Springfield) Illinois State Register*, February 28, 1937, 8.

71. When once discussing the ease with which a person could emulate President Lincoln's signature, Robert Lincoln stated, "This I knew myself because several times as a boy to amuse myself I used to write his ordinary signature so well that I think it would have passed muster with himself." RTL to Isaac Markens, January 5, 1917, folder 5, RTL Papers, CHM.

72. C. Hamilton, *Great Forgers and Famous Fakes*, 34–36.

73. E. R. Donehoo, interview, "A Bright Boy: Young Abe Lincoln's Youthful Modesty and Manliness," *Pittsburgh (PA) Commercial Gazette*, March 6, 1890, clipping, RTL Collection, Hildene Archives.

74. Ibid.

75. RTL to James G. Blaine, telegrams, September 1 and 11, 1889, reel 156, vol. 163, Dispatches from United States Ministers to Great Britain, 1889–93, National Archives, copies, Goff Papers; "Jack Lincoln Is Dead," *Chicago Tribune*, March 6, 1890, 5. Minister Lincoln left London on September 2 and returned on September 10.

76. One family letter suggests that Jack's cut may not have been an accident but the fault of his teacher, Madame Passa, using corporal punishment against her students. "I have had a great fear to [write to you] lest you might in some way blame Madame Passa," Minnie Chandler wrote to Mary Harlan Lincoln after Jack's death. "It is so hard to understand why the *rod* should be so applied." Minnie Chandler to Mary Lincoln, August 13, 1890, Chandler Papers.

77. RTL to James G. Blaine, November 2, 1889, telegram, reel 156, vol. 163, Dispatches from United States Ministers to Great Britain, 1889–93, National Archives, copies, Goff Papers.

78. Robert T. Lincoln, interview, "Minister Lincoln's Son Ill," *Chicago Tribune*, November 10, 1889, 1; RTL to Henry White, Versailles, France, November 8, 1889, Henry White Papers, Columbia University; RTL to James G. Blaine, Versailles, France, November 14, 1889, reel 11, General Correspondence, Blaine Family Papers.

79. "Saved from the Under-Tow," *New York Times*, September 11, 1881, 8.

80. RTL to John Hay, March 23, 1882, reel 8, Hay Papers, Brown University; RTL to "my dear Aunt," Chicago, November 4, 1884, HM 39283, RTL papers, Huntington Library; Juhl, *James Harlan and Robert Todd Lincoln Families' Mount Pleasant Memories*, 32.

81. RTL to John Hay, Versailles, France, December 20, 1889, reel 8, Hay Papers, Brown University; RTL to Robert McCormick, Versailles, France, November 26, 1889, folder 3, box 238, RTL Papers, CHM.

82. RTL to Robert McCormick, Versailles, France, November 28 and 30 and December 1, 1889, folder 3, box 238, RTL Papers, CHM; RTL to James G. Blaine, December 7, 1889, telegram, reel 156, vol. 163, Dispatches from United States Ministers to Great Britain, 1889–93, National Archives, copies, Goff Papers; RTL to James G. Blaine, London, December 12, 1889, LB, 14:20:77–78.

83. RTL to James G. Blaine, December 16, 1889, telegram, reel 156, vol. 163, Dispatches

from United States Ministers to Great Britain, 1889–93, National Archives, copies, Goff Papers; RTL to Robert McCormick, Versailles, France, December 15, 1889, folder 3, box 238, RTL Papers, CHM. Lincoln returned to Versailles on December 16.

84. RTL to James G. Blaine, December 30, 1889, telegram, reel 156, vol. 163, Dispatches from United States Ministers to Great Britain, 1889–93, National Archives, copies, Goff Papers; "Young Lincoln Growing Better," *Chicago Tribune*, December 27, 1889, 5; "Minister Lincoln's Son," *Chicago Tribune*, December 29, 1889, 4; John Hay to RTL, Washington, December 22, 1889, in Hay, *Letters of John Hay*, 2:184.

85. RTL to John Hay, London, January 7, 1890, reel 8, Hay Papers, Brown University; RTL to Robert McCormick, Versailles, France, January 10, 1890, and RTL to Eugene Hale, London, January 21, 1890, folder 3, box 238, RTL Papers, CHM; RTL to James G. Blaine, January 7 and 9, 1890, telegram, reel 157, vol. 163, Dispatches from United States Ministers to Great Britain, 1889–93, National Archives, copies, Goff Papers.

86. RTL to Robert McCormick, Versailles, France, January 12, 1890, folder 3, box 238, RTL Papers, CHM.

87. H. Webster Jones to Robert McCormick, Versailles, France, January 13, 1890, ibid.

88. RTL to Henry White, Paris, January 13, 1890, RTL Papers, ALPL, also in "Death in the Family," 1.

89. Ibid., 1, 4.

90. Mary "Mamie" Lincoln to Mrs. Robert McCormick, folder 3, box 238, RTL Papers, CHM.

91. H. Webster Jones to Robert McCormick, Versailles, France, January 13, 15, and 19, 1890, ibid.

92. For a description of the trip, see "Young Abraham Lincoln's Illness," *Chicago Tribune*, January 20, 1890, 5.

93. Charles Isham to Robert McCormick, Versailles, France, January 15, 1890, and RTL to Eugene Hale, London, January 21, 1890, and H. Webster Jones to Robert McCormick, London, January 28, 1890, folder 3, box 238, RTL Papers, CHM; RTL to James G. Blaine, January 18 and 28, 1890, telegrams, reel 157, vol. 163, Dispatches from United States Ministers to Great Britain, 1889–93, National Archives, copies, Goff Papers.

94. RTL to Robert McCormick, London, February 5, 1890, folder 3, box 238, RTL Papers, CHM.

95. RTL to John Hay, London, February 14, 1890, reel 8, Hay Papers, Brown University.

96. Isham interview, "Young Abraham Lincoln," *New York Times*, February 28, 1890, 3.

97. H. Webster Jones to Robert McCormick, London, February 15 and 21, 1890, folder 3, box 238, RTL Papers, CHM.

98. "Young Abraham Lincoln," *New York Times*, February 28, 1890, 3; "Young Lincoln Not Dead," *New York Times*, February 28, 1890, 1.

99. "Jack Lincoln Is Dead," *Chicago Tribune*, March 6, 1890, 5.

100. Letter of Henry White to his wife, quoted in Nevins, *Henry White*, 73. See also Henry White to James G. Blaine, March 5, 1890, telegram, reel 157, vol. 163, Dispatches from United States Ministers to Great Britain, 1889–93, National Archives, copies, Goff Papers.

101. Condolence letters are located in letter file K and calling cards and funeral cards located in box "Cards Left at American Embassy during RTL Term," RTL Papers, ALPL.

102. "Young Lincoln Is Dead," *Washington Post*, March 6, 1890, 1; "Young Lincoln's Death," *New York Times*, March 6, 1890, 1; "Sympathy for Minister Lincoln," *Chicago Tribune*, March 7, 1890, 5.

103. Abraham Lincoln II death certificate, copy, in Henderson, "Abraham Lincoln II," 55.

104. H. Webster Jones, letter, quoted in "Illness of Master Jack Lincoln," *Chicago Elite News*, February 15, 1890, clipping in folder 3, box 238, RTL papers, CHM; Edward Isham, interview, "Jack Lincoln Dead," *Boston Globe*, March 6, 1890, 8; "Jack Lincoln Is Dead," *Chicago Tribune*, March 6, 1890, 5; editorial, *Fort Worth (TX) Gazette*, March 24, 1890, 4.

105. Shutes, *Lincoln and the Doctors*, 127; Dr. Irving S. Cutter to Paul Angle, August 21, 1939, folder 3, box 238, RTL Papers, CHM. John A. Menaugh, "Death of Abraham Lincoln II: How the Emancipator's Grandson Passed," *Chicago Tribune*, March 3, 1940, J1.

106. William G. Beale to Mary Harlan Lincoln, n.d. [probably March 6 or 71890], letter file K, RTL Papers, ALPL (emphasis in original). The *Washington Post* reported that Robert "expressed a very earnest sorrow that he had permitted himself to be influenced to accept the position." "Young Lincoln Is Dead," *Washington Post*, March 6, 1890, 1.

107. Ellen H. Simpson to Robert and Mary Lincoln, Philadelphia, March 7, 1890, letter file K, RTL Papers, ALPL; "Jack Lincoln Is Dead," *Chicago Tribune*, March 6, 1890, 5; "Death of Abraham Lincoln," *Sun* (New York), March 6, 1890, 3; "Funeral of Young Abraham Lincoln," *Chicago Tribune*, March 8, 1890, 2; untitled newspaper clipping, box "Correspondence," RTL Papers, ALPL. That the Lincolns were considered Presbyterians, were regular attendees at the Second Presbyterian Church in Chicago (where Robert was a trustee but not officially a member) and especially that Jack was baptized are items previously unknown.

108. Henry White to James G. Blaine, March 6, 1890, telegram, reel 157, vol. 163, Dispatches from United States Ministers to Great Britain, 1889–93, National Archives, copies, Goff Papers; "Young Lincoln's Funeral," *New York Times*, March 8, 1890, 1; "Young Lincoln's Grave," *New York Press*, March 8, 1890, clipping, RTL Collection, Hildene Archives; "The Late Mr. Abraham Lincoln," n.d., clipping, box "Correspondence," RTL Papers, ALPL.

109. Unfortunately, White did not tell his wife exactly what Lincoln said about his mother. Henry White to his wife, quoted in Nevins, *Henry White*, 73. The original letter could not be located in the Henry White Papers in Columbia University or the Library of Congress.

110. "Sympathy for Minister Lincoln," *Chicago Tribune*, March 7, 1890, 5.

111. RTL to John Hay, London, April 8, 1890, reel 8, Hay Papers, Brown University.

112. RTL to John Nicolay, London, April 8, 1890, folder January–June 1890, box 5, Nicolay Papers.

113. Untitled editorial, *American*, March 5, 1890, clipping, Abraham Lincoln II memoriams, RTL Collection, Hildene Archives.

114. Untitled editorial, *Washington Post*, March 6, 1890, 4.

115. RTL to Edward M. Paxson, April 5, 1890, in "Abraham 'Jack' Lincoln, II—1873–1890," 3.

20. "Minister Lincoln Was Quietness Personified"

1. "President Lincoln's Widow," *New York Tribune*, May 22, 1875, 6.

2. Edward Isham, interview, "Distressed by the Sad News," *Chicago Tribune*, March 6, 1890, 5.

3. E. R. Donehoo, interview, "A Bright Boy: Young Abe Lincoln's Youthful Modesty and Manliness," *Pittsburgh (PA) Commercial Gazette*, March 6, 1890, clipping, RTL Collection, Hildene Archives. See also "Minister Lincoln's Great Loss," *Chicago Tribune*, March 6, 1890, 4.

4. "Mr. Lincoln's Future," *New York Times*, March 7, 1890, 1; "Minister Lincoln Will Not Resign," *Chicago Tribune*, March 11, 1890, 5.

5. RTL to James G. Blaine, London, March 21, 1890, reel 11, Blaine Family Papers; RTL to James G. Blaine, March 21, 1890, telegram, LB, 14:20:85, also in reel 157, vol. 163, Dispatches from United States Ministers to Great Britain, 1889–93, National Archives, copies, Goff Papers. See also Henry White to John Hay, March 22, 1890, reel 12, Hay Papers, Brown University.

6. RTL to James G. Blaine, London, March 21, 1890, reel 11, Blaine Family Papers.

7. RTL to John Hay, London, April 8, 1890, reel 8, Hay Papers, Brown University.

8. RTL to James G. Blaine, April 22, 1890, LB, 14:20:87–88.

9. "Mrs. Robert T. Lincoln in the City," *Chicago Tribune*, August 16, 1890, 3; "Mrs. Lincoln Reaches Home," *Chicago Inter Ocean*, August 20, 1890, 2.

10. Henry White to John Hay, July 4, 1890, reel 12, Hay Papers, Brown University.

11. RTL to William Walter Phelps, April 21, 1890, HM 27433, RTL Collection, Huntington Library. For a witness recollection of Robert's grief, see also Martha Freeman Esmond to Julia Boyd, Chicago, April 28, 1891, in Herma Clark, "When Chicago Was Young," *Chicago Tribune*, September 17, 1939, G4.

12. RTL to F. M. Williams, London, April 7, 1890, MC 2000.3, folder 12, box 1, George Burt Lincoln Family Papers. The death mask has never been found.

13. The bust of Abraham Lincoln II is now in the collection of the Abraham Lincoln Presidential Library.

14. RTL to John Hay, London, April 8, 1890, reel 8, Hay Papers, Brown University. Reproductions of the portrait of Jack are in the collections of the Abraham Lincoln Presidential Library and Hildene.

15. RTL to O. M. Hatch September 10, 1890, LB, 14:20:146–47, and RTL to Clinton Conkling, September 10, 1890, LB, 14:20:148–49; Lincoln Monument Association resolution, October 18, 1890, box 3, National Lincoln Monument Association Papers, 1885–95. "It is the arrangement I would make, under the peculiar circumstances, if the tomb of my father were, as would usually be the case, in my care, but I trust that it may be understood that I know that the monument was not erected or arranged for such a purpose and that I would abandon the desire if it does not seem proper to each member of the Association that the arrangement should be entered upon," Robert wrote.

16. "Minister Lincoln Arrives in New York with His Son's Remains," *Chicago Tribune*, November 6, 1890, 12; "Passengers on the Ocean," *New York Times*, November 6, 1890, 8; "Robert T. Lincoln at Home," *New York Times*, November 6, 1890, 8.

17. RTL to Clinton Conkling, September 10, 1890, LB, 14:20:146–47.

18. "Mr. Lincoln's Sad Errand," *New York Times*, November 9, 1890, 1. The *Chicago Tribune* story of the event quoted Lincoln as saying, "My friends, I thank you for being with me here on this sorrowful occasion." "Minister Lincoln's Sad Mission Over," *Chicago Tribune*, November 9, 1890, 9. See also RTL to O. M. Hatch, December 13, 1890, LB, 13:19:135.

19. "Minister Lincoln's Vacation," *New York Times*, January 5, 1891, 1.

20. Willson, *America's Ambassadors to England*, 399–400.

21. See years 1889 to 1893 in *Papers Relating to the Foreign Relations of the United States*.

22. "International Questions," *New York Times*, October 22, 1889, 4; "That New Extradition Treaty," *Chicago Tribune*, January 11, 1890, 2; "After Fleeing Criminals: Extradition Treaty with England Ratified," *New York Times*, February 19, 1890, 1; "Experiences of the Boston Police under the New Treaty with England," *New York Tribune*, November 24, 1891, 3.

23. See the "Report of the Commissioners of the United States" in *International Monetary Conference at Brussels*.

24. For an explanation and examination of gold and silver currency usages throughout the world and their international effects, see Russell, *International Monetary Conferences.*

25. RTL to James G. Blaine, London, August 11, 1891, reel 32, series 1, Harrison Papers.

26. RTL to Samuel Dana Horton, January 24, 1892, Samuel Horton Papers.

27. RTL to James G. Blaine, London, January 27 and May 28, 1892, reels 34 and 35, series 1, Harrison Papers.

28. The extensive correspondence of Minister Lincoln regarding the monetary conference can be found throughout reels 32, 34–36, series 1, Harrison Papers. See also RTL to James G. Blaine, London, February 17, 1892, reel 11, Blaine Family Papers.

29. "Good Will Result," *Chicago Tribune*, October 17, 1892, 2. "Personally I am a believer in bimetallism on some basis to be approved of by the concurrence of those best able to consider the subject," Lincoln stated in October 1892. "For I think that with gold alone as a standard, international currency is inadequate and is likely to become more so. . . . However, I should personally deplore an attempt on the part of the United States alone to adopt the free coinage of silver, without the assistance of those European nations whose aid is essential." "Minister Lincoln Here," *New York Times*, October 17, 1892, 8.

30. Tyler, *Foreign Policy of James G. Blaine*, 302.

31. The Bering Sea issue has been extensively written about, especially as part of Blaine's foreign policy. For excellent treatments, see Tyler, *Foreign Policy of James G. Blaine*, 302–45; Foster, *Diplomatic Memoirs*, 2:20–31; G. Hamilton, *Biography of James G. Blaine*, 659–72; Campbell, "Anglo-American Crisis in the Bering Sea, 1890–1891," 393–414.

32. Lord Salisbury to Sir Julian Pauncefote, March 28, 1890, in Campbell, "Anglo-American Crisis," 398.

33. "Minister Lincoln Arrives in London," *New York Sun*, January 17, 1891, 1; "Behring Sea," *San Francisco Morning Call*, January 29, 1891, 1.

34. RTL to James G. Blaine, August 20 and 23 and September 13, 1890, telegrams, reel 158, Dispatches from United States Ministers to Great Britain, 1889–93, National Archives, copies, Goff Papers.

35. For examples of articles about the situation, see "The Bering Sea Dispute," *New York Times*, May 8, 1891, 5; "The Behring Sea Dispute," *New York Sun*, May 29, 1891, 2; "The Bering Sea Letters," *New York Times*, June 2, 1891, 1; "Close Season for Seals," *New York Times*, June 9, 1891, 4. For some of Lincoln's correspondence and updates to Blaine, see RTL to James G. Blaine, January 24, June 6 and 10, 1891, and January 6, 1892, in *Papers Relating to the Foreign Relations of the United States*, (1892), 533–38. See also RTL to Blaine, May 30, 1891, reel 31, series 1, Harrison Papers; Crapol, *James G. Blaine*, 131–32.

36. The Monroe Doctrine, formulated in 1823 by President James Monroe, articulated three main concepts regarding American policy in the Western Hemisphere: separate spheres of influence for the Americas and Europe and noncolonization and nonintervention by European countries in the Western Hemisphere.

37. James G. Blaine to Henry White, Washington, December 30, 1889, in *Papers Relating to the Foreign Relations of the United States* (1891), 322.

38. James G. Blaine to RTL, Washington, May 1 and 6, 1890, in *Papers Relating to the Foreign Relations of the United States*, (1891), 337, 339.

39. RTL to James G. Blaine, May 5, 28, and June 25, 1890, in *Papers Relating to the Foreign Relations of the United States*, (1891), 337–38, 340–42.

40. "Admiral Walker's Mission," *New York Sun*, September 12, 1892, 5.

41. For an excellent survey of the dispute, see Cleveland, *Venezuelan Boundary Controversy*. See also Tyler, *Foreign Policy of James G. Blaine*, 80–90; Nevins, *Henry White*, 107–20.

42. "News from Abroad," *Washington, DC, Critic*, February 6, 1891, 1; "Miss Smith

Denies It," *Chicago Tribune*, February 8, 1891, 2; "Lincoln at the Play," *New York Morning Journal*, February 8, 1891, clipping, RTL Collection, Hildene Archives.

43. Martha Freeman Esmond to Julia Boyd, Chicago, April 28, 1891, in Herma Clark, "When Chicago Was Young," *Chicago Tribune*, September 17, 1939, G4; "Mrs. Lincoln Goes Abroad," *Chicago Inter Ocean*, February 26, clipping, RTL Collection, Hildene Archives; "Current Foreign Topics," *New York Times*, March 6, 1891, 5; "Mrs. Lincoln and Daughters," *Sacramento (CA) Record-Union*, March 6, 1891, 1; "American Ladies at Court," *New York Times*, March 14, 1891, 1; untitled article, *New York Sun*, March 14, 1890, 7; "Platform of the Liberals," *Omaha (NE) Bee*, March 14, 1890, 1.

44. "Latest News from Europe," *New York Sun*, June 7, 1891, 1.

45. "The Fourth at Mr. Lincoln's," *New York World*, July 5, 1891, and untitled article, *New York Advertiser*, July 5, 1891, clippings, RTL Collection, Hildene Archives; "Latest News from Europe," *New York Sun*, July 5, 1891, 1; "London's American Colony," *New York Times*, July 26, 1891, 1.

46. For the story of the second secretary vacancy, see Robert McCormick to James G. Blaine, London, May 16, 1890, reel 11, and James G. Blaine to RTL, August 8, 1890, reel 7, Blaine Family Papers; RTL to John Hay, London, June 22 and 26, 1891, reel 8, Hay Papers, Brown University; Robert McCormick to James G. Blaine, July 23, 1891, reel 160, Dispatches from United States Ministers to Great Britain, 1889–93, National Archives, copies, Goff Papers; "Mr. McCormick Coming Home," *New York World*, May 31, 1891, clipping, RTL Collection, Hildene Archives.

47. Larz was an excellent secretary and in many ways treated as a son by Minister Lincoln. "He is one of the finest types of the American gentleman I have ever seen," Robert later wrote to Larz's father. When General Anderson died in Switzerland in 1892, Lincoln offered Larz not only time off the job but also any funds he may have needed for the trip. "You must for the present devote yourself to your family, without regard for the Legation," Lincoln wrote to Larz. RTL to Nicholas Anderson, August 1891, quoted in I. Anderson, *Larz Anderson*, 69; RTL to Larz Anderson, September 19, 1892, in I. Anderson, *Letters and Journals of General Nicholas Longworth Anderson*, 35.

48. "Remorse and Suicide," *Chicago Herald*, December 17, 1891, and "Lincoln's Thieving Butler," *Chicago Inter Ocean*, December 19, 1891, clippings, RTL Collection, Hildene Archives; "Lincoln's Butler's Suicide," *New York Times*, December 19, 1891, 1; Martin, *Things I Remember*, 197–98.

49. Minister Robert T. Lincoln London Visitors Books, 1889–93, 3 vols., 1975.56.1–3, Hildene Archives. See also John Hay to RTL, May 2, 1891, reel 3, Hay Papers, LOC; Henry Adams to Elizabeth Cameron, London, October 1, 1892, in Ford, *Letters of Henry Adams*, 23; Anderson, *Letters and Journals of General Nicholas Longworth Anderson*, 307; Anderson, *Larz Anderson*, 97; "Lincoln and Isham," *New York Journal*, May 3, 1891, and untitled article, *New York World*, May 31, 1891, and "Astor's Honeymoon," *New York Journal*, May 10, 1891, clippings, RTL Collection, Hildene Archives.

50. Edward W. Matthews to RTL, London, May 25, 1891, and "The United States Minister's Speech," *Chart and Compass Sailors' Magazine*, June 1891, 166–168, items 1891.4.1 and 1891.4.2, RTL Collection, Hildene Archives.

51. For 1891 correspondence between Minister Lincoln and Secretary Blaine on the copyright issue, see *Papers Relating to the Foreign Relations of the United States* (1893), 220–24.

52. "British Authors Rejoice," *New York Times*, July 17, 1891, 1; "The Copyright Law," *Hartford (CT) Courant*, July 17, 1891, 1.

53. "A Lunch on the New York," *New York Times*, March 8, 1893, 8; "A Luncheon on the New York," *New York Tribune*, March 8, 1893, 2.

54. I. Anderson, *Larz Anderson*, 89.

55. Lincoln Isham, "Charles Isham," Isham Family Papers, copy in Hildene Archives.

56. C. J. King, *Four Marys and a Jessie*, 130.

57. Isham diaries, quoted in C. J. King, *Four Marys and a Jessie*, 129.

58. Previous authors have stated erroneously that First Secretary of Legation Henry White held an engagement banquet for the couple. The story is based on a newspaper article announcing both the engagement and the Whites' ball. A reading of the article, however, makes clear that the two incidents were separate, written in separate paragraphs, although part of the same news story about current events in London. "London's American Colony," *New York Times*, July 26, 1891, 1.

59. "Week in Social Circles," *Chicago Tribune*, July 26, 1891, 30; "Minister Lincoln's Daughter to be Wedded in London," *Los Angeles Times*, July 26, 1891, 5; "Isham-Lincoln," *St. Paul (MN) Globe*, July 26, 1891, 7.

60. "Lincoln-Isham," n.d., clipping, RTL Collection, Hildene Archives.

61. I. Anderson, *Larz Anderson*, 75–76.

62. "Marriage of Miss Lincoln," *New York Herald* Cable—Special to the *Bee*, *Omaha (NE) Bee*, September 3, 1891, 1.

63. Ibid. See also "Miss Lincoln's Wedding," *New York Times*, September 3, 1891, 4; "Miss Lincoln a Bride," *Washington Post*, September 3, 1891, 1; "Wedded at Brompton," *Chicago Tribune*, September 3, 1891, 5; Osmond, "P.E.O.'s Wedding in London," 10–11.

64. Charles Isham and Mary Lincoln marriage license, August 19, 1891, and marriage certificate September 2, 1891, copies, RTL Collection, Hildene Archives.

65. Jessie Lincoln to James Harlan, New York, June 9, 1892, item 2009.2.1, RTL Collection, Hildene Archives.

66. Strangely, the boy's true legal name is unknown for certain. Tradition bolstered by statements from family friends states that his full name was Abraham Lincoln Isham, although he always was known as just Lincoln Isham. The boy's name was reported at various times throughout his life to be "Abraham Lincoln Isham"—in honor of his dead uncle and paternal great-grandfather—and "Robert Lincoln Isham"—in honor of his grandfather—in addition to just "Lincoln Isham." His birth certificate has not been found. This author believes his full name is Abraham Lincoln Isham, which would have been a tribute both to his uncle Jack, dead barely two years and adored by Mamie Isham, as well as a tribute to great Lincoln family ancestry, which both Mamie and Charles Isham revered. Whether the boy's legal name is Abraham or Robert, he always preferred to be called Lincoln Isham, which is the name on his marriage certificate and his gravestone. His family nickname was "Linc." Noel Parmentel Jr., telephone interview by author, February 3, 2010; Harry J. Dunbaugh, "Robert Todd Lincoln: Lawyer, Executive, and Public Servant," speech before the Fortnightly, May 2, 1962, folder 2, RTL papers, CHM.

67. RTL to Charles Isham, London, June 11, 1892, folder 11, RTL Papers, CHM; RTL to "My dear Marston," New Hampshire, July 4, 1893, 1994–079 (M), New Hampshire Historical Society.

68. RTL to Mrs. [Potter] Palmer, Chicago, November 1, 1892, folder 1, RTL papers, CHM.

69. RTL to "My dear Marston," London, January 24, 1893, 1994–079 (M), New Hampshire Historical Society.

70. "Minister Lincoln Spoken of for the Vacant Secretaryship," *Sacramento (CA) Record-Union*, February 5, 1891, 1; "Robert T. Lincoln for Mayor," *Chicago Inter Ocean*, March 14, 1891, 1; "Comment about Noble," *Fort Worth (TX) Gazette*, June 4, 1891, 11; "Washington Letter," *Kirksville (MO) Weekly Graphic*, June 5, 1891, 2; "Minister Lincoln's Guests,"

New York Times, June 20, 1891, 5; "To Succeed Mr. Blaine," *New York Times*, June 26, 1892, 4.

71. "Gossip from the Capitol," *Chicago Tribune*, August 9, 1890, 7.

72. Waddington, *Letters of a Diplomat's Wife*, 340.

73. "Presidential Speculations," 18.

74. "Robert Todd Lincoln: The Best Man in Sight to Head the Republican Ticket," *Washington Post*, April 17, 1892, 4.

75. "Political Notes," *New York Times*, April 9, 1892, 4.

76. "Republican Prospect," 482.

77. "Harrison Wins the Prize," *New York Times*, June 11, 1892, 1; Eaton, *Presidential Timber*, 123.

78. RTL to Charles Isham, June 11, 1892, folder 11, RTL Papers, CHM; "Minister Lincoln Is Pleased," *New York Times*, June 11, 1892, 5.

79. RTL to President Benjamin Harrison, London, September 21, 1892, reel 36, series 1, Harrison Papers.

80. Lincoln requested a sixty-day leave of absence on September 21 and sailed for America on October 5. RTL to John W. Foster, September 21 and October 5, 1892, reel 163, Dispatches from United States Ministers to Great Britain, 1889–93, National Archives, copies, Goff Papers.

81. "Minister Lincoln Here," *New York Times*, October 17, 1892, 8; "Minister Lincoln," *Los Angeles Times*, October 17, 1892, 1; "Minister Lincoln Going West," *New York Times*, October 18, 1892, 8.

82. "Told by Lincoln," *Chicago Tribune*, October 25, 1892, 1; "The Two Meetings Last Evening," *Chicago Inter Ocean*, October 25, 1892, 4; RTL to Benjamin Harrison, Chicago, October 24, 1892, reel 37, series 1, Harrison Papers.

83. "Great Enthusiasm at Quincy" and "Quincy Hears Robert Lincoln," October 26, 1892, clippings, RTL Collection, Hildene Archives; "Wanted to Hear Lincoln," *Chicago Inter Ocean*, October 27, 1892, 2; "Abraham Lincoln's Son," *Hartford (CT) Courant*, October 28, 1892, 8.

84. "Ovations to Mr. Lincoln," *Terre Haute (IN) Express*, November 4, 1892, clipping, RTL Collection, Hildene Archives.

85. "Minister Lincoln at the Capitol," *New York Tribune*, December 21, 1892, 2; "Reception to Minister Lincoln," *Chicago Tribune*, December 24, 1892, 2; "Minister Lincoln Will Sail Wednesday," *Chicago Inter Ocean*, December 26, 1892, 2; "Telegraphic Brevities," *Hartford (CT) Courant*, January 5, 1893, 1; RTL to John W. Foster, January 5, 1893, reel 164, Dispatches from United States Ministers to Great Britain, 1889–93, National Archives, copies, Goff Papers.

86. RTL to John W. Foster, February 25, 1893, reel 164, Dispatches from United States Ministers to Great Britain, 1889–93, National Archives, copies, Goff Papers.

87. Walter Q. Gresham to RTL, Washington, March 30, 1893, in "Mr. Lincoln's Resignation Accepted," *New York Tribune*, March 31, 1893, 2.

88. Robert T. Lincoln interview, "Each Called on the Other," *New York Times*, May 15, 1893, 1.

89. Howe, *James Ford Rhodes*, 121.

90. Untitled editorial, *Hartford (CT) Courant*, March 31, 1893, 4.

91. "Latest News from Europe," *New York Sun*, March 12, 1893, 7.

92. RTL to John W. Foster, May 4, 1893, reel 165, Dispatches from United States Ministers to Great Britain, 1889–93, National Archives, copies, Goff Papers; "Lincoln Calls at

Windsor," *Los Angeles Times*, May 5, 1893, 1; "Minister Lincoln Goes to Windsor," *Hartford (CT) Courant*, May 5, 1893, 1.

93. RTL to "My dear Pulester," London, May 5, 1893, RTL Papers, ACPL.

21. "What Would His Father Say?"

1. A former clerk in the Isham, Lincoln, and Beale law firm later remembered that during the World's Fair in summer 1893, "seldom a day passed that our office did not receive a visit from one or more veterans of the Civil War, whose one and only request was to be permitted to step into Mr. Lincoln's office and look around so as to tell the folks back home they had been in the private office of the son of their great Commander-in-Chief." B. A. Levett to Ruth Painter Randall, New York, January 15, 1956, folder "Robert Lincoln," box 72, Randall Family Papers; "Robert T. Lincoln Arrives in Chicago," *Chicago Tribune*, June 1, 1893, 5; "Eulalie Meets Chicago's 400," *New York Times*, June 10, 1893, 5; "In Lasting Bronze," *Chicago Tribune*, June 23, 1893, 1.

2. "Graduation Day at Harvard," *New York Times*, June 29, 1893, 9; "Denounced by Robert Lincoln," *Chicago Tribune*, June 29, 1893, 1; "Central States," 22; G. B. Hill, *Harvard College by an Oxonian*, 105–6.

3. RTL to "My dear Marston," New Hampshire, July 4, 1893, accession number 1994–079 (M), New Hampshire Historical Society.

4. RTL to John Nicolay, Chicago, December 6, 1894, box 5, Nicolay Papers.

5. "Robert T. Lincoln Returns," *Chicago Herald*, November 8, 1890, 3; "Minister Lincoln," *Deseret News* (Salt Lake City, UT), December 19, 1890, 1; "The British Minister Traveling in Horse Cars," *Chicago Tribune*, February 21, 1891, clipping, RTL Collection, Hildene Archives; "United States a Parsimonious Employer," *Wall Street Journal*, February 17, 1906, 6; "Holland's Letter," *Wall Street Journal*, February 10, 1912, 1; "Holland's Letter," *Wall Street Journal*, March 31, 1913, 1.

6. RTL, "Abstract of Commercial National Bank Account," LB, 13:19:164. Records for Robert Lincoln's other bank accounts are not listed in his letterpress books and could not be found.

7. RTL, "Deposits made since March 23, 1893," LB, 13:19:171.

8. "Chicago's Exclusive 300," *New York Times*, January 11, 1897, 1. For a full list of the group's membership, see "Chicago's Three Hundred," *New York Times*, January 13, 1897, 1.

9. "What Would His Dad Say?" *Springfield (IL) Republican*, reprinted in *Richmond (VA) Dispatch*, January 16, 1897, 4.

10. "General Railway Notes," *New York Times*, September 20, 1880, 2; "Methods of the Railroads," *New York Times*, September 9, 1881, 5.

11. See Steeples and Whitten, *Democracy in Desperation*; Lauck, *Causes of the Panic of 1893*.

12. Husband, *Story of the Pullman Car*; Lindsay, *Pullman Strike*, 19–24.

13. George Pullman, interview, "George M. Pullman's City," *New York Sun*, December 9, 1883, 2. For an excellent study of the town, see Buder, *Pullman*.

14. "The Story of Pullman," prepared for distribution at the 1893 World's Fair, quoted in Husband, *Story of the Pullman Car*, 95.

15. George Pullman, interview, "George M. Pullman's City," *New York Sun*, December 9, 1883, 2.

16. U.S. Strike Commission, *Report on the Chicago Strike*, xxii.

17. Folder 109, box 2, series 3, record group 9, Pullman Company Archives. For full narrative details of the Pullman Strike of 1894, see the U.S. Strike Commission, *Report*

on the Chicago Strike. Key passages of the report are in Warne, *Pullman Boycott of 1894*. For the best secondary treatment, see Lindsay, *Pullman Strike*. Unless otherwise noted, the details of the strike come from these sources.

18. Ibid.

19. "Mr. Pullman Will Not Confer," *New York Times*, July 5, 1894, 2.

20. Folder 109, box 2, series 3, record group 9, Pullman Company Archives.

21. The *Chicago Herald* claimed that Lincoln "spends practically all his time in the office of the palace car magnate" and accompanied Pullman whenever he left Chicago and that the two men were "constant and inseparable companions." Lincoln's constant travel away from Chicago from May through July makes the newspaper's claims unlikely. "Pullman's Legal Advisor," *Chicago Herald*, reprinted in *Daily Herald* (Brownsville, TX), November 6, 1894, 2. For Robert's movements, see RTL to the editor, *Century Magazine*, Chicago, March 22, 1894, RTLFP; RTL to Manning P. Brown, Chicago, March 24, 1894, RTL papers, ACPL; Henry White to John Hay, May 2, 1894, reel 12, Hay Papers, Brown University; RTL to James Arthur Tufts, Chicago, May 22, 1894, RTL Collection, Hildene Archives; RTL to William Roscoe Thayer, Rye Beach, New Hampshire, July 21, 1894, bMS Am 1081 (1060), William Roscoe Thayer Papers; "Great Time Made by a Swimmer," *Chicago Tribune*, July 29, 1894, 11.

22. "Statement by Mr. Pullman," *New York Times*, July 14, 1894, 1; "Up among the Thousand Islands," *Chicago Tribune*, July 22, 1894, 11.

23. "Mr. Pullman Returning Home," *Pullman (IL) Herald*, August 31, 1894, 2.

24. Testimony of George M. Pullman, U.S. Strike Commission, *Report on the Chicago Strike*, 528–59; "Mr. Pullman on the Stand," *New York Times*, August 28, 1894, 8.

25. Charles Sweet to George Pullman, August 30, 1894, in Chapin, "Infamous Pullman Strike," 196–97.

26. Charles Sweet to George Pullman, November 12, 1894, in ibid.

27. "Debs Testifies in His Own Behalf," *New York Times*, February 7, 1895, 5; "Pullman Explains His Absence," *Chicago Tribune*, February 14, 1895, 5; Lindsey, *Pullman Strike*, 303.

28. The only papers concerning the Pullman strike in Robert Lincoln's voluminous letterpress books are written to George Pullman by his personal secretary, Charles Sweet. None of the letters mention Robert Lincoln in any way. For the Sweet-Pullman correspondence, see LB, 17:24:452, 18:25:92, 100–130. For an excellent article written from this correspondence, see Chapin, "Infamous Pullman Strike," 179–98.

29. Quoted in "A Cock and Bull Story," *Chicago Tribune*, November 17, 1894, 12.

30. Quoted in untitled article, *Chicago Tribune*, December 9, 1894, 12.

31. "Pullman's Legal Advisor," *Chicago Herald*, in *Daily Herald* (Brownsville, TX), November 6, 1894, 2.

32. The *Wall Street Journal* said Lincoln was chosen president because his "actual resultful work in complex law and business situations had proved his capacity and concentrating disposition." "Bye-the-Bye in Wall Street," *Wall Street Journal*, May 7, 1932, 8.

33. RTL to John Hay, Chicago, January 20, 1896, reel 8, Hay Papers, Brown University.

34. Coates, "Sons of Recent Presidents of the United States," 618.

35. "Are Sons of Great Sires," *Chicago Chronicle*, November 28, 1897, clipping, RTL Collection, Hildene Archives.

36. Untitled article, *Morning Call* (San Francisco) November 23, 1894, 6; untitled editorial, *Chicago Inter Ocean*, December 10, 1894, 6.

37. RTL to William Lincoln Shearer, New Hampshire, July 24, 1894, in Darrin, "Lincoln Family Friendship," 214.

38. RTL to William Lincoln Shearer, Chicago, April 30, 1895, in ibid., 214–15.

39. "Gen. James Makes a Prediction," *New York Times*, June 25, 1894, 8; "Lincoln for the Presidency," *New York Times*, May 17, 1895, 5.

40. Untitled article, *Washington Post*, November 13, 1895, 6; "Robert Lincoln as a Candidate," *Washington Post*, January 17, 1896, 10.

41. "Soldiers Monument Is Dedicated," *Chicago Tribune*, October 8, 1896, 1–2; Robert T. Lincoln speech at Galesburg, Illinois, October 7, 1896, galley proof, T1896.10.07, RTL Papers, ALPL.

42. For the definitive account of the debates and their meaning, see Davis and Wilson, *Lincoln Douglas Debates*.

43. "Great Day at Knox," *Chicago Tribune*, October 8, 1896, 1; "Lincoln and Douglas Debate," *(Springfield) Illinois State Journal*, October 8, 1896, 1.

44. *Speech of Hon. Robert T. Lincoln*.

45. "Great Day at Knox," *Chicago Tribune*, October 8, 1896, 1.

46. "Roosevelt Speaks Here Tonight," *Chicago Tribune*, October 15, 1896, 2.

47. Lincoln spoke in Minnesota at Duluth on October 22, Minneapolis on October 23, and St. Paul on October 24. He spoke in Illinois at Marshall on October 27, Shelbyville on October 28, Centralia on October 29, and Danville on October 30. His final two speeches were in Indianapolis and South Bend, Indiana, on October 30 and 31, respectively. His appearances were covered extensively in the major newspapers of each visited city as well as in the Chicago newspapers.

48. RTL to John Hay, Chicago, November 1, 1896, reel 8, Hay Papers, Brown University.

49. Mariah Vance worked as a daytime housekeeper, cook, and sometime nurse for the Lincolns from about 1850 until they left for Washington in 1861. In 1903, Mariah told the *(Springfield) Illinois State Journal* in an interview that she had known Abraham Lincoln since he was "a struggling young lawyer" and worked for his family, as well as the family of Dr. John Todd, Mary Lincoln's uncle. The day before the Lincolns left for Washington, Vance packed their belongings, cleaned the house, closed the windows, locked the doors, and returned the key to the president-elect at the Chenery House hotel, where the family stayed that night. "Oldest Person Born in County," *(Springfield) Illinois State Journal*, July 13, 1903, 5; Temple, "Mariah (Bartlett) Vance," part 1, 1, 3, 7, part 2, 1–2, 4–5, 8. Vance is the best-known servant from the Lincoln home in Springfield because of the publication of her supposed reminiscences called *Lincoln's Unknown Private Life* in 1995, although the book was subsequently discredited.

50. "Robert Lincoln Misunderstood, Cannon Asserts," *New York Herald Tribune*, July 27, 1926, 5. Newspaper coverage of the Danville, Illinois, rally did not mention Robert Lincoln's visit to Vance. "Closing Rallies for Republicans," *Chicago Tribune*, October 31, 1896, 2; "Big Tent: Robert T. Lincoln and Clark E. Carr: Speaking Today at Fairgrounds in LaPearl's Big Circus Tent," *Danville (IL) Daily News*, October 30, 1896, 1, 2; "Hon. Robert T. Lincoln," *Danville (IL) Daily News*, November 2, 1896, 2.

51. RTL to "My dear Hodson," January 1, 1897, reel 8, Hay Papers, Brown University.

52. "McKinley in Town Today," *Chicago Tribune*, December 17, 1896, 1; "Major McKinley Visit," *Hartford (CT) Courant*, December 19, 1896, 1.

53. RTL to John Hay, Chicago, February 28, 1897, reel 8, Hay Papers, Brown University.

54. Record group 15, Pullman Estate Papers. See also "Pullman Will Is In" and "Text of the Will in Full," *Chicago Tribune*, October 28, 1897, 1, 2.

55. Four boxes of executors' correspondence (series 1, record group 15) are in the Pullman Company Archives, Newberry Library. A survey of the correspondence clearly shows that Robert Lincoln was the executor in charge.

56. RTL to Henry White, Chicago, December 11, 1899, White Papers; "Executors Get

$425,000 Fee," *New York Times*, January 6, 1900, 1; "Pullman Estate Nearly $14,000,000," *New York Tribune*, January 6, 1900, 6.

57. "Talk of a New Head," *Chicago Tribune*, October 20, 1897, 3.

58. Martha Freeman Esmond to Julia Boyd, Chicago, November 13, 1897, in Herma Clark, "When Chicago Was Young," *Chicago Tribune*, November 11, 1945, E4; "Talk of a New Head," *Chicago Tribune*, October 20, 1897, 3. Chicago businessmen believed this to be the case as well.

59. Untitled article, *New York Times*, October 21, 1897, 7; "Olney and Frye," *Boston Globe*, October 21, 1897, 9.

60. Statement, Pullman Palace Car Company, November 11, 1897, RTL Papers, ALPL.

61. "Name R. T. Lincoln," *Chicago Tribune*, November 12, 1897, 5.

62. Cullom, *Fifty Years of Public Service*, 125.

63. RTL to C. A. Griscom, November 17, 1897, and RTL to William Lincoln Shearer, December 23, 1897, LB, 33:54:14, 49.

64. RTL to Charles L. Mills, May 3, 1884, LB, 11:16:165; "The Navy Takes to Water," *Chicago Daily News*, in *Omaha (NE) Bee*, October 15, 1884, 2.

65. "They Elope: Ex-Minister Lincoln's Daughter and Warren Beckwith Wed in Milwaukee," *Milwaukee (WI) Journal*, November 11, 1897, 1.

66. "Beckwith a Baseball Dude," *New York Times*, November 14, 1897, 4.

67. "Jessie Lincoln Elopes," *Chicago Tribune* November 11, 1897, 1; "Parents Objected," *Boston Globe*, November 12, 1897, 5.

68. Marriage certificate, Warren Beckwith and Jessie Lincoln, November 10, 1897, and O. P. Christian [the clergyman who performed Jessie's marriage] to RTL, Milwaukee, Wisconsin, November 13, 1897, RTLFP, copies, RTL Collection, Hildene Archives. For a detailed story of the elopement, see "They Elope: Ex-Minister Lincoln's Daughter and Warren Beckwith Wed in Milwaukee," *Milwaukee (WI) Journal*, November 11, 1897, 1. See also Olson, "Lincoln's Granddaughter Eloped to Milwaukee."

69. "Jessie Lincoln Elopes," *Chicago Tribune* November 11, 1897, 1.

70. Robert asked a friend, possibly Norman Ream, to investigate the marriage and verify its legality. Ream reported that "all legal requisites were complied with." R [Norman Ream?] to L [RTL], n.d., RTLFP, copy in RTL Collection, Hildene Archives; "Parents Objected," *Boston Globe*, November 12, 1897, 5.

71. "Beckwith Still in the Dark," *Chicago Tribune*, November 12, 1897, 5.

72. Warren Beckwith to Jessie Beckwith, Aurora, Illinois, November 11, 1897, RTLFP, copy in RTL Collection, Hildene Archives.

73. "Still True to Football," *New York Times*, November 13, 1897, 2.

74. "Mrs. Beckwith Goes West," *New York Times*, November 15, 1897, 1; "Lincoln-Beckwith Marriage," *New York Times*, November 17, 1897, 1.

75. "Beckwith Saved the Day," *New York Tribune*, November 18, 1897, 4.

76. "Independent Mr. Beckwith," *New York Times*, November 16, 1897, 1; "Lincoln-Beckwith Marriage," *New York Times*, November 17, 1897, 1.

22. "I Am Now a Vermont Farmer!"

1. "Spain's Legal Responsibility," *New York Times*, February 22, 1898, 2.

2. "He Opened His Mouth," *Mt. Pleasant (IA) News*, February 24, 1898, clipping, RTL file, Harlan-Lincoln House Collection. See also "Responsibility of Spain," *New York Times*, March 29, 1898, 7.

3. "Spanish Report Positive" and "Mine Wrecked the Maine," *New York Times*, March 26, 1898, 1.

4. "Will Be a Ball Player," *St. Paul (MN) Globe*, March 4, 1898, 5; "Beckwith to Pitch for Duluth," *New York Times*, March 11, 1898, 2; "Pitcher Beckwith Released," *New York Times*, March 30, 1898, 7.

5. "A Pitcher of Cannon Balls," *Kansas City (MO)Journal*, May 4, 1898, 5.

6. *Roster and Record of Iowa Soldiers*, 6:404; "Made Ill by Tainted Meat," *Chicago Tribune*, June 2, 1898, 3.

7. John Hay to Theodore Roosevelt, London, July 27, 1898, in Thayer, *Life and Letters of John Hay*, 2:337.

8. "Robert Lincoln's Daughter a Mother," *Chicago Tribune*, August 23, 1898, 5; "News in Brief," *Mount Vernon (IA) Hawkeye*, September 2, 1898, 3.

9. Juhl, *James Harlan and Robert Todd Lincoln*, 51.

10. RTL to Henry White, Chicago, December 11, 1899, Henry White Papers, Columbia University.

11. "Sacramento Is Installed in First Position," *San Francisco Call*, April 13, 1899, 11; "Said of the Players," *Minneapolis (MN) Journal*, September 30, 1901, 9; Warren Beckwith, interview by Seymour Korman, "Lincoln Family Story Turns Up a New Chapter," *Chicago Tribune*, March 20, 1952, 18; Juhl, *James Harlan and Robert Todd Lincoln*, 51.

12. RTL to Emily Helm, Chicago, March 27, 1898, folder 7, RTL Papers, CHM.

13. Charles Sweet to Edgar T. Welles, April 16, 1898, LB, 33:54:175.

14. RTL to Henry S. Huidekoper, Chicago, May 21, 1898, RTLFP.

15. RTL to O. A. Sprague, July 7, 1898, LB, 33:55:250; "Sanitary Commission Election," *New York Times*, July 17, 1898, 3; "Robert Lincoln Is Re-Elected," *New York Times*, October 14, 1898, 10.

16. RTL to Mrs. J. Y. Scammon, December 23, 1898, and RTL to Clinton Conkling, March 5, 1899, LB, 33:55:341, 367.

17. Yvonne C. Fettweis, manager, Christian Science Church History, to Jo King, July 13, 1993, Hildene Archives; Temple, *Abraham Lincoln*, 413.

18. Mary Baker Eddy to Jessie Lincoln, July 7, 1891, and Sept. 14, 1893, Hildene Archives; Jessie Lincoln to Mary Baker Eddy, Little Boar's Head, New Hampshire, August 22, 1893, shelf #688, series CH, First Church of Christ Scientist Archives; *Painting a Poem*, 131.

19. RTL to Clinton Conkling, March 5, 1899, LB, 33:55:367.

20. RTL to H. C. Hulbert, June 26, 1899, LB, 33:55:468.

21. "Ex-Senator Harlan Dying," *New York Times*, October 2, 1899, 2; "Death List of the Day," *New York Times*, October 6, 1899, 7; "Ex-Senator Harlan Dead," Associated Press, in *St. Paul (MN) Globe*, October 6, 1899, 4.

22. RTL to Henry White, Chicago, December 11, 1899, Henry White Papers, Columbia University; [Harlan funeral], *Mt. Pleasant (IA) News*, October 9, 1899, in Juhl, *James Harlan and Robert Todd Lincoln*, 54–55.

23. "Last of a Lincoln Cabinet," *Philadelphia Times*, reprinted in *Omaha (NE) Bee*, October 10, 1899, 6.

24. "Mrs. R. T. Lincoln Her Father's Heir," *New York Times*, October 14, 1899, 7; McMurtry, "Harlan-Lincoln Tradition," 9. Mary donated her father's house to Iowa Wesleyan University in 1907, where it was used for a time as the home of the college president. Today, the university still owns the Harlan-Lincoln Home and runs it as a historical site.

25. RTL to Henry White, Chicago, December 11, 1899, Henry White Papers, Columbia University. The Pullman-Wagner merger was constantly in the national news from October 18 to 21, 1899. For examples, see "Pullman-Wagner Merger," *New York Times*, October 20, 1899, 2; "Wagner Merges in Pullman," *Chicago Tribune*, October 21, 1899, 9; "Pullman Combine Ratified," *New York Times*, December 6, 1899, 13.

26. "Pullman Company Meets," *New York Times*, October 20, 1899, 2; "Wagner Merges in the Pullman," *Chicago Tribune*, October 21, 1899, 1; "President of New Pullman Company," *New York Tribune*, December 10, 1899, 6.

27. Previous stories claim that Robert was invited by President McKinley to attend the exposition, although I have found no primary evidence to support it. Robert had been invited by the president and board of directors of the Pan-American Exposition to attend the opening dedication on May 20, 1901, which Robert declined, although he replied that he hoped "to have the pleasure of visiting the Exposition this summer." So Robert Lincoln may not have been invited by McKinley at all, it may have been another amazing coincidence that he had chosen that weekend to visit the exposition. RTL to Secretary of the Committee on Ceremonies, Pan-American Exposition, May 13, 1901, and RTL to John A. Dillon, Deal, New Jersey, September 5, 1901, LB, 35:58:113, 193; "Rejoicing in Buffalo," *New York Tribune*, September 9, 1901, 2.

28. Charles Sweet to RTL c/o J. K. Bennett, Chicago, September [6], 1901, LB, 24:37:82. This telegram is actually dated September 7, but this is obviously an error.

29. "The Milburn Home," *New York Times*, September 7, 1901, 6.

30. "Story of an Eyewitness," *New York Times*, September 8, 1901, 1.

31. "How the Deed Was Done," "How the President Is Being Cared For," and "Dr. Mann's Operation on President McKinley," *New York Times*, September 7, 8, and 9, 1901, 1.

32. "Rejoicing in Buffalo," *New York Tribune*, September 9, 1901, 2; "Universal Rejoicing Over President's Progress," *New York Times*, September 9, 1901, 1; "McKinley Passing Danger Line," *Chicago Tribune*, September 9, 1901, 1.

33. There have been numerous variations of the story of exactly where Robert Lincoln was when McKinley was shot. These include that he was: on the train to Buffalo, just off the train at the Buffalo station, just entered the grounds of the Pan-American Exposition, among the crowd in front of the Temple of Music, inside the Temple of Music, within hearing of the shot, standing near the president, within sight of the shooting, and simply "nearby." "Lincoln's Son Dies in His Sleep at 82," *New York Times*, July 27, 1926, 1; "R. T. Lincoln, President's Son, 82, Dies," *Hartford (CT) Courant*, July 27, 1926, 5; "The Son of Abraham Lincoln," 36; Lucius C. Harper, "Dustin' Off the News," *Chicago Defender*, February 18, 1939, 1; Carroll, "Lincoln Jinx," 89–90; Ferguson, "Man Marked," 143; Dunbaugh, "Robert Todd Lincoln"; "Saw Three Presidents Killed," n.d., clipping, RTLFP.

34. "Lincoln's Son Dies in His Sleep at 82," *New York Times*, July 27, 1926, 1; "R. T. Lincoln, President's Son, 82, Dies," *Hartford Courant*, July 27, 1926, 5; "Saw Three Presidents Killed," n.d., clipping, RTLFP.

35. On February 25, 1902, Robert attended a White House dinner in honor of Prince Henry of Prussia, and on May 30, 1922, he attended the dedication of the Lincoln memorial, which included President Harding and former President Taft. Robert's presidential "curse" and his supposed reactions to it have been repeated time and again in numerous books and articles about bizarre historical facts and presidential trivia. Writer Sarah Vowell, in her book about the first three presidential assassinations, even hilariously dubbed Robert Lincoln "Jinxy McDeath." *Assassination Vacation*, 236.

36. RTL to Theodore Roosevelt, New York, September 18, 1901, bMS Am 1540 (547), Theodore Roosevelt Papers, Houghton Library; also in frames 15483–84, reel 19, series 1, Roosevelt Papers, LOC.

37. Theodore Roosevelt to RTL, September 20, 1901, page 14, reel 327, vol. 31, series 2, Roosevelt Papers, LOC.

38. Robert did not go to Manchester with his mother and brother in 1863 as previous

historians have claimed. "Personal," *Lowell (NH) Daily Citizen and News*, August 14, 1863, 2; "Personal," *Daily Constitutional Union* (Washington, DC), August 17, 1863, 2; "Local Intelligence," *Manchester (NH) Journal*, August 25, September 1 and 8, 1863, 3.

39. Robert's first verifiable return to Manchester after 1864 occurred in 1895, when he and twenty-year-old daughter Jessie were guests at Ormsby Hill. "Manchester," *Manchester (NH) Journal*, July 25, 1895, 3; "Personal," *Mt. Pleasant (IA) Journal*, July 27, 1895.

40. Robert Lincoln returned to Manchester as a guest at Ormsby Hill in September 1896, August 1900, and August 1901. "Manchester," *Manchester (NH) Journal*, September 3, 1896, August 23, 1900, and August 22, 1901, 3.

41. RTL to Mrs. George Pullman, March 3, 1902, LB, 35:59:429–30; "Edward S. Isham Dead," *New York Times*, February 18, 1902, 9; "Edward S. Isham, Lawyer, Is Dead," *Chicago Tribune*, February 18, 1902, 7; "Funeral of Edward S. Isham," *New York Tribune*, February 21, 1902, 7.

42. "Manchester," *Manchester (NH) Journal*, August 28, 1902, 3; RTL to Charles Sweet and RTL to Equinox House, telegrams, New York, August 18, 1902, RTL to Charles Isham, September 15, 1902, and RTL to Edward Isham Jr., September 17, 1902, LB, 36:60:60, 70, 79–80.

43. RTL to E. C. Orvis, October 18, 1902, and Memorandum of Deed of Conveyance from Frank H. Walker to Robert T. Lincoln, n.d., and RTL Petition to the Trustees of the Village of Manchester, Vermont, October 13, 1904, Hildene Construction Records, 1904.1.4.1–.4, Hildene Archives; "Lincoln Buys Country Seat," *Washington Post*, October 26, 1902, 3; "Note and Comment," *Hartford (CT) Courant*, October 28, 1902, 10; RTL to T. S. Peck, October 29, 1902, LB, 36:60:129; "Note and Comment," *Hartford (CT) Courant*, October 9, 1903, 10.

44. RTL to John J. McCook, December 28, 1903, RTL Papers, ALPL.

45. Ibid.; RTL to Norman Ream, October 1, 1903, LB, 36:61:439. The local newspaper said, "Honorable Robert T. Lincoln is proving to be quite a farmer. He has one of the finest dairies in the state consisting of 36 fine Jersey cows and butter sells in the cities for from $.40 to $.50 a pound." Clipping, *Manchester (NH) Journal*, July 14, 1904, RTL Collection, Hildene Archives.

46. RTL to Thomas Nelson Page, Manchester, Vermont, July 12, 1904, Page Papers.

47. Every room had a button system that, when pushed, would ring a bell and show an indicator flag to announce which station was in need.

48. In addition to these two major costs, between 1903 and 1905 Lincoln also made vast expenditures for the landscaping, gardening, surveying, road and fence construction, water and sewage construction and services, farming, hauling, furniture and interior decorating purchases, as well as the labor costs included in all these endeavors. Add to all this the purchase price of $32,000 for his five hundred acres of land between 1902 and 1903, and the total cost of the building of Hildene can be estimated to be a *minimum* of $250,000—which roughly equates to about $5 million in twenty-first-century value.

49. The name *Hildene* is a combination of two Middle English words meaning "hill and valley."

50. Contract between the Aeolian Company and Robert T. Lincoln, June 30, 1908, and other documents relating to the organ, D.1975.40 and 2009.37.02, RTL Collection, Hildene Archives.

51. Robert Lincoln's library at Hildene still contains about thirty books on astronomy. RTL to David Peck Todd, Manchester, Vermont, June 26, 1909, folder 190, box 5, series 1, David Peck Todd Papers.

52. RTL to W. W. Campbell, March 8, 1909, LB, 42:73:260.

53. RTL to F. J. Sherrer, May 20, July 8 and July 18, 1907, RTL to G. L. Woodcock, June 1, 1907, and RTL to Francis A. Houston, July 3, 1907, LB, 40:68:108–9, 126–27, 160, 170–71, 195.

54. RTL to William E. Reed, March 8, 1909, and RTL to W. W. Campbell, March 8, 1909, LB, 42:73:257, 260; RTL to David Peck Todd, Chicago, April 30, 1910, folder 190, box 5, series 1, David Peck Todd Papers. The blueprints for Robert Lincoln's observatory can be found in 1975.6.1, RTL Collection, Hildene Archives. The new observatory was constructed by the Warner & Swasey Company of Cleveland, Ohio.

55. RTL to Nicholas Murray Butler, New York, June 16, 1913, box 234, Nicholas Murray Butler Papers.

56. Robert's drafting tools still are at Hildene (records box 2008.26 and items 2007.34, 2007.34.1, 2007.34.1.1, and 2007.34.2), as are all the correspondence and records concerning the construction of the house and everything on the grounds, records 1904.1.1–.17. For Robert's correspondence on surveying the grounds for fencing, see Hildene Construction Records, folder 1904.1.5, Hildene Archives; RTL to Norman Ream, Manchester, Vermont, September 7, 1903, and RTL to Charles S. Forbes, September 14, 1904, LB, 36:61:486, 489.

57. Untitled notice, *Mt. Pleasant (IA) News*, July 21, 1904.

58. RTL to Charles Isham, Manchester, Vermont, August 20, 1904, folder 11, RTL papers, CHM.

59. *James C. Whitford v. Mrs. Robert T. Lincoln*, Claim for Damages, October 11, 1900, and Motion for More Specific Statement, October 27, 1900, box 417, Henry County Probate Court Records. The Lincolns later settled out of court. RTL to Babb and Babb, Attorneys, February 23, 1901, LB, 35:58:43.

60. The Associated Press wire story was printed in numerous newspapers, for examples, see "Jessie Lincoln's Love Was Fleeting," *Los Angeles Times*, December 22, 1900, 15. See also "Mrs. W. Beckwith Divorced," *New York Times*, December 22, 1900, 1. For verification of Peggy's bout of scarlet fever, see RTL to A. R. Keen, September 30, 1903, LB, 36:61:436.

61. "Jessie Lincoln Beckwith Separated from Her Husband," *New York Evening World*, December 21, 1900, 1.

62. Mary Harlan Lincoln to RTL, December 29, 1906, RTLFP, copy, RTL Collection, Hildene Archives.

63. Warren Beckwith, interview by Seymour Korman, "Lincoln Family Story Turns Up a New Chapter," *Chicago Tribune*, March 20, 1952, 18. See also Mary Harlan Lincoln to RTL, November 26, 1906, and Ann Dodge to Jessie Lincoln Beckwith, Mount Pleasant, Iowa, May 1, 1915, RTLFP, copies in Hildene Archives.

64. "Daughter with Lincoln," *New York Times*, February 5, 1907, 6; "Mr. Lincoln Not Surprised," *New York Herald*, February 5, 1907, clipping, RTLFP, copies in RTL Collection, Hildene Archives.

65. H. A. Ambler to Mrs. Warren Beckwith, Mount Pleasant, Iowa, February 12, 1907, and Divorce Decree, *Warren W. Beckwith v. Jessie Beckwith*, District Court of Henry County, Iowa, February 12, 1907, RTLFP, copies in RTL Collection, Hildene Archives; "To Divorce R. T. Lincoln's Daughter," *New York Tribune*, February 3, 1907, 9; "Beckwith Seeks Divorce," *Washington (DC) Herald*, February 3, 1907, 3; "A Lincoln Divorced," *New York Times*, February 13, 1907, 1; "Divorces Kin of Lincoln," *Chicago Tribune*, February 13, 1907, 6.

66. Warren Beckwith, interview by Seymour Korman, "Lincoln Family Story Turns Up a New Chapter," *Chicago Tribune*, March 20, 1952, 18.

67. William G. Beale to Mary Harlan Lincoln, December 24, 1906, and January 5,

1907, W. I. Babb to Mary Harlan Lincoln, Aurora, Illinois, n.d., and July 15, 1907, and W. I. Babb to RTL, February 25, 1907, RTLFP, copies in RTL Collection, Hildene Archives.

68. Mary wrote to her husband at the end of 1906, "I agree with you that this Jessie affair had better be settled now without too much delay." The letter also shows that Robert and Mary were willing to adopt Jessie's kids if necessary to prevent Warren obtaining custody in the event of her death. Mary Lincoln to RTL, December 29, 1906, RTLFP, copy in RTL Collection, Hildene Archives.

69. Warren Beckwith, interview by Seymour Korman, "Lincoln Family Story Turns Up a New Chapter," *Chicago Tribune*, March 20, 1952, 18.

70. "Good Year for the Pullman Company," *Chicago Tribune*, October 19, 1900, 12.

71. RTL to O. S. A. Sprague, May 15, 1900, LB, 34:56:242–43.

72. "Pullman Dividend a Record," *New York Times*, November 16, 1906, 13.

73. C. F. Anderson, *Freemen Yet Slaves under 'Abe' Lincoln's Son*, 4.

74. Ibid., 35.

75. Charles Sweet to C. F. Anderson, Chicago, December 21, 1903, in ibid., 13.

76. S. Laing Williams to Booker T. Washington, November 3, 1903, quoted in Harlan and Smock, *Booker T. Washington Papers*, 7:324n.1.

77. Booker T. Washington to Francis Jackson Garrison, February 22, 1904, in ibid., 7:446.

78. Lincoln stated that either way the customer would pay: if wages were increased, then ticket prices would increase and porters would receive less tips, if any tips at all. Robert T. Lincoln testimony, in U.S. Senate, Commission on Industrial Relations, Document no. 415, 64th Cong., 1st Sess., *Industrial Relations*, 10:9663–81. Lincoln's testimony was national news; for example see, "Public Put First in R.R. Service," *Washington Star*, May 5, 1915, 2; "Lincoln Talks on Tips," *Washington Post*, May 5, 1915, 2; "Lincoln Defends Tipping of Porters," *New York Times*, May 5, 1915, 22; "Will Robert T. Lincoln Be the Second Emancipator?" *Chicago Defender*, May 8, 1915, 1.

79. The Powell story is particularly well known and damning. Powell declared in his autobiography that during the summer of 1926, while a college student, he worked at the Equinox House in Manchester, Vermont, as a bellhop and witnessed firsthand that Robert Lincoln "hated Negroes." Powell claimed that Lincoln would arrive at the Equinox every night for dinner, and "whenever a negro put his hand on the car door to open it, Mr. Lincoln took his cane and cracked him across the knuckles." Since Powell had extremely light skin color, he was made Robert's personal bellhop because he looked white. The story is impossible because Lincoln died in summer 1926 and was ill most of the year. Also, Lincoln had a cook on staff at Hildene, and that plus his health makes it unbelievable that he went to the Equinox "nightly" for dinner. More specifically, however, Robert's Manchester tailor, Fred Nickelwhite (the master tailor at the Equinox), actually witnessed the event and consistently denied the story. According to Nickelwhite, Robert chided a black Equinox employee for touching his new Packard car because it had just been polished—Lincoln would have, and did, chastise any employee, black or white, who left a smudge or mark on the car. Powell, who was an acolyte of the Pullman Company–hating Asa Philip Randolph and was not present during the incident, seized on and transmogrified the event to paint the story of racism he wanted to convey. Powell, *Adam by Adam*, 33; Fred Nickelwhite, oral history taken by Nate Boone, Manchester, Vermont.

80. The War Department and Pullman records are all that exist to explain Robert's feelings about African Americans. None of his personal letters, or family letters, say anything on the issue.

81. The yearly revenue figures for the Pullman Company were reported every year in

the *New York Times* after each board of directors meeting, generally in late October or early November. See also "Newspaper Specials," *Wall Street Journal*, January 20, 1908, 2.

82. Lincoln was unanimously elected a member of the Equitable board of directors in December 1897, but he never attended any meetings or had anything to do with the company. "It was regarded as a mere compliment," he once explained. RTL to E. A. Angier, January 16, 1905, LB, 35:64:79, and RTL to Henry D. Estabrook, December 11, 1905, LB, 38:65:462–63.

83. "Robert T. Lincoln for Chairman of Directors," *New York World*, June 3, 1905, 3; "Two of Committee Won't Serve," *New York Tribune*, June 4, 1905, 1; "Lincoln May Head Equitable Board," *New York Times*, June 4, 1905, 3. For a study of the Panic of 1907, see Bruner and Carr, *Panic of 1907*.

84. "Lincoln Would Decline," *Hartford (CT) Courant*, June 5, 1905, 1.

85. RTL to Norman Ream, June 8, 1905, and RTL to William Alexander, June 9, and to [illegible], June 12, 1905, LB, 38:65:309, 315, 321; "Advised to Resign," *New York Tribune*, June 8, 1905, 1. For the complete story of the Equitable controversy, see Rousmaniere, *Life and Times of the Equitable*, 88–105; Beard, *After the Ball*, 207–33.

86. RTL to Charles W. Eliot, February 27, 1902, box 51, UAI 5.150, Eliot Papers; "Prince Henry at Chicago," *New York Times*, February 25, 1902, 1; "Lincoln Paid Tribune by Prince," *Chicago Tribune*, March 5, 1902, 3; "He Meets the Captains of Industry," 538–40.

87. RTL to Colonel McCook, May 14, 1900, LB, 34:56:238; "Some Views from Idaho," *New York Tribune*, June 18, 1900, 3.

88. RTL to W. J. Arkell, October 6, 1900, LB, 34:57:320.

89. Charles Sweet to RTL, Chicago, June 21, 1904, LB, 26:41:68.

90. RTL to O. S. A. Sprague, May 15, 1900, LB, 34:56:242–43.

91. RTL to H. H. Porter, October 21, 1901, LB, 35:58:225.

92. RTL telegrams to Mrs. John A. Dillon and Arthur Dillon, Chicago, October 14–16, 1902, LB, 36:60:108, 110, 116.

93. RTL to Emily Helm, May 13, 1905, folder 7, RTL Papers, CHM.

94. RTL to Emily Helm, January 26, 1906, and RTL to Richard Watson Gilder, February 12, 1906, Folders 2 and 7, RTL Papers, CHM.

95. "Marshall Field Dead," *Wall Street Journal*, January 17, 1906, 8; Tebbel, *Marshall Fields*, 94, 111–12; Dunbaugh, "Robert Todd Lincoln," 16.

96. RTL to William O. Stoddard, Augusta, Georgia, March 5, 1908, RTL Papers, ACPL.

97. RTL to Franklin MacVeagh, Manchester, Vermont, September 17, 1908, LB, 41:71:328.

98. RTL to William O. Stoddard, Augusta, Georgia, March 5, 1908, RTL Papers, ACPL.

23. "My Filial Gratitude Cannot Find Adequate Expression"

1. Schwartz, *Abraham Lincoln and the Forge of National Memory*, 113. I highly recommend this book in its entirety for an unparalleled examination of the creation and growth of Abraham Lincoln's national apotheosis. See also M. D. Peterson, *Lincoln in American Memory*, especially pages 175–94 for a discussion of the centennial.

2. "Abraham Lincoln," *Chicago Tribune*, February 7, 1909, J4.

3. Illinois Senate Joint Resolution no. 22, October 8, 1907, in *Lincoln Centennial*, 4.

4. "City, Greatest in Lincoln Memory, to Pay Tribute Today" and "The Day's Program," *(Springfield) Illinois State Journal*, February 12, 1909, 1, 3; *Lincoln Centennial*, 7–9; "Lincoln Centennial," 27–30; MacChesney, *Abraham Lincoln*, 183–85.

5. RTL to Walter Ranger, Commissioner of Public Schools, Providence, Rhode Island, February 10, 1909, LB, 42:72:151.

6. "A Lesson from Lincoln," *Providence (RI) Journal*, February 12, 1900, clipping, RTL Collection, Hildene Archives. For two examples, RTL to "My Little Friends," March 30, 1898, LB, 33:54:158, and RTL to Edward H. Stitt, principal, Public School no. 89, February 5, 1900, LB, 34:56:156.

7. Robert kept scores of copies of the pamphlet he subsidized and sent them out to anyone with an interest in the subject. The Hildene Archives retain thirty-six copies of Robert's personal cache of pamphlets. J. G. Nicolay, "Lincoln's Gettysburg Address," 596–609.

8. RTL to James H. Canfield, April 22, 1908, RTL Papers, ALPL, and January 30 and February 23, 1909, LB, 42:72:81–82, 198. See also RTL to W. H. Siviter, February 5, 1909, RTL Papers, ACPL; RTL to Darwin C. Pavey, February 9, 1909, RTL Papers, ALPL; "Relics at Columbia," *New York Tribune*, February 12, 1909, 2. When first contacted about contributing to the Columbia exhibit, Robert replied to the librarian, James H. Canfield, "I am going to say to you frankly that this business is beginning to appall me somewhat, for not a day passes that I do not receive one or more communications from most varied points of view, but all relating to this subject." Robert decided to loan a handful of his father's papers to the exhibit and was most pleased at the result.

9. M. Johnson, "Who Stole the Gettysburg Address?" 18.

10. RTL to General James B. Aleshire, April 26, 1909, telegram, and April 26, 1909, LB, 42:73:388–90, 396.

11. RTL to General James B. Aleshire, May 5, 1909, HM 25273, RTL Letters, Huntington Library.

12. RTL to General James B. Aleshire, May 5, 1909, and RTL to Major William H. Lambert, May 5, 1909, HM 25273, RTL Letters, Huntington Library.

13. Abraham Lincoln to Mrs. Lydia Bixby, Washington, November 21, 1864, in Basler et al., *Collected Works*, 8:116–17, and in series 3, General Correspondence, Abraham Lincoln Papers, LOC.

14. Arthur M. Bixby to David C. Mearns, August 31, 1948, box 81, Mearns Papers; "Grandson Believes Bixby Letter Lost," *New York Times*, August 9, 1925, 18.

15. Robert T. Lincoln to James H. Canfield, February 25, 1909, LB, 42:72:217–18.

16. The first letter from Robert that mentioned his search for the original Bixby letter was to General Charles H. T. Collis, January 27, 1902, RTL Papers, ALPL. Robert later stated that he began his search after the death of John G. Nicolay on September 26, 1901. RTL to Isaac Markens, January 5, 1917, folder 5, RTL Papers, CHM.

17. James H. Canfield to RTL, March 1, 1909, quoted in Bullard, "Again, the Bixby Letter," 27.

18. Burlingame, "New Light on the Bixby Letter," 59–71. Burlingame later expanded, revised, and renamed the article to "The Authorship of the Bixby Letter," in *At Lincoln's Side*, 169–84.

19. For a full examination and transcription of this new evidence, see Emerson, "New Evidence from an Ignored Voice," 86–116.

20. Lincoln to Markens, February 24, 1917, folder 5, RTL Papers, CHM (emphasis added). A second, earlier letter by Robert's secretary also states, "[I]n response to inquiries some years ago by Mr. [Robert] Lincoln, both Mr. Nicolay and Mr. Hay stated that they had never seen any draft or copy of this letter to Mrs. Bixby." Frederic N. Towers to Colonel John Tweedale, April 22, 1908, RTL Papers, ALPL.

21. Frederic Towers to *New York Evening Post*, August 8, 1925, Towers to Perriton Maxwell, August 19, 1925, and Towers to A. J. Gordon, October 3, 1925, RTL Collection, Hildene Archives.

22. RTL to Reverend Howard H. Russell, July 6, 1903, LB, 36:61:456.

23. This most likely stemmed from Maynard, *Was Abraham Lincoln a Spiritualist?*

24. The same story of Robert's comment on the subject was published in newspapers around the country. For example, see "Personal Gossip," *New York Times*, August 31, 1893, 4. RTL's correspondence with Harry Houdini contains five letters between February and October 1925, RTL Collection, Hildene Archives.

25. RTL to William Kellogg, LB, 42:73:277–78.

26. On February 9, 1864, Matthew Brady took the photo of a seated President Lincoln. RTL to Arthur F. Hall, August 3, 1905, photo included, RTL Papers, ACPL. Robert also gave his blessing and good wishes to the Abraham Lincoln Mutual Life Insurance Company of Philadelphia, Pennsylvania, when its president informed him of the use of Robert's father's name for the company. RTL to R. F. Whitmer, July 24, 1907, LB, 40:68:212.

27. "Abraham Lincoln's Portrait," *New York Times*, December 31, 1902, 3; "Lincoln's Final Conquest," *Hartford (CT) Courant*, December 26, 1902, 15.

28. RTL to Dean Pierrel, May 26, 1908, RTL Papers, ALPL.

29. "Exeter Gets $100,000," *New York Tribune*, March 26, 1909, 1.

30. RTL to H. B. Ledyard, January 7, 1909, LB, 42:72:157.

31. "I took this course from the start, for I felt that if I attended on one occasion it would be very difficult to refrain from accepting a similar invitation at another time, and that consequently on that day, I would always have long journeys to make," Robert once wrote. RTL to Francis D. Tandy, January 10, 1910, RTL Papers, ALPL.

32. RTL to Edward M. Paxon, May 9, 1905, LB, 38:64:249.

33. RTL to J. Otis Humphrey, January 4, 1909, LB, 41:71:492.

34. It was quite an occasion for Mary Harlan Lincoln to attend the Springfield celebration since she disliked public appearances even more than her husband. "Mrs. Lincoln is going down with me, but she will much prefer not to take part whatever in any formal matters," Robert explained. "But in a general way, as I am not nearly in good trim as I would like to be, she proposes to keep an eye on me, which is very good of her and will probably be very good for me." RTL to Clinton Conkling, February 8, 1909, LB, 42:72:125–26.

35. Charles Sweet to Clinton Conkling, January 29 and February 4, 1909, LB, 29:48:543–44, 547–49.

36. He sent the association a check for $200 for the costs. RTL to J. Otis Humphrey, January 21, 1909, folder 1, SC-1708, Humphrey Papers.

37. Charles Sweet to Clinton Conkling, January 29 and February 4, 1909, LB, 29:48:543–44, 547–549; RTL to Charles H. Schwepps, February 5, 1909, LB, 42:72:118.

38. RTL to William J. Bryan, February 5, 1909, LB, 42:72:116.

39. RTL to Abram Wakeman Jr., November 28, 1908, LB, 41:71:430–31.

40. The same story was published in newspapers around the country, apparently from the original reporting of the Associated Press. For example see, "Lincoln Honored by Three Nations," *New York Times*, February 13, 1909, 3.

41. "At Springfield," 363.

42. "Springfield Pays Homage to Memory of Her First Citizen," *(Springfield) Illinois State Journal*, February 13, 1909, 3.

43. RTL to James R. E. Van Cleave, February 19, 1909, LB, 42:72:182. See also RTL to J. J. Jusserand, March 17, 1909, and RTL to Clinton Conkling, May 28, 1909, LB, 42:73:291, 498; RTL to J. Otis Humphrey, October 20, 1909, SC 1708, Humphrey Papers; RTL to Francis D. Tandy, January 10, 1910, RTL Papers, ALPL.

44. RTL to William E. Reed, February 20, 1909, and RTL to Emory Speer, February 23, 1909, LB, 42:72:184, 194.

45. "Robert Lincoln Read Inquirer," n.d., clipping, RTL Collection, Hildene Archives.

46. RTL to Reverend James W. Lee, Chicago, February 20, 1909, RTLFP. Robert's letter to Lee was printed in the book edition of Lee's speech, in Lee, *Abraham Lincoln*.

47. RTL to John M. Hays, et al., March 14, 1904, LB, 37:63:251, Robert told another correspondent that in his own travels throughout the south, he was always treated with kindness, which he believed was intended in part "to exhibit in most cases a feeling very gratifying to me in regard to my father's memory." RTL to J. S. Bassett, April 25, 1905, LB, 38:64:217.

48. RTL to George Du Relle, May 14, 1909, LB, 42:73:427.

49. RTL to Hardin Helm Herr, May 24, 1909, RTL to Major Thomas Hays, May 24, 1909, RTL to [illegible], May 24, 1909, and RTL to Henry Watterson, May 25, 1909, LB, 42:73:461, 462, 471–72, 474.

50. "Lincoln's Son Overcome," *New York Times*, June 1, 1909, 1; "Heat Fells Robert Lincoln," *Chicago Tribune*, June 1, 1909, 1; "Taft a New Lincoln?" *Washington Post*, June 2, 1909, 4. The Associated Press wrote a story solely on Robert's distress that was published in newspapers across the country. For example, "R. T. Lincoln Suffers from Intense Heat," *Pensacola (FL) Journal*, June 1, 1909, 1.

51. RTL to J. Otis Humphrey, Washington, February 1, 1913, folder 2, SC 1708, Humphrey Papers.

52. RTL to Mary Harlan Lincoln, June 1, 1909, LB, 42:73:508. Robert said much the same thing to a reporter the next day in Chicago. "Robert Lincoln Fully Recovered," *New York Tribune*, June 2, 1909, 6.

53. RTL to John Wesley Hill, Chicago, June 5, 1909, Hill Papers.

54. RTL to Otis M. Mather, June 2, 1909, LB 42:73:512; RTL to Richard Lloyd Jones, June 16, 1909, RTL Papers, ALPL.

55. Barnard, "Sculptor's View of Lincoln," 21.

56. Taft, "Presentation Address," 57–58.

57. "Statue of Lincoln Hailed as True Art," *New York Times*, September 27, 1917, 13.

58. RTL to William Howard Taft, Washington, March 22, 1917, box 372, series 3, Taft Papers.

59. William Howard Taft to RTL, April 3, 1917, vol. 60, series 8, Taft Letterbooks, Taft Papers.

60. "Had No Money for St. Gaudens Lincoln," *New York Times*, January 3, 1918, 8.

61. "Mistake in Bronze," 211–20.

62. "Lincoln: Was He a Slouch?" 416–17.

63. "Not the Real Lincoln," *New York Times*, August 26, 1917, 22.

64. "Mr. Barnard's 'Lincoln' Once More," *Art World*, October 1917, 7–11. The letters of Robert Lincoln and Joseph Choate were also printed in "Defends Criticism of Lincoln Statue," *New York Times*, September 28, 1917, 11.

65. Copies of the Taft letter were distributed around the country; Robert had a printed circular made for his press package of the Conkling letter, a copy of which remains in the ALPL, Clinton Conkling to RTL, Springfield, Illinois, April 27, 1917.

66. Frederick Hill Meserve to F. Wellington Ruckstuhl, New York, November 19, 1917, in "Letter from Frederick Hill Meserve," 200.

67. RTL to F. Wellington Ruckstuhl, Hildene, September 3, 1917, HM 8414, RTL Letters, Huntington Library; RTL to Isaac Markens, Hildene, August 28, 1917, folder 5, RTL Papers, CHM; also printed in Angle, *Portrait of Abraham Lincoln in Letters by His Oldest Son*, 41. See also "The Lincoln Statue," *London Times*, September 27, 1917, 5.

68. "Lincoln's Statue for London," *London Times*, September 24, 1917, 7; "The Caricature of Lincoln," *Washington Post*, January 2, 1918, 6; "Barnard Lincoln," 32–33; Raymond, "Barnard Lincoln," 72–73.

69. "Barnard Statue of Lincoln," 649.

70. RTL to Isaac Markens, Hildene, September 14, 1917, folder 5, RTL Papers, CHM; also printed in Angle, *Portrait of Abraham Lincoln*, 43–44.

71. RTL to Judd Stewart, Hildene, October 18, 1917, HM 8430, RTL Letters, Huntington Library; George Gray Barnard to RTL, April 14, 1917, RTL Papers, ALPL.

72. "Barnard Statue of Lincoln," 241.

73. RTL to F. Wellington Ruckstuhl, Hildene, October 3, 1917, HM 8425, RTL Collection, Huntington Library.

74. "Barnard's Statue Is Again Opposed," *New York Times*, January 1, 1918, 17.

75. RTL to F. Wellington Ruckstuhl, Hildene, January 17, 1918, HM 8460, RTL Collection, Huntington Library.

76. On February 8, Robert declared, "I think matters are going on extremely well and I now have no doubt as to the solution"; on February 22 he also wrote that he had "little doubt" that the Saint-Gaudens statue would be sent to London in place of the Barnard. RTL to Judd Stewart, Washington, February 8, 1918, and RTL to F. Wellington Ruckstuhl, Washington, February 22, 1918, HM 8465 and HM 8467, RTL Collection, Huntington Library.

77. "Report to Academy on Lincoln Statue," *New York Times*, December 22, 1918, 9. See also "Memorandum for President Butler, in re: St. Gaudens Statue of Abraham Lincoln," December 12, 1938, box 234, Nicholas Murray Butler Papers.

78. "Lincoln Statue for London," 60–61. For further reading on the Barnard statue controversy, see also Dickson, "George Grey Barnard's Controversial Lincoln," 8–23; M. D. Peterson, *Lincoln in American Memory*, 208–214; Moffatt, *Errant Bronzes*; B. Schwartz, *Abraham Lincoln*, 271–76; Percoco, *Summers with Lincoln*, 48–86.

79. RTL to F. Wellington Ruckstuhl, Hildene, September 22, 1917, HM 8423, RTL Letters, Huntington Library; Nicholas Murray Butler to RTL, December 31, 1918, box 234, Nicholas Murray Butler Papers.

80. RTL to Nicholas Murray Butler, Washington, December 17, 1920, box 234, Nicholas Murray Butler Papers.

81. Nicholas Murray Butler to RTL, December 21, 1920, ibid.

82. RTL to Nicholas Murray Butler, Washington, January 8, 1919, ibid.

83. Ibid., December 17, 1920.

84. Anna Chittenden Thayer, "My Interview with Robert Lincoln, September 1922," Anna Gansevoort Chittenden Thayer Memoirs.

24. "I Am Now Enjoying Life"

1. Robert wrote to a friend in February 1906, "For something like a year I have found my nerves going back on me, and one thing with another—the culmination being Mr. [Marshall] Field's death—put me in such shape that I was ordered away from work." By June, he told his aunt he was "improving very greatly." RTL to Richard Watson Gilder, Augusta, Georgia, February 12, 1906, folder 2, RTL Papers, CHM, and RTL to Emily Helm, June 8, 1906, copy, RTL Collection, Hildene Archives.

2. "To Ask More Stock," *New York Tribune*, November 10, 1906, 9; "From the Papers," *Wall Street Journal*, November 12, 1906, 2; "Capital Is $100,000,000," *Los Angeles Herald*, November 15, 1906, 5.

3. "Pullman Head Will Retire," *Chicago Tribune*, April 20, 1911, 13; "Personal," *Wall*

Street Journal, April 20, 1911, 8; "Runnells Succeeds Lincoln," *New York Times*, May 19, 1911, 13; "J. S. Runnells Pullman Head," *Chicago Tribune*, May 19, 1911, 9.

4. RTL to George H. Thacher, May 9, 1912, portfolio 1, no. 21, Alfred Withal Stern Collection of Lincolniana.

5. "Pullman Profits Lower," *New York Times*, October 22, 1911, 16.

6. These statistics can be found in the company's annual reports, as reported in the *New York Times* and other newspapers.

7. "Some Pullman Figures," *Hartford(CT) Courant*, October 19, 1914, 14.

8. "Commonwealth Edison," *Wall Street Journal*, February 25, 1914, 6.

9. "Robert Todd Lincoln, 1843–1926," 4.

10. RTL to Charles Munroe, September 23, 1911, and RTL to Mary Harlan Lincoln, October 11, 1911, LB, 45:79:261, 292, 297. Robert sold his Chicago house for $65,000, closing the deal on October 11, 1911.

11. RTL to Charles Munroe, September 23, 1911, LB, 45:79:261, 297.

12. RTL to Cordelia Jackson, Hildene, August 3, 1918, RTL Papers, ACPL. Robert purchased a complete set of the Georgetown Historical Society Reports to see if his house ever was mentioned and found the original boundary marker buried in the garden. The house is today known as the Laird-Dunlop House, after the builder, Laird, and the second owner, Laird's son-in-law, U.S. Circuit Court Judge James Dunlop. It is well known also by its former longtime owner, Ben Bradlee, former editor of the *Washington Post*. Bradlee described the house in his memoir as "simply the most beautiful house I had ever seen." "Son of Lincoln, 82, Returns to Palatial Capital Home," *Washington Star*, November 22, 1925, clipping, RTL Collection Hildene Archives; Bradlee, *Good Life*, 458–59.

13. Margaret Wade, "Mainly about People," *Los Angeles Times*, October 17, 1911, 16.

14. "Back to Washington," *Pittsburgh (PA) Post-Gazette*, October 22, 1911, 34.

15. RTL to Mrs. E. A. Lawton, Washington, April 8, 1916, box 19, Anderson Papers.

16. One of Robert's former secretaries, Andrew P. Federline, supposedly said his employer had "fits of depression and melancholy," similar to his father, and during these periods sought refuge in his observatory. Federline claimed that Mrs. Lincoln feared her husband would commit suicide and "always" asked the secretary to stay with him. Margaret A. Flint to Ruth Painter Randall, Springfield, Illinois, November 12, 1955, folder "Robert Lincoln," box 72, Randall Family Papers.

17. *Centennial History of the Ekwanok County Club*, 150.

18. RTL to O. S. A. Sprague, May 15, 1900, LB, 34:56:242–43; RTL to Norman Ream, December 4, 1905, LN, 38:65:452.

19. Dunbaugh, "Robert Todd Lincoln," 16.

20. *Centennial History of the Ekwanok County Club*, 150.

21. Macdonald, *Scotland's Gift*, 131–33.

22. "Golf," *New York Tribune*, August 15, 1901, 4.

23. RTL to Mr. Corton, October 19, 1905, RTL Collection, Hildene Archives. Ainsworth, "Where the Golf Championship Will Be Played," 16. Robert was elected president of the Chicago Golf Club for that year.

24. Ekwanok County Club Board of Governors, resolution on the death of Robert T. Lincoln, 1926, *Centennial History of the Ekwanok County Club*, 154.

25. RTL to Charles B. Macdonald, April 20, 1905, LB, 38:64:195; RTL to Charles B. Macdonald, July 20, 1907, and RTL to James A. Stillman, July 20, 1907, LB, 40:68:200, 204; "National Golf Course," *New York Tribune*, May 25, 1908, 6; Macdonald, *Scotland's Gift*, 175–77.

26. Lincoln to Macdonald, quoted in Macdonald, *Scotland's Gift*, 177–78.

27. RTL to C. Herbert Windeler, Manchester, Vermont, September 14 and 24, 1908, LB, 41:71:325, 341.

28. Butler, *Across the Busy Years*, 2:379–80, 423.

29. "R. T. Lincoln, Emancipator's Son, Dies at 82," *New York Tribune*, July 27, 1926, 5.

30. The telescope is now part of the club's historical collection. *Centennial History of the Ekwanok County Club*, 152.

31. Ibid., 153; "Golf Stars at Ekwanok," *New York Times*, August 1, 1918, 12.

32. "Golf Boom Coming, All Due to Taft," *New York Times*, November 22, 1908, S2.

33. "Progress of the World," 387.

34. "President Leaves Beverly for Auto Tour of Vermont," *Christian Science Monitor*, October 5, 1912, 26; "Taft Satisfied with Trend to Him," *New York Times*, October 7, 1912, 6; "President Taft in Manchester," *Manchester (VT) Journal*, October 10, 1912, clipping, RTL Collection, Hildene Archives.

35. William Howard Taft to RTL, Pointe-au-Pic, Canada, August 5, 1913, Taft Letterbooks, vol. 5, series 8, Taft Papers.

36. "Tafts Guests of Lincolns," *Los Angeles Times*, September 6, 1913, 13; "Lincoln Entertains the Tafts," *New York Times*, September 8, 1913, 3; "Ex-President Taft in Manchester," *Manchester (VT) Journal*, September 11, 1913, clipping, RTL Collection, Hildene Archives; William Howard Taft to RTL, September 11, 1913, RTL Collection, Hildene Archives; RTL to William Howard Taft, September 17, 1913, box 259, series 3, Taft Papers.

37. The place was known at the time as the Munson House; now it is a bed-and-breakfast named the 1811 House. *Manchester (VT) Journal*, June 1 and July 4, 1905, clippings, RTL Collection, Hildene Archives.

38. RTL to Mrs. Lawton, August 2, 1905, box 19, Anderson Papers.

39. RTL to General Beverly H. Robertson, Manchester, Vermont, September 23, 1907, LB, 40:69:305.

40. The screen still is located in Hildene.

41. RTL to S. B. Elliot, Manchester, July 30 and August 1, 1907, LB, 40:68:226–27, 234.

42. RTL to Mrs. George Orvis, September 22, 1925, RTL Collection, Hildene Archives; C. J. King, *Four Marys*, 158.

43. "Manchester-in-Mountains," *New York Times*, August 29, 1909, sec. 6, p. 1.

44. Ibid., July 23, 1911; Jon Booth reminiscence, in "Happy Birthday Bud," 2.

45. RTL to S. M. Felton, Manchester, Vermont, July 16, 1907, LB, 40:68:183–85.

46. Noel E. Parmentel Jr., telephone interview with the author, February 3, 2010.

47. Jessie Beckwith wedding invitation to Emily Helm, folder 3, box 3, Emily Todd Helm Papers; an unaddressed wedding invitation is in the Hildene Archives; "Jessie Lincoln Remarries," and "R. T. Lincoln's Daughter Is Bride Again," *New York Herald*, June 23, 1915, clippings, RTL Collection, Hildene Archives.

48. RTL to Emily Helm, June 12, 1915, folder 8, RTL Papers, CHM.

49. Frank Edward Johnson to Mary Harlan Lincoln, March 15, 1915, RTLFP, copy in RTL Collection, Hildene Archives.

50. Frank Edward Johnson to RTL, Havana, Cuba, April 18, 1921, RTLFP, copy in Hildene Archives.

51. Mary Harlan Lincoln (quoting Robert Lincoln) to Jessie Lincoln Beckwith Johnson, June 10, 1921, RTL Collection, Hildene Archives.

52. "Granddaughter of Lincoln to Wed a Randolph," *Chicago Tribune*, December 30, 1926, 1.

53. In 1919, Robert established trust funds for both his daughters. For Mary Lincoln

Isham's trust, he deposited 375 shares of Commonwealth Edison stock worth slightly more than $38,000 and 1,000 shares of National Biscuit stock worth $85,000. For Jessie Lincoln Johnson's trust, he deposited 1,000 shares of Commonwealth Edison stock worth $101,750 and 1,000 shares of National Biscuit stock worth $85,000. Jessie received more because her father knew she was less frugal, and often irresponsible, with her finances. "R. T. Lincoln Stocks Up $1,000,000 since 1917," *New York Times*, February 14, 1930, 44; "Estate of Robert Todd Lincoln," in Owen, *Reports of the United States Board of Tax Appeals*, 336.

54. Robert achieved this increase by depositing another 1,250 shares of Commonwealth Edison stock, worth more than $100,000, into Jessie's trust fund. RTL to Jessie Lincoln Beckwith Johnson, Manchester, Vermont, July 6, 1920, and Jessie Lincoln Beckwith Johnson to RTL, Washington, July 18, 1920, RTLFP, copies in Hildene Archives; "R. T. Lincoln Stocks Up $1,000,000 since 1917," *New York Times*, February 14, 1930, 44.

55. "Gives Out Lincoln Letter," *Lexington (KY) Herald*, April 29, 1912, 6; "Roosevelt Assailed by Robert Lincoln," *New York Times* April 29, 1912, 2; "Robt. T. Lincoln Hits Roosevelt," *Chicago Times*, April 29, 1912, 4. President Taft made public Robert's entire letter during a campaign stop in Newark, New Jersey, after which the letter was published in newspapers across America.

56. "Lincoln and Roosevelt," *New York* Times, April 30, 1912, 10; J. C. Levi, "Lincoln and Roosevelt," letter to the editor, *New York Times*, May 1, 12; Henry C. Weeks, "Robert T. Lincoln for President," letter to the editor, *New York Times*, May 3, 1912, 10.

57. RTL to George H. Thacher, May 9, 1912, portfolio 1, no. 21, Alfred Withal Stern Collection of Lincolniana; Walter Trohan, "To Lincoln's Son, Golf Came First," *Chicago Tribune*, September 16, 1957, clipping, RTL Collection, Hildene Archives; Noel A. Dunderdale, "Robert Lincoln's Refusal to Run," *Chicago Tribune*, September 24, 1957, 24.

58. RTL to James H. Wilson, Manchester, Vermont, July 8, 1912, folder "Robert Lincoln," box 14, Wilson Papers.

59. "The Robert Lincoln Boom," *Los Angeles Times*, June 16, 1912, 12; "Roosevelt Firm For Ousting Men Seated by Fraud," *Chicago Tribune*, June 17, 1912, 1; "First Fight in Convention Likely over Temporary Chairmanship," *New York Times*, June 18, 1912, 1.

60. Walter Trohan, "To Lincoln's Son, Golf Came First," *Chicago Tribune*, September 16, 1957, clipping, RTL Collection, Hildene Archives.

61. "Might Have Barred Taft's Nomination," *New York Times*, June 1, 1924, 1.

62. RTL to James H. Wilson, Manchester, Vermont, May 4 and July 8, 1912, folder "Robert Lincoln," box 14, Wilson Papers.

63. "Taft Fund Was $904,828," *New York Times*, December 3, 1912, 24.

64. "President Taft in Manchester," *Manchester (VT) Journal*, October 10, 1912, clipping, RTL Collection, Hildene Archives.

65. "Man of Many Myths." The ad was published in newspapers across the country. For example, see *Grand Rapids (MI) Press*, October 20, 1916, 22.

66. RTL to Alice James, Manchester, Vermont, November 22, 1916, bMS Am 1928 (197), James Papers.

67. "War Loan Means U.S. Prosperity," *Philadelphia Inquirer*, October 18, 1915, 2; "The Anglo-French Loan," *London Times*, October 19, 1915, 15; Van Alstyne, "Private American Loans to the Allies, 1914–1916," 180–93.

68. RTL to Emily Helm, August 8, 1917, folder 7, RTL Papers, CHM.

69. Charles Isham diary, Isham Family Papers.

70. "Just Comment," *Miami Herald Record*, March 24, 1918, 20.

71. "Introducing Mrs. Cincinnatus," *Wyoming State Tribune*, April 3, 1918, 4.

72. RTL to Alice James, Washington, May 12, 1919, bMS Am 1928 (97), James Papers.

73. RTL to Mrs. E. A. Lawton, box 19, Anderson Papers.

74. RTL to Mrs. E. A. Lawton, box 19, Anderson Papers; RTL to Emily Helm, Manchester, Vermont, July 21, 1919, folder 8, RTL papers, CHM.

75. RTL to W. H. Chapple, Washington, April 11, 1917, RTL Collection, Hildene Archives.

76. The transfer was not made until 1902, and for the previous year, the papers had actually been partly in a Washington bank vault and partly in the possession of Nicolay's daughter Helen. RTL to John Hay, November 8, 1901, LB, 35:58:241, and RTL to John Hay, May 26, 1902, LB, 36:60:11. For a more complete and detailed history of the papers, see Mearns, *Lincoln Papers*, 1:89–109, and Hickey, "Robert Todd Lincoln and the 'Purely Private' Letters of the Lincoln Family," 166–79.

77. RTL to John Hay, October 19, 1904, reel 8, Hay Papers, Brown University.

78. Robert was quite naturally saddened by the death of his friend of nearly fifty years and attended the funeral in Cleveland. Years later he wrote, "What a wonderful man John Hay was!—the most charming man I ever met." "John Hay Is Buried with Simple Honors," *New York Times*, July 6, 1905, 9; RTL to Edward Everett Hale, March 19, 1909, LB, 42:73:300.

79. RTL to Andrew H. Allen, October 13, 21, and 28, 1905, LB, 38:65:355, 379, 387; RTL to Helen Nicolay, Washington, March 23, 1918, RTL Collection, ACPL.

80. Robert mentioned Sweet's overseeing of the papers numerous times in his correspondence, for example, see, RTL to Herbert Putnam, Manchester, Vermont, July 20, 1906, LB, 39:67:251, RTL to James Schouler, Manchester, Vermont, October 22, 1908, LB, 41:71:370; RTL to Frederic Bancroft, Manchester, Vermont, May 13 and June 10, 1912, Bancroft Papers.

81. For example, in 1909, Robert gave Frederick Dent Grant the original draft of President Lincoln's 1864 speech to Ulysses S. Grant making him lieutenant general of the army, as well as Grant's reply. RTL to Frederick Grant, February 10, 1909, LB, 42:72:143.

82. RTL to Herbert Putnam, Librarian of Congress, January 6, 1902, LB, 35:59:333.

83. RTL to Albert D. Hager, Washington, August 27, 1882, in Angle, *Chicago Historical Society*, 112.

84. RTL to Herbert Putnam, Manchester, Vermont, July 20, 1906, LB, 39:67:251.

85. Herbert Putnam to RTL, March 28, 1910, in Mearns, *Lincoln Papers*, 1:95–96.

86. Charles Moore, memorandum, May 6, 1919, in Mearns, *Lincoln Papers*, 1:100–101; "End of Lincoln Trunk Mystery," *New York Times*, June 13, 1926, XX13.

87. Robert himself used the term *safekeeping* regarding the transfer. RTL to Judd Stewart, Washington, January 8, 1920, HM 8480, Huntington Library; "Deed of Gift of Manuscripts and Private Papers of President Lincoln by His Son, Robert Todd Lincoln," January 23, 1923, file 75, cont. 4, part 2, RTLFP. That same year, Robert wrote into his will that the papers in the Library of Congress be given to the American people in the event of his death. "History of the Lincoln Papers in Library of Congress"; Mearns, *Lincoln Papers*, 1:101–2.

88. Appleton Griffin, acting librarian, to Charles Moore, acting chief of manuscripts, May 7, 1919, internal memo, RTLFP. For a complete index and survey of correspondence regarding the Library of Congress acquisition of the Lincoln papers from Robert Lincoln, beginning in 1902, see St. George L. Sioussat, chief of division of manuscripts, Library of Congress, to David C. Mearns, director of reference department, Library of Congress, March 21, 1947, box 85, Mearns Papers.

89. "Deed of Gift of Manuscripts and Private Papers of President Lincoln by His Son,

Robert Todd Lincoln," January 23, 1923, and St. George L. Sioussat to David C. Mearns, internal Library of Congress memorandum, April 1, 1947, and David C. Mearns to the Librarian of Congress, "Property Rights, Lincoln Manuscripts and the Seward Heirs," July 17, 1951, Mearns Papers; RTL deed of gift to Library of Congress, January 23, 1923, also in file 75, cont. 4, part 2, RTLFP.

90. Herbert Putnam to RTL, Washington, January 23, 1923, file 75, cont. 4, part 2, RTLFP.

91. RTL to Nicholas Murray Butler, April 24, 1924, Butler to RTL, April 21, 1924, and Butler to Herbert Putnam, December 1, 1938, box 234, Nicholas Murray Butler Papers; Albert Beveridge to Nicholas Murray Butler, April 19 and 23, 1924, and Butler to Beveridge, April 21 and 25, 1924, folder "Nicholas Murray Butler," cont. 286, Beveridge Papers; Frederic Towers to Jessie Lincoln Randolph, March 21, 1947, letter file A, RTL Papers, ALPL.

92. Robert also refused access to historians William E. Barton, Lord Charnwood, Emanuel Hertz, and William E. Dodd of the University of Chicago, all for the same reason. Albert Beveridge to RTL, December 27, 1922 and January 15, 1923, and RTL to Albert Beveridge, Washington, January 23, 1923, folder "L," cont. 290, Lincoln Correspondence, Beveridge Papers; William E. Dodd to RTL, January 28, 1925, and Dodd to Norman Frost [Lincoln attorney], February 20, 1925, RTL Collection, Hildene Archives; Emanuel Hertz to Norman Frost, April 17, 1925, and Frost to Hertz, April 18, 1925, RTL Collection, Hildene Archives; "End of Lincoln Trunk Mystery," *New York Times*, June 13, 1926, XX13.

93. RTL "Deed of Gift of Manuscripts and Private Papers of President Lincoln by His Son, Robert Todd Lincoln," January 23, 1923, file 75, cont. 4, part 2, RTLFP.

94. RTL to Herbert Putnam, January 16, 1926, file 75, cont. 4, part 2, RTLFP.

95. Frederic Towers to Katherine Helm, May 7, 1926, RTL Collection, Hildene Archives; Mary Harlan Lincoln to Herbert Putnam, Librarian of Congress, April 16, 1928, and Putnam to Mrs. Lincoln, April 18, 1928, and Frederic Towers [writing for Mary Harlan Lincoln] to W. A. Evans, April 21, 1930, file 75, cont. 4, part 2, RTLFP; Mearns, *Lincoln Papers*, 1:106.

96. David Davis to the Heirs of Robert T. Lincoln, February 11, 1927, and Frederic Towers [writing for Mary Harlan Lincoln] to David Davis, February 15, 1927, RTL Collection, Hildene Archives; Mary Harlan Lincoln to Dr. Jameson, Manchester, Vermont, July 19, 1929, and Frederic Towers [writing for Mary Harlan Lincoln] to W. A. Evans, April 21, 1930, file 75, cont. 4, part 2, RTLFP.

97. Butler, *Across the Busy Years*, 2:375–76, originally published in Butler, "Lincoln and Son," *Saturday Evening Post*, February 11, 1939, 23. Butler also told the story to Emmanuel Hertz in 1937, who included it in the introduction to his 1938 book. Hertz, *Hidden Lincoln*, 17–18.

98. For a complete examination of the paper-burning story of Butler and its numerous permutations through the years, see Mearns, *Lincoln Papers*, 1:121–36.

99. For example, see Schwartz, "Roasting Lincoln's Letters," 4–5.

100. James T. Hickey, curator of the Illinois Historical Society's Lincoln Collection, interviewed one of Robert Lincoln's secretaries, Andrew P. Federline, as well as Robert's Manchester, Vermont, attorney, James B. Campbell, who both stated they witnessed paper-burning at Hildene, but both adamantly believed the letters were Robert's own correspondence, not anything from his father. Hickey, "Robert Todd Lincoln and the 'Purely Private' Letters of the Lincoln Family," 174–78.

101. Hickey, "Robert Todd Lincoln and the 'Purely Private' Letters of the Lincoln Family," 166–79.

102. RTL to David Davis, Chicago, November 16, 1866, folder A-109, box 7, DDFP.

103. Mary Lincoln to Mary Jane Welles, July 11, 1865, in Turner and Turner, *Mary Todd Lincoln*, 257.

25. "He Simply Went to Sleep"

1. Legend states that the top hat Robert wore that day was one of his father's, which the son wore as a sign of filial homage.

2. William Howard Taft to RTL, May 23, 1922, box 514, series 3, Taft Papers.

3. "50,000 See Lincoln Memorial Presented to Nation," *Washington Star*, May 31, 1920, 4.

4. For historical background of the memorial's creation see, Lincoln Memorial Commission, *Lincoln Memorial Commission Report*; "Memorial to Abraham Lincoln," 247–57.

5. For details on the memorial itself, see Henry Bacon, "Lincoln Memorial," and Charles Moore, "Daniel Chester French's Statue of Lincoln," in "Memorial to Abraham Lincoln," 253–57; Duffield, "Dedication of the Lincoln Memorial," 552–56.

6. RTL to William Howard Taft, Manchester, Vermont, November 7 and 20, 1913, box 263, series 3, and January 18, 1914, box 269, series 3, and Taft to Lincoln, November 9 and 27, 1913, and January 19, 1914, Taft Letterbooks, vols. 8, 9, and 12, series 8, and January 12, 1914, box 269, series 3, Taft Papers.

7. "In Tribute to Lincoln," *Washington Post*, February 13, 1915, 5; "Lincoln Memorial Cornerstone Laid," *Los Angeles Times*, February 13, 1915, 12.

8. Daniel Chester French to RTL, April 26, May 1 and 12, September 18 and 26, 1916, reel 18, Daniel Chester French Papers; RTL to Clinton Conkling, Washington, November 24, 1917, folder 10, box 2, Conkling Family Papers.

9. C. S. Ridley to RTL, December 6, 1920, Section A-7: General Permits, Lincoln Memorial Commission Files, RG 42, NARA.

10. For an excellent article on efforts to kill the memorial, see Susan Mandel, "The Lincoln Conspirator," *Washington Post*, February 3, 2008, W14.

11. RTL to John W. Dwight, Washington, April 18, 1916, series 1, General Correspondence 1833–1916, Abraham Lincoln Papers, LOC. Dwight's widow gave the Lincoln manuscript to her husband's hometown library in Dryden, New York, in 1926. In 2009, the library sold the speech through Christie's auction house for $3.4 million in order to fund a building addition and general endowment. Oder, "Small Upstate New York Library Earns $3 Million from Lincoln Manuscript Sale"; "Abraham Lincoln's 1864 Victory Speech."

12. President Warren G. Harding to Chief Justice William H. Taft, April 26, 1922, RTL Collection, Hildene Archives; William Howard Taft to RTL, April 27 and May 23, 1922, and Lincoln to Taft, April 28, 1922, box 514, series 3, Taft Papers.

13. RTL letter quoted in Aaron Hardy Ulm, "Lincoln's Silent Son," *Leslie's Weekly*, February 11, 1922, 185, and in "Son of Lincoln, 82, Returns to Palatial Capital Home," *Washington Star*, November 22, 1925, clipping, RTL Collection, Hildene Archives. I have been unable to locate Robert's original manuscript letter.

14. "Harding, Taft Praise Lincoln at His Shrine," *Chicago Tribune*, May 31, 1922, 1.

15. "Memorial Day for Lincoln," *St. Petersburg (FL) Evening Independent*, May 30, 1922, 1, 12.

16. RTL to F. Wellington Ruckstuhl, Hildene, November 1, 1917, HM 8438, Letters, RTL Collection, Huntington Library.

17. Edward F. Bryant to RTL, August 25, 1925, RTL Collection, Hildene Archives.

18. Mearns, *Lincoln Papers*, 1:108–9. Unfortunately, Mearns does not cite from where he acquired this story, nor do his personal papers or book research notes at the Library of Congress illuminate his source.

19. "Appreciation of Robert Todd Lincoln."

20. Frederic Towers, writing for Mary Harlan Lincoln, to Lieutenant Colonel Clarence Sherrill, August 15, 1925, and Sherrill to Towers, September 9, 1926, RTL Collection, Hildene Archives; President Calvin Coolidge to RTL, White House, December 29, 1925, and RTL to Coolidge, Washington, December 31, 1925, folder 7, K box 5, William H. Townsend Collection; Mary H. Lincoln to Laura Hollister, March 14, 1926, Lincoln Collection, ALPL.

21. K. Helm, *True Story of Mary.*

22. For one specific description of his activities, see "Son of Lincoln," *Washington Star,* November 22, 1925, clipping, RTL Collection, Hildene Archives.

23. For example, see "Women Preparing Annual Flower Show in Green Mountains," *New York Tribune,* August 6, 1922, 5.

24. Owen, *Reports of the United States Board of Tax Appeals,* 337.

25. Mary Harlan Lincoln to Walter Sylvester Hertzog, Manchester, Vermont, November 18, 1923, Mary Harlan Lincoln Autograph File; Mary H. Lincoln to Laura Hollister, Lincoln Collection, ALPL.

26. Owen, *Reports of the United States Board of Tax Appeals,* 337; Horace Young to RTL, March 18, 1925, 1923.64, RTL Collection, Hildene Archives.

27. RTL to Emily Helm, Washington, March 19, 1920, folder 8, RTL papers, CHM.

28. RTL to Alice James, Manchester, Vermont, October 18, 1921, RTL Collection, Philips Exeter Academy Archives.

29. Aaron Hardy Ulm, "Lincoln's Silent Son," *Leslie's Weekly,* February 11, 1922, 184.

30. "As It Looks to Me," *Salt Lake Telegram,* July 1, 1920, 16.

31. "Robert T. Lincoln," *Detroit Free Press,* reprinted in *Los Angeles Times,* May 1, 1921, 3:46. See also "Son of Lincoln," *Washington Star,* November 22, 1925, clipping, RTL Collection, Hildene Archives; RTL to J. Keeley, October 17, 1925, RTL Papers, ALPL.

32. Editorial, "Why Not in Limelight?" *Lexington Herald,* July 30, 1916, 3.

33. "Crowds at Stations Cheer Lloyd George on Way to Canada," *New York Times,* October 7, 1923, 1; "Lloyd George Told of Lincoln by Abe's Son," *Chicago Tribune,* October 7, 1923, 3.

34. Ibid.

35. Owen, *Reports of the United States Board of Tax Appeals,* 338.

36. Ibid., 335–36. The government later investigated the legality of this action.

37. RTL to George Thacher, May 19, 1926, RTL Collection, Hildene Archives.

38. Henry B. Rankin to George A. Dondero, June 26, 1926, RTL Collection, Hildene Archives. Henry B. Rankin was a Springfield banker who claimed to have been a student in the Lincoln-Herndon Law Office in the 1850s. He published two books, *Personal Recollections of Abraham Lincoln* and *Intimate Character Sketches of Abraham Lincoln.* Historian Michael Burlingame argues convincingly, however, that Rankin never lived in Springfield in the 1850s nor studied in the Lincoln-Herndon Law Office but merely wanted to write himself into the Lincoln lore. "'Hard-Hearted Conscious Liar and an Oily Hypocrite,'" 389–98.

39. Frederic Towers to Dr. Samuel Adams, July 29, 1926, RTL Collection, Hildene Archives.

40. Owen, *Reports of the United States Board of Tax Appeals,* 338.

41. Mary Harlan Lincoln to Katherine Helm, 4:05 P.M., July 26, 1926, telegram, private collection.

42. Frederic Towers to B. H. Helm, telegram, 4:05 P.M., July 26, 1926, private collec-

tion; Keys interview, "Body of Son of Martyred President to Rest in Tomb," *(Springfield) Illinois State Journal Register*, July 27, 1926, 1.

43. Coolidge Pays High Tribute to Son of Lincoln," *Los Angeles Times*, July 28, 1926, 2.

44. "Kellogg Praises Public Career of Robert Lincoln," *New York Herald Tribune*, July 27, 1926, 5.

45. "Robert Lincoln Misunderstood, Cannon Asserts," *New York Herald Tribune*, July 27, 1926, 5.

46. General Orders No. 16, U.S. War Department, copy, RTL Collection, Hildene Archives.

47. "Body of Son of Martyred President to Rest in Tomb," *(Springfield) Illinois State Journal*, July 27, 1926, 1.

48. Statement on the death of Robert Lincoln, Board of Directors, Mark Skinner Library, RTL Collection, Hildene Archives; "Robert Todd Lincoln Memorial," 33; Dunbaugh, "Robert Todd Lincoln; "Tribute to Last Lincoln to be Paid by Chicago Bar," n.d., clipping, Lincoln Children Vertical File; "Illinois Bell Telephone," *Wall Street Journal*, July 31, 1926, 11.

49. RTL obituary, *Pullman News*, August 1926, 113, clipping, record group 15, Pullman Company Archives.

50. "Robert T. Lincoln," *New York Herald Tribune*, July 27, 1926, 16.

51. "Lincoln's Son Dies in His Sleep at 82," *New York Times*, July 27, 1926, 1.

52. For an example of the Associated Press story, see "Robert T. Lincoln, Son of President, Dies at Age of 83," *Washington Post*, July 27, 1926, 3.

53. "Chicago Friend Relates Anecdotes of Robert Lincoln," *Chicago Tribune*, July 27, 1926, 6.

54. "Son of Abraham Lincoln," 36.

55. "Mr. R. T. Lincoln," *London Times*, July 27, 1926, 11.

56. "Robert Todd Lincoln," *Boston Herald*, July 27, 1926.

57. Frederic Towers to Katherine Helm, Manchester, Vermont, August 24, 1926, F box 3, William H. Townsend Papers.

58. These arrangements included hiring the undertaker to do the embalming and layout, hiring the hearse, and purchasing the casket and the flowers, the total cost of which was nearly $1,000. Undertaker's ledger, Manchester, Vermont, July 27, 1926, entry 51, p. 73, RTL Collection, Hildene Archives.

59. "Simple Rites Honor Robert T. Lincoln," *New York Times*, July 29, 1926, 19.

60. Sermon of Reverend D. Cunningham-Graham, August 1, 1926, RTL Collection, Hildene Archives; "Robert Lincoln Rites Marked by Simplicity," *Washington Post*, July 29, 1926, 7.

61. Robert T. Lincoln Last Will and Testament, October 17, 1919, copy, RTL Collection, Hildene Archives; "R. T. Lincoln's Widow Is Bequeathed Estate," *Washington Post*, August 18, 1926, 20; "R. T. Lincoln's Will Filed," *New York Times*, August 18, 1926, 20; "Lincoln Will Filed," *New York Times*, September 14, 1926, 29; "Newspaper Specials," *Wall Street Journal*, September 15, 1926, 11.

62. Money for his grandchildren is mentioned in Jessie Lincoln Randolph to Mary Harlan Lincoln, n.d. [October 1936], RTLFP, copy, RTL Collection, Hildene Archives.

63. The story was national news. For examples, see "Lincoln Letters Given U.S. by Son Hidden until 1947," *Chicago Tribune*, July 27, 1926, 6; "Left Father's Letters a Gift to the Nation," *New York Times*, July 27, 1926, 4.

64. "Editorial of the Day: The Lincoln Letters," *Indianapolis News*, reprinted in *Chicago Tribune*, August 5, 1926, 8; "Kind but Misguided," 143.

65. "Son of Abraham Lincoln," 42.

66. "May Inter Son of R. T. Lincoln Beside Father," *(Springfield) Illinois State Journal*, October 1926, clipping, RTL folder, Lincoln Drawer, RTL Vertical File.

67. C. R. Miller to Mary Harlan Lincoln, Springfield, Illinois, September 2, 1926, and Frederic Towers, writing for Mrs. Lincoln, to C. R. Miller, September 8, 1926, RTL Collection, Hildene Archives.

68. "Tribute to Last Lincoln to Be Paid by Chicago Bar," n.d., clipping, Lincoln Children Vertical File.

Epilogue: "His Own Place in the Sun"

1. RTL to Honorable O. M. Hatch, London, September 10, 1890, box 3, National Lincoln Monument Association Papers, 1885–95, also in LB, 14:20:148–49 (emphasis in original).

2. RTL to Clinton Conkling, London, September 10, 1890, LB, 14:20:146–47 (emphasis in original).

3. RTL to Nicholas Murray Butler, Manchester, Vermont, November 15, 1922, box 234, Nicholas Murray Butler Papers.

4. Mary Harlan Lincoln to Katherine Helm, n.d., Mary G. Townsend Collection (emphasis in original). This letter was first revealed and published in Swick and McCreary, "His Own Place in the Sun," 3–6.

5. Untitled article, Associated Press, October 21, 1926, clipping, folder 2, RTL Papers, CHM; *Manchester (VT) Journal*, October 28, 1926, clipping, RTL Collection, Hildene Archives. The Manchester, Vermont, undertaker's records show services and fees related to transporting the body arranged on October 20 and paid on November 11, 1926. Manchester, Vermont, undertaker's ledger, October 20, 1926, entry 71, 78, RTL Collection, Hildene Archives.

6. Mary Harlan Lincoln to Katherine Helm, n.d., Mary G. Townsend Collection.

7. Robert Todd Lincoln Report of Interment, Arlington National Cemetery Records, copy in RTL Collection, Hildene Archives. The Reverend Joseph Sizoo of the New York Avenue Presbyterian Church in Washington later declared that he presided over a secret dedication ceremony at Robert's final interment. His description of the event, however, is so outlandish and incredible as to be unbelievable. Among other things, he states that Mary Harlan Lincoln kept the event secret from her daughters, which she never would have done, and he gets the date of the interment wrong by more than fourteen months. Edgington, *History of the New York Avenue Presbyterian Church*, 266–75.

8. Agreement of Mrs. RTL with James E. Fraser, July 1928, RTLFP.

9. "Memorial at Grave to Honor Son of Great Emancipator," *Washington Star*, July 31, 1928, clipping, RTL Collection, Hildene Archives.

10. "Lincoln's Son to Be Buried at Arlington," *(Springfield) Illinois State Journal*, October 22, 1926, 1; "Body of Abraham Lincoln II May Be Removed from City to Arlington Cemetery," *(Springfield) Illinois State Journal*, September 1, 1929, clipping, RTL Collection, Hildene Archives; "Body of Lincoln's Grandson Will Be Moved to Arlington," *Chicago Tribune*, September 7, 1929, 3; "To Reinter Lincoln's Grandson," *New York Times*, September 8, 1929, N5; Babb, "Robert Todd Lincoln's Milwaukee Friend," 66. Nearly one dozen letters between Frederic Towers (writing for Mary Harlan Lincoln), Lincoln's attorney Max Babb, and Springfield attorney Logan Hay, a member of the Lincoln Tomb Commission, concerning Jack's removal from Springfield are in the RTLFP.

11. Robert Todd Lincoln Report of Interment, Arlington National Cemetery Records, copy, RTL Collection, Hildene Archives.

12. "Obtain Permit to Move the Body of R. T. Lincoln's Son," *(Springfield) Illinois State Journal*, May 23, 1930, 1; "To Send Body of Son of R. T. Lincoln to Arlington Today," *(Springfield) Illinois State Journal*, May 25, 1930, 1; "Abraham Lincoln to Be Buried in East," *(Springfield) Illinois State Register*, May 25, 1930, 5; "Lincoln Crypts," *(Springfield) Illinois State Journal*, November 8, 1931, TS, RTLFP; "Belated Honor at Arlington," *Washington Post*, February 10, 1984, A1; "Rescue from Anonymity," *New York Times*, February 10, 1984, A20; Bigler, *In Honored Glory*, 56.

13. RTL to Emily Helm, Manchester, Vermont, July 21, 1919, folder 8, RTL Papers, CHM; "Washington Society," *Chicago Tribune*, October 22, 1929; Frederic Towers to Max Babb, December 16, 1931, RTLFP.

14. "Manchester," July 28, 1927, clipping, and A. R. Frost to Mrs. Robert T. Lincoln, New York, August 1, 1927, and trust agreement between Mary Harlan Lincoln and the Ekwanok Country Club, October 8, 1928, RTL Collection, Hildene Archives.

15. "Mrs. Lincoln Gives Letters to Library," *Washington Star*, February 3, 1927, clipping, and Frederic Towers, writing for Mary Harlan Lincoln, to David Davis, February 15, 1927, RTL Collection, Hildene Archives; "Lincoln Bibles Placed in Library of Congress," *New York Times*, April 22, 1928, 29; receipt for donated materials from Mary Harlan Lincoln to the Library of Congress, October 2, 1928, Frederic Towers to Dr. Herbert Putnam, Librarian of Congress, October 3, 1928, and Mary Harlan Lincoln to Dr. John Franklin Jameson, July 19, 1929, RTLFP.

16. "Mrs. Lincoln, Widow of President's Son," *New York Times*, April 1, 1937, 24; "Famous Healy Portrait of Lincoln Left to Nation by Widow of His Son," *New York Times*, April 10, 1937, 21; "Lincoln Portrait by Healy Slated for White House," *Christian Science Monitor*, April 10, 1937, 7; ["Mrs. Robert Lincoln"], 10; Frederic N. Towers to Franklin D. Roosevelt, Washington, December 28, 1938, RTL Papers, ALPL.

17. Lincoln Isham to Jessie Lincoln Randolph, October 1938, and Mary Lincoln Isham death certificate, November 22, 1938, RTL Collection, Hildene Archives; "Mrs. Isham Dies," *New York Times*, November 22, 1938, 24.

18. "Mrs. R. J. Randolph, Lincoln Descendant," *New York Times*, January 6, 1948, 23.

19. "Lincoln Isham Is Married," *Chicago Tribune*, September 3, 1919, 13; "Lincoln's Great-Grandson Marries New York Girl," *New York Times*, September 4, 1919, 2.

20. Lincoln Isham autobiographical statement, Hildene Archives; "Four Lincoln Items Given to Library," *New York Times*, February 12, 1958, 56; "Twenty-Nine Lincoln Checks Given to Library of Congress," *Washington Post*, June 25, 1959, A14; "Lincoln Kin Gives Books to Library," *Washington Post*, May 31, 1960, B1.

21. Isabel Parris, interview by C. J. King, in C. J. King, *Four Marys*, 151.

22. "Mary Lincoln Beckwith, Lincoln Kin, in Vermont," *Boston Globe*, July 12, 1975, clipping, RTL Collection, Hildene Archives. She made this statement originally in 1961.

23. "Kin of Lincoln Hits Pressing of Integration," *Chicago Tribune*, February 13, 1963, 3; C. J. King, *Four Marys*, 199.

24. "Missile Ship Launched," *New York Times*, May 15, 1960, 2.

25. Peggy Beckwith, diary entry, May 14, 1960, RTL Collection, Hildene Archives.

26. Mary Lincoln Beckwith certificate of death, Vermont Department of Health, Local File 231, copy, RTL Collection, Hildene Archives.

27. "Church Left $450,000 by Lincoln Kin," United Press International, n.d., clipping, Hildene Archives; Keelan, *Robert Todd Lincoln's Hildene*. Church policy was to "dispose of" donated property. The threat of Hildene's destruction roused local Manchester, Vermont, residents to form the nonprofit group Friends of Hildene Inc. and purchase the

house and grounds. The Friends established Hildene as a privately run historic site, which it remains today.

28. Louise Hutchinson, "102 Years after Lincoln Died: A Call on His Great-Grandson," *Chicago Tribune*, April 16, 1967, A1.

29. "Gettysburg Holds Memorial Today," *New York Times*, November 19, 1933, N1; "Kin Views Fair's Lincoln," *Chicago Tribune*, September 23, 1964, A2.

30. "Lincoln Memorabilia Donated to Illinois," *New York Times*, October 10, 1976, 25.

31. "Kin Views Fair's Lincoln," *Chicago Tribune*, September 23, 1964, A2.

32. "Lincoln's Last Descendant Self-Styled 'Spoiled Brat,'" United Press International, in *Anchorage Daily News*, December 27, 1985, A5; "Obituary," *Los Angeles Times*, December 27, 1985, A32; Hickey, "Robert Todd Lincoln Beckwith."

33. Robert Todd Lincoln Beckwith death certificate, Commonwealth of Virginia, file no. 85–043942, copy, Hildene Archives; "R. Todd Beckwith Dies," *Washington Post*, December 26, 1985, B6; "Last Descendant of Lincoln, 81 Years Old, Dies in Virginia," *New York Times*, December 26, 1985, D12.

34. The one book more responsible than any other for destroying Robert's reputation is Baker, *Mary Todd Lincoln*. See also Schreiner, *Trials of Mrs. Lincoln*; Croy, *Trial of Mrs. Abraham Lincoln*; Rhodes and Jauchius, *Trial of Mary Todd Lincoln*.

35. "A Friend's Tribute," *Manchester (VT) Journal*, n.d., clipping, RTL Papers, ALPL.

36. "As It Looks to Me," *Salt Lake (UT) Telegram*, July 1, 1920, 16.

Bibliography

Archives and Collections

America Singing: Nineteenth-Century Song Sheets. American Memory, Rare Book and Special Collections Division, Library of Congress.
Anderson, Robert. Papers. Manuscript Division, Library of Congress.
Arnold, Isaac N. Collection. Chicago History Museum.
Arthur, Chester A., Papers. Library of Congress.
Ashland: The Henry Clay Estate, Lexington, Kentucky.
Bailhache Family Papers. Abraham Lincoln Presidential Library, Springfield, Illinois.
Bancroft, Frederic. Papers. Rare Book and Manuscript Library, Butler Library, Columbia University.
Barbee, David Rankin. Papers. Georgetown University Archives.
Batavia Historical Society, Batavia, Illinois.
Bates, David Homer. Papers. Abraham Lincoln Presidential Library, Springfield, Illinois.
Bates, David Homer. Papers. Library of Congress.
Bayard, Thomas F., Papers. Library of Congress.
Bennett, James Gordon. Papers. Rare Book, Manuscript, and Special Collections, Duke University.
Beveridge, Albert J. Papers. Library of Congress.
Black, Elizabeth (Mrs. William M.). Diary. Abraham Lincoln Presidential Library, Springfield, Illinois.
Black, Jeremiah S., Papers. Library of Congress.
Blaine, James G., Family Papers. Library of Congress.
Borglum, Gutzun. Papers. Library of Congress.
Boyd, William Kenneth. Papers. Rare Book, Manuscript, and Special Collections, Duke University.
Butler, Benjamin F., Papers. Library of Congress.
Butler, Nicholas Murray. Papers. Rare Book and Manuscript Library, Butler Library, Columbia University.
Chandler, Minnie. Papers. Abraham Lincoln Presidential Library, Springfield, Illinois.
Cleveland, Grover. Papers. Library of Congress.
Conkling, Clinton. Papers. Archives and Manuscript Division, Sterling Memorial Library, Yale University.
Conkling Family Papers. Abraham Lincoln Presidential Library, Springfield, Illinois.
Conley, Benjamin. Papers. Rare Book, Manuscript, and Special Collections, Duke University.
Council Bluffs, Iowa, Public Library.
Crawford Family Papers. Georgetown University Archives.
Davis, David, Family. Papers. Abraham Lincoln Presidential Library, Springfield, Illinois.
Davis, David. Papers. Chicago History Museum.
Dawes, Henry L., Papers. Library of Congress.
Dispatches. U.S. Ministers to Great Britain. 1889–93. National Archives and Records Administration, Washington, DC.

Edwards, Albert S., Papers. Abraham Lincoln Presidential Library, Springfield, Illinois.
Edwards, Elizabeth Parker Todd. Letters. Abraham Lincoln Presidential Library, Springfield, Illinois.
Edwards, Ninian W., Papers. Abraham Lincoln Presidential Library, Springfield, Illinois.
Eliot, Charles W. Papers. Harvard University Archives.
Esbjorn, C. M., Papers. Special Collections Library, Augustana College, Rock Island, Illinois.
Federal Land Surveyors' Field Notes. Vols. 110–17 (1820–21). Manuscripts, Illinois State Archives, Springfield, Illinois.
Felton, Cornelius. Papers. Harvard University Archives.
First Church of Christ Scientist Archives, Boston, Massachusetts.
French, Benjamin B., Family Papers. Library of Congress.
French, Daniel Chester. Papers. Library of Congress.
Friend, Henry C. Papers. Abraham Lincoln Presidential Library, Springfield, Illinois.
Fuller, Melville Weston. Papers. Library of Congress.
Garfield, James A. Papers. Library of Congress.
Garfield, Lucretia Randolph. Papers. Library of Congress.
Goff, John. Papers. Archives, Hildene, the Lincoln Family Home. Manchester, Vermont.
Governor's Files. May 1901–October 1901. Illinois State Archives.
Grant, Ulysses S., Papers. Library of Congress.
Green, Adeline Ellery (Burr) Davis. Papers. Rare Book, Manuscript, and Special Collections, Duke University.
Gurley Family Papers. Abraham Lincoln Presidential Library, Springfield, Illinois.
Hale Family Papers. Sophia Smith Collection, Smith College, Northampton, Massachusetts.
Halford, Elijah Walker. Papers. Library of Congress.
Harlan-Lincoln House Collection. Iowa Wesleyan College Archives, Mount Pleasant, Iowa.
Harrison, Benjamin. Papers. Library of Congress.
Harvard College Course Catalog. 1860–61, 1861–62, 1862–63, 1863–64. Harvard University Archives.
Harvard College Papers. Harvard University Archives.
Harvard Faculty Records, 1861–65. Harvard University Archives.
Harvard University Admission Records. Harvard University Archives.
Harvard University Entrance Examinations, 1836–1925. Harvard University Archives.
Hatch, Ozias M., Papers. Abraham Lincoln Presidential Library, Springfield, Illinois.
Hay, John. Papers. Library of Congress.
Hay, John Milton. Collection. John Milton Hay Library, Brown University.
Hayes, Rutherford B., Papers. Rutherford B. Hayes Presidential Center, Spiegel Grove, Fremont, Ohio.
Helm, Emily Todd. Papers. Special Collections, Kentucky Historical Society, Frankfort.
Henry, Anson G., Papers. Abraham Lincoln Presidential Library, Springfield, Illinois.
Henry County Probate Court Records. Mount Pleasant, Iowa.
Herndon-Weik Collection of Lincolniana. Manuscript Division, Library of Congress.
Hickey, James T., File. Archives, Hildene, the Lincoln Family Home. Manchester, Vermont.

Hildene, the Lincoln Family Home. Archives. Friends of Hildene Inc., Manchester, Vermont.
Hill, John Wesley. Papers. Rare Book and Manuscript Library, Butler Library, Columbia University.
Horton, Lydiard Heneage. Papers. Rare Book and Manuscript Library, Butler Library, Columbia University.
Horton, Samuel. Papers. Rare Book and Manuscript Library, Butler Library, Columbia University.
Houghton Mifflin Company Papers. Manuscript Collections, Houghton Library, Harvard University.
Howe, M. A. DeWolfe. Papers. Manuscript Collections, Houghton Library, Harvard University.
Humphrey, J. Otis. Papers. Abraham Lincoln Presidential Library, Springfield, Illinois.
Huntington, George L., Family Papers. Library of Congress.
Huntington, Henry E., Library, San Marino, California.
Illinois Regional Archives Depository, University of Illinois, Springfield.
Isham Family Papers. Chicago History Museum.
Isham, Lincoln, and Beale Law Firm. Records. Chicago History Museum.
James, William. Papers. Manuscript Collections, Houghton Library, Harvard University.
Johnson, Andrew. Papers. Library of Congress.
King, Horatio. Papers. Library of Congress.
Lamon, Ward Hill. Papers. Henry E. Huntington Library, San Marino, California.
Letters Received by the Commission Branch of the Adjutant General's Office, 1863–70. National Archives and Records Administration, Washington, DC.
Lincoln, Abraham. Collection. Abraham Lincoln Presidential Library, Springfield, Illinois.
———. Collection. Allen County Public Library, Fort Wayne, Indiana.
———. Collection. Archives and Manuscript Division, Sterling Memorial Library, Yale University.
———. Collection. General Collection. Beinecke Rare Book and Manuscript Library, Yale University.
———. Collection. John Hay Library, Brown University.
———. Collection. Manuscript Collections, Houghton Library, Harvard University.
———. Collection. Phillips Exeter Academy Archives, Exeter, New Hampshire.
———. Papers. Library of Congress.
———. Papers. Western Reserve Historical Society, Cleveland, Ohio.
Lincoln, Abraham, Library and Museum, Harrogate, Tennessee.
Lincoln Centennial Association Papers. Manuscript Division, Abraham Lincoln Presidential Library, Springfield, Illinois.
Lincoln Collection. Howard Gotlieb Archival Research Center, Boston University.
Lincoln Collection. Lincoln College Museum, Lincoln, Illinois.
Lincoln Collection. Miscellaneous Manuscripts, Department of Special Collections, University of Chicago Library.
Lincoln, George Burt, Family Papers. Dickinson College Archives, Carlisle, Pennsylvania.
Lincoln Home National Historic Site, Springfield, Illinois.
Lincoln, Mary Harlan. Autograph File. Manuscript Collections, Houghton Library, Harvard University.

Lincoln, Mary Todd, House. Lexington, Kentucky.
Lincoln, Mary Todd. Insanity File. Lincoln Financial Foundation Collection. Allen County Public Library, Fort Wayne, Indiana.
———. Papers. Allen County Public Library, Fort Wayne, Indiana.
———. Vertical File. Sangamon Valley Collection. Lincoln Library, Springfield, Illinois.
Lincoln Memorial Commission. Files. National Archives and Records Administration, Washington, DC.
Lincoln, Robert Todd. Collection and Archives. Archives, Hildene, the Lincoln Family Home. Manchester, Vermont.
———. Collection. Henry E. Huntington Library, San Marino, California.
Lincoln, Robert Todd. Biographical File. Harvard University Archives.
———. Collection. Phillips Exeter Academy Archives, Exeter, New Hampshire.
———. Letterpress Books. Abraham Lincoln Presidential Library, Springfield, Illinois.
———. Papers. Abraham Lincoln Presidential Library, Springfield, Illinois.
———. Papers. Allen County Public Library, Fort Wayne, Indiana.
———. Papers. Chicago History Museum.
———. Papers. Manuscript Collections, Houghton Library, Harvard University.
———. Papers. Western Reserve Historical Society, Cleveland, Ohio.
———. Vertical File. Sangamon Valley Collection. Lincoln Library, Springfield, Illinois.
Lincoln, Robert Todd, Family Papers. Manuscript Division, Library of Congress.
Lincoln Shrine. Redlands, California.
Logan, John A., Family Papers. Library of Congress.
Lowell, James Russell. Papers. Manuscript Collections, Houghton Library, Harvard University.
Markens, Isaac. Collection. American Jewish Historical Society, New York, New York.
McClellan, Colonel George B., Papers. Library of Congress.
McKinley, William. Papers. Library of Congress.
McLellan, Charles W. Unpublished memoirs. Private collection.
Mearns, David C. Papers. Library of Congress.
Miscellaneous Manuscript Collection. Archives and Manuscript Division, Sterling Memorial Library, Yale University.
Morris Family Papers. Connecticut Historical Society Museum, Hartford.
National Lincoln Monument Association Papers. Abraham Lincoln Presidential Library, Springfield, Illinois.
New Hampshire Historical Society, Concord, New Hampshire.
Nicolay, John G., Papers. Library of Congress.
Office of the Tama County Recorder, Toledo, Iowa.
Oglesby, Richard J., Papers. Abraham Lincoln Presidential Library, Springfield, Illinois.
Page, Thomas Nelson. Papers. Rare Book, Manuscript, and Special Collections, Duke University.
Palfrey Family Papers. Manuscript Collections, Houghton Library, Harvard University.
Palfrey Family Papers. Special Collections, Hill Memorial Library, Louisiana State University, Baton Rouge.
Perkins, George W. Papers. Rare Book and Manuscript Library, Butler Library, Columbia University.
Pinkerton National Detective Agency. Records. Library of Congress.

Plimpton, George A., Papers. Rare Book and Manuscript Library, Butler Library, Columbia University.
Pratt, William Moody. Diaries. Special Collections and Digital Programs, University of Kentucky Libraries, Lexington.
Pritchard, Myra, Family. Papers. Private collection.
Pullman Company. Archives. Newberry Library, Chicago.
Randall [James G. and Ruth Painter] Family Papers. Library of Congress.
Records of Harvard College Class of 1864. Harvard University Archives.
Records of the Office of the Secretary of War. Vols. 92 and 187. National Archives and Records Administration, Washington, DC.
Ridgely, Anna (Hudson). Journal. Manuscript Division, Abraham Lincoln Presidential Library, Springfield, Illinois.
Roosevelt, Theodore. Papers. Library of Congress.
———. Papers. Manuscript Collections, Houghton Library, Harvard University.
Rosenthal, Albert. Papers. Archives of American Art, Smithsonian Institution, Washington, DC.
Second Presbyterian Church. Archives. Chicago.
Seward, William H. Papers. Library of Congress.
Shea, John Gilmary. Papers. Georgetown University Archives.
Sheridan, Philip H., Papers. Manuscript Division. Library of Congress.
Sibley, John Langdon. Diary. Harvard University Archives.
Smalley, George W., Papers. Library of Congress.
Staff Papers. Records of the Adjutant General's Office, War Department, National Archives and Records Administration, Washington, DC.
Stanton, Edwin L. Papers, Special Collections, Hill Memorial Library, Louisiana State University, Baton Rouge.
Stern, Alfred Whital, Collection of Lincolniana. Rare Book and Special Collections Division, Library of Congress.
Storm, Colton. Papers. Library of Congress.
Stuart-Hay Family Papers. Abraham Lincoln Presidential Library, Springfield, Illinois.
Sumner, Charles. Papers. Manuscript Collections, Houghton Library, Harvard University.
Symington, Evelyn Wadsworth. Collection. Library of Congress.
Taft, William Howard. Papers. Library of Congress.
Tarbell-Lincoln, Ida M., Collection. Pelletier Library, Allegheny College, Meadeville, Pennsylvania.
Telegrams Collected by the Office of the Secretary of War. 1861–82. National Archives and Records Administration, Washington, DC.
Telegrams Received by Government Officials, Mainly of the War and Navy Departments. National Archives and Records Administration, Washington, DC.
Thayer, Anna Gansevoort Chittenden. Memoirs. Guilford Free Public Library, Guilford, Connecticut.
Thayer, William Roscoe. Papers. Manuscript Collections, Houghton Library, Harvard University.
Todd, David Peck. Papers. Archives and Manuscript Division, Sterling Memorial Library, Yale University.
Todd, John B. S., Papers. Manuscript Division. Abraham Lincoln Presidential Library, Springfield, Illinois.

Townsend, Mary G., Collection. Private collection.
Townsend, William H., Collection. Special Collections and Digital Programs, University of Kentucky Libraries, Lexington.
Trumbull Family Papers. Clements Library, University of Michigan.
Trumbull, Lyman. Papers. Manuscript Division. Abraham Lincoln Presidential Library, Springfield, Illinois.
Trumbull, Walter. Papers. Rare Book, Manuscript, and Special Collections, Duke University.
Tyler, John. Papers. Library of Congress.
U.S. Secret Service. Daily Reports of Operatives. Records. National Archives II, Silver Spring, Maryland.
———. Description and Information of Criminals. General Register. National Archives II, Silver Spring, Maryland.
Union Staff Officer Files, 1861–66. Records of the Adjutant General's Office, War Department. National Archives and Records Administration, Washington, DC.
Vermont Historical Society, Barre, Vermont.
Waite, Morrison R., Papers. Library of Congress.
Washington during the Civil War: The Diary of Horatio Nelson Taft, 1861–1865. Library of Congress.
Watkins, Samuel C. G., Collection. Archives and Manuscript Division, Sterling Memorial Library, Yale University.
Weik, Jesse. Papers. Manuscript Division, Abraham Lincoln Presidential Library, Springfield, Illinois.
Welles, Gideon. Papers. Connecticut Historical Society Museum, Hartford.
———. Papers. Library of Congress.
White, Henry. Papers. Library of Congress.
———. Papers. Rare Book and Manuscript Library, Butler Library, Columbia University.
White, Horace. Papers. Abraham Lincoln Presidential Library, Springfield, Illinois.
Wickliffe-Preston Papers. Special Collections and Digital Programs, University of Kentucky Libraries, Lexington.
Willard, Charles W., Papers. Vermont Historical Society, Barre, Vermont.
Williams, Margaret D., Collection. Library of Congress.
Wilson, James Harrison. Papers. Library of Congress.

Newspapers

American Ballot, and Rockingham County Intelligencer (Exeter and Portsmouth, NH)
Anchorage Daily News
Atlanta Constitution
Atlanta Democrat and Cape May County Register
Aurora (IL) Beacon-News
Baltimore Sun
Bloomington (IL) Pantagraph
Boston Daily Advertiser
Boston Daily Journal
Boston Evening Transcript
Boston Globe
Boston Transcript
Brooklyn (NY) Eagle

Cambridge (MA) Chronicle
Charleston (SC) Courier
Chicago Daily Journal
Chicago Defender
Chicago Herald
Chicago Inter Ocean
Chicago Journal
Chicago Post and Mail
Chicago Times
Chicago Tribune
Christian Advocate (New York)
Christian Recorder
Christian Science Monitor
Cincinnati Commercial
Commercial Advertiser (New York)
Council Bluffs (IA) Nonpareil
Critic, The (Washington, DC)
Daily Central City (CO) Register
Daily Cleveland Herald
Daily Evening Bulletin (San Francisco, California)
Daily Herald (Brownsville, Texas)
Daily Miners' Register (Central City, Colorado)
Daily Ohio Statesman (Columbus)
Danville (IL) Daily News
Danville (IL) Vermilion County Press
Deseret News (Salt Lake City, Utah)
Evening Independent, The (St. Petersburg, Florida)
Evening World (New York)
Fort Worth Gazette
Frank Leslie's Illustrated Newspaper
Georgia Weekly Telegraph
Grand Rapids (MI) Press
Graphic, The (London)
Harper's Weekly
Hartford (CT) Courant
Hartford (CT) Daily Courant
Illinois Journal
Illinois State Register
Illinois Weekly Journal (Springfield)
Independent, The (New York)
Kansas City Journal
Lexington (KY) Herald
Lexington (KY) Observer and Reporter
Lexington (KY) Weekly Press
Literary Digest
Literary Digest
London Times
Los Angeles Herald
Los Angeles Times

Los Angeles Times
Louisville Daily Journal
Lowell (MA) Daily Citizen and News
Manchester (VT) Journal
Memphis Daily Avalanche
Miami Herald Record
Milwaukee Journal
Milwaukee Sentinel
Minneapolis Journal
Morning Courier (Springfield, Illinois)
Morning Oregonian (Portland, Oregon)
Mount Vernon (IA) Hawkeye
Mountain Democrat (Placerville, Nevada)
Mt. Pleasant (IA) Journal
Mt. Pleasant (IA) News
National Republican (Washington, DC)
New Orleans Times
New York Commercial Advertiser
New York Evangelist
New York Evening Mail
New York Herald
New York Herald Tribune
New York Observer and Chronicle
New York Times
New York Tribune
New York World
New-Hampshire Sentinel (Keene, New Hampshire)
New-Hampshire Statesman (Concord, New Hampshire)
Ohio Farmer (Cleveland)
Omaha (NE) Bee
Penny Illustrated Paper (London)
Pensacola (FL) Journal
Philadelphia Inquirer
Phoenix (AZ) Weekly Herald
Pittsburgh Post-Gazette
Portland Oregonian
Portsmouth (NH) Journal of Literature and Politics
Pullman Herald
Pullman News, The
Richmond Dispatch
Sacramento Record-Union
Salt Lake Telegram
San Francisco Bulletin
San Francisco Call
Sangamo Journal (Springfield, Illinois)
Semi-Weekly Mississippian (Jackson, MS)
St. Louis Globe-Democrat
St. Paul (MN) Globe
Sterling Republican and Gazette

Sun, The (New York)
United Press International
Wall Street Journal
Washington (DC) Herald
Washington National Intelligencer
Washington Post
Washington Star
Weekly Graphic (Kirksville, Missouri)
Weekly Mississippian (Jackson, MS)
Wyoming State Tribune

Books and Articles

"Abraham 'Jack' Lincoln, II—1873–1890." *Lincoln Newsletter* 7, no. 3 (summer 1988): 3.
Account of the Triennial and Sexennial Meetings of the Class of 1865 (Yale College), An. New York: Taintor, 1875.
Adams, Charles Francis. *Charles Francis Adams 1835–1915: An Autobiography.* Boston: Houghton Mifflin, 1916.
———. *Theodore Lyman and Robert Charles Winthrop, Jr.: Two Memoirs Prepared by Charles Francis Adams for the Massachusetts Historical Society.* Cambridge: Wilson, 1906.
Adams, Henry. *The Education of Henry Adams: An Autobiography.* Boston: Houghton Mifflin, 1918.
Adrienne. "Our Washington Letter." *Prairie Farmer,* 43, no. 9, March 2, 1872, 67.
Ainsworth, Ernest D. "Where the Golf Championship Will Be Played." *Town and Country,* June 3, 1905, 16.
Alexander, E. P. "Lee at Appomattox: Personal Recollections of the Break-Up of the Confederacy." *Century Magazine,* 63, no. 6, April 1902, 921–31.
Allen, Thomas Gaskell, Jr., and William Lewis Sachtleben. "Across Asia on Bicycle." *Century,* 48, no. 1, May 1894, 83–98.
Ames, Mary Clemmer. *Ten Years in Washington: Life and Scenes in the National Capital as a Woman Sees Them.* Hartford, CT: Worthington, 1873.
Anderson, C. F. *Freemen Yet Slaves under 'Abe' Lincoln's Son, or Service and Wages of Pullman Porters.* Self-published, 1904.
Anderson, Isabel, ed. *Larz Anderson: Letters and Journals of a Diplomat.* New York: Revell, 1940.
———. *Letters and Journals of General Nicholas Longworth Anderson.* New York: Revell, 1942.
Andreas, A. T. *History of Chicago.* 3 vols. Chicago: Self-published, 1884–86. Reprint, New York: Arno, 1975. References are to the 1975 edition.Andrews, Wayne. *Battle for Chicago.* New York: Harcourt, Brace, 1946.
Angle, Paul M. *The Chicago Historical Society, 1856–1956.* New York: Rand McNally, 1956.
———. *Here I Have Lived: The Story of Lincoln's Springfield, 1821–1865.* New Brunswick, NJ: Rutgers University Press, 1935.
———, ed. *A Portrait of Abraham Lincoln in Letters by His Oldest Son.* Chicago: Chicago Historical Society, 1968.
Annual Catalogue of the Officers and Students of Ill. State University, Springfield, Ill., 1858–1859. Springfield, IL: Richards, 1859.

Annual Report of the Chief Signal Officer of the Army to the Secretary of War for the Year 1884. Washington, DC: GPO, 1884.
Annual Report of the Chief Signal Officer, United States Army, to the Secretary of War for the Fiscal Year Ending June 30, 1882. 2 parts. Washington, DC: GPO, 1883.
Annual Report of the Secretary of War. 4 vols. Washington, DC: GPO, 1881.
Annual Report of the Secretary of War for the Year 1882. 4 vols. Washington, DC: GPO, 1882.
Annual Report of the Secretary of War for the Year 1883. 4 vols. Washington, DC: GPO, 1883.
"Appreciation of Robert Todd Lincoln, An." *Lincoln Lore*, 296, December 10, 1934.
Arnold, Isaac N. *Life of Abraham Lincoln*. Lincoln: University of Nebraska Press, 1994. First published in 1884.
Arthur W. Windett v. the Connecticut Mutual Life Insurance Co. Brief and argument. Appellate Court of Illinois, 1st dist., October term, 1887, term 129, gen. no. 2740. Chicago: Barnard & Gunthorp, 1888.
"At Springfield." *Outlook*, 91, no. 8, February 20, 1909, 363.
Ayres, Philip W. "Lincoln as a Neighbor." *American Review of Reviews* 57, no. 2 (February 1918): 183–85.
Babb, Irving T. "Robert Todd Lincoln's Milwaukee Friend: Max Babb of Allis-Chalmers." *Milwaukee History*, summer 1984, 62–68.
Babcock, Bernie. *Booth and the Spirit of Lincoln*. New York: Grosset & Dunlap, 1925.
Babeuf's Directory of Springfield, Illinois, and Business Mirror for 1881–1882, J. Springfield, IL: Babeuf, 1881.
Badeau, Adam. *Grant in Peace from Appomattox to Mount McGregor: A Personal Memoir*. Hartford: Scranton, 1887.
Baker, Jean H. *Mary Todd Lincoln: A Biography*. New York: Norton, 1987.
Baldwin, Joseph Glover. *The Flush Times of Alabama and Mississippi: A Series of Sketches*. New York: Appleton, 1853.
Baldwin, Martin T. "A Personal Experience with Jack Lincoln." *Journal of the Illinois State Historical Society* 51, no. 1 (spring 1958): 97.
Bales, Richard F. *The Great Chicago Fire and the Myth of Mrs. O'Leary's Cow*. Jefferson, NC: McFarland, 2002.
Bancroft, Frederic, ed. *Speeches, Correspondence and Political Papers of Carl Schurz*. 6 vols. New York: Negro Universities Press, 1969. First published in 1913.
Barnard, George Grey. "The Sculptor's View of Lincoln." In *Barnard's Lincoln: The Gift of Mr. and Mrs. Charles P. Taft to the City of Cincinnati*, 21–32. Cincinnati: Stewart & Kidd, 1917.
"Barnard Lincoln, The." *American Magazine of Art* 9, no. 1, November 1917, 32–33.
"Barnard Statue of Lincoln, The." *American Review of Reviews*, 56, no. 6, December 1917, 649.
"Barnard Statue of Lincoln, The." *Outlook*, October 17, 1917, 241.
Barnes, John S. "With Lincoln from Washington to Richmond in 1865." *Appleton's Magazine*, 1907. Reprint, *Magazine of History* 41, no. 1, extra no. 161, rare Lincolniana no. 39 (1930): 37–56.
Barton, William E. *The Life of Abraham Lincoln*. 2 vols. Indianapolis: Bobbs-Merrill, 1925.
———. *The Soul of Abraham Lincoln*. New York: Doran, 1920.
Basler, Roy P., ed. *The Collected Works of Abraham Lincoln Supplement, 1832–1865*. Contributions to American Studies 7. Westport, CT: Greenwood Press, 1974.

Basler, Roy P., ed., and Dolores Pratt and Lloyd A. Dunlap, asst. eds. *The Collected Works of Abraham Lincoln*. 9 vols. New Brunswick, NJ: Rutgers University Press, 1953–55.

Batchelder, Samuel F. *Bits of Harvard History*. Cambridge: Harvard University Press, 1923.

Bateman, Newton, editor-in-chief, Paul Selby, asst. ed., and Francis Shonkwiler, ed. *Historical Encyclopedia of Illinois*. 2 vols. Chicago: Munsell, 1915.

Bates, David Homer. *Lincoln in the Telegraph Office*. 1907. Reprint, Lincoln: University of Nebraska Press, 1995.

Bayne, Julia Taft. *Tad Lincoln's Father*. 1931. Reprint, Lincoln: University of Nebraska Press, 2001.

Beall, Edmond. "Recollections of the Assassination and Funeral of Abraham Lincoln." *Journal of the Illinois State Historical Society* 5, no. 4 (January 1913): 489–90.

Beard, Patricia. *After the Ball*. New York: HarperCollins, 2003.

Bell, Charles H. *History of the Town of Exeter, New Hampshire*. Boston: Farwell, 1888.

Bell, Clark. "The American Government and People and the English Home Secretary." Vol. 6. *The Medico-Legal Journal*, 588. New York: Medico-Legal Journal, 1899.

———. "Rights of American Girls Who Marry Foreigners." *Albany Law Journal* 60, no. 1 (August 5, 1899): 72–74.

Bell, William Gardner. *Secretaries of War and Secretaries of the Army: Portraits & Biographical Sketches*. Washington, DC: Center of Military History, U.S. Army, 1992.

Benedict, E. C. "Edwin Booth." *Valentine's Manual of Old New York*, n.s., 6 (1922): 175–84.

Benedict, Michael Les. *The Impeachment and Trial of Andrew Johnson*. 1973. Reprint, New York: Norton, 1999.

Beveridge, Albert J. *Abraham Lincoln, 1809–1858*. 4 vols. Standard Library Edition. Cambridge: Riverside Press, 1928.

Bigler, Philip. *In Honored Glory: Arlington National Cemetery: The Final Post*. Arlington, VA: Vandamere Press, 1987.

Biographical Sketches of the Leading Men of Chicago. Chicago: Wilson & St. Clair, 1868.

Bishop, Jim. *The Day Lincoln Was Shot*. New York: Harper and Brothers, 1955.

Bispham, William. "Memories and Letters of Edwin Booth." *Century Illustrated Magazine*, 47, no. 1, November 1893, 132–39.

Black, George N. "Reminiscences of the First Presbyterian Church Sabbath School." In *Seventy-Fifth Anniversary of the Organization of the First Presbyterian Church*. Springfield, IL: First Presbyterian Church, 1903.

"Blaine and Conkling and the Republican Convention of 1880." *McClure's Magazine*, 14, no. 3, January 1900, 281–86.

Blair, Albert. "Abraham Lincoln Visit to Exeter in 1860." *Bulletin of the Phillips Exeter Academy*, 16, no. 2, July 1920, 4–5.

Blair, Edward Tyler. *A History of the Chicago Club*. Chicago: Donnelley, 1898.

Blake, Victoria. *Mrs. Maybrick: Crime Archive*. Washington, DC: National Archives, 2008.

Bliss, D. W. "The Story of President Garfield's Illness." *Century*, 23, no. 2, December 1881, 299–306.

Bolster, Jeffrey W., ed. *Cross-Grained and Wiley Waters: A Guide to the Piscataqua Maritime Region*. Portsmouth: Randall, 2002.

Borreson, Ralph. *When Lincoln Died*. New York: Appleton-Century, 1965.

Bowen, Walter S., and Harry Edward Neal. *The United States Secret Service*. New York: Chilton, 1960.

Boyden, Anna L. *War Reminiscences, or, Echoes from Hospital and White House*. Boston: D. Lothrop, 1887.

Bradlee, Ben. *A Good Life: Newspapering and Other Adventures*. New York: Simon & Schuster, 1995.

Braude, Ann. *Radical Spirits: Spiritualism and Women's Rights in Nineteenth Century America*. Boston: Beacon Press, 1989.

Brayman, Mason. *Revised Statutes of the State of Illinois*. Springfield, IL: Walters & Weber, 1845.

Brewster, Paul G. "Specimens of Folklore from Southern Indiana." *Folklore*, 47, no. 4, December 1936, 363.

Briggs, Emily Edson. *The Olivia Letters: Being Some History of Washington City for Forty Years as Told by the Letters of a Newspaper Correspondent*. New York: Neale, 1906.

Brigham, Johnson. *James Harlan*. Iowa City, IA: State Historical Society, 1913.

Brooks, Noah. "A Boy in the White House." *St. Nicholas: An Illustrated Monthly for Young Folks*, 10, no. 1, November 1882, 57–65.

———. "Personal Reminiscences of Lincoln." *Scribner's Monthly*, 15, no. 5, March 1878, 681.

———. *Washington in Lincoln's Time*. Edited by Herbert Mitgang. New York: Rinehart, 1958.

Brown, E. E. *The Life and Public Services of James A. Garfield*. Boston: Guerley, 1881.

Brown, Harry James, and Frederick D. Williams, eds. *Diary of James A. Garfield*. 4 vols. East Lansing: Michigan State University Press, 1981.

Bruner, Robert F., and Sean D. Carr. *The Panic of 1907: Lessons Learned from the Market's Perfect Storm*. Hoboken, NJ: Wiley, 2007.

Bryan, Wilhelmus Bogart. *A History of the National Capital*. 2 vols. New York: Macmillan, 1916.

Buder, Stanley. *Pullman: An Experiment in Industrial Order and Community Planning, 1880–1930*. Urban Life in America Series. New York: Oxford University Press, 1967.

Bullard, F. Lauristan. "Again, the Bixby Letter." *Lincoln Herald* 53, no. 2 (summer 1951): 26–27, 37.

———. "The Magnanimity of Abraham Lincoln." *Proceedings of the Massachusetts Historical Society* 69 (October 1947–May 1950): 296–97.

———. *Tad and His Father*. Boston: Little, Brown, 1915.

["Mrs. Robert Lincoln."] *Bulletin of the Abraham Lincoln Association* 48, no. 1 (June 1937): 10.

Bullock, John M. "President Lincoln's Visiting Card." *Century Magazine*, 55, no. 4, February 1898, 565–71.

Burial records. Oak Ridge Cemetery, Springfield, Illinois.

Burlingame, Michael, ed. *Abraham Lincoln: The Observations of John G. Nicolay and John Hay*. Carbondale: Southern Illinois University Press, 2007.

———, ed. *At Lincoln's Side: John Hay's Civil War Correspondence and Selected Writings*. Carbondale: Southern Illinois University Press, 2000.

———. "'A Hard-Hearted Conscious Liar and an Oily Hypocrite': Henry B. Rankin's Reliability as a Lincoln Informant." In Weik, *Real Lincoln*, 389–98.

———. *The Inner World of Abraham Lincoln*. Urbana: University of Illinois Press, 1994.

———, ed. *Lincoln Observed: The Civil War Dispatches of Noah Brooks*. Baltimore: Johns Hopkins University Press, 1998.

———. *Lincoln's Journalist: John Hay's Anonymous Writings for the Press, 1860–1864.* Carbondale: Southern Illinois University Press, 1998.
———. "Lincolns' Marriage: 'A Fountain of Misery, of a Quality Absolutely Infernal.'" In Burlingame, *Inner World of Abraham Lincoln*, 268–355.
———. "Mary Todd Lincoln's Unethical Conduct as First Lady." In Burlingame, *At Lincoln's Side*, 185–203.
———. "New Light on the Bixby Letter." *Journal of the Abraham Lincoln Association* 16, no. 1 (winter 1995): 59–71.
———, ed. *An Oral History of Abraham Lincoln: John G. Nicolay's Interviews and Essays.* Carbondale: Southern Illinois University Press, 1996.
Busbey, William H. "A Coming Man." *Continent: An Illustrated Weekly Magazine*, 5, no. 111, March 26, 1884, 1.
Busey, Samuel C. *Personal Reminiscences and Recollections of Forty-Six Years' Membership in the Medical Society of the District of Columbia, and Residence in This City.* Philadelphia: Dornan, 1895.
Butler, Nicholas Murray. *Across the Busy Years: Recollections and Reflections.* 2 vols. New York: Scribner's, 1940.
———. "Lincoln and Son." *Saturday Evening Post*, February 11, 1939, 23, 63–66.
Cadwallader, Sylvanus. *Three Years with Grant.* Edited by Benjamin P. Thomas. New York: Knopf, 1955.
Calnek, Anthony. *The Hasty Pudding Theatre: A History of Harvard's Hairy-Chested Heroines.* New York: A. D. C., 1986.
Campbell, Charles S., Jr. "The Anglo-American Crisis in the Bering Sea, 1890–1891." *Mississippi Valley Historical Review* 48, no. 3 (December 1961): 393–414.
Cansler, Loman D. "Madstones and Hydrophobia." *Western Folklore* 23, no. 2 (April 1964): 95–105.
"Captain Lincoln Episode, The." *Lincoln Lore*, 1410, April 16, 1956.
Carpenter, Francis B. *Six Months at the White House.* New York: Hurd, 1866.
Carroll, Sidney. "The Lincoln Jinx." *Coronet*, 23, no. 4, February 1948, 89–90.
Cashman, Sean Dennis. *American in the Gilded Age.* New York: New York University Press, 1993.
Catton, Bruce. *A Stillness at Appomattox.* New York: Doubleday, 1953.
Centennial History of the Ekwanok County Club. Manchester, VT: Ekwanok Country Club, 2000.
Centennial History of the Harvard Law School: 1817–1917. Cambridge: Harvard Law School Association, 1918.
"Central States." *American Lawyer* 1, no. 8 (August 1893): 22.
Chambrun, Marquis Adolphe de. *Impressions of Lincoln and the Civil War: A Foreigner's Account.* Translated by General Aldebert de Chambrun. New York: Random, 1952.
Chandler, William E. *President Chester A. Arthur: Address by William E. Chandler at Fairfield, Vt., on August 19, 1903.* Concord, NH: Rumford, 1903.
Chapin, John R. "The Infamous Pullman Strike as Revealed by the Robert Todd Lincoln Collection." *Journal of the Illinois State Historical Society* 74, No. 3 (autumn 1981): 179–98.
Chaplin, Jeremiah, and J. D. Chaplin. *Life of Charles Sumner.* Boston: Lothrop, 1874.
Chapman, A. S. "The Boyhood of John Hay." *Century Magazine*, 78, no. 3, July 1909, 445–46.
Cleveland, Grover. *The Venezuelan Boundary Controversy.* Princeton, NJ: Princeton University Press, 1913.

"Close of Another Lincoln Generation, The." *Lincoln Lore*, 979, January 12, 1948.
Coates, Foster. "The Sons of Recent Presidents of the United States." *Chautauquan*, 25, no. 6 (September 1897): 617–24.
Coddington, Edwin B. *The Gettysburg Campaign: A Study in Command*. 1963. Reprint, New York: Touchstone, 1997.
Colbert, Elias, and Everett Chamberlin. *Chicago and the Great Conflagration*. Cincinnati: Vent, 1872.
"Contingency of 'Inability,' The." *Century*, 23, no. 1, November 1881, 144–45.
Cox, William J. "Abraham Lincoln in Exeter, Feb. 29–Mar. 5, 1860." *Phillips Exeter Bulletin*, 56, no. 3, February 1960, 2.
Crapol, Edward P. *James G. Blaine: Architect of Empire*. Biographies in American Foreign Policy 4. Wilmington, DE: Scholarly Resources, 2000.
Craughwell, Thomas J. *Stealing Lincoln's Body*. Cambridge: Belknap, 2007.
Cromie, Robert. *The Great Chicago Fire*. Nashville: Rutledge Hill, 1994.
Crook, William. *Through Five Administrations: Reminiscences of Colonel William H. Crook*. Edited by Margarite Spalding Gerry. New York: Harper, 1910.
Crosbie, Laurence M. *The Phillips Exeter Academy: A History*. Norwood, MA: Plimpton, 1924.
Croy, Homer. *The Trial of Mrs. Abraham Lincoln*. New York: Duell, 1962.
Cullom, Shelby M. *Fifty Years of Public Service*. Chicago: McClurg, 1911.
Cunningham, Frank H. *Familiar Sketches of the Phillips Exeter Academy and Surroundings*. Boston: Osgood, 1883.
Currey, Josiah Seymour. *Chicago: Its History and Its Builders*. 5 vols. Chicago: Clarke, 1912.
———. *Manufacturing and Wholesale Industries of Chicago*. 3 vols. Chicago: Poole, 1918.
Curtis, Francis. *The Republican Party: A History of Its Fifty Years' Existence and a Record of Its Measures and Leaders, 1854–1904*. 2 vols. New York: Putnam's, 1904.
Cuthbert, Norma B., ed. *Lincoln and the Baltimore Plot, 1861: From Pinkerton Records and Related Papers*. San Marino, CA: Huntington Library, 1949.
Darrin, Charles V. "A Lincoln Family Friendship." *Journal of the Illinois State Historical Society* 44, no. 3 (autumn 1951): 210–17.
Davis, Eugene. *Proceedings of the Republican National Convention: Held at Chicago, Illinois, Wednesday, Thursday, Friday, Saturday, Monday, and Tuesday, June 2d, 3d, 4th, 5th, 7th and 8th, 1880*. Chicago: Jeffery, 1881.
Davis, George T. M. *Autobiography of the Late Col. George T. M. Davis*. New York: Jenkins and McCowan, 1891.
Davis, Rodney O., and Douglas L. Wilson, eds. *The Lincoln Douglas Debates*. Urbana: University of Illinois Press, 2008.
"Death in the Family, A: Abraham Lincoln II 'Jack' (1873–1890)." *For the People*, 9, no. 3, autumn 2007, 1, 4.
Dennett, Tyler. *John Hay: From Poetry to Politics*. New York: Dodd, Mead, 1934.
———, ed. *Lincoln and the Civil War in the Diaries and Letters of John Hay*. 1939. Reprint, New York: Da Capo, 1988.
Depew, Chauncey M. *My Memories of Eighty Years*. New York: Scribner's, 1924.
Detzer, David. *Allegiance: Fort Sumter, Charleston, and the Beginning of the Civil War*. New York: Harcourt, 2001.
Dewey, Richard. "The Jury Law for Commitment of the Insane in Illinois (1867–1893), and Mrs. E. P. W. Packard, Its Author, also Later Developments in Lunacy Legislation in Illinois." *American Journal of Insanity* 69 (January 1913): 571–84.

DeWitt, Edward Nicholas. "Concerning Eyes." *American Journal of Nursing* 38, no. 8 (August 1938): 893–98.

Dickson, Harold E. "George Grey Barnard's Controversial Lincoln." *Art Journal* 27, no. 1 (autumn 1967): 8–23.

Dingley, Edward N. *The Life and Times of Nelson Dingley, Jr.* Kalamazoo, MI: Ihling, 1902.

"DKE Heritage." *Delta Kappa Epsilon.* http://www.dke.org (July 2007).

Dobyns, Kenneth W. *The Patent Office Pony: A History of the Early Patent Office.* Fredericksburg, VA: Sergeant Kirkland's Museum and Historical Society, 1994.

Dodge, H. Augusta, ed. *Gail Hamilton's Life in Letters.* 2 vols. Boston: Lee and Shepard, 1901.

Donald, David. *Lincoln's Herndon.* New York: Knopf, 1948.

———. *Lincoln Reconsidered.* New York: Knopf, 1969.

Doyle, Burton T., and Homer H. Swaney, comp. *Lives of James A. Garfield and Chester A. Arthur.* Washington, DC: Darby, 1881.

Duffield, J. W. "Dedication of the Lincoln Memorial." *Current History*, 16, no. 4, July 1922, 552–56.

Dunbaugh, Harry J. "Robert Todd Lincoln: Lawyer, Executive, and Public Servant." Speech before the Fortnightly, May 2, 1962, in folder 2, Robert Todd Lincoln Papers, Chicago History Museum.

Dunlevy, Hulburd. "Robert Todd Lincoln." *Green Bag: A Useless but Entertaining Magazine for Lawyers*, 1, no. 8, August 1889, 321–23.

Eaton, Herbert. *Presidential Timber: A History of Nominating Conventions, 1868–1960.* London: Free Press of Glencoe, 1964.

Edgington, Frank E. *History of the New York Avenue Presbyterian Church, 1803–1961.* Washington, DC: New York Avenue Presbyterian Church, 1961.

Edwards' New Chicago Directory. Chicago: Edwards, 1867.

Eisendrath, Joseph L., Jr. "Illinois' Oldest Memorial: The Stephen A. Douglas Monument." *Journal of the Illinois State Historical Society* 51, no. 2 (summer 1958): 127–48.

Eisenschiml, Otto. *In the Shadow of Lincoln's Death.* New York: Funk, 1949.

———. *Why Was Lincoln Murdered?* Boston: Little, Brown, 1937.

Eliot, Samuel A., ed. *Heralds of a Liberal Faith.* 4 vols. Boston: American Unitarian Society, 1910.

Emerson, Jason. "Aftermath of an Assassination: Recently Discovered Letters from the Days after Lincoln's Murder." *American History* 41, no. 2 (June 2006): 24–30, 74.

———. "How Booth Saved Lincoln's Life." *American History* 44, no. 1 (April 2005): 44–49.

———. *Lincoln the Inventor.* Carbondale: Southern Illinois University Press, 2009.

———. *The Madness of Mary Lincoln.* Carbondale: Southern Illinois University Press, 2007.

———. "New Evidence from an Ignored Voice: Robert Todd Lincoln and the Authorship of the Bixby Letter." *Lincoln Herald* 110, no. 2 (summer 2008): 86–116.

———. "New Mary Lincoln Letter Found." *Journal of the Illinois State Historical Society* 101, no. 3–4 (fall/winter 2008): 315–28.

———. "'Of Such Is the Kingdom of Heaven': The Mystery of Little Eddie." *Journal of the Illinois State Historical Society* 92, no. 3 (autumn 1999): 201–21.

———. "Perpetual Non-Candidate: Robert Todd Lincoln." *American History Magazine* 39, no. 5 (December 2004): 59–66.

———. "The Poetic Lincoln." *Lincoln Herald* 101, no. 1 (spring 1999): 4–12.

Evans, W. A. *Mrs. Abraham Lincoln: A Study of Her Personality and Her Influence on Abraham Lincoln*. New York: Knopf, 1932.
Evjen, Harry. "Illinois State University, 1852–1868." *Journal of the Illinois State Historical Society* 31, no. 1 (March 1938): 54–56.
Fanebust, Wayne. *The Missing Corpse: Grave Robbing a Gilded Age Tycoon*. Westport, CT: Praeger, 2005.
"Farewell Address, The." *Lincoln Lore*, 305, February 11, 1935.
Ferguson, Henry N. "A Man Marked." *Yankee*, February 1972, 143.
Field, Maunsell B. *Memories of Many Men and of Some Women*. New York: Harper, 1874.
Fleischner, Jennifer. *Mrs. Lincoln and Mrs. Keckly: The Remarkable Story of the Friendship between a First Lady and a Former Slave*. New York: Broadway, 2003.
Foner, Eric. *Reconstruction: America's Unfinished Revolution, 1863–1877*. New York: Harper & Row, 1988.
Ford, Worthington Chauncey, ed. *Letters of Henry Adams (1858–1891)*. Boston: Houghton Mifflin, 1930.
Fortieth Annual Report of the President of Harvard College to the Overseers, Exhibiting the State of the Institution for the Academic Year 1864–1865. Cambridge, MA: Welch, Bigelow, 1866. Available online at http://pds.lib.harvard.edu/pds/view/2574320?n=1625&s=4.
Foster, John W. *Diplomatic Memoirs*. 2 vols. Boston: Houghton Mifflin, 1909.
Foy, Eddie, and Harlow, Alvin F. "Clowning through Life." *Collier's* 78, no. 26, December 25, 1926, 15–16, 30.
Friedman, Jane M. *America's First Woman Lawyer: The Biography of Myra Bradwell*. Buffalo, NY: Prometheus, 1993.
Garraty, John A. *Henry Cabot Lodge: A Biography*. New York: Knopf, 1953.
Garrison, Lloyd McKin. "The HPC Theatre: An Historical Sketch." In *Hasty Pudding Club, an Illustrated History of the Hasty Pudding Club Theatricals*, 17–31. Cambridge, MA: Hasty Pudding Club, 1933.
Gattell, Frank Otto. *John Gorham Palfrey and the New England Conscience*. Cambridge: Harvard University Press, 1963.
Gemeroy, J. Conrad. "Strabismus in Children." *American Journal of Nursing* 41, no. 5 (May 1941): 516–17.
Gibbon, John. "Personal Recollections of Appomattox." *Century Magazine*, 63, no. 6, April 1902, 936–43.
Gilder, Rosamond, ed. *The Letters of Richard Watson Gilder*. Boston: Houghton Mifflin, 1916.
Gilliam, Nancy T. "A Professional Pioneer: Myra Bradwell's Fight to Practice Law." *Law and History Review* 5, no. 1 (spring 1987): 105–13.
Glaser, Lynn. *Counterfeiting in America: The History of an American Way to Wealth*. New York: Clarkson N. Potter, 1968.
Goff, John S. "The Education of Robert Todd Lincoln." *Journal of the Illinois State Historical Society* 53, no. 4 (winter 1960): 341–60.
———. *Robert Todd Lincoln: A Man in His Own Right*. Norman: University of Oklahoma Press, 1968.
Goltz, Carlos W. *Incidents in the Life of Mary Todd Lincoln*. Sioux City, IA: Deitch & Lamar, 1928.
Goode, J. Paul. *The Geographic Background of Chicago*. Chicago: University of Chicago Press, 1926.

Goodspeed, E. J. *History of the Great Fires in Chicago and the West.* New York: Goodspeed, 1871.
Goodspeed, Weston Arthur, and Daniel David Healy, eds. *History of Cook County, Illinois.* 2 vols. Chicago: Goodspeed, 1909.
Gookin, Frederick William. *The Chicago Literary Club: A History of Its First Fifty Years.* Chicago: Self-published, 1926.
Gordon, Malcolm S. *Massa Linkum's Boy.* Cincinnati: John Church, 1884. Copyright deposits, 1870–1885, America Singing: Nineteenth-Century Song Sheets, American Memory, Rare Book and Special Collections Division, Library of Congress.
Gould, E. W. *Fifty Years on the Mississippi.* St. Louis: Nixon-Jones, 1889.
Gould, Lewis L. *Grand Old Party: A History of the Republicans.* New York: Random, 2003.
Gouverneur, Marian. *As I Remember: Recollections of American Society during the Nineteenth Century.* New York: Appleton, 1911.
Graham, Anne E., Carol Emmas, and Keith Skinner. *The Last Victim: The Extraordinary Life of Florence Maybrick, Wife of Jack the Ripper.* London: Headline, 1999.
Grand Opening of the Northern Pacific Railway: Celebration at St. Paul, Minnesota, the Eastern Terminus, Sept. 3rd, 1883. St. Paul: Brown & Treacy, 1883.
Grant, Julia Dent. *The Personal Memoirs of Julia Dent Grant.* Edited by John Y. Simon. New York: Putnam's, 1975.
Grant, Ulysses S. *Personal Memoirs of U. S. Grant and Selected Letters 1839–1865.* New York: Library of America, 1990.
Greely, Adolphus W. *Three Years of Arctic Service.* 2 vols. New York: Scribner's, 1886.
Gresham, Matilda. *Life of Walter Q. Gresham: 1832–1895.* 2 vols. Chicago: Rand, McNally, 1919.
Gridley, Eleanor. "Presentation of Bronze Bust of Mrs. Myra Bradwell, First Woman Lawyer of Illinois." *Transactions of the Illinois State Historical Society* 38, no. 6 (May 1931).
Grimsley, Elizabeth Todd. "Six Months in the White House." *Journal of the Illinois State Historical Society* 19, nos. 3–4 (October 1926–January 1927): 43–73.
Guttridge, Leonard F. *Ghosts of Cape Sabine.* New York: Putnam's, 2000.
Hale, Edward Everett. "James Russell Lowell and His Friends." *Outlook* 60, no. 1 (September 3, 1898): 62–63.
———. *James Russell Lowell and His Friends.* Boston: Houghton Mifflin, 1899.
Hall, Newman. "My Impressions of America." *Broadway: A London Magazine*, n.s., 2 (March–August, 1869): 157.
Hamilton, Charles. *Great Forgers and Famous Fakes.* Lakewood, CO: Glenbridge, 1996.
Hamilton, Gail. *Biography of James G. Blaine.* Norwich, CT: Bill, 1895.
"Happy Birthday Bud." *Hildene Newsletter*, summer 1995, 2.
Harlan, George C. *Eyesight, and How to Care for It.* Philadelphia: Blakiston, 1882.
Harlan, Louis R., and Raymond W. Smock, eds. *The Booker T. Washington Papers.* 14 vols. Urbana: University of Illinois Press, 1972–89.
Harlow, Charles H. "Greely at Cape Sabine: Notes by a Member of the Relief Expedition." *Century*, 30, no. 1, May 1885, 77–91.
Harper, Robert S. *Lincoln and the Press.* New York: McGraw-Hill, 1951.
Harper, William Hudson, ed. *Chicago: A History and Forecast.* Chicago: Chicago Association of Commerce, 1921.
Harris, Gibson William. "My Recollections of Abraham Lincoln." *Woman's Home Companion*, November 1903, 9–11.

Harrison, Carter H. *Stormy Years: The Autobiography of Carter H. Harrison, Five Times Mayor of Chicago*. Indianapolis: Bobbs-Merrill, 1935.

Hart, Richard E. *Lincoln's Springfield: Abel W. Estabrook, Robert Todd Lincoln's Abolitionist Teacher*. Spring Creek Series. Springfield, IL: Abraham Lincoln Association, 2009.

———. *Lincoln's Springfield: Springfield's Early Schools, 1819–1860*. Spring Creek Series. Springfield, IL: Abraham Lincoln Association, 2008.

Hartley, Robert E. *Saving Yellowstone: The President Arthur Expedition of 1883*. Westminster, CO: Sniktau, 2007.

Harvard College Class of 1864 Secretary's Report. no. 6, 1864–89. Boston: Self-published, 1889.

Haselmayer, Louis A. *The Harlan-Lincoln Tradition at Iowa Wesleyan College*. Mount Pleasant: Iowa Wesleyan College, 1977.

Hasty Pudding Club. *An Illustrated History of the Hasty Pudding Club Theatricals*. Cambridge: Hasty Pudding Club, 1933.

Haupt, Herman. *Reminiscences of General Herman Haupt*. Milwaukee, WI: Wright, 1901.

Hay, John Milton. *Letters of John Hay and Extracts from Diary*. 2 vols. Washington, DC: Self-published, 1908.

Hayes, H. G., and C. J. Hayes. *A Complete History of the Life and Trial of Charles Julius Guiteau, Assassin of President Garfield*. Philadelphia: Hubbard, 1882.

Haynes, Jack Ellis. "The Expedition of President Chester A. Arthur to Yellowstone National Park in 1883." *Annals of Wyoming* 14, no. 1 (January 1942): 31–38.

Hays, Robert, ed. *Editorializing the "Indian Problem": The* New York Times *on Native Americans, 1860–1900*. Carbondale: Southern Illinois University Press, 1997.

"He Meets the Captains of Industry." *Independent* 54, no. 2779 (March 6, 1902): 538–40.

Helm, Edith Benham. *The Captains and the Kings*. New York: Putnam's, 1954.

Helm, Emily Todd. "Mary Todd Lincoln: Reminiscences and Letters of the Wife of President Lincoln." *McClure's Magazine* 11, no. 5, September 1898, 476–80.

———. "President Lincoln and the Widow of General Helm." Letter to the editor. *Century Magazine* 52, no. 2, June 1896, 318.

Helm, Katherine. *The True Story of Mary, Wife of Lincoln*. New York: Harper, 1928.

Henderson, Bob. "Abraham Lincoln II." *American History Illustrated*, 1, no. 8, December 1966, 54–55.

Hendrickson, Robert. *The Grand Emporiums: The Illustrated History of America's Great Department Stores*. New York: Stein, 1979.

Herndon, William, and Jesse Weik. *Herndon's Life of Lincoln*. Edited by Douglas L. Wilson and Rodney O. Davis. Urbana: University of Illinois Press, 2006.

Hertz, Emanuel. *The Hidden Lincoln: From the Letters and Papers of William H. Herndon*. New York: Viking, 1938.

———, ed. *Lincoln Talks: A Biography in Anecdote*. New York: Viking, 1939.

Hickey, James T. *The Collected Writings of James T. Hickey*. Springfield: Illinois State Historical Society, 1990.

———. "'Own the House Till It Ruins Me': Robert Todd Lincoln and His Parents' Home in Springfield." *Journal of the Illinois State Historical Society* 74, no. 4 (winter 1981): 279–96.

———. "Robert Todd Lincoln and the 'Purely Private' Letters of the Lincoln Family." In Hickey, *Collected Writings*, 166–79.

———. "Robert Todd Lincoln Beckwith." *Lincoln Newsletter*, 6, no. 6, spring 1986.

———. "Robert Lincoln on Artists and Sculptors of President Lincoln." Excerpt from a speech to the Chicago Civil War Round Table. *Lincoln Newsletter*, 7, no. 6, fall 1987, 1–3.

Hill, Frederick Trevor. *Lincoln the Lawyer*. New York: Century, 1906.

Hill, George Birkbeck. *Harvard College by an Oxonian*. New York: Macmillan, 1894.

Hill, Nancy. "The Transformation of the Lincoln Tomb." *Journal of the Abraham Lincoln Association* 27, no. 1 (winter 2006): 46–47.

Hirschhorn, Norbert. "Mary Lincoln's Suicide Attempt." *Lincoln Herald*, 104, no. 3, fall 2003, 92–98.

Hirshson, Stanley P. *Grenville M. Dodge: Soldier, Politician, Railroad Pioneer*. Bloomington: Indiana University Press, 1967.

History of Sangamon County, Ill. Chicago: Inter-state, 1881.

History of the Chicago Police. Chicago: Police Book Fund, 1887.

"History of the Lincoln Papers in Library of Congress." *Lincoln Lore*, 957, August 11, 1947.

Hoar, George F. *Autobiography of Seventy Years*. 2 vols. New York: Scribner's, 1903.

Hollister, O. J. *Life of Schuyler Colfax*. New York: Funk and Wagnalls, 1886.

Holzer, Harold, comp. and ed. *Dear Mr. Lincoln: Letters to the President*. Reading, MA: Addison-Wesley, 1993.

———. *Lincoln at Cooper Union: The Speech That Made Abraham Lincoln President*. New York: Simon & Schuster, 2004.

———, ed. *Lincoln's White House Secretary: The Adventurous Life of William O. Stoddard*. Carbondale: Southern Illinois University Press, 2007.

Holzer, Harold, and Frank J. Williams. *Lincoln's Deathbed in Art and Memory: The "Rubber Room" Phenomenon*. Gettysburg, PA: Thomas, 1998.

Houmes, Blaine V. "Lincoln & Booth: A Love Story?" *Manuscripts* 59, no. 1 (winter 2007): 5–11.

Howe, M. A. De Wolfe. *James Ford Rhodes: American Historian*. New York: Appleton, 1929.

Howell, John, ed. *Discoveries and Inventions: A Lecture by Abraham Lincoln Delivered in 1860*. San Francisco: Self-published, 1915.

Hoyt, J. G. *The Phillips Family and Phillips Exeter Academy*. Boston: Crosby, Nichols, 1858.

Hughes, Sarah Forbes, ed., *Letters and Recollections of John Murray Forbes*. 2 vols. Boston: Houghton Mifflin, 1899.

Huidekoper, H. S. *Personal Notes and Reminiscences of Lincoln*. Philadelphia: Bicking, 1896.

Hurb, Harvey B., ed. *Revised Statutes of the State of Illinois, 1887*. Chicago: Chicago Legal News, 1887.

Husband, Joseph. *The Story of the Pullman Car*. Chicago: McClurg, 1917.

Hutchinson, John M. "What Was Tad Lincoln's Speech Problem?" *Journal of the Abraham Lincoln Association* 30, no. 1 (winter 2009): 35–51.

"Illinois Farmer during the Civil War: Extracts from the Journal of John Edward Young, 1859–66, An." *Journal of the Illinois State Historical Society* 26, nos. 1 and 2 (April–July, 1933): 70–135.

"In Lighter Vein." *Continent* 5, no. 114, April 16, 1884, 512.

International Monetary Conference at Brussels. Washington, DC: GPO, 1893.

J. T. D. "Proposed National Monument to Abraham Lincoln at Springfield, Ill." *Scientific American*, n.s., 12, no. 23 (June 3, 1865): 357.

Jayne, William. "Personal Reminiscences of Abraham Lincoln." Address delivered before the Springfield chapter of the Daughters of the American Revolution, February 12, 1907, Lincoln Home, Springfield, Illinois. Privately printed, 1907.

Jeffers, H. Paul. *An Honest President: The Life and Presidencies of Grover Cleveland*. New York: Morrow, 2000.

Johnson, Arnold B. "Recollections of Charles Sumner." *Scribner's Monthly Magazine*, 10, no. 2, June 1875, 224–29.

Johnson, Charles B. *Illinois in the Fifties, or a Decade of Development, 1851–1860*. Illinois Centennial Edition. Champaign, IL: Flanigan-Pearson, 1918.

Johnson, David R. *Illegal Tender: Counterfeiting and the Secret Service in Nineteenth-Century America*. Washington, DC: Smithsonian Institution Press, 1995.

Johnson, Martin P. "Who Stole the Gettysburg Address?" *Journal of the Abraham Lincoln Association* 24, no. 2 (summer 2003): 1–19.

Jones, J. William. *Personal Reminiscences, Anecdotes, and Letters of Gen. Robert E. Lee*. New York: Appleton, 1875.

Journal of the Senate of the Thirty-Third General Assembly of the State of Illinois. Springfield, IL: Rokker, 1883.

Journey through the Yellowstone National Park and North-Western Wyoming. 1883. Photographs of the Party and Scenery along the Route Traveled, and Copies of Associated Press Dispatches Sent Whilst en Route. Washington, DC, GPO, 1883.

Juhl, Paul C. *The James Harlan and Robert Todd Lincoln Families' Mount Pleasant Memories*. Iowa City, IA: Brushy Creek, 2008.

Kaine, John Langdon. "Lincoln as a Boy Knew Him." *Century Monthly Magazine*, 85, February 1913, 557.

Karabell, Zachary. *Chester Alan Arthur*. American Presidents Series. New York: Holt, 2004.

Kauffman, Michael W. *American Brutus*. New York: Random, 2004.

Keckley, Elizabeth. *Behind the Scenes or, 30 Years a Slave and 4 Years in the White House*. 1868. Reprint, New York: Oxford University Press, 1988.

Keelan, Donald B. *Robert Todd Lincoln's Hildene and How It Was Saved*. Arlington, VT: Keelan, 2001.

"Kind but Misguided." *Independent*, 117, no. 3975, August 7, 1926, 143.

King, C. J. *Four Marys and a Jessie: The Story of the Lincoln Women*. Manchester, VT: Friends of Hildene, 2005.

King, Willard L. *Lincoln's Manager: David Davis*. Cambridge, MA: Harvard University Press, 1960.

Krueger, Lillian. "Mary Todd Lincoln Summers in Wisconsin." *Journal of the Illinois State Historical Society* 34, no. 2 (June 1941): 249–52.

Kunhardt, Dorothy Meserve. "An Old Lady's Lincoln Memories." *Life*, 46, no. 6, February 9, 1959, 57, 59–60.

Lamon, Ward H. *The Life of Abraham Lincoln*. 1872. Reprint, Lincoln: University of Nebraska Press, 1999.

———. *Recollections of Abraham Lincoln, 1847–1865*. Edited by Dorothy Lamon Teillard. 1911. Reprint, Lincoln: University of Nebraska Press, 1994.

Lancaster, Walter B. "Crossed Eyes in Children." *American Journal of Nursing* 50, no. 9 (September 1950): 535.

Langworthy, Henry Glover. "Eye Examination, Treatment and Operation." *American Journal of Nursing* 12, no. 10 (July 1912): 804.

Lauck, W. Jett. *The Causes of the Panic of 1893*. Boston: Houghton Mifflin, 1907.

Laws of the State of Illinois, Passed by the Sixteenth General Assembly, the Second Session, Commencing October 22, 1849. Springfield, IL: Lanphier, 1849.
Laws of the State of Illinois Passed by the Thirtieth General Assembly. Springfield, IL: Lusk, 1877.
Laws of the State of Illinois, Passed by the Thirty-Sixth General Assembly. Springfield, IL: Rokker, 1889.
Lee, James W. *Abraham Lincoln: A Tribute*. Self-published, 1909.
Leech, Margaret. *In the Days of McKinley*. New York: Harper, 1959.
Lentz, Harold H. *The Miracle of Carthage: History of Carthage College, 1847–1974*. Lima, OH: C. S. S., 1975.
"Letter from Frederick Hill Meserve." *Art World*, December 1917, 200.
Letters Received by the Commission Branch of the Adjutant General's Office. 1863–70. National Archives and Records Administration, Washington, DC.
Lewis, Lloyd. *Myths after Lincoln*. 1929. Reprint, New York: Readers Club, 1941.
"Lincoln, Abraham (1809–1865). Autograph Manuscript of His 1864 ELECTION VICTORY SPEECH as President, Delivered in Washington D.C. from the Window of the White House on the Evening of 10 November 1864." Sale 2263, lot 51. *Christie's*. http://www.christies.com/LotFinder/lot_details.aspx?from=searchresults&intObjectID=5176347&sid=2220373b-68c3-45e3-949e-97fadb05a754.
"Lincoln Again." *Century Illustrated Magazine*, 71, no. 1, November 1905, 158–59.
Lincoln Centennial. Springfield: Illinois Centennial Commission, 1909.
Lincoln Centennial Association Addresses: Third Annual Banquet. Springfield: Abraham Lincoln Association, 1911.
"Lincoln Centennial, The." *Journal of the Illinois State Historical Society* 2, no. 1 (April 1909): 27–30.
"Lincolniana: 'Every body likes to shake hands with him': Letters of Elbridge Atwood." *Journal of the Illinois State Historical Society* 72, no. 2 (May 1979): 139–42.
Lincoln Memorial Commission. *Lincoln Memorial Commission Report*. Senate Document no. 965, 62nd Congress, 3rd Session. Washington, DC: GPO, 1913.
"Lincoln, Miss Roby, and Astronomy." *Lincoln Lore*, 1349, February 14, 1955.
"Lincoln Statue for London, The." *Art and Archeology* 8, no. 1 (January–February 1919): 60–61.
"Lincoln: Was He a Slouch?" *Art World*, August 1917, 416–20.
Lindsay, Almont. *The Pullman Strike*. Chicago: University of Chicago Press, 1942.
"Living Dead Man." *Time*, 7, no. 10, March 8, 1926, 38–39.
Logan, Mrs. John A. *Reminiscences of a Soldier's Wife, an Autobiography*. New York: Scribner's, 1913.
Lomax, Elizabeth Lindsay. *Leaves from an Old Washington Diary, 1854–1863*. Edited by Lindsay Lomax Wood. New York: Jacobs, Golden Eagle, 1943.
Lowe, David W., ed. *Meade's Army: The Private Notebooks of Lt. Col. Theodore Lyman*. Kent: Kent State University Press, 2007.
Lupton, John A. "Abraham Lincoln: Pension Attorney." *Lincoln Newsletter*, 14, no. 4, winter 1996, 1, 7–8.
Lyon, Roger H. "College Recollections and Stories." *Harvard Register: An Illustrated Monthly*, 3, no. 3, March 1881, 183.
MacChesney, Nathan William, ed. *Abraham Lincoln: The Tribute of a Century*. Chicago: McClurg, 1910.
Macdonald, Charles Blair. *Scotland's Gift: Golf*. New York: Scribner's, 1928.
"Madstones." *Journal of American Folklore* 15, no. 59 (October 1902): 292–93.

"Man of Many Myths, The." Political advertisement. National Hughes Alliance. 1916.
Mansch, Larry D. *Abraham Lincoln, President-Elect: The Four Critical Months from Election to Inauguration*. Jefferson, NC: McFarland, 2005.
Marshal, Charles. "The Last Days of Lee's Army." *Century Magazine*, 63, no. 6, April 1902, 932–35.
Marszalek, John F. *Assault at West Point: The Court-Martial of Johnson Whittaker*. New York: Collier, 1972.
Martin, Frederick Townsend. *Things I Remember*. New York: Lane, 1913.
Maybrick, Florence. *Mrs. Maybrick's Own Story: My Fifteen Lost Years*. New York: Funk & Wagnalls, 1905.
Maynard, Nettie Colburn. *Was Abraham Lincoln a Spiritualist?* Philadelphia: Hartranft, 1891.
McClure, Alexander K. *Recollections of Half a Century*. Salem, MA: Salem Press, 1902.
McClure, J. B., ed. *Gen. Garfield: From the Log Cabin to the White House*. Chicago: Rhodes & McClure, 1881.
McCormack, Thomas J., ed. *Memoirs of Gustave Koerner, 1809–1896: Life Sketches Written at the Suggestion of His Children*. 2 vols. Cedar Rapids, IA: Torch Press, 1909.
McCoy, M. Garnett, ed. *Inauguration Day, March 4, 1861: A Young Detroit Girl's Witness to the Stirring Events in the City of Washington on the Day of Abraham Lincoln's First Inauguration as Revealed in a Letter to Her Sisters*. Detroit: Friends of the Detroit Public Library, 1960.
McCulloch, Hugh. *Men and Measures of Half a Century*. New York: Scribner's, 1889.
McElroy, Robert. *Grover Cleveland: The Man and the Statesman*. 2 vols. New York: Harper, 1923.
———. *Levi Parsons Morton: Banker, Diplomat and Statesman*. New York: Putnam's, 1930.
McLean, John M. "Eye Surgery." *American Journal of Nursing* 39, no. 5 (May 1939): 492.
McMurtry, R. Gerald. "The Harlan-Lincoln Tradition at Iowa Wesleyan College." *Lincoln Herald*, 48, no. 3, October 1946, 1–11.
Mearns, David C. *The Lincoln Papers: The Story of the Collection*. 2 vols. New York: Doubleday, 1948.
"Memorial to Abraham Lincoln, The." *Art and Archeology* 13, no. 6 (June 1922): 247–57.
Miers, Earl Schenck, ed. *Lincoln Day by Day: A Chronology, 1809–1865*. 3 vols. Dayton, OH: Morningside, 1991.
Miller, Richard F. *Harvard's Civil War: A History of the Twentieth Massachusetts Volunteer Infantry*. Hanover, NH: University Press of New England, 2005.
Miller, Virginia. "Dr. Thomas Miller and His Times." Transcript of a speech. *Records of the Columbia Historical Society, Washington, D.C.* 3 (1900): 303–23.
"Mistake in Bronze, A." *Art World*, June 1917, 211–20.
Moffatt, Frederick C. *Errant Bronzes: George Grey Barnard's Statues of Abraham Lincoln*. Cranbury, NJ: Associated University Presses, 1998.
Monaghan, Jay, comp. *Lincoln Bibliography, 1839–1939*. 2 vols. Collections of the Illinois State Historical Library Bibliographical Series 4. Springfield: Illinois State Historical Library, 1943.
Morison, Elting E., ed. *The Letters of Theodore Roosevelt*. 8 vols. Cambridge: Harvard University Press, 1951–54.
Morison, Samuel Eliot. *Three Centuries at Harvard: 1636–1936*. Reprint, Cambridge: Belknap Press of Harvard University Press, 2001. First published in 1936.

Mowry, Duane. "Robert T. Lincoln and James R. Doolittle: Interesting Political and Historical Letter from the James R. Doolittle Private Correspondence." *Journal of the Illinois State Historical Society* 13, no. 3 (October 1920): 464–75.
"Mr. Barnard's 'Lincoln' Once More." *Art World*, October 1917, 7–11.
"Mrs. Lincoln's Mental Collapse." *Lincoln Lore*, 1124, October 23, 1950.
Myra Bradwell v. State of Illinois. 83 U.S. 130 (1872).
Neely, Mark E., and R. Gerald McMurtry. *The Insanity File: The Case of Mary Todd Lincoln*. Carbondale: Southern Illinois University Press, 1986.
Nelson, Thomas Forsythe. "An Old Letter: Some Forgotten History of the City and the Man–Washington." *Records of the Columbia Historical Society, Washington, D.C.* 14 (1910): 25–48.
Nevins, Allan. *Henry White: Thirty Years of American Diplomacy*. New York: Harper and Brothers, 1930.
———, ed. *Polk: Diary of a President*. London: Longmans, Green, 1929.
"News of the School." *Bulletin of the Phillips Exeter Academy*, April 1921, 23.
Nicolay, Helen. *Lincoln's Secretary: A Biography of John G. Nicolay*. New York: Longmans, Green, 1949.
———. *Personal Traits of Abraham Lincoln*. New York: Century, 1912.
Nicolay, John G. "Lincoln's Gettysburg Address." *Century*, 47, no. 4, February 1894, 596–609.
Nicolay, John G., and John Hay. *Abraham Lincoln: A History*. 10 vols. New York: Century, 1890.
———. "Abraham Lincoln: A History—The Hampton Roads Conference." *Century*, 38, no. 6, October 1889, 846–52.
Norton, Smith. "The Four Men Whom I Saw in London." *Herald of Gospel Liberty*, 101, no. 41, October 14, 1909, 1292.
"Notable People of the Day." *Phrenological Journal and Science of Health* 87, no. 6 (June 1888): 305.
Nowland, James D. *Glory, Darkness and Light: History of the Union League Club of Chicago*. Evanston, IL: Northwestern University Press, 2004.
Nuhrah, Arthur G. "A Commission for Robert." *Lincoln Herald*, 66, no. 3, fall 1964, 143–48.
Oak Ridge Cemetery: Its History and Improvements, Rules and Regulations, National Lincoln Monument, and Other Monuments. Springfield, IL: Rokker, 1879.
Oder, Norman. "Small Upstate New York Library Earns $3 Million from Lincoln Manuscript Sale." *Library Journal*, February 13, 2009. Available online at http://www.libraryjournal.com/article/CA6637505.html.
Office of the Tama County Recorder. Toledo, Iowa.
Ogden, Robert Morris, ed. *The Diaries of Andrew D. White*. New York: Cornell University Library, 1959.
Oldroyd, Osborn H. *The Lincoln Memorial: Album of Immortelles*. New York: Carleton, 1883.
Olson, Lester W. "Lincoln's Granddaughter Eloped to Milwaukee." *Historical Messenger of the Milwaukee County Historical Society* 2, no. 4 (December 1955): 1–3.
Onstot, T. G. *Pioneers of Menard and Mason Counties*. Forest City, IL: Self-published, 1902.
"Open Letters—The Healy Portrait." *Century Magazine*, 77, no. 6, April 1909, 959.
Osmond, Mary, ed. "A P.E.O.'s Wedding in London." Reprint from October 1891, *P.E.O. Record* 100 (June 1998): 10–11.

Owen, Mabel M., ed. *Reports of the United States Board of Tax Appeals*. Vol. 24. Washington, DC: GPO, 1932.
Page, Edwin L. *Abraham Lincoln in New Hampshire*. Boston: Houghton Mifflin, 1929.
Painting a Poem: Mary Baker Eddy and James F. Gilman Illustrate Christ and Christmas. Twentieth-Century Biographers Series. Boston: Christian Science Society, 1998.
Palmer, John M. *The Bench and Bar of Illinois: Historical and Reminiscent*. 2 vols. Chicago: Lewis, 1899.
Papers Relating to the Foreign Relations of the United States. Washington, DC: GPO, 1890–94.
Parker, Dorothy. Introductory essay. In Elizabeth Keckley, *Behind the Scenes or, 30 Years a Slave and 4 Years in the White House*. The American Negro: His History and Literature Series. Reprint, New York: Arno Press and the New York Times, 1968.
"Patrick D. Tyrrell." In *History of the Chicago Police*, 892–93. Chicago: Police Book Fund, 1887.
Pease, Theodore Calvin, and James G. Randall, eds. *Diary of Orville Hickman Browning*. 2 vols. Springfield: Trustees of the Illinois State Historical Society, 1925, 1933.
Peavy, Linda, and Ursula Smith. *The Gold Rush Widows of Little Falls: A Story Drawn from the Letters of Pamelia and James Fergus*. St. Paul: Minnesota Historical Society Press, 1990.
Peck, J. M. *The Traveler's Directory for Illinois*. New York: Colton, 1839.
Pendel, Thomas F. *Thirty-Six Years in the White House*. Washington, DC: Neale, 1902.
Percoco, James A. *Summers with Lincoln: Looking for the Man in the Monuments*. New York: Fordham University Press, 2008.
Perkins, Jacob R. *Trails, Rails, and War: The Life of General G. M. Dodge*. Indianapolis: Bobbs-Merrill, 1929.
"Personal." *Harper's Bazaar*, 4, no. 27, July 8, 1871, 419.
"Personal." *Harper's Bazaar*, 4, no. 50, December 16, 1871, 787.
"Personal." *Harper's Weekly*, 21, No. 1092, December 1, 1877, 939.
"Personals." *Every Saturday: A Journal of Choice Reading*, December 23, 1871, 619.
Peskin, Allan. *Garfield: A Biography*. Kent, OH: Kent State University Press, 1978.
Petersen, William J. "Lincoln and Iowa." *Palimpsest* 41, no. 2 (February 1960): 87–89.
Peterson, Merrill D. *Lincoln in American Memory*. Oxford: Oxford University Press, 1994.
Pierce, Edward L., ed. *Memoirs and Letters of Charles Sumner*. 4 vols. Boston: Roberts Brothers, 1893.
Pinkerton, Allan. *History and Evidence of the Passage of Abraham Lincoln from Harrisburg, PA to Washington on the 22nd and 23rd of February, 1861*. 2nd ed. [New York:] Pinkerton National Detective Agency, 1892. First published in 1868.
Pinsker, Matthew. *Lincoln's Sanctuary: Abraham Lincoln and the Soldiers' Home*. New York: Oxford University Press, 2003.
"Plot to Steal the Lincoln Corpse, The." *Lincoln Lore*, 1611, May 1972.
Poole, Ernest. *The Bridge: My Own Story*. New York: Macmillan, 1940.
Poore, Benjamin Perley. *Reminiscences of Sixty Years in the National Metropolis*. 2 vols. Philadelphia: Hubbard Brothers, 1886.
Porter, D. D. *Incidents and Anecdotes of the Civil War*. New York: Appleton, 1885.
Porter, Horace. *Campaigning with Grant*. New York: Century, 1897.
———. "Campaigning with Grant: Preparing for the Last Campaign." *Century Magazine*, 54, no. 4, August 1897, 584–602.

"Postscript to the *Life Magazine* Article 'What Happened to Lincoln's Body.'" *Lincoln Lore*, 1502, April 1963, 4, and 1503, May 1963, 3.
Powell, Adam Clayton. *Adam by Adam: The Autobiography of Adam Clayton Powell.* Reprint, New York: Kensington, 1994. First published in 1971.
Power, John Carroll. *Abraham Lincoln: His Life and Public Services, Death and Great Funeral Cortege, with a History and Description of the National Lincoln Monument.* Chicago: Rokker, 1889.
———. *History of an Attempt to Steal the Body of Abraham Lincoln (Late President of the United States of America) Including a History of the Lincoln Guard of Honor, with Eight Years Lincoln Memorial Services.* Springfield, IL: Rokker, 1890.
Pratt, Harry E., comp. *Concerning Mr. Lincoln: In Which Abraham Lincoln Is Pictured as He Appeared to Letter Writers of His Time.* Springfield, IL: Abraham Lincoln Association, 1944.
———. *The Personal Finances of Abraham Lincoln.* Springfield, IL: Abraham Lincoln Association, 1943.
"President Lincoln as an Inventor." *Scientific American*, n.s., 12, no. 22 (May 27, 1865): 340.
"President Lincoln's Grandson." *Lincoln Lore*, 549, October 16, 1939.
President McKinley's Last Speech. New York: Malkan, 1901.
"Presidential Speculations." *Harper's Weekly*, 35, no. 1777, January 10, 1891, 18.
"Progress of the World, The." *American Review of Reviews* 43, no. 4 (April 1911): 387.
"Prominent Alumni from Yesterday. Big Names in DKE History: Robert Todd Lincoln '64 (1864), Alpha/Harvard." *Delta Kappa Epsilon*, 2011. http://www.dke.org/Heritage/Prominent_RTLincoln.
Prucha, Francis Paul. *The Great Father: The United States Government and the American Indians.* 2 vols. Lincoln: University of Nebraska Press, 1984.
Pulliam, John. "Changing Attitudes toward Free Public Schools in Ill. 1825–1860." *History of Education Quarterly* 7, no. 2 (summer 1967): 193–94.
Putnam, George Haven. *Abraham Lincoln: The People's Leader in the Struggle for National Existence.* New York: Putnam's, 1909.
———. *Memories of My Youth: 1844–1865.* New York: Putnam's, 1914.
———. "The Speech That Won the East for Lincoln." *Outlook*, February 8, 1922, 220–21.
Randall, Ruth Painter. *Lincoln's Sons.* Boston: Little, Brown, 1955.
———. *Mary Lincoln: Biography of a Marriage.* Boston: Little, Brown, 1953.
Rankin, Henry B. *Intimate Character Sketches of Abraham Lincoln.* Philadelphia: Lippincott, 1924.
———. *Personal Recollections of Abraham Lincoln.* New York: Putnam's, 1916.
Ray, I. "American Legislation on Insanity." *American Journal of Insanity* 21 (July 1864): 21–56.
Raymond, George L. "The Barnard Lincoln: An Open Letter." *American Magazine of Art* 9, no. 2, December 1917, 72–73.
Reeves, Thomas C. *Gentleman Boss: The Life of Chester Alan Arthur.* New York: Knopf, 1975.
———. "President Arthur in Yellowstone National Park." *Montana, the Magazine of Western History* 19, no. 3 (summer 1969): 18–29.
Reitano, Joanne. *The Tariff Question in the Gilded Age.* University Park: Pennsylvania State University Press, 1994.

"Reminiscences of Robert Lincoln and Abraham Lincoln." *Bulletin of the Phillips Exeter Academy*, 22, no. 3, August 1926, 8–9.
Renton, A. Wood. "Comparative Lunacy Law." *Journal of the Society of Comparative Legislation*, n.s., 1, no. 2 (July 1899): 266–67.
Report of Board of Officers to Consider an Expedition for the Relief of Lt. Greely and Party. Washington, DC: GPO, 1884.
Report of the Commission Created in Accordance with a Joint Resolution of Congress, Approved March 3, 1881, Providing for the Erection of a Monument at Yorktown, V.A., Commemorative of the Surrender of Cornwallis. Washington, DC: GPO, 1883.
Report of the Secretary of War; Being a Part of the Message and Documents Communicated to the Two Houses of Congress. 4 vols. Washington, DC: GPO, 1882.
Report of the Secretary of War; Being Part of the Message and Documents Communicated to the Two Houses of Congress at the Beginning of the Second Session of the Forty-Eighth Congress. 4 vols. Washington, DC: GPO, 1884.
Report of the Twenty-Sixth Annual Meeting of the American Bar Association. Philadelphia: Dando, 1903.
Republican Campaign Text Book for 1880, The. Washington, DC: Republican Congressional Committee, 1880.
"Republican Prospect, The." *Harper's Weekly*, 36, no. 1848, May 21, 1892, 482.
Revell, M. J. *Strabismus: A History of Orthoptic Techniques.* London: Barrie & Jenkins, 1971.
Rhodes, James, and Dean Jauchius. *The Trial of Mary Todd Lincoln.* Indianapolis: Bobbs-Merrill, 1959.
Rice, Allen Thorndike. *Reminiscences of Abraham Lincoln by Distinguished Men of His Time.* New and revised edition, New York: Harper & Brothers, 1909. First published in 1886 by North American.
Rice, Judith A. "Ida M. Tarbell: A Progressive Look at Lincoln." *Journal of the Abraham Lincoln Association* 19, no. 1 (winter 1998): 57–72.
Richardson, Albert D. *A Personal History of Ulysses S. Grant.* Boston: Guernsey, 1885.
Richardson, William L. "Robert Todd Lincoln." *Harvard Register: An Illustrated Monthly*, 3, no. 7 (July 1881): 378.
Riddle, Donald W. *Congressman Abraham Lincoln.* Urbana: University of Illinois Press, 1957.
Roberts, Octavia. *Lincoln in Illinois.* Boston: Houghton Mifflin, 1918.
"Robert T. Lincoln as a Law Student." *Chicago Legal News* 1, no. 3 (October 17, 1868): 21.
"Robert Todd Lincoln." *Harvard College Class of 1864 Secretary's Report.* No. 6. 1864–89. Boston: Self-published, 1889.
"Robert Todd Lincoln, 1843–1926." *John Crerar Library Quarterly* 16, no. 3 (September 1945): 4.
"Robert Todd Lincoln Beckwith." *Lincoln Newsletter*, 6, no. 6, spring 1986.
"Robert Todd Lincoln Could Tickle the Keys." *News from Historic Hildene* 6, no. 3, autumn 1982, 4.
"Robert Todd Lincoln: Memorial." In *The John Crerar Library Thirty-Second Annual Report for the Year 1926*, 33. Chicago: Board of Directors, 1927.
Robinson, Michael F. *The Coldest Crucible: Arctic Exploration and American Culture.* Chicago: University of Chicago Press, 2006.
Rogers, Henry Munroe. *Memories of Ninety Years.* Boston: Houghton Mifflin, 1928.

Rogers, Patricia H., Charles Sullivan, and the staff of the Cambridge Historical Commission. *A Photographic History of Cambridge*. Cambridge: MIT Press, 1984.
Rosner, Robert S. "Newer Concepts of Strabismus." *Ohio State Medical Journal* 43 (September 1947): 921–25.
Ross, Rodney A. "Mary Todd Lincoln: Patient at Bellevue Place, Batavia." *Journal of the Illinois State Historical Society* 63, no. 1 (1970): 5–34.
Roster and Record of Iowa Soldiers in Miscellaneous Organizations of the Mexican War, Indian Campaigns, War of the Rebellion, and the Spanish-American and Philippine Wars. 6 vols. Des Moines: Iowa General Assembly, 1911.
Rotundo, E. Anthony. *American Manhood*. New York: Basic Books, 1993.
Rousmaniere, John. *The Life and Times of the Equitable*. New York: Equitable, 1995.
Ruckstuhl, F. Wellington. "Lincoln: Was He a Slouch?" *Art World*, August 1917, 416–17.
———. "A Mistake in Bronze." *Art World*, June 1917, 211–20.
———. "Mr. Barnard's 'Lincoln' Once More." *Art World*, October 1917, 7–11.
Russell, Henry B. *International Monetary Conferences*. New York: Harper, 1898.
Ryan, Bernard. *The Poisoned Life of Mrs. Maybrick*. New York Penguin Books, 1976.
Sandburg, Carl. *Abraham Lincoln: The Prairie Years*. 2 vols. New York: Harcourt, Brace, 1926.
———. *Chicago Poems*. New York: Holt, 1916.
Sandburg, Carl, and Paul M. Angle. *Mary Lincoln: Wife and Widow*. New York: Harcourt, Brace, 1932.
Sawislak, Karen. *Smoldering City: Chicagoans and the Great Fire, 1871–1874*. Chicago: University of Chicago Press, 1995.
Sawyer, Alvah L. *A History of the Northern Peninsula of Michigan and Its People*. 3 vols. Chicago: Lewis, 1911.
Schama, Simon. *Dead Certainties: Unwarranted Speculations*. New York: Knopf, 1991.
Schley, W. S., and J. R. Soley. *The Rescue of Greely*. New York: Scribner's, 1885.
Schouler, James. "Lincoln at Tremont Temple." *Proceedings of the Massachusetts Historical Society* 42 (October 1908–June 1909): 81–82.
Schreiner, Samuel A. *The Trials of Mrs. Lincoln*. New York: Donald I. Fine, 1987.
Schwartz, Barry. *Abraham Lincoln and the Forge of National Memory*. Chicago: University of Chicago Press, 2000.
Schwartz, Thomas F. "'My stay on Earth, is growing very short,' Mary Todd Lincoln's Letters to Willis Danforth and Elizabeth Swing." *Journal of Illinois History* 6 (summer 2003): 125–36.
———. "Roasting Lincoln's Letters: What Did Robert T. Lincoln Burn?" *Lincoln Newsletter* 9, fall 1990, 4–5.
Schwartz, Thomas F., and Kim M. Bauer. "Unpublished Mary Todd Lincoln." *Journal of the Abraham Lincoln Association* 17, no. 2 (summer 1996): 1–21.
Scott, Kenneth. "Press Opposition to Lincoln in New Hampshire." *New England Quarterly* 21, no. 3 (September 1948): 326–41.
Seward, Frederick W. *Reminiscences of a War-Time Statesman and Diplomat*. New York: Putnam's, 1916.
Seymour, Silas M. *Incidents of a Trip through the Great Platte Valley to the Rocky Mountains*. New York: Van Nostrand, 1867.
Sherman, William Tecumseh. *Memoirs of Gen. W. T. Sherman, Written by Himself*. 2 vols. New York: Webster, 1892.
———. *Memoirs of William Tecumseh Sherman*. 2 vols. Foreword by B. H. Liddell Hart. Bloomington: Indiana University Press, 1957.

Shutes, Milton H. *Lincoln and the Doctors: A Medical Narrative of the Life of Abraham Lincoln*. New York: Pioneer, 1933.
———. "Mortality of the Five Lincoln Boys." *Lincoln Herald*, 57, no. 1–2, spring–summer 1955, 3–11.
Simon, John Y., ed. *The Papers of Ulysses S. Grant*. 31 vols. Carbondale: Southern Illinois University Press, 1967–.
Smith, Richard Norton. *The Colonel: The Life and Legend of Robert R. McCormick*. Boston: Houghton Mifflin, 1997.
Snively, E. A. "James M. Davidson." *Journal of the Illinois State Historical* Society 9 no. 2 (July 1916): 187.
Snow, Florence. *Pictures on My Wall: A Lifetime in Kansas*. Lawrence: University of Kansas Press, 1945.
Snow, Marshall S. "Abraham Lincoln—A Personal Reminiscence." *Bulletin of the Phillips Exeter Academy* 5, no. 3, September 1909, 30.
"Some Intimate Glimpses into the Private Lives of the Members of the Robert Lincoln Family." *Lincoln Lore*, 1525, March 1965.
"Son of Abraham Lincoln, The." *Literary Digest*, August 14, 1926, 36, 41–42.
Sorenson, Mark. "The Ill. State Library: 1818–1870." *Illinois Libraries* 81, no. 1 (winter 1999): 35–36.
Sotos, John G. *The Physical Lincoln Sourcebook: An Annotated Medical History of Abraham Lincoln and His Family*. Printing 1.1a. Mt. Vernon, VA: Mt. Vernon Book Systems, 2008.
Speech of Hon. Robert T. Lincoln Made at the Celebration of the Thirty-Eighth Anniversary of the Lincoln-Douglas Debate, Galesburg, Ill., October 7, 1896. Hancock, NY: Herald, 1921.
Speech of Mr. Lincoln, of Illinois, on the Reference of the President's Message, in the House of Representatives, Wednesday, January 14, 1848. Washington, DC: Gideon, 1848.
Speer, Bonnie Stahlman. *The Great Abraham Lincoln Hijack*. Norman, OK: Reliance Press, 1997.
Springfield City Directory for 1857–1858. Compiled by B. Winters & Co. Springfield, IL: S. H. James, 1857.
Starr, John W. *Abraham Lincoln's Religion in His Eldest Son's Estimation*. Self-published, 1926.
Steell, Willis. "Mrs. Abraham Lincoln and Her Friends." *Munsey's Magazine*, 40, no. 5, February 1909, 617–23.
Steeples, Douglas, and David O. Whitten. *Democracy in Desperation: The Depression of 1893*. Westport, CT: Greenwood Press, 1998.
Steers, Edward, Jr. *Blood on the Moon*. Lexington: University Press of Kentucky, 2001.
Sterling, James T. "How Lincoln 'Lost' His Inaugural Address." *Lincoln Herald*, 45, no. 1, February 1943, 23–25.
Stevens, Walter B. *A Reporter's Lincoln*. Edited by Michael Burlingame. Lincoln: University of Nebraska Press, 1998.
Stoddard, Henry L. *As I Knew Them: Presidents and Politics from Grant to Coolidge*. New York: Harper, 1927.
Stoddard, William O. *Inside the White House in War Times*. Edited by Michael Burlingame. Lincoln: University of Nebraska Press, 2000.
Story, Ronald. "Harvard Students, the Boston Elite, and the New England Preparatory System, 1800–1876." *History of Education Quarterly* 15, no. 3 (autumn 1975): 281–98.

"Strange History Brought to Light: Rare Photos of Lincoln's Exhumation." *Life*, February 15, 1963, 85–88.
Stringer, Lawrence B., ed. *History of Logan County, Illinois*. 2 vols. Chicago: Pioneer, 1911.
Stronks, Jim. "Mary Todd Lincoln's Sad Summer in Hyde Park." *Hyde Park Historical Society Newsletter* 20, no. 1 (spring 1998). http://www.hydeparkhistory.org/mtlincoln.html.
Strozier, Charles B. "The Psychology of Mary Todd Lincoln." *Psychohistory Review* 17, no. 1 (1988): 11–24.
Sullivan, Robert. *The Disappearance of Dr. Parkman*. Boston: Little, Brown, 1971.
Sutton, Amy Louise. "Lincoln and Son Borrow Books." *Illinois Archives* 48, no. 6 (June 1966): 443–49.
Sutton-Kellerstrass, Amy Louise. "Lincoln and Son Borrow Books." *Lincoln Herald*, 69, spring 1967, 13–16.
Swick, Gerald D., and Donna D. McCreary. "His Own Place in the Sun." *Lincoln Lore*, 1853, summer 1998, 3–6.
Swisshelm, Jane Grey. *Half a Century*. Chicago: Jansen, McClurg, 1880.
Taft, William Howard. "Presentation Address." In *Barnard's Lincoln: The Gift of Mr. and Mrs. Charles P. Taft to the City of Cincinnati*, 33–58. Cincinnati: Stewart & Kidd, 1917.
Tarbell, Ida. *All in the Day's Work*. New York: Macmillan, 1939.
———. *The Life of Abraham Lincoln: Drawn from Original Sources and Containing Many Speeches, Letters and Telegrams Hitherto Unpublished*. 2 vols. New York: Doubleday and McClure, 1900.
Taylor, Eugene. *Shadow Culture: Psychology and Spirituality in America*. Washington, DC: Counterpoint, 1999.
Tebbel, John. *The Marshall Fields*. New York: Dutton, 1947.
Temple, Wayne C. *Abraham Lincoln: From Skeptic to Prophet*. Mahomet, IL: Mayhaven, 1995.
———. *Alexander Williamson: Friend of the Lincolns*. Racine, WI: Lincoln Fellowship of Wisconsin, 1997.
———. "Alexander Williamson—Tutor to the Lincoln Boys." *Address at Annual Meeting, Lincoln Fellowship of Wisconsin*, Historical Bulletin 26, 1971.
———. *By Square and Compass: Saga of the Lincoln Home*. 1984. Rev. ed. Mahomet, IL: Mayhaven, 2002.
———. "Herndon on Lincoln: An Unknown Interview with a List of Books in the Lincoln & Herndon Law Office." *Journal of the Illinois State Historical Society* 98, no. 1–2 (spring–summer 2005): 34–50.
———. "Lincoln's Admiration of Washington and His Visit to Mount Vernon." *Lincoln Herald*, 107, no. 2, summer 2005, 62–67.
———. *Lincoln's Connection with the Illinois & Michigan Canal, His Return from Congress in '48, and His Invention*. Springfield, IL: Illinois Bell, 1986.
———. "Lincoln's Route to Washington from Springfield in 1848." *Lincolnian*, 24, no. 6, July–August 2005, 7–8.
———. *Lincoln's Travels on the* River Queen. Mahomet, IL: Mayhaven, 2007.
———. "Mariah (Bartlett) Vance: Daytime Servant to the Lincolns, Part 1." *For the People: A Newsletter of the Abraham Lincoln Association*, 6, no. 4, winter 2004, 1, 3.
———. "Mariah (Bartlett) Vance: Daytime Servant to the Lincolns, Part 2." *For the*

People: A Newsletter of the Abraham Lincoln Association, 7, no. 1, spring 2005, 1–2, 4–5, 8.

———. "Mary Todd Lincoln's Travels." *Journal of the Illinois State Historical Society* 52, no. 1 (spring 1959): 180–94.

———. *Stephen A. Douglas: Freemason.* Bloomington, IL: Masonic Book Club, Illinois Lodge of Research, 1982.

———. "Thomas and Abraham Lincoln as Farmers." *Bulletin of the 55th Annual Meeting of the Lincoln Fellowship of Wisconsin*, no. 53, April 22, 1995.

———. "Will the Real E. E. Ellsworth Step Forward?" *Rail Splitter: A Journal for the Lincoln Collector*, 6, no. 4, spring 2001, 23.

Thacher, George H. "Lincoln and Meade after Gettysburg." *American Historical Review* 32 no. 2, (January 1927): 282–83.

Thayer, William Roscoe. *The Life and Letters of John Hay.* 2 vols. Boston: Houghton Mifflin, 1929.

Thirty-Ninth Annual Report of the President of Harvard College to the Overseers, Exhibiting the State of the Institution for the Academic Year 1863–1864. Cambridge: Welch, Bigelow, 1865. http://pds.lib.harvard.edu/pds/view/2574320?n=1625&s=4.

Thomas, Benjamin P. *Abraham Lincoln: A Biography.* New York: Knopf, 1953.

———. *Portrait for Posterity: Lincoln and His Biographers.* New Brunswick, NJ: Rutgers University Press, 1947.

Thompson, Isaac Grant, comp. *The Albany Law Journal.* Vol. 6. Albany, NY: Weed, Parsons, 1873.

Thomson, Helen. *Murder at Harvard.* Boston: Houghton Mifflin, 1971.

Thoron, Ward, ed. *The Letters of Mrs. Henry Adams.* Boston: Little, Brown, 1936.

Todd, Alden. *Abandoned: The Story of the Greely Arctic Expedition 1881–1884.* Reprint, Fairbanks: University of Alaska Press, 2001. First published in 1961.

Townsend, George Alfred. *Lincoln and His Wife's Home Town.* Indianapolis: Bobbs-Merrill, 1929.

———. *Lincoln and the Bluegrass.* Lexington: University of Kentucky Press, 1955.

———. "President Garfield and His Cabinet." *Frank Leslie's Popular Monthly*, 11, no. 5, May 1881, 4–6.

Trefousse, Hans L. *Andrew Johnson: A Biography.* New York: Norton, 1989.

Trial of John H. Surratt in the Criminal Court for the District of Columbia. 2 vols. Washington, DC: French and Richardson, 1867.

Turner, Justin G., and Turner, Linda Levitt. *Mary Todd Lincoln: Her Life and Letters.* New York: Knopf, 1972.

Tyler, Alice Felt. *The Foreign Policy of James G. Blaine.* Reprint, Hamden, CT: Archon Books, 1965. First published in 1927.

Tyrrell, Patrick D. "At A. T. Stewart's Tomb." *Flynn's*, 13, no. 3, February 20, 1926, 424–33.

———. "The Boscobel Coniackers." *Flynn's*, 12, no. 2, January 2, 1926, 235–45.

———. "A Chain of Circumstances." *Flynn's*, 12, no. 5, January 23, 1926, 706–14.

———. "The Lincoln Tomb Robbers—Part 1." *Flynn's*, 11, no. 3, November 28, 1925, 348–57.

———. "The Lincoln Tomb Robbers—Part 2." *Flynn's*, 11, no. 4, December 5, 1925, 578–85.

———. "More Queer Than Genuine." *Flynn's*, 13, no. 1, February 6, 1926, 108–15.

———. "Thieves' Syndicate." *Flynn's*, 12, no. 6, January 30, 1926, 840–48.

Unger, Irwin. *The Greenback Era: A Social and Political History of American Finance, 1865–1879*. Princeton, NJ: Princeton University Press, 1964.
U.S. Census Bureau. *Mortality Schedule for Springfield, Sangamon Co., Illinois*. 1850. Washington, DC, 1850.
U.S. Congress. *Congressional Globe*. 30th Cong., 1st Sess., n.s., no. 1 (1847–48).
———. *Congressional Globe*. 39th Cong., 1st Sess., (1865–66).
———. *Congressional Record*. 47th Cong. 1st Sess., (1882).
U.S. Senate. Commission on Industrial Relations. *Industrial Relations: Final Report and Testimony*. 11 vols. Washington, DC: GPO, 1916.
U.S. Strike Commission. *Report on the Chicago Strike, June–July, 1894*. Washington, DC: GPO, 1895.
Van Alstyne, Richard W. "Private American Loans to the Allies, 1914–1916." *Pacific Historical Review* 2, no. 2 (June 1933): 180–93.
Van Deusen, Glyndon G. *Thurlow Weed: Wizard of the Lobby*. Boston: Little, Brown, 1947.
Villard, Henry. *Lincoln on the Eve of '61*. Edited by Harold G. Villard and Oswald Garrison Villard. New York: Knopf, 1941.
———. *The Memoirs of Henry Villard, Journalist and Financier, 1835–1900*. 2 vols. Boston: Houghton Mifflin, 1904.
Volwiler, Albert T., ed. *The Correspondence between Benjamin Harrison and James G. Blaine, 1882–1893*. Philadelphia: American Philosophical Society, 1940.
Vowell, Sarah. *Assassination Vacation*. New York: Simon & Schuster, 2005.
Waddington, Mary Alsop King. *Letters of a Diplomat's Wife, 1883–1900*. London: Smith, Elder, 1903.
Walker, W. G. "The Development of the Free Public High School in Illinois during the Nineteenth Century." *History of Education Quarterly* 4, no. 4 (December 1964): 268–69, 271.
Wallace, Joseph. *Past and Present of the City of Springfield and Sangamon County, Illinois*. 2 vols. Chicago: Clarke, 1904.
Walling, Regis M., and N. Daniel Rupp, eds. *The Diary of Bishop Frederic Baraga: First Bishop of Marquette, Michigan*. Detroit, MI: Wayne State University Press, 2001.
Warne, Colston E., ed. *The Pullman Boycott of 1894: The Problem of Federal Intervention*. Problems in American Civilization Series. Boston: D. C. Heath, 1955.
War of the Rebellion, The: A Compilation of the Official Records of the Union and Confederate Armies. Edited by Robert N. Scott. Series 1, vol. 46. Washington, DC: GPO, 1895. 127 vols. Cited as *OR*.
Taft, Horatio Nelson. *Washington during the Civil War: The Diary of Horatio Nelson Taft, 1861–1865*. American Memory, Manuscript Division, Library of Congress. Available online at http://memory.loc.gov/ammem/tafthtml/tafthome.html.
Washington, John E. *They Knew Lincoln*. New York: E. P. Dutton, 1942.
Weed, Thurlow. *Autobiography of Thurlow Weed*. Edited by Harriet Weed. Boston: Houghton Mifflin, 1883.
Weik, Jesse W. *The Real Lincoln: A Portrait*. Lincoln: University of Nebraska Press, 2003. First published in 1922 by Houghton Mifflin.
Welles, Gideon. *Diary of Gideon Welles: Secretary of the Navy under Lincoln and Johnson*. 3 vols. Boston: Houghton Mifflin, 1911.
Wendt, Kristine Adams. "Mary Todd Lincoln: 'Great Sorrows' and the Healing Waters of Waukesha." *Wisconsin Academy Review* 38, no. 2 (spring 1992): 14–19.

Western Tourist and Immigrant's Guide through the States of Ohio, Michigan, Indiana, Illinois, and Missouri. New York: J. H. Colton, 1840.

Western Tourist and Immigrant's Guide through the States of Ohio, Michigan, Indiana, Illinois, and Missouri. New York: J. H. Colton, 1845.

Whitney, Henry Clay. *Life on the Circuit with Lincoln.* Boston: Estes and Lauriat, 1892.

"Franc B. Wilkie." *Sketches and Notices of the Chicago Bar.* Chicago: Sumner, 1871.

Williams, Frank J. "Robert Todd Lincoln and John Hay, Fellow Travelers." *Lincoln Herald*, 96, no. 1, spring 1994, 3–14.

Williams, Myron R. *The Story of Phillips Exeter.* Reprint, Exeter, NH: Phillips Exeter Academy, 2000. First published in 1957.

Willis, N. P. "The President's Son." *Littell's Living Age*, 933, April 19, 1862, 154.

Willson, Beckles. *America's Ambassadors to England, 1785–1928: A Narrative of Anglo-American Diplomatic Relations.* Manchester, NH: Ayer, 1969. First published in 1928.

Wilson, Douglas L. "Abraham Lincoln and 'That Fatal First of January.'" In *Lincoln before Washington: New Perspectives on the Illinois Years*, 99–132. Urbana: University of Illinois Press, 1997.

———. *Honor's Voice: The Transformation of Abraham Lincoln.* New York: Vintage Books, 1999.

Wilson, Douglas L., and Rodney O. Davis, eds. *Herndon's Informants: Letters, Interviews and Statements about Abraham Lincoln.* Urbana: University of Illinois Press, 1998.

Wilson, Frank J. "Plotting Ghouls of the Catacombs: My Favorite Detective Case." *True Detective Mysteries*, June 1941, 16–19, 84–89.

Wilson, James Grant, ed. *The Presidents of the United States: 1789–1894.* New York: Appleton, 1894.

Wilson, James Grant, and John Fiske, eds. *Appleton's Cyclopedia of American History.* 6 vols. New York: Appleton, 1900.

Wilson, Rufus Rockwell, comp. and ed. *Intimate Memories of Lincoln.* New York: Primavera, 1945.

———, ed. *Lincoln among His Friends: A Sheaf of Intimate Memories.* Caldwell, ID: Caxton, 1942.

———. *Washington: The Capital City.* 2 vols. Philadelphia: Lippincott, 1901.

Woldman, Albert A. *Lawyer Lincoln.* 1936. Reprint, New York: Carroll & Graf, 2001.

Index

The abbreviation *RL* is used for *Robert Lincoln* in subentries.

Jason Emerson is an independent historian from upstate New York. He is the author of *The Madness of Mary Lincoln* (2007; Illinois State Historical Society book of the year) and *Lincoln the Inventor* (2009) and is the editor of *The Dark Days of Abraham Lincoln's Widow, as Revealed by Her Own Letters*, by Myra Helmer Pritchard (2011). He has worked as a U.S. National Park Service ranger at the Lincoln Home National Historic Site, the Gettysburg National Military Park, and the Jefferson National Expansion Memorial and as a professional journalist and freelance writer. His articles and book reviews have appeared in numerous popular magazines and academic journals.